Dear French Teachers,

We take this opportunity to welcome you to our new program, **Discovering French**. In fact, this is really your program, for it has taken shape thanks to the suggestions, critiques, and encouragement we have received from the many hundreds of secondary school teachers who, over the years, have enjoyed success getting their students to communicate through *French for Mastery*. **Discovering French** emphasizes communication and stresses interpersonal relationships in meaningful cultural contexts. Some of the key features, which many of you requested, are:

- *Integrated technology to accompany each lesson*
- *Stronger emphasis on daily-life themes*
- *Active encouragement of cooperative learning*
- *Greater opportunity for self-expression*
- *Use of euro currency in activities*

There are, of course, many more new features which you will discover as you look through the book.

In conclusion, we should stress that our program is a *flexible* one which allows teachers to take into account the needs of their students and build their own curriculum focusing on specific skills or topics.

We wish you the best of success with **Discovering French!** It is our hope that for you and your students, teaching and learning French with this program will be an enjoyable as well as a rewarding experience.

Jean-Paul Valette   *Rebecca M. Valette*

Merci!

We would like to express our appreciation to the many **French for Mastery** teachers who responded to our surveys and who sent us suggestions for designing this new program. In particular, we would like to thank the following people who carefully read the manuscript as it was being developed, provided us with guidance and encouragement, and gave invaluable feedback as they used the program:

Steve Covey
*Sunnyvale Junior
  High School
Sunnyvale, CA*

Dianne Hopen
*Humboldt High School
St. Paul, MN*

Margie Ricks
*Dulles High School
Sugar Land, TX*

T. Jeffrey Richards
*Roosevelt High School
Sioux Falls, SD*

Frank Strell
*LaSalle-Peru Township
  High School
LaSalle, IL*

Patricia McCann
*Lincoln-Sudbury Regional
  High School
Sudbury, MA*

Susan Wildman
*Western Albemarle High School
Crozet, VA*

Andrea Henderson
*First Colony Middle School
Sugar Land, TX*

First level:

DISCOVERING FRENCH BLEU–
Première partie

DISCOVERING FRENCH BLEU–
Deuxième partie

DISCOVERING FRENCH–BLEU

Discovering French will help you

A Practical Approach to Proficiency

- **Comprehension of Authentic Language**
  Discovering French–Bleu brings into the classroom the voices and faces of dozens of young people, their families and their friends, introducing useful communicative phrases and expressions.

- **Awareness of Structure**
  In **Discovering French**, grammar, pronunciation, and spelling patterns are not only taught as an instructional goal, but rather are presented to help the students express themselves more clearly and correctly.

- **Guided Practice for Building Accuracy**
  Discovering French provides numerous opportunities for practice in guided communicative activities, carefully graded from easier to more challenging, thus letting the students gradually build up accurate language habits.

- **Cooperative Learning in Meaningful Context**
  Discovering French has been designed for pair and small-group work so that students can learn together.

- **Frequent Opportunity for Self-Expression**
  Students are given frequent opportunity to express themselves creatively with the language they have learned.

DISCOVERING FRENCH

Second level:
DISCOVERING FRENCH–BLANC

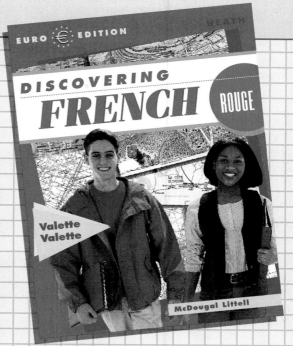

Third level:
DISCOVERING FRENCH–ROUGE

revitalize your French program!

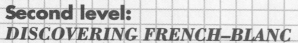

Technology you and your students will want to use

 Completely integrated video

 Choice of Laserdisc or Videocassette
Bar-coded access in TAE
for Laserdisc

 CD-ROM program directly keyed
to each lesson
CD-ROM student discs can be used
for individual practice at school or
at home

 Test Bank

 Writing Templates

A program that allows you to reach __all__ your students

 Multiple Intelligences

 Multicultural/ Global Awareness

 Interdisciplinary Connections

 Cooperative Practice and Learning Activities

 Varied Reading Materials

 Total Physical Response Suggestions

 Cyclical Re-entry and Review

 Language Games

PRINT

Student Text

Extended Teacher's Edition
A complete resource for point-of-use warm-ups, teaching notes, ancillary keying, multicultural expansion, lesson planning, TPR, critical thinking, cooperative learning and more.

Europak
Activities, games, maps, and overhead transparencies are provided to engage students in learning about the introduction of the euro.

Student Activity Book
Listening, speaking, reading and writing activities are provided to increase student time on task and reinforce classroom presentations.

Student Activity Book TAE

Video Activity Book
Activities for all 39 video modules provide both reinforcement and extension to encourage active viewing and focus on higher order thinking skills.

Communipak Copymasters
Pair/group communication activities in five different formats designed to encourage open-ended and spontaneous conversations.

Teaching Resources
Supplementary teaching support:

Internet Connections
Use the online activities on the McDougal Littell website (www.mcdougallittell.com) and see Internet Project suggestions throughout the Teacher's Edition.

Teaching to Multiple Intelligences
Specialized activities for encouraging success for all students, and professional development essays to expand the methodology of teaching to multiple intelligences in the modern language classroom.

Teacher-to-Teacher (Copymasters)
Classroom-proven games, puzzles, extension activities, technology resource suggestions and teaching tips in an easy-to-use format.

Lesson Plans
Suggestions for lesson planning, including block scheduling options.

Interdisciplinary/Community Connections
Thematically grouped interdisciplinary projects, including suggestions for connecting English/Language Arts, History, Math, Art, Music, Science, Technology, and the community.

Overhead Visual Copymasters
Complete blackline versions of all four-color overhead visuals, plus the new Situational/Conversation overheads. Suggested activities are also included.

Also included:

Answer Key to the Student Text and Communipak, Complete Video Script, Complete Cassette Script, Student Activity Book TAE

Components

AUDIOVISUAL

Integrated Video/Audio Videodisc/Audio

Complete integrated video, one module for each of the 36 lessons of the students text, plus three cultural video essays. Audio cassettes contain pronunciation, listening and speaking activities, and the sound-track of the video.

Also available in the following configurations:

 Videodisc/Audio CD Program

 Video/Audio CD Program

 Cassette Program only

 Audio CD Program only

 Video Program only

 Videodisc Program only

 Overhead Visuals and Copymasters

TECHNOLOGY

DF interactive CD-ROM Parts A, B and C
(Mac and Windows)

The only program to have won 4 national awards for excellence. Contains video, record/compare, journal, and creative dialogues and activities for every lesson of the student text, using the medium to its fullest extent.

Test Bank
(Mac and Windows)

Lesson Quizzes, Unit Tests and Comprehensive Tests (Semester Tests) in an easy-to-use computerized format, including A/B versions. Items may be modified, and new items or complete tests created.

Writing Templates
(Mac and Windows)

Writing Templates keyed to the Student Text provide additional writing practice including pre- and post-writing activities, and process writing skills development.

ASSESSMENT OPTIONS

Testing and Assessment Kit

ACHIEVEMENT TESTS

Lesson Quizzes

Unit Tests

 Portfolio Assessment

PROFICIENCY TESTS

 Listening Comprehension Performance Tests

Speaking Performance Test

Reading Performance Test

 Writing Performance Test

 Test Bank

 Cahier, Exploration

■ The **Table of Contents** provides quick access to the organization and structure of **DISCOVERING FRENCH.**

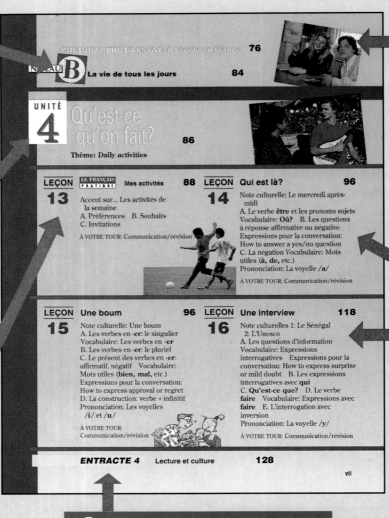

➤ Niveau B

After the introductory section, *Niveau A*, where students learn basic conversational skills, *Niveau B* begins the linguistic foundation for novice proficiency. Students practice real-life interactions and purposeful communication.

➤ Unité 4

Every unit develops a daily-life theme of interest to young people. Language is taught <u>in context,</u> enabling students to communicate with confidence about the theme.

➤ Leçon 13

The first lesson, *Le français pratique,* introduces the unit vocabulary in a meaningful thematic context.

➤ Cultural Photo Essay

À *l'école en France,* also available on video, provides students with direct experience of a French teen's life at home and at school, developing multicultural awareness and interdisciplinary connections.

➤ Leçons 14,15,16

The three *Langue et communication* lessons activate the basic vocabulary and structures in a variety of communicative contexts.

➤ Entracte

Motivating end-of-unit reading and writing extend the unit theme, recycle previously presented material and provide skill and strategy development in a cultural context.

Unit Walkthrough

■ The **Unit Opener** presents the unit theme and learning objectives.

➤ **Unité 4**
Qu'est-ce qu'on fait?

Photos of people and places students will encounter in the video illustrate the unit theme of "daily activities."

UNITÉ 4 Qu'est-ce qu'on fait?

LEÇON	**13**	Le français pratique: Mes activités
LEÇON	**14**	Qui est là?
LEÇON	**15**	Une boum
LEÇON	**16**	Une interview

THÈME ET OBJECTIFS

Daily activities

In this unit, you will be talking about the things you do every day, such as working and studying, as well as watching TV and listening to the radio.

You will learn . . .
- to describe some of your daily activities
- to say what you like and do not like to do
- to ask and answer questions about where others are and what they are doing

You will also learn . . .
- to invite friends to do things with you
- to politely accept or turn down an invitation

87

➤ **Lessons**

There are four thematically-linked lessons in each unit. Vocabulary presented in the first lesson *(Le français pratique)* is then used throughout the next three lessons as structure is taught, reinforcing the unit theme.

➤ **Thème et objectifs**

Students anticipate goals and outcomes in functions that relate to their daily lives. This anticipatory set allows students to see what they will later produce.

■ The **Lesson Opener** provides cultural and linguistic background through text and photos from the video, a visual briefing of the communicative contents of the lesson.

➤ Le français pratique

 This lesson presents the communicative focus and functional language of the lesson. Students immediately get and give information in French.

➤ Les activités de la semaine

VIDEODISC **CD-ROM**

The thematic presentation serves as an anticipatory set, introducing students to the lesson content. The video program provides additional cross-cultural interactions.

LEÇON 13

LE FRANÇAIS PRATIQUE

Mes activités

Accent sur ... Les activités de la semaine

French teenagers, as well as their parents, put a lot of emphasis on doing well in school. On the whole, French students spend a great deal of time on their studies. French schools have a longer class day than American schools, and teachers tend to assign quite a lot of homework.

However, French teenagers do not study all the time. They also watch TV and listen to music. Many participate in various sports activities, but to a lesser extent than young Americans. On weekends, French teenagers like to go out with their friends. Some go shopping. Others go to the movies. Many enjoy dancing and going to parties. Sunday is usually a family day for visiting relatives or going for a drive in the country.

■ **Au cinéma**
Des copains sont au cinéma.

■ **Au café**
Stéphanie est au café.

88 Unité 4

CULTURE

Une boum
Dominique et Stéphanie
sont à une boum.

**Le terrain de foot
au lycée Corot**
Des jeunes jouent au foot.

En classe
Marc et Patrick sont en classe.

➤ **Vocabulary in context**

VIDEODISC
CD-ROM

Photos taken from the video provide the
basis for video-modeled communicative
functions. Students are introduced to the
language patterns of the unit in an
authentic context.

➤ **Extended Teacher's Edition/TRP**

In the **Extended Teacher's Edition**, you'll find
additional photo culture notes, critical thinking
questions, and teaching strategies.

The **Teacher's Resource Package**
provides additional games and activities,
Interdisciplinary and Community Connections, suggestions and activities for
teaching to multiple intelligences, and *Internet Connection Notes*.

■ The ***Vocabulaire et communication*** sections of the *Français pratique* lessons present new conversational patterns by function.

➤ Vocabulary introduced by function

MULTIPLE INTELLIGENCES

New vocabulary and related conversational patterns are introduced in thematic context. All vocabulary is coded in yellow; functions are highlighted with a red triangle and darker yellow band.

➤ Activities to encourage success for all students

MULTIPLE INTELLIGENCES

Student-centered activities practice new vocabulary in contexts ranging from structured to open-ended self-expression. Additional practice is provided in the interactive video and video book, CD-ROM program, audio program, *Activity Book,* and *Communipak.* The Teacher's Edition indicates the focus for each activity (Communication: indicating preferences), and adds additional TPR and pair/group activities.

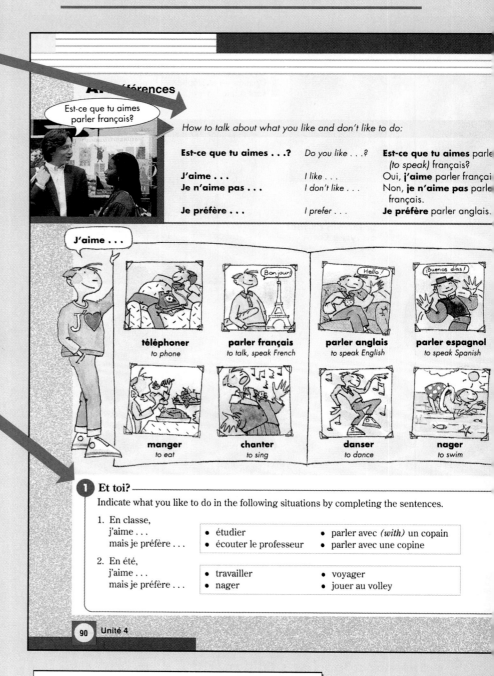

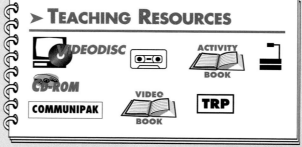

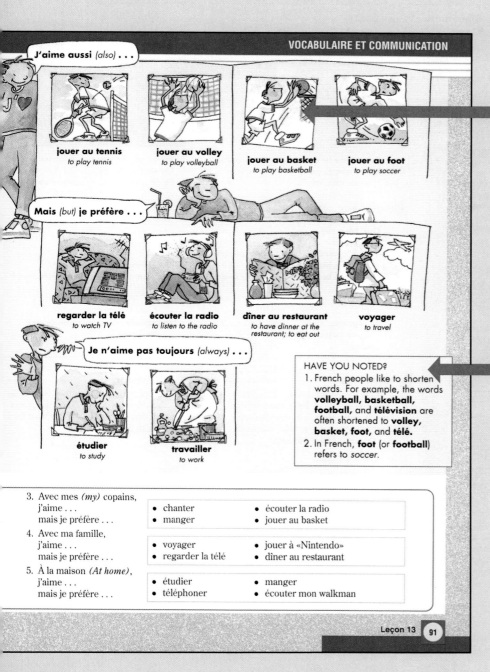

VOCABULAIRE ET COMMUNICATION

J'aime aussi *(also)* . . .

jouer au tennis
to play tennis

jouer au volley
to play volleyball

jouer au basket
to play basketball

jouer au foot
to play soccer

Mais *(but)* **je préfère** . . .

regarder la télé
to watch TV

écouter la radio
to listen to the radio

dîner au restaurant
to have dinner at the restaurant; to eat out

voyager
to travel

Je n'aime pas toujours *(always)* . . .

étudier
to study

travailler
to work

> **HAVE YOU NOTED?**
> 1. French people like to shorten words. For example, the words **volleyball, basketball, football,** and **télévision** are often shortened to **volley, basket, foot,** and **télé.**
> 2. In French, **foot** (or **football**) refers to *soccer.*

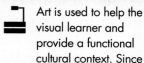

➤ Art-cued vocabulary

MULTIPLE INTELLIGENCES

Art is used to help the visual learner and provide a functional cultural context. Since the artists used in *DISCOVERING FRENCH* are actually French, students are exposed to authentic cultural detail in every drawing. All visuals are also available on overhead transparencies.

➤ Have you noted?

Additional language usage of interest to students is included in special notes throughout *DISCOVERING FRENCH.*

---

3. Avec mes *(my)* copains,
   j'aime . . .
   mais je préfère . . .

   - chanter
   - manger
   - écouter la radio
   - jouer au basket

4. Avec ma famille,
   j'aime . . .
   mais je préfère . . .

   - voyager
   - regarder la télé
   - jouer à «Nintendo»
   - dîner au restaurant

5. À la maison *(At home)*,
   j'aime . . .
   mais je préfère . . .

   - étudier
   - téléphoner
   - manger
   - écouter mon walkman

Leçon 13 **91**

■ Each *Français pratique* lesson moves through functional introduction of language practice activities, and culminates in the *À votre tour* review section.

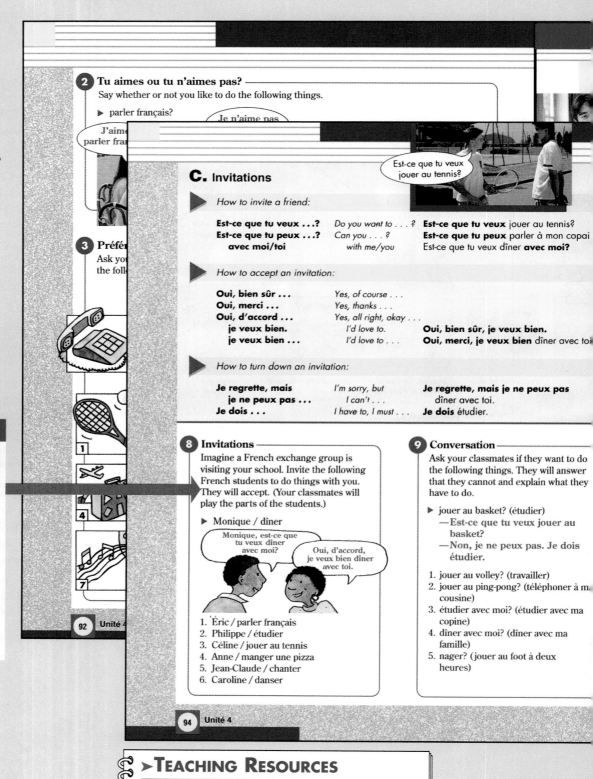

2 Tu aimes ou tu n'aimes pas?
Say whether or not you like to do the following things.

▶ parler français?

Je n'aime pas

J'aime
parler fra...

3 Préfér...
Ask you
the foll...

C. Invitations

Est-ce que tu veux
jouer au tennis?

How to invite a friend:

Est-ce que tu veux ...?   *Do you want to ... ?*   **Est-ce que tu veux** jouer au tennis?
Est-ce que tu peux ...?   *Can you ... ?*   **Est-ce que tu peux** parler à mon copai...
  avec moi/toi   *with me/you*   Est-ce que tu veux dîner **avec moi?**

How to accept an invitation:

Oui, bien sûr ...   *Yes, of course ...*
Oui, merci ...   *Yes, thanks ...*
Oui, d'accord ...   *Yes, all right, okay ...*
  je veux bien.   *I'd love to.*   **Oui, bien sûr, je veux bien.**
  je veux bien ...   *I'd love to ...*   **Oui, merci, je veux bien** dîner avec toi

How to turn down an invitation:

Je regrette, mais   *I'm sorry, but*   **Je regrette, mais je ne peux pas**
  je ne peux pas ...   *I can't ...*   dîner avec toi.
Je dois ...   *I have to, I must ...*   **Je dois** étudier.

8 Invitations
Imagine a French exchange group is visiting your school. Invite the following French students to do things with you. They will accept. (Your classmates will play the parts of the students.)

▶ Monique / dîner

Monique, est-ce que
tu veux dîner
avec moi?

Oui, d'accord,
je veux bien dîner
avec toi.

1. Éric / parler français
2. Philippe / étudier
3. Céline / jouer au tennis
4. Anne / manger une pizza
5. Jean-Claude / chanter
6. Caroline / danser

9 Conversation
Ask your classmates if they want to do the following things. They will answer that they cannot and explain what they have to do.

▶ jouer au basket? (étudier)
  —Est-ce que tu veux jouer au basket?
  —Non, je ne peux pas. Je dois étudier.

1. jouer au volley? (travailler)
2. jouer au ping-pong? (téléphoner à m... cousine)
3. étudier avec moi? (étudier avec ma copine)
4. dîner avec moi? (dîner avec ma famille)
5. nager? (jouer au foot à deux heures)

92   Unité 4

94   Unité 4

> **TEACHING RESOURCES**

VIDEODISC   **ACTIVITY BOOK**   **COMMUNIPAK**

CD-ROM

...hes)

How to talk about what you want, would like, and do not want to do:

COMMUNICATION ET RÉVISION

À votre tour!

1 Créa-dialogue

Ask your classmates if they want to do the following things with you. They will answer that they cannot and will give one of the excuses in the box.

> Est-ce que tu veux jouer au tennis avec moi?
>
> Non, je ne peux pas. Je dois travailler.

> ▶ jouer au tennis

1. jouer au basket
2. manger une pizza
3. regarder la télé
4. jouer au ping-pong
5. dîner au restaurant

Excuses:

étudier	dîner avec ma cousine
travailler	parler avec ma mère
téléphoner à une copine	chanter avec la chorale *(choir)*

2 Conversation dirigée

Philippe is phoning Stéphanie. Write out their conversation according to the directions. You may want to act out the dialogue with a classmate.

Philippe

			Stéphanie
asks Stéphanie how she is	➚	answers that she is fine	
asks her if she wants to eat out	➚	asks at what time	
says at 8 o'clock	➚	says that she is sorry but that she has to study	
says it is too bad (**Dommage!**)			

3 Expression personnelle

What we like to do often depends on the circumstances. Complete the sentences below saying what you like and don't like to do in the following situations.

▶ En hiver . . .
En hiver, j'aime regarder la télé. J'aime aussi jouer au basket. Je n'aime pas nager.

1. En été . . .
2. En automne . . .
3. Le samedi *(On Saturdays)* . . .
4. Le dimanche . . .
5. Le soir *(In the evening)* . . .
6. En classe . . .
7. Avec mes *(my)* amis . . .
8. Avec ma famille . . .

4 Composition

Write three things that you like to do and three things that you do not like to do.

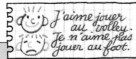

▶

> J'aime jouer au volley.
> Je n'aime pas jouer au foot.

5 Correspondance

This summer, you are going to spend two weeks in France. Your pen pal Philippe has written, asking what you like and don't like to do on vacation (**en vacances**). Write a postcard answering his questions.

▶

> Cher Philippe,
> En vacances,
> j'aime . . .
>
> PHILIPPE RAYMOND
> 12 AV. VICTOR HUGO
> PARIS 75116
> FRANCE

➤ Cyclical Re-entry and Review: À votre tour

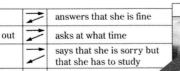

À votre tour activities recombine material from each lesson as well as previous units. These open-ended activities allow students to demonstrate what they can <u>do</u> with language and monitor their own progress through critical thinking and self-expression.

➤ Writing Portfolio

The writing activities encourage students to express their own thoughts and ideas and may be included in students' written Portfolio.

➤ Assessment Options

A wide variety of Assessment Options is available for monitoring and encouraging student progress.

TEST	Lesson Quizzes
	Unit Tests

PROFICIENCY TEST

	Listening Comprehension Performance Tests
	Speaking Performance Test
	Reading Performance Test
	Writing Performance Test
	Portfolio Assessment
CD-ROM	Cahier, Exploration
	Test Bank

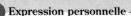

LEÇON 14 — Qui est là?

It is Wednesday afternoon. Pierre is looking for his friends

■ NOTE CULTURELLE

PIERRE: Où est Jacq
HÉLÈNE: Elle est à la
PIERRE: Et Jean-Clau
HÉLÈNE: Non, il n'est
PIERRE: Où est-il?
HÉLÈNE: Il est en ville
PIERRE: Et Nicole et
HÉLÈNE: Non, elles s
PIERRE: Alors, qui es
HÉLÈNE: Moi, je suis i
PIERRE: C'est vrai, tu
 je t'invite au
HÉLÈNE: Super! Pierr

● **Compréhension**—
Indicate where the fol

1. Jacqueline est . . .
2. Jean-Claude est . . .
3. Nicole et Sandrine
4. Hélène et Pierre s

96 Unité 4

LEÇON 15 — Une boum

Jean-Marc has been invited to a party. He is trying to

■ NO
CULTU

Une bou

JEAN-MARC: Dis, Bé
BÉATRICE: Bien sû
JEAN-MARC: Est-ce
BÉATRICE: Oui, je
JEAN-MARC: Et ta c
BÉATRICE: Non, el
JEAN-MARC: Alors,
BÉATRICE: Mais p
JEAN-MARC: Écoute
 je préfè
 C'est n

● **Compréhension:**
Read the following st
false (**C'est faux!**).

1. Béatrice aime dans
2. Elle danse bien.
e danse t

LEÇON 16 — Une interview

Nicolas is a reporter for *La Gazette des Étudiants*, the student newspaper. He has decided to write an article on the foreign students who attend his school. Today he is interviewing Fatou, a student from Senegal.

NICOLAS:	Bonjour, Fatou. Est-ce que je peux <u>te poser quelques questions</u>?	*ask you some questions*
FATOU:	Oui, bien sûr.	
NICOLAS:	Tu es <u>sénégalaise</u>, n'est-ce pas?	*Senegalese*
FATOU:	Oui, je suis sénégalaise.	
NICOLAS:	Où est-ce que tu habites?	
FATOU:	Je suis de Dakar, mais maintenant j'habite à Paris avec ma famille.	
NICOLAS:	<u>Pourquoi</u> est-ce que vous habitez à Paris?	*Why*
FATOU:	<u>Parce que</u> ma mère travaille pour l'Unesco.	*Because*
NICOLAS:	Est-ce que tu aimes Paris?	
FATOU:	J'adore Paris.	
NICOLAS:	<u>Qu'est-ce que tu fais le weekend</u>?	*What do you do on weekends*
FATOU:	Ça dépend! Je regarde la télé ou je joue au tennis avec <u>mes</u> copains.	*That* *my*
NICOLAS:	Merci beaucoup, Fatou.	
FATOU:	C'est <u>tout</u>?	*all*
NICOLAS:	Oui, c'est tout!	

■ **NOTES CULTURELLES**

1 Le Sénégal

Senegal is a country in western Africa, whose capital is Dakar. Its population includes twelve different tribes, all speaking their own dialects. Because of the historical and cultural ties between Senegal and France, French has been adopted as the official language.

Most of the people of Senegal are Muslims. Some common names are **Awa** and **Fatou** (for girls), **Babacar** and **Mamadou** (for boys).

118 Unité 4

➤ **Notes culturelles**

The illustrated cultural notes, coded in blue throughout the program, expand on the cultural content of the lesson opener. Further cultural expansion is also available on video, correlated at point-of-use in the Teacher's Edition (16.5 *Vignette culturelle: Le Sénégal*).

■ *Langue et communication* lesson openers present reading and culture as they re-cycle the communicative functions of the *Français pratique* vocabulary and provide grammar support and explanation.

LECTURE ET CULTURE

FATOU:	Bon. <u>Alors</u>, maintenant c'est mon <u>tour</u>!	*So / turn*
	Est-ce que je peux te poser une question?	
NICOLAS:	Bien sûr!	
FATOU:	Qu'est-ce que tu fais samedi?	
NICOLAS:	Euh . . . <u>je ne sais pas</u>.	*I don't know*
FATOU:	Alors, est-ce que tu veux <u>aller</u> à un concert	*to go*
	de musique africaine?	
NICOLAS:	Avec qui?	
FATOU:	Avec moi, bien sûr!	
NICOLAS:	D'accord! Où? <u>Quand</u>? Et à quelle heure?	*When*

2 L'Unesco

UNESCO (United Nations Educational Scientific and Cultural Organization) was founded in 1946 to promote international cooperation in education, science, and the arts. The organization has its headquarters in Paris and is staffed by people from all member countries.

Compréhension: Vrai ou faux?
Read the following statements and say whether they are true (**C'est vrai!**) or false (**C'est faux!**).

1. Fatou est française.
2. Elle habite à Paris.
3. Le père de Fatou travaille pour l'Unesco.
4. Le weekend, Fatou aime jouer au tennis.
5. Nicolas invite Fatou à un concert.
6. Fatou accepte l'invitation.

Leçon 16 119

> ➤ **Anticipatory Set:**
> **Lesson opener/video dialog**

VIDEODISC

CD-ROM

MULTIPLE INTELLIGENCES

The opening reading and/or video dialog provides an anticipatory set for the communicative functions and presentation of linguistic structures. You may vary your presentation of the new language according to the needs of your students, addressing a variety of learning styles.

> ➤ **Comprehension checks**

VIDEODISC

CD-ROM

Students can self-check their comprehension (both reading and listening) as receptive skills are developed.

A. Les questions d'information

The questions below ask for specific information and are called INFORMATION QUESTIONS. The INTERROGATIVE EXPRESSIONS in heavy print indicate what kind of information is requested.

—**Où** est-ce que tu habites?   *Where do you live?*
—J'habite **à Nice**.   *I live in Nice.*

—**À quelle heure** est-ce que vous dînez?   *At what time do you eat dinner?*
—Nous dînons **à sept heures**.   *We eat at seven.*

In French, information questions may be formed according to the pattern:

INTERROGATIVE EXPRESSION + **est-ce que** + SUBJECT + VERB . . . ?
À quelle heure   **est-ce que**   vous   trav... ?

→ **Est-ce que** becomes **est-ce qu'** before a vowel sound.
    Quand **est-ce qu'**Alice et Roger dînent?

→ In information questions, your voice rises on the interrog... the last syllable.

Quand est-ce que tu travailles?   À quelle heure ...

OBSERVATION: In casual conversation, French speakers frequ... placing the interrogative expression at the end of the sentenc... expression.

Vous habitez **où**?   Vous dînez **à qu**...

Vocabulaire: Expressions interrogatives		
où	*where?*	**Où** est-ce que vou...
quand?	*when?*	**Quand** est-ce que...
à quelle heure?	*at what time?*	**À quelle heure** e...
comment?	*how?*	**Comment** est-ce ...
pourquoi?	*why?*	—**Pourquoi** est-c...
parce que	*because*	—**Parce que** je v...

→ **Parce que** becomes **parce qu'** before a vowel sound.
    Juliette invite Olivier **parce qu'**il danse bien.

---

1 **Le Club International**

The president of the International Club wants to know where some of the members are from. The secretary tells her where each one lives.

▶ Sylvie (à Québec)
    LA PRÉSIDENTE: Où est-ce que Sylvie habite?
    LE SECRÉTAIRE: Elle habite à Québec.

1. Jacques (à Montréal)
2. Awa (à Dakar)
3. Marc et Frédéric (à Toulouse)
4. Jean-Pierre (à Genève)

B. Les expressions interrogatives avec *qui*

To ask about PEOPLE, French speakers use the following interrogative expressions:

qui?	*who(m)?*	**Qui** est-ce que tu invites au concert?
à qui?	*to who(m)?*	**À qui** est-ce que tu téléphones?
de qui?	*about who(m)?*	**De qui** est-ce que vous parlez?
avec qui?	*with who(m)?*	**Avec qui** est-ce que Pierre étudie?
pour qui?	*for who(m)?*	**Pour qui** est-ce que Laure organise la boum?

To ask *who is doing something*, French speakers use the construction:

qui + VERB . . . ?	
Qui habite ici?	*Who lives here?*
Qui organise la boum?	*Who is organizing the party?*

5 **Précisions** *(Details)*

Anne is telling Hélène what certain people are doing. She asks for more details. Play both roles.

▶ Alice dîne. (avec qui? avec une copine)

1. Jean-Pierre téléphone. (à qui? à Sylvie)
2. Frédéric étudie. (avec qui? avec un copain)
3. Madame Masson parle. (à qui? à Madame Bonnot)
4. Monsieur Lambert travaille. (avec qui? avec Monsieur Dumont)
5. Juliette danse. (avec qui? avec Georges)
6. François parle à Michèle. (de qui? de toi)

Alice dîne.
Elle dîne avec une copine.
Ah bon? Avec qui est-ce qu'elle dîne?

6 **Un sondage** *(A poll)*

Take a survey to find out how your classmates spend their free time. Ask who does the following things.

▶ écouter la radio
    Qui écoute la radio?

1. voyager souvent
2. aimer chanter
3. nager
4. aimer danser
5. regarder la télé
6. jouer au tennis
7. jouer au foot
8. travailler
9. regarder les clips *(music videos)*
10. parler italien
11. étudier beaucoup
12. visiter souvent New York

■ ***Langue et communication*** pages present grammatical structures in a variety of formats appropriate to varied learning styles, including model sentences, visual representations, cartoons, summary boxes, and charts.

E ET COMMUNICATION

colas meets
tudent. He wants
er. Play both roles.

ébec)
ce que tu habites?
à Québec.

ntréal)
s [*in*] une

ais? (toujours)
ais? (souvent)
tennis? (bien)

LANGUE ET COMMUN...

Questions

Prepare ... es with your classmates, using the information in the illustrations.

où?

▶ —Où est-ce que tu dînes?
—Je dîne à la maison.

 à la maison

 2. quand? — **en septembre**

 **3. comment?** BONJOUR! — **très bien**

4. avec qui? — **avec Denise**

 **1. à quelle heure?** — **à 8 heures**

 5. à qui? — **à mon cousin**

 6. de qui? BLA BLA BLA... — **de toi**

 **7. pour qui?** — **pour M. Lambert**

C. *Qu'est-ce que?*

Note the use of the interrogative expression **qu'est-ce que** *(what)* in the questions below.

Qu'est-ce que tu regardes?	Je regarde un match de tennis.
Qu'est-ce qu'Alice mange?	Elle mange une pizza.

To ask *what people are doing*, the French use the following construction:

qu'est-ce que + SUBJECT + VERB + . . . ?	**Qu'est-ce que** tu fais?
qu'est-ce qu' (+ VOWEL SOUND)	**Qu'est-ce qu'**elle fait?

La Boutique-Musique

People in Column A are at the Boutique-Musique, a local music shop. Use a verb from Column B to ask what they are listening to or looking at. A classmate will answer you, using an item from Column C.

A	B	C
tu	écouter?	une guitare
vous	regarder?	un poster
Alice		un compact (CD) de jazz
Éric		une cassette de rock
Antoine et Claire		un album de Paul Simon

Qu'est-ce qu'Éric écoute?

Il écoute un album de Paul Simon.

Leçon 16 **123**

➤ Presentations for all learning styles

MULTIPLE INTELLIGENCES

After students have become comfortable with material in context, formal charts help them analyze forms and structure.

➤ Vocabulary at Point of Use

Supplementary vocabulary, coded in yellow, offers students communicative functions for immediate implementation in dialogs. Inductive discovery teaching suggestions are provided in the Teacher's Edition.

D. Le verbe *faire*

Faire *(to do, make)* is one of the most useful French verbs. It is an IRREGULAR verb since it does no follow a predictable pattern. Note the forms of **faire** in the present tense.

faire *(to do, make)*	
je **fais**	Je **fais** un sandwich.
tu **fais**	Qu'est-ce que tu **fais** maintenant?
il/elle **fait**	Qu'est-ce que ton copain **fait** samedi?
nous **faisons**	Nous **faisons** une pizza.
vous **faites**	Qu'est-ce que vous **faites** ici?
ils/elles **font**	Qu'est-ce qu'elles **font** pour la boum?

Vocabulaire: Expressions avec *faire*

faire un match	to play a game (match)	Mes cousins **font un match** de tennis.
faire une promenade	to go for a walk	Caroline **fait une promenade** avec Olivier
faire un voyage	to take a trip	Ma copine **fait un voyage** en France.
faire attention	to pay attention	Est-ce que tu **fais attention** quand le professeur parle?

9 La boum de Juliette

Juliette's friends are helping her prepare food for a party. Use the verb **faire** to say what everyone is doing.

▶ Je . . . une crêpe.

Je fais une crêpe.

1. Nous . . . une salade.
2. Tu . . . une salade de fruits.
3. Vous . . . une tarte *(pie)*.
4. Cécile et Marina . . . un gâteau *(cake)*.
5. Christine . . . une pizza.
6. Marc . . . un sandwich.
7. Patrick et Thomas . . . une omelette.
8. Pierre et Karine . . . une quiche.

10 Qu'est-ce qu'ils font?

Read the descriptions below and say what the people are doing. Use the verb **faire** and an expression from the list below. Be logical.

un voyage   une promenade   une pizza   un match   attent*

▶ Madame Dumont est en Chine.
  Elle fait un voyage.

1. Nicolas travaille dans *(in)* un restaurant.
2. Nous sommes en ville.
3. Hélène et Jean-Paul jouent au tennis.
4. Je suis dans la cuisine *(kitchen)*.
5. Marc est dans le train Paris–Nice.
6. Vous jouez au volley.
7. Je suis dans le parc.
8. Monsieur Lambert visite Tokyo.
9. Nous écoutons le prof.

124 Unité 4

➤ **Learning About Language**

Special notes to students focus on strategies for authentic language production, explain terminology, and help students understand how language functions.

LANGUE ET COMMUNICATION

E. L'interrogation avec inversion

> ### Learning about language
>
> In conversational French, questions are usually formed with **est-ce que.** However, when the subject of the sentence is a pronoun, French speakers often use INVERSION, that is, they invert or reverse the order of the subject pronoun and the verb.
>
> REGULAR ORDER: **Vous parlez** français. INVERSION: **Parlez-vous** anglais?
> SUBJECT   VERB   VERB   SUBJECT

Look at the two sets of questions below. They both ask the same thing. Compare the position of the subject pronouns in heavy print.

Est-ce que **tu** parles anglais?	Parles-**tu** anglais?	*Do you speak English?*
Est-ce que **vous** habitez ici?	Habitez-**vous** ici?	*Do you live here?*
Où est-ce que **nous** dînons?	Où dînons-**nous?**	*Where are we having dinner?*
Où est-ce qu'**il** est?	Où est-**il?**	*Where is he?*

Inverted questions are formed according to the patterns:

YES / NO	VERB / SUBJECT PRONOUN . . . ?	
QUESTION	**Voyagez-vous**	souvent?

INFORMATION	INTERROGATIVE EXPRESSION + VERB / SUBJECT PRONOUN . . . ?	
QUESTION	**Avec qui travaillez-vous**	demain?

→ In inversion, the verb and the subject pronoun are connected by a hyphen.

OBSERVATION: In inversion, liaison is required before **il/elle** and **ils/elles.** If a verb in the singular ends on a vowel, the letter "**t**" is inserted between the verb and the subject pronoun so that liaison can occur:

Où travaille-t-il?	Où travaille-t-elle?
Avec qui dîne-t-il?	Avec qui dîne-t-elle?

Conversation
Get better acquainted with your class-mates by asking them a few questions. Use inversion.

▶ où / habiter? —Où habites-tu?
          —J'habite à (Boston).

1. à quelle heure / dîner?
2. à quelle heure / regarder la télé?
3. avec qui / parler français?
4. à qui / téléphoner souvent?
5. comment / nager?
6. avec qui / étudier?

▶ ▶

Prononciation   /y/

La voyelle /y/

Super!

The vowel sound /y/ – represented by the letter "**u**" – does not exist in English. Here is a helpful trick for producing this new sound.

First say the French word **si.** Then round your lips as if to whistle and say **si** with rounded lips: /sy/. Now say **si-per.** Then round your lips as you say the first syllable: **super!**

Répétez: /y/   **super   tu   étudie   bien sûr**
                Lucie   Luc
                Tu étudies avec Lucie.

➤ **Pronunciation**

Students practice in single "key" words and then in context. All pronunciation sections, coded in purple, are available in the audio program as well as on CD-ROM.

➤ What have students learned?

Culminating the lesson, the *À votre tour* activities provide opportunities for self/peer assessment of learning objectives in a variety of contextualized formats.

➤ Cooperative Practice

  Ideal for expanding students' use of language beyond the classroom setting, and communicating with others about daily life circumstances.

▶ Créa-dialogue

The *Créa-dialogue* format provides models to guide but not limit students' creative language use. Recombination and re-entry of previously learned material provides students with opportunities to demonstrate how well they can communicate in French.

COMMUNICA...

Créa-dialogue

Ask your classmates what they do on different days of the week. Carry out conversations similar to the model. Note: "??" means you can invent your own answers.

▶ ——Qu'est-ce que tu fais <u>lundi</u>?
——Je <u>joue au tennis</u>.
——Ah bon? À quelle heure est-ce que tu <u>joues</u>?
——<u>À deux heures</u>.
——Et avec qui?
——Avec <u>Anne-Marie</u>.

▶	lundi	mardi	mercredi	jeudi	vendredi	samedi	dimanche
TIVITÉ						??	??
QUELLE HEURE?	2 heures	6 heures	??	??	??	??	??
EC QUI?	avec Anne-Marie	avec un copain	??	??	??	??	??

▶ Written Self-expression

Students express thoughts and ideas in written form, providing material for their portfolios, and discovering how their knowledge of French has increased.

Faisons connaissance!
(Let's get acquainted!)

Get better acquainted with a classmate that you don't know very well. Ask questions in French. For instance:

- Where does he/she live?
- Does he/she study much at home?
- Does he/she speak French at home? (with whom?)
- Does he/she watch TV? (at what time?)
- Does he/she like to phone? (whom? [**à qui?**])

5 Interview

A famous rock star is visiting the United States. You are going to interview her for your school paper (perhaps even on the Internet!). Write out five questions you would want to ask the singer, addressing her as **vous**. For example, you may want to know . . .

- where she is singing
- why she is visiting your city
- how she is traveling
- how (well) she speaks English

Curiosité

Imagine that a French friend has just made the following statements. For each one, write down three or four related questions you could ask him or her.

Je joue au tennis.

Je dîne avec un copain.

oue au foot emain.

• Avec qui est-ce que tu joues?
• Où est-ce que vous jouez?
• À quelle heure est-ce que vous jouez?
• Pourquoi est-ce que vous jouez au foot?

Je fais une promenade.

J'organise une boum.

Leçon 16 **127**

▶ Assessment Options

The variety of assessment options provides opportunity for success for all students and all learning styles.

TEST Lesson Quizzes

Unit Tests

PROFICIENCY TEST

Listening Comprehension Performance Tests

Speaking Performance Test

Reading Performance Test

Writing Performance Test

Portfolio Assessment

CD-ROM Cahier, Exploration

Test Bank

■ The ***Entracte*** reading section, at the end of every unit, develops reading skills, cultural awareness, and vocabulary expansion in context.

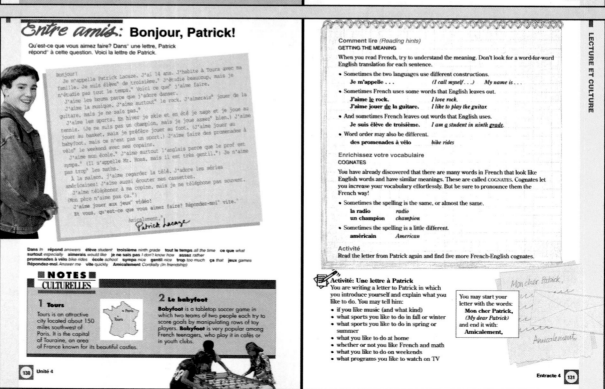

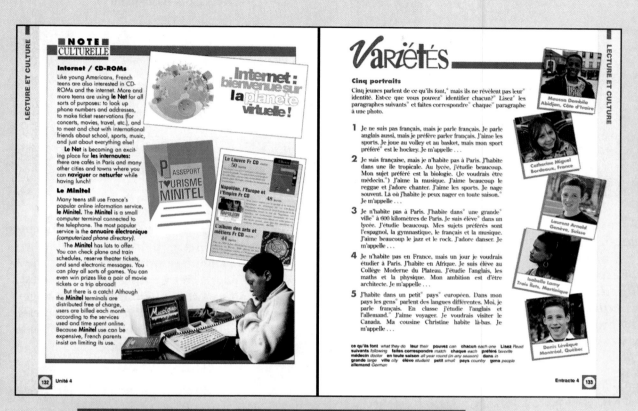

➤ Entracte: Development of Reading Skills

- Pre- and post-reading strategies and skill-building activities
- Reading comprehension hints
- Vocabulary enrichment techniques
- Advance organizers
- Authentic documents, letters, interviews, and surveys to encourage critical thinking and build rapid reading and information gathering skills
- Reading for pleasure and deriving meaning by word association build critical thinking skills

Here's what teachers using DISCOVERING FRENCH are saying . . .

"The best materials I have seen for multicultural instruction!"
—A. Burns, St. Thomas, V.I.

"...my teaching and my students' proficiency in French have been totally revitalized."
—F. Amo, Marquette, MI

"Discovering French allows my students to use French in real-life situations that are important to them. Discovering French gives them confidence to create dialogs using new expressions and vocabulary. They have a positive outlook on learning and speaking French."
—A. Morales, San Marcos, CA

"My students have become revitalized by your exciting new program. They instantly commented on the clarity of presentation. I am particularly thrilled with summary work presented in the À votre tour pages. It's exciting to have students work with one another, then proudly and eagerly present what they have created in these exercises... I'm so glad that there is a text like this available."
—V. Sachs, Morgan Hill, CA

"I love the...teaching techniques and suggestions throughout the series. Thanks for the help!"
—D. Wallace, Clover, SC

"My students are interacting with each other in French. They're having a good time communicating and their parents tell me they hear their children using French at home and on the phone! I love the total program and all the help for the teacher."
—F. Meyland, Clarkston, MI

Discovering French Teacher Network

If you would like to talk to a current **Discovering French** teacher, or become a member yourself, write to: **World Languages Product Manager**, McDougal Littell, 1560 Sherman Avenue, Evanston, IL 60201 or e-mail: Lori_Diaz@hmco.com.

World Connections Newsletter

As a **Discovering French** teacher, you are eligible to receive, free of charge, copies of our newsletter. The newsletter includes information articles on current pedagogical trends, new program features, teaching tips, and more. Sign up by writing to the address listed above.

"After 28 years of teaching, this is the first program I've used that is really complete, that has everything at hand, that doesn't require hours of preparing 'fun' and diverse activities or hours of test preparation. My students are enthusiastic and, even in level one, I'm so impressed with their confidence and willingness to speak French."
—P. Price, Sioux City IA

DISCOVERING FRENCH-BLEU

Guide to Teaching with
DISCOVERING FRENCH-*BLEU*

Special Features of
DISCOVERING FRENCH-*BLEU*

Articulation with DISCOVERING FRENCH

Discovering French is a carefully articulated three-level sequence of French instruction. Each level has its own special focus:

BLEU	Rudimentary communication with learned phrases Simple questions and answers: present tense Introduction to past narration	Level A (1-3) Level B (4-7) Level C (8-9)
BLANC	Creative conversation: asking and answering questions Basic narration in the past, using imperfect and passé composé Description and expression of simple comparisons Basic narration in the future Expression of simple conditions and wishes	Units 1-5 Unit 6 Unit 7 Unit 8 Units 8-9
ROUGE	Extended conversations: all tenses Past and future narration using complex sentences Expression of conditions in complex sentences Expression of emotions, wishes and hypotheses in complex sentences	Units 1, 4, 6, 10 Units 1, 3, 8 Units 5, 8 Units 2, 7, 9

The articulation of basic communication themes and topics is shown in the chart below. (Only the major entry and reentry points are shown. These themes and topics are recycled throughout the program in the various exercises, readings and communication activities.)

THEMES AND TOPICS	BLEU	BLANC	ROUGE
Greeting and meeting people	Niveau A: Unit 1	Reprise: Rappel 1	—
Time and weather	Niveau A: Unit 3	Reprise: Rappel 1	Unit 3
Family and friends; Family relationships	Niveau A: Unit 2	Unit 1	Reprise A; Unit 9
Food and restaurants	Niveau A: Unit 3 Niveau C: Unit 9	Units 1, 3	Reprise A
Money and shopping	Niveau A, Unit 3	Reprise: Rappel 2	Reprise B; Unit 4
School and education	Niveau A: À l'école	Reprise: Faisons Connaissance	Unit 10
Daily activities	Niveau B, Unit 4	Reprise: Rappel 3	Reprise A
Getting around the city	Niveau B: Unit 4 Niveau B: Unit 6	Unit 2	Unit 8
Describing oneself	Niveau B: Unit 5	Units 1, 7	Unit 1
Home and furnishings	Niveau B: Unit 5 Niveau B: Unit 6	Unit 6	Unit 6
Possessions and their description	Niveau B: Unit 5	Reprise: Rappel 2 Unit 2	Reprise A; Unit 2
Sports, fitness, daily routine	Niveau B: Unit 6	Units 5, 8	Unit 1
Medical and dental care	—	Unit 5	Unit 7
Clothing and personal appearance	Niveau B: Unit 7	Unit 7	Reprise A; Unit 4
Leisure activities, music, entertainment	Niveau C: Unit 8	Unit 4	Interlude 4
Vacation and travel	Niveau C: Unit 8	Unit 8	Reprise B; Unit 3
Transportation	Niveau C: Unit 8	Units 8, 9	Unit 5
Jobs and professions	—	Unit 1	Units 2, 10
Helping around the house	—	Unit 2	Unit 2
Nature and the environment	—	Unit 2	Unit 3
Services and repairs	—	—	Unit 4
Hotel accommodations	—	—	Unit 6

DISCOVERING FRENCH

FUNCTION	**F** BLEU	**F** BLANC	**F** ROUGE
Greeting people and socializing	Niveau A: Units 1, 2, 3	Reprise: Rappel 1	—
Talking about the present Asking and answering questions Describing people, places and things Describing future plans (Simple description)	Niveau B: Units 4, 5, 6, 7	Reprise: Rappels 2, 3; Unit 1	Reprise A
Narrating past events (Simple narration)	Niveau C: Unit 8	Unit 2	Reprise B
Discussing daily routines (Simple narration)	—	Unit 5	Unit 1
Describing people, places, things (Extended description)	Niveau C: Unit 9	Units 3, 4, 5	Reprise C Units 2, 4
Describing past conditions and narrating past events (Extended narration)	—	Unit 6	Reprise B Units 3, 7
Comparing and discussing people, things and actions (Complex description)	—	Unit 7	Units 6, 9
Discussing future events (Extended narration)	—	Unit 8	Unit 5, 8
Discussing hypothetical conditions and events (Complex discussion)	—	Unit 8	Units 5, 8
Expressing wishes and obligations (Direct statements)	—	Unit 9	Unit 2
Expressing doubts and emotions (Complex discussion)	—	—	Unit 7
Expressing cause and purpose (Complex discussion)	—	—	Unit 10

Organization of DISCOVERING FRENCH-BLEU

Basic Structure

The Student Text contains nine units and three illustrated photo essays which are grouped in three levels or *niveaux*.

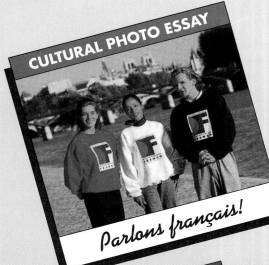

CULTURAL PHOTO ESSAY

Parlons français!

CULTURAL PHOTO ESSAY

À l'école en France

CULTURAL PHOTO ESSAY

À Paris

Cultural Photo Essay: *Parlons français!*

NIVEAU A Faisons connaissance!

Unité 1 Bonjour!

Unité 2 Les copains et la famille

Unité 3 Bon appétit!

Cultural Photo Essay: *À l'école en France*

NIVEAU B La vie de tous les jours

Unité 4 Qu'est-ce qu'on fait?

Unité 5 Le monde personnel et familier

Unité 6 En ville

Cultural Photo Essay: *À Paris*

Unité 7 Le shopping

NIVEAU C Le monde des jeunes

Unité 8 Le temps libre

Unité 9 Les repas

DISCOVERING FRENCH

INTRODUCTION

Niveau A begins the program immediately by introducing basic conversational skills without any formal presentation of structure.

Topics covered:

- greeting people
- introducing oneself
- talking about friends and family
- ordering in a café

Also:

- numbers 0–1,000
- telling time
- days of the week
- months and dates
- weather and seasons

CORE MATERIAL

Niveau B provides the linguistic base needed for basic communication skills. Emphasis is on asking and answering questions. (Students should complete these units.)

Topics covered:

- discussing daily activities and leisure pastimes
- talking about people and possessions
- getting around town
- describing where one lives
- shopping for clothes

FURTHER DEVELOPMENT

Niveau C introduces somewhat more complex language functions. (Although it is desirable to present these units, it is not critical to finish them since the material is reviewed and expanded in the first part of *Discovering French–Blanc.*)

Topics covered:

- describing weekend activities
- talking about vacation plans
- planning meals
- shopping for food

Focus on:

NIVEAU A Faisons connaissance!

A special feature of **DISCOVERING FRENCH**, Niveau A builds student confidence and paves the way for a successful French learning experience. It introduces students to a new cultural world, gets students speaking with confidence, and offers success for <u>all</u> students.

■ NIVEAU A gets students speaking French with confidence

The main focus in **Niveau A** is getting students to feel at ease with the sounds, rhythms and patterns of spoken French.

For American students, learning French presents a special challenge:
• On paper, French can look very similar to English:
  Roger visite Paris.
  Elisabeth préfère la musique classique.
• But spoken French is very different from English. And, for Americans, it certainly does not seem to sound the way it is written.

Learning French, unlike learning Spanish or German, means getting the sound and the rhythm and the melody of French into your head. Only when students feel comfortable with sounds and intonation patterns, are they ready to begin studying the language in a more formal way.

In **Niveau A**, students learn to carry out short conversations in French using basic phrases and expressions.

By the end of the first twelve lessons, students can…
• **greet people and introduce themselves and even spell out their names**
• **count, tell time, give the date, and describe the weather**
• **order something to eat or drink in a café or fast food restaurant**
• **find out people's names, ages, and where they are from**
• **find out what something costs**
• **pay in euro currency**

DISCOVERING FRENCH

■ NIVEAU A invites students to explore a new cultural world.

In **Niveau A** students discover that the study of French opens the doors to an exciting multi-ethnic, multi-cultural world. At the same time, they find out about some basic similarities and differences between French and American daily life patterns.

■ NIVEAU A introduces students to how French works.

While learning to talk to one another on everyday topics, students become familiar with two key features of the French language:

— the concept of gender and agreement of articles (*un garçon - une fille*)
— the concept of subject-verb agreement (*je suis - tu es*)

le garçon, la fille

The French equivalent of *the* has two basic forms: **le** and **la**.

	MASCULINE		FEMININE
	le garçon *the boy* **le** copain *the friend*		**la** fille *the girl* **la** copine *the friend*

NOTE: Both **le** and **la** become **l'** before a vowel sound.

un copain → le copain   une copine → la copine
un ami   → l'ami   une amie   → l'amie

■ NIVEAU A offers success for ALL learners.

Just as all students have learned their native language, so all students experience success with French in **Niveau A**. There are ample learning opportunities for ALL learners:

- MUSICAL/AUDITORY LEARNERS: video / audio cassettes / CD-ROM
- SPATIAL/VISUAL LEARNERS: video / overheads/ cartoons / CD-ROM
- KINESTHETIC LEARNERS: TPR activities
- LOGICAL/MATHEMATICAL LEARNERS: Student text/CD ROM/ Activity Book
- LINGUISTIC/PRINT LEARNERS: student text / Activity Book / Video Activity Book /Communipak (communication activities) / CD-ROM
- INTERPERSONAL/INTERACTIVE LEARNERS: pair work / communication activities
- INTERPERSONAL LEARNERS: Student Text (personalized activities)/Portfolios

Teaching Tip:

Time spent on Niveau A is time well spent!

Use the **Niveau A** videos, cassettes and CD-ROM program as frequently as you can so that the students feel at ease with the spoken language.

Once students are comfortable with the material in **Niveau A**, they will be able to assimilate the more challenging material of **Niveau B** and **Niveau C** with success and confidence.

Goals and Standards for Foreign Language Learning

Focus on:

General Background: Questions and Answers

■ *What are the Goals and Standards for Foreign Language Learning?*

Over the past several years, the federal government has supported the development of Standards in many K-12 curriculum areas such as math, English, fine arts, and geography. These Standards are "content" standards and define what students "know and are able to do" at the end of grades 4, 8 and 12. Moreover, the Standards are meant to be challenging, and their attainment should represent a strengthening of the American educational system.

In some subject matter areas, these Standards have formed the basis for building tests used in the National Assessment of Education Progress (NAEP). At that point, it was necessary to develop "performance" standards which define "how well" students must do on the assessment measure to demonstrate that they have met the content standards.

As far as states and local school districts are concerned, both implementation of the Standards and participation in the testing program are voluntary. However, the very existence of these standards is seen as a way of improving our educational system so as to make our young people more competitive on the global marketplace.

■ *How have the Goals and Standards for Foreign Language Learning been developed?*

In fall 1992, representatives of ACTFL (American Council on the Teaching of Foreign Languages), AATF (American Association of Teachers of French), AATG (American Association of Teachers of German), and AATSP (American Association of Teachers of Spanish and Portuguese) met to formulate a proposal for the establishment of Standards in foreign languages. In 1993, a joint proposal to create student standards at the K-12 level received funding from the U.S. Department of Education and the National Endowment for the Humanities, and the first part of the project to develop Goals and Standards for Foreign Language Learning was underway.

The K-12 Student Standards Task Force was formed and assigned the charge of creating generic foreign language standards. They prepared a comprehensive draft document which underwent several subsequent revisions, based on input from teachers across the country. In 1994, these new draft standards were piloted in six school districts across the United States, and the results of these programs were analyzed in the preparation of a final draft. In November 1995, the National Standards Project released its final report: **Standards for Foreign Language Learning: Preparing for the 21st Century.**[1] The chart below delineates the **Standards for the Learning of French.**

GOAL 1: COMMUNICATION **Communicate in French**	**Standard 1.1** *Interpersonal Communication* Students engage in conversations or correspondence in French to provide and obtain information, express feelings and emotions, and exchange opinions. **Standard 1.2** *Interpretive Communication* Students understand and interpret spoken and written French on a variety of topics. **Standard 1.3** *Presentational Communication* Students present information, concepts, and ideas in French on a variety of topics to an audience of listeners or readers.
GOAL 2: CULTURES **Gain Knowledge and Understanding of the Cultures of the French-speaking World**	**Standard 2.1** *Practices of Culture* Students demonstrate an understanding of the relationship between the practices and perspectives of the cultures of the French-speaking world. **Standard 2.2** *Products of Culture* Students demonstrate an understanding of the relationship between the products and perspectives of the cultures of the French-speaking world.
GOAL 3: CONNECTIONS **Use French to Connect with Other Disciplines and Expand Knowledge**	**Standard 3.1** *Making Connections* Students reinforce and further their knowledge of other disciplines through French. **Standard 3.2** *Acquiring Information* Students acquire information and recognize the distinctive viewpoints that are available only through the French language and French-speaking cultures.
GOAL 4: COMPARISONS **Develop Insight into the Nature of Language and Culture**	**Standard 4.1** *Language Comparisons* Students demonstrate understanding of the nature of language through comparisons of French and their native language. **Standard 4.2** *Cultural Comparisons* Students demonstrate understanding of the nature of culture through comparisons of French-speaking cultures and their own.
GOAL 5: COMMUNITIES **Participate in French-speaking Communities at Home and Around the World**	**Standard 5.1** *School and Community* Students use French both within and beyond the school setting. **Standard 5.2** *Lifelong Learning* Students show evidence of becoming lifelong learners by using French for personal enjoyment and enrichment.

[1] For more information on the National Standards project and its publications, contact: National Standards in Foreign Language Education, 6 Executive Plaza, Yonkers, NY 10701-6801; phone: (914) 963-8830

DISCOVERING FRENCH

■ **How are the Goals and Standards for Foreign Language Learning defined?**

The Goals and Standards for Foreign Language Learning contain five general goals which focus on communication, culture, and the importance of second language competence in enhancing the students' ability to function more effectively in the global community of the 21st century. These five goals, each with their accompanying standards, are shown in the chart on page 34. In the formal report, these standards are defined in greater detail with the addition of sample "progress indicators" or learning outcomes for grades 4, 8 and 12, and are illustrated with sample learning scenarios.

■ **How are these Standards for Foreign Language Learning being implemented?**

In March 1994, the "Goals 2000: Educate America Act" reaffirmed a core curriculum for American schools, and, more importantly, specifically listed foreign languages as one of ten "core" subject areas. The existence of Standards for Foreign Language Learning has encouraged states and school districts to strengthen their foreign language offerings and lengthen their course sequences. Although implementation is voluntary, many teachers are modifying their curricula so as to take into account those goals and standards which are most relevant to their programs.

Teaching to the Standards

The new Standards for Foreign Language Learning focus on the outcomes of long K-12 sequences of instruction. In most schools, however, French programs begin at the Middle School or Secondary level. With the **Discovering French** program, teachers can effectively teach towards these goals and standards while at the same time maintaining realistic expectations for their students.

Goal One: Communicate in French

From the outset, **Discovering French** students learn to communicate in French. In Niveau A of **DF-Bleu**, the focus is on understanding what French young people are saying (on video, cassette, and CD-ROM) and on exchanging information in simple conversations. In Niveau B of **DF-Bleu**, the oral skills are supplemented by the written skills, and students learn to read and express themselves in writing.

As students progress through **DF-Blanc** and **DF-Rouge**, they learn to engage in longer conversations, read and interpret more challenging texts, and understand French-language films and videos. Teachers who incorporate portfolio assessment into their programs will have the opportunity to keep samples of both written and recorded student presentations.

Goal Two: Gain Knowledge and Understanding of the Cultures ot the Francophone World

In **Discovering French**, students are introduced to the diversity of the French-speaking world. In **DF-Bleu**, the emphasis is on contemporary culture — in France, of course, but also in Quebec, the Caribbean, and Africa. Students learn to observe and analyze cultural differences in photographs and on the video program.

In **DF-Blanc**, the cultural material is expanded to include brief historical overviews, as well as presentations of contemporary reality. Cultural notes in the student text are expanded upon in the Extended Teacher Edition. In **DF-Rouge**, the cultural scope is significantly enlarged, since students have a much stronger command of French.

In the Student Text, they are introduced to historical background, literary works, artistic achievements, and contemporary problems (such as ecological and humanitarian concerns). Feature-length films also help students expand their cultural understanding.

Goal Three: Use French to Connect with Other Disciplines and Expand Knowledge

It is especially in **DF-Rouge** that students have the opportunity to use the French language to learn about history, art, music, social concerns and civic responsibilities. Topics suggested in the student text can be coordinated with colleagues across the school curriculum.

Goal Four: Develop Insight into the Nature of Language and Culture

From the outset, **Discovering French** draws the students' attention to the way in which French speakers communicate with one another, and how some of these French patterns differ from American ones (for example, shaking hands or greeting friends with a *bise*). Notes in the Extended Teacher Edition provide suggestions for encouraging cross-cultural observation. English and French usage is also compared and contrasted, as appropriate.

Goal Five: Use French to Participate in Communities at Home and Around the World

In **Discovering French**, beginning students are invited to exchange letters with French-speaking penpals. In addition, students are encouraged to participate in international student exchanges. The Extended Teacher Edition has a listing of addresses of organizations that can provide these types of services. In addition, teachers are given information on where to obtain French-language publications for their classes, and where to find French-language material on the Internet. In **DF-Rouge**, students are invited to discover French-language videos which in many parts of the country can be found in a local video store. As students experience the satisfaction of participating in authentic cultural situations, they become more confident in their ability to use their skills in the wider global community.

Introduction

Technology—whether software, CD-ROM, video or videodisc—provides additional resources, enrichment and excitement to the French classroom. *DISCOVERING FRENCH-Bleu* provides the most extensive technology resources currently available to make your teaching easier, more effective, and more enjoyable. Components include:

- Video/Audio Program
- Laserdisc Program
- Cassette or Audio CD Program
- CD-ROM Program
- Test Bank Program
- Writing Templates
- TRP: Internet Connection Notes

In order to select technology products that enhance and complement your own teaching style, consider the following checklist. Technology should always be the **means** to a more effective language presentation, and not an end in itself. In addition, good technology products should never be intimidating!

- ✔ Easy to use
- ✔ Fully integrated into the student text and teacher's materials
- ✔ Offer full use of the strongest features of each particular medium
- ✔ Interactive to motivate student interest
- ✔ Flexibly structured for individual and pair/group use
- ✔ Suitable for your particular teaching style

Integrating **well-designed** technology into the French curriculum gives both students and teachers access to the French-speaking world no matter **where** their classroom is located! The *DISCOVERING FRENCH* program provides technology components that are fun, practical, focused, and easy to use.

Unit–level Internet Projects can be found at the end of each unit on the following pages in Level 1: T33, T55, T75, T133, T185, T235, T291, T343, T397.

 ## CD-ROM

A well-produced CD-ROM program provides multimedia integration of all the best elements of a complete French program. Thus the linear access provided by using a textbook, a video segment, realia, or audio cassettes is combined into a single unified environment with simultaneous access to all these sources at once. Students are free to control the pace and sequence of instruction.

DISCOVERING FRENCH Interactive provides a blend of video, interactive activities, record features, and writing all in one simple format. This award-winning program is being used for individual, pair/group, and whole class work. Because of CD-ROM's unique combination of features, students are highly motivated to spend extra time in self-assessment activities, as well as creative development and extension of their listening, writing, and speaking skills. Each of the 36 CD-ROM modules also includes *Exploration* activities that may be saved on disk for teacher review or for inclusion in student portfolios.[1]

 ## Internet

Access to the Internet, and the World Wide Web, opens an exciting new environment for language teaching and learning. There are many Internet service providers in all areas of the country. Most of these services offer a trial period free of charge. Many universities also offer access to educational users.

The *DISCOVERING FRENCH* Teacher's Resource Package offers a unique feature: *Internet Connection Notes*, which contains practical technical information, useful addresses, and specially-designed Internet activities. You and your students can enjoy the benefits of being part of the global society, contacting schools and information sources throughout the French-speaking world.

If you would like to introduce additional technology vocabulary, see pages 82-83 of the Student Text or Teacher's Edition, as well as the Situational Overhead Visuals S1 and S2 and the accompanying copymaster activities.

Integrating the wide range of technology resources available in *DISCOVERING FRENCH* into your classroom can revitalize your teaching and provide you and your students with a personalized connection to French speakers worldwide.

---

[1] A useful general introduction to CD-ROM (hardware, software, general terminology) may be found in *CD-ROM for Schools, A Directory and Practical Handbook for Media Specialists*, Berger and Kinnell, Eight Bit Books, Wilton, CT ©1994

DISCOVERING FRENCH

 VIDEODISC Video and Videodisc

The *DISCOVERING FRENCH Video/Videodisc Program* motivates students from the first day of class, and provides a complete cultural and linguistic experience.

Objectives

- Foster multicultural awareness
- Develop listening comprehension skills using dozens of different voices in varied contexts
- Promote communication skills in real-life situations
- Encourage vocabulary acquisition in context
- Provide materials suitable for teaching to multiple intelligences, useful for all learning styles

Organization and Contents

- 39 video modules (one for each of the 36 lessons and 3 cultural video essays)
- Video script
- Audio CDs or audio cassettes, including listening and speaking activities and pronunciation exercises

Note: Additional activities are also available in the *Video Activity Book* (copymasters)

Easy access is provided by barcodes (for videodisc) and frame numbers (for videotapes) at point of use in the Extended Teacher's Edition, *Video Scripts*, and *Video Activity Books*.

TYPE OF SEGMENT	DESCRIPTION	STUDENT OBJECTIVE
Dialogue (type 1): script as presentation text	Video recording of one or several scenes	Develop listening comprehension
Dialogue (type 2): script not in student text	Video recording of one or several scenes	Develop listening comprehension
Mini-scenes: listening	Montage of candid interviews and short scenes focusing on a vocabulary theme or a selected conversational pattern	Develop listening comprehension and observe specific aspects of the French language used in authentic contexts
Mini-scenes: speaking	Structured situations, visually cued, in which students have the opportunity to use the patterns they have been hearing	Develop speaking proficiency in situational context
Vignette culturelle	Introduction to an aspect of French culture, often accompanied by a brief interview or dialogue	Observe cross-cultural similarities and differences and develop multicultural awareness

 Test Banks

Test banks or test generators allow teachers to compose or modify testing materials to accommodate individual needs as well as provide a source for "A" and "B" versions of tests and exams. The *DISCOVERING FRENCH Test Bank* provides copymaster A and B versions of the Lesson Quizzes, Unit Tests, and Comprehensive (Semester) Tests as well as the software capability to edit, create new items or create whole tests. Teachers may thus use the existing tests, adapt them by adding, deleting or changing items, or create a completely personalized testing program. This flexibility provides for the individual needs of many learning styles and helps to insure success for all students.

Writing Templates

The development of writing skills is an important step in preparing students to function in a multilingual society. The ability to express personal thoughts and feelings allows students to grow and mature intellectually. Cross-disciplinary connections to English, literature, history, math, art and music courses can be fostered as students develop their organizational, research, and writing skills.

The *DISCOVERING FRENCH* Writing Templates provide process writing development in many different formats. Materials are keyed to the unit themes of *DISCOVERING FRENCH*, and are appropriate to the language level of the students. The use of writing template software also encourages the inclusion of technology across the curriculum, and helps build life-long learning skills.

Scope and Sequence

The students' unit-by-unit progression through **Discovering French–Bleu** is represented on the following Scope and Sequence chart. (The numbers in parentheses refer to the lesson numbers.) This chart identifies the cultural theme of each unit and lists the main communication functions and activities, correlating them with the corresponding communication topics (thematic vocabulary) and linguistic goals (accuracy of expression).

In Niveau A, the emphasis is on oral communication, both listening comprehension and speaking. Grammar is not presented formally, but certain structural contrasts, such as gender distinctions, are pointed out.

In Niveaux B and C, the communication topics are expanded, and the lessons build on the four skills of listening, speaking, reading and writing. In a given unit, the bulk of the thematic vocabulary is presented in the first lesson (**le français pratique**), and then is re-entered and consolidated in the next three lessons as students increase their ability to handle the related communication functions. Grammar patterns are presented formally for reference, but are practiced in functional situations relating to the unit theme.

Unité 1 Bonjour!	CULTURAL CONTEXT Meeting people	
COMMUNICATION FUNCTIONS AND ACTIVITIES **Comprehension and Self-expression**	**COMMUNICATION TOPICS** **Thematic Vocabulary**	**LINGUISTIC GOALS** **Accuracy of Expression**
■ *Meeting people* • Introducing oneself (1) • Spelling one's name (1) • Asking someone's name (1) • Saying where you are from (2)	• Adjectives of nationality (2)	• L'alphabet (1) • **Français / française** (2)
■ *Greeting people* • Saying hello (1) • Asking how people feel (3) • Saying good-bye (3)	• Expressions with **ça va** (3)	
■ *Talking about time* • Asking for the time (4) • Indicating the time (4) • Saying when certain events are scheduled (4)	• Counting 0 to 10 (1) • Counting 10 to 20 (2) • Counting 20 to 60 (3) • Expressions of time (4)	

DISCOVERING FRENCH

Unité 2 Les copains et la famille	**CULTURAL CONTEXT** Talking about people	
COMMUNICATION FUNCTIONS AND ACTIVITIES Comprehension and Self-expression	**COMMUNICATION TOPICS** Thematic Vocabulary	**LINGUISTIC GOALS** Accuracy of Expression
■ *Talking about other people* • Pointing people out (5) • Finding out someone's name (6) • Saying where a person is from (6)	• People (5)	• **Un garçon / une fille** (5) • **Le garçon / la fille** (6)
■ *Introducing one's family (7)* • Giving their names (6) • Giving their ages (7)	• Family members (7) • Counting 60 to 79 (5) • Counting 80 to 100 (6)	• **Mon cousin / ma cousine** (7) • **Ton cousin / ta cousine** (7)
■ *Talking about dates* • Asking the day of the week (8) • Giving the date (8) • Talking about birthdays (8)	• Days of the week (8) • Months of the year (8)	

Unité 3 Bon appétit!	**CULTURAL CONTEXT** Having a snack in France	
■ *Saying you are hungry (9)* • Offering a friend something to eat (9) • Asking a friend for something to eat (9)	• Foods (9)	• **Un sandwich / une pizza** (9)
■ *Saying you are thirsty (10)* • Ordering a beverage in a café (10) • Asking an adult for something to eat or drink (10)	• Beverages (10)	• **S'il te plaît / s'il vous plaît** (10)
■ *Paying at a café in France* • Asking what something costs (11) • Asking a friend to lend you money (11)		
■ *Talking about the weather (12)*	• Weather expressions (12) • Seasons (12)	

C'EST TA SOEUR?

NON, C'EST MON FRÈRE.

30 JUIN 8 MAI 4 MARS 21 NOVEMBRE

Unité 4 Qu'est-ce qu'on fait?   CULTURAL CONTEXT Daily activities at home, at school, on weekends

COMMUNICATION FUNCTIONS AND ACTIVITIES Comprehension and Self-expression	COMMUNICATION TOPICS Thematic Vocabulary	LINGUISTIC GOALS Accuracy of Expression
■ *Describing daily activities* • What people do and don't do (13) • What people like to do and don't like to do (13) • What you want and don't want to do (13)	• Daily activities (13) • Expressions with **faire** (16)	• Subject pronouns (14) • Verb + infinitive (15) • The negative **ne... pas** (14) • Regular **-er** verbs (15) • The verb **faire** (16)
■ *Talking about where people are*	• Places (14)	• The verb **être** (14)
■ *Finding out what is going on* • Asking yes/no questions (14) • Asking information questions (16)	• Question words (16)	• Yes/no questions with **est-ce que** (14) • Information questions with **est-ce que** (16) • Questions with inversion (16)
■ *Inviting friends to do things with you* • Extending an invitation (13) • Accepting an invitation (13) • Turning down an invitation (13)		• Verb + infinitive (15)
■ *Expanding one's conversational skills* • Answering yes/no questions (14) • Expressing approval or regret (15) • Expressing mild doubt or surprise (16)	• Affirmative and negative expressions (14)	

Unité 5 Le monde personnel et familier   CULTURAL CONTEXT People and their possessions

■ *Describing yourself and others* • Physical appearance (17) • Age (17, 18) • Character traits (19) • Nationality (19)	• People (17) • Adjectives of physical description (17) • Adjectives of personality (19) • Adjectives of nationality (19) • Adjectives of aspect (20)	• Singular and plural nouns (18) • Definite and indefinite articles (18) • The expression **avoir... ans** (18) • Adjective formation (19) • Adjective position (19, 20) • Use of **c'est** and **il est** (20)
■ *Describing your room* • What is in it (17) • Where things are located (17)	• Room furnishings (17) • Prepositions of place (17)	• The expression **il y a** (17)
■ *Talking about possessions* • Things that one owns and doesn't own (17, 18) • Whether they work or not (17) • Where they were made (19) • What they look like (20)	• Everyday objects (17) • Color (20) • Aspect (20)	• The verb **avoir** (18) • The negative article **pas de** (18)
■ *Expanding one's conversational skills* • Getting someone's attention (20) • Making generalizations (18) • Talking about regular events (18) • Expressing opinions (20) • Contradicting a negative statement or question (18) • Introducing a conclusion (19)	• Attention getters (20) • Expressions of opinion (20)	• Use of the definite article: in general statements (18) to indicate repeated events (18) • Impersonal **c'est** (20)
OPTIONAL: ■ *Talking about past events (18, 19, 20)*		• Conversational introduction: answering questions in the **passé composé** (18, 19, 20)

DISCOVERING FRENCH

Unité 6 En ville	CULTURAL CONTEXT City life—the home, the family and urban activities	
COMMUNICATION FUNCTIONS AND ACTIVITIES **Comprehension and Self-expression**	**COMMUNICATION TOPICS** **Thematic Vocabulary**	**LINGUISTIC GOALS** **Accuracy of Expression**
■ *Describing your city* • Streets and public buildings (21) • Places you often go to (22) • How you get around (22)	• City places and buildings (21) • Transportation (22)	• The verb **aller** (22) • Contractions with **à** (22)
■ *Finding your way around* • Asking and giving directions (21) • Indicating the floor (24)	• Giving directions (21)	• Ordinal numbers (24)
■ *Describing your home and your family* • Your address (21) • The inside and outside of your home (21) • Your family (24)	• Neighborhood (21) • Rooms of the house (21) • Family members (24)	• The expression **chez** (22) • Stress pronouns (23) • The construction noun + **de** + noun (23) • Possession with **de** (24) • Possessive adjectives (24)
■ *Making plans to do things in town* • What you are going to do (22) • Asking others to come along (23) • Saying where you have been (23)	• Activities: sports, games, etc. (23)	• **Aller** + infinitive (22) • The verb **venir** (23) • Contractions with **de** (23)
■ *Expanding one's conversational skills:* • Contradicting someone (23) • Expressing doubt (24) • Expressing surprise (23)		
OPTIONAL: ■ *Talking about past events (21, 22, 23, 24)*		• Conversational introduction: answering questions in the **passé composé** (21, 22, 23, 24)

Unité 7 Le shopping	CULTURAL CONTEXT Buying clothes	
■ *Talking about clothes* • What people are wearing (25) • Whether the clothes fit (25) • What they look like (25, 27) • What one's preferences are (25)	• Clothing and accessories (25) • Descriptive adjectives (25) • Adjectives **beau**, **nouveau**, **vieux** (27) • Expressions of opinion (25)	• The verb **mettre** (26) • The verb **préférer** (26) • The demonstrative **ce** (26) • The interrogative **quel?** (26)
■ *Discussing shopping plans* • Where to go (25, 28) • What to buy (26)	• Stores that sell clothes (25) • Verbs like **vendre** (28)	• The verb **acheter** (26) • Regular **-re** verbs (28) • The pronoun **on** (28)
■ *Buying clothes* • Asking for help (25) • Finding out prices (25, 28) • Deciding what to choose (27) • Comparing items (27) • Talking about what you need and what you like (28) • Giving advice (28)	• Numbers 100–1000 (25) • Money-related expressions (28) • Verbs like **choisir** (27) • Expressions **avoir besoin de** and **avoir envie de** (28)	• Regular **-ir** verbs (27) • The verb **payer** (28) • Comparisons (27) • The imperative (28)
■ *Expanding one's conversational skills* • Emphasizing a remark (26) • Indicating approval (28) • Introducing an opinion (27)		
OPTIONAL: ■ *Talking about past events (25, 26, 27, 28)*		• Conversational introduction: answering questions in the **passé composé** (25, 26, 27, 28)

Unité 8 Le temps libre
CULTURAL CONTEXT Leisure-time activities

COMMUNICATION FUNCTIONS AND ACTIVITIES Comprehension and Self-expression	COMMUNICATION TOPICS Thematic Vocabulary	LINGUISTIC GOALS Accuracy of Expression
■ *Discussing leisure activities* • Going out with friends (29) • Sports (29) • Helping around the house (29) • How you and others feel (30) • Things you never do (32)	• Common weekend activities (29) • Individual summer and winter sports (29) • Household chores (29)	• **Faire de** + sport (29) • Expressions with **avoir** (30) • **Ne... jamais** (32)
■ *Describing vacation travel plans* • Travel dates (29, 32) • How to travel (29) • How long to stay (29, 31) • What to see (31)	• French holidays (29) • Means of transportation (29) • Divisions of time (29) • Periods of future time (31) • Verbs of movement (32)	• The verb **voir** (31)
■ *Narrating what happened* • What you did and didn't do (30, 31) • Where you went and when you returned (32) • The sequence in which you did these things (30) • Remaining vague about certain details (32)	• Adverbs of sequence (30) • Periods of past time (31)	• **Passé composé** of **-er** verbs (30) • **Passé composé** of **-ir** verbs (31) • **Passé composé** of **-re** verbs (31) • **Passé composé** of irregular verbs (31) • **Passé composé** with **être** (32) • **Quelqu'un, quelque chose** and their opposites (32)

Unité 9 Les repas
CULTURAL CONTEXT Food and meals

■ *Talking about your favorite foods* • What you like and don't like (33) • What you can, should and want to eat (33, 34, 35)	• Names of foods and beverages (33) • Verbs of preference (33)	• The verb **vouloir** (34) • The verbs **pouvoir** and **devoir** (35)
■ *Shopping for food* • Making a shopping list (33) • Interacting with vendors (33) • Asking prices (33)	• Quantities (33) • Fruits and vegetables (33)	• Partitive article (34)
■ *Planning a meal* • Asking others to help you (35) • Setting the table (33)	• Meals (33) • Verbs asking for service (35) • Place setting (33)	• Pronouns **me**, **te**, **nous**, **vous** (35) • Pronouns with commands (35)
■ *Eating out with friends* • Ordering food (33) • Asking the waiter/waitress to bring things for others (36) • Talking about people you know (35) • Talking about what others have said or written (36)	• Verbs using indirect objects (36)	• The verb **prendre** (34) • The verb **boire** (34) • The verb **connaître** (36) • The verbs **dire** and **écrire** (36) • Pronouns **le**, **la**, **les**, **lui**, **leur** (36)

Pacing Suggestions

General Guidelines

This section answers some of the questions which are frequently raised by teachers using the program for the first time.

■ *At what pace should my classes proceed through* **Discovering French–Bleu?**

There is no single answer to this question. Your optimum pacing will depend on many factors, including the number of contact hours per week, the age of the students, and their language aptitude.

The typical school year consists of 180 class days; however, it is more realistic to plan on only 160 full periods of French instruction to make allowance for semester exams and for the less productive days before and after vacations, as well as field days, fire drills, and other unpredictable events.

The chart on pages 44-45 shows three suggested time budgets.

■ *What types of lesson plans fit the following suggested time budgets?*

These time budgets are based on the premise that the typical class lesson plans will include a 5 to 10 minute warm-up (video viewing, TPR activity, communication questions, etc.), a brief presentation of new material, and three to five learning activities of various sorts. It may not always be possible, or even advisable, to do every activity in the program. However, since the emphasis in **Discovering French–Bleu** is on high-frequency vocabulary, structures and conversation patterns, students will always have the opportunity to consolidate their mastery of new material in subsequent lessons.

■ *What if students say the pace is too fast?*

Student performance tends to rise to meet teacher expectations. (If the athletic coach did not push the players to do rapid pushups and running drills, the team would never be in shape to win a game.) By encouraging students to move ahead a bit more quickly, we actually will enhance their sense of accomplishment.

■ *What is the suggested time budget for junior high classes that have daily periods of only 20 to 30 minutes?*

For classes with short periods, you can select either *Formula 1* or *Formula 2* and spread it across two years. For each lesson or section, double the suggested time budget. For example, if the chart suggests 2 days for a given lesson, you would plan for 4 days.

- With *Formula 1,* your students would do Units 1 through 5 in the first year, and Units 6 through 9 in the second year.
- With *Formula 2,* your students would complete Units 1 to 4 (and begin Unit 5) in the first year, and then do Units 5 to 7 (and parts of Unit 8) in the second year.

■ *What about middle school classes that meet only two or three times a week?*

Depending on the age of the students, you may want to schedule **Discovering French– Bleu** over three years. In the first year, the students would complete Niveau A: Units 1, 2 and 3. In the second year, they would do most of Niveau B: Units 4, 5 and 6. In the third year, they would do Units 7, 8 and 9, thus finishing Niveau B and completing Niveau C.

What is the difference between the three formulas?

- *Formula 1* is for ninth and tenth grade classes in a standard curriculum where classes meet about 50 minutes a day. Typically these students will be doing some homework on a daily basis. Next year these students will move quickly through the opening chapters of **Discovering French– Blanc** and finish the book by June.
- *Formula 2* is for seventh, eighth and ninth grade students in classes that meet 40 to 50 minutes a day. Students will not always be given daily homework assignments. Next year these students will move more slowly through the opening chapters of **Discovering French–Blanc** and complete three-quarters of the book by the end of the year.
- *Formula 3* is for high school honors classes. Next year these students will move through **Discovering French–Blanc** at a more rapid pace, again allowing for additional enrichment and vocabulary expansion activities.

Can Discovering French-Bleu *be adapted to block scheduling?*

There are many different types of block scheduling and concentrated curricula being used in schools across the country. The actual pacing of the material will depend on the nature of the program and the available time blocks.

In order to develop effective lessons plans for longer class periods (e.g., 75 minutes or 90 minutes), it is important to allow for a wide variety of activities. In addition to the activities in the basic Student Text, it is helpful to include as many of the following ancillary configurations as possible:

- CD-ROM work stations where students in pairs or small groups can work independently
- Video (or laserdisc) areas where students can view the video several times and do the activities in the Video Workbook
- A class set of Activity Books and a cassette player so that students can do the recorded activities, either as a full class or in a listening area of the room
- A class set of Communipak Workbooks so that students can engage in a variety of guided interactive pair activities.
- Several Answer Keys so that students in triads can do the activities in the Student Text, with two students performing the dialogues and the third student following in the Answer Key and acting as language consultant.

Suggested Time Budgets

NIVEAU A, B, C	Formula 1 (days)	Formula 2 (days)	Formula 3 (days)
	For classes that meet five times a week and plan to finish the entire book: Niveau A, Niveau B, and Niveau C.	For classes that plan to finish Niveau A and Niveau B, plus a light introduction to Unit 8.	For classes that plan to finish the entire book and incorporate additional enrichment activities.
Total Days	**160**	**161**	**148**

NIVEAU A	Formula 1 (days)	Formula 2 (days)	Formula 3 (days)
	For classes that meet five times a week and plan to finish the entire book: Niveau A, Niveau B, and Niveau C.	For classes that plan to finish Niveau A and Niveau B, plus a light introduction to Unit 8.	For classes that plan to finish the entire book and incorporate additional enrichment activities.
CULTURAL PHOTO ESSAY **Parlons français!**	**2**	**2**	**2**
UNITÉ 1			
Leçon 1	2	3	2
Leçon 2	2	3	2
Leçon 3	2	2	1
Leçon 4	2	2	2
À votre tour/ review	1	2	1
Unit test 1	1/2	1/2	1/2
Entracte 1	1/2	1/2	1/2
Unité 1 Total	**10**	**13**	**9**
UNITÉ 2			
Leçon 5	2	2	1
Leçon 6	2	2	1
Leçon 7	2	3	2
Leçon 8	2	3	2
À votre tour/ review	1	2	1
Unit Test 2	1/2	1/2	1/2
Entracte 2	1/2	1/2	1/2
Unité 2 Total	**10**	**13**	**8**
UNITÉ 3			
Leçon 9	2	3	2
Leçon 10	2	3	2
Leçon 11	2	2	1
Leçon 12	1	2	1
À votre tour/ review	1	2	1
Unit Test 3	1	1	1
Entracte 3	1	1	1
Unité 3 Total	**10**	**14**	**9**
NIVEAU A Total	32	42	28

NIVEAU B	Formula 1 (days)	Formula 2 (days)	Formula 3 (days)
	For classes that meet five times a week and plan to finish the entire book: Niveau A, Niveau B, and Niveau C.	For classes that plan to finish Niveau A and Niveau B, plus a light introduction to Unit 8.	For classes that plan to finish the entire book and incorporate additional enrichment activities.
CULTURAL PHOTO ESSAY **À l'école en France**	**2**	**2**	**2**
UNITÉ 4			
Leçon 13	4	5	3
Leçon 14	4	5	4
Leçon 15	5	6	4
Leçon 16	4	5	4
Review	1	2	1
Unit Test 4	1	1	1
Entracte 4	1	2	1
Unité 4 Total	**20**	**26**	**18**
UNITÉ 5			
Leçon 17	5	6	5
Leçon 18	6	7	5
Leçon 19	4	5	4
Leçon 20	4	5	4
Review	1	2	1
Unit Test 5	1	1	1
Entracte 5	1	2	1
Unité 5 Total	**22**	**28**	**21**
UNITÉ 6			
Leçon 21	4	5	4
Leçon 22	5	6	4
Leçon 23	4	5	4
Leçon 24	4	5	4
Review	1	2	1
Unit Test 6	1	1	1
Entracte 6	1	2	1
Unité 6 Total	**20**	**26**	**19**
CULTURAL PHOTO ESSAY **À Paris**	**2**	**2**	**2**
UNITÉ 7			
Leçon 25	4	5	4
Leçon 26	4	5	4
Leçon 27	4	4	3
Leçon 28	5	6	4
Review	1	2	1
Unit Test 7	1	1	1
Entracte 7	1	2	1
Unité 7 Total	**20**	**25**	**18**
NIVEAU B Total	**86**	**109**	**80**

NIVEAU C	Formula 1 (days)	Formula 2 (days)	Formula 3 (days)
	For classes that meet five times a week and plan to finish the entire book: Niveau A, Niveau B, and Niveau C.	For classes that plan to finish Niveau A and Niveau B, plus a light introduction to Unit 8.	For classes that plan to finish the entire book and incorporate additional enrichment activities.
UNITÉ 8			
Leçon 29	4	3	3
Leçon 30	5	3	4
Leçon 31	4	3	4
Leçon 32	4	—	4
Review	1	1/2	1
Unit Test 8	1	1/2	1
Entracte 8	1	—	1
Unité 8 Total	**20**	**10**	**18**
UNITÉ 9			
Leçon 33	5	—	5
Leçon 34	5	—	5
Leçon 35	4	—	4
Leçon 36	5	—	5
Review	1	—	1
Unit Test 9	1	—	1
Entracte 9	1	—	1
Unité 9 Total	**22**	**—**	**22**
NIVEAU C Total	**42**	**10**	**40**

F Pedagogical Resource Guide

This part of the front matter focuses on some current educational approaches and indicates how they can be implemented with **Discovering French**. These include: TPR (Total Physical Response), Cooperative Learning, Critical Thinking, Portfolio Assessment, and the French Spelling Reform of 1990.

Introducing TPR into the Classroom

General Background: Questions and Answers

■ *What is TPR?*

TPR (or Total Physical Response) is an approach to second language learning developed by James Asher over twenty-five years ago.[1] The key premise of the TPR approach is that listening comprehension provides the most effective introduction to second-language learning. More specifically, TPR proponents point out that listening activities in which students respond physically in some way (moving around, pointing, handling objects, etc.) are not only excellent ways of establishing comprehension of new phrases, but material learned in this manner is remembered longer. This explains why students learn the parts of the body more quickly by playing "Simon Says" than by repeating the same vocabulary words after the teacher.

■ *How is a typical TPR activity structured?*

In a typical TPR activity, the teacher gives commands to the students, either as a full class, a small group, or individually. Traditionally, the TPR activity consists of four steps:

Step 1. Group performance with a teacher model The teacher gives a command and then performs the action. The students listen, watch and imitate the teacher. Three to five new commands are presented in this way.

Step 2. Group performance without a teacher model When the teacher feels the students understand the new phrases, he or she gives the command without moving. It is the students who demonstrate their comprehension by performing the desired action. If the students seem unsure about what to do, the teacher will model the action again.

Step 3. Individual performance without a teacher model Once the group can perform the new commands easily, the teacher gives these commands to individual students. If an individual student does not remember a given command, the teacher calls on the group to perform the command. It is important to maintain a relaxing atmosphere where all students feel comfortable.

Step 4. Individual performance of a series of commands When the class is comfortable with the new commands, the teacher gives an individual student a series of two or more commands. This type of activity builds retention and encourages more careful listening.

These four steps are repeated each time new commands are introduced. As the TPR activities progress, the new commands are intermingled with those learned previously.

■ *How many new commands are introduced at any one time?*

Generally three to five new commands are introduced and then practiced. It is important not to bring in new items until all the students are comfortable with the current material. Practice can be made more challenging by giving the commands more rapidly.

■ *Is it necessary to have everyone perform all the commands?*

In a regular classroom, it is sometimes difficult to have an entire class performing all the commands. It may be easier to have smaller groups of students take turns coming to the front of the room to learn the new commands and have the rest of the class observe. (Asher found that by actively watching others perform the commands, students would also develop their listening comprehension.)

[1] For a complete introduction, consult James J. Asher, **Learning Another Language Through Actions: The Complete Teacher's Guidebook**, 2nd ed., l983 (Sky Oaks Productions, P.O. Box 1102, Los Gatos, CA 95031).

■ Must TPR activities relate directly to the content of the lesson?

Since TPR activities develop listening comprehension skills through movement and the use of props, they can be planned independently of the lesson content. Basically there are two kinds of TPR activities:

- *Text-related activities.* These activities introduce material which will be immediately activated in the corresponding lesson of the book. The TPR activity helps students build their listening comprehension before being asked to produce this new material in speaking and writing. Then, when students are presented with this material formally, they can concentrate on details such as pronunciation and spelling because they will already know what all the new words mean.
- *Comprehension-expansion activities.* These activities are designed to expand the students' listening proficiency and introduce vocabulary and structures which will not be formally presented until later in the program. Since TPR is fun, and since the material presented is not formally "tested," TPR can be effectively used for vocabulary expansion and for anticipatory introduction of new material. For example, verbs of movement and classroom objects can be presented via TPR early in the course.

■ How are TPR activities usually scheduled into the lesson plan?

TPR activities can be planned at the beginning of the hour as a warm-up, or may be introduced in the middle or at the end of the period as a change of pace. It is usually best to use TPR for no more than ten minutes per class period.

■ How do I prepare for a TPR activity?

Before beginning a TPR activity, it is very important to plan which commands you are going to use and what new vocabulary you are going to introduce. You may want to write these out on an index card or on self-adhesive note paper which you can stick into your textbook. As you lead the activity, you will need to be able to vary the sequence of the commands and give them rapidly and fluidly. If students have difficulty with certain commands, be sure to repeat them frequently.

■ How and when do I introduce TPR to my students?

TPR activities can be introduced on the first day of class. You will find three initial TPR activities described on the next page.

■ How do I plan additional TPR activities in the course of the year?

Sample TPR activities for **Discovering French–Bleu** are suggested in the Extended Teacher's Edition and prefaced with the symbol: **TPR** . You may also want to develop activities of your own.[2] A list of sample commands is given on page 49. An illustrated vocabulary listing of common classroom objects may be found on page 83 of the Student Text.

[2] For helpful classroom advice, consult Ramiro Garcia, **Instructor's Notebook: How to Apply TPR for Best Results,** 1985. See also Francisco L. Cabello, **Total Physical Response in First Year Spanish,** 1985. (Both available from Sky Oaks Productions.)

F Initial TPR Activities

The following three TPR activities are designed to introduce students to this type of listening comprehension activity.

TPR ACTIVITY 1
Comprehension-expansion: movements

PROPS: Several chairs

■ Tell the class: "Listen and see how much you understand of what I am saying.
Levez-vous. Asseyez-vous. Levez-vous. Marchez. Arrêtez. Sautez. Tournez-vous. Marchez. Asseyez-vous."
Students will look blank. Then say: "In ten minutes you will understand everything I said."

■ Bring out a chair, sit down and instruct the students: "Listen carefully and do what I do. Do not speak. Just try to understand."
"Levez-vous." [Teacher gets up. If necessary, motions to class to get up.]
"Asseyez-vous." [Teacher sits down.]
"Levez-vous." [Teacher stands up again.]
"Sautez." [Teacher jumps in place.]
"Sautez." [Teacher jumps again.]
"Asseyez-vous." [Teacher sits down.]
Repeat the sequence for the class to perform but do not move unless the class seems to need the action modelled again.

■ Place several chairs in the front of the classroom and call for volunteers. This time only the volunteers respond while the others watch. Three new commands are added. The teacher models the actions.
"Levez-vous." [Teacher gets up.]
"Marchez." [Teacher walks.]
"Arrêtez." [Teacher stops.]
"Marchez." [Teacher walks again.]
"Arrêtez." [Teacher stops.]
"Sautez." [Teacher jumps.]
"Tournez-vous." [Teacher makes a half turn.]
"Marchez." [Teacher walks back to chair.]
"Arrêtez." [Teacher stops in front of chair.]
"Tournez-vous." [Teacher makes a half turn.]
"Asseyez-vous." [Teacher sits down.]
Repeat the new commands and have the volunteers act them out. Then call on other volunteers. Vary the order of the commands and increase the pace as students show that they understand. For variety, unexpected commands can be given, such as **"asseyez-vous"** where there is no chair and students have to sit on the floor.

■ At the end of the TPR activity, read the original list of commands so that students realize how much they have learned.

TPR ACTIVITY 2
Comprehension-expansion: classroom and furniture

PROPS: Classroom furniture

■ Begin TPR Activity 2 by reviewing the commands of TPR Activity 1. If necessary, model the actions again.

■ Introduce new movements, telling students to go to the door, to the desk, to the window, etc.
"Allez à la porte."
"Allez à la table."
"Allez à la fenêtre."
"Allez au tableau."

■ Tell the whole class to point out the new objects.
"Montrez la porte."
"Montrez le tableau." etc.

TPR ACTIVITY 3
Comprehension-expansion: classroom objects

PROPS: Classroom objects (books, notebooks, pencils, pens, etc.)

Place several objects on a table in full view of the class. Call up two or three student volunteers and tell them to point out and touch various objects:
"Montrez le livre."
"Touchez le cahier."
"Montrez le crayon."
"Touchez le stylo." etc.

■ Have students put similar objects on their desks and follow the commands together with the volunteers.

■ At the end of the TPR activity, give individual students some simple series of commands drawing from all expressions they have learned so far.
"Pierre, lève-toi, va à la table et touche le cahier." etc.

Note: An illustrated vocabulary listing of common classroom objects is on page 83 of the student text as well as on Transparency 50.

Sample TPR Commands

Here is a listing of some sample commands in both the **"tu"** and the **"vous"** forms. As a teacher, you have two options:

■ You can use the formal **"vous"** form for both group and individual commands.

■ You can address the class and small groups with the plural **"vous"** form and then address individual students as **"tu."**

MOVEMENTS

Stand up.	**Lève-toi.**	**Levez-vous.**
	Debout.	**Debout.**
Sit down.	**Assieds-toi.**	**Asseyez-vous.**
Walk.	**Marche.**	**Marchez.**
Jump.	**Saute.**	**Sautez.**
Stop.	**Arrête.**	**Arrêtez.**
Turn around.	**Tourne-toi.**	**Tournez-vous.**
Turn right/left.	**Tourne à droite/à gauche.**	**Tournez à droite/à gauche.**
Go ...	**Va (au tableau).**	**Allez (à la fenêtre).**
Come ...	**Viens (au bureau).**	**Venez (au tableau).**
Raise ...	**Lève (la main).**	**Levez (le bras).**
Lower ...	**Baisse (la tête).**	**Baissez (les yeux).**

POINTING OUT AND MANIPULATING OBJECTS

Point out ...	**Montre (le cahier).**	**Montrez (le livre).**
Touch ...	**Touche (la porte).**	**Touchez (la fenêtre).**
Pick up / Take ...	**Prends (le crayon).**	**Prenez (le stylo).**
Put ...	**Mets (le livre sur la table).**	**Mettez (le cahier sous la chaise).**
Take away ...	**Enlève (le livre).**	**Enlevez (le cahier).**
Empty ...	**Vide (le sac).**	**Videz (la corbeille).**
Give ...	**Donne (la cassette à Anne).**	**Donnez (le disque à Paul).**
Give back ...	**Rends (la cassette à Marie).**	**Rendez (le disque à Michel).**
Pass ...	**Passe (le stylo à Denise).**	**Passez (le crayon à Marc).**
Keep ...	**Garde (la cassette).**	**Gardez (la cassette).**
Open ...	**Ouvre (la porte).**	**Ouvrez (le livre).**
Close ...	**Ferme (la fenêtre).**	**Fermez (le cahier).**
Throw ...	**Lance (la balle à Jean).**	**Lancez (le ballon à Claire).**

ACTIVITIES WITH PICTURES AND VISUALS

Look at ...	**Regarde (la carte).**	**Regardez (le plan de Paris).**
Look for/Find ...	**Cherche (la Suisse).**	**Cherchez (la tour Eiffel).**

PAPER OR CHALKBOARD ACTIVITIES

Draw ...	**Dessine (une maison).**	**Dessinez (un arbre).**
Write ...	**Écris (ton nom).**	**Écrivez (votre nom).**
Erase ...	**Efface (le dessin).**	**Effacez (la carte).**
Color ...	**Colorie (le chat en noir).**	**Coloriez (le chien en jaune).**
Put an "x" on ...	**Mets un "x" sur (le garçon).**	**Mettez un "x" sur (la fille).**
Circle ...	**Trace un cercle autour de (la chemise rouge).**	**Tracez un cercle autour de (la jupe blanche).**
Cut out ...	**Découpe (un coeur).**	**Découpez (un cercle).**

F Cooperative Learning and Cooperative Practice

General Background: Questions and Answers

■ What is Cooperative Learning?

The term Cooperative Learning is used to describe classroom environments where students work together in small groups to accomplish specific objectives. Rather than studying alone and competing for grades assigned on a curve, students help one another attain group goals. In addition to mastering new subject matter, students also acquire social skills and learn to assess how well their group is functioning.[3]

■ What are the basic elements of Cooperative Learning?

Although there are several models for Cooperative Learning, they all tend to share the following features:

- *Mutual goals.* Students in small groups work together to attain a common goal. Each student within a group may have different tasks and/or responsibilities, but they all receive the same reward (grade, certificate, bonus points, etc.) at the end of the project.
- *Heterogeneous grouping.* Groups contain students of differing abilities. High achievers and low achievers both try to do their best because they are interdependent with one another.
- *Individual accountability.* Students in the group are also held individually accountable for learning material presented. There may be individual exams or grading of individual assignments.
- *Social interaction.* By working together, students learn to communicate effectively and to share responsibility.

■ Can the basic Cooperative Learning model be applied to French classes?

This is an important question. As has historically been the case with many educational innovations, the research studies in Cooperative Learning have focused on subject areas such as math, social studies and language arts, where students communicate with one another in English. Moreover, it is in English that students read material from various reference sources and acquire additional knowledge. In elementary French classes, on the other hand, students are dependent on the teacher to provide the basic instruction. It is the teacher who knows the language, who models the phrases to be learned, who selects comprehensible input (videos, tapes, readings, realia), and who plans activities at the linguistic level of the students. Since the goal of the French course is to have students communicate in French, the Cooperative Learning model is most appropriate at the advanced levels, once students have the needed linguistic skills. At the early levels, students will tend to interact in English and therefore Cooperative Learning activities must be carefully selected.

The section on page 51 suggests some sample Cooperative Learning activities that can be used effectively with **Discovering French–Bleu**.

■ Can paired activities and small group work be considered as Cooperative Learning?

Not really. Paired activities and small group work are usually examples of *Cooperative Practice*.

■ What is Cooperative Practice?

Cooperative Practice is a term used to describe language practice and language acquisition activities in which students interact with one another. These activities take place after the teacher has presented the new material. Cooperative Practice activities are usually much narrower in scope than the traditional Cooperative Learning activities. The group goal may simply be to complete a specific exercise or brief communication task. For certain types of activities, there may be differentiation of tasks. There is usually no group grade given. Individual assessment in the form of a quiz may be delayed until the end of a lesson.

■ What is the advantage of Cooperative Practice?

The advantage of Cooperative Practice is that students are directly involved in French language activities. Whereas during traditional practice activities, it is the teacher who elicits responses either chorally or individually, during Cooperative Practice, it is the students themselves who ask and answer questions. During Cooperative Practice activities, the teacher can circulate, offering assistance and making corrections privately rather than publicly.

■ How can Cooperative Practice be incorporated into Discovering French classes?

The section on page 51 gives suggestions for introducing Cooperative Practice activities into the classroom.

[3] For an excellent introduction to this topic, see the 1990 monograph by Eileen Veronica Hilke entitled **Cooperative Learning.** This publication (subtitled Fastback 299) can be obtained from the Phi Delta Kappa Educational Foundation, P. O. Box 789, Bloomington, IN 47402-0789 ($.90).

Types of Cooperative Learning Activities

This section describes three types of Cooperative Learning activities which can be used effectively with **Discovering French– Bleu**. Further suggestions are found in the Extended Teacher's Edition preceded by the symbol:

Small group homework correction

Students get together in heterogeneous groups of 4 or 5 to check the homework assignment. Each student is responsible for correcting his or her own paper. If the group cannot decide on the right response, they can ask the teacher for help. Students receive full homework credit if all team members have corrected all their errors. Points are taken off for uncorrected mistakes.

Note: To be sure that students do not do their homework during class or copy it from a teammate during the correction activity, the teacher can check that the homework sheets have been completed as the students enter the classroom.

Group homework correction has several advantages:

• Students learn from correcting their own work. In small groups they are more willing to ask their peers for explanations. Since all members of the group have a stake in getting the assignment right, they are not reluctant to request help when necessary.

• By relegating the homework correction activity to the last five or ten minutes of the class hour, the teacher has more class time available for communication activities.

• The teacher's out-of-class homework correction work is reduced to simply glancing over each paper and entering a notation in the grade book.

Team games

Certain sentence-building activities in the Student Text can be easily adapted to Cooperative Learning. The students are randomly divided into teams of 3 or 4. (This may be done numerically by counting off in French, alphabetically by middle initial, sequentially by month of birth, etc.) Each team is given a sheet of paper. When the signal to begin is given, the first student on the team writes a sentence incorporating the suggested phrases. Teammates check to be sure the sentence is correct. Then the paper is passed to the next student who writes the second sentence, and so forth. At the end of the time limit, the team that has the most correct sentences is declared the winner and receives a small reward (such as less homework or extra credit points).

Cross-cultural observation

Students are divided into teams of 3 or 4. The teacher plays a segment of a **Discovering French** video module, and asks the students to look for cross-cultural similarities and differences between what they see and similar situations in the United States. Each team puts together a list of what the members have observed. If time allows, the video may be shown several times. Then the teams take turns sharing the observations they have noted. The team with the highest number of correct observations wins a reward.

Note: To encourage individual accountability, the teacher may give a brief follow-up quiz where students list as many observations as they can remember.

Types of Cooperative Practice Activities

There are many possibilities for incorporating Cooperative Practice into the French classroom. Here are a few guidelines and suggestions. Activities which lend themselves readily to Cooperative Practice are indicated in the Extended Teacher's Edition with the symbol:

Cooperative pair activities

Students each team up with a partner to do the speaking exercises in the textbook.

• For the dialogue activities, each partner plays a role.

• For the practice activities, one person gives the cue and the other supplies the response.

• For personal questions, one student reads the question, and the other student replies.

Halfway through the cooperative pair activity, roles are reversed.

Note: Pair activities work best when students know exactly what is expected of them. Especially with beginning classes, it is often most effective to go over an activity rapidly with everyone, eliciting full-class or half-class choral responses, and then have students practice the entire exercise once more in pairs.

Cooperative practice in trios

In trio activities, students divide into groups of three. Two students engage in a paired speaking activity, such as a role-play exercise or a dialogue. The third student is given a copy of the corresponding answers (taken from the **Discovering French** Answer Key) and makes sure the others respond accurately. Then roles are rotated for the next activity.

Note: In trio activities, students take the responsibility for correcting one another in a supportive way. While two students focus on speaking, the third student practices reading and critical listening skills.

F Critical Thinking

General Background: Questions and Answers

■ *What is meant by the term Critical Thinking?*

Critical Thinking, which some trace to John Dewey in the early part of this century, is an educational trend that has elicited a great deal of interest in recent years.[4] Typically, teaching is divided into two areas: skills and dispositions.

■ *What are Critical Thinking skills?*

Critical Thinking skills or abilities relate to the cognitive functions of analysis, synthesis and evaluation. Some commonly cited Critical Thinking skills are the ability to formulate questions, to observe patterns, to identify assumptions, to clarify problems, to use logic, and to weigh judgments.

■ *What are Critical Thinking dispositions?*

Dispositions or attitudes constitute the affective aspect of Critical Thinking. They include using one's critical thinking skills, being open-minded, remaining impartial, suspending judgment, questioning one's own views, and recognizing the complexity of the real world and its problems.

■ *How can the teaching of Critical Thinking be incorporated in beginning foreign language classes?*

As one would expect, current educational research has focused on the teaching of logic and the introduction of Critical Thinking skills into subject areas taught in English, such as math, science, social studies, reading and writing. However, even though the main focus of beginning language classes is the acquisition of basic communication skills, students can be introduced to Critical Thinking skills as they make cross-cultural comparisons and as they learn to analyze how language functions. Once their linguistic base is broadened, they can sharpen their Critical Thinking skills while increasing their reading and listening comprehension and learning to express themselves with greater precision in speaking and writing.

■ *How does* Discovering French *encourage the teaching of Critical Thinking?*

The manner in which **Discovering French–Bleu** fosters the development of both Critical Thinking skills and dispositions is described in the next two sections. Specific suggestions for Critical Thinking activities are given in the Extended Teacher's Edition preceded by the symbol:

Strengthening Critical Thinking Skills

Discovering French–Bleu uses four main types of activities to develop Critical Thinking skills. (Since Critical Thinking is an open-ended process, suggestions for these activities are often given in the Teacher's Edition rather than in the Student Text.)

Observing Cross-Cultural Similarities and Differences

With **Discovering French** students have frequent opportunity to observe aspects of another culture with which they are unfamiliar.

- Obviously, the richest point of departure for cross-cultural observations is the **Discovering French Video**. Suggestions for activities of this type are given in the Extended Teacher's Edition.
- In the Student Textbook, the cultural notes and numerous photographs can also lead to reflection and analysis.
- In the *Vive la différence!* readings in certain *Entracte* sections, students answer questions about their own preferences and then compare their responses with those of French students their own age.

Noticing Linguistic Similarities and Differences

The study of a second language helps students think critically about how English works. As they compare English and French, they begin to recognize that concepts exist independently of the words with which they are expressed.

- In *Learning about Language* boxes, students acquire the terminology to talk about language. (See Student Text, p.98)
- Where appropriate, English and French are contrasted graphically to show that there is not a word-for-word correspondence between the two languages. (See Student Text, p.109)

[4] For an informative overview, see Mellen Kennedy, Michelle B. Fisher and Robert H. Ennis, "Critical Thinking: Literature Review and Needed Research" in Lorna Idol and Beau Fly Jones, eds., **Educational Values and Cognitive Instruction: Implications for Reform,** North Central Regional Educational Laboratory, 1991, pp. 11–40. (Published by Lawrence Erlbaum Assoc., 365 Broadway, Hillsdale, NJ)

Using Logic

Certain types of activities in **Discovering French** require the students to use logic to arrive at the appropriate responses.

- In *Allô!* activities, students make logical deductions as they match questions with their corresponding answers. (See Student Text, p.126, Act.1)
- In more challenging activities, students are given the responses and are asked to determine which questions were asked. (See Student Text, p.126, Act.2)
- Certain types of completion activities ask the students to think logically as they select an appropriate response. (See Student Text, p.124, Act.10)

Developing Reading Skills

In the *Entracte* sections, students have the opportunity to work with a variety of different types of readings.

- Critical thinking skills are often incorporated into the pre-reading and post-reading activities.
- The *Comment lire* sections encourage students to use critical thinking skills as they learn to read French for comprehension.

Strengthening Critical Thinking Dispositions

Although it is difficult to change attitudes through teaching materials alone, **Discovering French–Bleu**, with the support and guidance of the teacher, encourages students to broaden their views.

Developing a Multi-Cultural World View

Film is a powerful medium for expanding student horizons. Through multiple critical viewings of the **Discovering French** video modules, students will become more open-minded and less judgmental about cross-cultural differences between France and the United States. They will slowly begin to shed a monocultural world view and become more accepting of cultural diversity.

Appreciating Linguistic Diversity

As students listen to the more than one hundred different French voices on the cassette program and see these speakers on the video, they will begin to recognize the diversity of the French linguistic world.

Breaking Away from a Monolingual Mode of Expression

As students learn to observe how the French language works and how it compares to English, they will begin to see that similar concepts are expressed differently in the two languages. Moreover, they will start to realize that to make oneself understood in a second language, one must adopt the characteristics of that language.

F Portfolio Assessment

General Background: Questions and Answers

■ **What is Portfolio Assessment?**

Portfolio Assessment is a means of evaluating academic progress by collecting the best work a student has produced in the course of the term. This portfolio of material is kept on file in the school to be used as the basis for final grades and other evaluation.

■ **What are the key features of Portfolio Assessment?**

Although the features of Portfolio Assessment vary somewhat from program to program, the following are quite characteristic:

- Students are given clear instructions as to the steps required in the preparation of the portfolio piece or pieces.
- Students maintain a formal log or notebook which contains outlines and early drafts of the written work.
- Students are encouraged to work cooperatively in pairs or teams to edit and polish their final pieces.
- The final portfolio piece is presented in a "formal" format (e.g., written in ink, typed, printed by computer).
- Students often have the opportunity to read one another's pieces.
- Students may be graded on the "process" (that is, how carefully they have gone through the suggested steps in preparing their piece) as well as the "product" (the piece itself).

■ **What are the benefits of Portfolio Assessment?**

Since traditional tests, be they achievement tests or proficiency tests, evaluate performance at a specific point in time, they are often associated with a feeling of pressure which may affect how well a student does. Even if pressure is not a factor, the grades on traditional tests are always subject to Standard Error, that is, some students do better than expected on a test while others do worse.

With Portfolio Assessment, students have longer periods of time to work on the material for which they will be evaluated and feel less overwhelmed. In selecting pieces for their portfolios, they each have the opportunity to interact with the teacher, who helps them choose their best work.

The Portfolio itself is of educational benefit. As students compare portfolio pieces done early in the year with work produced later, they see their own improvement and can take pride in their progress.

Furthermore, with the Portfolio pieces, the teacher also has a selection of carefully prepared language samples to show families on Parent-Teacher night.

Finally, a system of Portfolio Assessment helps schools evaluate their programs because it provides a basis of comparing learning outcomes over time as well as between classes.

■ **Does Portfolio Assessment replace traditional assessment?**

Usually Portfolio Assessment is used to supplement, but not replace traditional assessment, which usually includes formal tests, quizzes, class participation, homework, and so forth. In classes that have adopted Portfolio Assessment, a given percent of the student's grade is determined by the portfolio pieces.

■ **In what form can Portfolio Assessment be adapted to French classes?**

Traditionally, Portfolio Assessment procedures have been developed for language arts and social studies classes, where students prepare written reports and essays in English. In French classes, Portfolio Assessment would ideally contain examples of both oral and written French since there is an emphasis on speaking as well as writing skills.

Implementing Portfolio Assessment

Although Portfolio Assessment in French classes has traditionally not been introduced until the second or third year, once students have a stronger command of the language, the format of **Discovering French–Bleu** is such that teachers can have students prepare individual portfolios from the beginning of instruction.

For each unit (or every other unit), students can polish one of the *À votre tour* activities for inclusion in their portfolio. For Units 1 to 3, these will be oral conversations. Beginning with Unit 4, the teacher has the option of assigning either an oral or a written piece, or both. Obviously, at this beginning level, the pieces will be brief and limited to known vocabulary and structures. However, over the course of the year, the pieces will become more complex and students will have the satisfaction of seeing how much progress they have made.

Preparing the Oral Portfolio

The preparation of an oral portfolio piece requires careful planning.

- The first step is to decide on format: whether to record the oral portfolio on audiocassette or videocassette. This decision will obviously depend on the audio-visual support available. It is also possible to use audiocassettes for some units and videocassettes for others.
- The next step is the selection of the specific conversation to be prepared and recorded. Depending on the level of the class, you may opt for a structured conversation (such as a *Conversation dirigée* or *Créa-dialogue,* where there is a recorded model in the Cassette Program) or a more open-ended one (for which there is no recorded model).
- The third step is to match each person with a conversational partner. You may let students select their own partners, you may assign them by pairing stronger students with weaker students, or you may determine the pairs randomly by picking numbers.

Once the task has been assigned and the partners selected, the students work together to prepare and record a "preliminary draft" of their conversation. (Even if the final version is to be on videocassette, this preparatory step can be done on audiocassette.)

Then students get together in groups of four and take turns listening to and correcting their two recorded conversations. If they have questions, they can ask the teacher's advice. The purpose of this step is to suggest ways of improving the final portfolio recording which will be graded.

Finally, the students in pairs make their final recordings, which are then placed in the portfolio. (See Student Text, p. 31, Act.5)

Preparing the Written Portfolio

The preparation of a piece for the written portfolio is similar, in its general outline, to that of the recorded portfolio piece, but with two major differences: (1) there is no need for audio-visual logistics, and (2) students submit their pieces individually, rather than in pairs.

Beginning with Niveau B, the students learn to express themselves in writing. The *À votre tour* sections, which, beginning with Unit 4, appear at the end of each lesson, always have suggestions for written self-expression. For each unit, the teacher will select one topic (or a choice of two or three) for the portfolio piece.

Students prepare their first drafts, and then work in small groups editing and correcting one another's work. If necessary, they may ask the teacher for assistance. (If desired, the students may prepare a second modified draft which is turned in to the teacher for correction.)

Each student then incorporates the suggestions received into a final draft, which is rewritten in formal form and placed, together with the early drafts, in the individual portfolio. (See Student Text, p.105, Act.4)

Sharing the Portfolio Contents

An important by-product of Portfolio Assessment is that students can share their work with others. There are many ways this can be done.

- Video-taped portfolio pieces can be shown to the entire class. If appropriate, classes in a school system can exchange video portfolios.
- Written portfolio pieces can be "published" in a class newsletter. If appropriate, certain pieces can be selected for a school-wide newsletter or a department bulletin board.
- Portfolio pieces can be the basis of pen pal exchanges or class correspondence with a matched school in a French-speaking country.

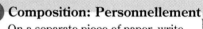

5 Composition: Personnellement

On a separate piece of paper, write where you are and where you are not at each of the following times.

▶ à 9 heures du matin

- à 4 heures
- à 7 heures du soir
- samedi
- dimanche
- en juillet

F The Euro Currency

When did France adopt the euro?

France officially changed its currency system on January 1, 1999. It replaced the franc, the monetary unit which it had been using for about 200 years, by the **euro**, the common currency adopted by eleven different European countries. The fixed conversion rate between the two currencies was set at:

    1 euro = 6.56 francs (more precisely, 6.55957 francs)
To help French people adjust to this major change in their habits, the French government decided that its citizens could use both the old franc and the new euro for a period of three years.

    During this transition period, bills and coins denominated in francs would remain in use, but French people could choose to pay their bills either in francs or euros when using their checkbooks or their credit cards. In shops, every price had to be labeled both in francs and in its equivalent in euros, and every invoice had to be written in both currencies. For certain transactions, however, such as the purchase of stocks and bonds, prices would be given only in euros. The new euro bills and coins would be issued on January 1, 2002, and the old franc currency would be completely withdrawn from circulation on July 1, 2002. After that date, the euro would be the only legal currency of France.

What is the value of the euro?

The euro has the same value in every European country where it has been adopted; that is, one euro in France is the same as one euro in Germany or Italy or Spain. However, the euro fluctuates in value against the other currencies of the world. As of January 1, 2000, the value of the euro was about 1.1 US dollar. For classroom activities, students can be told roughly to equate 1 euro to 1 dollar (unless the exchange rather between the two currencies deviates substantially from this parity).

How is the Euro symbolized and what are its divisions?

The euro is abbreviated EUR and its symbol resembles the Greek letter epsilon (for "Europa"), crossed by two horizontal bars: €
The euro is divided into 100 cents which, in France, can be called **cents** or **centimes**.

What does the euro currency consist of and what do the bills and coins look like?

The euro currency consists of 7 different bills and 8 different coins, as depicted on the facing page.

- The 7 bills are of different colors and different sizes, with the size increasing with the value of each bill: 5 euros (gray), 10 euros (red), 20 euros (blue), 50 euros (orange), 100 euros (green), 200 euros (yellow), 500 euros (purple). The design of the euro bills was created by an Austrian artist and is identical for all countries using the euro.
The doors, windows and archways pictured on the front (or recto) of the bills symbolize economic opportunity and the opening to new ideas. The bridges which constitute the main motif of the back (or verso) of the bills evoke the strong ties between the European countries represented on the right. These architectural and engineering features are not real buildings or bridges, but rather represent different styles from the oldest (5 euros) to the most modern (500 euros) associated with the various periods in European history.

- The 8 coins (1, 2, 5, 10, 20, 50 cents and 1 and 2 euros) have the same image on the recto (or "head") side in all the countries using the euro currency. The verso (or "tail") side, however, features national symbols typical of the country in which they are minted. For the French coins, the 1, 2 and 5 cent coins represent the face of "**Marianne**," symbol of the French Republic. The 10, 20 and 50 cent coins bear the letters "**RF**" (for **République Française**) and an effigy of "**La Semeuse**" (a woman sowing seeds) who has traditionally been another symbol of France. The 1 and 2 euro coins feature a tree of life together with the letters "**RF**" and the French motto "**Liberté, Egalité, Fraternité**."

Radio gonflable
pour emporter à la plage
ou à la piscine, en PVC
18,14€

Sac à dos
multipoche avec
compartiment en mousse
pour ordinateur
75,46€

Ordinateur de poche
édition limitée, léger, petit,
se loge facilement dans
un sac à main
730,23€

Stylo-bille
embout Plasmium
liquide, qui prend la
forme des doigts
3,26€ PIÈCE

How does one pronounce prices in euros?

In French, the word **euro** is pronounced /øro/. When counting, the usual rules of liaison apply. The basic liaison patterns are as follows:

un/ⁿ/ euro	six/ᶻ/ euros	vingt/ᵗ/ euros
deux/ᶻ/ euros	sept/ᵗ/ euros	cent/ᵗ/ euros
trois/ᶻ/ euros	huit/ᵗ/ euros	deux cents/ᶻ/ euros
quatre euros	neuf/ᵛ/ euros	mille euros
cinq/ᵏ/ euros	dix/ᶻ/ euros	deux mille euros

Where can I get more information on the euro?

The official French information site for the euro is to be found on the Internet at:

www.elysee.fr/euro/index.htm

Another informative site is maintained at:

www.laposte.fr/euro

What about the "old" franc?

Students should be familiar with the franc since they will discover its existence in texts and films prior to the year 2000, which, of course, includes the bulk of French literature and cinema. For this reason, while we have updated the student text to the new euro standard, we have kept the use of the franc in the video. As the occasions arise, students should be encouraged to convert francs into euros. To arrive at a close approximation, the following simple arithmetic operation may be used:

EXAMPLE: What is the euro equivalent of 240 francs?

a) write down the price in francs:	240
b) divide the price by 2:	+ 120
c) add the two sums:	360
d) divide the result by 10:	36
ANSWER	**240 francs = 36 euros**

How can one use the euro in the classroom?

Because the creation of the euro represents a significant development on the international economic scene, students should be encouraged to use it as early as possible. A special transparency featuring the euro currency has been prepared and should be used to familiarize the students with the design of the bills and the coins. This transparency can also be used as a copymaster to create black-and-white "paper money" which can be distributed to the students and used in traditional classroom activities, such as shopping, buying food, auctioning possessions, guessing the prices of items, etc.

F Reference Information

Brief Directory of Useful Addresses

From time to time, classroom teachers of French find themselves in need of professional support. This section gives the names and addresses of selected organizations and the type of assistance they might be able to provide.

Professional Language Organizations

Professional language organizations offer a wide variety of services and support to their membership.

■ AATF (American Association of Teachers of French)

As an AATF member:

- you will receive subscriptions to the *French Review* and the *AATF National Bulletin.*
- you will be able to attend local, regional and national AATF meetings where you can share ideas and meet new colleagues.
- you have the opportunity to apply for one of the many summer scholarships to France and Quebec offered to AATF members.
- you may sponsor a chapter of the *Société Honoraire de Français* at your school so that your students will then be eligible to compete for the ten annual $500 study abroad travel grants and participate in the SHF creative writing contest.
- you can have your students participate in the National French Contest and be considered for local, regional and national awards.
- you can obtain pen pals for your students through the *Bureau de Correspondance Scolaire.*

For membership information, write:
AATF-Mailcode 4510, Dept. of Foreign Languages
Southern Illinois University, Carbondale, IL 62901-4510
Phone: (618) 453-5731. http://aatf.utsa.edu

■ ACTFL (American Council on the Teaching of Foreign Languages)

As an ACTFL member:

- you will receive subscriptions to the *Foreign Language Annals* and the *ACTFL Bulletin.*
- you will be able to attend the annual ACTFL convention where you can share ideas and meet new colleagues.
- you have the opportunity to apply for one of the ACTFL summer scholarships to France.

For membership information, contact:
ACTFL, 6 Executive Plaza
Yonkers, NY 10701-6801
Phone: (914) 963-8830

The ACTFL office will also be able to let you know whom to contact to join your local state foreign language association, and how you can get information about regional language meetings.

Governmental Organizations

■ Alliance Française

The Alliance Française is a French organization dedicated to the promotion of French language and culture. In addition to language courses, most Alliance Française centers sponsor a variety of cultural and educational events.

To obtain the address of the Alliance Française nearest you, write:
Alliance Française, Délégation générale
2819 Ordway St., NW
Washington, DC 20008-1346
Phone: 1 (800) 6-FRANCE
         (202) 966-9740

■ French Cultural Services

The French Cultural Services are very supportive of French teaching in the United States. For more information, contact the French Cultural Officer at the French Consulate nearest you or write the New York office.

To obtain information about available French cultural materials, write:
Services Culturels de France
934 Fifth Avenue
New York, NY 10021
Phone: (212) 606-3688

■ Quebec Delegation

The Province of Quebec has official delegations in many of the large cities. Many of these Delegations are eager to work with French teachers to promote the teaching of French and closer contacts with Quebec.

Publications

■ *News from France*

News from France is a biweekly English-language publication containing a review of news and trends from France. It is distributed free of charge.

To be placed on the mailing list, write:
French Embassy Press and Information Service
4101 Reservoir Road, NW
Washington, DC 20007-2182
Phone: (202) 944-6000
http://www.info.France.usa.org

■ *Update*

Update is a publication of the Quebec Government which appears every three months. It is distributed free of charge.

Contact your regional delegation to be placed on the mailing list.

■ *Journal français d'Amérique*

The *Journal français d'Amérique* is a biweekly French-language newspaper published in San Francisco. Special group subscription rates are available to schools.

To receive a sample issue which also contains subscription information, write:
Journal français d'Amérique
P.O. Box 1522
Martinez, CA 94553-6500
Phone (800) 851-7785

Other Useful Addresses

■ *Sister Cities International*

If your town has a Sister City in a French-speaking country, you might want to explore the possibility of initiating a youth or education exchange program. If your town does not yet have a French-speaking Sister City, you might want to encourage your community to set up such an affiliation.

For information on both youth exchanges and the establishment of a sister-city association, contact:
Sister Cities International
Suite 2501
1300 Pennsylvania Ave. NW
Washington, DC 20004
Phone: (202) 312-1200

■ *Nacel Cultural Exchanges*

If you have students who would like to host a French-speaking student for a month during the summer, or who would themselves like to stay with a family in France or Senegal, have them contact the non-profit organization **Nacel.**

For information on summer homestays, write:
Nacel Cultural Exchanges
3410 Federal Drive, Suite 101
St. Paul, MN 55122
Phone: (612) 686-0080
http://www.nacel.ca

Cultural Reference Guide

Topic	Student text page	ETE note page	Video module
Animals			
domestic animals	46, 54	T45, T46, T54, T151	M 7, M 21
wild animals	173, 185		
Arts			
French contributions	7	T7	
la Maison des Jeunes			VC 23
See also: Cinema, Museums, Music and concert halls			
Attitudes and values			
cars	171		VC 20
cinema	42, 235	T307	
cuisine and food	59, 68, 346, 371	T56, T78, T371	
fashion	246, 266, 288		
friendship	34, 37, 136, 161, 180		VC 5
money	66, 136, 275, 290–291, 296		VC 11
music	42, 329	T310	M 32, VC 32
quality of life	296, 307		
school	88	T297	
Birthdays	47, 50, 337		M 8
Cafés	56, 59, 63, 211	T57, T62, T89, T101, T119, T371	M 9, VC 9, M 11, VC 14
ordering beverages	63	T351	M 10, VC 10, M 11
tipping	63		
Cars	171	T171	M 20, VC 20
drivers license	171		VC 20
parking		T146	M 20
Cinema			
French actors and actresses	232, 233	T233	
movies	88, 230, 234–235, 296	T89	M 4, M 29, VC 30
Cities			
Abidjan, Côte d'Ivoire	3, 133		
Angers, France		T189	
Annecy, France			M 29
Bordeaux, France	133, 188		
Bruxelles, Belgique	341	T341	
Chamonix, France	255	T6	
Dakar, Sénégal	118		M-A, M 16, VC 16
Deauville, France	250	T356, T380, T381	M 36
Fort-de-France, Martinique	19		M-A
Genève, Suisse	133		M-A
Grenoble, France	188, 338		
La Rochelle, France	33		
Le Havre, France	342		

Topic	Student text page	ETE note page	Video module
Lille, France	188		M 21
Lyon, France	188	T188, T343	M 21
Marseille, France	188, 392	T188	M 21
Montpellier, France	33, 149	T149	
Montréal, Canada	41, 133, 254	T41, T121, T192, T254, T309	M-A, VC 6
Nantes, France	188		
New Orleans, Louisiana		T206	
Nice, France	188, 255, 338		
Nîmes, France	286	T338	
Orléans, France	33		
Paris, France	33, 119, 137, 188, 199, 236–243	T188, T212, T342	M-C
Québec, Canada	3, 393	T192, T277	M-A, VC 6
Savigny-sur-Orge	76, 77	T77	
Strasbourg, France	149, 188	T149	M 21
Toulon, France	188, 343	T343	M 21
Toulouse, France	2, 182, 188	T182	
Tours, France	130	T190, T199	M 21
Trois Îlets, Martinique	133	T394	
Versailles, France	221	T221	
City life			
apartment buildings	220, 221, 242	T195	M 24, VC 24
châteaux	189, 221		M 21
churches	238	T191	M-A, M 21
libraries			M 21
la Maison des Jeunes			VC 23
neighborhoods	191		
parks	189		M 21
public buildings	189, 191, 199, 236–241	T191, T197	M 21
shopping malls			M 21, VC 27
street names	190	T193	
See also Cafés, Museums, Restaurants			
Clothing and personal appearance			
Fashion	247, 286	T248	M 25, VC 25, M 26, M 27
Shopping for clothes	248–250, 252, 266	T248, T250	M 25, VC 25, M 26, M 27, VC 27
Communications			
le Minitel et l'Internet	132, 189	T132	
post office	189	T189	
telephone		T374, T386	VC 13
writing letters	131, 183		
Concerts: *See* **Music**			
Cuisine			
Creole cuisine	394, 395		
French terminology	348, 371		
making **crêpes**	396–397	T370	VC 35

Topic	Student text page	ETE note page	Video module
Currency: *See* **Money**			
Cycling: *See* **Sports**			
Daily activities	78, 88, 128	T78	M 13, M 14, M 15, M 16, M 30
See also: School, Leisure activities			
Earning a living			M 28, VC 28
part-time jobs	275		
Ethnic diversity	136	T3, T137, T229	M-A, M 2, VC 2, M 19, VC 19
Exchange programs		T42	
Family			
family members	44, 45, 223	T45, T223	M 7, VC 7
family occasions	45, 180, 307	T45	VC 7
helping at home	296		M 29, M 34
vacations	45, 305		M 29, M 36
Fashion			
clothing	246, 248–250, 266, 286		M 25. VC 25, M 26, M 27
Fast foods and snacks			
la bonbonnière		T57	M 9
la boulangerie	56	T189	M 9
la crêperie	396		VC 33
la croissanterie			M 33
fast-food restaurants	56, 59, 371	T57, T59, T349	M 9, M 14, M 33
la pâtisserie	56		M 9
street vendors	56, 58		VC 9
See also: Cafés			
Food	59, 350–351, 355, 359	T107, T189, T342, T347, T350, T351, T359, T369, T381	M 33, VC 34, M 35, M 39
beverages	63, 64, 351	T63, T64, T92, T351, T346	M 10
des biscottes			
la bouillabaisse	392		
le camembert	392		
les crêpes	59, 396–397	T357, T396	M 35
un croque-monsieur		T60	
desserts	351		
ice cream		T59, T101, T119, T137, T275	
le pâté	380	T107	
les pizzas		T58	M 9
sandwiches	59, 60	T60, T119	VC 9, M 25
See also: Cafés, Fast food, Restaurants, School cafeteria			
France	6		M-A, VC 2, VC 12
See also: Cities, Geography, Population, Regions			
French Canada	3	T311, T347	M-A, VC 6
"Alouette"	74	T74	
le château Frontenac	393	T277, T393	
French language in Canada		T17, T21, T49, T171, T190, T248, T298, T317, T348, T351, T393	
See also: Cities: Montreal, Quebec, French-speaking world: Quebec			

Topic	Student text page	ETE note page	Video module
French-speaking world		T5	
Algeria	2, 5, 340	T5, T341	M-A, VC 19
Belgium	5, 340, 341		M-A
Cambodia	2, 4, 136	T2, T136	M-A, VC 19
Cameroun		T229	
Congo		T229	
Congo (Democratic Republic)	5	T5	M-A
Côte d'Ivoire	3, 5	T5, T229	M-A
Haiti	3, 4		M-A
Laos	136	T136	
Lebanon	4		
Louisiana	4		
Luxembourg	5		M-A
Madagascar	5	T5	M-A
Mali		T229	
Morocco	5	T5	M-A
New England	4		
North Africa	3, 5, 136	T5, T136	M-A
Québec	3, 4, 41, 340, 393	T280, T347	M-A, M 6
Sénégal	5, 118	T5, T118, T229	M-A, M 16, VC 16
Switzerland	2, 5		M-A
Tunisia	5	T5	M-A
Vietnam	3, 4, 136	T136	M-A
See also: Regions and overseas departments			
Friends: *See* **Interpersonal relations**			
Geography			
Alps	7, 255	T6, T71	VC 12
beaches	6–7		VC 12, M 29, M 36, VC 36
France	6–7		M-A, M 2, VC 2, VC 12, M 19, VC 19
Pyrénées	7	T6, T54	VC 12
Greetings			
la bise	12		M 1, VC 1, M 6,
formality	23, 98	T23	M 3, VC 3
forms of address	23		
greetings	12, 23, 24, 30	T15, T23	M 1, M 3, VC 1, M 6
handshake	12		
introductions			M 2
History and historical sites			
French-Indian Wars		T33	
Gallo-Roman Period	7, 343	T7, T16, T49, T188	
Lascaux caves		T7	
Louisiana Purchase		T33	
Normandy landing	342		
Nouvelle France	33	T33, T393	
Vikings		T39	
Holidays and traditions			
birthdays	47, 50, 337		VC 8
French flag			M 20
French holidays	301	T300, T301	
le Quatorze Juillet	103, 301, 343	T103, T199, T301	
Housing and the home			
apartment buildings	220, 221	T195	M 24, VC 24
bedrooms of French teens		T215	M-B, VC 17
floor plan	195	T195	

Topic	Student text page	ETE note page	Video module
Cardin, Pierre	246		
Champlain	33		
Chanel, Coco	246, 286	T245, T286	
Colette		T7	
Chirac, Jacques		T169	
Corot, Jean-Baptiste	80		M-B
Curie, Marie and Pierre		T67	
Debussy, Claude		T7	
Depardieu, Gérard	233	T233	
Dior, Christian	246, 247		
Dubuque	33		
Duluth	33		
Eiffel, Gustave		T20	
Gauguin		T7	
Goldman, Jean-Jacques	169		
Hugo, Victor	190	T7	
Jolliet	33		
Lacoste, René	286	T286	
La Fayette	33, 190		
Lambert, Christophe	233	T233	
LaSalle	33		
Louis XIV	33, 221		
Marquette	33		
Masséna		T193	
Matisse		T7	
Molière		T193	
Monet, Claude	240	T240	
Moulin, Jean		T193	
Napoléon	33, 238, 343	T35, T213, T238	
Noah, Yannick	169		
Pascal, Blaise		T193	
Pompidou, Georges		T240	
Ravel		T7	
Rampal, Jean-Pierre		T7	
Renoir, Auguste	240	T7, T240	
Rousseau		T7	
Rykiel, Sonia	246		
Saint Laurent, Yves	246		
Saint Louis	33		
Sartre, Jean-Paul		T7	
Sully, Duc de		T193	
Toulouse-Lautrec, Henri de	240	T240	
Vuarnet, Jean	286	T141, T286	
Voltaire		T7	
Wilson, Woodrow	190		
Population			
ethnic backgrounds	136	T137	
France	136		
Paris	236		
United States		T136	
Québec	340	T280, T347	
description and population	41		VC 6
Radio		T135	M 13
Reading and literature			
bookstores		T161	M 17, M 26
comics	16, 55	T135	
French literature	7	T129	
libraries			M 22
Paris-Match		T312	
reading for pleasure	180, 230, 296		
Regions and departments of France	7		M-A, VC 12
Alsace	7, 149	T6	VC 12
Bretagne	7, 396		

Topic	Student text page	ETE note page	Video module
Champagne	392	T392	
Corsica	342		
Côte d'Azur		T6	VC 12
DOM-TOM		T19	VC 2
French Guiana		T7, T21	VC 2
Guadeloupe	4, 394	T229, T303	VC 2
Martinique	2, 4, 19, 340, 394	T18, T19, T229	M-A, VC 2
New Caledonia	4		VC 2
Normandie	7, 250, 342	T39, T342	
Provence	7		VC 12
Réunion			VC 2
St. Pierre et Miquelon		T4	VC 2
Savoie			VC 12
Tahiti	4, 338		VC 2
Touraine	7, 130	T6	VC 12
Religion	136	T191	
Restaurants			
Guide Michelin		T68	
ordering from a menu	352, 357, 393	T62, T395	
types of restaurants	68, 371	T357	M 21, M 33, M 35
School			
le bac		T80, T282 T297	
cafeteria	18, 160, 359	T80, T345, T359	M 2, M-B
le cartable		T97	
classes, class schedules	79, 88, 157	T15, T89	M-B
le collège	81, 107	T15, T138	M 1, M 2, M 3
entrance exams		T297	
foreign languages	79, 136		M-B
getting to school	78, 232		M 3, M 22
homework	78, 88, 319	T373	M 8, M-B, M 15, M 29, M 30, M 31
le lycée	80, 81, 107	T138	M-B
la rentrée	14, 15		M 1
report cards	81	T81	
teachers	180		M 1, M 3, M-B, M 27
Wednesday afternoon	79, 97		M 30
Shopping for clothes	248–250, 252, 266, 286, 289	T248, T250	
catalog shopping	265, 287		
clothing stores and boutiques	246–247	T254, T266	M 25, VC 25, M 26, M 27
department stores	246, 256	T254, T257, T263	M 25, M 26, VC 26, M 27
discount stores	246, 247		VC 25
Les Galeries Lafayette	226, 246, 286	T152, T213, T237, T246, T262	M 25
le Marché aux puces	246, 247, 253, 288		VC 25
window-shopping	266	T267	M 25
Shopping for food		T355	
going shopping	189		M 33
les grandes surfaces	288	T288	
le marché	355	T345, T355	VC 33
specialty shops	189	T355	
supermarkets	189, 355	T351	VC 33, M 34

HEATH

DISCOVERING FRENCH

BLEU

Jean-Paul Valette
Rebecca M. Valette

McDougal Littell
Evanston, Illinois • Boston • Dallas

Teacher Consultants

Steve Covey, *Sunnyvale Junior High School, California*
Andrea Henderson, *First Colony Middle School, Texas*
Dianne Hopen, *Humboldt High School, Minnesota*
Patricia McCann, *Lincoln-Sudbury High School, Massachusetts*
T. Jeffrey Richards, *Roosevelt High School, South Dakota*
Margie Ricks, *Dulles High School, Texas*
Frank Strell, *La Salle-Peru Township High School, Illinois*
Susan Wildman, *Western Albemarle High School, Virginia*

McDougal Littell wishes to express its heartfelt appreciation to **Gail Smith,** Supervising Editor for *DISCOVERING FRENCH.* Her creativity, organizational skills, determination and sheer hard work have been invaluable in all aspects of the program, including the award winning *DISCOVERING FRENCH* CD-ROM.

Illustrations

Yves Calarnou
Jean-Pierre Foissy
Élisabeth Schlossberg

Printed in the United States of America
International Standard Book Number: 0-618-03504-4

1 2 3 4 5 6 7 8 9 10 –VHP– 06 05 04 03 02 01 00

Lycée Jean-Baptiste Corot

MERCI

Special thanks to the students and staff of
• **Collège Eugène Delacroix,** *Paris*
• **Lycée Jean-Baptiste Corot,** *Savigny-sur-Orge*
for their cooperation and assistance.

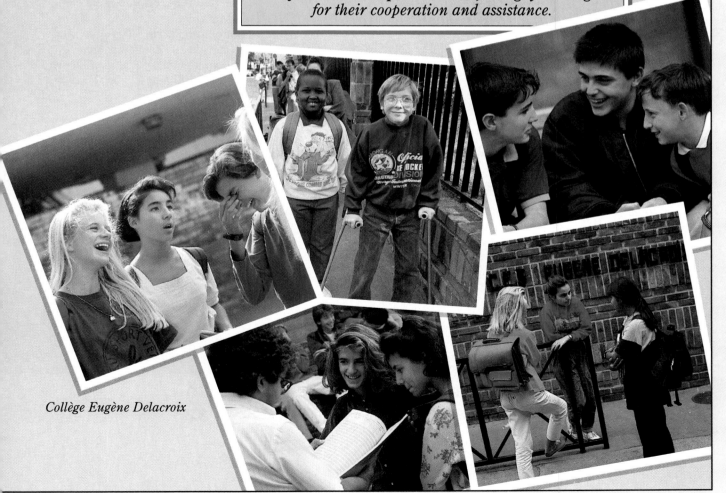

Collège Eugène Delacroix

Contents

UNITÉ 1 Bonjour!   12

Introduction culturelle: Salutations
Thème: Getting acquainted

iv

vii

ix

x

Parlons français!

Chers amis,

Welcome to DISCOVERING FRENCH and congratulations on your choice of French as a foreign language!

There are many reasons why people decide to learn French. Some people choose French because they plan to visit Canada or Europe or French-speaking Africa. Others want to learn to read articles or books written in French. Still others study French because in their work, they will come into contact with French speakers or because their own family is of French or French-American heritage. And there are many people who learn French for pleasure: They want to enjoy French films and French music, and they like French poetry and French art.

There is another reason for studying French that you have perhaps not thought about. As you learn another language, you develop a better understanding of your own language and how it works. You also develop a better appreciation of your own country and culture as you expand your world view and discover the various French-speaking areas of the globe. You will discover cultural similarities and differences, and you will realize how much French civilization has contributed to our life in the United States.

And, of course, everyone will agree that studying a foreign language also helps us get to know and communicate with people from other cultures. By speaking French, you will be in touch with the many millions of people who use that language in their daily lives. These French speakers **(les francophones)** represent a wide variety of ethnic and cultural backgrounds. As you will see, they live not only in France and other parts of Europe but also in Africa, in North and South America, in Asia . . . in fact, on all continents!

On the pages of this book and in the accompanying video, you will meet many young people who speak French. Listen carefully to what they say and how they express themselves. They will help you understand not only their language but also the way they live.

Bonne chance!

Jean-Paul Valette   *Rebecca M. Valette*

Bienvenue!

France is a country of Western Europe with a population of close to 60 million people. On the map of the world, France may look tiny when compared to such giant countries as the United States, Canada, China, India, Russia or Australia. Yet, in spite of its relatively small size and population, France plays a major role in world affairs. It is a founding member of the United Nations and one of the five permanent members of the Security Council, along with the United States, Great Britain, Russia and China. As such, it must approve and can veto any decision taken by this world organization.

Economically, France is a highly developed nation, and its citizens enjoy one of the highest standards of living in the world. It is a pioneer and leader in many advanced technological and scientific fields, such as pharmaceutical and medical research, aeronautics and space exploration, rapid urban transportation, electronics, software engineering, and telecommunications.

The France of 2000 draws much of its prosperity and vitality from its integration into an economically unified Europe. **The European Union** (or **Union européenne**, as it is called in French), has taken nearly fifty years to build, but now has become a reality for nearly 400 million people. The first steps occurred in the 1950s when the leaders of France and Germany, two countries which had historically been very bitter enemies, decided to form a zone of free exchange between themselves and their immediate neighbors. At first the European Union had only six members, but now it includes fifteen countries of western, northern and southern Europe.

In addition to forming a powerful economic bloc, the creation of the European Union has provided many benefits for the citizens of its member countries and especially for its young people who can study, work and travel in any country of their choice within the Union without needing a passport, visa or permit of any kind. When shopping, they use the euro, the common European currency which has replaced the local currencies since 2002 and has the same value no matter in which country it is earned or spent. The creation of the euro is useful not only for Europeans, but also for the millions of American tourists who visit Europe every year and who no longer have to convert dollars into French francs, francs into German marks, marks into Italian liras, and liras into Spanish pesetas as they travel from country to country.

°2000 = deux mille

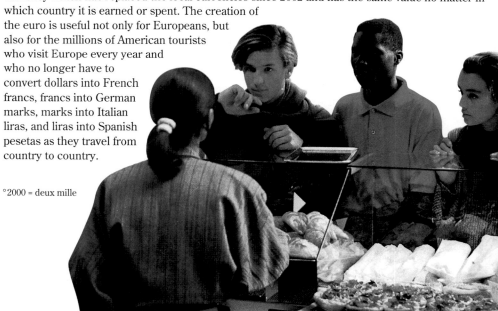

■ ### Some facts about the European Union

• Population: nearly 400 million people

• 15 member countries (11 of which use the "euro" as their national currency)

• 11 official languages (French, English, German, Spanish, Italian, Portuguese, Dutch, Danish, Finnish, Swedish, and Greek)

• European anthem: "Ode to Joy" by Beethoven

• European holiday: May 9 (This date commemorates the speech given on May 9, 1950, by the French statesman Robert Schuman in which he strongly advocated economic cooperation among France, Germany, and other European partners.)

■ **French sources of information on the euro:**

www.elysee.fr/euro

www.laposte.fr/euro

The European flag floats next to the French flag on many French public buildings. It consists of a circle of twelve yellow stars on a blue background. The number "12" does not represent the number of member countries, but is a symbol of strength and unity.

▲ The French flag consists of three vertical bands in blue, white and red. It is known to the French as **le tricolore**.

■ **Photo note**
The photo in the center shows the authors with a group of French **lycéens**. This picture was taken at the **Place Igor Stravinski** near the **Centre Pompidou** in Paris. The church in the background is the **église Saint Merri**.

◄ In 2000 the euro replaced the French franc as the national currency of France. The verso (or back) of each euro bank note has, on the left, the picture of a bridge which symbolizes the strong links between the member countries shown on the right.

Mlle Élise DuROCHER
8, rue des Grandes-Écoles
B.P. 377
86000 Poitiers
France

Mlle Sophie ANTOINE
12, rue Voltaire
75008 Paris

PAR AVION

◄ The euro is divided into 100 **cents** or **centimes**. Its symbol is the capital letter "E" (for **Europa**) formed by a partial circle crossed with two horizontal bars.

THE COUNTRIES OF THE EUROPEAN UNION

ORIGINAL MEMBERS	NEW MEMBERS	
Belgium	Austria	Ireland
France	Denmark*	Portugal
Germany	Finland	Spain
Italy	Great Britain*	Sweden*
Luxembourg	Greece*	
Netherlands		

In 1999, all of the above countries voted to use the euro as their national currency, except for the four marked with an asterisk (*).

▲ The first French stamp celebrating the euro and denominated in both the new currency (0,46 euro) and the old currency (3,00 francs).

1

A.4 Des francophones aux États-Unis
(5:48–7:38 min.)

■ This video segment has brief interviews with several French speakers in the U.S., including Dr. Phan (#12).

VIDEODISC Disc 1, Side1
10773–14190

Parlons français!

CULTURAL THEME:

The French-speaking world

VIDEO ESSAY:
Parlons français!
Total time: 7:01 min.
(Counter: 00:40 min.)

A.1 **Introduction**
(00:55–1:27 min.)
A.2 **La France**
(1:28–3:14 min.)
A.3 **Le monde francophone**
(3:15–5:47 min.)
A.4 **Des francophones aux États-Unis**
(5:48–7:38 min.)

VIDEODISC Disc 1, Side 1
1575–14190

Parlons français!

*T*he people portrayed on these pages represent many different backgrounds. Some live in France, some in the United States. They are from Europe, Africa, Asia, and North America. They do, however, have one thing in common. They all speak French. Let's meet them.

1
Sophie Lafont, 14, is from Toulouse, a city in southern France. She is a student at the Lycée Saint-Exupéry. (A **lycée** is the equivalent of an American high school.)

2
Philippe Martin, 15, lives in Paris and goes to the Collège Eugène Delacroix.

3
Stéphanie Malle, 14, also lives in Paris and attends the Collège Eugène Delacroix. Her family is from Martinique, a French island in the Caribbean.

4
Ahmed Belkacem, 14, lives in Lyon, France, and goes to the Lycée Jean Moulin. His parents are from Algeria and speak French and Arabic. Ahmed, who was born in France, speaks only French.

5
Fredy Vansattel, 20, lives near Lausanne, a city in French-speaking Switzerland. He is a student at the well-known École Hôtelière. In addition to French, Fredy also speaks English and German.

6
Prak Maph, 15, left Cambodia with his family when he was four. He lives in Paris and goes to the Lycée Claude Monet. Maph speaks French as well as Khmer, the national language of Cambodia.

2

■ **If students ask**
Prak Maph (#6): In Cambodia, the family name is always given first, and is then followed by the individual's name.

📖 **Pre-reading**
Have students look at the pictures of the various French-speakers.
Without reading the text, have them try to guess which countries these people are from.

Post-reading
Ask students to pick a person from the the text whom they would like to meet. Why would they like to talk to that person? What questions might they want to ask?

7

Amélan Konan, 13, lives in Abidjan, a large city in Ivory Coast, a country of West Africa. Amélan goes to the Collège Moderne Voltaire, where many of the teachers are from France. Amélan is fluent in both French and Baoulé, the tribal language that she speaks with her relatives.

8

Pauline Lévêque, 14, is from Quebec City in the province of Quebec, in Canada. Pauline goes to the École Louis-Jolliet. She speaks both French and English, but she prefers to speak French with her friends and family.

9

Moustapha Badid is a French athlete of North African origin who lives in Paris. At age 23, he won the wheelchair title at the Boston Marathon and established a world record in the event. In that same year, he also won an Olympic gold medal. He speaks French, Arabic, and some English.

10

Dr. Michèle Klopner, a clinical psychologist, grew up in Haiti, where her family resides. She came to the United States to study at the University of Michigan and Rutgers University. Dr. Klopner speaks French, Haitian Creole, and English. She uses all these languages in her work at the Cambridge Hospital in Cambridge, Massachusetts.

11

Marie-Christine Mouis was born in Canada of a French father and a Canadian mother. At the age of 16, Marie-Christine joined the Paris Opera Ballet, becoming the youngest dancer in the world's oldest ballet company. She was the principal ballerina of the Boston Ballet for ten years.

12

Dr. Larry Phan was born in Vietnam. At the age of ten, he went to France, where he received his high school education. In 1976, he came to the United States to pursue a medical career. He attended the University of California and Tufts School of Dental Medicine. Dr. Phan is on the staff of the Children's Hospital in Boston.

ACTIVITÉS CULTURELLES

1. On a world map or globe, locate the cities and countries of origin for each of the people pictured.
2. Do you know any people in your community who have French names or people who speak French? Where are their families originally from?

Using the video

In the Video Essay **Parlons français,** students are introduced to French speakers from around the world. Play the entire module as an introduction to the program, and more specifically, as an introduction to the photo essay.

Multi-culturalism

From the outset, students will discover that French is spoken not only in Europe, but also in Africa, Asia, and the Americas.

French-speakers represent many different ethnic groups and a broad variety of cultural traditions.

Bonjour, le monde français!

■ **Cultural note:** There are also two small French islands in the Atlantic, off the Canadian coast: Saint-Pierre and Miquelon. Since 1985, Saint-Pierre and Miquelon **(Saint-Pierre-et-Miquelon)** are considered as a "collectivité territoriale" and not as a "département."

■ **Cultural note:** In May 1997, newly appointed president of Zaire Laurent Kabila renamed his country the Democratic Republic of Congo **(la République Démocratique du Congo** or **le Congo démocratique).**

*I*n today's world, French is an international language spoken daily by more than 100 million people. French is understood by another 100 million in many countries and regions of the globe.

IN NORTH AMERICA

■ In Canada, about one third of the population speaks French. These French speakers live mainly in the province of Quebec **(le Québec)**. They are descendants of French settlers who came to Canada in the 17th and 18th centuries.

■ In the United States, French is understood and spoken in many families whose French and French-Canadian ancestors came to Louisiana **(la Louisiane)** and New England **(la Nouvelle-Angleterre)** at various times in our history.

■ In the Caribbean, French and Creole are spoken in the Republic of Haiti **(Haïti)**. French is also spoken on the islands of Martinique **(la Martinique)** and Guadeloupe **(la Guadeloupe)**; the inhabitants of these two islands are French citizens.

IN OTHER PARTS OF THE WORLD

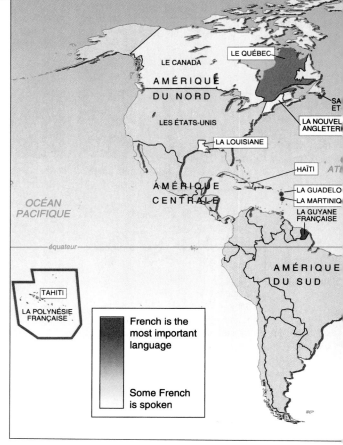

- LE CANADA
- LE QUÉBEC
- AMÉRIQUE DU NORD
- LES ÉTATS-UNIS
- SA ET
- LA NOUVEL ANGLETERI
- LA LOUISIANE
- HAÏTI
- AMÉRIQUE CENTRALE
- OCÉAN PACIFIQUE
- LA GUADELO
- LA MARTINIQ
- LA GUYANE FRANÇAISE
- équateur
- AMÉRIQUE DU SUD
- TAHITI
- LA POLYNÉSIE FRANÇAISE

French is the most important language

Some French is spoken

■ French is spoken as far away as Tahiti **(Tahiti)** and New Caledonia **(la Nouvelle-Calédonie)**, two French territories in the South Pacific.

■ In the Middle East, French is still taught and spoken in Lebanon **(le Liban)**.

■ French is also used and understood by many Vietnamese and Cambodian families who have left their countries **(le Viêt-nam, le Cambodge)** to settle in other parts of the world.

4

IN EUROPE

French is not only spoken in France **(la France)** but also in parts of Belgium **(la Belgique)**, Switzerland **(la Suisse)**, and Luxembourg **(le Luxembourg)**.

IN AFRICA

French is an important language in countries which have strong commercial and cultural ties to France.

■ In Western and Central Africa, about 20 countries have adapted French as their official language.

These countries include Senegal **(le Sénégal)**, the Ivory Coast **(la Côte d'Ivoire)**, and the Democratic Republic of Congo **(la République démocratique du Congo)**. French is also spoken on the large island of Madagascar **(Madagascar)**.

■ In North Africa, French is understood and spoken by many people of Algeria **(l'Algérie)**, Morocco **(le Maroc)**, and Tunisia **(la Tunisie)**. More than two million people from these countries have emigrated to France and have become French citizens.

■ **Cultural note:** Two African countries are named after the Congo River, one of the longest rivers in the world. In size, **la République démocratique du Congo** is the largest French-speaking country of Africa. It was known as **le Congo belge** before its independence in 1960, and as **le Zaïre** until 1997. Its eastern neighbor, **le Congo,** is a former French colony.

Cultural expansion
Names of African countries where French is an important language (capitals are given in parentheses):
Algérie (Alger)
Bénin (Porto-Novo)
Burkina Faso (Ouagadougou)
Burundi (Bujumbura)
Cameroun (Yaoundé)
Congo (Brazzaville)
Congo, République démocratique (Kinshasa)
Côte-d'Ivoire (Yamoussoukro)
Djibouti (Djibouti)
Gabon (Libreville)
Guinée (Conakry)
Madagascar (Antananarivo)
Mali (Bamako)
Maroc (Rabat)
Mauritanie (Nouakchott)
Niger (Niamey)
République Centrafricaine (Bangui)
Ruanda [Rwanda] (Kigali)
Sénégal (Dakar)
Tchad (N'Djamena)
Togo (Lomé)
Tunisie (Tunis)

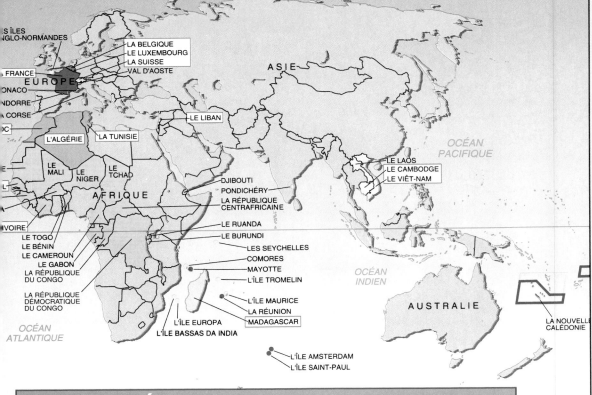

ACTIVITÉS CULTURELLES

1. Name at least six African countries where French is spoken. Find out the capital of each country. (Source: atlas, encyclopedia)
2. Collect clippings from newspapers and magazines in which a French-speaking country is mentioned. Try to find one clipping for each of the areas on the map.

NOTE: You may also wish to refer to the reference map of the French-speaking world on pages R2–R3.

Bonjour, la France!

■ **Photo culture notes**
Pictures described clockwise:
Eguisheim, Alsace
The small village of Eguisheim is located on the **Route des vins** near **Colmar.**
Note the fountain and the typical half-timbered Alsatian houses with their sloped roofs.

Les Alpes et Chamonix
Chamonix is located in a valley in the Alps at the foot of the **Massif du Mont Blanc.** (Mont Blanc is the highest mountain in Europe.) Chamonix is a famous ski resort. The first Winter Olympics were held there in 1924.

Menton et la Côte d'Azur
Menton is located on the French Riviera, or **la Côte d'Azur,** just east of Monaco. The Côte d'Azur stretches about 100 miles along the Mediterranean, from the Toulon area to the Italian border. For the French, the Côte d'Azur is their favorite summer vacation place.

Les Pyrénées
The **Pyrénées** are a high mountain chain which separates France from Spain (**l'Espagne**).

Le Château d'Azay-le-Rideau
This castle, located in **la Touraine,** is one of the many **Châteaux de la Loire** which were built by the French kings nearly 500 years ago.

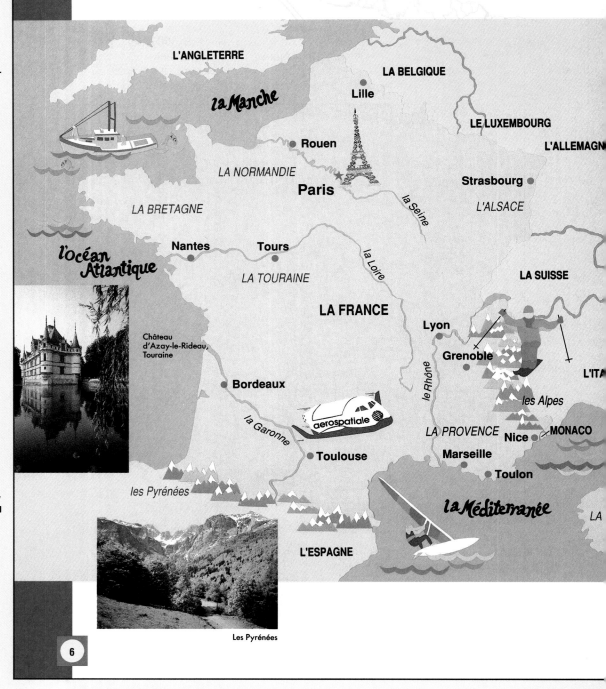

Château d'Azay-le-Rideau, Touraine

Les Pyrénées

6

Classroom project
You might have students prepare a bulletin board display about France using maps, postcards, travel brochures, etc.

Eguisheim, Alsace

Les Alpes, Chamonix

Menton, Côte d'Azur

*B*efore starting your study of French, you may be interested in learning a few facts about France.

■ In area, France is the second-largest country in Western Europe.

■ Economically, France is one of the most developed countries of the world with a sophisticated high-tech industry.

■ France is the only European country with a space exploration program. French communication satellites provide 400 million Europeans with direct TV transmission.

■ France is a country with a strong cultural tradition. French philosophers, writers, and artists have influenced our ways of thinking and looking at the world.

■ France has a long history reaching back through Roman times into distant prehistory.

■ Geographically, France is a very diversified country with the highest mountains in Europe **(les Alpes et les Pyrénées)** and an extensive coastline along the Atlantic **(l'océan Atlantique)** and the Mediterranean **(la Méditerranée)**.

■ France consists of many different regions which have maintained their traditions, their culture, and—in some cases—their own language. Some of the traditional provinces are Normandy and Brittany **(la Normandie et la Bretagne)** in the west, Alsace **(l'Alsace)** in the east, Touraine **(la Touraine)** in the center, and Provence **(la Provence)** in the south.

ACTIVITÉS CULTURELLES

1. Find the countries which have a common border with France. What are their capitals? (Source: atlas, encyclopedia)
2. Imagine that you are spending a year in France. Where would you go if you wanted to ski in the winter? Which provinces would you want to visit in the summer if you wanted to swim in the Atlantic? in the Mediterranean? Are there any particular parts of France you would like to explore?

NOTE: You may also wish to refer to the reference map of France on page R4.

7

■ **Cultural notes**
• **Size:** In area, one can compare France to:
  (a) 4/5 of Texas, or
  (b) Wyoming plus Oregon, or
  (c) New England plus New York, Pennsylvania and Ohio.
• **Technology:** The French Ariane rockets are launched from French Guiana **(la Guyane française)** in South America.
• **French cultural tradition:**
  Philosophers: Voltaire, Montesquieu, Rousseau, Jean-Paul Sartre
  Writers: Victor Hugo, Albert Camus, Colette, Baudelaire
  Musicians: composers Debussy and Ravel, flutist Jean-Pierre Rampal
  Artists: Gauguin, Renoir, Matisse
• **Pre-history:** the Cro-Magnon caveman and the caves of Lascaux
• **Roman times:** Julius Caesar conquered France (Gaul) in 43 B.C.; one can still visit the Roman ruins in Provence: Nîmes, Orange, Pont du Gard.

■ **Activités culturelles**
Answers:
1. Belgium (Brussels)
   Luxembourg (Luxembourg)
   Germany (Berlin)
   Switzerland (Bern)
   Italy (Rome)
   Spain (Madrid)
2. Skiing: les Alpes, les Pyrénées
   Swimming in the Atlantic: La Bretagne, La Normandie
   Swimming in the Mediterranean: La Provence

Bonjour! Je m'appelle ...

■ **English equivalents of French boys' names:**
Alain (Alan)
André (Andrew)
Antoine (Anthony)
Christophe (Christopher)
Édouard (Edward)
Étienne (Steven)
François (Francis, Frank)
Frédéric (Frederick)
Geoffroy (Jeffrey)
Guillaume (William)
Henri (Henry)
Jacques (James)
Jean (John)
Julien (Julian)
Laurent (Lawrence)
Marc (Mark)
Matthieu (Matthew)
Michel (Michael)
Olivier (Oliver)
Philippe (Phillip)
Pierre (Peter)
Raoul (Ralph)

Here is a list of some traditional French names. As you begin your study of the French language, you may want to "adopt" a French name from the list.

Alain	Geoffroy	Mathieu
Albert	Georges	Michel
André	Grégoire	Nicolas
Antoine	Guillaume	Olivier
Bernard	Henri	Patrick
Bertrand	Jacques	Paul
Charles	Jean	Philippe
Christophe	Jean-Claude	Pierre
Daniel	Jean-François	Raoul
David	Jean-Louis	Raymond
Denis	Jean-Paul	Richard
Dominique	Jérôme	Robert
Édouard	Joseph	Roger
Éric	Julien	Samuel
Étienne	Laurent	Simon
François	Marc	Thomas
Frédéric		

8

Teaching note: Choosing French names

Let students adopt a new French identity. Some may want to find a French version of their English name.

Others may want to pick a completely original name.

If some students do not want to choose a French name, teach them how to pronounce their own name with a French accent.

■ **English equivalents of French girls' names:**
Andrée (Andrea)
Cécile (Cecilia)
Diane (Diana)
Éléonore (Eleanor)
Émilie (Emily)
Françoise (Frances)
Hélène (Helen)
Jeanne (Jean)
Laure (Laura)
Lise (Lisa)
Lucie (Lucy)
Marguerite (Margaret)
Marie (Mary)
Marthe (Martha)
Michèle (Michelle)
Monique (Monica)
Nathalie (Natalie)
Suzanne (Susan)
Sylvie (Sylvia)
Thérèse (Teresa)
Virginie (Virginia)

Alice	Éléonore	Marthe
Andrée	Élisabeth	Michèle
Anne	Émilie	Monique
Anne-Marie	Florence	Nathalie
Barbara	Françoise	Nicole
Béatrice	Hélène	Patricia
Brigitte	Isabelle	Pauline
Caroline	Jeanne	Rachel
Catherine	Judith	Renée
Cécile	Juliette	Rose
Charlotte	Karine	Sophie
Christine	Laure	Stéphanie
Claire	Lise	Suzanne
Corinne	Louise	Sylvie
Delphine	Lucie	Thérèse
Denise	Marguerite	Véronique
Diane	Marie	Virginie
Dominique	Marie-Christine	

Jean?	*Guillaume?*	*Georges?*
Henri?	*Philippe?*	*François?*
Jacques?	*Charles?*	*Michel?*
Sébastien?	*Gérard?*	*Paul?*
Jean-Paul?	*Pierre?*	*Marc?*
Lucien?	*Jean-Pierre?*	*Luc?*
	André?	

Nathalie

9

Teaching note: Pronunciation

Read the above lists aloud and have
students repeat the names after you.
    Be sure they always let the accent fall
on the last syllable of each name.

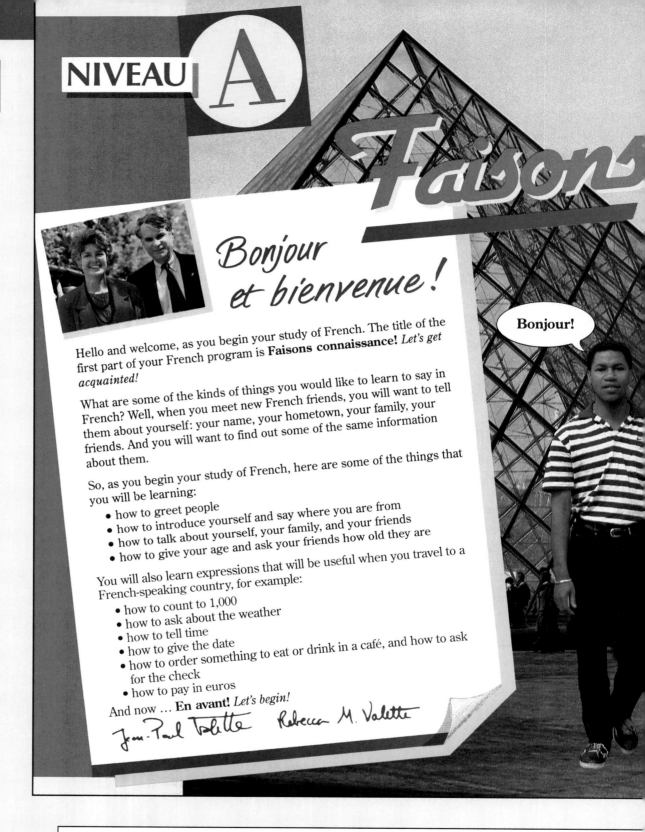

NIVEAU **A**

Faisons

Bonjour et bienvenue!

Hello and welcome, as you begin your study of French. The title of the first part of your French program is **Faisons connaissance!** *Let's get acquainted!*

What are some of the kinds of things you would like to learn to say in French? Well, when you meet new French friends, you will want to tell them about yourself: your name, your hometown, your family, your friends. And you will want to find out some of the same information about them.

So, as you begin your study of French, here are some of the things that you will be learning:

- how to greet people
- how to introduce yourself and say where you are from
- how to talk about yourself, your family, and your friends
- how to give your age and ask your friends how old they are

You will also learn expressions that will be useful when you travel to a French-speaking country, for example:

- how to count to 1,000
- how to ask about the weather
- how to tell time
- how to give the date
- how to order something to eat or drink in a café, and how to ask for the check
- how to pay in euros

And now ... **En avant!** *Let's begin!*

Jean-Paul Valette   *Rebecca M. Valette*

Bonjour!

Overview of Niveau A

Niveau A begins **Discovering French — Bleu** with a focus on oral communication, both listening comprehension and speaking. Basic conversational skills are introduced without a formal presentation of structure.

New conversational patterns are grouped by function in the **Pour communiquer** sections.

Students will learn how to greet people, introduce themselves, talk about their friends and family, and even order in a café.

Telling time, talking about the days of the week, months and dates, the weather and seasons, and the numbers from 0-1,000 are introduced.

The first three lessons of each Niveau A unit develop simple conversational exchanges. The fourth lesson, subtitled **Le français pratique,** focuses on a specific communication topic.

Unité 1

MAIN THEME:
Getting acquainted

➤ Teaching Resources

Technology/Audio Visual

 VIDEO/VIDEODISC

Unité 1, Modules 1–4
1. La rentrée
2. Tu es français?
3. Salut! Ça va?
4. Le français pratique: L'heure

 DFi A,
CD-ROM Modules 1-4
Exploration 1

 Writing Template
Unité 1

 Unité 1, Leçons 1, 2, 3,
CD 4

1, 2a, 2b, 2c, 3, 4,
5, 6
Situational S3, S4

Print

Answer Key, Cassette Script,
Video Script, Overhead
Visuals Copymasters

Activity Book, pp. 3–32
Activity Book TAE

Video Activity Book pp. 1–13

Communipak, pp. 1–16

Teacher's Resource Package

 Teacher-to-Teacher:
Games, Additional
Activities

 Interdisciplinary
Connections:
Projects Book

 Teaching to Multiple
Intelligences in the
Modern Language
Classroom

 Internet Connections
www.mcdougallittell.com

T12

UNITÉ
1 Bonjour!

INTRODUCTION
culturelle

Salutations *(Greetings)*

How do you greet people in the United States? You may nod or smile. With adults, you may shake hands when you are introduced for the first time.

In France, people shake hands with friends and acquaintances each time they see one another, and not only to say hello but also when they say good-bye. Among teenagers, boys shake hands with boys. Girls kiss each other on the cheeks two or three times. (This is called **une bise**). Boys and girls who are close friends also greet each other with **une bise.**

LEÇON	1	La rentrée

LEÇON	2	Tu es français?

LEÇON	3	Salut! Ça va?

LEÇON	4	Le français pratique: L'heure

 12

Unit overview

COMMUNICATION GOALS: Students will learn greetings and basic phrases. They will also learn how to count and tell time. LINGUISTIC GOALS: Students will begin to recognize what French sounds like and learn how French words are pronounced.

CRITICAL THINKING GOALS: Students will encounter the concept of linguistic differences. They will discover that often there is no word-for-word correspondence between French and English.
CULTURAL GOALS: Students will discover that in France people greet one another and interact differently than in the U.S.

THÈME ET OBJECTIFS

Getting acquainted

In this unit, you will be meeting French people.

You will learn . . .
- to say hello and good-bye
- to introduce yourself and say where you are from

You will also learn . . .
- to count to 60
- to tell time

TPR **TPR Suggestion**
Activities 1, 2, 3
(see Front Matter)

■ **Teaching notes:**
- **TPR (or Total Physical Response)** activities provide an excellent channel for introducing spoken French into the classroom. For many students, the demonstration of comprehension via physical movement enhances the ability to remember the new language.
- The Teacher Front Matter explains what TPR is and presents several initial TPR activities designed to introduce basic classroom commands and familiarize students with this type of activity. Throughout the book, suggestions for specific TPR activities will be given at the bottom of the page of this Teacher Edition.

🌐 **Cross-cultural observation**
Have students study each picture carefully, looking at the young people, their dress, and their way of greeting one another.
- Which elements in the pictures seem to be definitely French?
- Which elements could also be American?

Pacing

Try to move through this unit rather quickly, concentrating on listening and speaking.

In Niveau B, the students will encounter the same vocabulary again. At that time they will be expected to master the material in writing.

➤ Assessment Options

ACHIEVEMENT TESTS	**PROFICIENCY TESTS**	**Test Bank, Unit 1**

ACHIEVEMENT TESTS

Lesson Quizzes 1–4 pp. 43–50
   Test Cassette A, Side 1

Unit Test 1

 Portfolio Assessment
   pp. T30–31
   Activities 1–6

PROFICIENCY TESTS

 Listening Comprehension
   Performance Test, p. 27
   Test Cassette C, Side 1

 Speaking Performance Test, p. 9

 Reading Comprehension
   Performance Test, p. 13

Writing Performance Test, p. 35

 Test Bank, Unit 1
   Version A or B

CD-ROM **DFi A,**
   Exploration 1
   Cahier, Créa-dialogue

MODULE 1:
La rentrée
Total time: 3:42 min.
(Counter: 7:50 min.)

1.1 **La rentrée**
(7:58–8:50 min.)
1.2 **Mini-scenes: Meeting people**
(8:51–10:09 min.)
1.3 **Vignette culturelle: Bonjour!**
(10:10–11:28 min.)

VIDEODISC Disc 1, Side 2
1580-8116

■ **Comprehension practice:** Play the entire module through as an introduction to the lesson.

1.1 La rentrée
(7:58–8:50 min)

VIDEODISC Disc 1, Side 2
1585–3309

 Leçon 1, Section 1

LEÇON 1

La rentrée

This is the first day of school. Students are greeting their friends and meeting new classmates.

Bonjour! Je m'appelle Philippe.

Et moi, je m'app[elle] Stéphanie.

« —Bonjour! Je m'appelle Philippe.
—Et moi, je m'appelle Stéphanie. »

Je m'appelle Marc. Et toi?

Moi, je m'appelle Isabelle.

Comment t'appelles-tu?

Je m'appelle Nath[alie]

« —Je m'appelle Marc. Et toi?
—Moi, je m'appelle Isabelle. »

« —Comment t'appelles-tu?
—Je m'appelle Nathalie.
—Bonjour.
—Bonjour. »

14 Unité 1

Using the video and the cassettes

For each lesson of Niveau A, the opening text corresponds to part 1 of the video. Similarly, the first section of the cassette program contains the video sound track of the scene with its varied and authentic voices. (See Front Matter for complete description.)

First play the entire video module through as an introduction to the lesson. Have students observe how young people greet one another in France.

Then play the opening scene several more times and have students practice repeating the new phrases.

POUR *COMMUNIQUER*

Bonjour!

How to say hello:

Bonjour!	*Hello!*	—**Bonjour,** Nathalie! —**Bonjour,** Jean-Paul!

How to ask a classmate's name:

Comment t'appelles-tu?	*What's your name?*	— **Comment t'appelles-tu?**
Je m'appelle . . .	*My name is . . .*	— **Je m'appelle** Stéphanie.

OTHER EXPRESSIONS		
moi	*me*	**Moi,** je m'appelle Marc.
et toi?	*and you?*	**Et toi,** comment t'appelles-tu?

■ NOTES ■ CULTURELLES

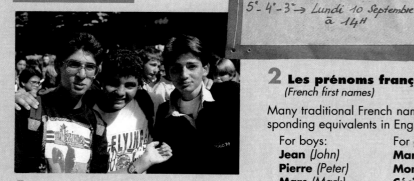

1 La rentrée *(Back to school)*

French and American students have about the same number of days of summer vacation. In France, summer vacation usually begins at the end of June and classes resume in early September. The first day back to school in fall is called **la rentrée.**

2 Les prénoms français
(French first names)

Many traditional French names have corresponding equivalents in English.

For boys:	For girls:
Jean *(John)*	**Marie** *(Mary)*
Pierre *(Peter)*	**Monique** *(Monica)*
Marc *(Mark)*	**Cécile** *(Cecilia)*
Philippe *(Philip)*	**Alice**
Nicolas *(Nicholas)*	**Caroline**

Often the names **Jean** and **Marie** are combined in double names such as **Jean-Paul** and **Marie-Christine.** In recent years, names of foreign origin, like **Dimitri** and **Karine,** have become quite popular.

Leçon 1 **15**

Pour communiquer

■ **Language note:** Literally, **bonjour** means *good day* and corresponds to *good morning* or *good afternoon.*
In the evening, **bonjour** may be replaced by **bonsoir** *(good evening).*
Bonne nuit *(good night)* is used when someone is going to bed. Also: **Comment est-ce que tu t'appelles?**

■ **Language note:** When speaking among themselves, French people often use CASUAL SPEECH. Since these forms are spoken (and not written), they are not formally presented in the students' textbook. If you wish, you may introduce them orally in class for recognition. For example, to ask someone's name in casual French one may say: **Tu t'appelles comment?** or **Comment tu t'appelles?**

Notes culturelles

There are four grades in a French **collège:**
• **sixième** (sixth grade),
• **cinquième** (seventh grade),
• **quatrième** (eighth grade) and
• **troisième** (ninth grade).

🌐 **Cross-cultural observation:** Have students look at the photograph of the sign.
What is the date of **la rentrée?** [Monday, September 10]
At what time do the students in **sixième** report? [9:00 AM]
And the students in **cinquième, quatrième,** and **troisième?** [2:00 PM]
Which group does not have class in the afternoon? [students in sixième]
(At this point, you may wish to review the 24-hour system of telling time.)

TPR 🏃 **Total Physical Response**

Some teachers like to develop initial listening comprehension skills using Total Physical Response techniques.

For a brief description of this approach and instructions for three beginning activities, see the general discussion in the Front Matter.

**1.2 Mini-scenes:
Meeting people**
(8:51–10:09 min.)

VIDEODISC   Disc 1, Side 2
3838–5699

🔲 **Leçon 1, Section 2**

---

1 EXCHANGES: greetings

---

2 COMMUNICATION: identifying oneself

■ Chain activity in small groups: Student 1 asks Student 2 his/her name. Then Student 2 asks the name of Student 3, and so on.
Je m'appelle [Stéphanie]. Et toi? Moi, je m'appelle [David]. Et toi? etc.

---

3 COMMUNICATION: asking someone's name

---

4 PRACTICE: greetings

■ **Teaching suggestion:** Model the correct pronunciation of the names so that students can pronounce them with a French accent.

▷ **L'alphabet**

🔲 **Leçon 1, Section 3**

T16

Bonjour!
Je m'appelle
Astérix.

1 **Bonjour!**
Say hello to the student nearest to you.

▶
Bonjour!   Bonjour!
Bonjour!

2 **Je m'appelle . . .**
Introduce yourself to your classmates.

▶ **Je m'appelle (Paul).**
▶ **Je m'appelle (Denise).**

3 **Et toi?**
Ask a classmate his or her name.

▶ —**Comment t'appelles-tu?**
  —**Je m'appelle (Christine).**

4 **Bonjour, les amis!** *(Hello everyone!)*
Say hello to the following students.

▶ **Bonjour, Marc!**

▶  **Marc**

 Juliette

 **Jean-Paul**

 **Isabelle**

 Philippe

 **François**

 Stéphanie

 **Nathalie**

L'alphabet

A	B	C	D	E	F	G	H	I	J	K	L
a	bé	cé	dé	e	effe	gé	hache	i	ji	ka	elle

 Unité 1

Teaching the alphabet
Say each letter of the alphabet and have students repeat as you write it on the board. Then, have a volunteer come and point to the letters as you say them in random order. The others can point to the corresponding letters in their textbook.

Game: "Le pendu"
Play hangman in French using the names of famous people or well-known places, or French products available in the United States.

Les signes orthographiques (Spelling marks)

French uses accents and spelling marks that do not exist in English. These marks are part of the spelling and cannot be left out.

In French, there are four accents that may appear on vowels.

´	**l'accent aigu** (acute accent)	Cécile, Stéphanie
`	**l'accent grave** (grave accent)	Michèle, Hélène
^	**l'accent circonflexe** (circumflex)	Jérôme
¨	**le tréma** (diaeresis)	Noël, Joëlle

There is only one spelling mark used with a consonant. It occurs under the letter "**c**."

‚	**la cédille** (cedilla)	François

---

5 La rentrée

It is the first day of class. The following students are introducing themselves. Act out the dialogues with your classmates.

▶ Hélène et Philippe

Moi, je m'appelle Philippe.

...e m'appelle Hélène. Et toi?

1. Stéphanie et Marc
2. Cécile et Frédéric
3. Michèle et François
4. Béatrice et Joël
5. Céline et Jérôme

Les nombres de 0 à 10

0	1	2	3
zéro	un	deux	trois

4	5	6	7
quatre	cinq	six	sept

8	9	10
huit	neuf	dix

6 Numéros de téléphone

Imagine you are visiting a family in Quebec. Give them your American phone number in French.

▶ 617-963-4028   six, un, sept — neuf, six, trois — quatre, zéro, deux, huit

M	N	O	P	Q	R	S	T	U	V	W	X	Y	Z
emme	enne	o	pé	ku	erre	esse	té	u	vé	double vé	ixe	i grec	zède

---

▶ Les signes orthographiques

Language notes:

• The acute accent ☐ occurs only on **e** to show it is pronounced /e/.
• The grave accent ☐ occurs mainly on **e** to show it is pronounced /ɛ/, and in the words **à**, **là**, and **où**.
• The circumflex ☐ can occur on all vowels; often the corresponding English word has an "s": **forêt**, **hôpital**, **mât**.
• The diaeresis ☐ is placed on the second of two vowels to show that they are pronounced separately: **naïf**.
• The c-cedilla ☐ is used before **a, o, u** to show it is pronounced /s/: **ça, garçon, reçu**. Otherwise, **c** before **a, o, u** is pronounced /k/: **café, collège, culturel**.
• **Note:** Accent marks are often not placed on capital letters. In this book, however, we will show accents on capital letters to make it easier for students.

5 EXCHANGES: making introductions

▷ Les nombres de 0 à 10

🔲 Leçon 1, Section 4

■ **Speaking activity:** To practice the numbers 0-10, knock loudly on your desk. Have the students identify the number of knocks in French. For example: (toc! toc!) **Deux!**, etc.

■ **If students ask:**
un nombre = number or numeral, in the mathematical sense
un numéro = number, in a series; e.g., phone number, house number

6 COMMUNICATION; giving one's telephone number

■ **Cultural note:** In Quebec, as in the United States, phone numbers are given digit by digit.

TPR 🏃 **Numbers 0 to 10**

With your right hand, demonstrate the numbers 0 to 5 as you say them:
  Voici 0. [closed fist]
  Voici 1. [thumb extended]
  Voici 2. [thumb and index finger] ...

Have students respond to commands with the same gestures:
  Montrez-moi 0, 1, 2 ...
Practice the numbers in random order:
  Montrez-moi 3, 5, 2, ...
Continue with numbers 6 through 10, using both hands.

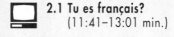

LEÇON 2 Tu es français?

It is the opening day of school and several of the students meet in the cafeteria (**la cantine**) at lunchtime. Marc discovers that not everyone is French.

Tu es français?

Oui, je suis français.

MARC: Tu es français?
JEAN-PAUL: Oui, je suis français.

MARC: Et toi, Patrick, tu es français aussi?
PATRICK: Non! Je suis américain. Je suis de Boston.

Non! Je suis américain.

MARC: Et toi, Stéphanie, tu es française ou américaine?
STÉPHANIE: Je suis française.
MARC: Tu es de Paris?
STÉPHANIE: Non, je suis de Fort-de-France.
MARC: Tu as de la chance!

Je suis française.

MARC: Are you French?
JEAN-PAUL: Yes, I'm French.

MARC: And you, Patrick, are you French too?
PATRICK: No! I'm American. I'm from Boston.

MARC: And you, Stéphanie, are you French or American?
STÉPHANIE: I'm French.
MARC: Are you from Paris?
STÉPHANIE: No, I'm from Fort-de-France.
MARC: You're lucky!

 Unité 1

POUR COMMUNIQUER

Tu es de Denver?

How to talk about where people are from:

| **Tu es de ...?** | *Are you from ...?* | —**Tu es de** Denver? |
| **Je suis de ...** | *I'm from ...* | —Non, **je suis de** Dallas. |

How to talk about one's nationality:

| **Tu es ...?** | *Are you ...?* | —Pierre, **tu es** français? |
| **Je suis ...** | *I am ...* | —Oui, **je suis** français. |

Les nationalités

	français	française
	anglais	anglaise
	américain	américaine
	canadien	canadienne

OTHER EXPRESSIONS

oui	*yes*	Tu es français? **Oui,** je suis français.
non	*no*	Tu es canadien? **Non,** je suis américain.
et	*and*	Je suis de Paris. **Et** toi?
ou	*or*	Tu es français **ou** canadien?
aussi	*also, too*	Moi **aussi,** je suis française.

LA MARTINIQUE

B A L A T A
jardin botanique

NOTE CULTURELLE

Fort-de-France et la Martinique

Fort-de-France is the capital of Martinique, a small French island in the Caribbean. Because Martinique is part of the French national territory, its inhabitants are French citizens. Most of them are of African origin. They speak French as well as a dialect called **créole.**

Martinique is also known as the Island of the Flowers (**l'Île aux Fleurs**) because of its warm tropical climate and magnificent vegetation. In the winter months, it attracts thousands of European and American tourists.

Leçon 2 **19**

Pour communiquer

🖳 **Transparency 4**
US, Canada, England, France

▨ This is the students' first introduction to adjective agreement, and should be kept as simple as possible. The key objective is that students hear the sound differences and pronounce the masculine and feminine forms correctly.

▨ **Pronunciation:** Be sure students notice that the final consonant sound (/z/, /n/) is pronounced in the feminine forms but is silent in the masculine forms.

Note culturelle

🖥 **2.3 Vignette culturelle: Qui est français?**
(14:36–18:48 min.)

◉ **IDEODISC** Disc 1, Side 2
13679–21306

‖‖‖‖‖‖‖‖‖‖‖‖‖‖‖‖

🌐 **Cultural note:** As students have learned in the first photo essay (pp. 1–9), the French national territory extends beyond continental France (**la France métropolitaine**). Martinique is one of the four French overseas departments (**Départements d'Outre-Mer**).

Listening comprehension activity

Read the following eight sentences.
Have students raise their hands (or stand) if the sentence refers to a girl.

Tu es français?	**Tu es américaine?**
Tu es canadienne?	**Tu es anglaise?**
Tu es anglais?	**Tu es américain?**
Tu es française?	**Tu es canadien?**

▷ **français, française**

🔲 Leçon 2, Section 2

1 COMMUNICATION: identifying oneself

■ **Pronunciation:** If your students are from a city that begins with a vowel sound, have them use **d'**: **Je suis d'(Atlanta).** (The concept of elision is presented formally in Niveau B, Lesson 14.)

2 ROLE PLAY: discussing where people are from

🖥 **2.2 Mini-scenes: Finding out where people are from** (13:02–14:35 min.)

VIDEODISC Disc 1, Side 2
10900–13651

‖‖‖‖‖‖‖‖‖‖‖‖‖‖‖‖

■ **Extra speaking activity:** Ask students to pretend they are a famous person. Have them introduce themselves to the class, say where they are from, and give their nationalities. For example: **Je m'appelle Margaret Thatcher. Je suis de Londres et je suis anglaise.** (Be sure the students only use English, French, American, or Canadian personalities.)

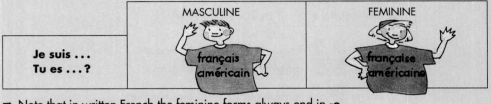

français, française

Names of nationalities may have two different forms, depending on whom they refer to:

	MASCULINE	FEMININE
Je suis . . . **Tu es . . . ?**	français américain	française américaine

➡ Note that in written French the feminine forms always end in **-e**.

1 Et toi?
Give your name, your nationality, and your city of origin.

> Bonjour!
> Je m'appelle Bob Jones.
> Je suis américain.
> Je suis de Providence.

> Bonjour!
> Je m'appelle Linda Carlson.
> Je suis américaine.
> Je suis de Boston.

20 Unité 1

2 Français ou française?
You meet the following young people. Ask them if they are French. A classmate will answer you, as in the model. (Be sure to use **français** with boys and **française** with girls.)

▶ —Sophie, tu es française?
—Oui, je suis française. Je suis de Strasbourg.

1. Jean-Pierre
Sophie
Paris
Strasb
2. Paul
3. Éric
Lyon
5. Nicol
Bordeaux
4. Michèle
Marsei

Cooperative pair practice

In cooperative pair practice, students do activities together with a partner. (See Front Matter for a complete description.)

Introduce the class to Cooperative Pair Practice with Act. 2 and 3. Be sure each student has a partner.

First do the exercise with the entire class, having half the group give the first cue, and the other half the response.

Then let the students do the same activity again in pairs. For the odd numbered cues, Student A asks the question and Student B responds. For the even-numbered cues, the roles are reversed.

3 Quelle nationalité? *(Which nationality?)*

Greet the following young people and find out each one's nationality. A classmate will answer you, according to the model.

▶ —Bonjour, Marc. Tu es canadien?
—Oui, je suis canadien. Je suis de Montréal.

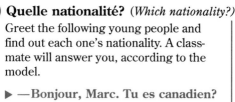

Marc
Montréal

1. Claire
Québec

2. Patrick
Boston

3. Denise
Liverpool

4. Donna
Memphis

5. Paul
Cambridge

Les nombres de 10 à 20

10 dix	**11** onze	**12** douze
13 treize	**14** quatorze	**15** quinze
16 seize	**17** dix-sept	**18** dix-huit
19 dix-neuf	**20** vingt	

4 La fusée Ariane

(The Ariane rocket)

Give the countdown for the lift-off of the French rocket Ariane, from 20 to 0.

Prononciation

Les lettres muettes *(Silent letters)*

In French, the last letter of a word is often not pronounced.

Paris

- Final "**e**" is always silent.
  Répétez: **Sophie̶ Philippe̶ Stéphanie̶ anglaise̶ française̶
  onze̶ douze̶ treize̶ quatorze̶ quinze̶ seize̶**

- Final "**s**" is almost always silent.
  Répétez: **Paris̶ Nicolas̶ Jacques̶ anglais̶ français̶ trois̶**

- The letter "**h**" is always silent.
  Répétez: **H̶élène H̶enri T̶homas Nat̶halie Cat̶herine**

Leçon 2   21

3 ROLE PLAY: discussing one's nationality

■ **Language note:** People from the province of Quebec will often say:
Je suis québécois(e).

▷ **Les nombres de 10 à 20**

🔊 Leçon 2, Section 3

▪ **Pronunciation:** Note the pronunciation of **vingt** /vɛ̃/.

4 PRACTICE: numbers 0 to 20

■ **Language note:** In French, a *countdown* is **un compte à rebours.**

■ **Cultural note:** All the French Ariane rockets are launched from Kourou in French Guiana (South America). France is the only country in Europe with an ongoing space program.

Prononciation

🔊 Leçon 2, Section 4

- Have students pronounce the French /r/ in Paris as if they were clearing their throats.
- In later lessons, students will encounter a few common words where the final "s" is pronounced: **un fils̲, mars̲, tennis̲**
- The letters "ph" represent the sound /f/, as in English: **Philippe, Stéphanie.**
- The letters "ch" usually represent the sound /ʃ/, as in: **Chicago, Michèle.**
- The letters "chr" represent the sound /kr/ as in: **Christophe, Christine.**

TPR 🏃 Numbers 11 to 20

PROPS: index cards with numbers 11 to 20
Place the first five index cards on the chalkboard tray. Point to the numbers as you name them: **11, 12, 13, 14, 15.**

Have students come forward to point out and touch the numbers as you name them.
X, montre le 12. Touche le 15.

Present the second five cards.
Place all cards randomly on the tray. Ask students to pass numbers to their classmates.
Y, prends le 20 et donne-le à Z.

MODULE 3:
Salut! Ça va?
Total time: 4:35 min.
(Counter: 19:05 min.)

3.1 **Salut! Ça va?**
(19:10–19:45 min.)
3.2 **Mini-scenes: Greeting people**
(19:46–22:19 min.)
3.3 **Vignette culturelle: Bonjour ou Salut?**
(22:20–23:26 min.)

VIDEODISC Disc 1, Side 2
21710–29879

■ **Comprehension practice:** Play the entire module through as an introduction to the lesson.

3.1 Salut! Ça va?
(19:10–19:45 min.)

VIDEODISC Disc 1, Side 2
21717–22783

▭ Leçon 3, Section 1

Salut! Ça va?

On the way to school, François meets his friends.

Salut, Isabelle!

Ça va! Merci!

Salut! Ça va?

Salut, Nathalie! Ça va?

Ça va bien! Et toi?

Moi aussi!

Ça va, Philippe?

Ah non! Z
Ça va ma

François also meets his teachers.

Bonjour, monsieur.

Bonjour, François.

Bonjour, madame.

Bonjour, François.

Bonjour, mademoiselle.

Bon
Fran

Monsieur Masson   **Madame Chollet**   **Mademoiselle Lad**

After class, François says good-bye to his teacher and his friends.

Au revoir, mademoiselle.

Au revoir, François.

Au revoir, Nathalie.

Au revoir, François.

22 Unité 1

Setting the scene

Ask students how they greet their teachers when they meet them before school or in the hall.

Have them watch the video to see if French students greet their teachers with the same formality or informality.

POUR
COMMUNIQUER

Salut!

How to greet a friend or classmate:

Salut!   *Hi!*

How to greet a teacher or another adult:

Bonjour!   *Hello!*

Bonjour, monsieur.
Bonjour, madame.
Bonjour, mademoiselle.

How to say good-bye:

Au revoir!   *Good-bye!*

Au revoir, Philippe.
Au revoir, monsieur.

➔ In written French, the following abbreviations are commonly used:

    M. Masson   Monsieur Masson
    Mme Chollet   Madame Chollet
    Mlle Lacour   Mademoiselle Lacour

➔ Young people often use **Salut!** to say good-bye to each other.

■ NOTE ■ CULTURELLE

Bonjour ou Salut?

French young people may greet one another with **Bonjour,** but they often prefer the less formal **Salut.** When they meet their teachers, however, they always use **Bonjour.** French young people are generally much more formal with adults than with their friends. This is especially true in their relationships with teachers, whom they treat with great respect.

    Have you noticed that in France adults are addressed as **monsieur, madame,** or **mademoiselle?** The last name is almost never used in greeting people.

Pour communiquer

▨ **Language note:** When used alone, the titles **monsieur, madame,** and **mademoiselle** are not capitalized.

▨ **Casual speech:** Young people often use **salut** or the Italian **ciao** / tʃau / to say good-bye.

▨ **If students ask:** the French have no equivalent for "Ms." Instead they usually use **Madame.**

Abbreviations
- When an abbreviation includes only the first letter of a word, a period is used:
  Monsieur = M.
- When an abbreviation consists of the first and last letters of a word, no period is needed:
  Madame = Mme,
  Mademoiselle = Mlle

Note culturelle

In France, young people almost never call adults by their first names.

💻 **3.3 Vignette culturelle: Bonjour ou Salut?** (22:20–23:36 min.)

VIDEODISC   Disc 1, Side 2
27511–29879

Teaching strategy: Greeting adults

To activate **Monsieur, Madame,** and **Mademoiselle,** give names of other teachers in your school. Ask students to imagine they see these people in the hall. Have them greet the teachers in French.

Mrs. Mills – **Bonjour, Madame!**
Mr. Tower – **Bonjour, Monsieur!**
Miss Swenson – **Bonjour, Mademoiselle!**

1 **Bonjour ou salut?**

You are enrolled in a French school. Greet your friends and teachers.

▶ **Salut, Sophie!**

▶ **Bonjour, mademoiselle!**

Sophie

Mademoiselle Pinot

1. Anne

2. Monsieur Masson

3. Nathalie

4. Marc

5. Madame Albert

6. Mademoiselle Boucher

POUR *COMMUNIQUER*

How to ask people how they feel:

| —**Ça va?** | *How are you? How are things going? How's everything?* |
| —**Ça va!** | *(I'm) fine. (I'm) okay. Everything's all right.* |

| **Ça va . . .** | **très bien** | **bien** | **comme ci, comme ça** | **mal** | **très mal** |

How to express one's feelings of frustration and appreciation:

| **Zut!** | *Darn!* | **Zut!** Ça va mal! | **Merci!** | *Thanks!* | Ça va, **merci.** |

➡ **Ça va?** *(How are you?)* is an informal greeting that corresponds to the following expressions:

Comment vas-tu? (when addressing a friend)
   Bonjour, Paul. Comment vas-tu?
Comment allez-vous? (when addressing an adult)
   Bonjour, madame. Comment allez-vous?

2 **Dialogue**

Exchange greetings with your classmates and ask how they are doing.

▶ —**Salut, (Thomas)! Ça va?**
   —**Ça va! Et toi?**
   —**Ça va bien. Merci.**

24 Unité 1

Teaching note: Spoken and written numbers

The emphasis in Niveau A is on functional language use. In order to get around in a French-speaking country, it is very important to be able to understand and use numbers in communicative situations.

At the basic level, students need a great deal of practice in order to understand and use numbers easily.

As a challenge activity, some students may want to learn to spell the numbers, but spelling is not necessary at this level. Most French people use digits to write numbers, especially numbers over 20.

3 Situations

Sometimes we feel good and sometimes we don't. How would you respond in the following situations?

▶ You have the flu.
—Ça va?
—Ça va mal!

1. You just received an "A" in French.
2. You lost your wallet.
3. Your uncle gave you five dollars.
4. Your grandparents sent you a check for 100 dollars.
5. You bent the front wheel of your bicycle.
6. Your parents bought you a new bicycle.
7. Your little brother broke your walkman.
8. It's your birthday.
9. You have a headache.
10. You just had an argument with your best friend.
11. Your favorite baseball team has just lost a game.
12. Your French teacher has just canceled a quiz.

4 Ça va?

How would the following people answer the question **Ça va?**

▶▶▶▶▶▶▶▶▶▶▶▶▶▶▶▶▶▶▶▶▶▶▶▶

Les nombres de 20 à 60

20 vingt	30 trente	40 quarante
vingt et un	trente et un	quarante et un
vingt-deux	trente-deux	quarante-deux
vingt-trois	trente-trois	quarante-trois
. . .	. . .	. . .
vingt-neuf	trente-neuf	quarante-neuf

50 cinquante   60 soixante

cinquante et un
cinquante-deux
cinquante-trois
. . .
cinquante-neuf

➡ Note the use of **et** in numbers with **un**: **vingt et un.**

5 Loto

Read out loud the numbers on the French Loto tickets.

LOTO N°21 TIRAGE DU JEUDI 11 AVRIL tirage gagnez jusqu'à 65 000€
13 21 37 42 55 59

LOTO N°43 TIRAGE DU LUNDI 3 JUIN tirage gagnez jusqu'à 65 000€
16 20 29 31 48 56   2€ TAC TAC

Prononciation

Les consonnes finales
(Final consonants)

1 2 3
un̸ deux̸ trois̸

In French, the last consonant of a word is often not pronounced.

• Remember: Final "**s**" is usually silent.
 Répétez: **trois̸ français̸ anglais̸**

• Most other final consonants are usually silent.
 Répétez: **Richard̸ Albert̸ Robert̸ salut̸ américain̸ canadien̸ bien̸ deux̸**

EXCEPTION: The following final consonants are usually pronounced: "**c**," "**f**," "**l**," and sometimes "**r**."
 Répétez: **Éric Daniel Lebeuf Pascal Victor**

However, the ending **-er** is usually pronounced /e/.
 Répétez: **Roger̸ Olivier̸**

---

3 ROLE PLAY: expressing one's feelings

4 PRACTICE: selecting an appropriate response

▷ **Les nombres de 20 à 60**

⊙─⊙ **Leçon 3, Section 3**

▪ **Pronunciation:** Remind students that there is no liaison after et:/ 31 / trãteɛ̃ /, etc.

▪ **Speaking activity:** Have the class say numbers in series.
• counting by 3s: 30 - 33 - 36 - 39 - 42 - 45 - 48 - 51…
• by 4s: 28 - 32 - 36 - 40 - 44…
• by 5s: 25 - 30 - 35 - 40 - 45…

5 PRACTICE: reading numbers up to 60

▪ **Listening comprehension:** Read a number from one of the tickets and have students indicate whether the number appears on ticket A or B.

Prononciation

⊙─⊙ **Leçon 3, Section 4**

▪ **Exceptions**
• The final consonant is pronounced in **zut!** and numbers used in counting like **six**, **sept**, **huit**, **dix**.
• The "r" in **monsieur** is silent.

▪ **Memory aid:** These final consonants are found in the word: **CaReFuL**.

TPR 🏃 Numbers and prepositions

PROPS: Index cards for 10, 20, 30, 40, 50, 60 Spread out the index cards on a table. Place three cards in a row on the chalktray.
 Je mets les nombres 10-20-30 en ligne droite.
Then have students perform similar actions.
 X, mets les nombres 40-50-60 en ligne droite.

Introduce new numbers with **après** (after).
 Maintenant, je mets le 30 après le 20.
 Y, mets le 10 après le 30. …
Similarly introduce **avant** (before), **derrière** (behind), **devant** (in front of).
 Je mets le 40 avant le 10. …
 Je mets le 50 derrière le 20. …
 Je mets le 60 devant le 40. …

MODULE 4:
Le français pratique:
L'heure
Total time: 8:56 min.
(Counter: 23:47 min.)

4.1 Un rendez-vous
(24:06–24:26 min.)
4.2 Mini-scenes:
Telling time
(24:36–28:44 min.)
4.3 À quelle heure
est le film?
(28:45–29:04 min.)
4.4 Mini-scenes:
Indicating at what
time an event occurs
(29:15–29:34 min.)
4.5 Vignette culturelle:
L'heure officielle
(29:35–32:01 min.)

■ **Comprehension practice:** Play
the entire module through as an
introduction to the lesson.

Pour communiquer

4.1 Un rendez-vous
4.2 Mini-scenes:
Telling time
(24:06–28:44 min.)

  Leçon 4, Section 1

T26

L'heure

A. Un rendez-vous

Jean-Paul and Stéphanie are sitting in a café.
Stéphanie seems to be in a hurry to leave.

STÉPHANIE:	Quelle heure est-il?
JEAN-PAUL:	Il est trois heures.
STÉPHANIE:	Trois heures?
JEAN-PAUL:	Oui, trois heures.
STÉPHANIE:	Oh là là. J'ai un rendez-vous avec David dans vingt minutes. Au revoir, Jean-Paul.
JEAN-PAUL:	Au revoir, Stéphanie. À bientôt!

STÉPHANIE:	*What time is it?*
JEAN-PAUL:	*It's three o'clock.*
STÉPHANIE:	*Three o'clock?*
JEAN-PAUL:	*Yes, three o'clock.*
STÉPHANIE:	*Uh, oh! I have a date with David in twenty minutes. Good-bye, Jean-Paul.*
JEAN-PAUL:	*Good-bye, Stéphanie. See you soon!*

Il est huit heures!

POUR COMMUNIQUER

How to talk about the time:

Quelle heure est-il?   *What time is it?*
Il est . . .   *It's . . .*

une heure	deux heures	trois heures	quatre heures	cinq heures	six heures

sept heures	huit heures	neuf heures	dix heures	onze heures	midi	min

26 Unité 1

☀ Warm-up: Reviewing numbers

Have the students each write their phone
numbers on a slip of paper and place
them in a box.
 Draw the first number and read it out
loud (Quebec style: digit by digit).

 The student whose number is read
stands up and recites his/her phone
number back. Then that student comes
forward, draws a new number, and reads
it aloud. The game continues until no
numbers are left in the box.

1 Quelle heure est-il?

Ask your classmates what time it is.

Quelle heure est-il?

Il est quatre heures.

2 L'heure d'été *(Daylight savings time)*

Philippe forgot to set his watch ahead for daylight savings time, so he is an hour off. Isabelle gives him the correct time.

▶ PHILIPPE: **Il est sept heures.**
ISABELLE: **Mais non, il est huit heures!**

➡ Although *o'clock* may be left out in English, the expression **heure(s)** must be used in French when giving the time.

It's ten. (It's ten o'clock.)   **Il est dix heures.**

➡ To distinguish between A.M. and P.M., the French use the following expressions:

du matin	*in the morning*	Il est dix heures **du matin.**
de l'après-midi	*in the afternoon*	Il est deux heures **de l'après-midi.**
du soir	*in the evening*	Il est huit heures **du soir.**

NOTE DE PRONONCIATION: In telling time, the NUMBER and the word **heure(s)** are linked together. Remember, in French the letter "**h**" is always silent.

une heure   deux heures   trois heures   quatre heures   cinq heures   six heures

sept heures   huit heures   neuf heures   dix heures   onze heures

---

🌀 **TPR** 🏃 **Telling time**

PROP: Clock with movable hands

Move the hands of the clock to show the hours and give the corresponding times.

Quelle heure est-il? Il est une heure.
Il est deux heures. etc.

Call on individual students to move the hands of the clock as you give the time.

Il est cinq heures.
X, viens ici. Montre-nous cinq heures.

🔲 **Leçon 4, Section 2**

1 PRACTICE: asking and telling the time

1. Il est trois heures.
2. Il est six heures.
3. Il est une heure.
4. Il est neuf heures.
5. Il est onze heures.
6. Il est midi.
7. Il est minuit.

2 ROLE PLAY: talking about time

1. cinq heures / six heures
2. dix heures / onze heures
3. huit heures / neuf heures
4. deux heures / trois heures
5. midi / une heure

■ **If students ask:** French uses **mais** *(but)* for emphasis, much as English uses *why*.
Compare: **Mais non!** *Why no!*

💻 **4.5 Vignette culturelle: L'heure officielle** (29:35–32:01 min.)

VIDEODISC Disc 1, Side 2
40505–45016

🌐 **Cross-cultural observation**
As is described in the video, the French use a 24-hour clock on timetables and TV schedules:
1 P.M. = 13h (treize heures)
8 P.M. = 20h (vingt heures)
• To go from P.M. to the 24-hour clock, add 12 hours:
   1 P.M. = 1 + 12 = 13 heures
• To go from the 24-hour clock to P.M., simply subtract 12 hours:
   20 heures = 20 – 12 = 8 P.M.

🔲 **Leçon 4, Section 6**
(optional)

4.3 À quelle heure est le film?

4.4 Mini-scenes: Indicating at what time an event occurs

4.5 Vignette culturelle: L'heure officielle (28:45–32:01 min.)

VIDEODISC Disc 1, Side 2
38992–45016

 Leçon 4, Section 3

■ **If students ask:** To refer to *clock time*, the French use the word **heure:**
Quelle heure est-il?
To talk about *time* in the general sense, they use the word **temps:**
Nous avons le temps.

Pour communiquer

 Transparency 6
Clock face

 Leçon 4, Section 4

■ **Language notes:**
• Since people use digits when writing out times, students at the basic level do not need to spell these phrases out. (Therefore, the spelling **demi** as in **midi et demi**, is not presented here.)

• **Expansion:** You may want to introduce **moins** + *minutes*, as in **deux heures moins dix.** At the basic level, students can simply say **une heure cinquante.** This is becoming more and more common with the increased use of digital clocks in France.

T28

B. À quelle heure est le film?

Stéphanie and David have decided to go to a movie.

STÉPHANIE: Quelle heure est-il?
DAVID: Il est trois heures et demie.
STÉPHANIE: Et à quelle heure est le film?
DAVID: À quatre heures et quart.
STÉPHANIE: Ça va. Nous avons le temps.

STÉPHANIE: *What time is it?*
DAVID: *It's three-thirty (half past three).*
STÉPHANIE: *And at what time is the movie?*
DAVID: *At four-fifteen (quarter past four).*
STÉPHANIE: *That's okay. We have time.*

POUR COMMUNIQUER

À quelle heure est le dîner?

How to ask at what time something is scheduled:

À quelle heure est ...?   *At what time is . . . ?*
—À quelle heure est le concert?   *At what time is the concert?*
—Le concert est à huit heures.   *The concert is at eight.*

How to say that you have an appointment or a date:

J'ai un rendez-vous à ...   *I have an appointment (a date) at . . .*   **J'ai un rendez-vous à deux heures.**

How to indicate the minutes:

Il est . . .   dix heures dix   six heures vingt-cinq   sept heures trente-cinq   deux heures cinquante-deux

How to indicate the half hour and the quarter hours:

 et quart   **et demie**   **moins le quart**

 Il est une heure **et quart.**   Il est deux heures **et demie.**   Il est trois heures **moins le quart.**

28 Unité 1

TPR 🏃 **Quarter hours and minutes**

PROP: clock with movable hands

Model the quarter hours and minutes, moving the hands on the clock.
Il est trois heures et quart. etc. Have students show the times on the clock.
X, montre-nous cinq heures dix.

Send two students to the board to write the times as you say them.
Y et Z, venez au tableau. Il est dix heures vingt. Écrivez l'heure. [Students write: "10h20".] Students at their desks can also write down the times.

3 L'heure

Give the times according to the clocks.

▶ **Il est une heure et quart.**

4 À quelle heure?

Ask your classmates at what time certain activities are scheduled. They will answer according to the information below.

▶ 8 h 50   le film

—À quelle heure est le film?
—Le film est à huit heures cinquante.

1. 7 h 15   le concert
2. 2 h 30   le match de football *(soccer)*
3. 3 h 45   le match de tennis
4. 5 h 10   le récital
5. 7 h 45   le dîner

Musée d'Orsay
Festival de cinéma
12h15

5 Rendez-vous

Isabelle has appointments with various classmates and teachers. Look at her notebook and act out her dialogues with Philippe.

▶ ISABELLE: **J'ai un rendez-vous avec Marc.**
PHILIPPE: **À quelle heure?**
ISABELLE: **À onze heures et demie.**

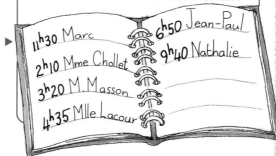

11h30 Marc
2h10 Mme Chollet
3h20 M. Masson
4h35 Mlle Lacour
6h50 Jean-Paul
9h40 Nathalie

6 À la gare *(At the train station)*

You are at the information desk of a French train station. Travelers ask you the departure times for the following trains. Answer them according to the posted schedule.

▶ le train de Nice

À quelle heure est le train de Nice?

Le train de Nice est à six heures dix.

DÉPARTS			
NICE	◆ 6 h 10	TOULON	◆ 9 h 35
LYON	◆ 7 h 15	COLMAR	◆ 10 h 40
CANNES	◆ 7 h 30	TOULOUSE	◆ 10 h 45
TOURS	◆ 8 h 12	MARSEILLE	◆ 10 h 50
DIJON	◆ 8 h 25	BORDEAUX	◆ 10 h 55

Leçon 4   **29**

---

3 PRACTICE: telling time

1. Il est deux heures trente (deux heures et demie).
2. Il est trois heures quarante cinq (quatre heures moins le quart).
3. Il est quatre heures quinze (quatre heures et quart).
4. Il est six heures trente (six heures et demie).
5. Il est dix heures quarante-cinq (onze heures moins le quart).

EXCHANGES: asking and answering questions about **4** time of events

■ **If students ask**
• The "h" dividing the hours from the minutes in French stands for **heures** and corresponds to the colon used in English.
• U.S. football is **le football américain.**

☰ **Leçon 4, Section 5**

EXCHANGES: discussing **5** appointment times

ROLE PLAY: asking and answering questions about **6** train schedules

■ **Variation** (easier format):
— À quelle heure est le train de Nice?
— À six heures dix.

🌐 Geography skills

PROP: Transparency 1

As a warm-up, have individual students point to the cities in Act. 6 on the transparency.
X, viens ici et montre-nous Nice. [Voici Nice.]

Have the other students point to the same cities on the map of France in their book, p. R4.

À votre tour 1

MAIN TOPIC:

Recapitulation and review

1 COMPREHENSION

1-a	4-c
2-f	5-d
3-e	6-b

🔲 AVT 1, Section 1

2 GUIDED ORAL EXPRESSION

🔲 AVT 1, Section 2

■ **Speaking practice**
- Play the cassette, stopping after each question to elicit various student answers.
- Play the cassette activity straight through, having students whisper their answers quickly in the pauses.
- Play the cassette again, pointing to individual students to give their answers in the pauses.

3 GUIDED ORAL EXPRESSION

Sample dialogue:
JP: Bonjour
J: Bonjour. Ça va?
JP: Oui, ça va.
J: Comment t'appelles-tu?
JP: Je m'appelle Jean-Pierre. Et toi?
J: Je m'appelle Janet.
JP: Tu es anglaise?
J: Non, je suis américaine.
JP: Tu es de New York?
J: Non, je suis de San Francisco.

🔲 AVT 1, Section 3

T30

---

1 **Nathalie et Marc**

It is the first day of school. Nathalie is talking to Marc and you hear parts of their conversation. For each of Nathalie's greetings or questions, select Marc's reply from the suggested responses on the right.

1 Salut!
2 Ça va?
3 Comment t'appelles-tu?
4 Tu es français?
5 Quelle heure est-il?
6 Au revoir!

a. Bonjour!
b. Au revoir!
c. Non, je suis canadien.
d. Il est deux heures moins le quart.
e. Marc Boutin.
f. Oui, ça va bien! Merci!

2 **Et toi?**

You and Nathalie meet at a sidewalk café. Respond to her greetings and questions.

1. Salut! Ça va?
2. Comment t'appelles-tu?
3. Tu es canadien (canadienne)?
4. Quelle heure est-il?
5. Oh là là. J'ai un rendez-vous dans *(in)* dix minutes. Au revoir.

3 **Conversation dirigée**

Two students, Jean-Pierre and Janet, meet on the Paris-Lyon train. With a partner, compose and act out their dialogue according to the suggested script.

Jean-Pierre

says hello	⇄	responds and asks how things are
says things are fine	⇄	asks him what his name is
says his name is Jean-Pierre . . . asks her name	⇄	says her name is Janet
asks her if she is English	⇄	says no and responds that she is American
asks her if she is from New York	→	replies that she is from San Francisco

Janet

 Unité 1

À votre tour

The communicative activities in this section move from closely structured (Act. 1) to more open-ended (Act. 5).

Select those activities which are most appropriate for your students. You may or may not wish to do them all.

👥👥 Cooperative practice

Pair work: Students do the activities in pairs. For Act. 1, 3, and 4, they can check their work by listening to the cassette tape.

Trios: Students work in groups of 3. Two students perform a dialogue. The third reads the Answer Key and acts as monitor.

4 Minidialogues

Create original dialogues on the basis of the pictures below.

1. David et Nicole

2. Monsieur Bertin et Mademoiselle Laval

3. Florence et Alain

4. Jean-Pierre et Sylvie

5. Thomas et Nicole

5 En scène

With a classmate, act out the following scene.

CHARACTERS:
You and a French exchange student

SITUATION:
You are at a party and meet a French exchange student who is happy to respond to your greetings and questions.

- Greet the student.
- Ask how things are going.
- Introduce yourself and ask his/her name.
- Ask if he/she is French.
- Ask if he/she is from Paris.
- Say good-bye.

6 Les nombres

1. Select any number between 0 and 15 and give the next five numbers in sequence.

2. Select a number between 1 and 9. Use that number as a starting point and count by tens to 60.

▶ deux

douze, vingt-deux, trente-deux, etc.

4 GUIDED ORAL EXPRESSION

Sample dialogues:
1. D: Salut, Nicole.
   N: Salut, David.
2. M. B: Bonjour, mademoiselle.
   Mlle L: Bonjour, monsieur.
3. F: Bonjour, Alain. Ça va?
   A: Non, ça va mal.
4. JP: Salut, Sylvie. Ça va?
   S: Ça va très bien.
5. T: Je suis français. Et toi? Tu es américaine?
   N: Oui, je suis américaine. Je suis de Chicago. Et toi?
   T: Moi, je suis de Lyon.

🔲 **AVT 1, Section 4**

■ **Listening practice:** Play the sample exchanges.

■ **Cooperative practice:** Have students in pairs prepare their own exchanges.

5 GUIDED ORAL EXPRESSION

6 GUIDED ORAL EXPRESSION

📓 Oral portfolios

For an introduction to oral portfolio assessment, see the Front Matter for a complete description.

Divide the class into pairs. Either assign all students the same activity, or let each pair select an activity at the appropriate level of challenge.

Have the pairs prepare their dialogues and make an audio (or video) recording. (Be sure they introduce themselves on the recording: **Je m'appelle X. Moi, je m'appelle Y.**)

If time allows, play all the recordings for the entire class. Store the cassettes as part of each student's oral portfolio.

Entracte 1

OBJECTIVES:

- Reading skills development
- Development of cultural awareness

Oui, vous parlez français!

OBJECTIVE:
- Reading simple signs

■ **Teaching strategy:**
Read each sign aloud. Have students raise their hands if the French word is spelled exactly like its English cognate.

■ **Pronunciation practice**
- Have students repeat the words on the signs after you (or after the cassette). Be sure they use an even rhythm and that they accent the <u>last</u> syllable only.
  parking muni<u>ci</u>pal
  office de tou<u>ris</u>me
- Ask which two of the English equivalent words are accented on the last syllable. (hotel, garage)

■ **Cultural note:** In France, toilets are often identified with the letters WC (water closet) plus the picture of a man or woman. Sometimes the following abbreviations are used:
- men: **H** (hommes) or **M** (messieurs)
- women: **F** (femmes) or **D** (dames)

Oui, vous parlez *français!*

Yes, you speak French! If you were visiting a French city, you would be able to understand many of the signs around you.

Look at the words on the following signs and compare them to their English equivalents. Which ones are spelled exactly the same? Which ones are spelled a little differently? What are the differences?

Pre-reading

Read the signs aloud to the class, with books closed. How many words can the class understand?

Then have students open their books and read the signs. They will probably understand them all. Play the cassette again as students read along.

Post-reading

Explain to students that words which look the same in both languages are called COGNATES. Stress that cognates in two languages are always <u>pronounced differently</u>.

La présence **FRANÇAISE** en Amérique

Between 1600 and 1750, the French explored large parts of Canada and the United States, which they called **La Nouvelle France** (*New France*). Today many American towns have French names, as you will see on the map below.

LA NOUVELLE FRANCE

Can you match the French place names on the map with their English equivalents?

Almost an Island	Beautiful Mountain	Flowering (place)	Saint Mary's Waterfall
The Barn	Beautiful View	Good City	and Rapids
Barred	Bottom of the Lake	High Land	Stick
Beautiful City	Clear Water	Small Hill	Strait
Beautiful Fork	Flat City	Red Pole	Wooded (place)
Beautiful Fountain			

Un jeu (game)

Many American cities were also named after:

- French people (such as King Louis XIV and his patron Saint Louis, General La Fayette, Napoleon, and of course, explorers like Champlain, Jolliet, Marquette, La Salle, Duluth, Dubuque)
- French cities (such as Paris, Montpellier, La Rochelle, Orléans)

In teams of three or four, see how many cities with French names you can locate on a map of the United States.

Entracte 1 (33)

Pre-reading activity

As an introduction to this selection, read the names of the cities aloud, first as they are said in America and then as they would be pronounced in France. Which ones sound most similar in the two languages?

Post-reading activity

Un jeu is a cooperative learning game.
VARIATION: Have students do their research as homework, and then have the teams pull together their answers in class the next day.
Un jeu can also be assigned for extra credit, or be developed into a wall map.

➤ Teaching Resources

Technology/Audio Visual

 VIDEO/VIDEODISC

Unité 2, Modules 5-8
5. Copain ou copine?
6. Une coïncidence
7. Les photos d'Isabelle
8. Le français pratique: Le jour et la date

 CD-ROM **DFi A,**
Modules 5-8
Exploration 2

 Writing Template
Unité 2

Unité 2, Leçons 5, 6, 7, 8

7, 8, 9
Situational S5, S6

Print

Answer Key, Cassette Script, Video Script, Overhead Visuals Copymasters

Activity Book, pp. 35-60
Activity Book TAE

Video Activity Book pp. 17-29

Communipak, pp. 17-36

Teacher's Resource Package

 Teacher-to-Teacher:
Games, Additional Activities

 Interdisciplinary Connections:
Projects Book

 Teaching to Multiple Intelligences in the Modern Language Classroom

 Internet Connections
www.mcdougallittell.com

T34

UNITÉ

2 Les copains et la famille

INTRODUCTION
culturelle

L'amitié *(Friendship)*

Is friendship important to you? Friendship is very important to French teenagers. Of course, there are various levels of friendship and different types of friends: classmates whom we see every day in school, friends with whom we spend time outside of school, and the few special friends who are always there when we need them and who will remain our friends for the rest of our lives. As you will see, the French have different words to describe these various relationships.

LEÇON	**5**	**Copain ou copine?**
LEÇON	**6**	**Une coïncidence**
LEÇON	**7**	**Les photos d'Isabelle**
LEÇON	**8**	**Le français pratique: Le jour et la date**

34

Unit overview

COMMUNICATION GOALS: Students will learn to introduce family and friends. They will also learn to identify dates and days of the week.
LINGUISTIC GOALS: The focus of this unit is on spoken French. Students learn about liaison and nasal vowels.

CRITICAL THINKING GOALS: Students begin to observe how gender influences form in French by contrasting masculine and feminine articles **un/une, le/la, mon/ma, ton/ta.**
CULTURAL GOALS: Students will become aware of the French concept of friendships and the importance of the French heritage in Québec, Canada.

THÈME ET OBJECTIFS

Talking about people

In this unit, you will be talking about people you know. You will learn . . .
- to identify friends, family, and relatives
- to say how old you are and find out someone's age
- to talk about birthdays and holidays

You will also learn . . .
- to count from 60 to 1,000
- to give the date and the day of the week

Copain ou copine?

In French, there are certain girls' and boys' names that sound the same. Occasionally this can be confusing.

Leçon 5

MAIN TOPICS:

Pointing out people and finding out who they are

MODULE 5:
Copain ou copine?
Total time: 3:23 min.
(Counter: 32:13 min.)

5.1 **Dialogue: Copain ou copine?**
(32:54–33:31 min.)
5.2 **Mini-scenes: Listening — Pointing out people**
(33:32–34:22 min.)
5.3 **Vignette culturelle: La bande des copains**
(34:23–35:31 min.)

IDEODISC Disc 2, Side 1
1565–7587

■ **Comprehension practice:** Play the entire module through as an introduction to the lesson.

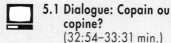
5.1 Dialogue: Copain ou copine?
(32:54–33:31 min.)

IDEODISC Disc 2, Side 1
1565–3864

  Leçon 5, Section 1

Scène 1. Philippe et Jean-Paul

Philippe is at home with his friend Jean-Paul. He seems to be expecting someone. Who could it be . . . ? The doorbell rings.

PHILIPPE: Tiens! Voilà Dominique!
JEAN-PAUL: Dominique? Qui est-ce? Un copain ou une copine?
PHILIPPE: C'est une copine.

Dominique? Qui est-ce? Un copain ou une copine?

Scène 2. Philippe, Jean-Paul, Dominique

PHILIPPE: Salut, Dominique! Ça va?
DOMINIQUE: Oui, ça va! Et toi?
JEAN-PAUL: *(thinking)* C'est vrai! C'est une copine!

Salut, Dominique! Ça va?

Scene 1. *Philippe and Jean-Paul*
PHILIPPE: *Hey! There's Dominique!*
JEAN-PAUL: *Dominique? Who's that? A boy(friend) or a girl(friend)?*
PHILIPPE: *A girl(friend).*

Scene 2. *Philippe, Jean-Paul, Dominique*
PHILIPPE: *Hi, Dominique! How's everything?*
DOMINIQUE: *Fine! And you?*
JEAN-PAUL: *(thinking) It's true! She is a girlfriend!*

36 Unité 2

Setting the stage

Ask students to think of names for boys and girls that sound the same.

For example: Kim, Lynn, Marty, Bobby/Bobbie, Gene/Jean.

In French, also, there are many boy's and girl's names that are pronounced alike.

Names spelled the same:
Dominique, Claude.
Names spelled differently:
René/Renée, André/Andrée, Joël/Joëlle, Noël/Noëlle, Michel/Michèle, Daniel/Danielle, Gabriel/Gabrielle, Frédéric/Frédérique.

POUR COMMUNIQUER

> Tiens! Voilà Caroline! C'est une copine!

How to introduce or point out someone:

Voici . . . — *This is . . . , Here come(s) . . .*

Voilà . . . — *This (That) is . . . , There's . . .*

Voici Jean-Paul.
Voici Nathalie et François.
Voilà Isabelle.
Voilà Philippe et Dominique.

How to find out who someone is:

Qui est-ce? — *Who's that? Who is it?*
C'est . . . — *It's . . . , That's . . . , He's . . . , She's . . .*

—**Qui est-ce?**
—**C'est** Patrick. **C'est** un copain.

How to get someone's attention or to express surprise:

Tiens! — *Look! Hey!*

Tiens, voilà Dominique!

Les personnes			
un garçon	boy	**une fille**	girl
un ami	friend (male)	**une amie**	friend (female)
un copain	friend (male)	**une copine**	friend (female)
un monsieur	gentleman	**une dame**	lady
un prof	teacher	**une prof**	teacher

NOTE CULTURELLE

Amis et copains

French young people, like their American counterparts, enjoy spending time with their friends. They refer to their friends as **un ami** (for a boy) and **une amie** (for a girl) or — more commonly — as **un copain** or **une copine.** Note that the words **copain, copine** can also have special meanings. When a boy talks about **une copine,** he is referring to a friend who is a girl. However, when he says **ma** *(my)* **copine,** he may be referring to his girlfriend. Similarly, a girl would call her boyfriend **mon copain.**

Leçon 5 (37)

Pour communiquer

■ **Language note:** The expression **voilà** may also mean *That is, There is, There are.*
One can say: **C'est qui? Qui c'est?**

 **Transparency 7**
Les personnes

5.2 Mini-scenes: Pointing out people
(33:32–34:22 min.)

VIDEODISC Disc 2, Side 1
3890–5380

Note culturelle

5.3 Vignette culturelle: La bande des copains
(34:23–35:31 min.)

 VIDEODISC Disc 2, Side 1
5400–7587

■ **Cultural note:** There are several ways of referring to one's boyfriend or girlfriend:
• **mon petit ami, ma petite amie** (though these terms are not as commonly used as several years ago)
• **mon petit copain, ma petite copine**
• **mon ami, mon amie**
The possessive is used to signal a more personal relationship.

■ **Language note:**
Un prof/une prof. In casual speech, both teachers and students in France use the terms **un prof** and **une prof.** These expressions are easier for beginners and are therefore introduced here in Niveau A. The more formal term **un professeur,** which refers to both men and women, is introduced in Niveau B, Lesson 17.

TPR 🏃 **Nouns with un/une**

PROPS: Transparency 7
Red and blue index cards
Model new words on the transparency.
   Voici un garçon. Voici une fille. ...
Have students come point out the words.
   X, viens ici. Montre-nous une fille.
Distribute two cards to each student.

Voici "un". [Hold up the blue card.]
Voici "une". [Hold up the red card.]
As you make statements using the new words, have students hold up their cards.
C'est un copain. Levez la carte bleue.
C'est une amie. Levez la carte rouge.
C'est un ami. [blue cards.]

un garçon, une fille

In French, all NOUNS are either MASCULINE or FEMININE.
Nouns referring to boys or men are almost always MASCULINE.
   They are introduced by **un** *(a, an).*
Nouns referring to girls or women are almost always FEMININE.
   They are introduced by **une** *(a, an).*

MASCULINE		FEMININE	
un garçon	*a boy*	**une** fille	*a girl*
un ami	*a friend (male)*	**une** amie	*a friend (female)*

1 **Copain ou copine?**
Say that the following people are your friends. Use **un copain** or **une copine,** as appropriate.

▶ **Christine est une copine.**

Christine

1. Alice

2. Marie-Jeanne

3. Éric

4. David

5. Sylvie

2 **Les amis**
The same young people are visiting your school. Point them out to your classmates, using **un ami** or **une amie,** as appropriate.

▶ —**Tiens, voilà Christine!**
  —**Qui est-ce?**
  —**C'est une amie.**

3 **Un ou une?**
Identify the people below by completing the sentences with **un** or **une.**

1. Voici . . . fille.
2. Voilà . . . garçon.
3. Voici . . . dame.
4. C'est . . . amie.
5. Olivier est . . . ami.
6. Jean-Paul est . . . copain.
7. Cécile est . . . copine.
8. Voici Mlle Lacour. C'est . . . prof.
9. Voici M. Masson. C'est . . . prof.
10. Voici Mme Chollet. C'est . . . prof.

4 À la fenêtre *(At the window)*

You and a friend are walking down the street and you see the following people at their windows. Identify them in short dialogues.

▶ —Tiens, voilà un monsieur!
—Qui est-ce?
—C'est Monsieur Mercier. ▶

Monsieur Mercier

 1. Nicole

  2. Mademoiselle Lasalle

 3. Éric

 4. Madame Albert

 5. Monsieur Lavie

6. Alain

Les nombres de 60 à 79

60 soixante

61 soixante et un	66 soixante-six
62 soixante-deux	67 soixante-sept
63 soixante-trois	68 soixante-huit
64 soixante-quatre	69 soixante-neuf
65 soixante-cinq	

70 soixante-dix

71 soixante et onze	76 soixante-seize
72 soixante-douze	77 soixante-dix-sept
73 soixante-treize	78 soixante-dix-huit
74 soixante-quatorze	79 soixante-dix-neuf
75 soixante-quinze	

➡ Note that in counting from 70 to 79, the French continue adding numbers to 60:

   70 = 60 + 10   71 = 60 + 11   72 = 60 + 12, etc.

5 Numéros de téléphone

Read aloud the phone numbers of Jean-Paul's friends in Paris.

▶ Philippe
   zéro un,
   quarante-deux,
   soixante et un,
   dix-neuf,
   soixante-quinze

Philippe   01.42.61.19.75
Martine   01.41.33.64.79
Michèle   01.42.56.76.62
Stéphanie 01.45.68.77.35
François   01.49.78.13.62

Prononciation

La liaison

Pronounce the following words:

un ami

un ami   un Américain   un Anglais   un artiste

In general, the "n" of **un** is silent. However, in the above words, the "n" of **un** is pronounced as if it were the *first* letter of the next word. The two words are *linked* together in LIAISON.

Liaison occurs between two words when the second one begins with a VOWEL SOUND, that is, with "a", "e", "i", "o", "u", and sometimes "h" and "y".

➡ Although liaison is not marked in written French, it will be indicated in your book by the symbol ‿ where appropriate.

Contrastez et répétez:

LIAISON: **un ami   un Américain   un Italien   un artiste**

NO LIAISON: **un copain   un Français   un Canadien   un prof**

Leçon 5 **39**

⊠ Game: Mini-loto (Numbers 60–79)

PREPARATION: Write the numbers from 60–79 on slips of paper (or use commercial bingo numbers).

   Have students draw a tic-tac-toe grid and fill the nine squares with numbers of their choice between 60 and 79.

Call out the numbers as you draw the slips in random order. When a student has three numbers in a row in any direction, have him/her call out "Loto."

---

4 ROLE PLAY: discussing the identity of people

■ Encourage varied responses.

▷ **Les nombres de 60 à 79**

⊟ Leçon 5, Section 3

▨ **If students ask:** From 1 to 60, French uses the Roman system of counting by 10s. However, from 60 to 100, the French count by scores (or 20s). This system was brought to England and Normandy in the tenth century by the Vikings or Norsemen.

▨ **Pronunciation:** Remind students that there is no liaison after **et**: **soixante et un, soixante et onze.**

5 PRACTICE: reading numbers up to 79

■ **Cultural note:** Paris phone numbers consist of 10 digits read in groups of two. The first two digits for Paris are always 01.

■ **Listening comprehension:** Have students close their books. Slowly dictate the numbers from the phone list. Then have students open their books to correct their work as you read the numbers once more.

Prononciation

⊟ Leçon 5, Section 4

■ **Pronunciation:** You may want to point out that similar linking occurs in English after *an*: *an apple, an uncle, an hour.*

■ **If students ask:** Adjectives of nationality are capitalized when they are used as nouns referring to people.

MODULE 6:
Une coïncidence
Total time: 4:42 min.
(Counter: 35:42 min.)

6.1 **Dialogue:**
Une coïncidence
(36:07–36:36 min.)
6.2 **Mini-scenes: Listening**
— Describing people
(36:37–38:16 min.)
6.3 **Vignette culturelle:**
Le Québec
(38:17–40:20 min.)

VIDEODISC Disc 2, Side1
7868–16231

|||||||||||||||||||||||||||||||||||||

■ **Comprehension practice:** Play the entire module through as an introduction to the lesson.

6.1 **Dialogue:**
Une coïncidence
(36:07–36:36 min.)

VIDEODISC Disc 2, Side1
7870–9429

|||||||||||||||||||||||||||||||||||||

 Leçon 6, Section 1

Une coïncidence

Isabelle is at a party with her new Canadian friend Marc. She wants him to meet some of the other guests.

Tu connais la fille là-bas?

Non. Qui est-ce?

C'est une copine. Elle s'appelle Juliette Savard.

Elle est française?

Non, elle est canadienne. Elle est de Montréal.

Moi aussi!

Quelle coïncidence!

ISABELLE: *Do you know the girl over there?*
MARC: *No. Who is she?*
ISABELLE: *She's a friend. Her name is Juliette Savard.*

MARC: *Is she French?*
ISABELLE: *No, she's Canadian. She is from Montreal.*
MARC: *Me too!*
ISABELLE: *What a coincidence!*

☀ Warm-up and review: Nationalities

PROP: Transparency 4

Ask students to give names to the 8 people, and write these names on the transparency next to each of the figures.

Pointing to the figures, have the students identify them.

Qui est-ce? [C'est Marie.]

Then, having the students take the role of the figure, ask their nationalities.

Marie, tu es française?
[Oui je suis française.]
Marie, tu es anglaise?
[Non, je suis française.]

POUR *COMMUNIQUER*

> Tu connais la dame?

> Oui, elle s'appelle Madame Leblanc.

How to inquire about people:

Tu connais . . . ?	*Do you know . . . ?*	**Tu connais** Jean-Paul?

How to describe people and give their nationalities:

Il est . . .	*He is . . .*	**Il est** canadien.
Elle est . . .	*She is . . .*	**Elle est** canadienne.

How to find out another person's name:

Comment s'appelle . . . ?	*What's the name of . . . ?*	**Comment s'appelle** le garçon?
		Comment s'appelle la fille?
Il s'appelle . . .	*His name is . . .*	**Il s'appelle** Marc.
Elle s'appelle . . .	*Her name is . . .*	**Elle s'appelle** Juliette.

■ NOTE ■ CULTURELLE

Montréal et la province de Québec

In population, metropolitan Montreal is the second-largest city in Canada. After Paris, it is also the second-largest French-speaking city in the world.

Montreal is located in the province of Quebec, where French is the official language. In fact, French speakers represent over 90% of the population. These people are the descendants of French settlers who came to Canada in the 17th and 18th centuries. If you visit Montreal, you will discover that the people of Quebec **(les Québécois)** are very proud of their heritage and dedicated to maintaining French as their language.

Leçon 6   **41**

Pour communiquer

 6.2 Mini-scenes:
Describing people
(36:37–38:16 min.)

VIDEODISC   Disc 2, Side 1
9460–12426

 Leçon 6, Section 2

■ **Language note:** Current usage often replaces **la dame/le monsieur** with **la/cette femme/ le/ce/monsieur**.

Note culturelle

 6.3 Vignette culturelle:
Le Québec
(38:17–40:20 min.)

VIDEODISC   Disc 2, Side 1
12435–16231

■ **If students ask:** The largest city in Canada is Toronto.

■ **Photo culture notes**
Le Vieux Montréal
Place Jacques Cartier in the heart of Old Montreal. The building in the background behind the statue is the Hôtel de Ville. It is here that Charles de Gaulle made his famous proclamation "Vive le Québec! Vive le Québec libre!"

Lookout, Parc Mont Royal
This park, located in the middle of Montreal, affords city dwellers a place for biking, picnicking, hiking, and cross-country skiing. A popular spot is **Lac des Castors** (Lake of the Beavers) where Montrealers can go paddleboating in the summer and ice-skating in the winter.

▷ **le garçon, la fille**

📼 Leçon 2, Section 2

If students ask
- The dropping of a final "e" (or "a," in the case of **la**) is called ELISION.
- A word that begins with **a, e, i, o,** or **u** is said to begin with a VOWEL SOUND.

1 PRACTICE: asking about people, using definite article

2 EXCHANGES: identifying people

■ **Expansion:** Have each student bring in a picture of a known personality:
- **Tu connais ce monsieur?** (holding up picture of a man)
- **Oui, c'est Bill Cosby. (Non, qui est-ce?)**

3 EXCHANGES: discussing people's names

■ **Teaching note:** Students should learn to understand the numbers and pronounce them correctly. They should not be expected to spell the numbers. (See notes and activities on page 25.)

T42

BONJOUR!

TU CONNAIS LE MONSIEUR?

OUI, IL S'APPELLE ONCLE SAM. IL EST AMÉRICAIN.

le garçon, la fille

The French equivalent of *the* has two basic forms: **le** and **la.**

MASCULINE		FEMININE	
le garçon	*the boy*	**la** fille	*the girl*
le copain	*the friend*	**la** copine	*the friend*

NOTE: Both **le** and **la** become **l'** before a vowel sound.

un copain → le copain   une copine → la copine
un ami → l'ami   une amie → l'amie

1 **Qui est-ce?**

Ask who the following people are, using **le, la,** or **l'.**

▶ une prof   1. un monsieur   3. une fille   5. un prof   7. une amie
Qui est la prof?   2. une dame   4. un garçon   6. un ami

2 **Tu connais . . . ?**

Ask your classmates if they know the following people. They will answer that they do.

▶ une dame / Madame Vallée

Tu connais la dame?

Oui, c'est Madame Vallée.

1. un prof / Monsieur Simon
2. un garçon / Christophe
3. une fille / Sophie
4. une dame / Mademoiselle Lenoir
5. une prof / Madame Boucher
6. un monsieur / Monsieur Duval

3 **Comment s'appelle . . . ?**

Ask the names of the following people, using the words **le garçon, la fille.** A classmate will respond.

▶ —**Comment s'appelle la fille?**
   —**Elle s'appelle Stéphanie.**

| Stéphanie | 1. Marc | 2. Juliette | 3. Franç |
| 4. Jean-Paul | 5. Nathalie | 6. Philippe | 7. Isabe |

42 Unité 2

4 Français, anglais, canadien ou américain?

Give the nationalities of the following people.

▶ Jewel?
Elle est américaine.

1. le prince Charles?
2. Céline Dion?
3. Juliette Binoche?

4. Gwyneth Paltrow?
5. Pierre Cardin?
6. Matt Damon?

7. Oprah Winfrey?
8. Tom Cruise?
9. Hugh Grant?

Les nombres de 80 à 1000

80 quatre-vingts

81 quatre-vingt-un	86 quatre-vingt-six
82 quatre-vingt-deux	87 quatre-vingt-sept
83 quatre-vingt-trois	88 quatre-vingt-huit
84 quatre-vingt-quatre	89 quatre-vingt-neuf
85 quatre-vingt-cinq	

90 quatre-vingt-dix

91 quatre-vingt-onze	96 quatre-vingt-seize
92 quatre-vingt-douze	97 quatre-vingt-dix-sept
93 quatre-vingt-treize	98 quatre-vingt-dix-huit
94 quatre-vingt-quatorze	99 quatre-vingt-dix-neuf
95 quatre-vingt-quinze	

100 cent   1000 mille

➔ Note that in counting from 80 to 99, the French add numbers to the base of **quatre-vingts** (fourscore):

$$80 = 4 \times 20 \qquad 90 = 4 \times 20 + 10$$
$$85 = 4 \times 20 + 5 \qquad 99 = 4 \times 20 + 19$$

---

5 Au téléphone

In France, the telephone area code (**l'indicatif**) is always a four-digit number. Your teacher will name a city (**une ville**) from the chart. Give the corresponding area code.

▶ Nice? **C'est le zéro quatre quatre-vingt-treize.**

VILLE	INDICATIF
Albi	0563
Avignon	0490
Cannes	0493
Dijon	0380
Marseille	0491
Montpellier	0467
Nancy	0383
▶ Nice	0493
Nîmes	0466
Rennes	0299
Saint-Tropez	0494
Strasbourg	0388
Vichy	0470

Prononciation   /ɛ̃/

La voyelle nasale /ɛ̃/

In French, there are three nasal vowel sounds:

/ɛ̃/ **cinq** (5)   /ɔ̃/ **onze** (11)   /ɑ̃/ **trente** (30)

Practice the sound /ɛ̃/ in the following words. Note that this vowel sound can have several different spellings.

➔ Be sure not to pronounce an "**n**" or "**m**" after the nasal vowel.

Répétez:
"in"   ci**n**q qui**n**ze vi**n**gt vi**n**gt-ci**n**q quatre-vi**n**gt-qui**n**ze
"ain"   américai**n** Alai**n** copai**n**
"(i)en"   bie**n** canadie**n** tie**n**s!
"un"   u**n**

Tien**s! Voilà Alai**n**. Il est américai**n**.   E**t** Julie**n**? Il est canadie**n**.**

5

cinq

---

4 DESCRIPTION: discussing people's nationalities

1. anglais	6. américain
2. canadienne	7. américaine
3. française	8. américain
4. américaine	9. anglais
5. français	

▶ **Les nombres de 80 à 1000**

🔲 **Leçon 6, Section 3**

■ **Pronunciation:** There is no liaison between **quatre-vingt** and the numbers **un, huit, onze**.

■ **Language note:** **Mille** is presented for recognition. Numbers between 100 and 1000 are <u>not</u> activated.

If students ask:

101 **cent un**	102 **cent deux**
111 **cent onze**	120 **cent vingt**

5 COMPREHENSION: identifying telephone area codes

■ **Variation:** Quel est l'indicatif de Nice?

■ **Map work:** You may want to have students locate these cities on a map of France (p. R4 in the student text or on Transparency 1).

■ **Cultural note:** As of October 1996, French telephone numbers have 10 digits, beginning with 01, 02, 03, 04 or 05. Paris numbers always begin with <u>01</u>. (Ex: 01 43 56 96 00) If you are calling from the U. S., however, you do <u>not</u> use the 0. (Ex: 33 <u>1</u> 43 56 96 00) The 33 is France's "country code" for long distance dialing.

Prononciation

🔲 **Leçon 6, Section 4**

■ **Pronunciation:** Some French people still distinguish between /ɛ̃/ **(in)** and /œ̃/ **(un)**. However, most French speakers use only the nasal vowel /ɛ̃/. For simplicity, we are not introducing the nasal /œ̃/ at this level.

MODULE 7:
Les photos d'Isabelle
Total time: 5:32 min.
(Counter: 40:30 min.)

7.1 Dialogue: Les photos d'Isabelle
(40:45–41:16 min.)
7.2 Monologue: La famille d'Isabelle
(41:17–42:33 min.)
7.3 Mini-scenes: How old are you?
(42:34–44:13 min.)
7.4 Vignette culturelle: La famille française: un mariage
(44:14–45:57 min.)

VIDEODISC Disc 2, Side 1
16443–26301

7.1 Dialogue: Les photos d'Isabelle
(40:45–41:16 min.)

VIDEODISC Disc 2, Side 1
16447–17796

Leçon 7, Section 1

Les photos d'Isabelle

Isabelle is showing her family photo album to her friend Jean-Paul.

ISABELLE: Voici ma mère.
JEAN-PAUL: Et le monsieur, c'est ton père?
ISABELLE: Non, c'est mon oncle Thomas.
JEAN-PAUL: Et la fille, c'est ta cousine?
ISABELLE: Oui, c'est ma cousine Béatrice. Elle a seize ans.
JEAN-PAUL: Et le garçon, c'est ton cousin?
ISABELLE: Non, c'est un copain.
JEAN-PAUL: Un copain ou ton copain?
ISABELLE: Dis donc, Jean-Paul, tu es vraiment trop curieux!

ma mère

mon oncle Thomas

ma cousine Béatrice

??

ISABELLE: *This is my mother.*
JEAN-PAUL: *And the man, is he your father?*
ISABELLE: *No, that's my uncle Thomas.*
JEAN-PAUL: *And the girl, is she your cousin?*
ISABELLE: *Yes, that's my cousin Béatrice. She's sixteen.*

JEAN-PAUL: *And the boy, is he your cousin?*
ISABELLE: *No, that's a friend.*
JEAN-PAUL: *A friend or a boyfriend?*
ISABELLE: *Hey there, Jean-Paul, you are really too curious!*

44 Unité 2

☀ Warm-up and review: Copains et copines

Ask questions about students in the class:
[Point to a girl] **Qui est-ce?** [C'est Anne.]
Est-ce que c'est un garçon ou une fille?
[C'est une fille.]
C'est un copain ou une copine?
[C'est une copine.]

Address a boy in the class:
Et toi, est-ce qu'Anne est une copine ou ta copine?
[C'est une copine. or: C'est ma copine.]
Ask similar questions about other students.

POUR COMMUNIQUER

Voici mon chien Malice.

How to introduce your family:

Voici mon père.   *This is my father.*
Et voici ma mère.   *And this is my mother.*

La famille *(Family)*

un frère	brother	**une soeur**	sister
un cousin	cousin	**une cousine**	cousin
un père	father	**une mère**	mother
un oncle	uncle	**une tante**	aunt
un grand-père	grandfather	**une grand-mère**	grandmother

Les animaux domestiques *(Pets)*

MIAOU   OUAF OUAF

un chat   **un chien**

■ NOTE ■ CULTURELLE

La famille française

When you and your friends talk about your families, you usually are referring to your brothers, sisters, and parents. In French, however, **la famille** refers not only to parents and children but also to grandparents, aunts, uncles, cousins, as well as a whole array of more distant relatives related by blood and marriage.

Since the various members of a family often live in the same region, French teenagers see their grandparents and cousins fairly frequently. Even when relatives do not live close by, the family finds many occasions to get together: for weekend visits, during school and summer vacations, on holidays, as well as on special occasions such as weddings and anniversaries.

Leçon 7 45

Pour communiquer

💻 **7.2 Monologue: La famille d'Isabelle**
(41:17–42:33 min.)

VIDEODISC Disc 2, Side 1
17835–20097

🔲 Leçon 7, Section 2

📇 **Transparency 8**
Family tree

Supplementary vocabulary

FAMILY
un beau-père	*stepfather*
une belle-mère	*stepmother*
un beau-frère	*stepbrother*
une belle-soeur	*stepsister*
un demi-frère	*halfbrother*
une demi-soeur	*halfsister*

PETS
un hamster /ɛamstɛr /,	no liaison
un cochon d'Inde	*Guinea pig*
un poisson rouge	*goldfish*
une souris blanche	*white mouse*
un oiseau	*bird*
une perruche	*parakeet*
un serpent	*snake*

Note culturelle

💻 **7.3 Vignette culturelle: La famille française: un mariage**
(44:14–45:57 min.)

VIDEODISC Disc 2, Side 1
23143–26301

🌐 **Cross-cultural observation**
Ask students if they have ever attended a wedding. Discuss the similarities and differences between French and American weddings, pointing out especially the dual ceremony (church/**mairie**) in France.

TPR 🏃 The family

PROP: Transparency 8
Describe the various family relationships, pointing to the transparency.

> **François Mallet est le père de Véronique.**
> **M. Mallet est aussi le père de Frédéric....**

Ask students to point out family members.

> **X, viens à l'écran. Montre-nous la cousine de Catherine. ...**

FOLLOW-UP: Ask the names of people.

> **Comment s'appelle le frère de Véronique?**
> [Il s'appelle Frédéric Mallet.]

▷ **mon cousin, ma cousine**

▢ **Teaching notes**
- This lesson provides an initial introduction to adjective AGREEMENT with the singular forms **mon/ma** and **ton/ta**.
- It is important that students learn to differentiate clearly between the pronunciation of **mon** and **ma**, **ton** and **ta**. They should pronounce the "n" of **mon** and **ton** only in liaison.
- In Niveau B, students will encounter all the forms of the possessive adjectives (Lesson 24).

1 PRACTICE: talking about friends, relatives, and pets

■ **Pronunciation:** album /albɔm/

2 COMMUNICATION: discussing the names of relatives, friends, and pets

---

Petit commentaire

The French people love pets, especially cats and dogs. What is important is the animal's personality and friendliness rather than its pedigree. Some common names given to animals are:

Minou, Pompon, Fifi (cats)
Titus, Milou, Médor (dogs)

C'EST TA SOEUR?
NON, C'E MON FRÈ

mon cousin, ma cousine

The French equivalents of *my* and *your* have the following forms:

MASCULINE			FEMININE	
mon cousin	*my cousin (male)*		**ma** cousine	*my cousin (female)*
mon frère	*my brother*		**ma** soeur	*my sister*
ton cousin	*your cousin (male)*		**ta** cousine	*your cousin (female)*
ton frère	*your brother*		**ta** soeur	*your sister*

➔ Note that the feminine **ma** becomes **mon** and the feminine **ta** becomes **ton** before a vowel sound. Liaison is required.

une amie → **mon** amie **ton** amie

1 **L'album de photos**
You are showing a friend your photo album. Identify the following people, using **mon** and **ma**, as appropriate.

▶ cousine Jacqueline   **Voici ma cousine Jacqueline.**

1. frère	5. père	9. copine Pauline	13. chien Toto
2. soeur	6. mère	10. amie Florence	14. chat Minou
3. tante Monique	7. copain Nicolas	11. grand-mère Michèle	15. cousine Sophie
4. oncle Pierre	8. ami Jérôme	12. grand-père Robert	

2 **Comment s'appelle . . . ?**
Ask your classmates to name some of their friends, relatives, and pets. They can invent names if they wish.

▶ le copain

Comment s'appelle ton copain?
Mon copain s'appelle Bob.

1. l'oncle	4. la cousine	7. la grand-mère
2. la tante	5. la copine	8. le chien
3. le cousin	6. le grand-père	9. le chat

 46 Unité 2

☀ **Warm-up and review: Numbers**

Divide the class in half: side A and side B. Point to side A and say a number. Then point to side B and say another number. Students on the side with the higher number raise their hands.

A – 22. B – 35. [Students on Side B raise their hands.]
A – 89. B – 64. [Students on Side A raise their hands.]

POUR
COMMUNIQUER

COMMUNICATION

> Quel âge as-tu?

> J'ai treize ans.

How to find out how old a friend is:

Quel âge as-tu?	*How old are you?*	—**Quel âge as-tu?**
J'ai . . . ans.	*I'm . . . (years old).*	—**J'ai treize ans.**

How to ask about how old others are:

—**Quel âge a ton père?**	*How old is your father?*
—**Il a quarante-deux ans.**	*He is 42 (years old).*
—**Quel âge a ta mère?**	*How old is your mother?*
—**Elle a trente-neuf ans.**	*She is 39 (years old).*

➡ Although *years old* may be left out in English, the word **ans** must be used in French when talking about someone's age.
Il a vingt ans. *He's twenty. (He's twenty years old.)*

---

3 Quel âge as-tu? ─────────
Ask your classmates how old they are.

▶ —**Quel âge as-tu?**
—**J'ai (treize) ans.**

4 Joyeux anniversaire! ─────
(Happy birthday!)
Ask your classmates how old the following people are.

▶ —**Quel âge a Stéphanie?**
—**Elle a quatorze ans.**
Stéphanie

1. **Éric** 2. **Mademoiselle Doucette** 3. **Monsieur Boucher**

4. **Madame Dupont** 5. **Monsieur Camus** 6. **Madame Simon**

▶ ▶ ▶ ▶ ▶ ▶ ▶ ▶ ▶ ▶ ▶ ▶ ▶ ▶ ▶ ▶ ▶

5 Curiosité ─────
Find out the ages of your classmates'
friends and relatives. If they are not sure,
they can guess or invent an answer.

▶ la copine —**Quel âge a ta copine?**
—**Ma copine a (treize) ans.**

1. le père	4. la tante	7. le grand-père
2. la mère	5. le cousin	8. la grand-mère
3. l'oncle	6. la cousine	

Prononciation /ã/ /ɔ̃/

Les voyelles nasales /ã/ et /ɔ̃/

tante oncle

The letters "**an**" and "**en**" usually
represent the nasal vowel /ã/. Be
sure not to pronounce an "**n**" after the nasal vowel.

Répétez: **ans tante grand-père français
anglais quarante cinquante
trente comment Henri Laurent**

The letters "**on**" represent the nasal vowel /ɔ̃/. Be sure
not to pronounce an "**n**" after the nasal vowel.

Répétez: **non mon ton bonjour oncle
garçon onze**

Contrastez: **an—on tante—ton onze—ans
Mon oncle François a trente ans.**

Pour communiquer

▪ **Photographs:** On the beach at Deauville

 7.3 Mini-scenes: How old are you? (42:34–44:13 min.)

VIDEODISC Disc 2, Side 1 20140–23121

▭▭ Leçon 7, Section 3

▪ **If students ask:** Literally, these sentences mean: *What age do you have? I have thirteen years.*

3 COMMUNICATION: asking how old someone is

4 PRACTICE: discussing people's ages

▪ **Listening comprehension:** Ask the ages of these people in random order. Students write down the number of the corresponding birthday cake.
Qui a soixante-quatre ans? (4)
Qui a trente-deux ans? (3)
Qui a dix-huit ans? (1)
Qui a quatre-vingt-trois ans? (6)
Qui a vingt-cinq ans? (2)
Qui a soixante-quinze ans? (5)

5 COMMUNICATION: discussing friends' and relatives' ages

Prononciation

▭▭ Leçon 7, Section 4

▪ **Pronunciation:**
• The combination **ien** is pronounced /jɛ̃/: **bien**
• Remind students that they should not pronounce an "n" after the nasal vowel.

Teaching strategy: Ages

PROP: Transparency 8
Ask students to determine the ages of the people on the transparency.
  –**Quel âge a Frédéric?**
  – [Student X]: **Il a quinze ans.**
  – **Vous êtes d'accord?** *Do you agree?*

Write "15" in the box next to Frédéric. Have students assign ages to the other members of the family.
Then ask questions about the transparency.
  Qui a quarante ans?
  Quel âge a la soeur de Frédéric?

T47

MODULE 8:
**Le français pratique:
Le jour et la date**
Total time: 5:47 min.
(Counter: 46:08 min.)

8.1 **Dialogues:**
A. Quel jour est-ce?
(46:45–47:11 min.)
B. Anniversaire
(47:12–47:34 min.)
8.2 **Mini-scenes:**
Dates and birthdays
(47:35–50:04 min.)
8.3 **Vignette culturelle:**
Joyeux anniversaire!
(50:05–51:48 min.)

VIDEODISC Disc 2, Side1
26533–26791

8.1 **Dialogue: A. Quel
jour est-ce?**
(46:45–47:11 min.)

VIDEODISC Disc 2, Side1
26535–2902

 Leçon 8, Section 1

**LE FRANÇAIS
PRATIQUE**

LEÇON 8

Le jour et la date

Super! Demain, c'est samedi!

A. Quel jour est-ce?

For many people, the days of the week are not all alike.

Dialogue 1. Vendredi

PHILIPPE: Quel jour est-ce?
STÉPHANIE: C'est vendredi.
PHILIPPE: Super! Demain, c'est samedi!

Dialogue 2. Mercredi

NATHALIE: Ça va?
MARC: Pas très bien.
NATHALIE: Pourquoi?
MARC: Aujourd'hui, c'est mercredi.
NATHALIE: Et alors?
MARC: Demain, c'est jeudi! Le jour de l'examen.
NATHALIE: Zut! C'est vrai! Au revoir, Marc.
MARC: Au revoir, Nathalie. À demain!

Demain, c'est jeudi! Le jour de l'examen.

Dialogue 1. *Friday*

PHILIPPE: *What day is it?*
STÉPHANIE: *It's Friday.*
PHILIPPE: *Great! Tomorrow is Saturday!*

Dialogue 2. *Wednesday*

NATHALIE: *How are things?*
MARC: *Not very good.*
NATHALIE: *Why?*
MARC: *Today is Wednesday.*

NATHALIE: *So?*
MARC: *Tomorrow is Thursday! The day of the exam.*
NATHALIE: *Darn! That's right! Good-bye, Marc.*
MARC: *Good-bye, Nathalie. See you tomorrow!*

48 Unité 2

☀ **Warm-up and review: Ça va?**

Ask students how they are feeling, reviewing the expressions from Lesson 3. For example:

Bonjour, X. Ça va?
[Oui, ça va très bien.]
Et toi, Y, ça va bien ou ça va mal?
[Ça va mal.]

Z, demande à W si ça va.
[–Bonjour W, ça va?
–Ça va comme ci, comme ça.]

POUR COMMUNIQUER

How to talk about days of the week:

Quel jour est-ce? — *What day is it?*
  Aujourd'hui, c'est mercredi. — *Today is Wednesday.*
  Demain, c'est jeudi. — *Tomorrow is Thursday.*

How to tell people when you will see them again:

À samedi! — *See you Saturday!*
À demain! — *See you tomorrow!*

À samedi!

Les jours de la semaine *(Days of the week)*

lundi	*Monday*	**vendredi**	*Friday*	**aujourd'hui**	*today*
mardi	*Tuesday*	**samedi**	*Saturday*	**demain**	*tomorrow*
mercredi	*Wednesday*	**dimanche**	*Sunday*		
jeudi	*Thursday*				

---

1 **Questions**

1. Quel jour est-ce aujourd'hui?
2. Et demain, quel jour est-ce?

2 **Un jour de retard** *(One day behind)*
Georges has trouble keeping track of the date. He is always one day behind. Monique corrects him.

▶ samedi

Aujourd'hui, c'est samedi?

Non, aujourd'hui, c'est dimanche!

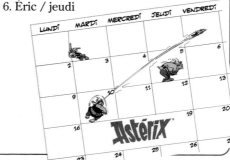

1. lundi   3. jeudi   5. dimanche
2. mardi   4. vendredi   6. mercredi

3 **Au revoir!**
You are on the phone with the following friends. Say good-bye and tell them when you will see them.

▶ Christine / lundi
  Au revoir, Christine. À lundi.

1. David / dimanche
2. Roger / samedi
3. Delphine / mercredi
4. Sophie / vendredi
5. Alain / mardi
6. Éric / jeudi

LUNDI   MARDI   MERCREDI   JEUDI   VENDREDI

Astérix

Leçon 8   **49**

Language note: Days of the week

You may wish to tell your students that the days are named for the Roman gods. The suffix **di** comes from the Latin **dies** (day).

  lun-di   (moon-day)
  mar-di   (Mars-day)
  mercre-di   (Mercury-day)

  jeu-di   (Jupiter-day)
  vendre-di   (Venus-day)
  same-di   (Saturn-day)
Dimanche comes from the Latin **Dominus** (the Lord).

Pour communiquer

■ **Language note:** Also:
Quel jour sommes-nous?
Quel jour est-on?

■ **Casual speech:** One can say:
C'est quel jour?
On est quel jour?

Supplementary vocabulary

À bientôt!   *See you soon!*

▷ **Les jours de la semaine**

Leçon 8, Section 2

■ **Cultural note:** On French calendars, the week traditionally begins with **lundi**. On Canadian calendars, however, the week begins with **dimanche**.

■ **If students ask:** The days of the week are usually not capitalized in French.

1 COMMUNICATION: stating today's and tomorrow's dates

2 EXCHANGES: getting the date right

■ **Variation:** Philippe is one day ahead.
– Aujourd'hui, c'est samedi?
– Non, aujourd'hui, c'est vendredi.

3 ROLE PLAY: telling people good-bye and when you will see them again

■ **Challenge** (dialogue format):
– Au revoir, Christine.
– Au revoir. À lundi.

VIDEODISC Disc 2, Side1
29038–33609

Leçon 8, Section 3

■ **If students ask:** Explain that **si** *(yes)* is used to respond to a negative statement or question.

8.2 Mini-scenes: Dates and birthdays
(47:35–50:04 min.)

VIDEODISC Disc 2, Side1
29080–33610

Leçon 8, Section 4

 Transparency 9
Calendar

■ **Language note:** To ask for the date, one can also say:
Quel jour est-ce?
Quel jour est-on? or
Quel jour sommes-nous?

■ **If students ask:** The months are usually not capitalized in French.

B. Anniversaire

François and Isabelle are on their way to Nathalie's birthday party. As they are talking, François wants to know when Isabelle's birthday is.

FRANÇOIS: C'est quand, ton anniversaire?
ISABELLE: C'est le 18 mars!
FRANÇOIS: Le 18 mars? Pas possible!
ISABELLE: Si! Pourquoi?
FRANÇOIS: C'est aussi mon anniversaire.
ISABELLE: Quelle coïncidence!

FRANÇOIS: *When is your birthday?*
ISABELLE: *It's March 18!*
FRANÇOIS: *March 18? That's not possible!*
ISABELLE: *Yes, it is! Why?*
FRANÇOIS: *It's my birthday too.*
ISABELLE: *What a coincidence!*

POUR COMMUNIQUER

Quelle est la date?

How to talk about the date:

Quelle est la date?	*What's the date?*
C'est le 12 (douze) octobre.	*It's October 12.*
C'est le premier juin.	*It's June first.*

How to talk about birthdays:

| —**C'est quand, ton anniversaire?** | *When is your birthday?* |
| —**Mon anniversaire est le 2 (deux) mars.** | *My birthday is March 2.* |

Les mois de l'année *(Months of the year)*			
janvier	**avril**	**juillet**	**octobre**
février	**mai**	**août**	**novembre**
mars	**juin**	**septembre**	**décembre**

 50 Unité 2

Casual speech

In French, casual speech is often heard, but rarely written. (This is like English, where people often say: *You coming?* and write: *Are you coming?*)

In this textbook, students are introduced to standard written French.

Some forms of casual speech are so common that they have been accepted into general usage. Two examples of this are **un prof** and **jouer au foot.**

In this lesson, students learn the casual **C'est quand, ton anniversaire?** which is simpler than **Quand est-ce, ton anniversaire?**

La date

To express a date in French, the pattern is:

le	+	NUMBER	+	MONTH
le		11 (onze)		novembre
le		20 (vingt)		mai

EXCEPTION: The first of the month is **le premier.**

➡ In front of numbers, the French use **l'** (and never **l'**): **le onze, le huit.**

➡ Note that when dates are abbreviated in French, the day always comes first.

2 / **8**   **le deux** août   **1** / **11**   **le premier** novembre

Les Backstreet Boys
à Paris
Au Parc des Princes
le 23 juin

4 **Anniversaires**
Ask your classmates when their birthdays are.

— C'est quand, ton anniversaire?
— Mon anniversaire est le 3 février.

5 **Quelle est la date?**
Ask what the date is.

▶ —Quelle est la date?
—C'est le douze septembre.

12 SEPTEMBRE

1 30 JUIN **2** 8 MAI **3** 4 MARS **4** 21 NOVEMBRE **5** 1 AVRIL **6** 25 AOÛT

6 **Dates importantes**
Give the following dates in French.

▶ Noël *(Christmas):* 25/12   C'est le vingt-cinq décembre.

1. le jour de l'An *(New Year's Day):* 1/1
2. la fête *(holiday)* de Martin Luther King: 15/1
3. la Saint-Valentin: 14/2
4. la Saint-Patrick: 17/3
5. la fête nationale américaine: 4/7
6. la fête nationale française: 14/7
7. la fête de Christophe Colomb: 12/10

Leçon 8   **51**

▷ **La date**

🔘 Leçon 8, Section 5

■ **Language Note**
With dates, you may introduce the years beginning with 2000:

2000	deux mille
2001	deux mille un
2002	deux mille deux, etc.

Aujourd'hui, nous sommes le dix décembre deux mille....

■ **Language note:** Also: **le un** (when **un** is a number and not a pronoun).

■ **Language note:** Abbreviations of dates may also be punctuated with hyphens or periods.
• The months are sometimes expressed in roman numerals: **le 2.VIII.**
• Note: **le premier** may be abbreviated as **le 1er.**

4 COMMUNICATION: discussing birthdays

■ **Variation**
Have students walk around the room grouping themselves according to the month of their birth.
– C'est quand, ton anniversaire?
– Mon anniversaire est le 1er mai. Et toi?
As a follow-up, begin with January, and have students in each group give their birthdays before sitting back down.

5 EXCHANGES: asking today's date

6 PRACTICE: telling the date of certain events

Project: Calendars

You may wish to have your students prepare a calendar of the month of their next birthday. Have them label the month, the days of the week, and their birthday in French. Ask them to illustrate the top of the calendar with an original drawing.

This activity is particularly appropriate for younger learners.

À votre tour 2

MAIN TOPICS:

Recapitulation and review

1 COMPREHENSION

1-h	4-g	7-f
2-d	5-e	8-a
3-c	6-b	

▭▭ AVT 2, Section 1

2 GUIDED ORAL EXPRESSION

▭▭ AVT 2, Section 2

3 GUIDED ORAL EXPRESSION

Sample answers:
C: Nathalie, tu connais la fille?
N: Oui, c'est une amie (une copine).
C: Comment s'appelle ton amie (ta copine)?
N: Elle s'appelle Michèle Lafontaine.
C: Elle est canadienne?
N: Oui. Elle est de Québec.
C: Quelle coïncidence! Moi aussi, je suis de Québec.

▭▭ AVT 2, Section 3

À votre tour!

1 Nathalie et Philippe

Nathalie is talking to Philippe and you hear parts of their conversation. For each of Nathalie's questions, select Philippe's response from the suggested answers.

Qui est-ce?¹
C'est ta soeur?²
Quel âge as-tu?³
C'est quand, ton anniversaire?⁴
Quel âge a ton oncle?⁵
Tu connais Stéphanie?⁶
Comment s'appelle ta prof de français?⁷
Quel jour est-ce aujourd'hui?⁸

a. Vendredi.
b. Oui, c'est une copine.
c. Quinze ans.
d. Non, c'est ma cousine.
e. Quarante-cinq ans.
f. Elle s'appelle Madame Doucette.
g. Le dix-huit décembre.
h. C'est mon cousin Christophe.

2 Et toi?

You have just met Nathalie at a party. Answer her questions.

1. Quel âge as-tu?
2. Quel âge a ton copain (ta copine)?
3. C'est quand, ton anniversaire?
4. C'est quand, l'anniversaire de ton copain (ta copine)?
5. Comment s'appelle le (la) prof de français?

3 Conversation dirigée

Nathalie and Christophe are in a café. Christophe sees another girl that Nathalie seems to know. He wonders who she is.

Christophe				Nathalie
	asks Nathalie if she knows the girl	→	says she does and that she is a friend	
	asks Nathalie the name of her friend	→	says that her name is Michèle Lafontaine	
	asks if she is Canadian	→	says yes and adds that she is from Quebec City **(de Québec)**	
	says what a coincidence **(Quelle coïncidence!)** and adds that he is also from Quebec City			

52 Unité 2

À votre tour

This section is similar to the *À votre tour* of Unit 1 (see Teacher notes, page 30).

As before, you will want to select those activities which are most appropriate for your students. Encourage students to work cooperatively in pairs and trios.

▰ Portfolio assessment

If you began Oral portfolio assessment in Unit 1 (see Teacher notes, page 31), you may have your students prepare a second audio (or video) recording to go with Unit 2. But you may prefer to wait until Unit 3, and only do portfolio recordings every other unit.

1 Ma famille *(My family)*

You are showing your friends a picture of your family. Introduce everyone, giving their ages.

▶ **Voici ma soeur. Elle a douze ans.**

5 En scène

With a classmate, act out the following scene.

CHARACTERS:
You and a French guest

SITUATION:
You are in France. Your French friends have invited you to a picnic. You meet one of the guests and have a conversation.

- Greet the guest.
- Introduce yourself and ask the guest's name.
- Tell the guest how old you are and ask his/her age.
- Tell the guest the date of your birthday and ask the date of his/her birthday.
- *(The guest waves to a friend.)* Ask the guest the name of his/her friend.
- *(It is the end of the picnic.)* Say good-bye.

6 Le loto

Loto is a French version of Bingo. Read out loud the numbers on your board.

À votre tour **53**

4 GUIDED ORAL EXPRESSION

5 GUIDED ORAL EXPRESSION

6 NUMBERS

Game: Loto

PREPARATION: Have your students make French Loto cards by drawing a grid with 27 squares and selecting fifteen numbers between 1 and 90. Place numbers between 1 and 10 in the first column, numbers between 11 to 20 in the second column, etc.

Each horizontal row must contain five numbers.

PLAY: Call out random numbers from 1 to 90, as in bingo. The first student to completely cover a horizontal row of five wins. This student then reads the numbers aloud so that they can be checked.

OBJECTIVES:

- Development of cross-cultural awareness
- Vocabulary expansion

Les bruits français

OBJECTIVE:
- Learning that speakers of other languages may interpret sounds differently

■ **Expansion**
- **le coq** *(rooster)*: **cocorico**
  le cheval *(horse)*: **hî - hî - hî...**
  le mouton *(sheep)*: **mè-è-è-è**
  le poisson *(fish)*: **glou glou**
  l'oiseau *(bird)*: **cui cui**
- **dog:** also **ouah ouah**

■ **Photo culture notes**
La campagne française
The scene is a rural landscape typical of southwestern France (**les Pyrénées**).
The farm (**la ferme**) is over 300 years old. Have students note:
- the main building (**le logis principal**)
- the square tower (**la tour carrée**)
- the barn (**la grange**)
- the wood shed (**la remise à bois**)
In the field there are rolled bales of hay (**les bottes de foin**) which will be stored in the barn for winter.

LES BRUITS FRANÇAIS *(French sounds)*

People in various countries can hear the same noises and interpret them differently. Notice how the French express certain common sounds.

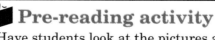

📖 Pre-reading activity
- Have students look at the pictures and give the corresponding English equivalents for the sounds and animal noises.
- Model the sounds in French and have student repeat them. (Note that in **cot-cot-codèt,** the final "t's" are pronounced.)

Post-reading activities
- For each sound, have students vote whether they think the English version or the French version is closer to reality.
- If some students in the class are from other cultures, ask how these sounds are expressed in their languages.

ASTÉRIX en action

Astérix and his friends lead an action-packed life. Can you match the sounds with the corresponding cartoon frames?

a CRAAAC!

b POM POM! POM!

c RRROAÂOOO! GRRRAOOR!

d GLOU! GLOU! GLOU! GLOU! GLOU!

e TATARARA TATA!

f PAFFF!

1 From ASTÉRIX LE GAULOIS

2 From ASTÉRIX GLADIATEUR

AU NOM DE CÉSAR, OUVREZ!

3 From ASTÉRIX CHEZ LES BRETONS

4 From ASTÉRIX CHEZ LES BRETONS

5 From ASTÉRIX GLADIATEUR

6 From ASTÉRIX LE GAULOIS

© 1991 LES ÉDITIONS ALBERT RENÉ/GOSCINNY-UDERZO

Entracte 2   55

Astérix en action

OBJECTIVES:
• Interpreting sounds
• Becoming familiar with a popular French cartoon character

■ **Teaching hint:**
• Model the sounds and have students repeat them.
• If necessary, clarify the pictures:
(1) Astérix is drinking the magic potion that gives him power.
(2) A Roman soldier leaves only his sandals and molars behind as a punch from Astérix sends him flying.
(3) Someone is pounding at the door and shouting: "Open up, in the name of Caesar!"
(4) Obélix has just kicked in the door.
(5) The lions are entering the ring to fight the gladiators.
(6) Roman soldiers are sounding reveille.

UNITÉ 2 INTERNET PROJECT

Students may use the Internet to find international holidays for the twelve months of the year. They can start with the link available below, or use the alternate given. Students may wish to create and display poster-size calendars with an international holiday featured for each day of the week. To expand this activity, have students generate new links by using the search engine of their choice and the keywords **"fêtes légales"; "jours fériés"; (French names of specific holidays)**.

One-World Global Calendar
http://www.zapcom.net/phoenix.arabeth/1world.html

ALTERNATE
Worldwide Holidays and Events
http://www.classnet.com/holidays

📖 **Pre-reading activity**
• Ask students if they remember who Astérix is. (If not, turn back to page 16.)
• Point out that the Gauls **(les Gaulois)** get their strength from drinking a magic mistletoe potion (picture 1).
• Obélix (picture 4) is Astérix's strong and dependable companion.

Post-reading activity
Ask students how they would translate these frames into English.

UNITÉ

3 Bon appétit!

INTRODUCTION

culturelle

Bon appétit!

Where do you go when you want something to eat or drink? Maybe to a fast-food restaurant or an ice cream place?

French teenagers also have a large choice of places to go when they are hungry or thirsty. Some go to a bakery **(une boulangerie)** or a pastry shop **(une pâtisserie)** to buy croissants, éclairs, or other small pastries. Some may buy pizzas, crepes, hot dogs, or ice-cream cones from street vendors. Still others may go to a fast-food restaurant **(un fast-food).** But the favorite place to get something to eat or drink is the café. There are cafés practically everywhere in France. As you will see, the café plays an important role in the social life of all French people.

LEÇON	**9**	**Tu as faim?**
LEÇON	**10**	**Au café**
LEÇON	**11**	**Ça fait combien?**
LEÇON	**12**	**Le français pratique: Le temps**

56

Unit overview

COMMUNICATION GOALS: Students will learn to order something to eat or drink in a café or fast-food restaurant. They will also learn to talk about weather.

LINGUISTIC GOALS: Students will begin to acquire features of the French sound system, particularly rhythm, stress, intonation, and the French / r /.

CRITICAL THINKING GOALS: Students will discover that all nouns — even those referring to things — have gender. They will observe that in French *it* is expressed as either **il** or **elle.**

CULTURAL GOALS: Students will become aware of types of eating establishments and the French monetary system.

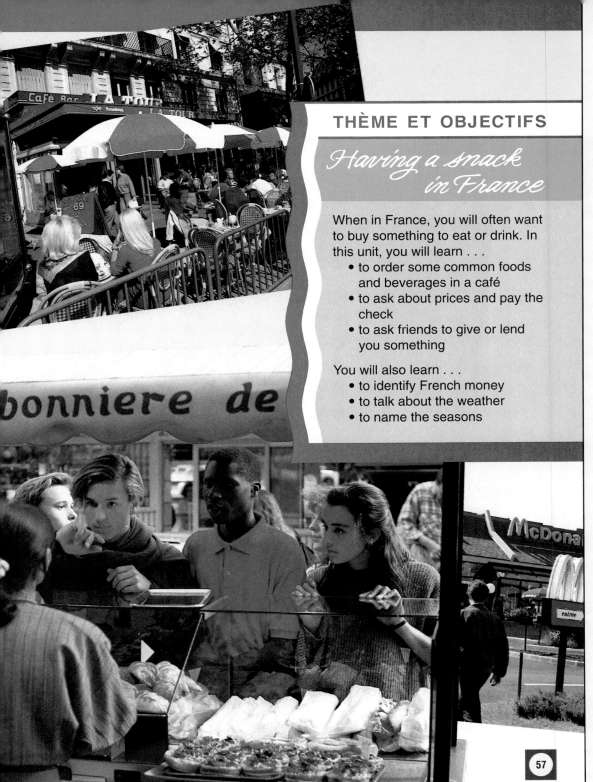

THÈME ET OBJECTIFS

Having a snack in France

When in France, you will often want to buy something to eat or drink. In this unit, you will learn . . .

- to order some common foods and beverages in a café
- to ask about prices and pay the check
- to ask friends to give or lend you something

You will also learn . . .

- to identify French money
- to talk about the weather
- to name the seasons

57

■ **Language note:** The expression **Bon appétit!** is used as people sit down to eat. It means *Enjoy the meal!*

■ **Photo culture notes**
La bonbonnière
This photo, taken in a Parisian department store, shows a stand that sells **croissants**, **sandwiches**, and **pâtisseries**. It is called **La bonbonnière** or "candy box."

Les fast-foods
Fast food restaurants (**les fast-foods**, or technically, **les restaurants de restauration rapide**) have multiplied in France in recent years and are now very popular with French teenagers. One can order:

- hamburgers (**des hamburgers**)
- hotdogs (**des saucisses, des hot dogs**)
- French fries (**des frites**)
- salads (**des salades**), and sometimes
- pastry (**des pâtisseries**)

A typical meal at a fast food restaurant costs about 6 euros (or about $6).
In addition to McDonald's and Burger King, there are also other chains, like Quick, Free Time, Le Duff, and La Croissanterie.

■ **Language Note:** The term for "drive-up" at fast-food restaurants like McDonald's is **service au volant** (service at the steering wheel).

Pacing

Try to move through this unit rather quickly, focusing on listening and speaking.

In later lessons, students will encounter the same vocabulary again. At that time they will be expected to master the material in writing.

MODULE 9:
Tu as faim?
Total time: 6:15 min.
(Counter: 52:02 min.)**9.1**

Dialogue: **Tu as faim?**
(52:29–53:01 min.)
9.2 Mini-scenes:
Ordering food
(53:03–55:15 min.)
9.3 Vignette culturelle:
Qu'est-ce qu'on mange?
(55:16–58:13 min.)

VIDEODISC Disc 2, Side 2
1570–12756

■ **Comprehension practice:** Play the entire module through as an introduction to the lesson.

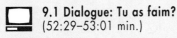 **9.1 Dialogue: Tu as faim?**
(52:29–53:01 min.)

VIDEODISC Disc 2, Side 2
1570–3317

 Leçon 9, Section 1

■ **Photo culture note**
Les pizzas
In France, pizzas are sold:
• at pizzerias (**une pizzéria**)
• at certain bakeries (**une boulangerie**)
• at deli shops (**une charcuterie**).
One can buy individual mini-pizzas about 5 inches in diameter.
Pizzas may be made with:
• cheese (**du fromage**)
• anchovies (**des anchois**)
• pepperoni (**du chorizo**)
• green peppers (**des poivrons**)
• mushrooms (**des champignons**)
Note the sign for take-out pizza
(**pizza à emporter**).

T58

LEÇON 9

Tu as faim?

Pierre, Philippe, and Nathalie are on their way home from school. They stop by a street vendor who sells sandwiches and pizza. Today it is Pierre's turn to treat his friends.

Scène 1. Pierre et Nathalie

PIERRE: Tu as faim?
NATHALIE: Oui, j'ai faim.
PIERRE: Tu veux un sandwich ou une pizza?
NATHALIE: Donne-moi une pizza, s'il te plaît.
PIERRE: Voilà.
NATHALIE: Merci.

Scène 2. Pierre et Philippe

PIERRE: Et toi, Philippe, tu as faim?
PHILIPPE: Oh là là, oui, j'ai faim.
PIERRE: Qu'est-ce que tu veux? Un sandwich ou une pizza?
PHILIPPE: Je voudrais un sandwich . . . euh . . . et donne-moi aussi une pizza.
PIERRE: C'est vrai! Tu as vraiment faim!

Scene 1. Pierre and Nathalie

PIERRE: Are you hungry?
NATHALIE: Yes, I'm hungry.
PIERRE: Do you want a sandwich or a pizza?
NATHALIE: Give me a pizza, please.
PIERRE: Here you are.
NATHALIE: Thanks.

Scene 2. Pierre and Philippe

PIERRE: And you, Philippe, are you hungry?
PHILIPPE: Oh yes, I'm hungry.
PIERRE: What do you want? A sandwich or a pizza?
PHILIPPE: I would like a sandwich . . . er . . . and give me a pizza too.
PIERRE: It's true! You are really hungry!

58 Unité 3

🌐 Cross-cultural observation

Have students look at the foods pictured in *Pour communiquer*.

The only word that may be unfamiliar to them is **frites** (French fries).

Model the words and have students repeat them with a French accent.

Ask students the following questions:

• Which of the food names are originally American words?
• Which of the food names are French?
• Which food name is Italian?
• What are the similarities and differences in where French teens shop for food and what they eat?

POUR COMMUNICER

How to say that you are hungry:

J'ai faim.	*I'm hungry.*
Tu as faim?	*Are you hungry?*

J'ai faim!
Tu as faim?

How to offer a friend something:

Tu veux . . . ?	*Do you want . . .?*
Qu'est-ce que tu veux?	*What do you want?*

Tu veux un sandwich?
Qu'est-ce que tu veux? Un sandwich ou une pizza?

How to ask a friend for something:

Je voudrais . . .	*I would like . . .*
Donne-moi . . .	*Give me . . .*
S'il te plaît . . .	*Please . . .*

Je voudrais un sandwich.
Donne-moi une pizza.
S'il te plaît, François, donne-moi une pizza.

Les nourritures *(Foods)*

un croissant

un sandwich

un steak

un steak-frites

un hamburger

un hot dog

une salade   une pizza   une omelette   une crêpe   une glace

NOTE CULTURELLE

Les jeunes et la nourriture

In general, French teenagers eat their main meals at home with their families. On weekends or after school, however, when they are with friends, they often stop at a fast-food restaurant or a café for something to eat.

At fast-food restaurants, French teenagers order pretty much the same types of foods as Americans: hamburgers, hot dogs, and pizza.

At a café, teenagers may order a croissant, a sandwich, or a dish of ice cream. Some favorite sandwiches are ham (**un sandwich au jambon**), Swiss cheese (**un sandwich au fromage**), or salami (**un sandwich au saucisson**). And, of course, they are made with French bread, which has a crunchy crust. Another traditional quick café meal is a small steak with French fries (**un steak-frites**).

Leçon 9 **59**

Pour communiquer

📺 **9.2 Mini-scenes: Ordering food**
(53:03–55:15 min.)

VIDEODISC Disc 2, Side 2
3332–7337

📼 Leçon 9, Sections 2, 3

■ **Photo culture note**
Le cornet de glace
Vendors usually sell ice cream in cones (**un cornet**).

■ **Pronunciation:** Be sure the students say the American words with a French accent: nasal "a" and no "n" or "m" in **sandwich,** **hamburger;** no liaison and a silent "h" in **un hotdog.**

🖨 Transparency 10
Foods

Supplementary vocabulary

une salade verte,	une tarte *pie*
de tomates	un gâteau *cake*
une glace à la	un éclair
vanille, au chocolat	

Note culturelle

📺 **9.3 Vignette culturelle: Qu'est-ce qu'on mange?**
(55:16–58:13 min.)

VIDEODISC Disc 2, Side 2
07355–12756

■ **Cultural note:** In France, **les fast-food** are located in downtown areas and shopping malls. They often have only stand-up counters.

TPR Foods

PROPS: Pictures of the foods (above)

Present the French names of the foods.
[Hold up "croissant."] **Voici un croissant.**
[Hold up "sandwich."] **Voici un sandwich.**

Est-ce que c'est un croissant? [Non.]
Est-ce que c'est un sandwich? [Oui.]
Have students distribute the "foods."
X, prends le croissant et donne-le à Y.
Qui a le croissant? [Y.]
You may give more complex commands.
X, prends une pizza et un steak.
Donne la pizza à Y et le steak à Z.

Petit commentaire

Two popular sandwiches sold in cafés are **le croque-monsieur** and **le croque-madame**.

The **croque-monsieur** is a grilled ham and cheese sandwich made with American-style bread.

The **croque-madame** is similar, but with a fried egg on top.

Petit commentaire

In France, sandwiches are traditionally very simple: a piece of French bread with a slice of ham or cheese. Usually sandwiches are not made with mayonnaise or lettuce.

un sandwich, une pizza

You may have noted that the names of some foods are masculine and others are feminine. In French, ALL NOUNS, whether they designate people or things, are either MASCULINE or FEMININE.

MASCULINE NOUNS		FEMININE NOUNS	
un sandwich	**le** sandwich	**une** pizza	**la** pizza
un croissant	**le** croissant	**une** salade	**la** salade

1 EXCHANGES: offering food and making a selection

■ **Variation:** To simplify this activity, have students choose one of the two foods in each item.
– **Donne-moi une pizza, s'il te plaît.**
– **Voilà.**
– **Merci.**

■ **Challenge** (dialogue format):
– **Tu as faim?**
– **Oui, j'ai faim.**
– **Tu veux un hamburger?**
– **Oui, donne-moi un hamburger, s'il te plaît.**

1 Au choix *(Your choice)*

Offer your classmates a choice between the following items. They will decide which one they would like.

▶ une pizza ou un sandwich?

1. un hamburger ou un steak?
2. un hot dog ou un sandwich?
3. une salade ou une omelette?
4. un steak-frites ou une pizza?
5. une crêpe ou un croissant?
6. une glace à la vanille ou une glace au chocolat?

Qu'est-ce que tu veux? Une pizza ou un sandwich?

Donne-moi un sandwich s'il te plaît.

2 COMMUNICATION: ordering food

1. un sandwich
2. une salade
3. une pizza
4. une glace
5. une omelette
6. un steak-frites

2 Au café

You are in a French café. Ask for the following dishes.

▶ Je voudrais un croissant.

Cooperative pair practice
Activities 1, 3

T60

Listening practice: Gender identification

PROPS: Red and blue index cards for each student

Quickly read aloud sentences containing masculine and feminine nouns. Have the students hold up the blue card for masculine nouns and the red card for feminine nouns.

1. **Voici une salade.** [R]
2. **Voici le sandwich.** [B]
3. **Voici la glace.** [R]
4. **Voici une crêpe.** [R]
5. **Voici un steak.** [B]
6. **Voici le croissant.** [B]
7. **Voici la pizza.** [R]
8. **Voici un hot dog.** [B]

3 Tu as faim?

You have invited French friends to your home. Ask if they are hungry and offer them the following foods.

▶ — Tu as faim?
— Oui, j'ai faim.
— Tu veux un hamburger?
— Oui, merci.

4 Qu'est-ce que tu veux?

Say which foods you would like to have in the following circumstances.

▶ You are very hungry.

Je voudrais un steak-frites.

1. You are at an Italian restaurant.
2. You are on a diet.
3. You are a vegetarian.
4. You are having breakfast.
5. You would like a dessert.
6. You want to eat something light for supper.

3 ROLE PLAY: offering food and accepting it

1. une pizza
2. un steak
3. un sandwich
4. un hot dog
5. une glace
6. une crêpe

4 COMPREHENSION: selecting food according to specific circumstances

Prononciation

L'intonation

When you speak, your voice rises and falls. This is called INTONATION. In French, as in English, your voice goes down at the end of a statement.

Voici un steak . . . et une salade.

However, in French, your voice rises after each group of words in the middle of a sentence. (This is the opposite of English, where your voice drops a little when you pause in the middle of a sentence.)

Répétez: **Je voudrais une pizza.**

Je voudrais une pizza et un sandwich.

Je voudrais une pizza, un sandwich et un hamburger.

Voici un steak.

Voici un steak et une salade.

Voici un steak, une salade et une glace.

Prononciation

Leçon 9, Section 4

Sounding French

A key outcome of Niveau A is that students begin to "sound French" so that they can be easily understood by French speakers.

One of the most important parts of "sounding French" is to acquire the intonation patterns of the language.

An effective technique is to have students say English sentences using French intonation. Use English equivalents of the above sentences to practice. For example:
I would like a pizza.
I would like a pizza and a sandwich.
I would like a pizza, a sandwich, and a hamburger.

MODULE 10:
Au café
Total time: 5:25 min.
(Counter: 58:24 min.)

10.1 Dialogue: Au café
(58:40–59:24 min.)
10.2 Mini-scenes: Saying please
(59:25–1:01:25 min.)
10.3 Vignette culturelle: Qu'est-ce qu'on boit?
(1:01:26–1:03:45 min.)

VIDEODISC Disc 2, Side 2
12998–22696

■ **Comprehension practice:** Play the entire module through as an introduction to the lesson.

10.1 Dialogue: Au café
(58:40–59:24 min.)

VIDEODISC Disc 2, Side 2
12998–14782

Leçon 10, Section 1

■ **Language notes**
• When calling a waiter, one may also say **"Garçon!"** It is becoming common, however, to use the more polite **"Monsieur!"**
• The traditional term **un garçon** is slowly being replaced by **un serveur.**
• A waitress is **une serveuse.**

■ **Photo culture note**
Le garçon de café
French waiters (**un garçon de café**) are usually dressed formally: black pants, white shirt and bow tie, vest or jacket.

Au café

This afternoon Jean-Paul and Isabelle went shopping. They are now tired and thirsty. Jean-Paul invites Isabelle to a café.

Tu as soif?

Vous désirez, mademoiselle?

Scène 1. Jean-Paul, Isabelle

JEAN-PAUL: Tu as soif?
ISABELLE: Oui, j'ai soif.
JEAN-PAUL: On va dans un café? Je t'invite.
ISABELLE: D'accord!

Scène 2. Le garçon, Isabelle, Jean-Paul

LE GARÇON: Vous désirez, mademoiselle?
ISABELLE: Un jus d'orange, s'il vous plaît.
LE GARÇON: Et pour vous, monsieur?
JEAN-PAUL: Donnez-moi une limonade,* s'il vous plaît.

C'est pour vous, mademoiselle?

Scène 3. Le garçon, Isabelle, Jean-Paul

LE GARÇON: *(à Isabelle)* La limonade, c'est pour vous, mademoiselle?
JEAN-PAUL: Non, c'est pour moi.
LE GARÇON: Ah, excusez-moi. Voici le jus d'orange, mademoiselle.
ISABELLE: Merci.

Scene 2. *The waiter, Isabelle, Jean-Paul*
WAITER: *May I help you, Miss?*
ISABELLE: *An orange juice, please.*
WAITER: *And for you, Sir?*
JEAN-PAUL: *Give me a "limonade," please.*

Scene 1. *Jean-Paul, Isabelle*
JEAN-PAUL: *Are you thirsty?*
ISABELLE: *Yes, I'm thirsty.*
JEAN-PAUL: *Shall we go to a café? I'm treating (inviting) you.*
ISABELLE: *Okay!*

Scene 3. *The waiter, Isabelle, Jean-Paul*
WAITER: *The "limonade" is for you, Miss?*
JEAN-PAUL: *No, it's for me.*
WAITER: *Oh, excuse me. Here is the orange juic*
ISABELLE: *Thank you.*

*Une limonade is a popular inexpensive soft drink with a slight lemon flavor.

☀ **Warm-up and review: Forms of address**

PROPS: Magazine pictures of individual men, women, and teenagers.

Have students greet one another saying:
– **Salut, X! Comment vas-tu?**
– **Ça va très bien (comme ci, comme ça).**
Hold up the magazine pictures; point out that students do not know these people.

Ask them to greet each person in the picture formally:
Bonjour, madame (monsieur, mademoiselle). Comment allez-vous?
Then have them observe how people address one another in the café scene from the video.

POUR
COMMUNIQUER

> Donnez-moi une limonade, s'il vous plaît!

How to say that you are thirsty:

J'ai soif.	*I'm thirsty.*
Tu as soif?	*Are you thirsty?*

How to order in a café:

Vous désirez?	*May I help you?*	**—Vous désirez?**
Je voudrais . . .	*I would like . . .*	**—Je voudrais** un Perrier.

How to request something . . .

from a friend:	*from an adult:*	
S'il te plaît, donne-moi . . .	**S'il vous plaît, donnez-moi . . .**	*Please, give me . . .*

➡ Note that French people have two ways of saying *please*. They use
   s'il te plaît with friends, and
   s'il vous plaît with adults.
As we will see later, young people address their friends as **tu** and adults that they do not know very well as **vous.**

Les boissons *(Beverages)*

...oda	un jus d'orange	un jus de pomme	un jus de tomate	un jus de raisin*	une limonade	un café	un thé	un chocolat

■ NOTE ■
CULTURELLE

Le café

The café is a favorite gathering place for French young people. They go there not only when they are hungry or thirsty but also to meet their friends. They can sit at a table and talk for hours over a cup of coffee or a glass of juice. French young people also enjoy mineral water and soft drinks, which they order by brand name (**un Coca, un Orangina, un Pepsi, un Schweppes, un Perrier).** In a French café, a 15% service charge is included in the check. However, most people also leave some small change as an added tip.

*Jus de raisin** is a golden-colored juice made from grapes.

Pour communiquer

10.2 Mini-scenes: Using **s'il vous plaît** and **s'il te plaît** (59:25–1:01:25 min.)

VIDEODISC Disc 2, Side 2
14800–18392

Leçon 10, Section 2

■ **Language note:** Literally, **tu as soif** means *you have thirst.*

Transparency 11
Beverage

Supplementary vocabulary

un café crème *coffee with cream*
un jus d'ananas *pineapple juice*
un jus de pamplemousse
   grapefruit juice
un citron (une orange) pressé(e)
   *freshly squeezed lemon
   (orange) juice, served with
   water and sugar on the side*

Note culturelle

■ **Photo culture note**
On the table is a bottle of Badoit, a French mineral water.

10.3 Vignette culturelle: Qu'est-ce qu'on boit? (1:01:26–1:03:4 min.)

VIDEODISC Disc 2, Side 2
18408–22696

TPR Beverages

PROPS: Transparency 11
red and blue transparency markers
Point out beverages on the transparency.
   Voici un café. Voici un soda. etc.
Have students point out beverages.
   X, viens ici. Montre-nous un café.
Hold up the blue and the red markers.

Voici un stylo bleu et un stylo rouge.
Si vous entendez <u>un</u>, prenez le stylo
   bleu. Si vous entendez <u>une</u>, prenez
   le rouge.
Dessinez un cercle autour de la
   boisson.
Écoutez. "Je voudrais un thé."
   [Draw a blue circle around the tea.]

1 EXCHANGES: offering and selecting beverages

Leçon 10, Section 3

2 ROLE PLAY: placing an order at a café

1. un chocolat
2. une limonade
3. un jus de pomme
4. un thé
5. un café
6. un jus de tomate

■ **Variation** (more basic):
You may want to do the exercise quickly with the whole class, having students give just a one-sentence response:
Un jus d'orange, s'il vous plaît.
Then have students in pairs practice the dialogue format as indicated in the text.

Leçon 10, Section 4

1 **Tu as soif?**

You have invited a French friend to your house. You offer a choice of beverages and your friend (played by a classmate) responds.

▶ un thé ou un chocolat?
—**Tu veux un thé ou un chocolat?**
—**Donne-moi un chocolat, s'il te plaît.**

1. un thé ou un café?
2. une limonade ou un soda?
3. un jus de pomme ou un jus d'orange?   4. un jus de raisin ou un jus de tomate?

2 **Au café**

You are in a French café. Get the attention of the waiter **(Monsieur)** or the waitress **(Mademoiselle)** and place your order. Act out the dialogue with a classmate.

Game: C'est logique?

PREPARATION: Prepare 2 bags of cards:
• (Bag A: 10 cards) On 5 cards, write **J'ai faim.** On the other 5, write **J'ai soif.**
• (Bag B: 21 cards) Begin each card with **Je voudrais, Donne-moi,** or **Donnez-moi** and add a food or beverage from pp. 59 and 63.

Divide the class into two teams: **logique** and **illogique.**

A player from each team comes up. One reads a card from Bag A, the other reads one from Bag B. If the sentences fit logically, the **logique** team earns a point. If not, a point goes to the **illogique** team. For example: **J'ai soif. Donne-moi une pizza. = illogique**

3 Que choisir? *(What to choose?)*

You are in a French café. Decide what beverage you are going to order in each of the following circumstances.

▶ You are very thirsty.
S'il vous plaît, une limonade (un jus de pomme) . . .

1. It is very cold outside.
2. You do not want to spend much money.
3. You like juice but are allergic to citrus fruits.
4. It is breakfast time.
5. You have a sore throat.

4 La faim et la soif *(Hungry and thirsty)*

You are having a meal in a French café. Order the food suggested in the picture. Then order something to drink with that dish. A classmate will play the part of the waiter.

Note: **Et avec ça?** means *And with that?*

1
2
3
4

Vous désirez?
Je voudrais un steak-frites.

Et avec ça?
Un Orangina, s'il vous plaît.

Prononciation

L'accent final

In French, the rhythm is very even and the accent always falls on the *last* syllable of a word or group of words.

Répétez:
Philippe   Thomas   Alice   Sophie   Dominique

un café   **Je voudrais un café.**
une salade   **Donnez-moi une salade.**
un chocolat   **Donne-moi un chocolat.**

ŭn chŏcŏlāt

If you want French people to understand you, the most important thing is to speak with an even rhythm and to stress the last syllable in each group of words. (Try speaking English this way: people will think you have a French accent!)

Leçon 10   **65**

Sounding French

Along with intonation, one of the most important parts of "sounding French" is to acquire the rhythm and stress patterns of the language.

An effective technique is to let students mimic a French accent in English. Have them speak in a staccato rhythm, ending each group of words with a longer syllable, and using rising intonation at the end of phrases in the middle of a sentence.

In-the-French-lan-GUAGE↗
all-syl-la-bles-are-e-VEN↗
ex-cept-the-last-ONE↗
which-gets-the-ac-CENT.↘

MODULE 11:
Ça fait combien?
Total Time: 5:04 min.
(Counter: 1:03:56 min.)

11.1 Dialogue: Ça fait combien?
(1:04:12–1:04:45 min.)
11.2 Mini-scenes: Asking what one owes
(1:04:46–1:06:17 min.)
11.3 Vignette culturelle: L'argent français
(1:06:18–1:08:55 min.)

VIDEODISC   Disc 2, Side 2
22935–31946

■ **Teaching Note**
The prices quoted in the dialogue are given in **euros** in the student text, but have remained in **francs** in the video so that students can learn about the currency system used in France through spring 2002. To familiarize students with the euro currency, use the transparency from the Europak which depicts the euros and the coins. For more information on the euro currency, see front matter p. 56.

■ **Comprehension practice:** Play the entire module through as an introduction to the lesson.

 11.1 Dialogue: Ça fait combien?
(1:04:12–1:04:45 min.)

VIDEODISC   Disc 2, Side 2
22938–24395

 Leçon 11, Section 1

T66

LEÇON 11 Ça fait combien?

At the café, Jean-Paul and Isabelle have talked about many things. It is now time to go. Jean-Paul calls the waiter so he can pay the check.

JEAN-PAUL: S'il vous plaît?
LE GARÇON: Oui, monsieur.
JEAN-PAUL: Ça fait combien?
LE GARÇON: Voyons, un jus d'orange, 4 euros, et une limonade, 3 euros. Ça fait 7 euros.
JEAN-PAUL: 7 euros   . . . Très bien . . . Mais, euh . . . Zut! Où est mon porte-monnaie . . . ? Dis, Isabelle, prête-moi 10 euros, s'il te plaît.

Dis, Isabelle, prête-moi 10 euros, s'il te plaît.

JEAN-PAUL: *Excuse me? (Please?)*
WAITER: *Yes, Sir.*
JEAN-PAUL: *What do I owe you? (How much does that make?)*
WAITER: *Let's see, one orange juice, 4 euros, and one "limonade" 3 euros. That comes to (makes) 7 euros.*

JEAN-PAUL: *7 euros . . . Very well . . . But, uh . . . Darn! Where is my wallet . . . ? Hey, Isabelle, loan me 10 euros, please.*

■ NOTE ■
CULTURELLE

L'argent européen *(European money)*

France uses the euro (**l'euro**) as its monetary unit. The euro is the common currency of eleven European countries and has the same value in each country. It is divided into 100 **cents,** also called **centimes** or **eurocentimes** in France. The euro-currency consists of bills and coins. The 7 euro bills are of different colors and different sizes, the greater the value, the larger the bill: 5, 10, 20, 50, 100, 200, and 500 euros. The face of a euro bill shows an archway, door or window to symbolize opportunity and opening to new ideas. The bridge on the back of each bill emphasizes the strong links among the various European countries shown in the map underneath the bridge. The 8 euro coins are issued in the following values: 1, 2, 5, 10, 20, and 50 cents, and 1 and 2 euros.

Prior to 2002, the French used the **franc** as their national currency. Unlike the euro, the franc could be used only in France.

☀ **Warm-up: Numbers**

Teach the students the following phrase:
Combien font deux plus deux?
(Note that the "s" on **plus** is pronounced /plys/.)
   Have the class solve arithmetic problems.

Combien font quatorze plus seize?
[Trente] or
[Quatorze plus seize font trente.]

POUR COMMUNIQUER

C'est combien?

How to ask how much something costs:

C'est combien?	How much is it?	**—C'est combien?**
Ça fait combien?	How much does that come to (make)?	**—Ça fait combien?**
Ça fait . . .	That's . . . , That comes to . . .	**—Ça fait** 10 euros.
Combien coûte . . . ?	How much does . . . cost?	**—Combien coûte** le sandwich?
Il/Elle coûte . . .	It costs . . .	**—Il coûte** 5 euros.

How to ask a friend to lend you something:

Prête-moi . . .	Lend me . . . , Loan me . . .	**Prête-moi** 30 euros, s'il te plaît.

➡ Note that masculine nouns can be replaced by **il** and feminine nouns can be replaced by **elle.**

Voici **une glace.**	**Elle** coûte 2 euros.	*It costs 2 euros.*
Voici **un sandwich.**	**Il** coûte 5 euros.	*It costs 5 euros.*

Leçon 11   **67**

Pour communiquer

11.2 Mini-scenes: Asking what one owes (1:04:46–1:06:17 min.)

VIDEODISC   Disc 2, Side 2   24397–27170

▭▭ **Leçon 11, Sections 2, 3**

■ **Language note:** In asking for prices, the casual speech forms given are much more common than **Combien est-ce que c'est?** or **Combien est-ce que ça fait?**

■ **Pronunciation Note**
To practice counting in euros, refer to front matter, p. 56.

■ **Cultural Note**
The exchange rate between the dollar and the euro fluctuates daily. For the purposes of the activities, an exchange rate of 1 dollar = 1 euro can be used, unless there is a substantial variation in that parity.
In addition to France, the countries which use the euro as their monetary unit are: Austria, Belgium, Finland, Germany, Ireland, Italy, Luxembourg, the Netherlands, Portugal, and Spain.

Game

Divide the class into teams A and B. Two players come forward.

Player A asks a math question.

If player B answers correctly, both teams get a point.

If player B is wrong, and player A can answer his/her own question correctly, team A gets a point.

Then the next two players have their turn. This time player B asks the question. Etc.

Petit commentaire
The **Guide Michelin**, the classic guide to restaurants in France, annually grants "stars" for outstanding cuisine. About 575 restaurants are given one star, 85 restaurants receive two stars, and about 20 truly outstanding restaurants are awarded the coveted three stars.

Petit commentaire
*French people of all ages love to eat out, and French restaurants have the reputation of offering the best cuisine in the world. Of course, there are all kinds of restaurants for all kinds of budgets, ranging from the simple country inn (**l'auberge de campagne**) with its hearty regional food to the elegant three-star restaurant (**restaurant trois étoiles**) with its exquisite—and expensive—menu.*

1 PRACTICE: asking someone for a loan

1 S'il te plaît . . .

You have been shopping in Paris and discover that you did not exchange enough money. Ask a friend to loan you the following sums.

▶ 10 euros
S'il te plaît, prête-moi dix euros.

1. 20 euros	4. 60 euros	7. 85 euros
2. 30 euros	5. 75 euros	8. 90 euros
3. 45 euros	6. 80 euros	9. 95 euros

2 EXCHANGES: asking how much things cost

📇 **Transparency 12**
Menu from "Le Select"

■ **Teaching note:** You may wish to project Transparency 12 as students do the activities on this page.

2 Décision

Before ordering at a café, Stéphanie and Émilie are checking the prices. Act out the dialogues.

▶ le chocolat

Combien coûte le chocolat?

Il coûte deux euros cinquante.

1. le thé
2. le jus d'orange
3. la salade de tomates
4. la glace à la vanille
5. le café
6. le steak-frites
7. le hot dog
8. l'omelette
9. la salade mixte
10. le jus de raisin

LE SELECT

BOISSONS

café	2€
chocolat	2€50
thé	2€80
limonade	3€
jus d'orange	3€50
jus de raisin	3€

GLACES

glace au chocolat	2€50
glace à la vanille	2€50

SANDWICHS

sandwich au jambon	4€
sandwich au fromage	4€

ET AUSSI . . .

steak-frites	5€25
salade mixte	3€50
salade de tomates	4€
omelette	5€25
hot dog	3€50
croissant	3€50
pizza	4€50

LE SELECT
P. SOULIE
CAFÉ RESTAURANT*
Tél. 01.45.22.46.29
30, boulevard des Batignolles 75017 Paris

■ **Realia note:**
Ask the students:
Comment s'appelle le café/restaurant? [Le Select]
Quel est le numéro de téléphone? [C'est le 01.45.22.46.29]

Project: Un menu

Using the "Le Select" menu as a model, have the students prepare menus in French. They should include the name, address, and telephone number of the café/restaurant and illustrate with original drawings or cut-out pictures.

Display the finished products on the bulletin board and/or around the room. If you choose to have your students do the Challenge activity on p. T73, they can use the menus in their café conversations.

3 Ça fait combien?

You have gone to Le Select with your friends and have ordered the following items. Now you are ready to leave the café, and each one wants to pay. Check the prices on the menu for Le Select, and act out the dialogue.

▶ — Ça fait combien, s'il vous plaît?
▶ — Ça fait deux euros cinquante.
— Voici deux euros cinquante.
— Merci.

1   2   3   4   5

4 Au «Select»

You are at Le Select. Order something to eat and drink. Since you are in a hurry, ask for the check right away. Act out the dialogue with a classmate who will play the part of the waiter/waitress.

Monsieur, s'il vous plaît!

Vous désirez?

Je voudrais un sandwich au jambon et un café. Ça fait combien?

Ça fait 6 euros.

1. (un croissant) 2 euros 50
2. (une pizza) 4 euros 50
3. (un sandwich) 3 euros 50
4. (un jus d'orange) 4 euros 50
5. (un thé) 2 euros 80

4 ROLE PLAY: ordering something to eat and drink

Prononciation

🔊 Leçon 11, Section 4

■ **Pronunciation:** If students have trouble producing the sound, it is better for them to identify the French "r" with an American "h" sound than with an American "r."

Classroom Notes

Prononciation

La consonne «r»   /r/

The French consonant "**r**" is not at all like the English "**r**."
It is pronounced at the back of the throat. In fact, it is similar to the Spanish "jota" sound of José.

Marie

Répétez: **Marie   Paris   orange   Henri**
           franc   très   croissant   fromage
           bonjour   pour   Pierre   quart
           Robert   Richard   Renée   Raoul

           Marie, prête-moi trente euros.

Leçon 11   **69**

Leçon 12

MAIN TOPIC:

Talking about the weather

MODULE 12:
**Le français pratique:
Le temps**
Total time: 5:38 min.
(Counter: 1:09:07 min.)

12.1 Dialogue: Le temps
(1:09:21–1:09:51 min.)
**12.2 Mini-scenes:
Talking about weather**
(1:09:52–1:11:45 min.)
**12.3 Vignette culturelle:
La géographie de la
France**
(1:11:46–1:14:42 min.)

VIDEODISC   Disc 2, Side 2
32275–42351

Comprehension practice: Play
the entire module through as an
introduction to the lesson.

12.1 Dialogue: Le temps
(1:09:52–1:11:45 min.)

VIDEODISC   Disc 2, Side 2
32278–33582

 Leçon 12, Section 1

T70

LE FRANÇAIS
PRATIQUE

LEÇON 12

Le temps

It is nine o'clock Sunday morning. Cécile and her brother Philippe have planned a picnic for the whole family. Cécile is asking about the weather.

> Quel temps fait-il?
>
> Il fait mauvais.
>
> Zut, zut et zut!
>
> Papa va nous inviter au restaurant.

CÉCILE: Quel temps fait-il?
PHILIPPE: Il fait mauvais!
CÉCILE: Il fait mauvais?
PHILIPPE: Oui, il fait mauvais! Regarde!
Il pleut!
CÉCILE: Zut, zut et zut!
PHILIPPE: !!!???
CÉCILE: Et le pique-nique?
PHILIPPE: Le pique-nique? Ah oui, le pique-nique! . . .
Écoute, ça n'a pas d'importance.
CÉCILE: Pourquoi?
PHILIPPE: Pourquoi? Parce que Papa va
nous inviter au restaurant.
CÉCILE: Super!

CÉCILE: *How's the weather?*
PHILIPPE: *It's bad!*
CÉCILE: *It's bad?*
PHILIPPE: *Yes, it's bad! Look! It's raining!*
CÉCILE: *Darn, darn, darn!*
PHILIPPE: *!!!???*
CÉCILE: *And the picnic?*
PHILIPPE: *The picnic? Oh yes, the picnic! .
Listen, it's not important (that ha
no importance).*
CÉCILE: *Why?*
PHILIPPE: *Why? Because Dad is going to
take us out (invite us) to a
restaurant.*
CÉCILE: *Great!*

70 **Unité 3**

☀ Warm-up and review: Months and dates

Have the class name the months of the year as you write their abbreviations across the top of the chalkboard.

Then go around the class asking all the students to give their birthdays.
Sue, c'est quand, ton anniversaire?
[Sue: C'est le 21 août.]

Write the student's name and abbreviated birthdate under the appropriate month.
[août]   Sue: le 21/8.
Have students read the dates. Ask:
C'est quand, l'anniversaire de Sue?
NOTE: In a class of 25 the odds are 50/50 that two people will share the same birthday.

POUR COMMUNIQUER

Quel temps fait-il?

How to talk about the weather:

Quel temps fait-il?   *How's the weather?*

Il fait beau.

Il fait bon.

Il fait chaud.

Il fait frais.

Il fait froid.

Il fait mauvais.

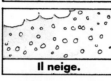

Il pleut.

Il neige.

Les saisons *(Seasons)*

le printemps	spring	**au printemps**	in (the) spring
l'été	summer	**en été**	in (the) summer
l'automne	fall, autumn	**en automne**	in (the) fall
l'hiver	winter	**en hiver**	in (the) winter

1 Ta région

Tell Cécile what the weather is like in your part of the country.

▶ en juillet

En juillet, il fait chaud.

1. en août
2. en septembre
3. en novembre
4. en janvier
5. en mars
6. en mai

2 Les quatre saisons

Describe what the weather is like in each of the four seasons in the following cities.

▶ à Miami

En été, il fait chaud.
En automne, il fait chaud
aussi. En hiver, il fait frais.
Au printemps, il fait bon.

Miami

1. à Chicago	4. à Boston
2. à San Francisco	5. à Seattle
3. à Denver	6. à Dallas

Leçon 12 71

TPR Weather

PROPS: Transparency 13

Teach the weather expressions by pointing to the pictures on the overhead.

**Quel temps fait-il? Il fait beau.
Et maintenant, quel temps fait-il?
Il pleut.
Est-ce qu'il fait beau?** [Non.]

Have students point out the weather.

**X, viens ici. Montre-nous le temps.
Il pleut.** [points to rain]
Il neige. [points to snow] etc.

Pour communiquer

12.2 Mini-scenes: Talking about the weather
(1:09:52–1:11:45 min.)

VIDEODISC Disc 2, Side 2
33605–36982

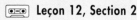

▭ **Leçon 12, Section 2**

Transparency 13
Weather

■ **Language note:** Contrast:
Il fait beau. *It's beautiful weather, the sun is out.*
Il fait bon. *It's nice weather, comfortable, warm.*

■ **Expansion:**
Il fait <u>très</u> beau, <u>très</u> froid, etc.

■ **Pronunciation notes**
• Be sure students do not pronounce the silent letters in **temps** and **printemps.**
• Be sure students make the following liaisons:
en hiver, en été, en automne.

1 COMMUNICATION: talking about the weather

■ **Variation** (dialogue format):
– Quel temps fait-il en juillet?
– Il fait chaud.

2 DESCRIPTION: giving details about the weather

12.3 Vignette culturelle: La géographie de la France
(1:11:46–1:14:42 min.)

VIDEODISC Disc 2, Side 2
37002–42351

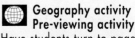

🌐 **Geography activity
Pre-viewing activity**
Have students turn to pages 6–7 and locate the following provinces on the map of France: Touraine, Alsace, Savoie, Provence.

À votre tour!

1 COMPREHENSION

 AVT 3, Section 1

2 ORAL EXPRESSION

AVT 3, Section 2

3 GUIDED ORAL EXPRESSION

Sample answer:
G: Bonjour, mademoiselle! Vous désirez?
S: (Donnez-moi, Je voudrais) un croissant, s'il vous plaît. Combien coûte un jus d'orange?
G: (Un jus d'orange coûte) 3 euros.
S: (Donnez-moi, Je voudrais) un jus d'orange, s'il vous plaît!... (Monsieur,) s'il vous plaît! Ça fait cambien?
G: (Ça fait) 8 euros 50.
S: Voici 10 euros.
G: Merci, mademoiselle.

AVT 3, Section 3

1 Isabelle et Jean-Paul

Isabelle is talking to Jean-Paul. You hear parts of their conversation. For each of Isabelle's questions, select Jean-Paul's response from the suggested answers.

1. Tu as faim?
2. Tu veux un jus de pomme?
3. Combien coûte le café au Café Français?
4. Quel temps fait-il?
5. Quelle est ta saison favorite?

a. Il fait chaud.
b. Trois euros.
c. Oui, merci, j'ai soif.
d. C'est le printemps.
e. Oui, je voudrais un sandwich.

2 Et toi?

Now Isabelle is phoning you. Answer her questions.

1. Quel temps fait-il aujourd'hui?
2. Quel temps fait-il en hiver?
3. Quelle est ta saison favorite?

3 Conversation dirigée

Stéphanie is in a café called Le Petit Bistrot. The waiter is taking her order. With a partner, compose and act out a dialogue according to the script suggested below.

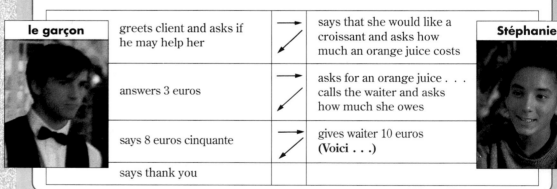

le garçon			**Stéphanie**
	greets client and asks if he may help her	says that she would like a croissant and asks how much an orange juice costs	
	answers 3 euros	asks for an orange juice . . . calls the waiter and asks how much she owes	
	says 8 euros cinquante	gives waiter 10 euros **(Voici . . .)**	
	says thank you		

À votre tour

For specific teaching suggestions, see the Teacher Notes in Unit 1, page 30.

You will want to select those activities which are most appropriate for your students. Encourage them to work in pairs and in trios (where one has the Answer Key).

The first 3 activities are on audiocassette.
Act. 1: Play Section 1 of the cassette so that students can check their answers.
Act. 2: Play Section 2 and have students answer the spoken questions orally.
Act. 3: Play Section 3 as a model. Then have students act out their own dialogues.

4 Au café

You are in a French café. Call the waiter/waitress and order the following items. A classmate will play the part of the waiter/waitress.

▶ —Monsieur (Mademoiselle), s'il vous plaît!
—Vous désirez?
—Un croissant, s'il vous plaît!
(Donnez-moi un croissant, s'il vous plaît!)
(Je voudrais un croissant, s'il vous plaît!).

5 En scène

With two classmates, act out the following scene.

CHARACTERS:

You, a French friend, and the waiter in the café

SITUATION:

A French friend has been showing you around Paris. You invite your friend to a café and discover too late that you have not changed enough money. Your friend will respond to your questions.

• Ask your friend if he/she is thirsty.
• Ask if he/she wants a soft drink.
• Ask if he/she is hungry.
• Ask if he/she wants a sandwich.
• When the waiter comes, your friend orders and you ask for a croissant and a cup of hot chocolate.
• Ask the waiter how much everything is.
• Ask your friend to please lend you 20 euros.

6 La date, la saison et le temps

Look at the calendar days. For each one, give the date, the season, and the weather.

▶ C'est le dix avril.
C'est le printemps.
Il pleut.

  1  2   3   4   5

---

4 GUIDED ORAL EXPRESSION

1. une glace
2. une pizza
3. un chocolat
4. un jus de raisin
5. un steak-frites

■ **Challenge:** You are leaving the café and want to know what you owe. Your classmate will invent a reasonable price.

– **Monsieur/Mademoiselle, s'il vous plaît! Ça fait combien?**
– **Ça fait trois euros trente.**

5 GUIDED ORAL EXPRESSION

6 GUIDED ORAL EXPRESSION

1. Il neige. C'est l'hiver.
2. Il fait chaud. C'est l'été.
3. Il fait mauvais. (Il fait frais.) C'est l'automne.
4. Il fait beau. C'est le printemps.
5. Il fait frais. C'est l'automne.

Portfolio assessment

For more specific guidelines, see the Teacher Notes in Unit 1, page 31.

The café conversations of the **Challenge** activity on the right could be recorded for the oral portfolio.

Challenge activity

Students in groups of 3 or 4 prepare original café conversations. One person is the waiter, and the others are teenage customers who are talking to one another. Encourage them to use expressions they learned in Units 1 and 2: greetings, introductions, time, etc.

Entracte 3

OBJECTIVES:

- Development of cross-cultural awareness
- Vocabulary expansion

Une chanson: Alouette

OBJECTIVES:

- Introducing a popular French-Canadian folksong
- Introducing parts of the body

Cultural note: In Canada, the lark was formerly hunted as a game bird. In this song, the cook is plucking the bird's feathers before preparing to roast it.

English equivalent
Lark, sweet lark,
I will pluck you
I will pluck your head ...

I will pluck your beak ...
your neck...
your wing ...
your back ...
your legs ...
your tail ...

Une chanson: Alouette

Alouette *(The Lark)* is a popular folksong of French-Canadian origin. As the song leader names the various parts of the bird's anatomy, he points to his own body. The chorus repeats the refrain with enthusiasm.

Alouette

le bec   la tête   le cou

1. Alouette, gentille alouette,
   Alouette, je te plumerai.

   Je te plumerai la tête,
   Je te plumerai la tête.

   Et la tête—et la tête
   Alouette—Alouette
   Oh oh oh oh

2. Alouette, gentille alouette
   Alouette, je te plumerai.

   Je te plumerai le bec,
   Je te plumerai le bec.

   Et le bec—et le bec
   Et la tête—et la tête
   Alouette—Alouette
   Oh oh oh oh

3. Je te plumerai le cou . . .
4. Je te plumerai les ailes . . .
5. Je te plumerai le dos . . .
6. Je te plumerai les pattes . . .
7. Je te plumerai la queue . . .

74

Québec

Pre-reading activity

Ask how many students know the song "Alouette."

- What country is the song from?
- What kind of bird is an **alouette?**
- What is the song all about?

Post-reading activity

Ask students if they know other French songs. Perhaps they can sing "Frère Jacques."
Frère Jacques / Dormez-vous? / Sonnez les matines. / Din din don. / (Are you sleeping / Brother John? / Morning bells are ringing / Ding dang dong)

T74

Les parties du corps

(Parts of the body)

l'oeil (les yeux)
le nez
la bouche
les cheveux
la tête
l'oreille
le cou
le dos
le bras
le ventre
la main
la jambe
le pied

Un jeu   Jacques a dit

The French sometimes play a game called **Jacques a dit** *(Jim said)*. The rules are the same as the English game of Simon Says. Everyone stands up to play.

The game leader says: **Jacques a dit: Les mains sur la tête!** placing her hands on her head. The other players also place their hands on their head.

Then the game leader may say: **Les mains sur le dos!** placing her hands on her back. This time, however, the other players should not move, because the game leader did not first say **Jacques a dit.** Any player that did move must sit down.

The game continues until only one player is left standing.

Entracte 3 **75**

Les parties du corps

OBJECTIVE:
• Learning parts of the body

■ **Game: Vrai ou faux?** When the teacher mentions a part of the body and points to it correctly, students respond by saying **vrai.** When the teacher points to the wrong part of the body, students respond by saying **faux.** E.g.,
Voici ma jambe (point to leg)
  vrai
Voici mon pied. (point to arm)
  faux

■ **Expansion**
Les mains sur les épaules (shoulders).
Les mains sur la taille (waist).
Les mains sur les genoux (knees).

 **UNITÉ 3
INTERNET PROJECT**

Students may use the Internet to find out about popular French soft drinks and beverage manufacturers. They can start with the links available below, or use the alternate given. To expand this activity, have students generate new links by using the search engine of their choice and the keywords "boissons gazeuses"; "eaux minérales"; *(French brandnames for specific soft drinks).*

Evian
http://www.evian.fr/

Coca Cola Belgium
http://www.cocacola.be/

ALTERNATE
Perrier
http://www.perrier.com/

TPR Parts of the body

PROP: Halloween skeleton
Introduce the class to the skeleton, to whom you have given a name.
  Qui est-ce? C'est mon ami Victor.
Shake hands with the skeleton.
  Je donne la main à Victor.

Call on individual students to come up.
  X, viens ici et donne la main à Victor.
  Touche-lui l'épaule.
  Montre-nous sa bouche. ...
OPTIONAL: Have students contort Victor.
  Y, viens et mets-lui le pied sur la tête.
  Mets-lui la main gauche sur le cou.

VIDEO ESSAY:
À l'école en France
Total time: 5:35 min.
(Counter: 00:40 min.)

B.1 Visite avec Nathalie Aubin
(00:53–1:37 min.)

B.2 Le lycée Jean-Baptiste Corot
(1:39–4:09 min.)

B.3 Mini-scenes: Quel est ton sujet favori?
(4:10–4:43 min.)

B.4 Conclusion de la visite
(4:44–6:11 min.)

VIDEODISC Disc 1, Side 1
14393–24450

À l'école en France

BONJOUR, Nathalie!

Bonjour!
Je m'appelle Nathalie Aubin.
J'ai 15 ans et j'habite° à Savigny-sur-Orge
avec ma famille. (Savigny est
une petite° ville° à 20 kilomètres
au sud° de Paris.)
J'ai un frère, Christophe, 17 ans,
et deux soeurs, Céline, 13 ans,
et Florence, 7 ans.
Mon père est programmeur.
(Il travaille° à Paris.)
Ma mère est dentiste.
(Elle travaille à Savigny.)
Je vais au lycée Jean-Baptiste
Corot.
Je suis élève° de seconde°
Et vous?

Nathalie

j'habite *I live* **petite** *small* **ville** *city* **sud** *south*
travaille *works* **élève** *student* **seconde** *tenth grade*

76

🖥 Using the video

This Video Essay, **À l'école en France,**
was filmed at the Lycée Jean-Baptiste
Corot in Savigny-sur-Orge, near Paris.
Play the entire module as an introduction
to the photo essay.

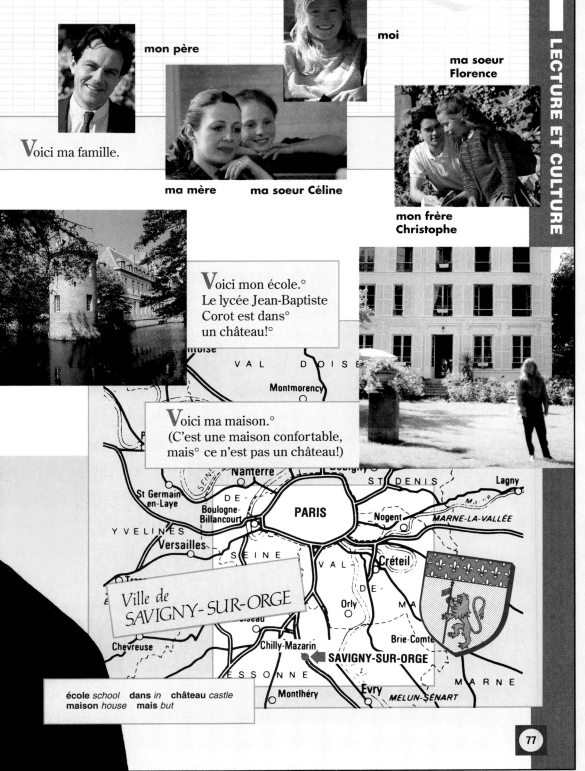

mon père

moi

ma soeur
Florence

Voici ma famille.

ma mère   ma soeur Céline

mon frère
Christophe

Voici mon école.°
Le lycée Jean-Baptiste
Corot est dans°
un château!°

Voici ma maison.°
(C'est une maison confortable,
mais° ce n'est pas un château!)

Ville de
SAVIGNY-SUR-ORGE

SAVIGNY-SUR-ORGE

école *school*   dans *in*   château *castle*
maison *house*   mais *but*

77

■ **Photo culture note**
Savigny-sur-Orge
The construction of the **R.E.R.**
(**Réseau Express Régional**), a fast
commuter train, has brought
Savigny-sur-Orge within easy
commuting distance of Paris. It
takes only half an hour to get from
Savigny to the center of the
capital.
Like most French towns, Savigny-
sur-Orge has its coat of arms (**un
écusson**) which you can see on the
map. Along the upper band you
can see the **fleur-de-lis** which is
the symbol of the former French
kings. It appears on the coat of
arms of **l'Île de France** (the region
around Paris).

🧠🧠 Cooperative learning

After showing the video, have students in
groups discuss the similarities and
differences between their school and the
Lycée Corot. Let each group name a
recorder (**secrétaire**) who will list their
findings.

As a full class activity, ask the
recorders to read their lists and compare
the findings. Which group was most
observant?

As a follow-up, you may want to play
the video a second time.

VIDEODISC Disc 1, Side1
14676–24450

■ **Un jour de classe** is based on the above video segments.

■ **Cultural note**
Le dîner
Note that the Aubin family has dinner at 7:30. French people eat later than Americans, usually not before 7:00 and often as late as 8:30. **Le dîner** is generally a lighter meal than the **le déjeuner** (which is served at noon.) In France, dinner is always a family meal, a time for children and parents to talk about how they spent the day.

Un jour de classe

Le matin

À la maison

Nathalie gets up every morning at seven. After a light breakfast (toasted bread with butter and jam, hot chocolate), she leaves for school.

Nathalie sur sa mobylette

Since she does not live too far from her lycée, she goes there on her moped **(sa mobylette).** Students who live farther away take the school bus.

La classe de sciences-

Nathalie arrives at school at about 8:25, five minutes before her first class. Today, Thursday, her first class is economics **(les sciences économiques),** which is her favorite subject.

L'après-midi

À la cantine

At 12:30, Nathalie goes to the school cafeteria **(la cantine)** for lunch. As in American schools, the food is served cafeteria-style. During lunch break, Nathalie meets with her friends from other classes.

La classe d'anglais

Classes start again at two o'clock. Today they finish at four.

Après les classes

Depending on when her last class ends, Nathalie either goes home right after school or participates in one of the many school clubs.

Le soir

Dans la salle à manger

The Aubins have dinner around 7:30. Everyone helps with the kitchen chores. Today it is Christophe's turn.

Nathalie dans sa chambre

Nathalie does her homework after dinner. She usually has about one or two hours of homework every night. When she is finished, she reads or listens to cassettes for a while, then goes to bed around 11 P.M.

L'emploi du temps

LYCÉE JEAN-BAPTISTE COROT

Étudiante: AUBIN, Nathalie

	LUNDI	MARDI	MERCREDI	JEUDI	VENDREDI	SAMEDI
8h30 à 9h30	Histoire	Allemand		Sciences économiques		
9h30 à 10h30	Anglais	Français	Anglais	Sciences physiques	Allemand	Français
10h30 à 11h30	Sport	Français	Sciences économiques	(13h30) Maths	Latin	Français
11h30 à 12h30	Français	Latin	Maths	(13h30)		Latin
13h00 à 14h00					Sciences physiques	Histoire ou Civilisation
14h00 à 15h00	Sciences physiques	Maths				
15h00 à 16h00	Géographie	Maths		Allemand		
16h00 à 17h00	Civilisation	Anglais		Histoire		

■ NOTE ■ CULTURELLE

Le programme scolaire

At the lycée, all students take a certain number of required subjects. These include French, math, one foreign language, history and geography, physical sciences, natural sciences, and physical education. Depending on their career plans, French students also have to choose among certain electives: a second foreign language, economics, computer science, biology, music.

Here are some of the subjects taught in French secondary schools. How many can you identify?

le français	**l'histoire**	**les maths**
l'anglais	**la géographie**	**la biologie**
l'espagnol	**les sciences**	**la physique**
l'allemand	**économiques**	**la chimie**
le latin	**l'éducation civique** *(civics)*	**l'informatique** *(computer science)*
	la musique	
	le dessin	**les sciences naturelles**
	l'éducation physique	**la philosophie**

ACTIVITÉS CULTURELLES

1. Look carefully at Nathalie's class schedule. You may have noted certain differences between the French and the American school systems.
   - French students have more class hours than American students. How many hours of classes does Nathalie have each week?
   - French students learn more foreign languages than American students. In France, the study of foreign languages is compulsory. What languages is Nathalie learning?
   - French students usually have Wednesday afternoon free. Does Nathalie have school on Saturday morning? on Saturday afternoon?
2. Write out your own class schedule in French.

79

B.2 Le lycée Jean-Baptiste Corot

B.3 Mini-scenes: Quel est ton sujet favori? (1:39–4:43 min.)

VIDEODISC Disc 1, Side 1
16124–21652

■ You may want to play these two segments again, having students focus on the school itself rather than on Nathalie.

un pastel de Corot

Jean-Baptiste Corot

Like many French schools, the lycée Jean-Baptiste Corot of Savigny-sur-Orge is named after a famous French person. Jean-Baptiste Corot is a 19th century painter, remembered especially for his landscapes.

The lycée Jean-Baptiste Corot is both very old and very modern. It was created in the 1950's on the grounds of a historical castle dating from the 12th century. The castle, which serves as the administrative center, is still surrounded by a moat. The lycée itself has many modern facilities which include:

- **les salles de classe** *(classrooms)*
- **la cantine** *(cafeteria)*
- **le stade** *(stadium)* **et le terrain de sport** *(playing field)*

Plan du lycée Jean-Baptiste Corot

une salle de classe

la cantine

le terrain de sport

■ **If students ask:** On the background map, the student cafeteria (**la cantine**) is labeled **réfectoires élèves.**
Another wing of the same building houses the **réfectoire professeurs** where the teachers take their meals.

Cultural background: Le baccalauréat

Students must pass a two-part competitive national exam in order to earn their **baccalauréat** (or **bac**) which gives them entrance to the university.

- The first part, which focuses on French, is administered at the end of **première.**

- The second part, given at the end of **terminale,** focuses on the students' area of academic concentration. Students have the choice of several options.

NOTES CULTURELLES

1 L'école secondaire

There are two types of secondary schools in France:

- **le collège,** which corresponds to the U.S. middle school (grades 6 to 9)
- **le lycée,** which corresponds to the U.S. high school (grades 10 to 12)

On the following chart, you will notice that each grade **(une classe)** is designated by a number (as in the United States): **sixième (6e), cinquième (5e), quatrième (4e),** etc. However, the progression from grade to grade is the opposite in France. The secondary school begins in France with **sixième** and ends with **terminale.**

École	Classe	Âge des élèves	Équivalent américain
Le collège	sixième (6e) cinquième (5e) quatrième (4e) troisième (3e)	11–12 ans 12–13 ans 13–14 ans 14–15 ans	*sixth grade* *seventh grade* *eighth grade* *ninth grade*
Le lycée	seconde (2e) première (1re) terminale	15–16 ans 16–17 ans 17–18 ans	*tenth grade* *eleventh grade* *twelfth grade*

2 Le bulletin de notes

At the end of each term, French students receive a report card **(le bulletin de notes),** which must be signed by their parents. Most schools assign grades on a scale of 0 (low) to 20 (high). Most teachers also write a brief evaluation of the student's progress in each subject.

Here is a report card for the first semester.

ACTIVITÉ CULTURELLE

1. What is the name of the student?
2. What is the name of his school?
3. What grade is he in?
4. What is his best subject? What grade did he get?
5. What is his weakest subject? What grade did he get?
6. How many foreign languages is he studying? Which ones?

■ **Le bulletin de notes**
Have students guess the meanings of the abbreviations on the report card:
Math. = Mathématiques
Sc. Phys. = Sciences physiques
Sc. Nat. = Sciences naturelles

■ **Vocabulary**
une appréciation *comment*
le proviseur *principal*
le proviseur adjoint *vice principal*
le conseiller principal d'éducation *guidance counselor*
le professeur principal *homeroom teacher*

■ **Activité culturelle**
Answers:
1. Picard
2. Lycée Jean-Baptiste Corot
3. seconde (tenth grade)
4. English; 16 (A)
5. French; 11 (C)
6. two; English and German

Baccalauréat L (série littéraire):
   French literature and Foreign Languages
Baccalauréat ES (série économique sociale):
   Economics and Social Studies
Baccalauréat F (série scientifique):
   Mathematics, Physical and Natural Sciences, and Technology

Expressions pour la classe

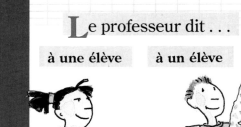

L e professeur dit . . .

à une élève   à un élève   **Écoutez!**   à la classe

Regarde! *(Look!)*	**Regardez!**
Regarde la vidéo.	**Regardez la vidéo.**
Écoute! *(Listen!)*	**Écoutez!**
Écoute la cassette *(tape).*	**Écoutez la cassette.**
Parle! *(Speak!)*	**Parlez!**
Parle plus fort *(louder).*	**Parlez plus fort.**
Réponds! *(Answer!)*	**Répondez!**
Réponds à la question.	**Répondez à la question.**
Répète! *(Repeat!)*	**Répétez!**
Répète la phrase *(sentence).*	**Répétez la phrase.**
Lis! *(Read!)*	**Lisez!**
Lis l'exercice.	**Lisez l'exercice.**
Écris! *(Write!)*	**Écrivez!**
Écris dans ton cahier.	**Écrivez dans vos cahiers.**

Prends *(Take)*	une feuille de papier.		**Prenez**	une feuille de papier.
	un crayon			un crayon
Ouvre *(Open)*	ton livre.		**Ouvrez**	vos livres.
	la porte			la porte
Ferme *(Close)*	ton cahier.		**Fermez**	vos cahiers.
	la fenêtre			la fenêtre

Viens! *(Come!)*	**Venez!**
Viens ici.	**Venez ici.**
Va! *(Go!)*	**Allez!**
Va au tableau.	**Allez au tableau.**
Lève-toi! *(Stand up!)*	**Levez-vous!**
Assieds-toi! *(Sit down!)*	**Asseyez-vous!**

Apporte-moi *(Bring me)*		**Apportez-moi**	
Donne-moi *(Give me)*	ton devoir.	**Donnez-moi**	vos devoirs.
Montre-moi *(Show me)*		**Montrez-moi**	

 82

Quelques objets

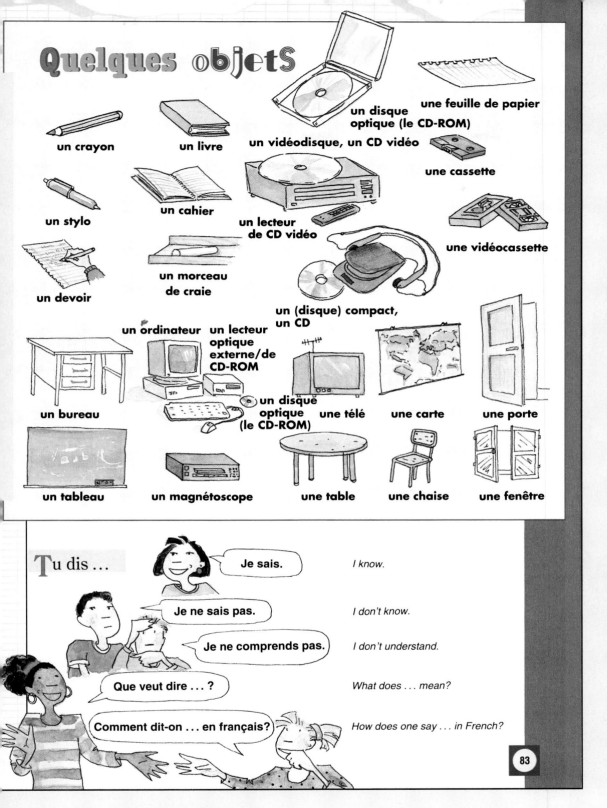

un crayon

un livre

un disque optique (le CD-ROM)

une feuille de papier

un vidéodisque, un CD vidéo

une cassette

un stylo

un cahier

un lecteur de CD vidéo

une vidéocassette

un devoir

un morceau de craie

un (disque) compact, un CD

un ordinateur

un lecteur optique externe/de CD-ROM

un bureau

un disque optique (le CD-ROM)

une télé

une carte

une porte

un tableau

un magnétoscope

une table

une chaise

une fenêtre

Tu dis …

Je sais.	I know.
Je ne sais pas.	I don't know.
Je ne comprends pas.	I don't understand.
Que veut dire … ?	What does … mean?
Comment dit-on … en français?	How does one say … in French?

(83)

TPR 🏃 Classroom objects

You may want to introduce these words with TPR activities (see Front Matter).
Montrez-moi une feuille de papier. etc.
Mettez un stylo sur la feuille de papier.
Mettez un livre sur le stylo.
Mettez un morceau de craie sur le bureau.

Include additional technology vocabulary as an expansion.

NIVEAU **B**

La vie de

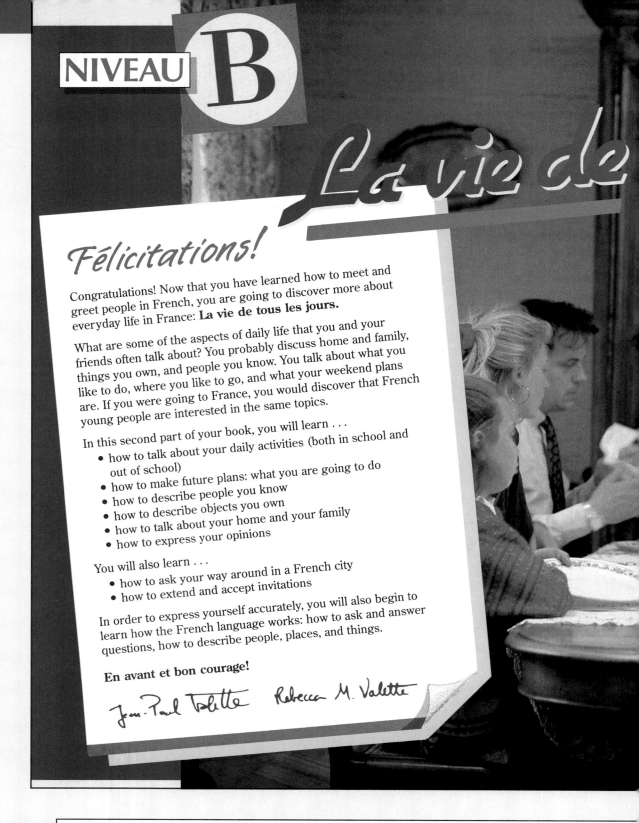

Félicitations!

Congratulations! Now that you have learned how to meet and greet people in French, you are going to discover more about everyday life in France: **La vie de tous les jours.**

What are some of the aspects of daily life that you and your friends often talk about? You probably discuss home and family, things you own, and people you know. You talk about what you like to do, where you like to go, and what your weekend plans are. If you were going to France, you would discover that French young people are interested in the same topics.

In this second part of your book, you will learn . . .
- how to talk about your daily activities (both in school and out of school)
- how to make future plans: what you are going to do
- how to describe people you know
- how to describe objects you own
- how to talk about your home and your family
- how to express your opinions

You will also learn . . .
- how to ask your way around in a French city
- how to extend and accept invitations

In order to express yourself accurately, you will also begin to learn how the French language works: how to ask and answer questions, how to describe people, places, and things.

En avant et bon courage!

Jean-Paul Valette   *Rebecca M. Valette*

Overview of Niveau B

Niveau B contains the core of **Discovering French — Bleu.** Students will be acquiring the linguistic foundation needed for basic communication skills: the ability to ask and answer questions and the ability to use French creatively for self-expression.

In particular, in Niveau B there will be:
- a shift from primarily oral practice (which characterized Niveau A) to a four-skills approach including reading and writing,
- a focus on basic French sentence patterns and high frequency vocabulary,

tous les jours

85

- an introduction to critical thinking about language and how the French language works,
- an emphasis on communicative interaction, with numerous role play and dialogue activities.

Unité 4

MAIN THEME:
Daily Activities

Qu'est-ce qu'on fait?

Unit overview

COMMUNICATION GOALS: Students will learn to talk about their daily activities and how to extend and respond to invitations.
LINGUISTIC GOALS: The primary focus is on the present tense (affirmative, negative) and question formation.

CRITICAL THINKING GOALS: Students are introduced to the concept of subject-verb agreement and the importance of verb endings in French.
CULTURAL GOALS: This unit focuses on the daily activities of French young people: school and homework, as well as sports and leisure activities.

THÈME ET OBJECTIFS

Daily activities

In this unit, you will be talking about the things you do every day, such as working and studying, as well as watching TV and listening to the radio.

You will learn . . .
- to describe some of your daily activities
- to say what you like and do not like to do
- to ask and answer questions about where others are and what they are doing

You will also learn . . .
- to invite friends to do things with you
- to politely accept or turn down an invitation

87

Cross-cultural observation
All of these pictures were taken in France.
As usual, have students look at the photos and answer the following questions:
- Could any of them have been taken in the United States?
- Why or why not?
- Which elements in the pictures seem to be definitely French?

■ **Photo culture note: L'armoire**
Note the **armoire** *(wardrobe)* in the top picture. Traditionally French homes have few closets, so most rooms have free-standing **armoires** which are used to store clothes, linen, dishes, and so forth.

Pacing

Beginning with Unit 4, the lessons are longer and there is a dual emphasis on both oral and written skills.

For specific suggestions on pacing, turn to the Front Matter.

► **Assessment Options**

ACHIEVEMENT TESTS

Lesson Quizzes 13-16 pp. 67-74
Test Cassette A, Side 2

Unit Test 4

 Portfolio Assessment pp. T95, Activities 1-5; pp. T104-105, Activities 1-5; pp. T116-117, Activities 1-5; pp. T126-127, Activities 1-6

PROFICIENCY TESTS

 Listening Comprehension Performance Test, p. 33
Test Cassette C, Side 2

 Speaking Performance Test, p. 21

 Reading Comprehension Performance Test, p. 22

Writing Performance Test, p. 43

 Test Bank, Unit 4 Version A or B

 DFi B, Exploration 4 Cahier, Créa-dialogue

Leçon 13

MAIN TOPICS:

**Describing daily
activities
Offering and
receiving invitations**

MODULE 13:
**Le français pratique:
Mes activités**
Total time: 5:56 min.
(Counter: 6:24 min.)

**13.1 Mini-scenes: Listening
— J'aime téléphoner**
(7:22–8:04 min.)
**13.2 Mini-scenes: Speaking
— Tu aimes écouter la
radio?** (8:05–9:07 min.)
**13.3 Mini-scenes: Listening
— Invitations**
(9:08–9:24 min.)
13.4 Dialogue: Tennis
(9:25–10:32 min.)
**13.5 Vignette culturelle:
Le téléphone**
(10:33–12:15 min.)

VIDEODISC Disc 3, Side 1
1558–12171

▮ **Comprehension practice:** Play
the entire module through as an
introduction to the lesson.

LEÇON ## 13

**LE FRANÇAIS
PRATIQUE**

Mes activités

Accent sur ... Les activités de la semaine

French teenagers, as well as their
parents, put a lot of emphasis on
doing well in school. On the whole,
French students spend a great deal of
time on their studies. French schools
have a longer class day than American
schools, and teachers tend to assign quite a
lot of homework.

However, French teenagers do not study all
the time. They also watch TV and listen to
music. Many participate in various sports
activities, but to a lesser extent than young
Americans. On weekends, French teenagers
like to go out with their friends. Some go
shopping. Others go to the movies. Many
enjoy dancing and going to parties. Sunday
is usually a family day for visiting relatives or
going for a drive in the country.

▮ **Au cinéma**
Des copains sont au cinéma.

▮ **Au café**
Stéphanie est au café.

88 **Unité 4**

🖳 Using the video

Beginning with this lesson, there is more
variety in the sequencing of the video
modules.
 Play the entire module through as an
introduction to the cultural themes and
new linguistic material of the lesson.

The various parts of the video are closely
correlated to specific sections in the
lesson. Notes in the Teacher Edition
(prefaced with the video logo) indicate
points at which you may want to use
certain video segments.

Une boum
Dominique et Stéphanie
sont à une boum.

**Le terrain de foot
au lycée Corot**
Des jeunes jouent au foot.

En classe
Marc et Patrick sont en classe.

■ **Photo culture notes**

Au cinéma
The Danton movie theater in the Latin Quarter of Paris is showing "Cyrano" and "La Gloire de mon père" (My Father's Glory). Note the neon arrows that tell people where to line up to buy tickets for each movie.

Au café
French cafés traditionally have wicker chairs.

Une boum
Note the moldings on the walls and ceiling. These are traditional design elements in older French homes and apartments.

■ **Language note:** French teens also use the words **une soirée** and **une fête** to refer to a party.

Lycée Corot
For more information about the Lycée Corot, turn to pages 76–83.

En classe
Traditionally, French students are required to have different bound notebooks for each subject.

Teaching strategy: Le français pratique

Beginning with Niveau B, the first lesson of each unit introduces the communication theme and the related vocabulary. All of these new words and phrases are then re-entered in a variety of situations in the remainder of the unit.

Try to move rather quickly through *Le français pratique* because students will have ample opportunity to master the new material as they do the many activities in the next three lessons.

COMMUNICATIVE FUNCTION:
Expressing likes and
dislikes

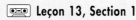 Transparencies 14A, 14B
Verbs

Leçon 13, Section 1

Pronunciation practice: This
cassette activity models the new
vocabulary in sentence context.

Looking ahead: In this lesson,
students will become familiar with
the meaning of these verbs in the
infinitive form.
  In Lesson 15, they will learn how
to use them in the present tense.

COMMUNICATION:
indicating preferences

1

■ Oral introduction
- Model the options in each question for listening comprehension, asking for a show of
hands.
  En classe, qui aime étudier?
  Qui aime écouter le pro-
  fesseur?
  Qui préfère parler avec un
  copain?
  Qui préfère parler avec une
  copine?
- Ask individual students who
have raised their hands to
respond orally:
  X, en classe, est-ce que tu
  aimes étudier?
  X: Oui, j'aime étudier.

T90

A. Préférences

Est-ce que tu aimes parler français?

How to talk about what you like and don't like to do:

Est-ce que tu aimes . . .?	Do you like . . .?	**Est-ce que tu aimes** parler *(to speak)* français?
J'aime . . .	I like . . .	Oui, **j'aime** parler français.
Je n'aime pas . . .	I don't like . . .	Non, **je n'aime pas** parler français.
Je préfère . . .	I prefer . . .	**Je préfère** parler anglais.

J'aime . . .

| **téléphoner** | **parler français** | **parler anglais** | **parler espagnol** |
| to phone | to talk, speak French | to speak English | to speak Spanish |

| **manger** | **chanter** | **danser** | **nager** |
| to eat | to sing | to dance | to swim |

1 **Et toi?**

Indicate what you like to do in the following situations by completing the sentences.

1. En classe,
   j'aime . . .
   mais je préfère . . .
   - étudier
   - écouter le professeur
   - parler avec *(with)* un copain
   - parler avec une copine

2. En été,
   j'aime . . .
   mais je préfère . . .
   - travailler
   - nager
   - voyager
   - jouer au volley

TPR **Everyday activities**

PROPS: Transparencies 14a and 14b
  Develop a gesture for each verb.
Model the sentences in the verb charts and
have the class mimic the action with you.
  J'aime téléphoner. [Gesture "dialing"]
  J'aime manger. [Gesture "eating"]
  J'aime jouer au foot. [Gesture "kicking"]

Say sentences with students acting out
verbs. Have students point out the actions
on the transparency:
  X, montre-nous l'action: J'aime
  chanter. etc.
Have students repeat each sentence with
you as they gesture the action. Do the
action and have the class say the sentence.

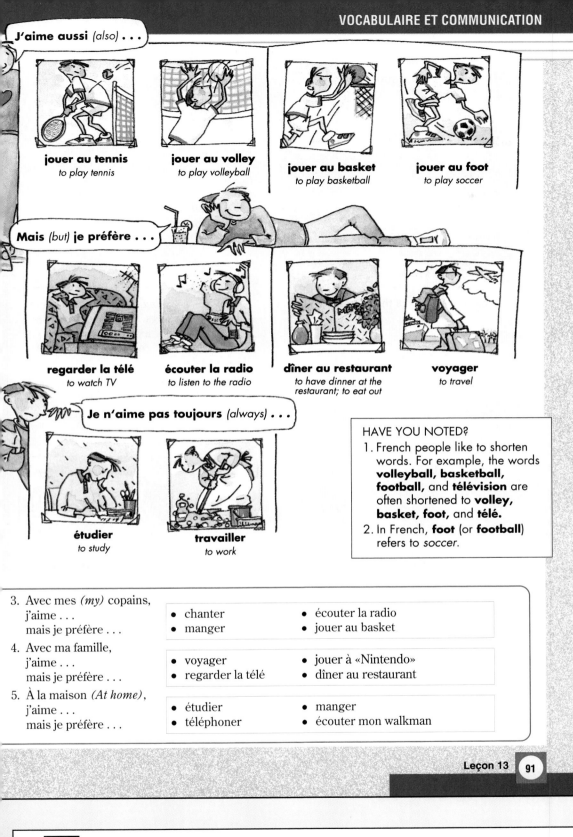

J'aime aussi *(also)* . . .

jouer au tennis
to play tennis

jouer au volley
to play volleyball

jouer au basket
to play basketball

jouer au foot
to play soccer

Mais *(but)* **je préfère** . . .

regarder la télé
to watch TV

écouter la radio
to listen to the radio

dîner au restaurant
to have dinner at the restaurant; to eat out

voyager
to travel

Je n'aime pas toujours *(always)* . . .

étudier
to study

travailler
to work

HAVE YOU NOTED?

1. French people like to shorten words. For example, the words **volleyball, basketball, football,** and **télévision** are often shortened to **volley, basket, foot,** and **télé.**

2. In French, **foot** (or **football**) refers to *soccer*.

---

3. Avec mes *(my)* copains, j'aime . . .
mais je préfère . . .

4. Avec ma famille, j'aime . . .
mais je préfère . . .

5. À la maison *(At home)*, j'aime . . .
mais je préfère . . .

- chanter
- manger

- écouter la radio
- jouer au basket

- voyager
- regarder la télé

- jouer à «Nintendo»
- dîner au restaurant

- étudier
- téléphoner

- manger
- écouter mon walkman

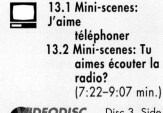

13.1 Mini-scenes: J'aime téléphoner
13.2 Mini-scenes: Tu aimes écouter la radio?
(7:22–9:07 min.)

VIDEODISC   Disc 3, Side 1
3232–6435

   Leçon 13, Sections 2, 3

Classroom Notes

👀 Cooperative group practice

As a preparation for group work, first introduce Activity 1 orally. (See side note.)

Then divide the class into groups, each with a recorder (**un/une secrétaire**).

Individual group members take turns indicating their preferences (Act. 1).

En classe, je préfère étudier.

The **secrétaire** tallies the group's responses.

#1. La majorité préfère étudier. (La majorité préfère écouter le professeur.)

The results can be reported back to the class, or handed in to the teacher.

2 Tu aimes ou tu n'aimes pas?

Say whether or not you like to do the following things.

▶ parler français?

J'aime parler français.

Je n'aime pas parler français.

1. parler anglais?
2. étudier?
3. danser?
4. chanter?
5. jouer au basket?
6. jouer au tennis?
7. regarder la télé?
8. dîner au restaurant?
9. manger?
10. travailler?
11. écouter la radio?
12. téléphoner?

3 Préférences

Ask your classmates if they like to do the following things.

▶ —Est-ce que tu aimes téléphoner?
—Oui, j'aime téléphoner. (Non, je n'aime pas téléphoner.)

4 Dialogue

Philippe is asking Hélène if she likes to do certain things. She replies that she prefers to do other things. Play both roles. Note: "??" means you can invent an answer.

▶ PHILIPPE: **Est-ce que tu aimes nager?**
HÉLÈNE: **Oui, mais je préfère jouer au tennis.**

92 Unité 4

Teaching note: Writing activities

Beginning with Unit 4, students will be developing both their writing and speaking skills. Activities which lend themselves to written (as well as oral) practice will be signaled in the Teacher Edition with a paper and pencil symbol.

The Student Activity Book provides a wide variety of additional writing activities.

B. Souhaits *(Wishes)*

Je voudrais voyager en France.

How to talk about what you want, would like, and do not want to do:

Je veux ...	I want . . .	**Je veux** parler français.
Je voudrais ...	I would like . . .	**Je voudrais** voyager en France.
Je ne veux pas ...	I don't want . . .	**Je ne veux pas** étudier aujourd'hui.

5 **Ce soir** *(Tonight)*

Say whether or not you want to do the following things tonight.

▶ étudier?
Oui, je veux étudier.
(**Non, je ne veux pas étudier.**)

1. parler français?
2. travailler?
3. jouer au ping-pong?
4. chanter?
5. danser?
6. regarder la télé?
7. écouter la radio?
8. dîner avec une copine?
9. parler à *(to)* mon frère?
10. téléphoner à mon cousin?

6 **Weekend**

Caroline and her friends are discussing their weekend plans. What do they say they would like to do?

▶ CAROLINE: **Je voudrais jouer au tennis.**

▶ **Caroline**
1. **Jérôme**
2. **Monique**
3. **Jean-Louis**
4. **Céline**
5. **Patrick**

7 **Trois souhaits** *(Three wishes)*

Read the list of suggested activities and select the three that you would like to do most.

parler français
parler espagnol
parler avec *(with)* Oprah Winfrey
dîner avec le Président
dîner avec Tom Cruise

voyager avec ma cousine
voyager en France
chanter comme *(like)* Will Smith
jouer au tennis avec Venus Williams
jouer au basket comme Michael Jordan

▶ **Je voudrais parler espagnol.**
Je voudrais chanter comme Will Smith.
Je voudrais voyager en France.

COMMUNICATIVE FUNCTION: expressing wishes

 5 COMMUNICATION: indicating what you want/don't want to do

■ **Language note:** In French, one must say **téléphoner à,** *to phone "to" someone.*

 6 DESCRIPTION: indicating what people would like to do

1. nager
2. dîner au restaurant
3. danser
4. jouer au basket
5. écouter la radio

■ **Challenge:** Add **Et toi?**
The next student replies with an alternative activity.
Caroline: **Je voudrais jouer au tennis. Et toi?**
Élève A: **Je voudrais jouer au foot (chanter, etc.).**

 7 COMMUNICATION: indicating what you would like to do

■ **Variation:** Have students substitute other names in their responses.
Je voudrais parler avec Oprah Winfrey.

■ **Variation:** Have the students select the three activities they would like to do <u>least</u>. Then have them compare their responses with a partner.
Je ne voudrais pas voyager avec ma cousine., etc.

T93

Section C

COMMUNICATIVE FUNCTION:
Extending invitations

13.3 Mini-scenes:
Invitations
(9:08–9:24 min.)

VIDEODISC Disc 3, Side 1
6455–6946

Leçon 13, Sections 3, 4

---

8 ROLE PLAY: extending and
accepting invitations

■ **Challenge:** Students can use
other phrases as they accept the
invitations: e.g., **D'accord / Oui,**
merci / Oui, bien sûr.

9 EXCHANGES: extending
and refusing invitations

13.4 Dialogue: Tennis?
(9:25–10:32 min.)

VIDEODISC Disc 3, Side 1
6975–8984

Leçon 13, Section 5

Cooperative
pair practice
Activities 8, 9

C. Invitations

Est-ce que tu veux
jouer au tennis?

▶ How to invite a friend:

Est-ce que tu veux …?	Do you want to . . . ?	**Est-ce que tu veux** jouer au tennis?
Est-ce que tu peux …?	Can you . . . ?	**Est-ce que tu peux** parler à mon copain?
avec moi/toi	with me/you	Est-ce que tu veux dîner **avec moi?**

▶ How to accept an invitation:

Oui, bien sûr …	Yes, of course . . .	
Oui, merci …	Yes, thanks . . .	
Oui, d'accord …	Yes, all right, okay . . .	
je veux bien.	I'd love to.	**Oui, bien sûr, je veux bien.**
je veux bien …	I'd love to . . .	**Oui, merci, je veux bien** dîner avec toi.

▶ How to turn down an invitation:

Je regrette, mais	I'm sorry, but	**Je regrette, mais je ne peux pas**
je ne peux pas …	I can't . . .	dîner avec toi.
Je dois …	I have to, I must . . .	**Je dois** étudier.

---

8 Invitations

Imagine a French exchange group is
visiting your school. Invite the following
French students to do things with you.
They will accept. (Your classmates will
play the parts of the students.)

▶ Monique / dîner

Monique, est-ce que
tu veux dîner
avec moi?

Oui, d'accord,
je veux bien dîner
avec toi.

1. Éric / parler français
2. Philippe / étudier
3. Céline / jouer au tennis
4. Anne / manger une pizza
5. Jean-Claude / chanter
6. Caroline / danser

9 Conversation

Ask your classmates if they want to do
the following things. They will answer
that they cannot and explain what they
have to do.

▶ jouer au basket? (étudier)
—Est-ce que tu veux jouer au
basket?
—Non, je ne peux pas. Je dois
étudier.

1. jouer au volley? (travailler)
2. jouer au ping-pong? (téléphoner à ma
cousine)
3. étudier avec moi? (étudier avec ma
copine)
4. dîner avec moi? (dîner avec ma
famille)
5. nager? (jouer au foot à deux
heures)

Teaching the video dialogue

For Lesson 13, the video (part 4) and the
cassette program (part 5) contain a series
of conversations.
Step 1: Set the scene. Tell students: In
this scene Jean-Claude is looking for a
tennis partner. **Regardez. (Écoutez.)**
Step 2: Play the video/cassette segment.

Step 3: Have students in small groups try
to recall the scenes.
Écrivez l'invitation de Jean-Claude
et les réponses de ses amis.
Step 4: Play the segment again to let
groups check their work.
Step 5: Compare the group answers.

À votre tour!

1 Créa-dialogue

Ask your classmates if they want to do the following things with you. They will answer that they cannot and will give one of the excuses in the box.

> ▶ jouer au tennis

Est-ce que tu veux jouer au tennis avec moi?

Non, je ne peux pas. Je dois travailler.

1. jouer au basket
2. manger une pizza
3. regarder la télé
4. jouer au ping-pong
5. dîner au restaurant

Excuses:
étudier	dîner avec ma cousine
travailler	parler avec ma mère
téléphoner à une copine	chanter avec la chorale *(choir)*

2 Conversation dirigée

Philippe is phoning Stéphanie. Write out their conversation according to the directions. You may want to act out the dialogue with a classmate.

Philippe

Stéphanie

asks Stéphanie how she is	→	answers that she is fine	
asks her if she wants to eat out	→	asks at what time	
says at 8 o'clock	→	says that she is sorry but that she has to study	
says it is too bad **(Dommage!)**			

3 Expression personnelle

What we like to do often depends on the circumstances. Complete the sentences below saying what you like and don't like to do in the following situations.

> ▶ En hiver . . .
> En hiver, j'aime regarder la télé.
> J'aime aussi jouer au basket.
> Je n'aime pas nager.

1. En été . . .
2. En automne . . .
3. Le samedi *(On Saturdays)* . . .
4. Le dimanche . . .
5. Le soir *(In the evening)* . . .
6. En classe . . .
7. Avec mes *(my)* amis . . .
8. Avec ma famille . . .

4 Composition

Write three things that you like to do and three things that you do not like to do.

> ▶
> *J'aime jouer au volley.*
> *Je n'aime pas jouer au foot.*

5 Correspondance

This summer, you are going to spend two weeks in France. Your pen pal Philippe has written, asking what you like and don't like to do on vacation **(en vacances)**. Write a postcard answering his questions.

> ▶
> *Cher Philippe,*
> *En vacances,*
> *j'aime . . .*
>
> PHILIPPE RAYMOND
> 12 AV. VICTOR HUGO
> PARIS 75116
> FRANCE

1 GUIDED ORAL EXPRESSION

▭ Leçon 13, Section 6

2 GUIDED ORAL EXPRESSION

P: (Salut, Stéphanie.) Ça va?
S: Oui, ça va (merci).
P: Tu veux dîner au restaurant?
S: À quelle heure?
P: À 8 heures.
S: Je regrette, mais je dois étudier.
P: Dommage!

▭ Leçon 13, Section 7

🖥 **13.5 Vignette culturelle:**
Le téléphone
(10:33–12:15 min.)

3 ORAL EXPRESSION

4 WRITTEN SELF-EXPRESSION

5 WRITTEN SELF-EXPRESSION

■ **Cooperative reading practice:**
Have students prepare a writing activity for homework. Then, in class, divide students into small groups and let them read one another's compositions.

À votre tour

Beginning with this lesson, the **À votre tour** sections have both oral and written communication activities.

Depending on your goals and objectives, you may or may not wish to assign all of the activities in the **À votre tour** section.

📁 Portfolio assessment

Beginning with Unit 4, students may start a Written Portfolio (see Front Matter for a complete description).

You will perhaps want to do only one oral portfolio recording and one written composition per unit. In this lesson, a good written portfolio topic is Act. 5.

MODULE 14:
Où est Jean-Claude?
Total time: 5:02 min.
(Counter: 12:28 min.)

14.1 Mini-scenes: Listening — Je suis en classe
(13:02–13:30 min.)
14.2 Mini-scenes: Speaking — Où sont-ils?
(13:31–14:44 min.)
14.3 Dialogue: Où est Jean-Claude?
(14:45–15:52 min.)

VIDEODISC Disc 3, Side 1
12425–21435

■ **Comprehension practice:** Play the entire module through as an introduction to the lesson.

 Leçon 14, Section 1

COMPREHENSION

1. (b) à la maison
2. (c) en ville
3. (d) au restaurant
4. (a) au café

■ **Oral comprehension:** Read each statement and have students indicate whether it is true (**vrai**) or false (**faux**).
1. Jacqueline est à la maison. (vrai)
2. Jean-Claude est à la maison. (faux)
3. Nicole est au restaurant. (vrai)
4. Sandrine est au cinéma. (faux)
5. Hélène est au café. (vrai)

T96

LEÇON 14 Qui est là?

It is Wednesday afternoon. Pierre is looking for his friends but cannot find anyone. Finally he sees Hélène at the Café Bellevue and asks her where everyone is.

PIERRE:	Où est Jacqueline?	*Where*
HÉLÈNE:	Elle est à la maison.	*at home*
PIERRE:	Et Jean-Claude? Il est là?	*here*
HÉLÈNE:	Non, il n'est pas là.	
PIERRE:	Où est-il?	
HÉLÈNE:	Il est en ville avec une copine.	*in town*
PIERRE:	Et Nicole et Sandrine? Est-ce qu'elles sont ici?	*here*
HÉLÈNE:	Non, elles sont au restaurant.	
PIERRE:	Alors, qui est là?	*So*
HÉLÈNE:	Moi, je suis ici.	
PIERRE:	C'est vrai, tu es ici! Eh bien, puisque tu es là, je t'invite au cinéma. D'accord?	*true / since* *I'll invite you to the movies*
HÉLÈNE:	Super! Pierre, tu es un vrai copain!	*real*

● **Compréhension**

Indicate where the following people are by selecting the appropriate completions.

1. Jacqueline est . . .   a) au café
2. Jean-Claude est . . .   b) à la maison
3. Nicole et Sandrine sont . . .   c) en ville
4. Hélène et Pierre sont . . .   d) au restaurant

96 Unité 4

Setting the stage
You may want to introduce the opening text by having students listen to the cassette recording with their books closed. They will hear a conversation between Pierre and Hélène. Pierre is looking for **Jacqueline, Jean-Claude,** and **Nicole et Sandrine.**

Draw three sets of stick figures (a girl, a boy, two girls) and identify them, as above.

Then label line drawings of three places: **en ville, au restaurant, à la maison.**

Tell students they are to listen to the conversation carefully and determine who is where.

NOTE CULTURELLE

Le mercredi après-midi

French high school students do not have classes on Wednesday afternoons. They use this free time to go out with their friends or to catch up on their homework. For some students, Wednesday afternoon is also the time for music and dance lessons as well as sports club activities. However, in contrast to the United States, many French schools have classes on Saturday mornings.

Leçon 14 97

Note culturelle

For more information about the French school system, turn to the photo essay on pp. 76–81, **À l'école en France**.

■ Photo culture note
Le cartable
In France, students often carry their books and school supplies in a **cartable** (a large briefcase).

14.4 Vignette culturelle: Au café
(15:53–17:26 min.)

VIDEODISC   Disc 3, Side 1
18594–21435

 Cross-cultural observation: After showing the video segment, have students in pairs make a list of similarities and differences between the French **café** and similar places where teens go in the United States.

🖥 Using the video

In many lessons of Niveau B, like this one, the video dialogue is different from the one in the opening text. (This is visually indicated by the presence of cartoon characters in the opening photograph.)

You may still want to play the entire video as an introduction to the lesson, because it develops the communication themes and highlights the new structures.

The video logos in the Teacher Edition will let you know where to use specific video segments.

Section A

COMMUNICATIVE FUNCTION:
Identifying people and
where they are

↩ **Re-entry and review:**
Remind students that they have
already been using the singular
forms of **être:**
Je suis américain.
Tu es français.
Il est canadien.

■ **Pronunciation note:** There is
usually liaison after **est:**
Elle **est** ici.
Liaison is optional after other
forms of **être:**
Ils **sont** ici. or
Ils **sont** ici.

■ **If students ask:** The pronouns
il and **elle** may also mean *it.*
Remind them that in Niveau A
they used sentences like:
[le sandwich] **Il coûte 3 euros.**

■ **Learning aid:** Always use
vous with people you address as
Monsieur, Madame, or
Mademoiselle.

■ **Teaching tip:** Use Transparency 16 (subject pronouns) as
a visual aid to present and
practice verb forms throughout
this program.

A. Le verbe *être* et les pronoms sujets

Être *(to be)* is the most frequently used verb in French. Note the forms of **être** in the
chart below.

	être	*to be*	
SINGULAR	je **suis** tu **es** il/elle **est**	*I am* *you are* *he/she is*	Je **suis** américain. Tu **es** canadienne. Il **est** anglais.
PLURAL	nous **sommes** vous **êtes** ils/elles **sont**	*we are* *you are* *they are*	Nous **sommes** à Paris. Vous **êtes** à San Francisco. Ils **sont** à Genève.

➡ Note the liaison in the **vous** form:
  Vous êtes français?
➡ Note the expression **être d'accord** *(to agree):*
  —Tu **es** d'accord   *Do you agree*
    avec moi?   *with me?*
  — Oui, je **suis d'accord!**   *Yes, I agree.*

TU or *VOUS?*

When talking to ONE person, the French have two
ways of saying *you:*

  • **tu** ("familiar *you*") is used to talk to someone
    your own age (or younger) or to a member of
    your family
  • **vous** ("formal *you*") is used when talking to
    anyone else

When talking to TWO or more people, the French
use **vous.**

Learning about language

The words **je** *(I),* **tu** *(you),* **il** *(he),* **elle**
(she), etc. are called SUBJECT PRONOUNS.

  • SINGULAR pronouns refer to one
    person (or object).
  • PLURAL pronouns refer to two or
    more people (or objects).

The VERB **être** *(to be)* is IRREGULAR because
its forms do not follow a predictable
pattern.

A chart showing the subject pronouns
and their corresponding verb forms is
called a CONJUGATION.

REMINDER: You should use . . .
  • **vous** to address your teacher
  • **tu** to address a classmate

Teaching note: Learning styles

Since different students have different
learning styles, **Discovering French**
presents French structures in several
ways:
• STRUCTURES IN CONTEXT (in dialogues)
— for those who learn best by hearing
and repeating.

• CHARTS AND BRIEF EXPLANATIONS
— for those who need to understand a
pattern before practicing it.
• CARTOON DRAWINGS (where appropriate)
— for those who find it helpful to visual-
ize a concept in picture form.

ILS or ELLES?

The French have two ways of saying *they:*

- **ils** refers to two or more males or to a mixed group of males and females
- **elles** refers to two or more females

Ils sont à Paris. Ils sont à Bordeaux.

Ils sont à Lyon. Elles sont à Nice.

1 PRACTICE: saying where people are

1 En France

The following students are on vacation in France. Which cities are they in?

▶ Alice . . . à Nice.　**Alice est à Nice.**

1. Philippe . . . à Toulon.
2. Nous . . . à Paris.
3. Vous . . . à Marseille.
4. Je . . . à Lyon.
5. Tu . . . à Tours.
6. Michèle et Francine . . . à Lille.
7. Éric et Vincent . . . à Strasbourg.
8. Ma cousine . . . à Toulouse.
9. Mon copain . . . à Bordeaux.

Vocabulaire: *Où?*

Où est Cécile?	*Where is Cécile?*		
Elle est . . .	**ici** *(here)*	**là** *(here, there)*	**là-bas** *(over there)*
	à Paris *(in Paris)*	**à** Boston	**à** Québec
	en classe *(in class)*	**en ville** *(downtown, in town, in the city)*	
	en vacances *(on vacation)*	**en** France *(in France)*	
	au café *(at the café)*	**au restaurant**	**au cinéma** *(at the movies)*
	à la maison *(at home)*		

---

2 À Nice

Catherine is spending her summer vacation in Nice at the home of her pen pal Stéphanie Lambert. Catherine has met many different people and is asking them various questions. Complete her questions with **Tu es** or **Vous êtes,** as appropriate.

▶ (Stéphanie's brother) . . . en vacances?
Tu es en vacances?

▶ (Monsieur Lambert) . . . de *(from)* Tours?
Vous êtes de Tours?

1. *(Mélanie, a friend of Stéphanie's)* . . . canadienne?
2. *(Olivier, Stéphanie's boyfriend)* . . . souvent *(often)* avec Stéphanie?
3. *(Monsieur Tardif, the neighbor)* . . . en vacances?
4. *(the mailman)* . . . de Nice?
5. *(Frédéric, Stéphanie's young cousin)* . . . souvent à Nice?
6. *(a woman in the park)* . . . française?
7. *(a little girl at the beach)* . . . en vacances?
8. *(a man reading* Time *magazine)* . . . américain?

Leçon 14　99

▷ Vocabulaire

Transparency 15
Où sont-ils?

14.1 Mini-scenes: Je suis en classe
14.2 Mini-scenes: Où sont-ils? (13:02–14:44 min.)

VIDEODISC.　Disc 3, Side 1
12425–16529

Leçon 14, Sections 2, 3

2 COMPREHENSION: using tu and vous

■ **If students ask:** In French, the word for vacation (**les vacances**) is always plural.

TPR ✍ In France

PROPS: signs: Paris, Bordeaux, Lyon, Nice
Place signs dividing class into 4 "cities."
　Voici Paris. Voici Bordeaux. etc.
Ask in which city students are.
　Où est X? [À Bordeaux.]
　Où sont Y et Z? [À Paris.]

Then have students move around.
　X, où es-tu? [À Bordeaux.]
　Lève-toi et va à Nice.
　Où es-tu maintenant? [À Nice.] …
　Y et Z, levez-vous et allez à Lyon.
　Où êtes-vous? [À Lyon.] …
Optional, with full answers:
　[Je suis à Nice.]

■ **TPR Variation:**
Use places from the **Vocabulaire** section: **en classe, au café, au cinéma, à la maison**…

T100

---

3 Où sont-ils?

Corinne is wondering if some of the people she knows are in certain places. Tell her she is right, using **il, elle, ils,** or **elles** in your answers.

▶ —Ta cousine est à Chicago?
—Oui, **elle est à Chicago.**

▶ —Pierre et Vincent sont au café?
—Oui, **ils sont au café.**

1. Stéphanie est à Lyon?
2. Monsieur Thomas est à San Francisco?
3. Suzanne et Monique sont à Genève?
4. Cécile et Charlotte sont au café?

5. Ta sœur est en ville?
6. Ton cousin est en vacances?
7. Claire, Alice et Éric sont au cinéma?
8. Monsieur et Madame Joli sont à Montréal?

4 Où?

You want to know where certain people are. A classmate will answer you on the basis of the illustrations.

▶ —Où est Céline?
—Elle est à New York.

Céline

1. Daniel | **2. Caroline** | **3. Jean-Louis**

4. Robert | **5. Florence** | **6. Hélène** | **7. Julien**

B. Les questions à réponse affirmative ou négative

The sentences on the left are statements. The sentences on the right are questions. These questions are called YES/NO QUESTIONS because they can be answered by *yes* or *no*. Note how the French questions begin with **est-ce que.**

STATEMENTS	YES/NO QUESTIONS	
Stéphanie est ici.	**Est-ce que** Stéphanie est ici?	*Is Stéphanie here?*
Tu es français.	**Est-ce que** tu es français?	*Are you French?*
Paul et Marc sont au café.	**Est-ce que** Paul et Marc sont au café?	*Are Paul and Marc at the café?*
Tu veux dîner avec moi.	**Est-ce que** tu veux dîner avec moi?	*Do you want to have dinner with me?*

Yes/no questions can be formed according to the pattern:

est-ce que + STATEMENT?	**Est-ce que** Pierre est ici?
↓	
est-ce qu' (+ VOWEL SOUND)	**Est-ce qu'**il est en ville?

Teaching note: Elision

The dropping of the final letter (usually "e") of a one-syllable word, as in **que → qu'**, is called ELISION.

Students have seen examples of elision already with **le, la → l'**. In this lesson they will also encounter **ne → n'** and **de → d'**.

The term "elision" is not used in the student text. Note, however, that words which have an elision form will be pointed out in the appropriate grammar sections.

➡ In yes/no questions, the voice goes up at the end of the sentence.

Est-ce que Paul et Florence sont au café?

➡ In casual conversation, yes/no questions can be formed without **est-ce que** simply by letting your voice rise at the end of the sentence.

Tu es français?   Cécile est en ville?

OBSERVATION: When you expect someone to agree with you, another way to form a yes/no question is to add the tag **n'est-ce pas** at the end of the sentence.

Tu es américain, **n'est-ce pas?**	*You are American, **aren't you?***
Tu aimes parler français, **n'est-ce pas?**	*You like to speak French, **don't you?***
Vous êtes d'accord, **n'est-ce pas?**	*You agree, **don't you?***

5 Nationalités

You are attending an international music camp. Ask about the nationalities of the other participants.

▶ Marc/canadien?   **Est-ce que Marc est canadien?**

1. Jim/américain?   3. Paul et Philippe/français?   5. vous/anglais?   7. Ellen et Carol/
2. Luisa/mexicaine?   4. tu/canadien?   6. Anne/française?   américaines?

Expressions pour la conversation

How to answer a yes/no question:

Oui!	*Yes!*	**Non!**	*No!*
Mais oui!	*Sure!*	**Mais non!**	*Of course not!*
Bien sûr!	*Of course!*		
Peut-être . . .	*Maybe . . .*		

6 Conversation

Ask your classmates the following questions. They will answer, using an expression from **Expressions pour la conversation**.

▶ Ton cousin est français?

1. Ta mère est à la maison?
2. Ta cousine est en France?
3. Ton copain est en classe?
4. Tu veux dîner avec moi?
5. Tu veux jouer au tennis avec moi?

Mais oui!   (Mais non!)

Alice, est-ce que ton cousin est français?

Leçon 14 **101**

Teaching note: Tag questions

You may want to point out to students that it is very easy to ask tag questions in French because there is only one tag:
n'est-ce pas?
This expression literally means
is it not so?

In English, on the other hand, tags are many and complex:
You will come, *won't you?*
You didn't refuse, *did you?* etc.
The multiplicity of tags makes French students feel that English is at times a difficult language to learn.

■ **Pronunciation:** As in English, your voice goes up at the end of the tag.

5 PRACTICE: asking questions about nationality

↩ **Re-entry and Review:** Nationalities from Lesson 2.

■ **Challenge:** Answer each question affirmatively.
– Est-ce que Marc est canadien?
– Oui, il est canadien.
Note: Help students differentiate between singular and plural in items 4 and 5:
4. Oui, je suis...
5. Oui, nous sommes...

■ **Variation:** Formulate tag questions with n'est-ce pas.
Marc est canadien, n'est-ce pas?

Supplementary vocabulary

Bien sûr que oui!
    Why of course!
Bien sûr que non!
    Why of course not!

6 COMMUNICATION: asking personal questions

■ **Photo culture note**
Un café à Paris
The two girls are having ice cream which in France is usually served with a wafer (**une gaufrette**).
In the background you can see cone-shaped folded parasols.

■ **Language note:** Ne → n' is another example of elision.

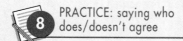

7 DESCRIPTION: answering questions in the negative

■ **Expansion:** Continue your answer with a positive statement.
– **Est-ce que tu es français?**
– **Non, je ne suis pas français(e). Je suis américain(e).**

8 PRACTICE: saying who does/doesn't agree

C. La négation

Compare the affirmative and negative sentences below:

AFFIRMATIVE	NEGATIVE	
Je **suis** américain.	Je **ne suis pas** français.	*I'm not French.*
Nous **sommes** en classe.	Nous **ne sommes pas** en vacances.	*We are not on vacation.*
Claire **est** là-bas.	Elle **n'est pas** ici.	*She is not here.*
Vous **êtes** à Paris.	Vous **n'êtes pas** à Lyon.	*You are not in Lyon.*
Tu **es** d'accord avec moi.	Tu **n'es pas** d'accord avec Marc.	*You do not agree with Marc.*

Negative sentences are formed as follows:

SUBJECT + **ne** + VERB + **pas** . . .
↓
n' (+ VOWEL SOUND)

Éric et Anne **ne** sont **pas** là.

Michèle **n'est pas** avec moi.

Je suis en classe.
Je **ne** suis **pas** à la maison.

7 **Non!**

Answer the following questions negatively.

▶ —Est-ce que tu es français (française)?
—**Non, je ne suis pas français (française).**

1. Est-ce que tu es canadien (canadienne)?
2. Est-ce que tu es à Québec?
3. Est-ce que tu es à la maison?
4. Est-ce que tu es au café?
5. Est-ce que tu es en vacances?
6. Est-ce que tu es au cinéma?

8 **D'accord**

It is raining. François suggests to his friends that they go to the movies. Say who agrees and who does not, using the expression **être d'accord.**

▶ ☹ Philippe **Philippe n'est pas d'accord.** ▶ ☺ Hélène **Hélène est d'accord.**

1. ☺ nous
2. ☺ je
3. ☹ tu
4. ☺ Patrick et Marc
5. ☹ Claire et Stéphanie
6. ☹ vous
7. ☺ ma copine
8. ☹ mon frère

 Cooperative pair practice
Activity 8

Speaking practice
PROP: Transparency 15 with names written in the boxes below each picture.
Point to the picture of the café.
Qui est-ce? [C'est Sophie.]
Est-ce que Sophie est au café?
[Mais oui, elle est au café.]
Similarly introduce each picture.

Then practice negatives. Point to Sophie.
Qui est-ce? C'est Marc?
[Non, ce n'est pas Marc. C'est Sophie.]
Est-ce que Sophie est en classe?
[Non, elle n'est pas en classe.]
Est-ce que Sophie est à la maison?
[Mais non, elle n'est pas à la maison.]
Où est Sophie? [Elle est au café.]

Vocabulaire: Mots utiles *(Useful words)*

à	at	Je suis **à** la maison **à** dix heures.
	in	Nous sommes **à** Paris.
de	from	Vous êtes **de** San Francisco.
	of	Voici une photo **de** Paris.
et	and	Anne **et** Sophie sont en vacances.
ou	or	Qui est-ce? Juliette **ou** Sophie?
avec	with	Philippe est **avec** Pauline.
pour	for	Je veux travailler **pour** Monsieur Martin.
mais	but	Je ne suis pas français, **mais** j'aime parler français.

➡ **De** becomes **d'** before a vowel sound:
   Patrick est **de** Lyon.   François est **d'**Annecy.

Fête Nationale
mardi 14 juillet
à 22h

PARIS

---

9 **Le mot juste** *(The right word)* ───

Complete the sentences below with the word in parentheses that fits logically.

1. Monsieur Moreau est en France. Aujourd'hui, il est . . . Lyon. (à/de)
2. Martine est canadienne. Elle est . . . Montréal. (de/et)
3. Florence n'est pas ici. Elle est . . . Jean-Claude. (et/avec)
4. Alice . . . Paul sont au restaurant. (avec/et)
5. Jean-Pierre n'est pas à la maison. Il est au café . . . au cinéma. (ou/et)
6. J'aime jouer au tennis . . . je ne veux pas jouer avec toi. (ou/mais)
7. Je dois travailler . . . mon père. (pour/à)

10 **Être ou ne pas être** *(To be or not to be)*

We cannot be in different places at the same time. Express this according to the model.

▶ Aline est en ville. (ici)
   Aline n'est pas ici.

1. Frédéric est là-bas. (à la maison)
2. Nous sommes en classe. (au restaurant)
3. Tu es à Nice. (à Toulon)
4. Vous êtes au café. (au cinéma)
5. Jérôme est avec Sylvie. (avec Catherine)
6. Juliette et Sophie sont avec Éric. (avec Marc)

Prononciation   /a/

La voyelle /a/

The letter "**a**" alone always represents the sound /a/ as in the English word *ah*. It never has the sound of "*a*" as in English words like *class*, *date*, or *cinema*.

chat

Répétez: **ch<u>a</u>t ç<u>a</u> v<u>a</u> <u>à</u> l<u>a</u> l<u>à</u>-b<u>a</u>s <u>a</u>vec <u>a</u>mi voil<u>à</u>
cl<u>a</u>sse c<u>a</u>fé s<u>a</u>l<u>a</u>de d<u>a</u>me d<u>a</u>te M<u>a</u>d<u>a</u>me C<u>a</u>n<u>a</u>d<u>a</u>

<u>A</u>nne est <u>a</u>u C<u>a</u>n<u>a</u>d<u>a</u> <u>a</u>vec M<u>a</u>d<u>a</u>me L<u>a</u>v<u>a</u>l.

■ **Language note:** You may wish to point out the spelling difference between **ou** *(or)* and **où** *(where)*:
   Où est Juliette?
   Au café **ou** au cinéma?

■ **Cultural realia:**
Ask your students:
– What event is taking place in Paris? [the national holiday]
– What is the date of this event? [Tuesday, July 14]
– **Quelle est la date de la Fête Nationale?** [le mardi 14 juillet]
– **À quelle heure est la fête?** [À 22h.]

COMPREHENSION: choosing prepositions and conjunctions **9**

DESCRIPTION: saying where people are not **10**

14.3 Dialogue: Où est Jean-Claude? (14:45–15:52 min.)

VIDEODISC Disc 3, Side1
16549–18572

Leçon 14, Section 5

Prononciation

Leçon 14, Section 6

💻 Listening game: Où est Jean-Claude?

Prepare a cloze version of the video/cassette script of *Où est Jean-Claude?* with selected words deleted.

   Play the video or the cassette dialogue.

   Divide the class into teams of three and distribute one script to each team. The teams all try to fill in as many

missing words as they can remember. Replay the video/cassette, pausing after each sentence so that the teams can try to complete their texts.

   Have teams exchange and correct their scripts. The team with the most correct completions is the winner.

COMPREHENSION

1
COMPREHENSION

1-c	4-e
2-d	5-b
3-a	

 Leçon 14, Section 7

2
COMPREHENSION

1. au cinéma
2. en vacances
3. au restaurant (au café)
4. à la maison
5. en vacances

Classroom Notes

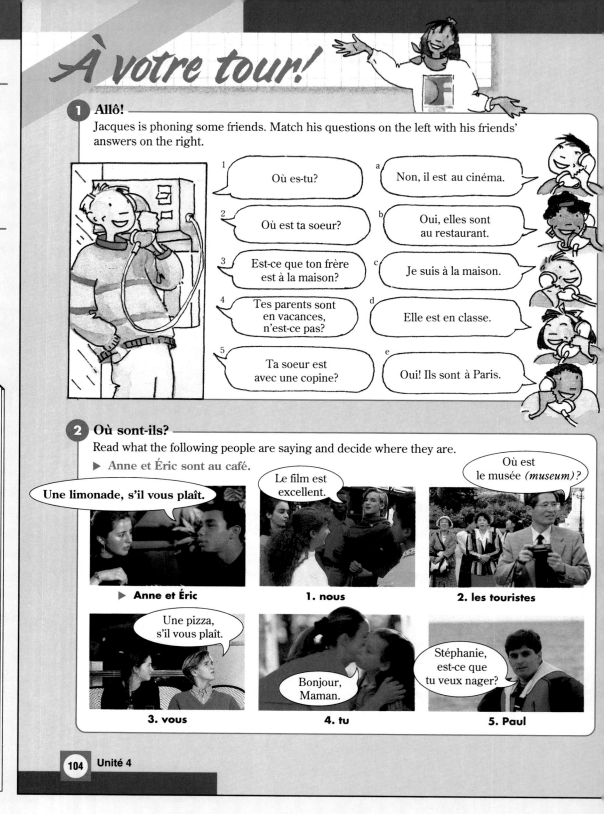

À votre tour!

1 Allô!

Jacques is phoning some friends. Match his questions on the left with his friends' answers on the right.

1 Où es-tu?

a Non, il est au cinéma.

2 Où est ta soeur?

b Oui, elles sont au restaurant.

3 Est-ce que ton frère est à la maison?

c Je suis à la maison.

4 Tes parents sont en vacances, n'est-ce pas?

d Elle est en classe.

5 Ta soeur est avec une copine?

e Oui! Ils sont à Paris.

2 Où sont-ils?

Read what the following people are saying and decide where they are.

▶ Anne et Éric sont au café.

Une limonade, s'il vous plaît.

Le film est excellent.

Où est le musée *(museum)*?

▶ **Anne et Éric**

1. nous

2. les touristes

Une pizza, s'il vous plaît.

Bonjour, Maman.

Stéphanie, est-ce que tu veux nager?

3. vous

4. tu

5. Paul

104 Unité 4

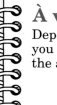

À votre tour

Depending on your goals and objectives, you may or may not wish to assign all of the activities in the **À votre tour** section.

👥 Cooperative practice

Act. 1 and 3 lend themselves to cooperative pair practice.

For Act. 3, you may prefer to have students work in trios, with two performing while the other holds the Answer Key and acts as a monitor.

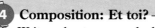

3 Créa-dialogue

You are working for a student magazine in France. Your assignment is to interview tourists who are visiting Paris. Ask them where they are from. (Make sure to address the people appropriately as **tu** or **vous**.) Remember: The symbol "??" means you may invent your own responses.

Nationalité	Villes *(Cities)*	
▶ anglaise	Londres? *(London)* Liverpool	

▶ — Bonjour. <u>Vous êtes anglaise</u>?
— Oui, je suis <u>anglaise</u>.
— Est-ce que <u>vous êtes</u> de <u>Londres</u>?
— Mais non, je ne suis pas de <u>Londres</u>. Je suis de <u>Liverpool</u>.

Nationalité	Villes	
1 américaine	New York? Washington	
2 canadien	Québec? Montréal	
3 française	Paris? Nice	
4 mexicain	Mexico? Puebla	
5 ??	?? ??	
6 ??	?? ??	

4 Composition: Et toi?

Write a short paragraph about yourself and your friends.

1. Say what city you are from. **(Je suis de . . .)**
2. Say what city your father or your mother is from. **(Mon père /ma mère est de . . .)**
3. Say where one of your friends is from. **(Mon copain /ma copine . . .)**
4. Name an activity you like to do with a friend. **(J'aime . . . avec . . .)**
5. Name an activity you want to do with two friends. **(Je veux . . .)**
6. Name an activity you would like to do with one of your relatives. **(Je voudrais . . .)**

5 Composition: Personnellement

On a separate piece of paper, or on a computer, write where you are and where you are not at each of the following times.

▶ à 9 heures du matin
- à 4 heures
- à 7 heures du soir
- samedi
- dimanche
- en juillet

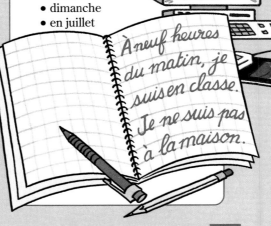

À neuf heures du matin, je suis en classe. Je ne suis pas à la maison.

3 GUIDED ORAL EXPRESSION

🔊 **Leçon 14, Section 8**

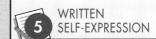

4 WRITTEN SELF-EXPRESSION

5 WRITTEN SELF-EXPRESSION

Classroom Notes

📁 Portfolio assessment

You will probably select only one speaking activity and one writing activity to go into the students' portfolios for Unit 4.

In this lesson, Act. 3 lends itself well to an oral portfolio recording. Act. 4 and 5 are both good writing portfolio topics.

(Encourage your students to invent their own responses as in items 5 and 6 in Act. 3.)

Une boum

Jean-Marc has been invited to a party. He is trying to decide whether to bring Béatrice or Valérie. First he talks to Béatrice.

Leçon 15

MAIN TOPIC:

Talking about one's activities

MODULE 15:
Une boum
Total time: 4:50 min.
(Counter: 17:36 min.)

**15.1 Mini-scenes: Listening
— J'étudie**
(17:51–18:51 min.)

**15.2 Mini-scenes: Listening
— Tu téléphones?**
(18:52–19:25 min.)

**15.3 Mini-scenes: Speaking
— Est-ce qu'il travaille?**
(19:26–20:27 min.)

**15.4 Dialogue: Jean-Paul à
la boum**
(20:28–21:21 min.)

**15.5 Vignette culturelle:
Une boum**
(21:22–22:16 min.)

 Disc 3, Side1
21659–30162

■ **Comprehension practice:** Play
the entire module through as an
introduction to the lesson.

 Leçon 15, Section 1

■ **Photo culture note**
La Défense
The new high-rise business center of
Paris is located at La Défense, in the
suburb of Nanterre west of the city.
L'Arche de la Défense, an actual
building housing many offices, was
inaugurated in 1989.

JEAN-MARC:	<u>Dis</u>, Béatrice, tu aimes danser?	*Hey*
BÉATRICE:	Bien sûr, j'aime danser!	
JEAN-MARC:	Est-ce que tu danses bien?	
BÉATRICE:	Oui, je danse très, <u>très bien</u>.	*very well*
JEAN-MARC:	Et ta cousine Valérie? Est-ce qu'elle danse bien?	
BÉATRICE:	Non, elle ne danse pas très bien.	
JEAN-MARC:	<u>Alors</u>, c'est Valérie <u>que</u> j'invite à la <u>boum</u>.	*So / that / party*
BÉATRICE:	Mais <u>pourquoi</u> elle? Pourquoi pas moi?	*why*
JEAN-MARC:	Écoute, Béatrice, <u>je ne sais pas</u> danser! <u>Alors</u>, je préfère inviter une fille qui ne danse pas très bien. C'est normal, non?	*don't know how / So*

● **Compréhension: Vrai ou faux?**

Read the following statements and say whether they are true (**C'est vrai!**) or false (**C'est faux!**).

1. Béatrice aime danser.
2. Elle danse bien.
3. Valérie danse très bien.
4. Jean-Marc invite Béatrice.
5. Il invite Valérie.

 COMPREHENSION

1. C'est vrai!
2. C'est vrai!
3. C'est faux!
4. C'est faux!
5. C'est vrai!

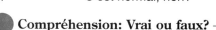
Setting the stage

Ask students if they organize informal
parties at home for their friends.
    What do they serve to eat and drink?
    What do they do? Talk? Dance? Sing?
Tell them that in this lesson they will
learn about French parties.

■ NOTE ■
CULTURELLE

Une boum

On weekends, French teenagers like to go to parties that are organized at a friend's home. Often the guests contribute something to the buffet: sandwiches or soft drinks. There is also a lot of music and dancing. (French teenagers love to dance!)

These informal parties have different names according to the age group of the participants. For students at a **collège** (or junior high), a party is sometimes known as **une boum** or **une fête.** For older students at a **lycée** (or high school), it is called **une soirée** or **une fête.**

■ **Photo culture notes**
The top buffet spread shows:
• potato chips (**des chips**)
• crackers (**des biscuits**)
• peanuts (**des cacahuètes**)
• little sandwiches with caviar or pâté (**des sandwiches au caviar et au pâté**)
• paper cups (**des timbales en papier**)

The bottom table contains:
• soft drinks (**des sodas**)
• apples (**des pommes**)
• bananas (**des bananes**)
• cheeses (**des fromages**)
• slices of cake (**des portions de gâteau**)

  15.5 **Vignette culturelle: Une boum** (21:22–22:16 min.)

 **VIDEODISC**   Disc 3, Side 1
28463–30162

🌐 Cross-cultural understanding

Have students watch the video (or look at the above photographs taken from the video scenes).

What kinds of similarities and differences do they notice between parties in France and parties that they go to?

T107

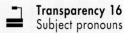
Transparency 16
Subject pronouns

15.1 Mini-scenes: J'étudie
15.2 Mini-scenes: Tu téléphones?
(17:51–19:25 min.)

VIDEODISC   Disc 3, Side 1
21659–24930

Leçon 15, Sections 2, 3

■ **Pronunciation:** You may want to point out that the singular forms of **-er** verbs all sound the same. There is a difference in spelling in the **tu**-form.

1 ROLE PLAY: getting acquainted

A. Les verbes en -er: le singulier

Many French verbs end in **-er** in the infinitive. Most of these verbs are conjugated like **parler** *(to speak)* and **habiter** *(to live)*. Note the forms of the present tense of these verbs in the singular. Pay attention to their endings.

> **Learning about language**
> The basic form of the VERB is the INFINITIVE:
> **jouer** *(to play)*   **travailler** *(to work)*
> In French dictionaries, verbs are listed by their infinitives.

INFINITIVE	parler	habiter	ENDINGS
STEM	parl-	habit-	
PRESENT TENSE (SINGULAR)	Je **parle** français. Tu **parles** anglais. Il / Elle **parle** espagnol.	J' **habite** à Paris. Tu **habites** à Boston. Il / Elle **habite** à Madrid.	-e -es -e

The present tense forms of -er verbs consist of two parts:

STEM + ENDING

- The STEM does not change. It is the infinitive minus **-er**:
  parler parl-   habiter habit-
- The ENDINGS change with the subject:
  je → -e   tu → -es   il / elle → -e

⇒ The above endings are silent.
⇒ **Je** becomes **j'** before a vowel sound.
  je parle   **j'**habite

> **Learning about language**
> Verbs conjugated like **parler** and **habiter** follow a *predictable pattern*.
> They are called REGULAR VERBS.

1 Curiosité

At the party, Olivier wants to learn more about Isabelle.
She answers his questions affirmatively. Play both roles.

Tu parles anglais?

Oui, je parle anglais.

▶ parler anglais?

1. parler espagnol?
2. habiter à Paris?
3. étudier ici?
4. jouer au volley?
5. jouer au basket?
6. chanter?

Cooperative pair practice
Activities 1, 2

Critical thinking about language

In this lesson, students are encouraged to think about how verbs work in French.

In Section A, they will learn the singular forms, which sound the same, but which are not all spelled the same.

In Section B, they will learn the plural forms with their endings, and notice how liaison helps link subject and verb together.

Finally in Section C, they will see the complete verb charts with both affirmative and negative forms. They will learn what a paradigm for regular verbs looks like, and how it can serve as a model.

Vocabulaire: Les verbes en *-er*

Verbs you already know:

chanter	*to sing*	**nager**	*to swim*
danser	*to dance*	**parler**	*to speak, talk*
dîner	*to have dinner*	**regarder**	*to watch, look at*
écouter	*to listen (to)*	**téléphoner**	*to phone, call*
étudier	*to study*	**travailler**	*to work*
jouer	*to play*	**voyager**	*to travel*
manger	*to eat*		

New verbs:

aimer	*to like*	Tu **aimes** Paris?
habiter	*to live*	Philippe **habite** à Toulouse?
inviter	*to invite*	J'**invite** un copain.
organiser	*to organize*	Sophie **organise** une **boum**/une **soirée**/une **fête** *(party).*
visiter	*to visit (places)*	Hélène **visite** Québec.

➡ **Regarder** has two meanings:

to look (at)	Paul **regarde** Cécile.
to watch	Cécile **regarde** la télé.

➡ Note the construction **téléphoner à:**

Hélène **téléphone**	**à**	Marc.
Hélène calls	. . .	*Marc.*

➡ Note the constructions with **regarder** and **écouter:**

Philippe **regarde**	. . .	Alice.
Philippe looks	*at*	*Alice.*

Alice **écoute**	. . .	le professeur.
Alice listens	*to*	*the teacher.*

---

2 **Quelle activité?**

Describe what the following people are doing by completing the sentences with one of the verbs below. Be logical in your choice of activity.

 chanter   écouter   parler   *travailler*   *manger*   voyager   regarder   inviter

1. Je . . . un sandwich. Tu . . . une pizza.
2. Tu . . . anglais. Je . . . français.
3. Éric . . . la radio. Claire . . . un compact (un CD).
4. Jean-Paul . . . la télé. Tu . . . un match de tennis.
5. M. Simon . . . en *(by)* bus. Mme Dupont . . . en train.
6. Nicolas . . . Marie à la boum. Tu . . . Alain.
7. Mlle Thomas . . . dans *(in)* un hôpital. Je . . . dans un supermarché *(supermarket).*
8. Mick Jagger . . . bien. Est-ce que tu . . . bien?

Leçon 15 **109**

▷ **Vocabulaire**

 Transparencies 14A, 14B, 17
Verbs

COMPREHENSION: saying what people are doing

2

1. mange / manges
2. parles / parle
3. écoute / écoute
4. regarde / regardes
5. voyage / voyage
6. invite / invites
7. travaille / travaille
8. chante / chantes

TPR Activities

Together with the class, develop gestures for the new verbs in the chart. E.g.:
aimer: hands across one's heart
habiter: arms over head in a "roof" shape

Review gestures you created for the other verbs (page T90).

J'habite à Paris. ["roof"gesture] …
Then address individual students directly.
X, tu danses bien. [X shows "dancing"]
Ask students what they are doing.
Y, qu'est-ce que tu fais?
[Y gestures "tennis"]
Est-ce que Y chante? [non]
Est-ce qu'il joue au tennis? [oui]

3 Le télescope

Curious Georges has set up a telescope to observe what his neighbors are doing. Describe each person's activity.

▶ **Monsieur Thomas dîne.**

4 Où sont-ils?

You want to know where the following people are. A classmate will answer, telling you where the people are and what they are doing.

▶ Jacques? (en classe/étudier)

Où est Jacques?

Il est en classe. Il étudie.

1. Pauline? (au restaurant/dîner)
2. Véronique? (à la maison/téléphoner)
3. Mme Dupont? (en ville/travailler)
4. M. Lemaire? (en France/voyager)
5. Jean-Claude? (à Paris/visiter la tour Eiffel)
6. André? (au Tennis Club/jouer au tennis)
7. Alice? (à l'Olympic Club/nager)

B. Les verbes en -er: le pluriel

Note the plural forms of **parler** and **habiter**, paying attention to the endings.

INFINITIVE	parler	habiter	ENDINGS
STEM	parl-	habit-	
PRESENT TENSE (PLURAL)	Nous **parlons** français. Vous **parlez** anglais. Ils/Elles **parlent** espagnol.	Nous **habitons** à Québec. Vous **habitez** à Chicago. Ils/Elles **habitent** à Caracas.	-ons -ez -ent

➡ In the present tense, the plural endings of **-er** verbs are:

nous → **-ons**   vous → **-ez**   ils/elles → **-ent**

➡ The **-ent** ending is silent.

➡ Note the liaison when the verb begins with a vowel sound:

Nous étudions.   Vous invitez Thomas.   Ils habitent en France.   Elles aiment Paris.

OBSERVATION: When the infinitive of the verb ends in **-ger**, the **nous**-form ends in **-geons**.

nager: nous na**geons**   manger: nous man**geons**   voyager: nous voya**geons**

TPR Subject pronouns

Teach students gestures for each pronoun.

Montrez-moi "je". [point to self]
  Montrez-moi "tu". [point straight ahead, somewhat down, as if to a child]
  Montrez-moi "il" ou "elle" [stretch one arm out to the side, hand open]

Add: **"nous"** [both hands point to self]
  "vous" [both hands point straight ahead]
  "ils/elles" [both arms stretched to side]
Have students identify subjects.
  Nous organisons une boum. ["nous"]
The subjects **il(s)/elle(s)** may be ambiguous.
  Il(s) joue(nt) au tennis. ["il" or "ils"]
Clarify: **Pierre joue au tennis.** ["il"]

5 Qui?

Stéphanie is speaking to or about her friends. Complete her sentences with **tu, elle, vous,** or **ils.**

▶ . . . étudient à Toulouse.
   Ils étudient à Toulouse.

1. . . . habitez à Tours.
2. . . . aime Paris.
3. . . . étudiez à Tours.
4. . . . aiment danser.
5. . . . organisent une boum.
6. . . . parlez espagnol.
7. . . . téléphone à Jean-Pierre.
8. . . . invites un copain.
9. . . . dîne avec Cécile.
10. . . . invitent Monique.

6 À la boum

At a party, Olivier is talking to two Canadian students, Monique and her friend. Monique answers yes to his questions.

▶ parler français?

Vous parlez français, n'est-ce pas?

Oui, nous parlons français.

1. parler anglais?   5. voyager en train?
2. habiter à Québec?   6. visiter Paris?
3. étudier à Montréal?   7. aimer Paris?
4. voyager en France?   8. aimer la France?

7 Le camp français

At summer camp, everything is organized according to a schedule. Describe the activities of the following campers by completing the sentences according to the illustrations.

▶ À cinq heures, Alice et Marc . . .   À cinq heures, Alice et Marc jouent au volley.

▶

1. À neuf heures, nous . . .   4. À sept heures, nous . . .
2. À quatre heures, vous . . .   5. À trois heures, Thomas et François . . .
3. À huit heures, Véronique et Pierre . . . 6. À six heures, vous . . .

8 Un voyage à Paris

A group of American students are visiting Paris. During their stay, they do all of the following things:

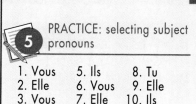

...yager en bus   téléphoner à un copain

visiter la tour Eiffel   dîner au restaurant

inviter une copine

Describe the trips of the following people.

▶ Jim   **Il voyage en bus, il visite la tour Eiffel . . .**

écouter un opéra

1. Linda   2. Paul et Louise   3. nous   4. vous

Leçon 15 **111**

5 PRACTICE: selecting subject pronouns

1. Vous   5. Ils   8. Tu
2. Elle   6. Vous   9. Elle
3. Vous   7. Elle   10. Ils
4. Ils

■ Be sure students make the liaison in 1, 3, 4, 5, and 10.

6 ROLE PLAY: getting to know people

■ **Variation:** Ask questions with **est-ce que**; respond with **bien sûr.**
– Est-ce que vous parlez français?
– Bien sûr, nous parlons français.

7 COMPREHENSION: describing what people do at various times of day

1. téléphonons
2. jouez au tennis
3. regardent la télé
4. dînons
5. jouent au basket
6. nagez

↩ **Re-entry and review:** Before doing this exercise you may want to review telling time (Lesson 4).

8 PRACTICE: describing activities on a trip

■ **Pronunciation: bus** /bys/

👥 Cooperative writing practice

Act. 8 lends itself to cooperative writing practice. First go through the entire model paragraph with the whole class.

Then group students in pairs and assign each pair a number (1, 2, 3, or 4). Each pair then writes out the paragraph corresponding to its number.

When all are done, have each pair pass its paper to the next pair. The pairs then read and check the new paragraph they have received. (For example, pair 2 passes its paper to pair 3 and reads the paper it receives from pair 1.)

Section C

COMMUNICATIVE FUNCTION:
Describing what people do
and don't do

15.3 Mini-scenes:
Est-ce qu'il travaille?
(19:26–20:27 min.)

 **IDEODISC** Disc 3, Side1
24959–26808

 Leçon 15, Section 4

Transparency 16
Subject pronouns

■ **Teaching tip:** You can make
large subject pronoun flash cards
by projecting the drawings from
the transparency onto heavy
paper and tracing the outlines
with markers. If desired, you can
label each drawing with the corresponding pronoun. Use these
cards throughout the program to
practice verb forms

■ **Language note:** Be sure students notice that the one word
parle in French may correspond
to two words in English:
is speaking, does speak.
Point out that *is* corresponds to
est only when it represents the
main verb.

C. **Le présent des verbes en *-er*: forme affirmative et forme négative**

FORMS

Compare the affirmative and negative forms of **parler.**

AFFIRMATIVE	NEGATIVE
je **parle**	je **ne parle pas**
tu **parles**	tu **ne parles pas**
il/elle **parle**	il/elle **ne parle pas**
nous **parlons**	nous **ne parlons pas**
vous **parlez**	vous **ne parlez pas**
ils/elles **parlent**	ils/elles **ne parlent pas**

REMEMBER: The negative form of the verb follows the pattern:

SUBJECT + **ne** + VERB + **pas**
↓
n' (+ VOWEL SOUND)

Il **ne** travaille **pas** ici.

Je **n'**invite **pas** Pierre.

Il **ne** travaille **pas**.

Ils **n'**écoutent **pas**.

Elle **ne** chante **pas** bien.

USES

In the present tense, French verbs have several English equivalents:

Je **joue** au tennis.
{ *I **play** tennis.*
{ *I **do play** tennis.*
{ *I am **playing** tennis.*

Je **ne joue pas** au tennis.
{ *I **do not play** tennis. (I **don't** play tennis.)*
{ *I am **not playing** tennis. (I'm **not playing** tennis.)*

Studying French helps you better appreciate
how the English language works.

112 Unité 4

Teaching note: Verb endings

Use Transparency 16 to help students
learn to spell the verb endings and say
the forms. First have the students
identify the pronoun cartoons (**je, tu,**...).

With a washable transparency marker,
write the forms of **dîner** below each
picture.

With a second color, box the endings.

Have students read the verbs aloud,
first in sequence (**je dîne, tu dînes,** ...)
and then randomly as you point to them
(**nous dînons, elle dîne,** ...).

Erase the forms of **dîner.** Have volunteers come write the forms of other verbs.

9 Non!

One cannot do everything. From the following list of activities, select at least three that you do *not* do.

▶ **Je ne joue pas au bridge.**

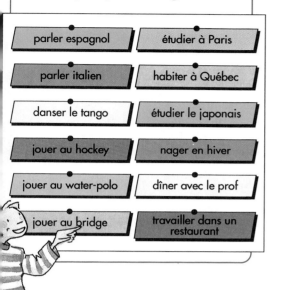

parler espagnol	étudier à Paris
parler italien	habiter à Québec
danser le tango	étudier le japonais
jouer au hockey	nager en hiver
jouer au water-polo	dîner avec le prof
jouer au bridge	travailler dans un restaurant

10 Pas aujourd'hui

Today the following people are tired and are not doing what they usually do. Express this according to the model.

▶ Pierre joue au tennis.
Aujourd'hui, il ne joue pas au tennis.

1. Je joue au foot.
2. Tu étudies.
3. Madame Simonet travaille.
4. Vous dînez à la maison.
5. Marc téléphone à Martine.
6. Nous nageons.
7. Jacques et Florence étudient.

11 Un jeu: Weekend!

On weekends, people like to do different things. For each person, pick an activity and say what that person does. Select another activity and say what that person does not do.

▶ **Antoine et Isabelle dansent.
Ils ne regardent pas la télé.**

je
tu
ma cousine
nous
Antoine et Isabelle
Monsieur Leblanc
Madame Jolivet
vous
le professeur

COMMUNICATION: stating activities that one does not do

9

Cooperative pair practice
• Use the cues as the basis of a poll.
• Divide the class into pairs, and have students interview one another to discover what their partners do and do not do.
  – **Tu joues au bridge?**
  – **Oui, je joue au bridge. (Non, je ne joue pas au bridge.)**

■ **Variation:** Use other subjects: **nous, tu, mon copain, ma copine.**

PRACTICE: saying what people are not doing today

10

COMPREHENSION: stating what people do and don't do

11

jouer au tennis
jouer au basket
regarder la télé
écouter la radio
travailler
étudier
danser
dîner au restaurant
nager

Classroom Notes

T113

Teaching tip: Have students notice the two-column (French-English) format in the **Vocabulaire** sections. Encourage them to practice the vocabulary by covering one of the two columns with a slip of paper and then saying or writing the corresponding expression in the other language. They can verify their responses by sliding the paper down the page as they go through the list.

COMMUNICATION: describing how well or often one does things

12

COMMUNICATION: expressing approval or regret

13

Variation: Address two or more students.
– Est-ce que vous chantez?
– Oui, nous aimons chanter. (Non, nous n'aimons pas chanter.)

Cooperative pair practice
Activity 13, 14

Vocabulaire: Mots utiles

bien	*well*	Je joue **bien** au tennis.
très bien	*very well*	Je ne chante pas **très bien.**
mal	*badly, poorly*	Tu joues **mal** au volley.
beaucoup	*a lot, much, very much*	Paul aime **beaucoup** voyager.
un peu	*a little, a little bit*	Nous parlons **un peu** français.
souvent	*often*	Charles invite **souvent** Nathalie.
toujours	*always*	Je travaille **toujours** en été.
aussi	*also, too*	Je téléphone à Marc. Je téléphone **aussi** à Véronique.
maintenant	*now*	J'étudie **maintenant.**
rarement	*rarely, seldom*	Vous voyagez **rarement.**

➡ In French, the above expressions _never_ come _between_ the subject and the verb. They usually come _after_ the verb. Compare their positions in French and English.

Nous parlons **toujours** français.   We **always** speak French.
Tu joues **bien** au tennis.   You play tennis **well.**

---

12 **Expression personnelle**

Complete the following sentences with an expression from the list below.

bien	mal	très bien	toujours	souvent	rarement	un peu	beaucoup

1. Je chante . . .
2. Je nage . . .
3. Je regarde . . . la télé.
4. Je mange . . .
5. Je voyage . . . en bus.
6. Le prof parle . . . français.
7. Nous parlons . . . français en classe.
8. Les Rolling Stones chantent . . .
9. Michael Jordan joue . . . au basket.
10. Les Yankees jouent . . . au baseball.

Expressions pour la conversation

Tu parles français?
Super!
Oui, je parle français.

How to express approval or regret:

| **Super!** | *Terrific!* | Tu parles français? **Super!** |
| **Dommage!** | *Too bad!* | Tu ne joues pas au tennis? **Dommage!** |

13 **Conversation**

Ask your classmates if they do the following things. Then express approval or regret, according to their answers.

▶ parler français? —Est-ce que tu parles français?
                 —Oui, je parle français. (Non, je ne parle pas français.)
                 —Super! (Dommage!)

1. parler espagnol?
2. jouer au tennis?
3. danser bien?
4. voyager beaucoup?
5. dîner souvent au restaurant?
6. inviter souvent ton copain?

D. La construction: verbe + infinitif

Note the use of the infinitive in the following sentences.

J'aime **parler** français.   *I like to speak French. I like speaking French.*
Nous aimons **voyager**.   *We like to travel. We like traveling.*

Tu n'aimes pas **étudier**.   *You don't like to study. You don't like studying.*
Ils n'aiment pas **danser**.   *They don't like to dance. They don't like dancing.*

To express what they like and don't like to do, the French use these constructions:

SUBJECT + PRESENT TENSE + INFINITIVE . . . of **aimer**		SUBJECT + **n'** + PRESENT TENSE + **pas** + INFINITIVE . . . of **aimer**		
Nous	**aimons** **voyager**.	Nous	**n'aimons pas**	**voyager**.

⇒ Note that in this construction, the verb **aimer** may be affirmative or negative:

AFFIRMATIVE: Jacques **aime** voyager.   NEGATIVE: Philippe **n'aime pas** voyager.

⇒ The above construction is used in questions: Est-ce que Paul **aime voyager?**

OBSERVATION: The infinitive is also used after the following expressions:

Je préfère . . .	*I prefer . . .*	**Je préfère travailler.**
Je voudrais . . .	*I would like . . .*	**Je voudrais voyager.**
Je (ne) veux (pas) . . .	*I (don't) want . . .*	**Je veux jouer** au foot.
Est-ce que tu veux . . .	*Do you want . . .*	**Est-ce que tu veux danser?**
Je (ne) peux (pas) . . .	*I can (I can't) . . .*	**Je ne peux pas dîner** avec toi.
Je dois . . .	*I have to . . .*	**Je dois étudier.**

4 Dialogue

Ask your classmates if they like to do the following things.

▶ chanter?
—Est-ce que tu aimes chanter?
—Oui, j'aime chanter.   (Non, je n'aime pas chanter.)

1. étudier?	4. danser?	7. nager en hiver?
2. voyager?	5. parler français en classe?	8. travailler le week-
3. téléphoner?	6. nager en été?	end *(on weekends)*?

5 Une excellente raison *(An excellent reason)*

The following people are doing certain things. Say that they like these activities.

▶ Thomas voyage.   **Il aime voyager.**

1. Monique chante.	7. Lise et Rose jouent au frisbee.
2. Charles étudie la musique.	8. Éric et Denis écoutent la radio.
3. Henri téléphone.	9. Nous travaillons.
4. Isabelle organise une boum.	10. Nous parlons espagnol.
5. Marc et Sophie nagent.	11. Vous regardez la télé.
6. Annie et Vincent dansent.	12. Vous mangez.

▶▶▶▶▶▶▶▶▶▶▶▶▶▶▶▶▶▶▶▶▶▶▶▶▶

Prononciation

Les voyelles /i/ et /u/

/u/ **o**ù?   /i/ **i**c**i**!

The vowel sounds /i/ and /u/ are easy to say. Remember to pronounce the French "i" as in **Mimi** and not as in the English *him.*

Répétez:
/i/   **i**c**i**   Ph**i**l**i**ppe   **i**l
    Mim**i**   S**y**lv**i**e   v**i**s**i**te
Ph**i**l**i**ppe v**i**s**i**te Par**i**s avec S**y**lv**i**e.

/u/   **o**ù   n**ou**s   v**ou**s
    éc**ou**te   j**ou**e   t**ou**j**ou**rs

V**ou**s j**ou**ez au f**oo**t avec n**ou**s?

Section D

COMMUNICATIVE FUNCTION: Talking about what people like and don't like to do

 15.4 Dialogue: Jean-Paul à la boum (20:28–21:21 min.)

 Disc 3, Side1 26829–28439

 Leçon 15, Section 5

14 COMMUNICATION: discussing likes and dislikes

■ **Expansion:** In the event of an affirmative answer, a follow-up question could be asked with **bien** or **souvent.**
Est-ce que tu chantes bien?

15 PRACTICE: saying what people like to do

■ **Challenge:** Continue the response by inventing an activity that the person does not like to do.
Il aime voyager mais il n'aime pas parler anglais.

Prononciation

■ /i/ Spelled **i, y.**
Be sure students pronounce /i/ like "ee" of *beet* and not the "i" of *bit.*
■ /u/ Spelled **ou, où.**

Jean-Paul à la boum

- Divide the class into teams of four.
- Play the video or the cassette segment *Jean-Paul à la boum.*
- Replay the first scene and pause so that each team can write as many phrases from the conversation as they can remember. Do the same for the second scene.

- Then play both scenes once more so the teams can try to complete their texts.
- Distribute a copy of the video/cassette script to each team so that they can circle all the phrases they listed correctly. Play the scenes a final time for confirmation.

1 COMPREHENSION

1-d   3-e   5-c
2-b   4-a

🔲 Leçon 15, Section 7

2 GUIDED ORAL EXPRESSION

jouer au tennis
écouter la radio
nager
voyager
chanter
regarder la télé
étudier
travailler

🔲 Leçon 15, Section 7

Classroom Notes

À votre tour!

1 Allô!

Sophie is phoning some friends. Match her questions on the left with her friends' answers on the right.

1. Est-ce que Marc est canadien?
2. Est-ce que tu joues au tennis?
3. Ton frère est à la maison?
4. Ta mère est en vacances?
5. Tu invites Christine et Juliette à la boum?

a. Non, elle travaille.
b. Oui, mais pas très bien.
c. Bien sûr! Elles aiment beaucoup danser.
d. Oui, il habite à Montréal.
e. Non, il dîne au restaurant avec un copain.

2 Créa-dialogue

Find out how frequently your classmates do the following activities. They will respond using one of the expressions on the scale.

NON	OUI		
	un peu →	souvent →	beaucoup

— **Robert**, est-ce que tu **joues au tennis**?
— Non, je **ne joue pas au tennis**.
— Est-ce que tu **écoutes la radio**?
— Oui, j'**écoute souvent la radio**.

À votre tour

Depending on your goals and objectives, you may or may not wish to assign all of the activities in the **À votre tour** section.

 Cooperative practice

In Act. 2, 3, and 4, you may want to have students work together in trios, with two performing and one consulting the Answer Key and acting as monitor.

Qu'est-ce qu'ils font?

(What do they do?)

Look at what the following students have put in their lockers and say what they like to do.

Éric aime jouer au tennis.
Il aime aussi . . .

4 Message illustré

Marc wrote about certain activities, using pictures. On a separate sheet, write out his description replacing these pictures with the missing words.

À la maison, ma soeur Catherine à une copine. Mon frère Éric ♪ ♫. En général, nous à sept heures et demie. Après° le dîner, mes° parents ☐. Moi, j' ☐ pour la classe de français. En vacances, nous ☒. Je ～. Éric et Catherine ☒. Parfois° mes parents au restaurant.

Après *After* **mes** *my* **Parfois** *Sometimes*

Point de vue personnel

Select one of the following situations. On a separate sheet of paper, or on a computer, write two things you do and one thing you do not do in that situation. Use complete sentences.

À la maison, . . .

c mes (my) ains, . . .

En classe, je . . .

En vacances, . . .

Avec mes Parents, . . .

Leçon 15 **117**

3 COMPREHENSION

Éric aime jouer au tennis et parler (étudier le) français.
Hélène et Anne aiment danser et écouter la radio.
Nous aimons jouer au basket et parler espagnol.
Vous aimez jouer au foot et nager.

4 COMPREHENSION

téléphone
écoute la radio
dînons
regardent la télé
étudie
n'étudions pas
nage
jouent au tennis
dînent

■ **Challenge: De nouveaux messages** Have students, alone or in pairs, prepare their own **messages illustrés** (complete with an answer key on the back). Let them exchange their messages with each other. On a separate sheet of paper, have them replace the pictures with the missing words and check their answers using the answer key provided.

5 WRITTEN SELF-EXPRESSION

📁 Portfolio assessment

You will probably only select one speaking activity and one writing activity to go into the students' portfolios for Unit 4.

In this lesson, Act. 2 can be the basis of an oral portfolio recording.

(You may want to use the **Challenge** version of Act. 4 for the written portfolio.)

MODULE 16:
Une interview
Total time: 6:12 min.
(Counter: 22:27 min.)

16.1 Mini-scenes: Listening — Où est-ce qu'il va?
(23:17–24:44 min.)

16.2 Mini-scenes: Listening — Qu'est-ce que tu fais?
(24:45–25:29 min.)

16.3 Mini-scenes: Speaking — Questions
(25:30–26:13 min.)

16.4 Dialogue: Une interview
(26:14–27:02 min.)

16.5 Vignette culturelle: Le Sénégal
(27:03–28:33 min.)

 Disc 3, Side 1
30430–41569

■ **Comprehension practice:** Play the entire module through as an introduction to the lesson.

 16.5 Vignette culturelle: Le Sénégal
(27:03–28:33 min.

 Disc 3, Side 1
38684–41569

🌐 **Cross-cultural observation:** Have students in pairs make a list of similarities and differences between Sénégal and the United States.

 Leçon 16, Section 5 (optional)

Une interview

Nicolas is a reporter for *La Gazette des Étudiants,* the student newspaper. He has decided to write an article on the foreign students who attend his school. Today he is interviewing Fatou, a student from Senegal.

NICOLAS: Bonjour, Fatou. Est-ce que je peux <u>te poser quelques questions</u>? *ask you some questions*

FATOU: Oui, bien sûr.

NICOLAS: Tu es <u>sénégalaise</u>, n'est-ce pas? *Senegalese*

FATOU: Oui, je suis sénégalaise.

NICOLAS: Où est-ce que tu habites?

FATOU: Je suis de Dakar, mais maintenant j'habite à Paris avec ma famille.

NICOLAS: <u>Pourquoi</u> est-ce que vous habitez à Paris? *Why*

FATOU: <u>Parce que</u> ma mère travaille pour l'Unesco. *Because*

NICOLAS: Est-ce que tu aimes Paris?

FATOU: J'adore Paris.

NICOLAS: <u>Qu'est-ce que tu fais le weekend</u>? *What do you do on weekends?*

FATOU: Ça dépend! Je regarde la télé ou je joue au tennis avec <u>mes</u> copains. *That / my*

NICOLAS: Merci beaucoup, Fatou.

FATOU: C'est <u>tout</u>? *all*

NICOLAS: Oui, c'est tout!

■ NOTES ■
CULTURELLES

1 Le Sénégal

Senegal is a country in western Africa, whose capital is Dakar. Its population includes twelve different tribes, all speaking their own dialects. Because of the historical and cultural ties between Senegal and France, French has been adopted as the official language.

Most of the people of Senegal are Muslims. Some common names are **Awa** and **Fatou** (for girls), **Babacar** and **Mamadou** (for boys).

Setting the scene

Ask students how many African countries they can name. Write these on the board. Do they remember which of these countries use French as an official language? Circle these countries. (If necessary, have them turn back to the photo essay on pages 1–9.)

Locate these French-speaking countries on the map.

In particular, have students locate Senegal and its capital city Dakar. Tell them that in this chapter they will meet a student from Dakar.

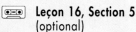

Note culturelle

 16.4 Dialogue: Une interview
(26:14–27:02 min.)

VIDEODISC Disc 3, Side 1
37224–38666

Leçon 16, Section 1

FATOU:	Bon. <u>Alors</u>, maintenant c'est mon <u>tour</u>! Est-ce que je peux te poser une question?	*So / turn*
NICOLAS:	Bien sûr!	
FATOU:	Qu'est-ce que tu fais samedi?	
NICOLAS:	Euh . . . <u>je ne sais pas</u>.	*I don't know*
FATOU:	Alors, est-ce que tu veux <u>aller</u> à un concert de musique africaine?	*to go*
NICOLAS:	Avec qui?	
FATOU:	Avec moi, bien sûr!	
NICOLAS:	D'accord! Où? <u>Quand</u>? Et à quelle heure?	*When*

2 L'Unesco

UNESCO (United Nations Educational Scientific and Cultural Organization) was founded in 1946 to promote international cooperation in education, science, and the arts. The organization has its headquarters in Paris and is staffed by people from all member countries.

● **Compréhension: Vrai ou faux?**
Read the following statements and say whether they are true (**C'est vrai!**) or false (**C'est faux!**).

1. Fatou est française.
2. Elle habite à Paris.
3. Le père de Fatou travaille pour l'Unesco.
4. Le weekend, Fatou aime jouer au tennis.
5. Nicolas invite Fatou à un concert.
6. Fatou accepte l'invitation.

Leçon 16 119

Photo culture note
Un café à Paris
On the table you can see:
• a ham and cheese sandwich (**un sandwich au jambon et au fromage**) made from half a loaf of French bread (**une baguette**).
• a plate of mixed vegetable salads (**des crudités**) including grated carrots (**des carottes râpées**) and beets (**des betteraves**).
In the background is a hotel (**un hôtel**). To the right is a confectionary (**une confiserie**) or shop specializing in home-made candies. The awning says **glacier**, indicating that the store makes its own ice cream.

 COMPREHENSION

1. C'est faux! Elle est sénégalaise.
2. C'est vrai!
3. C'est faux! La mère de Fatou travaille pour l'Unesco.
4. C'est vrai!
5. C'est faux! Fatou invite Nicolas (à un concert).
6. C'est faux! C'est Nicolas qui accepte l'invitation de Fatou.

Using the video

In this lesson, the opening text corresponds to the video interview. (This is why the student text has a photograph from the video rather than a cartoon montage.) However, the printed text is somewhat longer than the edited video/cassette version.

• First, have students follow in their books as you read the text aloud.
• Tell the class that the recorded version will not be exactly the same, and play it for them.
• Then play the video/cassette a second time. Have students find those sentences which are not in the recorded interview, and note those which have been modified.

A. Les questions d'information

The questions below ask for specific information and are called INFORMATION QUESTIONS. The INTERROGATIVE EXPRESSIONS in heavy print indicate what kind of information is requested.

—**Où** est-ce que tu habites?	***Where** do you live?*
—J'habite **à Nice.**	*I live **in Nice.***
—**À quelle heure** est-ce que vous dînez?	***At what time** do you eat dinner?*
—Nous dînons **à sept heures.**	*We eat **at seven.***

In French, information questions may be formed according to the pattern:

INTERROGATIVE EXPRESSION	+ **est-ce que**	+ SUBJECT	+ VERB . . . ?
À quelle heure	**est-ce que**	vous	travaillez?

➡ **Est-ce que** becomes **est-ce qu'** before a vowel sound.
　　Quand **est-ce qu'**Alice et Roger dînent?

➡ In information questions, your voice rises on the interrogative expression and then falls until the last syllable.

Quand est-ce que tu travailles?　　**À quelle heure** est-ce que vous dînez?

OBSERVATION: In casual conversation, French speakers frequently form information questions by placing the interrogative expression at the end of the sentence. The voice rises on the interrogative expression.

Vous habitez **où?**　　Vous dînez **à quelle heure?**

Vocabulaire: Expressions interrogatives

où	where?	**Où** est-ce que vous travaillez?
quand?	when?	**Quand** est-ce que ton copain organise une boum?
à quelle heure?	at what time?	**À quelle heure** est-ce que tu regardes la télé?
comment?	how?	**Comment** est-ce que tu chantes? Bien ou mal?
pourquoi?	why?	—**Pourquoi** est-ce que tu étudies le français?
parce que	because	—**Parce que** je veux voyager en France.

➡ **Parce que** becomes **parce qu'** before a vowel sound.
　　Juliette invite Olivier **parce qu'**il danse bien.

 ☀ Warm-up and review

PROP: Transparency 6 or clock with hands
　Review times by asking students at what time they do certain things. Then ask a classmate to show the corresponding time on the clock face.
Dis-moi, W, à quelle heure est-ce que tu dînes?

[Je dîne à six heures et quart.]
X, viens ici et montre-nous six heures et quart.
Y, à quelle heure est-ce que tu étudies? ...
Z, à quelle heure est-ce que tu écoutes la radio? ...

1 Le Club International

The president of the International Club wants to know where some of the members are from. The secretary tells her where each one lives.

▶ Sylvie (à Québec)

LA PRÉSIDENTE: **Où est-ce que Sylvie habite?**

LE SECRÉTAIRE: **Elle habite à Québec.**

1. Jacques (à Montréal)
2. Awa (à Dakar)
3. Marc et Frédéric (à Toulouse)
4. Jean-Pierre (à Genève)
5. Sophie et Michèle (à Nice)
6. Isabelle (à Paris)

2 Curiosité

At a party in Paris, Nicolas meets Béatrice, a Canadian student. He wants to know more about her. Play both roles.

▶ où / habiter? (à Québec)

NICOLAS: **Où est-ce que tu habites?**

BÉATRICE: **J'habite à Québec.**

1. où/étudier? (à Montréal)
2. où/travailler? (dans [*in*] une pharmacie)
3. quand/parler français? (toujours)
4. quand/parler anglais? (souvent)
5. comment/jouer au tennis? (bien)
6. comment/danser? (très bien)
7. pourquoi/être en France? (parce que j'aime voyager)
8. pourquoi/être à Paris? (parce que j'ai [*I have*] un copain ici)

Expression pour la conversation

How to express surprise or mild doubt:

Ah bon? *Oh? Really?* —Stéphanie organise une soirée.
                            —**Ah bon?** Quand?

---

3 Au téléphone

When Philippe phones his cousin Michèle, he likes to tell her what his plans are. She asks him a few questions. Play both roles.

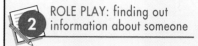

J'organise une soirée.

Samedi.

Ah bon? Quand est-ce que tu organises une soirée?

▶ organiser une soirée (quand? samedi)

1. organiser un pique-nique (quand? dimanche)
2. dîner avec Pauline (quand? lundi)
3. dîner avec Caroline (où? au restaurant Belcour)
4. regarder «Batman» (à quelle heure? à 9 heures)
5. jouer au tennis (quand? demain)
6. inviter Brigitte (où? à un concert)
7. parler espagnol (comment? assez bien)
8. étudier l'italien (pourquoi? je veux voyager en Italie)

4 Questions personnelles

1. Où est-ce que tu habites? *(name of your city)*
2. Où est-ce que tu étudies? *(name of your school)*
3. À quelle heure est-ce que tu dînes?
4. À quelle heure est-ce que tu regardes la télé?
5. Quand est-ce que tu nages?
6. Quand est-ce que tu joues au tennis? (en mai? en juillet?)
7. Comment est-ce que tu chantes? (bien? très bien? mal?)
8. Comment est-ce que tu nages?

Leçon 16 121

1 ROLE PLAY: discussing where people live

■ **Pronunciation:** Note that the "t" is not pronounced in **Montréal** since it is considered as the final consonant of a word: **Mont Réal** (*Mount Royal*).

2 ROLE PLAY: finding out information about someone

3 ROLE PLAY: asking for information

4 COMMUNICATION: answering personal questions

■ **Variation** (written self-expression):
Have students describe themselves by answering the questions in writing. They may vary the sequence of their answers and add additional information for extra credit.

Cooperative pair practice
Activities 1, 2, 3

T121

■ **Language note:** Unlike their English equivalents, the two words in expressions like **à qui** and **avec qui** cannot be separated.
Avec qui est-ce que tu travailles?
Who(m) do you work with?

■ **Casual speech:** In casual conversation, the entire interrogative expression may go to the end of the sentence:
Tu travailles avec qui?

■ **Language note:** In French as in English, the verb in **qui** questions is singular even if the expected answer is plural.
– **Qui joue au tennis?**
(Who is playing tennis?)
– **Paul et Monique.**

5 ROLE PLAY: finding out information about others

■ **Variation:** Use casual speech.
– **Alice dîne.**
– **Ah bon? Elle dîne avec qui?**
– **Avec une copine.**

6 COMMUNICATION: taking a survey

■ **Pronunciation:** clips /klips/

Note: **un clip** is a music video.

B. Les expressions interrogatives avec *qui*

To ask about PEOPLE, French speakers use the following interrogative expressions:

qui?	who(m)?	**Qui** est-ce que tu invites au concert?
à qui?	to who(m)?	**À qui** est-ce que tu téléphones?
de qui?	about who(m)?	**De qui** est-ce que vous parlez?
avec qui?	with who(m)?	**Avec qui** est-ce que Pierre étudie?
pour qui?	for who(m)?	**Pour qui** est-ce que Laure organise la boum?

To ask _who is doing something_, French speakers use the construction:

qui + VERB . . . ?	
Qui habite ici?	**Who** lives here?
Qui organise la boum?	**Who** is organizing the party?

5 **Précisions** *(Details)*
Anne is telling Hélène what certain people are doing. She asks for more details. Play both roles.

▶ Alice dîne. (avec qui? avec une copine)

1. Jean-Pierre téléphone. (à qui? à Sylvie)
2. Frédéric étudie. (avec qui? avec un copain)
3. Madame Masson parle. (à qui? à Madame Bonnot)
4. Monsieur Lambert travaille. (avec qui? avec Monsieur Dumont)
5. Juliette danse. (avec qui? avec Georges)
6. François parle à Michèle. (de qui? de toi)

Alice dîne.

Ah bon? Avec qui est-ce qu'elle dîne?

Elle dîne avec une copine.

6 **Un sondage** *(A poll)*
Take a survey to find out how your classmates spend their free time. Ask who does the following things.

▶ écouter la radio
Qui écoute la radio?

1. voyager souvent
2. aimer chanter
3. nager
4. aimer danser
5. regarder la télé
6. jouer au tennis
7. jouer au foot
8. travailler
9. regarder les clips *(music videos)*
10. parler italien
11. étudier beaucoup
12. visiter souvent New York

Cooperative pair practice
Activities 5, 7, 8

Game: Getting acquainted

On a separate sheet of paper, have each student copy the model and 12 cues of Act. 6.
 Students then move around asking classmates one by one if they do an activity on the list.

Annie: **Marc, est-ce que tu nages?**
Marc: **Oui, je nage.**
Annie writes Marc's name next to **nager**.
If Marc says no, Annie asks someone else.
 The first person to complete his/her sheet with 13 different names is the winner.

7 Questions

Prepare short dialogues with your classmates, using the information in the illustrations.

où?

à la maison

▶ —Où est-ce que tu dînes?
—Je dîne à la maison.

1. à quelle heure?

à 8 heures

2. quand?

en septembre

3. comment?

BONJOUR!

très bien

4. avec qui?

avec Denise

5. à qui?

à mon cousin

6. de qui?

BLA BLA BLA...

de toi

7. pour qui?

pour M. Lambert

C. Qu'est-ce que?

Note the use of the interrogative expression **qu'est-ce que** *(what)* in the questions below.

Qu'est-ce que tu regardes?   Je regarde un match de tennis.
Qu'est-ce qu'Alice mange?   Elle mange une pizza.

To ask *what* people are doing, the French use the following construction:

qu'est-ce que + SUBJECT + VERB + . . . ?	**Qu'est-ce que** tu fais?
↓	
qu'est-ce qu' (+ VOWEL SOUND)	**Qu'est-ce qu'**elle fait?

8 La Boutique-Musique

People in Column A are at the Boutique-Musique, a local music shop. Use a verb from Column B to ask what they are listening to or looking at. A classmate will answer you, using an item from Column C.

A	B	C
tu	écouter?	une guitare
vous	regarder?	un poster
Alice		un compact (CD) de jazz
Éric		une cassette de rock
Antoine et Claire		un album de Paul Simon

Qu'est-ce qu'Éric écoute?

Il écoute un album de Paul Simon.

Leçon 16   123

7 EXCHANGES: asking and answering questions

1. ... regardes la télé?
2. ... visites Paris?
3. ... parles français?
4. ... joues au tennis?
5. ... téléphones?
6. ... parles?
7. ... travailles?

■ **Expansion:** Have students make up their own answers to the questions.
– Où est-ce que tu dînes?
– Je dîne <u>au restaurant</u>. (etc.)

Section C

COMMUNICATIVE FUNCTION:
Asking what people are doing

■ **Casual speech:** Note how **quoi** is used instead of **qu'est-ce que** in casual questions.
Tu regardes quoi?
Alice mange quoi?

▢ **16.2 Mini-scenes:**
Qu'est-ce que tu fais?
16.2 Mini-scenes:
Questions
(24:45–26:13 min.)

VIDEODISC   Disc 3, Side1
34565–37198

▭ Leçon 16, Sections 3, 4

8 EXCHANGES: asking and answering questions

■ **Variation: Un jeu.** Have teams of students see how many correct dialogues they can write in five minutes.

■ **Teaching strategy:** Ask students what other irregular verb they have learned (**être**). Have them point out the similarities between **être** and **faire**: singular forms end in **-s, -s, -t; vous-**form ends in **-tes; ils-**form ends in **-ont.**

■ **Practice drill:** Have students practice sentences with **faire.**
Je fais une pizza.
(Tu) Tu fais une pizza. etc.
Qu'est-ce que je fais?
(Vous) Qu'est-ce que vous faites? etc.

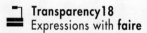
Transparency18
Expressions with **faire**

Supplementary vocabulary

faire un pique-nique
to have a picnic
faire un tour
to go for a short walk or ride
Note: **faire une promenade** may also mean *to go for a ride:* **faire une promenade à vélo, en voiture.** (This is re-entered in Lesson 22.)

↺ **Review:** Remind students that **faire** is used in many weather expressions.
Il fait beau. Il fait mauvais.

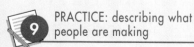
PRACTICE: describing what people are making

1. faisons	4. font	7. font
2. fais	5. fait	8. font
3. faites	6. fait	

COMPREHENSION: describing what people are doing

D. Le verbe *faire*

Faire *(to do, make)* is one of the most useful French verbs. It is an IRREGULAR verb since it does not follow a predictable pattern. Note the forms of **faire** in the present tense.

faire *(to do, make)*	
je **fais**	Je **fais** un sandwich.
tu **fais**	Qu'est-ce que tu **fais** maintenant?
il/elle **fait**	Qu'est-ce que ton copain **fait** samedi?
nous **faisons**	Nous **faisons** une pizza.
vous **faites**	Qu'est-ce que vous **faites** ici?
ils/elles **font**	Qu'est-ce qu'elles **font** pour la boum?

Vocabulaire: Expressions avec *faire*

faire un match	*to play a game (match)*	Mes cousins **font un match** de tennis.
faire une promenade	*to go for a walk*	Caroline **fait une promenade** avec Olivier.
faire un voyage	*to take a trip*	Ma copine **fait un voyage** en France.
faire attention	*to pay attention*	Est-ce que tu **fais attention** quand le professeur parle?

9 **La boum de Juliette**

Juliette's friends are helping her prepare food for a party. Use the verb **faire** to say what everyone is doing.

▶ Je . . . une crêpe.

Je fais une crêpe.

1. Nous . . . une salade.
2. Tu . . . une salade de fruits.
3. Vous . . . une tarte *(pie)*.
4. Cécile et Marina . . . un gâteau *(cake)*.
5. Christine . . . une pizza.
6. Marc . . . un sandwich.
7. Patrick et Thomas . . . une omelette.
8. Pierre et Karine . . . une quiche.

10 **Qu'est-ce qu'ils font?**

Read the descriptions below and say what the people are doing. Use the verb **faire** and an expression from the list below. Be logical.

un voyage   une promenade   une pizza   un match   attention

▶ Madame Dumont est en Chine.
Elle fait un voyage.

1. Nicolas travaille dans *(in)* un restaurant.
2. Nous sommes en ville.
3. Hélène et Jean-Paul jouent au tennis.
4. Je suis dans la cuisine *(kitchen)*.
5. Marc est dans le train Paris–Nice.
6. Vous jouez au volley.
7. Je suis dans le parc.
8. Monsieur Lambert visite Tokyo.
9. Nous écoutons le prof.

E. L'interrogation avec inversion

Section E

COMMUNICATIVE FUNCTION:
Asking questions

> ### Learning about language
>
> In conversational French, questions are usually formed with **est-ce que.** However, when the subject of the sentence is a pronoun, French speakers often use INVERSION, that is, they invert or reverse the order of the subject pronoun and the verb.
>
> REGULAR ORDER: **Vous parlez** français.   INVERSION: **Parlez-vous** anglais?
>   SUBJECT   VERB   VERB   SUBJECT

■ **Teaching note:** Inversion is taught mainly for recognition here. It is not emphasized in Book One.

Look at the two sets of questions below. They both ask the same thing. Compare the position of the subject pronouns in heavy print.

Est-ce que **tu** parles anglais?	Parles-**tu** anglais?	*Do you speak English?*
Est-ce que **vous** habitez ici?	Habitez-**vous** ici?	*Do you live here?*
Où est-ce que **nous** dînons?	Où dînons-**nous?**	*Where are we having dinner?*
Où est-ce qu'**il** est?	Où est-**il?**	*Where is he?*

Inverted questions are formed according to the patterns:

YES / NO	VERB / SUBJECT PRONOUN . . . ?	
QUESTION	**Voyagez-vous**	souvent?

INFORMATION	INTERROGATIVE EXPRESSION + VERB / SUBJECT PRONOUN . . . ?		
QUESTION	**Avec qui**	**travaillez-vous**	demain?

➡ In inversion, the verb and the subject pronoun are connected by a hyphen.

OBSERVATION: In inversion, liaison is required before **il/elle** and **ils/elles.** If a verb in the singular ends on a vowel, the letter "**t**" is inserted between the verb and the subject pronoun so that liaison can occur:

Où travaille-**t**-il?	Où travaille-**t**-elle?
Avec qui dîne-**t**-il?	Avec qui dîne-**t**-elle?

11 Conversation

Get better acquainted with your classmates by asking them a few questions. Use inversion.

▶ où / habiter? —Où habites-tu?
              —J'habite à (Boston).

1. à quelle heure / dîner?
2. à quelle heure / regarder la télé?
3. avec qui / parler français?
4. à qui / téléphoner souvent?
5. comment / nager?
6. avec qui / étudier?

▶ ▶ ▶ ▶ ▶ ▶ ▶ ▶ ▶ ▶ ▶ ▶ ▶ ▶ ▶ ▶ ▶ ▶ ▶ ▶

Prononciation   /y/

La voyelle /y/

The vowel sound /y/ – represented by the letter "**u**" – does not exist in English. Here is a helpful trick for producing this new sound.

Super!

First say the French word **si.** Then round your lips as if to whistle and say **si** with rounded lips: /sy/. Now say **si-per.** Then round your lips as you say the first syllable: **super!**

Répétez: /y/   **super   tu   étudie   bien sûr
                  Lucie   Luc
                  Tu étudies avec Lucie.**

11 COMMUNICATION:
getting acquainted

■ **Additional practice:** To practice inversion with **il/elle,** have the students redo Act. 5, p. 122 using inversion instead of **est-ce que.**
– Alice dîne.
– Ah bon? Avec qui dîne-t-elle?
– Elle dîne avec une copine.

Prononciation

🔲 Leçon 16, Section 6

■ **Teaching strategy:** If students have trouble producing /y/, have them pronounce the sound as /i/. They should not pronounce it as /u/.

1 COMPREHENSION

1-d 3-a 5-b
2-e 4-c 6-f

[cassette] Leçon 16, Section 7

2 COMPREHENSION

1. Où est-ce que tu habites?
2. À quelle heure est-ce que tu dînes?
3. Où est-ce que tu dînes/ vous dînez?
4. Qu'est-ce que tu manges?
5. Qu'est-ce que tu regardes?
6. Qui est-ce que tu invites?

Classroom Notes

À votre tour!

1 Allô!

Awa is phoning some friends. Match her questions on the left with her friends' answers on the right.

1. Qu'est-ce que tu fais?
2. Qu'est-ce que vous faites samedi?
3. Où est ton père?
4. Quand est-ce que tu veux jouer au tennis avec moi?
5. Qui est-ce que tu invites au cinéma?
6. Pourquoi est-ce que tu étudies l'anglais?

a. Il fait une promenade.
b. Ma cousine Alice.
c. Dimanche. D'accord?
d. J'étudie.
e. Nous faisons un match de tennis.
f. Parce que je voudrais habiter à New York.

2 Les questions

The following people are answering questions. Read what they say and figure out what questions they were asked.

Je chante très mal.

▶ Comment est-ce que tu chantes?

1. J'habite à Québec.
2. Je dîne à sept heures.
3. Nous dînons à l'Hippopotame.
4. Je mange une pizza.
5. Je regarde un film.
6. J'invite Catherine.

126 Unité 4

À votre tour

Depending on your goals and objectives, you may or may not wish to assign all of the activities in the **À votre tour** section.

👥 Cooperative practice

Act. 1–4 lend themselves to cooperative pair practice.

3 Créa-dialogue

Ask your classmates what they do on different days of the week. Carry out conversations similar to the model. Note: "??" means you can invent your own answers.

▶ —Qu'est-ce que tu fais <u>lundi</u>?
—Je <u>joue au tennis</u>.
—Ah bon? À quelle heure est-ce que tu <u>joues</u>?
—<u>À deux heures</u>.
—Et avec qui?
—Avec <u>Anne-Marie</u>.

GUIDED ORAL EXPRESSION

📼 Leçon 16, Section 8

	lundi	mardi	mercredi	jeudi	vendredi	samedi	dimanche
ACTIVITÉ	🎾	📝	〰️	🧹	🏀	??	??
À QUELLE HEURE?	2 heures	6 heures	??	??	??	??	??
AVEC QUI?	avec Anne-Marie	avec un copain	??	??	??	??	??

4 Faisons connaissance!

(Let's get acquainted!)

Get better acquainted with a classmate that you don't know very well. Ask questions in French. For instance:

- Where does he/she live?
- Does he/she study much at home?
- Does he/she speak French at home? (with whom?)
- Does he/she watch TV? (at what time?)
- Does he/she like to phone? (whom? [**à qui?**])

5 Interview

A famous rock star is visiting the United States. You are going to interview her for your school paper (perhaps even on the Internet!). Write out five questions you would want to ask the singer, addressing her as **vous**. For example, you may want to know . . .

- where she is singing
- why she is visiting your city
- how she is traveling
- how (well) she speaks English

4 GUIDED CONVERSATION

- Où est-ce que tu habites? (Où habites-tu?)
- Est-ce que tu étudies beaucoup à la maison? (Étudies-tu beaucoup à la maison?)
- Est-ce que tu parles français à la maison? (Parles-tu français à la maison?) (Avec qui?)
- Est-ce que tu regardes la télé? (Regardes-tu la télé?)
- Est-ce que tu aimes téléphoner? (Aimes-tu téléphoner?) (À qui?)

6 Curiosité

Imagine that a French friend has just made the following statements. For each one, write down three or four related questions you could ask him or her.

• Avec qui est-ce que tu joues?
• Où est-ce que vous jouez?
• À quelle heure est-ce que vous jouez?
• Pourquoi est-ce que vous jouez au foot?

Je joue au foot demain.

Je joue au tennis.

Je dîne avec un copain.

Je fais une promenade.

J'organise une soirée.

WRITTEN SELF-EXPRESSION

WRITTEN SELF-EXPRESSION

Leçon 16 127

📁 Portfolio assessment

You will probably only select one speaking activity and one writing activity to go into the students' portfolios for Unit 4.

In this lesson, Act. 3 and 4 are good oral portfolio conversation topics.

Entracte 4

Vive la différence!
Les activités quotidiennes

Nous sommes américains, français, anglais, canadiens . . . Nos° cultures ont° beaucoup de points communs, mais elles ne sont pas identiques.

Parlons° de la vie quotidienne.° Nous faisons les mêmes choses,° mais souvent nous faisons ces° choses un peu différemment.° Voici plusieurs° questions. Répondez° à ces questions. À votre avis,° quelles° sont les réponses des jeunes Français?°

1 Quel jour de la semaine est-ce que vous préférez?
- le lundi
- le vendredi
- le samedi
- le dimanche

Et les Français, quel jour est-ce qu'ils préfèrent?

3 Voici quatre sports. Quel sport est-ce que vous pratiquez le plus?°
- Je nage.
- Je joue au basket.
- Je fais du jogging.
- Je joue au football.

Et les jeunes Français, quel sport est-ce qu'ils pratiquent le plus?

5 En moyenne,° combien d'heures° par jour° est-ce que vous regardez la télé?
- une heure
- deux heures
- trois heures
- quatre heures ou plus°

Et les jeunes Français? Combien d'heures par jour est-ce qu'ils regardent la télé?

2 Pendant° la semaine, qu'est-ce que vous préférez faire quand vous n'étudiez pas?
- Je préfère regarder la télé.
- Je préfère lire.°
- Je préfère jouer au basket.
- Je préfère téléphoner à mes° copains.

Et les jeunes Français, qu'est-ce qu'ils préfèrent faire?

4 À quelle heure est-ce que vous dînez en général?
- entre° cinq heures et demie et six heures
- entre six heures et sept heures
- entre sept heures et huit heures
- après huit heures

Et les Français, à quelle heure est-ce qu'ils dînent?

6 Qu'est-ce que vous préférez regarder à la télé?
- les sports
- les films
- la publicité°
- les feuilletons°

Et les jeunes Français, qu'est-ce qu'ils préfèrent regarder?

> ***Et les Français?***
> 1. Ils préfèrent le samedi. 2. Ils préfèrent regarder la télé. 3. Ils jouent au football. 4. Ils dînent entre sept heures et huit heures. 5. Ils regardent la télé deux heures par jour. 6. Ils préfèrent regarder les films.

Nos *Our* **ont** *have* **Parlons** *Let's talk* **vie quotidienne** *daily life* **mêmes choses** *same things* **ces** *these* **différemment** *differently* **plusieurs** *several* **Répondez** *Answer* **À votre avis** *In your opinion* **quelles** *what* **jeunes Français** *young French people* **Pendant** *During* **lire** *to read* **mes** *my* **le plus** *the most* **entre** *between* **En moyenne** *On the average* **combien d'heures** *how many hours* **par jour** *per day* **plus** *more* **publicité** *commercials* **feuilletons** *series*

EN FRANCE

À la télé, ce weekend

In France, TV viewers have a choice of seven main channels: **TF1**, **France 2**, **France 3**, **Arte**, **La Cinq**, **M6**, and **Canal Plus**. (People who want to watch **Canal Plus** need to have a special decoding machine for which they pay a monthly fee.)

Note that in TV listings, times are expressed using a 24-hour clock. In this system, 8 P.M. is **20.00 (vingt heures)**; 10 P.M. is **22.00 (vingt-deux heures)**.

Imagine that you are spending a month in Paris with a French family. This Friday and Saturday you have decided to stay home and watch TV. Look at the program listings at the right.

Which programs would you like to watch on Friday? When do they start?

Which programs would you choose on Saturday evening? When do they start?

Your French hosts are soccer fans. What program would they want to watch and when? Which teams are playing? (Locate these cities on the map of France.)

What program is featured on **France 2** on Saturday evening? Who are the guests on this program? Do you know any of them?

How many different movies are being shown over the weekend? How many of these movies are American? Which movie would you choose to see? At what time and on which channel?

You are interested in watching a French TV series. Which program would you select? On which channel? According to its title, what kind of a series do you think it is?

SÉLECTION DE LA SEMAINE

	VEN	SAM
TF 1	**20.30** VARIÉTÉS **SALUT L'ARTISTE** Émission présentée par Yves Noël et Ophélie Winter **22.05** DOCUMENT **HISTOIRES NATURELLES**	**20.35** SPECTACLE **HOLIDAY ON ICE** Mis en scène par Jérôme Savary **22.10** SÉRIE **DANS LA CHALEUR DE LA NUIT**
2 France	**20.35** SÉRIE **HÔTEL DE POLICE LE GENTIL MONSIEUR** de Claude Barrois avec Cécile Magnet **23.20** FILM **ALICE DANS LES VILLES** de Wim Wenders	**20.40** VARIÉTÉS **CHAMPS-ÉLYSÉES** Invités: Ricky Martin, Juliette Binoche, Ben Affleck **22.25** SÉRIE **MÉDECINS DE NUIT**
3 France	**21.30** SÉRIE **LE MASQUE MADEMOISELLE EVELYNE** de Jean-Louis Fournier **23.45** CONCERT **MUSIQUES, MUSIQUE**	**20.35** JEUNESSE **SAMDYNAMITE** DESSINS ANIMÉS Série : **BATMAN** **22.25** ENTRETIEN **LE DIVAN** Pierre Dumayet
arte	**20.15** DOCUMENTAIRE **Cent ans de cinéma japonais** **23.20** MAGAZINE **Une vidéo inédite** de Lara Fabian	**20.40** SÉRIE **Comédie visuelle** **21.45** DOCUMENTAIRE **Le monde des animaux**
M6	**20.30** FILM TV **LE CINQUIÈME ÉLÉMENT** de Luc Besson avec Bruce Willis, Milla Jovovich **22.05** THÉÂTRE **LE SEXE FAIBLE**	**20.35** FILM TV **L'ÉCLOSION DES MONSTRES** de J. Piquer Simon avec Yan Sera **22.20** SÉRIE **LE COMTE DE MONTE-CRISTO**
CANAL+	**20.30** FOOTBALL **CAEN - TOULOUSE** Championnat de France 28ᵉ journée **22.40** FILM **MALCOM X** de Spike Lee	**20.30** FILM **ALIENS, LE RETOUR** de James Cameron avec Sigourney Weaver **22.45** FILM **UNE NUIT À L'ASSEMBLÉE NATIONALE** de Jean-Pierre Mocky

Entracte 4 ⟨129⟩

Pre-reading

Ask pairs of students to name their favorite TV programs.

Quelle est votre émission favorite? Nous aimons [Jeopardy].

Group reading activity

Divide the class into groups of 4 or 5. Each group must decide on which early and which late show they will watch each night. Then they report their decision to the class.

Vendredi nous allons regarder ... et ...
Samedi nous allons regarder ... et ...

Entre amis: Bonjour, Patrick!

Qu'est-ce que vous aimez faire? Dans° une lettre, Patrick répond° à cette question. Voici la lettre de Patrick.

Bonjour!
Je m'appelle Patrick Lacaze. J'ai 14 ans. J'habite à Tours avec ma famille. Je suis élève° de troisième.° J'étudie beaucoup, mais je n'étudie pas tout le temps.° Voici ce que° j'aime faire.

J'aime les boums parce que j'adore danser.

J'aime la musique. J'aime surtout° le rock. J'aimerais° jouer de la guitare, mais je ne sais pas.°

J'aime les sports. En hiver je skie et en été je nage et je joue au tennis. (Je ne suis pas un champion, mais je joue assez° bien.) J'aime jouer au basket, mais je préfère jouer au foot. (J'aime jouer au babyfoot, mais ce n'est pas un sport.) J'aime faire des promenades à vélo° le weekend avec mes copains.

J'aime mon école.° J'aime surtout l'anglais parce que le prof est sympa.° (Il s'appelle Mr. Ross, mais il est très gentil.°) Je n'aime pas trop° les maths.

À la maison, j'aime regarder la télé. J'adore les séries américaines! J'aime aussi écouter mes cassettes.

J'aime téléphoner à ma copine, mais je ne téléphone pas souvent. (Mon père n'aime pas ça.°)

J'aime jouer aux jeux° vidéo!
Et vous, qu'est-ce que vous aimez faire? Répondez-moi° vite.°

Amicalement,°
Patrick Lacaze

Dans *In* **répond** *answers* **élève** *student* **troisième** *ninth grade* **tout le temps** *all the time* **ce que** *what* **surtout** *especially* **aimerais** *would like* **je ne sais pas** *I don't know how* **assez** *rather* **promenades à vélo** *bike rides* **école** *school* **sympa** *nice* **gentil** *nice* **trop** *too much* **ça** *that* **jeux** *games* **Répondez-moi** *Answer me* **vite** *quickly* **Amicalement** *Cordially (In friendship)*

■ NOTES ■ CULTURELLES

1 Tours

Tours is an attractive city located about 150 miles southwest of Paris. It is the capital of Touraine, an area of France known for its beautiful castles.

2 Le babyfoot

Babyfoot is a tabletop soccer game in which two teams of two people each try to score goals by manipulating rows of toy players. **Babyfoot** is very popular among French teenagers, who play it in cafés or in youth clubs.

OBJECTIVE:
• Reading a longer text

■ Language notes
• Patrick writes in a casual style. Point out the shortened words:
un prof (professeur)
sympa (sympathique)
• When pronounced the French way, "Ross" sounds like **rosse** which is slang for *nasty.*

■ Questions sur le texte
1. Pourquoi est-ce que Patrick aime les boums?
2. Quelle sorte de musique est-ce qu'il aime?
3. Quels sports est-ce qu'il pratique en hiver? Et en été?
4. Comment est-ce qu'il joue au tennis?
5. Pourquoi est-ce qu'il aime l'anglais?
6. Qu'est-ce qu'il aime regarder à la télé?
7. À qui est-ce qu'il téléphone?
8. Pourquoi est-ce qu'il ne téléphone pas souvent?

■ Questions personnelles
1. Est-ce que tu aimes la musique? Quelle sorte de musique est-ce que tu aimes écouter?
2. Est-ce que tu joues d'un instrument?
3. Quels sports est-ce que tu pratiques en hiver? en été?
4. Est-ce que tu aimes ton école? Quels sujets est-ce que tu aimes? Quels sujets est-ce que tu n'aimes pas?
5. Est-ce que tu aimes étudier le français? (Pourquoi ou pourquoi pas?)
6. Est-ce que tu téléphones souvent? À qui? Est-ce que tu aimes téléphoner?

📖 Pre-reading
Ask if any of the students in the class have penpals.
   Est-ce que vous avez un correspondant ou une correspondante?
   Où habite votre correspondant(e)?
Tell them this is a letter from a French penpal.

Comment lire *(Reading hints)*
GETTING THE MEANING

When you read French, try to understand the meaning. Don't look for a word-for-word English translation for each sentence.

- Sometimes the two languages use different constructions.

  Je m'appelle . . .   *(I call myself . . .)*   *My name is . . .*

- Sometimes French uses some words that English leaves out.

  J'aime <u>le</u> rock.   *I love rock.*
  J'aime jouer <u>de</u> la guitare.   *I like to play the guitar.*

- And sometimes French leaves out words that English uses.

  Je suis élève de troisième.   *I am <u>a</u> student in ninth <u>grade</u>.*

- Word order may also be different.

  des promenades à vélo   *bike rides*

Enrichissez votre vocabulaire
COGNATES

You have already discovered that there are many words in French that look like English words and have similar meanings. These are called COGNATES. Cognates let you increase your vocabulary effortlessly. But be sure to pronounce them the French way!

- Sometimes the spelling is the same, or almost the same.

  la radio   *radio*
  un champion   *champion*

- Sometimes the spelling is a little different.

  américain   *American*

Activité
Read the letter from Patrick again and find five more French-English cognates.

Activité: Une lettre à Patrick
You are writing a letter to Patrick in which you introduce yourself and explain what you like to do. You may tell him:

- if you like music (and what kind)
- what sports you like to do in fall or winter
- what sports you like to do in spring or summer
- what you like to do at home
- whether or not you like French and math
- what you like to do on weekends
- what programs you like to watch on TV

> You may start your letter with the words:
> **Mon cher Patrick,**
> *(My dear Patrick)*
> and end it with:
> **Amicalement,**

Mon cher Patrick,

Amicalement,

■ **Additional cognates:**
adore
la musique
le rock
la guitare
les sports
le tennis
le weekend
les séries
mes cassettes
les maths...

Entracte 4   **131**

■ NOTE ■ CULTURELLE

Internet / CD-ROMs

Like young Americans, French teens are also interested in CD-ROMs and the internet. More and more teens are using **le Net** for all sorts of purposes: to look up phone numbers and addresses, to make ticket reservations (for concerts, movies, travel, etc.), and to meet and chat with international friends about school, sports, music, and just about everything else!

Le Net is becoming an exciting place for **les internautes:** there are cafés in Paris and many other cities and towns where you can **naviguer** or **netsurfer** while having lunch!

Le Minitel

Many teens still use France's popular online information service, **le Minitel.** The **Minitel** is a small computer terminal connected to the telephone. The most popular service is the **annuaire électronique** *(computerized phone directory).*

The **Minitel** has lots to offer. You can check plane and train schedules, reserve theater tickets, and send electronic messages. You can play all sorts of games. You can even win prizes like a pair of movie tickets or a trip abroad!

But there is a catch! Although the **Minitel** terminals are distributed free of charge, users are billed each month according to the services used and time spent online. Because **Minitel** use can be expensive, French parents insist on limiting its use.

Le Louvre Fr CD #06831
50 euros

Napoléon, l'Europe et l'Empire Fr CD
48 euros

L'album des arts et métiers Fr CD #06829
44 euros

  UNITÉ 4 INTERNET PROJECTS

Variétés

Cinq portraits

Cinq jeunes parlent de ce qu'ils font,° mais ils ne révèlent pas leur° identité. Est-ce que vous pouvez° identifier chacun?° Lisez° les paragraphes suivants° et faites correspondre° chaque° paragraphe à une photo.

Moussa Dembila
Abidjan, Côte d'Ivoire

1 Je ne suis pas français, mais je parle français. Je parle anglais aussi, mais je préfère parler français. J'aime les sports. Je joue au volley et au basket, mais mon sport préféré° est le hockey. Je m'appelle . . .

2 Je suis française, mais je n'habite pas à Paris. J'habite dans une île tropicale. Au lycée, j'étudie beaucoup. Mon sujet préféré est la biologie. (Je voudrais être médecin.°) J'aime la musique. J'aime beaucoup le reggae et j'adore chanter. J'aime les sports. Je nage souvent. Là où j'habite je peux nager en toute saison.° Je m'appelle . . .

3 Je n'habite pas à Paris. J'habite dans° une grande° ville° à 600 kilomètres de Paris. Je suis élève° dans un lycée. J'étudie beaucoup. Mes sujets préférés sont l'espagnol, la gymnastique, le français et la musique. J'aime beaucoup le jazz et le rock. J'adore danser. Je m'appelle . . .

4 Je n'habite pas en France, mais un jour je voudrais étudier à Paris. J'habite en Afrique. Je suis élève au Collège Moderne du Plateau. J'étudie l'anglais, les maths et la physique. Mon ambition est d'être architecte. Je m'appelle . . .

5 J'habite dans un petit° pays° européen. Dans mon pays les gens° parlent des langues différentes. Moi, je parle français. En classe j'étudie l'anglais et l'allemand.° J'aime voyager. Je voudrais visiter le Canada. Ma cousine Christine habite là-bas. Je m'appelle . . .

Catherine Miguel
Bordeaux, France

Laurent Arnold
Genève, Suisse

Isabelle Lamy
Trois Îlets, Martinique

Denis Lévêque
Montréal, Québec

ce qu'ils font *what they do* **leur** *their* **pouvez** *can* **chacun** *each one* **Lisez** *Read* **suivants** *following* **faites correspondre** *match* **chaque** *each* **préféré** *favorite* **médecin** *doctor* **en toute saison** *all year round (in any season)* **dans** *in* **grande** *large* **ville** *city* **élève** *student* **petit** *small* **pays** *country* **gens** *people* **allemand** *German*

OBJECTIVES:
• Reading at the paragraph level
• Developing logical thinking

UNITÉ 4 INTERNET PROJECT

American students will find that young French people have most of the same interests as they do. Have them investigate websites for French pop culture. To expand this activity, have students generate new links by using the search engine of their choice and the keywords "loisirs", "television + France"; "radio + French."

Loisirs (general)
http://www.europeonline.com/ fra/index.htm

ALTERNATE
Céline Dion
http://www.aloa.com/celine/ celine.html

Game: Cooperative pair reading

Be sure all students have their books closed. Divide the class into pairs. Each pair prepares a sheet of paper with the numbers 1 to 5.
Prenez une feuille de papier et écrivez les numéros 1, 2, 3, 4, 5.
When you give the signal, they are to turn to page 133 and do the reading activity, writing the five names next to the corresponding numbers.
The first pair to complete the list correctly is the winner.
Maintenant, tournez à la page cent trente-trois et commencez.

Teaching Resources

Technology/Audio Visual

 VIDEO/VIDEODISC

Unité 5, Modules 17-20
17. Le français pratique: Les personnes et les objets
18. Tu as un vélo?
19. Le copain de Mireille
20. La voiture de Roger

 CD-ROM **DFi B,**
Modules 17-20
Exploration 5

 Writing Template
Unité 5

 CD Unité 5, Leçons 17, 18,
19, 20

18, 19, 20, 21, 22, 23,
24, 25, 26, 27, 28, 29
Situational S11, S12

Print

Answer Key, Cassette Script,
Video Script, Overhead
Visuals Copymasters

Activity Book, pp. 125-162
Activity Book TAE

Video Activity Book pp. 61-82

Communipak, pp. 71-92

Teacher's Resource Package

 Teacher-to-Teacher:
Games, Additional
Activities

 Interdisciplinary
Connections:
Projects Book

 Teaching to Multiple
Intelligences in the
Modern Language
Classroom

 Internet Connections
www.mcdougallittell.com

T134

UNITÉ
5
Le monde personnel et familier

LEÇON 17 **Le français pratique:**
Les personnes et les objets

LEÇON 18 **Vive la différence!**

LEÇON 19 **Le copain de Mireille**

LEÇON 20 **La voiture de Roger**

Unit overview

COMMUNICATION GOALS: Students will learn to describe themselves and their family, friends, and personal possessions. LINGUISTIC GOALS: The focus is on the noun group: articles, nouns, and adjectives. The passé composé is introduced informally.

CRITICAL THINKING GOALS: Students are introduced to the concepts of gender and noun-adjective agreement. They learn to observe and apply these patterns in French.
CULTURAL GOALS: This unit presents the multi-cultural reality of contemporary France, while highlighting the common interests of French and American youth.

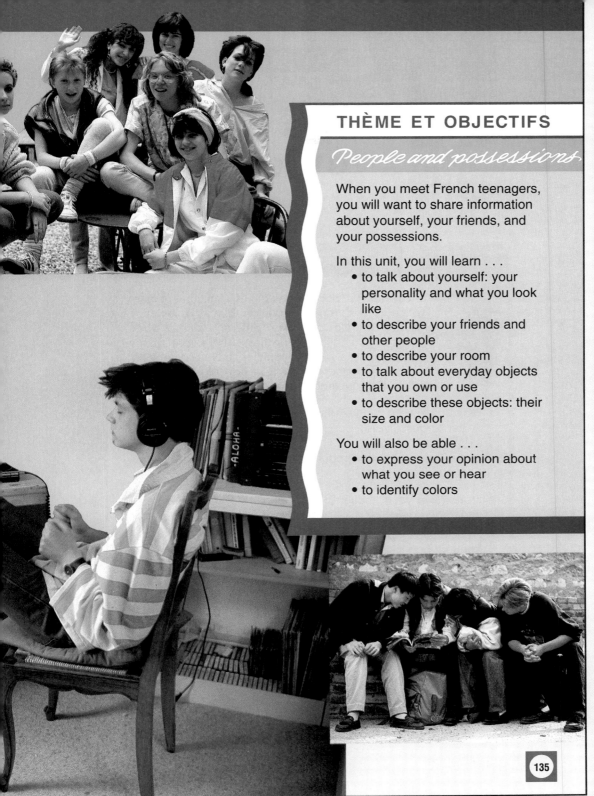

THÈME ET OBJECTIFS

People and possessions

When you meet French teenagers, you will want to share information about yourself, your friends, and your possessions.

In this unit, you will learn . . .
- to talk about yourself: your personality and what you look like
- to describe your friends and other people
- to describe your room
- to talk about everyday objects that you own or use
- to describe these objects: their size and color

You will also be able . . .
- to express your opinion about what you see or hear
- to identify colors

135

■ **Photo culture notes**
Le vélo
The student on the left is riding a mountain bike (**un vélo tout terrain: un VTT**). These bikes are very popular with French teenagers. In the school parking lot, one can also see many mopeds (**un vélomoteur**) and scooters (**un scooter**).

Le walkman
Like their American counterparts, French teenagers love to listen to music through headphones (**des écouteurs**) on their personal stereos (**un walkman**, or technically **un baladeur**).

Les bandes dessinées
On the bottom right, the students are looking at the latest comic book (**des bandes dessinées: des B.D.**). In France, there is a wide variety of **bandes dessinées** created for teens and young adults.

Pacing

Unit 5 reviews and expands considerably on Unit 2 of Niveau A. As in Unit 4, there is a dual emphasis on both oral and written skills.

For specific suggestions on pacing, turn to Section 7 in the Front Matter.

➤ Assessment Options

ACHIEVEMENT TESTS

Lesson Quizzes 17-20 pp. 75-82
  Test Cassette A, Side 2

Unit Test 5

 Portfolio Assessment pp. T147, Activities 1-4; pp. T158-159, Activities 1-6; pp. T168-169, Activities 1-6; pp. T178-179, Activities 1-5

PROFICIENCY TESTS

 Listening Comprehension Performance Test, p. 35
  Test Cassette C, Side 2

 Speaking Performance Test, p. 25

 Reading Comprehension Performance Test, p. 25

 Writing Performance Test, p. 46

Test Bank, Unit 5
  Version A or B

CD-ROM DFi B, Exploration 5
  Cahier, Créa-dialogue

Leçon 17

MAIN TOPIC:

Describing people and things

MODULE 17:
Le français pratique:
Les personnes et les objets
Total time: 6:58 min.
(Counter: 28:45 min.)

17.1 Mini-scenes: Listening — J'ai un walkman
(29:53–30:56 min.)

17.2 Mini-scenes: Speaking — Qu'est-ce que c'est?
(30:57–32:02 min.)

17.3 Dialogue: Tu as un walkman?
(32:03–33:01 min.)

17.4 Mini-scenes: Speaking — Où est-il?
(33:02–34:19 min.)

17.5 Vignette culturelle: La chambre de Catherine
(34:20–35:41 min.)

VIDEODISC Disc 3, Side 2
1562–14055

■ **Comprehension practice:** Play the entire module through as an introduction to the lesson.

■ **Cultural notes**
• The U.S. population is about 274 million.
• North Africa, French-speaking West Africa, Vietnam, Laos, and Cambodia were all former French colonies.
• Less than 20% of the U.S. population is under 20.

LE FRANÇAIS
PRATIQUE

LEÇON 17

Les personnes et les objets

Accent sur . . . Les Français

France has a population of 60 million people. France is a European country, but its population includes people of many different ethnic backgrounds and cultural origins. There are many French citizens whose families have come from North Africa and French-speaking West Africa, as well as from Vietnam, Laos, and Cambodia.

• France is a country of Catholic tradition, but it also has:
— the largest Jewish population of Western Europe (about 600,000 people).
— the largest Muslim population of Western Europe (about five million people).

• France is a young country. Thirty percent of its population is under the age of 20.

• French young people tend to be idealists. They believe in freedom and democracy. They also believe in friendship and family. In fact, they rank these values far above money and material success.

• French young people in general have a positive attitude toward Americans. They like American music and would enjoy visiting the United States.

• Because language study is required in French secondary schools, many French teenagers can communicate in a second language, such as English or German.

136 Unité 5

Setting the scene

Ask students what kinds of things they buy, other than food and clothes: school supplies, books, posters, cassettes, CDs, audio equipment, etc.

Ask what other possessions they have: a watch, a camera, a bicycle, etc.

As they watch Video Module 17, they will meet many French young people who will talk about their own possessions.

In the last segment, Olivier invites them to his room and points out some of his favorite things.

Au Café Montparnasse
Stéphanie parle avec ses amis.

Chez le marchand de glaces
Philippe est chez le marchand de glaces avec une copine.

À Paris
Des jeunes font une promenade sur les Champs-Élysées.

Chez des amis
Stéphanie écoute des disques avec un copain.

■ **Photo culture notes**
Montparnasse
At the turn of the century, the Montparnasse neighborhood on the Left Bank (**la rive gauche**) of Paris was the home to many artists, including Picasso, Modigliani, and Chagall. Renovated in the 1960s, the area is now dominated by the 52-floor Tour Maine-Montparnasse. Students and other visitors come to Montparnasse to explore its numerous cafés, restaurants, and movie theaters.

Les glaces
In France, one can buy ice cream (**une glace**) and sherbets (**un sorbet**) from street vendors or in specialized shops. Some pastry shops (**une pâtisserie**) also sell ice cream.
Favorite flavors of ice cream include:
coffee (**une glace au café**)
strawberry (**une glace aux fraises**)
raspberry (**un sorbet aux framboises**)
black currant (**un sorbet aux cassis**)

Les Champs-Élysées
Les Champs-Élysées is the most famous avenue of Paris and a favorite place for strolling with friends. The avenue runs from the **Arc de Triomphe** (in the picture) to the **Place de la Concorde**.

🌐 Multiculturalism in France

PROP: Transparency 2 (world map)

French society is becoming increasingly multicultural as the country attracts immigrants representing many different traditions and backgrounds.

On the world map on p. R2, have students find the main countries of origin of these French immigrant groups:

Les Arabes et les Musulmans:
   l'Algérie, la Tunisie, le Maroc
Les Africains: l'Afrique occidentale — la
   Côte d'Ivoire, le Sénégal, le Mali ...
Les Orientaux: le Viêt-nam, le
   Cambodge

Qui est-ce?

C'est un copain.

Section A

COMMUNICATIVE FUNCTION:
Describing people

⟲ **Review and expansion**:
Phrases from Niveau A.

▓ **Casual speech:** Questions can be formed using a rising intonation:
C'est qui?
Il/Elle s'appelle comment?
Il/Elle a quel âge?

▷ **Les personnes**

▓ **Language note:** The term **un étudiant (une étudiante)** refers to college students, although it is now sometimes used in talking about high school students, especially older ones. The traditional term for high school students is **un lycéen (une lycéenne)**.

▓ **Teaching strategy:** To help students differentiate between the sound of **un** and **une**, point to various students and ask:
Est-ce que c'est un élève ou une élève?
Est-ce que c'est un camarade ou une camarade?

A. La description des personnes

▶ *How to describe someone:*

Qui est-ce?
C'est un copain.

Comment s'appelle-t-il?
Il s'appelle Marc.

Quel âge a-t-il?
Il a seize ans.

Comment est-il?
Il est petit.
Il est blond.

Qui est-ce?
C'est une copine.

Comment s'appelle-t-elle?
Elle s'appelle Sophie.

Quel âge a-t-elle?
Elle a quinze ans.

Comment est-elle?
Elle est grande.
Elle est brune.

Les personnes

une **personne**

une **personne**

un **étudiant** (student)	une **étudiante**
un **élève** (pupil)	une **élève**
un **camarade** (classmate)	une **camarade**
un **homme** (man)	une **femme** (woman)
un **professeur,** un **prof** (teacher)	un **professeur,** une **prof**
un **voisin** (neighbor)	une **voisine**

➡ **Une personne** is always feminine whether it refers to a male or female person.
➡ **Un professeur** is always masculine whether it refers to a male or female teacher. However, in casual French, one distinguishes between **un prof** (male) and **une prof** (female).

TPR **Descriptive adjectives**
PROPS: Blue and red index cards

Give each student a blue and a red card. On the board, draw a stick figure of a boy (labeled Michel) and a girl (labeled Michelle).
Voici Michel. C'est un copain.
Et voilà Michelle. C'est une copine.

Hold a blue card next to Michel, and a red card next to Michelle.
La carte bleue est pour Michel.
La carte rouge est pour Michelle.
Read descriptions using new vocabulary and have students hold up the right card.
Michel est grand. [blue card]
Michelle est belle. [red card]
Michel(le) est jeune. [either: both cards]

La description physique

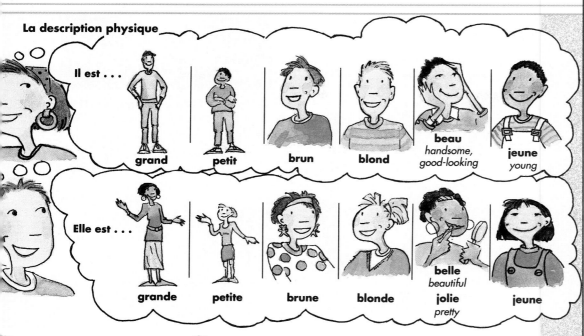

Il est . . .

grand — petit — brun — blond — **beau** *handsome, good-looking* — **jeune** *young*

Elle est . . .

grande — petite — brune — blonde — **belle** *beautiful* — **jolie** *pretty* — jeune

1 Oui ou non?

Describe the people below in affirmative or negative sentences.

▶ Michael Jordan / petit?
Michael Jordan n'est pas petit.

▶ Cameron Diaz / jolie?
Cameron Diaz est jolie.

1. Dennis Rodman / grand?
2. Leonardo DiCaprio / blond?
3. Dracula / beau?
4. mon copain / brun?
5. mon père / petit?
6. mon voisin / jeune?
7. Drew Barrymore / belle?
8. Meryl Streep / jeune?
9. Oprah Winfrey /grande?
10. ma copine / petite?
11. ma mère / brune?
12. ma voisine / jolie?

2 Vacances à Québec

You spent last summer in Quebec and have just had your photographs developed. Describe each of the people, giving name, approximate age, and two or three characteristics.

blond(e) petit(e)
brun(e) beau (belle)
grand(e) jeune

▶ Il s'appelle Alain.
Il est brun.
Il a seize ans.
Il n'est pas grand.
Il est petit.

▶ Alain

1. Anne-Marie   2. Jean-Pierre   3. Claire
4. Mademoiselle Lévêque   5. Madame Paquette   6. Monsieur Beliveau

Leçon 17 **139**

Game: Qui est-ce?

PROPS: Magazine pictures showing a variety of individuals with different looks

Tape the pictures across the chalkboard. Have the class identify each one. Write the names.
Voici une femme. Comment s'appelle-t-elle? [Elle s'appelle Mme Duroc.] …

Each student stands and describes one of the people without mentioning his/her name. The others try to guess who it is.
C'est une femme. Elle est blonde. Elle est grande. Elle n'est pas jeune. Qui est-ce? [C'est Madame Duroc.]
VARIATION: Use well-known personalities.

Qu'est-ce que c'est?

B. Les objets

▶ *How to identify something:*

Qu'est-ce que c'est?	*What is it? What's that?*	—**Qu'est-ce que c'est?**
C'est . . .	*It's . . . , That's . . .*	—**C'est** une radio.

▶ *How to say that you know or do not know:*

Je sais.	*I know.*
Je ne sais pas.	*I don't know.*

▶ *How to point out something:*

—**Regarde ça.**	*Look at that.*
—**Quoi?**	*What?*
—**Ça,** là-bas.	*That, over there.*

Quelques objets *(A few objects)*

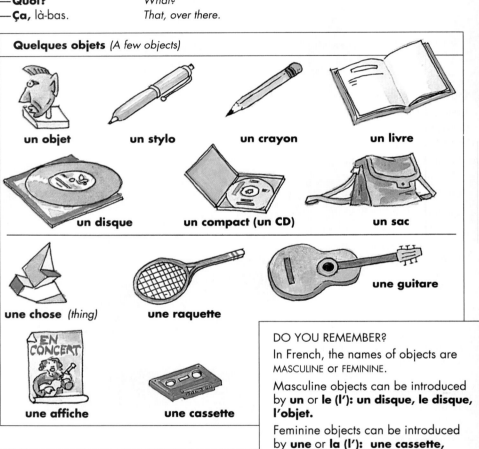

un objet · un stylo · un crayon · un livre

un disque · un compact (un CD) · un sac

une chose *(thing)* · une raquette · une guitare

une affiche · une cassette

> DO YOU REMEMBER?
> In French, the names of objects are MASCULINE or FEMININE.
>
> Masculine objects can be introduced by **un** or **le (l')**: **un disque, le disque, l'objet.**
>
> Feminine objects can be introduced by **une** or **la (l')**: **une cassette, la cassette, l'affiche.**

140 Unité 5

TPR Everyday objects

PROPS: Objects from the above vocabulary

Hold up the objects (or corresponding pictures), identifying them one by one.
 Voici un stylo.
 Voici une cassette. ...
Go over the objects, misidentifying some.

Voici un stylo. [holding a pencil]
Ah non, ce n'est pas un stylo.
Est-ce que c'est un livre? [non]
Est-ce que c'est un crayon? [oui]
Have students manipulate the objects.
X, viens ici. Montre-nous le sac.
Y, prends la raquette et donne-la à Z.

— QU'EST-CE QUE
C'EST QUE ÇA?
— QUOI?
— ÇA, LÀ-BAS!
— C'EST UNE TÉLÉ.

—OH LÀ LÀ, NON!
REGARDE! C'EST
UN EXTRA-
TERRESTRE!

3 Qu'est-ce que c'est?

Ask a classmate to identify the following objects.

est-ce que
c'est?

C'est un stylo.

4 S'il te plaît

Ask a classmate to give you the following objects.

▶ —S'il te plaît, donne-moi
   la cassette.
   —Voilà la cassette.
   —Merci.

▶

C'EST VUARNET!

VUARNET®
FRANCE

141

■ **Teaching strategy:** Have students note the use of **ça** and **quoi** in the cartoon at left.

3 DESCRIPTION: identifying objects

1. un livre
2. une affiche
3. une guitare
4. une raquette
5. un sac

■ **Variation:** Go around the classroom holding up or pointing to objects students can identify.
– **Regardez ça. Qu'est-ce que c'est?**
– **C'est [un crayon].**
– **Et ça? Qu'est-ce que c'est?**
– **C'est [un stylo].**

4 EXCHANGES: asking for things

1. le crayon
2. l'affiche
3. le livre
4. le disque
5. le compact (le CD)

■ **Realia note**
Jean Vuarnet, one of the best-known French skiers, was a gold medalist at the 1960 Winter Olympic Games. The company which bears his name manufactures sunglasses (**des lunettes de soleil**) and other sports accessories.

Cooperative
pair practice
Activities 3, 4

C. Les possessions personnelles

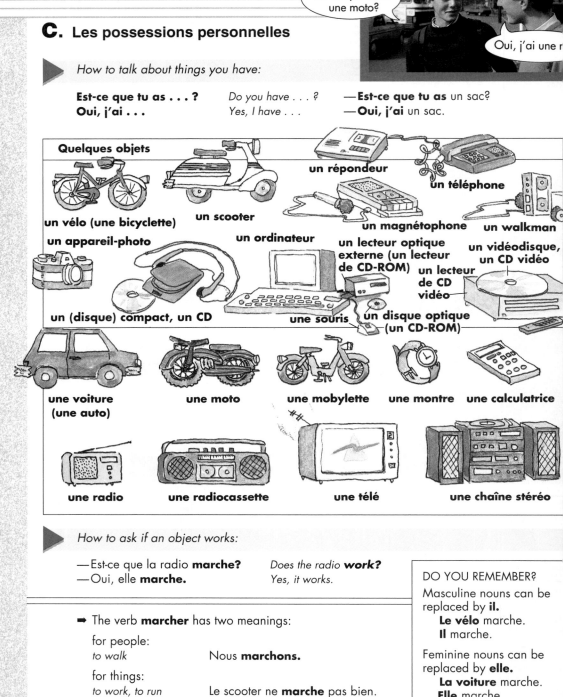

How to talk about things you have:

Est-ce que tu as . . . ?	*Do you have . . . ?*	—**Est-ce que tu as** un sac?
Oui, j'ai . . .	*Yes, I have . . .*	—**Oui, j'ai** un sac.

Quelques objets

un vélo (une bicyclette)
un scooter
un répondeur
un téléphone
un magnétophone
un walkman
un appareil-photo
un ordinateur
un lecteur optique externe (un lecteur de CD-ROM)
un lecteur de CD vidéo
un vidéodisque, un CD vidéo
un (disque) compact, un CD
une souris
un disque optique (un CD-ROM)
une voiture (une auto)
une moto
une mobylette
une montre
une calculatrice
une radio
une radiocassette
une télé
une chaîne stéréo

How to ask if an object works:

—Est-ce que la radio **marche?**	*Does the radio **work?***
—Oui, elle **marche.**	*Yes, it works.*

➡ The verb **marcher** has two meanings:

for people:
to walk   Nous **marchons.**

for things:
to work, to run   Le scooter ne **marche** pas bien.

DO YOU REMEMBER?

Masculine nouns can be replaced by **il.**
    Le vélo marche.
    Il marche.

Feminine nouns can be replaced by **elle.**
    La voiture marche.
    Elle marche.

142 Unité 5

Est-ce que tu as une moto?

Oui, j'ai une r

5 **Et toi?**

1. J'ai . . .
   (Name 3 objects you own.)
2. Je voudrais . . .
   (Name 3 things you would like to have.)
3. Pour Noël / Hanoukka, je voudrais . . .
   (Name 2 gifts you would like to receive.)

6 **Joyeux anniversaire**
(Happy birthday)

For your birthday, a rich aunt is giving you the choice between different possible gifts. Indicate your preferences.

▶ vélo ou scooter?

1. mobylette ou moto?
2. montre ou radio?
3. appareil-photo ou walkman?
4. radiocassette ou chaîne stéréo?
5. télé ou ordinateur?
6. magnétophone ou calculatrice?

Je préfère le vélo.

Je préfère le scooter.

7 **Qu'est-ce que tu as?**

Philippe asks Christine if she has the following objects. She says that she does. Play both roles.

▶ PHILIPPE: **Est-ce que tu as une guitare?**
CHRISTINE: **Oui, j'ai une guitare.**

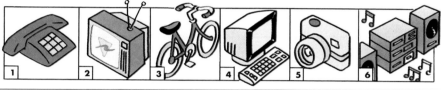

8 **Est-ce qu'il marche bien?**

Tell your classmates that you own the following objects. They will ask you if the objects are working. Answer according to the illustrations.

▶ —J'ai un vélo.
—Est-ce qu'il marche bien?
—Non, il ne marche pas bien.

▶ —J'ai une télé.
—Est-ce qu'elle marche bien?
—Oui, elle marche très bien.

Language note
The word **mobylette** was originally a brand name. The word has become the generic term for *motorbike* in French, replacing **vélomoteur.** Other common examples of brand names that have become generic terms are:

un frigidaire or un frigo (replacing **un réfrigérateur**)
un walkman (replacing **un baladeur**)
un bic (replacing **un stylo à bille**)

Cooperative pair practice
Activities 7, 8

17.3 Dialogue: Tu as un walkman?
(32:03–33:01 min.)

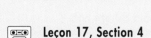 **VIDEODISC** Disc 3, Side 2
7488–9232

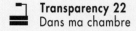 **Leçon 17, Section 4**

Looking ahead: Plural nouns are presented in Lesson 18.

Transparency 22
Dans ma chambre

Language note: Une chambre is a *bedroom*. The general word for *room* is **une pièce**.

Supplementary vocabulary

un meuble *piece of furniture*
un fauteuil *armchair*
un placard *closet*
un tapis *rug, carpet*
une bibliothèque *bookcase*
une étagère *shelf*
une commode *dresser*

Transparency 23
Les prépositions

D. Ma chambre *(My room)*

Dans ma chambre il y a une télé.

▶ **How to talk about what there is in a place:**

il y a	there is there are	Dans *(In)* ma chambre, **il y a** une télé. Dans le garage, **il y a** deux voitures.
est-ce qu'il y a . . . ?	*is/are there . . . ?*	**Est-ce qu'il y a** un ordinateur dans la classe?
qu'est-ce qu'il y a . . . ?	*what is there . . . ?*	**Qu'est-ce qu'il y a** dans le garage?

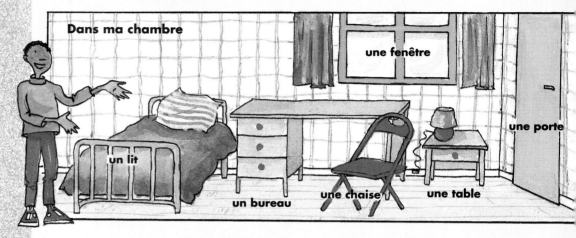

Dans ma chambre

une fenêtre

un lit · un bureau · une chaise · une table · une porte

▶ **How to say where something or someone is:**

Où est Félix?
Félix est . . .

dans le lit · sur le lit · sous le lit · devant le lit · derrière le lit

---

TPR **Location**

PROPS: Objects from the lesson

Demonstrate prepositions of place:
 Je mets le CD dans le sac.
 Je mets la raquette sur la chaise.
 Je mets la guitare sous la table.
 Je mets le stylo derrière le livre. ...

Have students move the objects around.
 X, viens ici. Mets la cassette dans le sac.
 Y, viens et mets le crayon devant le sac.
 Z, prends le livre et mets-le derrière le sac.

9 Qu'est-ce qu'il y a?

Describe the various objects that are in the pictures.

1. Sur la table, il y a . . .   2. Sous le lit, il y a . . .   3. Dans le garage, il y a . . .

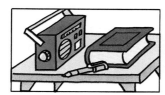 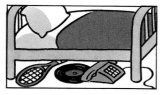 

10 Ma chambre

Describe the various objects (pieces of furniture and personal belongings) that are in your room.

▶ Il y a une radio, . . .
  Il y a aussi . . .

11 Où est le téléphone?

Michèle is looking for the telephone. Jean-Claude tells her where it is.

▶ MICHÈLE: **Où est le téléphone?**
  JEAN-CLAUDE: **Il est sur la table.**

12 C'est étrange! *(It's strange!)*

Funny things sometimes happen. Describe these curious happenings by selecting an item from Column A and putting it in one of the places listed in Column B.

> Il y a un éléphant sous le lit!

▶ Il y a . . .

A	B
un rhinocéros	dans la classe
un éléphant	sur le bureau
une girafe	sous la table
un crabe	sous le lit
une souris *(mouse)*	derrière la porte
un ami de King Kong	sur la tour Eiffel
	dans le jardin *(garden)*
un extra-terrestre	devant le restaurant

---

9 DESCRIPTION: saying where things are

1. une radio, un stylo et un livre
2. une raquette, un disque et un téléphone
3. un scooter, une voiture (une auto) et un vélo (une bicyclette)

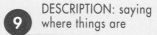

10 COMMUNICATION: describing one's room

11 ROLE PLAY: saying where something is

1. sur le bureau
2. sur la chaise
3. sous le lit
4. devant la fenêtre
5. derrière la porte

12 COMMUNICATION: describing improbable locations

■ **Expansion:** Have students invent other improbable statements using known vocabulary.

 17.4 **Mini-scenes: Où est-il?** (33:02–34:19 min.)

 VIDEODISC Disc 3, Side 2 9249–11559

 Leçon 17, Section 5

OPTIONAL: give more complex commands.
X, mets le crayon dans le sac.
Et puis mets le sac sous la chaise de Y.

Cooperative pair practice
Activity 11

VIDEODISC Disc 3, Side 2
11579–14055

 **Leçon 17, Section 6**

13 ROLE PLAY: asking where
things are

1. sur la table
2. derrière la chaise
3. dans le sac
4. devant la fenêtre
5. sur le bureau
6. devant la télé (sur la table)
7. sur le bureau
8. sur la table
9. sur la chaise

 COMPREHENSION:
14 describing where someone is

1. dans
2. sous
3. derrière
4. devant

■ **Cultural note**
La contractuelle is an auxiliary
police officer who is authorized to
write tickets (**une contravention**)
for illegally parked vehicles.
The traffic sign in the cartoon sig-
nals a no parking zone (**stationne-
ment interdit**).

 **Cooperative
pair practice**
Activity 13

T146

---

13 **La chambre de Nicole**
Florence wants to borrow a few things
from Nicole's room. Nicole tells her
where each object is.

▶ la raquette

1. la télé   6. le sac
2. la guitare   7. la radio
3. le livre   8. le compact
4. le vélo   9. la cassette
5. l'ordinateur

Où est la raquette?
Elle est sous le lit.

14 **Pauvre Monsieur Vénard** *(Poor Mr. Vénard)*
Today Monsieur Vénard left on vacation, but he soon ran out of luck. Describe the four
cartoons by completing the sentences below.

Le voyage de Monsieur Vénard

1. M. Vénard est
____ la voiture.

2. M. Vénard est
____ la voiture.

3. M. Vénard est
____ la voiture.

4. La contractuelle°
est ____ la voiture.

la contractuelle *meter maid*

À votre tour!

Créa-dialogue

Daniel is showing Nathalie his recent photographs, and she is asking questions about the various people. Create similar dialogues and act them out in class.

un copain

Éric/14

▶ —Qui est-ce?
—C'est <u>un copain</u>.
—Comment s'appelle-t-<u>il</u>?
—<u>Il</u> s'appelle <u>Éric</u>.
—Quel âge a-t-<u>il</u>?
—<u>Il</u> a <u>quatorze</u> ans.

1. une cousine	2. un camarade	3. une camarade	4. un voisin	5. une voisine	6. un professeur
Valérie/20	Philippe Boucher/13	Nathalie Masson/15	Monsieur Dumas/70	Madame Smith/51	Monsieur Laval/35

Conversation dirigée

Olivier is visiting his new friend Valérie. Act out the dialogue according to the instructions.

Olivier

asks Valérie if she has a boom box	⤵	answers affirmatively	**Valérie**
asks her if it works well	⤵	says that it works very well and asks why	
says he would like to listen to his new **(sa nouvelle)** cassette	→	says that the boom box is on the table in the living room **(le salon)**	

Mes possessions

Imagine that your family is going to move to another city. Prepare for the move by making a list of the objects you own. Use a separate sheet of paper.

4 Composition: Un objet

Write a short paragraph describing a real or an imaginary object. You may want to include a picture. (Use only vocabulary that you know.) You may begin your sentences with the following phrases:

▶ Voici mon/ma…
Il/Elle est…
Il/Elle marche (ne marche pas)…

---

1 GUIDED ORAL EXPRESSION

📼 Leçon 17, Section 7

2 GUIDED ORAL EXPRESSION

O: Est-ce que tu as une radio-cassette?
V: Oui.
O: Est-ce qu'elle marche bien?
V: Oui, elle marche très bien. Pourquoi?
O: Je voudrais écouter ma nouvelle cassette.
V: La radiocassette est sur la table dans le salon.

📼 Leçon 17, Section 8

3 WRITTEN SELF-EXPRESSION

4 WRITTEN SELF-EXPRESSION

À votre tour

Select those activities which are most appropriate for your students.

👥👥 Cooperative practice

In Act. 1 and 2, you may want to have students work cooperatively in trios, with two performing and one consulting the Answer Key and acting as monitor.

📁 Portfolio assessment

You will probably select only one speaking activity and one writing activity to go into the students' portfolios for Unit 5.

In this lesson, Act. 4 is an appropriate writing portfolio topic.

MODULE 18:
Tu as un vélo?
Total time: 5:14 min.
(Counter: 35:50 min.)

18.1 **Mini-scenes: Listening — Tu as un vélo?**
(36:23–37:04 min.)

18.2 **Mini-scenes: Listening — Qu'est-ce que tu as?**
(37:05–38:04 min.)

18.3 **Mini-scenes: Speaking — Est-ce que tu as un vélo?**
(38:05–39:11 min.)

18.4 **Dialogue: J'organise une boum**
(39:12–39:45 min.)

18.5 **Vignette culturelle: La mobylette**
(39:46–41:03 min.)

VIDEODISC Disc 3, Side 2
14316–23676

Lecon 18, Section 1

■ **Language note:** In French, **pas de** is often followed by a singular noun.
Il n'a pas de frère. =
He doesn't have a brother.
(He has no brothers.)

COMPREHENSION

1. Caroline et Jean-Pierre
2. Jean-Pierre
3. Jean-Pierre
4. Caroline et Jean-Pierre
5. Caroline
6. Jean-Pierre
7. Caroline et Jean-Pierre

LEÇON 18 Vive la différence

We are not necessarily like our friends. Caroline, a French girl from Montpellier, describes herself. She also talks about her friend Jean-Pierre.

Caroline

Jean-Pierre

Je m'appelle Caroline.
J'habite à Montpellier.
J'ai des frères.

J'ai un chien.

J'ai un scooter.

J'aime le cinéma.
J'aime les films de science-fiction.
J'aime les sports.
J'étudie l'anglais.

Il s'appelle Jean-Pierre.
Il habite à Strasbourg.
Il n'a pas de frère,
    mais il a des soeurs.

Il n'a pas de chien,
    mais il a deux horribles chats.

Il a une moto.

Il préfère le théâtre.
Il préfère les westerns.
Il préfère la musique.
Il étudie l'espagnol.

Jean-Pierre et moi, nous sommes très différents . . . mais nous sommes copains.
C'est l'essentiel, non?

● **Compréhension**

Answer the questions below with the appropriate names: **Caroline, Jean-Pierre,** or **Caroline et Jean-Pierre.**

1. Qui habite en France?
2. Qui a des soeurs?
3. Qui n'a pas de frère?
4. Qui a un animal domestique?
5. Qui aime jouer au volley?
6. Qui préfère écouter un concert?
7. Qui étudie une langue *(language)*?

Setting the scene

The theme of this opening text is that friends do not always have identical tastes and backgrounds. **Et toi?** encourages students to talk about their own similarities and differences.

Using the video

Video Module 18 prepares students to talk about various things they own. They will meet a wide variety of French people who will describe their possessions. The *Vignette culturelle* is about the moped.

Et toi?

Describe yourself and your best friend by completing the sentences below with a phrase of your choice.

1. J'ai . . .
   Mon copain (ma copine) a . . .
   - un frère
   - une soeur
   - des frères
   - des soeurs

2. J'ai . . .
   Mon copain (ma copine) a . . .
   - un chien
   - un chat
   - un perroquet *(parrot)*
   - un poisson rouge *(goldfish)*

3. J'ai . . .
   Mon copain (ma copine) a . . .
   - un vélo
   - une moto
   - un scooter
   - une mobylette

4. J'aime . . .
   Mon copain (ma copine) aime . . .
   - le cinéma
   - le théâtre
   - la musique
   - les sports

5. Je préfère . . .
   Mon copain (ma copine) préfère . . .
   - les westerns
   - les comédies
   - les films d'aventures
   - les films de science-fiction

6. J'étudie . . .
   Mon copain (ma copine) étudie . . .
   - l'espagnol
   - le français
   - l'italien
   - l'allemand *(German)*

7. Mon ami(e) et moi,
   nous sommes . . .
   - assez *(rather)* différent(e)s
   - très différent(e)s
   - assez semblables *(similar)*
   - très semblables

COMMUNICATION:
describing oneself and one's friend

■ **Teaching note:** If certain students need to answer items 1, 2, and 3 negatively, quickly introduce the construction **Je n'ai pas de** (frère, chien, vélo...).

NOTE CULTURELLE

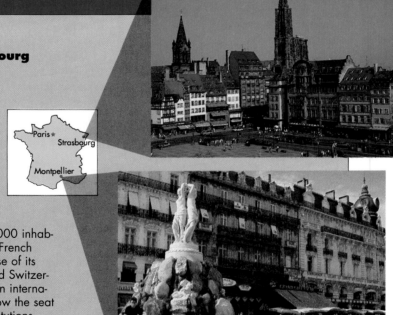

Montpellier et Strasbourg

Montpellier and Strasbourg are two very different cities.

- Montpellier is a city of more than 200,000 inhabitants located in southern France near the Mediterranean. It is an important university center with a School of Medicine founded in 1221.

- Strasbourg, a city of 255,000 inhabitants, is the capital of the French province of Alsace. Because of its location near Germany and Switzerland, it has always been an international city. Strasbourg is now the seat of important European institutions.

Note culturelle

■ **Photo culture notes**
Strasbourg
Since Strasbourg is the seat of the European Parliament (**le Parlement européen**), it is sometimes called **"la capitale de l'Europe"**. The photo shows the medieval section of the city, with its famous cathedral of pink sandstone and its picturesque half-timbered Alsatian buildings.

Montpellier
The photo of Montpellier shows **la Place de la Comédie** with its sidewalk cafés and **la Fontaine des Trois Grâces**, a fountain dating back to the 18th century.

Composition

Have students use the cues in **Et toi?** as a point of departure for writing a composition about themselves and one of their friends.

Suggest that they write their descriptions in two columns, using as a model Caroline's text on p. 148.

Review and expansion:
Students learned the singular
forms of **avoir** in Niveau A.
Point out that the plural form **ont**
is similar to **sont** and **font**.

■ **Teaching note:** Use flash
cards for subject pronouns and
known objects to practice the
forms of **avoir.**
On the chalkledge place 2 cards,
e.g., card [**nous**] + card [*tennis
racket*]
Response: **Nous avons une
raquette.**

1 PRACTICE: saying what
type of car people have

1. une Chevrolet
2. une Mercedes /mɛrsedɛs/
3. une Volvo
4. une Renault
5. une Jaguar
6. une Alfa Roméo

■ **Language note:** Makes of cars
are always feminine.

 2 COMMUNICATION: giving
people's ages

■ **Expansion:** Have students
guess the ages of well-known
sports and TV figures.

■ **Language note:** The French
always use **ans** after the number
when giving someone's age.

 3 EXCHANGES: offering,
accepting, and refusing food

 Re-entry and review: Foods
and **avoir faim/soif** from Lessons
9 and 10.

■ **Language note:** French people
say **merci** both to accept and
refuse something.

T150

A. Le verbe *avoir*

The verb **avoir** *(to have, to own)* is irregular. Note the forms of this verb in the present tense.

avoir	to have	
j' **ai**	I have	**J'ai** une copine à Québec.
tu **as**	you have	Est-ce que tu **as** un frère?
il/elle **a**	he/she has	Philippe **a** une cousine à Paris.
nous **avons**	we have	Nous **avons** un ordinateur.
vous **avez**	you have	Est-ce que vous **avez** une moto?
ils/elles **ont**	they have	Ils n'**ont** pas ton appareil-photo.

➡ There is liaison in the forms: **nous avons, vous avez, ils ont, elles ont.**

Vocabulaire: Expressions avec *avoir*

avoir faim	to be hungry	**J'ai faim.** Et toi, est-ce que tu **as faim?**
avoir soif	to be thirsty	Paul **a soif.** Sylvie n'**a** pas **soif.**
avoir . . . ans	to be . . . (years old)	**J'ai** 14 **ans.** Le prof **a** 35 **ans.**

1 **Les voitures**

The people below own cars made in
the countries where they live. Match
each car with its owner.

▶ Monsieur Sato habite à Tokyo.

Il a une Toyota.

une Alfa Roméo
une Jaguar
une Renault
une Chevrolet
une Volvo
une Mercedes
une Toyota

1. Tu habites à Boston.
2. Vous habitez à Munich.
3. Madame Ericson habite
à Stockholm.
4. J'habite à Paris.
5. Nous habitons à Oxford.
6. Mes cousines habitent à
Rome.

2 **Expression personnelle**

How old are the following
people? Complete the
sentences below. If you
don't know the exact age,
make a guess.

1. J'ai . . .
2. *(The student on your
right)* Tu as . . .
3. *(The teacher)* Vous . . .
4. Mon copain . . .
5. Ma copine . . .
6. La voisine . . .

3 **Faim ou soif?**

You are at a party with your classmates. Offer them
the following foods and beverages. They will accept or
refuse by saying whether they are hungry or thirsty.

1. une crêpe
2. un soda
3. un hamburger
4. un jus d'orange
5. un croissant
6. un jus de raisin
7. une pizza
8. un Perrier

▶ un sandwich
▶ une limonade

Tu veux
un sandwich?

Oui, merci!
J'ai faim.

(Non,
Je n'ai
fai

Tu veux une limonade?

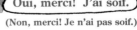

Oui, merci! J'ai soif.

(Non, merci! Je n'ai pas soif.)

Teaching note: Introducing the past tense

Once students learn the present tense
forms of **avoir,** you may want to introduce the PASSÉ COMPOSÉ for conversation
practice. (The tense is presented formally
in Unit 8.)

Beginning with this lesson, you will find
optional oral questions about past events.

To talk about what happened yesterday
(**hier**), the French use the PASSÉ COMPOSÉ:

> present of **avoir** + past participle

For **-er** verbs, the past participle ends in **-é**.
(You may want to use the chart on p. 309.)

B. Les noms et les articles: masculin et féminin

NOUNS

• Nouns designating PEOPLE
Nouns that designate male persons
are almost always *masculine:*

un garçon   un ami

Nouns that designate female persons
are almost always *feminine:*

une fille   une amie

➡ EXCEPTIONS:

une personne is always feminine (even when it refers to a male)
un professeur is always masculine (even when it refers to a woman)

• Nouns designating ANIMALS, OBJECTS, and THINGS
There is no systematic way to determine whether these nouns are
masculine or feminine. Therefore, it is very important to learn these
nouns with their articles.

MASCULINE:	**un** disque	**un** vélo	**un** ordinateur
FEMININE:	**une** cassette	**une** moto	**une** affiche

> ### Learning about language
> NOUNS are words that designate people, animals, objects, and things.
>
> In French, all nouns have GENDER: they are either MASCULINE or FEMININE.

ARTICLES

Note the forms of the articles in the chart below.

	MASCULINE		FEMININE			
INDEFINITE ARTICLE	**un**	*a, an*	**une**	*a, an*	**un** garçon	**une** fille
DEFINITE ARTICLE	**le**	*the*	**la**	*the*	**le** garçon	**la** fille

> ### Learning about language
> Nouns are often introduced by ARTICLES. In French, ARTICLES have the *same* gender as the nouns they introduce.

➡ Both **le** and **la** become **l'** before a vowel sound:

le garçon   l'ami
la fille   l'amie

> ### Learning about language
> Nouns may be replaced by PRONOUNS. In French, PRONOUNS have the *same* gender as the nouns they replace.

PRONOUNS

Note the forms of the pronouns in the chart below.

MASCULINE	**il**	*he* *it*	Où est **le** garçon? / Où est **le** disque?	**Il** est en classe. / **Il** est sur la table.
FEMININE	**elle**	*she* *it*	Où est **la** fille? / Où est **la** voiture?	**Elle** est en ville. / **Elle** est là-bas.

Leçon 18   151

Section B

COMMUNICATIVE FUNCTION: Designating people and things

■ **Language notes**
• For the more common farm animals, the gender of the noun does correspond to the sex of the animal:
un taureau, **une vache**.
• Be sure students understand that gender is linked to the NOUN and <u>not</u> to the object itself. For example, a *bicycle* can be referred to as <u>**une**</u> **bicyclette** or <u>**un**</u> **vélo**.

↩ **Re-entry and review:**
Definite and indefinite articles from Lessons 5 and 6; pronouns from Lessons 11 and 14.

🔆 **Critical thinking: pronouns**
Have students look at the sentences in the pronoun chart. How can they tell if **il** means *he* or *it*?
Il est en classe. *He is in class.*
Il est sur la table. *It is on the table.*
[They look at the context to see what **il** is referring to: **le garçon?** **le disque?**]
Similarly, how can they tell if **elle** means *she* or *it*?

Cooperative pair practice
Activity 3

Talking about past events

Let's talk about what you did yesterday.
▶ **Est-ce que tu as étudié hier?**
Oui, j'ai étudié hier.
(Non, je n'ai pas étudié hier.)
• **Est-ce que tu as étudié hier?**
• **Est-ce que tu as travaillé hier?**
• **Est-ce que tu as regardé la télé hier?**

• **Est-ce que tu as écouté la radio?**
• **Est-ce que tu as parlé français?**
• **Est-ce que tu as joué au tennis?**
• **Est-ce que tu as dîné au restaurant?**
• **Est-ce que tu as mangé un steak?**
(Reminder: use **pas de** in the negative.)
• **Est-ce que tu as mangé une omelette?**

4 Les célébrités

You and Jean-Pierre have been invited to a gala dinner attended by many American celebrities. Jean-Pierre asks you who each person is. Answer him using **un** or **une,** as appropriate.

▶ Katie Couric / journaliste

1. Peter Jennings / journaliste
2. Cameron Diaz / actrice
3. Matt Damon / acteur
4. Whoopi Goldberg / comédienne
5. Lauryn Hill / chanteuse *(singer)*
6. Michael Jordan / athlète
7. Denzel Washington / acteur
8. Will Smith / chanteur

5 Sur la table ou sous la table?

Caroline is looking for the following objects. Cécile tells her where each one is: on or under the table.

▶ walkman
CAROLINE: **Où est le walkman?**
CÉCILE: **Le walkman? Il est sur la table.**

1. ordinateur
2. sac
3. affiche
4. calculatrice
5. raquette
6. disque
7. radiocassette
8. télé

C. Les noms et les articles: le pluriel

Compare the singular and plural forms of the articles and nouns in the sentences below.

SINGULAR	PLURAL
Tu as **le disque?**	Tu as **les disques?**
Qui est **la fille** là-bas?	Qui sont **les filles** là-bas?
Voici **un livre.**	Voici **des livres.**
J'invite **une copine.**	J'invite **des copines.**

PLURAL NOUNS

In written French, the plural of most nouns is formed as follows:

SINGULAR NOUN + **s** = PLURAL NOUN

➡ If the noun ends in **-s** in the singular, the singular and plural forms are the same.
Voici **un Français.** Voici **des Français.**

➡ In spoken French, the final **-s** of the plural is always silent.

➡ NOTE: **des gens** *(people)* is always plural. Compare:

une personne	*person*	Qui est **la personne** là-bas?
des gens	*people*	Qui sont **les gens** là-bas?

4 EXCHANGES: identifying celebrities

■ **Expansion:** Have students suggest other names for each of the categories in Act. 4: e.g., **Katie Couric est une journaliste.**

5 ROLE PLAY: describing location

1. Il est sur la table.
2. Il est sur la table.
3. Elle est sur la table.
4. Elle est sous la table.
5. Elle est sous la table.
6. Il est sous la table.
7. Elle est sous la table.
8. Elle est sous la table.

■ **Expansion:** Use classroom objects.
– Où est le livre?
– Il est sur le bureau.

Section C

COMMUNICATIVE FUNCTION: Identifying people and things

■ **Language note:** Note the following plurals:
des appareils-photo
des chaînes stéréo
There is no "s" on **photo** or **stéréo** since these are shortened forms of **photographique(s)** and **stéréophonique(s).**

■ **Vocabulary note: gens** is masculine.

■ **Realia note**
The **Galeries Lafayette** is a well-known Parisian department store.

Cooperative pair practice
Activities 4, 5, 7

TPR Singular and plural forms

PROPS: Classroom objects

Point out either one or two common objects.
Voici un crayon.
Voici des crayons.
Voilà une fenêtre.
Voilà des fenêtres.
Où sont les livres? Où est le livre?

Then have individual students point out one or several objects.
X, montre-nous un stylo.
Maintenant, montre-nous des stylos.
Y, montre-nous le livre de français.
Où sont les livres de français?
Z, montre-nous des élèves.
Maintenant, montre-nous une élève.

SINGULAR AND PLURAL ARTICLES

The forms of the articles are summarized in the chart below.

	SINGULAR	PLURAL		
DEFINITE ARTICLE	**le (l')** *the* **la (l')**	**les** *the*	**les** garçons **les** filles	**les** ordinateurs **les** affiches
INDEFINITE ARTICLE	**un** *a, an* **une**	**des** *some*	**des** garçons **des** filles	**des** ordinateurs **des** affiches

➡ There is liaison after **les** and **des** when the next word begins with a vowel sound.

➡ **Des** corresponds to the English article *some*. While *some* is often omitted in English, **des** MUST be expressed in French. Contrast:

Il y a *There are*	**des** *some*	**livres sur la table.** *books on the table.*

Je dîne avec *I'm having dinner with*	**des** . . .	**amis.** *friends.*

6 Pluriel, s'il vous plaît

Give the plurals of the following nouns.

▶ une copine
des copines

▶ l'ami
les amis

1. un copain
2. une amie
3. un homme
4. une femme
5. un euro
6. une affiche
7. le voisin
8. l'élève
9. la cousine
10. le livre
11. l'ordinateur
12. la voiture

8 Qu'est-ce qu'il y a?

Explain what there is in the following places. Complete the sentences with **il y a** and a noun from the box. Be sure to use the appropriate articles: **un, une, des.** Be logical. Often several choices are possible.

▶ Dans le garage, . . .

Dans le garage, il y a une moto (des voitures . . .).

1. Sur le bureau, . . .
2. À la boum, . . .
3. Dans la classe, . . .
4. Au café, sur la table, . . .
5. Dans ma chambre, . . .
6. Dans la classe de maths, . . .

limonade   stylo   livres   affiches   moto
professeur   lit   croissants   voitures   filles
ordinateur   garçons   élèves   table

7 Shopping

You are in a department store in Montpellier looking for the following items. Ask the salesperson if he or she has these items. The salesperson will answer affirmatively.

▶ —Pardon, monsieur (madame). Est-ce que vous avez des sacs?
—Bien sûr, nous avons des sacs.

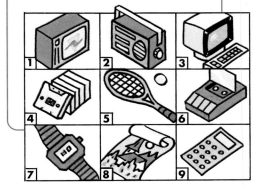

6 PRACTICE: plural articles and nouns

7 ROLE PLAY: asking for items in a store

1. des télés
2. des radios
3. des ordinateurs
4. des cassettes
5. des raquettes
6. des magnétophones
7. des montres
8. des affiches
9. des calculatrices

■ Be sure students make the required liaisons in items 3 and 8.

■ **Listening activity:** Read the following sentences aloud and have students mark whether the nouns are singular or plural.
Voici le professeur. [singular]
Voici les élèves. [plural], etc.

8 COMPREHENSION: saying where things are

Listening activity

Quickly read off sentences containing singular or plural articles. Have students raise one finger if they hear a singular article. Have them extend all fingers if they hear a plural article.
1. **Voici des copines.** [P]
2. **Voici le vélo.** [S]
3. **Voici une affiche.** [S]
4. **Voici les professeurs.** [P]
5. **Voici des ordinateurs.** [P]
6. **Voici un camarade.** [S]
7. **Voici les amis.** [P]
8. **Voici l'appareil-photo.** [S]

Section D

COMMUNICATIVE FUNCTION:
Expressing negation

18.1 Mini-scenes: Tu as un vélo?

18.2 Mini-scenes: Qu'est-ce que tu as?

18.3 Mini-scenes: Est-ce que tu as un vélo?
(36:23–39:11 min.)

 VIDEODISC Disc 3, Side 2
14453–20301

‖‖‖‖‖‖‖‖‖‖‖‖‖‖‖‖‖‖‖‖

Leçon 18, Sections 2, 3

---

9 EXCHANGES: discussing possessions

■ **Expansion:** Ask a third person to report the answer.
X a un ordinateur.
(X n'a pas d'ordinateur.)

■ **Variation** (with people):
1. un copain à Paris
2. une copine à Québec
3. un oncle très riche
4. des cousins à Strasbourg
5. des cousines à Montpellier

---

10 PRACTICE: saying what people don't have

■ **Language note:** Remind students that in French, the noun after **pas de** may be in the singular.
Je n'ai pas de copain à Lyon.
or: **Je n'ai pas de copains à Lyon.**

T154

D. L'article indéfini dans les phrases négatives

Compare the forms of the indefinite article in affirmative and negative sentences.

AFFIRMATIVE	NEGATIVE	
Tu as **un** vélo?	Non, je n'ai **pas de** vélo.	*No, I don't have a bike.*
Est-ce que Paul a **une** radio?	Non, il n'a **pas de** radio.	*No, he doesn't have a radio.*
Vous invitez **des** copains demain?	Non, nous n'invitons **pas de** copains.	*No, we are not inviting any friends.*

After a NEGATIVE verb:

> **pas + un, une, des** becomes **pas de**

➡ Note that **pas de** becomes **pas d'** before a vowel sound.
  Alice a un ordinateur. Paul n'a **pas d'**ordinateur.
  J'ai des amis à Québec. Je n'ai **pas d'**amis à Montréal.

➡ The negative form of **il y a** is **il n'y a pas:**
  Dans ma chambre,
    il y a une radio. **Il n'y a pas de** télé. *There is no TV.*
    il y a des affiches. **Il n'y a pas de** photos. *There are no photographs.*

➡ After **être,** the articles **un, une,** and **des** do NOT change.
  Philippe est un voisin. Éric n'est **pas un** voisin.
  Ce sont des vélos. Ce ne sont **pas des** mobylettes.

---

9 **Possessions**

Ask your classmates if they own the following.

▶ un ordinateur

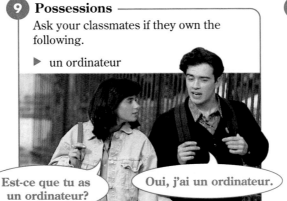

Est-ce que tu as un ordinateur?

Oui, j'ai un ordinateur.

(Non, je n'ai pas d'ordinateur.)

1. un appareil-photo
2. une moto
3. une mobylette
4. une clarinette
5. des disques de jazz
6. des affiches
7. un boa
8. un alligator
9. des hamsters

---

10 **Oui et non**

One cannot have everything. Say that the following people do not have what is indicated in parentheses.

▶ Paul a un vélo. (un scooter)
  Il n'a pas de scooter.

1. Julien a un scooter. (une voiture).
2. J'ai une radio. (une télé)
3. Vous avez des cassettes. (des compacts)
4. Vous avez des frères. (une soeur)
5. Nous avons un chien. (des chats)
6. Tu as des copains à Bordeaux. (des copains à Lyon)
7. Marc a un oncle à Québec. (un oncle à Montréal)
8. Nathalie a des cousins à San Francisco. (des cousins à Los Angeles)

154 Unité 5

Teaching strategy: Il y a with objects

PROP: Transparency 21

Using a transparency marker, draw an "X" through eight of the objects shown. Describe what is and is not in the picture. Point to the bicycle, saying: **Il y a un vélo.** Cross out the scooter: **Il n'y a pas de scooter.**

Continue, having students repeat after you. When eight items have been crossed out, ask questions about the transparency.
Est-ce qu'il y a une voiture?
  [Oui, il y a une voiture.]
Est-ce qu'il y a un ordinateur?
  [Non, il n'y a pas d'ordinateur.]

11 Le grenier *(The attic)*

Your friend is cleaning the attic. Ask if the following items are up there. Your friend (a classmate) will answer according to the illustration.

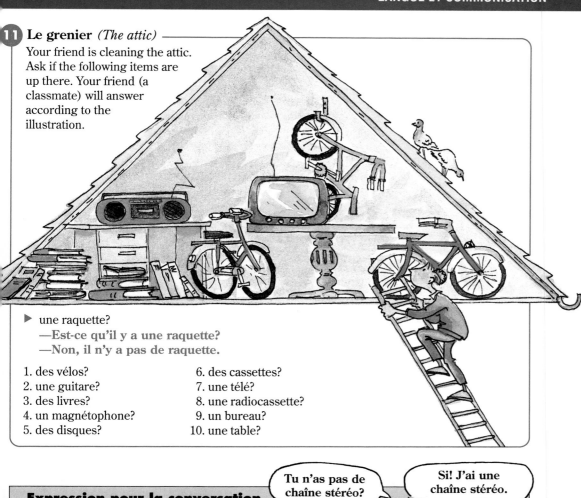

▶ une raquette?
—Est-ce qu'il y a une raquette?
—Non, il n'y a pas de raquette.

1. des vélos?
2. une guitare?
3. des livres?
4. un magnétophone?
5. des disques?
6. des cassettes?
7. une télé?
8. une radiocassette?
9. un bureau?
10. une table?

Expression pour la conversation

How to contradict a negative statement or question:

Si! *Yes!* —Tu n'as pas de chaîne stéréo?
—Si! J'ai une chaîne stéréo.

Tu n'as pas de chaîne stéréo?

Si! J'ai une chaîne stéréo.

12 Contradictions!

Contradict all of the following negative statements.

▶ Tu ne parles pas anglais! **Si, je parle anglais!**

1. Tu ne parles pas français!
2. Tu n'étudies pas!
3. Tu ne joues pas au basket!
4. Tu n'aimes pas les sports!
5. Tu n'aimes pas la musique!
6. Tu n'écoutes pas le professeur!

Leçon 18 155

11 EXCHANGES: locating objects

1. oui   6. non
2. non   7. oui
3. oui   8. oui
4. non   9. oui
5. non   10. oui

Transparency 24
Le grenier

12 PRACTICE: contradicting negative statements

↺ **Re-entry and review:** Verbs from Unit 4.

■ **Teaching strategy:** Have students contrast the negative question and response in the example with the following affirmative question and response:
– Tu as une chaîne stéréo?
– <u>Oui</u>, j'ai une chaîne stéréo.

18.4 Dialogue: J'organise une boum
18.5 Vignette culturelle: La mobylette (39:12–41:03 min.)

 Disc 3, Side 2
20322–23676

Cooperative pair practice
Activities 9, 11

■ **Language note:** Usually, English does not use articles to introduce abstract nouns or nouns used in a general sense.

■ **Realia note**
Have students read the sign: **J'aime le français.** (They may want to make similar signs of their own.)

COMMUNICATION: expressing likes and dislikes

■ **Teaching hint:** Model the new words and cognates, being sure that students pronounce them the French way.

COMPREHENSION: describing what people like

E. L'usage de l'article défini dans le sens général

In French, the definite article **(le, la, les)** is used more often than in English. Note its use in the following sentences.

J'aime **la musique.**	*(In general) I like* **music.**
Tu préfères **le tennis** ou **le golf?**	*(Generally) do you prefer* **tennis** *or* **golf?**
Pauline aime **les westerns.**	*(In general) Pauline likes* **westerns.**
Nous aimons **la liberté.**	*(In general) we love* **liberty.**

The definite article **(le, la, les)** is used to introduce ABSTRACT nouns, or nouns used in a GENERAL or COLLECTIVE sense.

13 **Expression personnelle**

Say how you feel about the following things, using one of the suggested expressions.

Je n'aime pas . . .
J'aime un peu . . .
J'aime beaucoup . . .

▶ Je n'aime pas la violence.

la musique	**le français**	**la violence**	**le théâtre**
la nature	**les maths**	**l'injustice**	**le cinéma**
les sports	**les sciences**	**la liberté**	**la danse**
le camping			**la photo**
			(photography)

14 **C'est évident!** *(It's obvious!)*

Read about the following people and say what they like. Choose the appropriate item from the list. (Masculine nouns are in blue. Feminine nouns are in red.)

▶ Cécile écoute des cassettes.
Cécile aime la musique.

art   cinéma   danse   français   musique   nature   tennis

1. Jean-Claude a une raquette.
2. Vous faites une promenade dans la forêt.
3. Les touristes visitent un musée *(museum)*.
4. Tu regardes un film.
5. Nous étudions en classe de français.
6. Véronique et Roger sont dans une discothèque.

F. L'usage de l'article défini avec les jours de la semaine

Compare the following sentences.

REPEATED EVENTS	SINGLE EVENT
Le samedi, je dîne avec des copains.	**Samedi,** je dîne avec mon cousin.
(On) Saturdays (in general), I have dinner with friends.	*(On) Saturday (that is, this Saturday), I am having dinner with my cousin.*

To indicate a repeated or habitual event, French uses the construction:

le + DAY OF THE WEEK

➡ When an event happens only once, no article is used.

15 Questions personnelles

1. Est-ce que tu étudies le samedi?
2. Est-ce que tu dînes au restaurant le dimanche? Si *(If)* oui, avec qui?
3. Est-ce que tu as une classe de français le lundi? le mercredi?
4. Est-ce que tu regardes les matchs de football américain le samedi? le dimanche?
5. Quel programme de télé est-ce que tu regardes le vendredi? le jeudi?
6. Est-ce que tu travailles? Où? *(Name of place or store)* Quand?

16 L'emploi du temps

	LUNDI	MARDI	MERCREDI	JEUDI	VENDREDI
9 h	français	physique	sciences	biologie	
10 h		histoire		maths	anglais
11 h	maths	sciences	anglais		français

The following students all have the same morning schedule. Complete the sentences accordingly.

▶ **Nous avons une classe de français le lundi . . .**

1. J'ai une classe de maths _____ .
2. Tu as une classe de sciences _____ .
3. Jacques a une classe de physique _____ .
4. Thérèse a une classe d'histoire _____ .
5. Vous avez une classe de biologie _____ .
6. Les élèves ont une classe d'anglais _____ .

Prononciation　　　　　　　　　　　　　　**le** /lə/　　**les** /le/

Les articles le et les

Be sure to distinguish between the pronunciation of **le** and **les**. In spoken French, that is often the only way to tell the difference between a singular and a plural noun.

le sac　　**les sacs**

Répétez:	/lə/	**le**	**le sac**	**le vélo**	**le disque**	**le copain**	**le voisin**
	/le/	**les**	**les sacs**	**les vélos**	**les disques**	**les copains**	**les voisins**

Leçon 18　**157**

Talking about past events

Let's talk about what you did last Saturday.

▶ **Est-ce que tu as étudié samedi dernier?**
Oui, j'ai étudié samedi dernier.
(Non, je n'ai pas étudié samedi dernier.)

• **Est-ce que tu as travaillé?**
• **Est-ce que tu as regardé la télé?**

• **Est-ce que tu as joué au basket?**
• **Est-ce que tu as organisé une boum?**
• **Est-ce que tu as dansé?**
• **Est-ce que tu as dîné au restaurant?**
• **Est-ce que tu as mangé un hot dog?** (Reminder: use **pas de** in the negative.)
• **Est-ce que tu as mangé une pizza?**

1 COMPREHENSION

1-c	4-a
2-f	5-e
3-b	6-d

🔲 **Leçon 18, Section 7**

2 ORAL EXPRESSION

1. une montre
2. un vélo
3. une radio
4. des disques
5. des affiches
6. un ordinateur
7. des compacts

Classroom Notes

À votre tour!

1 Allô!

Jean-Marc is phoning some friends. Match his questions on the left with his friends' answers on the right.

1. Quel âge a ton copain?
2. Est-ce qu'Éric a un scooter?
3. Où est l'appareil-photo?
4. Tu as des cassettes?
5. Est-ce que tu aimes étudier l'anglais?
6. Tu as soif?

a. Oui, mais je n'ai pas de magnétophone.
b. Il est sur la table.
c. Quatorze ans.
d. Oui, je voudrais une limonade.
e. Oui, mais je préfère l'espagnol.
f. Non, mais il a une moto.

2 Un sondage

A French consumer research group wants to know what things American teenagers own. Conduct a survey in your class asking who has the objects on the list. Count the number of students who raise their hands for each object, and report your findings on a separate piece of paper.

Qui a des cassettes?...
Quinze élèves
ont des cassettes.

UN SONDAGE

15

158 **Unité 5**

À votre tour

Depending on your goals and objectives, you may or may not wish to assign all of the activities in the **À votre tour** section.

👥👥 Cooperative practice

Act. 1, 3, and 4 lend themselves to cooperative pair practice. They can also be done in trios, with two students performing and the third acting as monitor and following along in the Answer Key.

3 Créa-dialogue

Ask your classmates if they like the following things. Then ask if they own the corresponding object.

	1. la musique	2. le jogging	3. les maths	4. la photo	5. les matchs de baseball	6. l'exercice

▶ —Tu aimes le tennis?
—Oui, j'aime le tennis.
(Non, je n'aime pas le tennis.)

—Tu as une raquette?
—Oui, j'ai une raquette.
(Non, je n'ai pas de raquette.)

4 Quelle est la différence?

Sophie went away with her family for the weekend and she took some of her belongings with her. Describe what is in her room on Friday and what is missing on Saturday.

VENDREDI

SAMEDI

▶ Il y a . . .

▶ Il n'y a pas de . . .

5 Inventaire *(Inventory)*

Write a short paragraph naming two things that may be found in each of the following places. Also indicate one thing that is usually not found in that place.

▶ Dans le salon, il y a une télé et des chaises. Il n'y a pas de lit.

- dans ma chambre
- dans mon sac
- dans le garage
- dans la rue *(street)*
- sur la table

6 Composition: Ma semaine

In a short paragraph, describe what you do (or do not do) regularly on various days of the week. Select three days and two different activities for each day. Use only vocabulary that you know. Perhaps you might want to exchange paragraphs with a friend by FAX or modem. ▶

Le lundi, j'ai une classe de français.
Je regarde «La roue de la fort...
(Wheel of Fort...

Le lundi, j'ai une classe de français. Je regarde « La roue de la fortune » (Wheel of Fortune) à la télé.

Le samedi, je n'étudie pas. Je dîne au restaurant avec mon copain.

3 GUIDED ORAL EXPRESSION

 Leçon 18, Section 8

4 COMPREHENSION

Vendredi: Il y a...

un bureau	un lit
une chaise	un sac
un appareil- photo	un chat une radiocassette
des crayons	une télé
des stylos	des disques
une chaîne stéréo	des cassettes une guitare
des compacts	une raquette
des livres	une affiche
un téléphone	

Samedi: Il n'y a pas...

d'appareil- photo	de compacts de radiocassette
de sac	de cassettes
de chat	de raquette

5 WRITTEN SELF-EXPRESSION

6 WRITTEN SELF-EXPRESSION

📁 Portfolio assessment

You will probably select only one speaking activity and one writing activity to go into the students' portfolios for Unit 5.

In this lesson, Act. 6 is a good written portfolio topic. You might also wish to use the composition suggested at the bottom of page T149.

MODULE 19:
Le copain de Mireille
Total time: 5:03 min.
(Counter: 41:11 min.)

19.1 Mini-scenes: Listening — Je suis américain
(41:43–42:00 min.)

19.2 Mini-scenes: Listening — Qui est-ce?
(42:01–42:55 min.)

19.3 Mini-scenes: Speaking — Comment sont-ils?
(42:56–43:55 min.)

19.4 Dialogue: Le copain de Mireille
(43:56–44:43 min.)

19.5 Vignette culturelle: La France et ses voisins
(44:44–46:13 min.)

 DEODISC   Disc 3, Side 2
23951–32981

19.4 Dialogue: Le copain de Mireille
(43:56–44:43 min.)

 DEODISC   Disc 3, Side 2
28863–30250

 Leçon 19, Section 1

 COMPREHENSION

1. une fille
2. Mireille Labé
3. oui
4. Oui! Elle est amusante, intelligente et sympathique.
5. oui
6. C'est Jean-Claude.

 T160

Le copain de Mireille

Nicolas and Jean-Claude are having lunch at the school cafeteria. Nicolas is looking at the students seated at the other end of their table.

NICOLAS:	Regarde la fille là-bas!	
JEAN-CLAUDE:	La fille blonde?	
NICOLAS:	Oui! Qui est-ce?	
JEAN-CLAUDE:	C'est Mireille Labé.	
NICOLAS:	Elle est <u>mignonne</u>!	*cute*
JEAN-CLAUDE:	Elle est aussi <u>amusante</u>, intelligente et <u>sympathique</u>.	*fun / nice*
NICOLAS:	Est-ce qu'elle a un copain?	
JEAN-CLAUDE:	Oui, elle a un copain.	
NICOLAS:	Il est sympathique?	
JEAN-CLAUDE:	Oui . . . Très sympathique!	
NICOLAS:	Et intelligent?	
JEAN-CLAUDE:	Aussi!	
NICOLAS:	Dommage! . . . Qui est-ce?	
JEAN-CLAUDE:	C'est moi!	
NICOLAS:	Euh . . . oh . . . Excuse-moi et <u>félicitations</u>!	*congratulations*

Compréhension

1. Qui est-ce que Nicolas regarde?
2. Comment s'appelle la fille?
3. Est-ce qu'elle est jolie?
4. Est-ce qu'elle a d'autres *(other)* qualités?
5. Est-ce qu'elle a un copain?
6. Qui est le copain de Mireille *(Mireille's boyfriend)*?

Setting the scene

The opening text introduces several students having lunch at the Lycée Corot. Not untypically, they are engaged in people-watching.

(For more background on this **lycée**, have students turn to pp. 76–81.)

To help students develop listening comprehension skills, have them keep their books closed as they watch the video (Section 4) or listen to the audiocassette version of the video soundtrack.

Then have them open their books and read the text.

■ NOTE ■ CULTURELLE

L'amitié *(Friendship)*

For the French, friendship is very important. It is high on the scale of values such as family, freedom, justice, love, and money.

What qualities do French young people expect in their friends? As in the United States, friends must be fun to be with, since French teenagers like to do things as a group with their **bande de copains.** Friends should be helpful and understanding because when French teenagers have a problem, they tend to talk to their friends before talking to their parents. And, of course, friends must be loyal, because the French tend to remain close to their high school friends for the rest of their lives.

■ **Photo culture note**
Les posters
In the bottom photo, French teenagers are looking at posters (**une affiche, un poster**) which are displayed in plastic cases outside a bookstore. The stand in the back has greeting cards (**une carte de voeux**).

Classroom Notes

 Multi-culturalism in France

The opening segments of Video Module 19 focus on the diversity of the French population. The final *Vignette culturelle* presents the various national origins of the people of contemporary France.

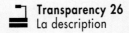 **Transparency 26**
La description

■ **Teaching hint:** Use Transparency 26 and the overlay to present the descriptive adjectives.

---

1 PRACTICE: adjective forms

■ **Language note:** Point out that nationalities are adjectives.

■ **Expansion** (dialogue format):
▶ **Jean-Claude est brun. (Nathalie)**
  – **Jean-Claude est brun.**
  – **Et Nathalie? Elle est brune?**
  – **Mais non, elle n'est pas brune.**

A. Les adjectifs: masculin et féminin

Compare the forms of the adjectives in heavy print as they describe masculine and feminine nouns.

MASCULINE	FEMININE
Le scooter est **petit.**	La voiture est **petite.**
Patrick est **intelligent.**	Caroline est **intelligente.**
L'ordinateur est **moderne.**	La télé est **moderne.**

In written French, feminine adjectives are usually formed as follows:

> MASCULINE ADJECTIVE + **-e** = FEMININE ADJECTIVE

⇒ If the masculine adjective ends in **-e,** there is no change in the feminine form.

  Jérôme est **timide.**   Juliette est **timide.**

⇒ Adjectives that follow the above patterns are called REGULAR adjectives. Those that do not are called IRREGULAR adjectives. For example:

  Marc est **beau.**   Sylvie est **belle.**
  Paul est **canadien.**   Marie est **canadienne.**

NOTE: French dictionaries list adjectives by their masculine forms. For irregular adjectives, the feminine form is indicated in parentheses.

NOTES DE PRONONCIATION:
- If the masculine form of an adjective ends in a silent consonant, that consonant is pronounced in the feminine form.
- If the masculine form of an adjective ends in a vowel or a pronounced consonant, the masculine and feminine forms sound the same.

DIFFERENT PRONUNCIATION		SAME PRONUNCIATION	
petit	petite	timide	timide
blond	blonde	joli	jolie
français	française	espagnol	espagnole

Learning about language

ADJECTIVES are words that describe people, places, and things.

In French, MASCULINE adjectives are used with masculine nouns, and FEMININE adjectives are used with feminine nouns. This is called NOUN-ADJECTIVE AGREEMENT.

---

1 **Vive la différence!**

People can be friends and yet be quite different. Describe the girls named in parentheses, indicating that they are not like their friends.

▶ Jean-Claude est brun. (Nathalie)
  Nathalie n'est pas brune.

1. Jean-Louis est blond. (Carole)
2. Paul est petit. (Mireille)
3. Éric est beau. (Marthe)
4. Jérôme est grand. (Louise)
5. Michel est riche. (Émilie)
6. André est français. (Lisa)
7. Antonio est espagnol. (Céline)
8. Bill est américain. (Julie)

TPR **Descriptions**

This is similar to the activity on p. 138.
PROPS: Blue and red index cards

On the board, draw a stick figure of a boy (labeled René) and a girl (labeled Renée).
  Voici René. C'est un voisin. [blue]
  Et ici Renée. C'est une voisine. [red]
Give each student a blue and a red card.

As you read descriptions using the new vocabulary, they raise the appropriate card.
  René est amusant. [blue card]
  Renée est mignonne. [red card]
  René(e) est timide. [either: both cards]
  Renée est assez sportive. [red card]
  René est très intelligent. [blue card] …

Vocabulaire: La description

ADJECTIFS

		Voici Jean-Claude.	Voici Mireille.
amusant	amusing, fun	Il est **amusant**.	Elle est **amusante**.
intelligent	intelligent	Il est **intelligent**.	Elle est **intelligente**.
intéressant	interesting	Il est **intéressant**.	Elle est **intéressante**.
méchant	mean, nasty	Il n'est pas **méchant**.	Elle n'est pas **méchante**.
bête	silly, dumb	Il n'est pas **bête**.	Elle n'est pas **bête**.
sympathique	nice, pleasant	Il est **sympathique**.	Elle est **sympathique**.
timide	timid	Il est **timide**.	Elle n'est pas **timide**.
gentil (gentille)	nice, kind	Il est **gentil**.	Elle est **gentille**.
mignon (mignonne)	cute	Il est **mignon**.	Elle est **mignonne**.
sportif (sportive)	athletic	Il est **sportif**.	Elle est **sportive**.

ADVERBES

assez	rather	Nous sommes **assez** intelligents.	
très	very	Vous n'êtes pas **très** sportifs!	

2 Oui ou non?

In your opinion, do the following people have the suggested traits? (Note: These traits are given in the masculine form only.)

Il est intéressant.

Il n'est pas intéressant.

▶ le prince Charles / intéressant? ▶

1. le Président / sympathique?
2. Martina Hingis / sportif?
3. ma copine / gentil?
4. Jennifer Aniston / mignon?
5. Oprah Winfrey / intelligent?
6. Einstein / bête?
7. Jay Leno / amusant?
8. le prof / méchant?

3 Descriptions

Select one of the following characters. Using words from the **Vocabulaire,** describe this character in two affirmative or negative sentences.

▶ Frankenstein
Il est très méchant.
Il n'est pas très mignon.

1. Tarzan   6. Wonder Woman
2. King Kong   7. Charlie Brown
3. Big Bird   8. Blanche-Neige *(Snow White)*
4. Batman   9. Garfield
5. Miss Piggy   10. Snoopy

4 L'idéal

Now you have the chance to describe your ideal people. Use two adjectives for each one.

1. Le copain idéal est . . . et . . .
2. La copine idéale est . . . et . . .
3. Le professeur idéal est . . . et . . .
4. L'étudiant idéal est . . . et . . .
5. L'étudiante idéale est . . . et . . .

Leçon 19 **163**

Game: Descriptions

Have students in pairs pick one of the characters in Act. 3 and write a description in two identical copies.

Then ask each pair to give one copy of the description to the pair on their left, and the other to the pair on their right.

Each pair now has two new descriptions to read. They read the two descrip-

tions and at the bottom of each they write down the name of the person they think is being described.

The descriptions are then returned to the "original authors." The winners are those pairs who had both copies of their descriptions identified correctly.

▷ Vocabulaire

📼 Leçon 19, Section 2

Pronunciation
gentil /ʒãti/
gentille /ʒãtij/

Language note: Adverbs like **assez** and **très** often modify adjectives. Note that liaison is required after **très**. In conversation, there is usually no liaison after **assez**.

Supplementary vocabulary

content ≠ triste *happy ≠ sad*
fort ≠ faible *strong ≠ weak*
riche ≠ pauvre *rich ≠ poor*
fatigué ≠ énergique *tired ≠ energetic*
génial ≠ stupide *brilliant ≠ dumb*
poli ≠ impoli *polite ≠ impolite*
drôle ≠ pénible *funny ≠ "a pain"*
optimiste ≠ pessimiste

sincère
indépendant
athlétique
dynamique

2 COMMUNICATION:
describing people

■ **Variation** (dialogue format):
– Est-ce que le prince Charles est intéressant?
– Oui, il est intéressant.
  (Non, il n'est pas intéressant.)

3 COMMUNICATION:
describing people

 4 COMMUNICATION:
describing ideal people

■ **Variation** (in the negative):
Le copain idéal n'est pas (méchant)...

■ **Expansion:** le père idéal, la mère idéale, le frère idéal, la soeur idéale

B. Les adjectifs: le pluriel

Compare the forms of the adjectives in heavy print as they describe singular and plural nouns.

SINGULAR	PLURAL
Paul est **intelligent** et **timide.**	Paul et Éric sont **intelligents** et **timides.**
Alice est **intelligente** et **timide.**	Alice et Claire sont **intelligentes** et **timides.**

In written French, plural adjectives are usually formed as follows:

> SINGULAR ADJECTIVE + **-s** = PLURAL ADJECTIVE

➡ If the masculine singular adjective already ends in **-s,** there is no change in the plural form.

Patrick est **français.** Patrick et Daniel sont **français.**
BUT: Anne est **française.** Anne et Alice sont **françaises.**

NOTE DE PRONONCIATION: Because the final **-s** of plural adjectives is silent, singular and plural adjectives sound the same.

SUMMARY: Forms of regular adjectives

	MASCULINE	FEMININE	also:
SINGULAR	**–** **grand**	**-e** **grande**	timide timide
PLURAL	**-s** **grands**	**-es** **grandes**	français françaises

5 **Une question de personnalité**

Indicate whether or not the following people exhibit the personality traits in parentheses. (These traits are given in the masculine singular form only. Make the necessary agreements.)

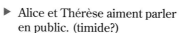
Elles ne sont pas timides.

▶ Alice et Thérèse aiment parler en public. (timide?)

1. Claire et Valérie sont très populaires. (amusant?)
2. Robert et Jean-Luc n'aiment pas danser. (timide?)
3. Catherine et Martine aiment jouer au foot. (sportif?)
4. Laure et Gisèle ont un «A» en français. (intelligent?)
5. Thomas et Vincent n'aiment pas le jogging. (sportif?)
6. Les voisins n'aiment pas parler avec nous. (sympathique?)

Talking about past events

Let's talk about what you did last summer.

▶ Est-ce que tu as voyagé l'été dernier?
Oui, j'ai voyagé l'été dernier.
(Non, je n'ai pas voyagé l'été dernier.)

• Est-ce que tu as visité Paris l'été dernier?
• Est-ce que tu as visité Québec?

• Est-ce que tu as étudié?
• Est-ce que tu as travaillé?
• Est-ce que tu as joué au volley?
• Est-ce que tu as joué au tennis?
• Est-ce que tu as nagé?
• Est-ce que tu as dîné au restaurant?

Vocabulaire: Les adjectifs de nationalité

américain	American	**italien (italienne)**	Italian
mexicain	Mexican	**canadien (canadienne)**	Canadian
français	French	**japonais**	Japanese
anglais	English	**chinois**	Chinese
espagnol	Spanish		
suisse	Swiss		

➡ Words that describe nationality are adjectives and take adjective endings.

Monsieur Katagiri est **japonais.**
Kumi et Michiko sont **japonaises.**

Expression pour la conversation

J'habite à Québec.

Alors, tu es canadien.

How to introduce a conclusion:

alors *so, then* —J'habite à Québec.
—**Alors,** tu es canadien!

6 Quelle nationalité? —

Your classmate wants to know more about the following people: where they live and what their nationality is. Act out the dialogues.

▶ —Où habitent Janet et Barbara?
—Elles habitent à San Francisco.
—Alors, elles sont américaines?
—Mais oui, elles sont américaines.

Janet et Barbara	1. Jim et Bob	2. Laure et Céline
San Francisco	Liverpool	Toulouse
américain	anglais	français
3. Luisa et Teresa	4. Éric et Vincent	5. ??
Madrid	Montréal	??
espagnol	??	??

7 Les nationalités —

Read the descriptions of the following people and give their nationalities.

▶ Silvia et Maria sont étudiantes à Rome.
   Elles sont italiennes.

1. Lise et Nathalie étudient à Québec.
2. Michael et Dennis sont de Liverpool.
3. Luis et Paco étudient à Madrid.
4. Isabel et Carmen travaillent à Acapulco.
5. Yoko et Liliko sont étudiantes à l'université de Tokyo.
6. Monsieur et Madame Chen habitent à Beijing.
7. Jean-Pierre et Claude sont de Genève.
8. Françoise et Sylvie travaillent à Paris.

Leçon 19 **165**

▷ Vocabulaire

🗐 **Transparency 27**
Les adjectifs de nationalité

🔁 **Review and expansion:**
Adjectives of nationality from Lesson 2.

▪ **Language note:** Remind students that adjectives of nationality are not capitalized in French.

Supplementary vocabulary

allemand *German*
hollandais *Dutch*
portugais *Portuguese*
libanais *Lebanese*
russe *Russian*
grec (grecque) *Greek*
égyptien(ne) *Egyptian*
israélien(ne) *Israeli*
brésilien(ne) *Brazilian*
péruvien(ne) *Peruvian*
coréen(ne) *Korean*
vietnamien(ne) *Vietnamese*

🖥 **19.1 Mini-scenes: Je suis américain**
19.2 Mini-scenes: Qui est-ce?
19.3 Mini-scenes: Comment sont-ils?
(41:43–44:43 min.)

VIDEODISC Disc 3, Side 2
24090–28829

▣ Leçon 19, Sections 3, 4, 5

6 EXCHANGES: discussing nationalities

7 COMPREHENSION: identifying nationality

1. canadiennes   5. japonaises
2. anglais   6. chinois
3. espagnols   7. suisses
4. mexicaines   8. françaises

Now you will learn to talk about what others did last summer.
(First ask one student what he/she did. Then ask the class to reaffirm.)

▶ **X, est-ce que tu as voyagé l'été dernier?**
Oui, j'ai voyagé.
(to the class) **Est-ce que X a voyagé?**
Oui, il a voyagé.

▶ **Z, est-ce que tu as visité Paris?**
Non, je n'ai pas visité Paris.
(to the class) **Est-ce que Z a visité Paris?**
Non, elle n'a pas visité Paris.

(Use the questions on the facing page.)

Section C

COMMUNICATIVE FUNCTION:
Using adjectives to describe
people and things

■ **Looking ahead:** Adjectives
which precede the noun will be
presented in Lesson 20.

■ **Realia note**
Ask students to read the penpal
ad.
• Was it written by a boy or a
girl? [a boy]
• How do you know? [from the
word **étudiant** and the masculine adjectives]
• Is the person looking for a male
or female penpal? [a female
penpal]
• How do you know? [from the
word **étudiante** and the feminine
adjectives]

OPTIONAL: Have students write their
own penpal ads.

NOTE: Please do *not* allow students
to use the address that appears in
the realia.

8 COMMUNICATION:
expressing preferences

9 PRACTICE: pointing out
similarities

C. La place des adjectifs

Note the position of the adjectives in the sentences on the right.

Philippe a une voiture.	Il a une voiture **anglaise.**
Denise invite des copains.	Elle invite des copains **américains.**
Voici un livre.	Voici un livre **intéressant.**
J'ai des amies.	J'ai des amies **sympathiques.**

In French, adjectives usually come AFTER the noun they
modify, according to the pattern:

ARTICLE	+	NOUN	+	ADJECTIVE
une		voiture		**française**
des		copains		**intéressants**

R.S.V.P.
Le Club de Correspondance

Étudiant français, 16 ans,
brun, grand, sportif,
assez intelligent, un peu
timide, voudrait
correspondre avec
étudiante américaine
sportive et sympathique.

Envoyez votre message à :
**Correspondants
13 rue de la Cerisaie
75004 Paris**

8 Préférences personnelles ——

For each person or object below, choose
among the characteristics in parentheses.
Indicate your preference.

▶ avoir un copain (sympathique,
intelligent, sportif)
**Je préfère avoir un copain
intelligent.**

1. avoir une copine (amusante,
mignonne, intelligente)
2. avoir un professeur (gentil,
intelligent, amusant)
3. avoir des voisins (sympathiques,
intéressants, riches)
4. avoir une voiture (moderne,
confortable, rapide)
5. avoir une calculatrice (japonaise,
américaine, française)
6. avoir une montre (suisse, japonaise,
française)
7. dîner dans un restaurant (italien,
chinois, français)
8. regarder un film (intéressant,
amusant, intelligent)
9. travailler avec des personnes
(gentilles, amusantes, sérieuses)
10. faire un voyage avec des gens
(amusants, riches, sympathiques)

9 Qui se ressemble . . . ——
(Birds of a feather . . .)
Say that the following people have
friends, relatives, or acquaintances with
the same personality or nationality.

▶ Claire est anglaise. (un copain)
Elle a un copain anglais.

1. Jean-Pierre est sympathique.
(des cousines)
2. La prof est intelligente. (des étudiants)
3. Madame Simon est intéressante.
(des voisines)
4. Alice est américaine. (des copines)
5. Véronique est amusante. (un frère)
6. Michel est sportif. (une soeur)
7. Pedro est espagnol. (des camarades)
8. Antonio est mexicain. (une copine)
9. Bernard est sportif. (un voisin)

Birds of a feather flock together.

Talking about past events

Let's talk about what you and your friends
did last weekend.
▶ **W et X, est-ce que vous avez étudié le
weekend dernier?
Oui, nous avons étudié.
(Non, nous n'avons pas étudié.)**
• **Est-ce que vous avez regardé la télé?**

• **Est-ce que vous avez joué au foot?**
• **Est-ce que vous avez joué au tennis?**
• **Est-ce que vous avez nagé?**
• **Est-ce que vous avez organisé une boum?**
• **Est-ce que vous avez invité des copains?**
• **Est-ce que vous avez dansé?**
• **Est-ce que vous avez chanté?**

10 Préférences internationales

Choose an item from Column A and indicate
your preference as to country of origin by
choosing an adjective from Column B. Be sure to
make the necessary agreement.

Je préfère
les voitures italiennes.

	A	B
	la musique	anglais
	la cuisine	américain
	les voitures	français
Je préfère . . .	les ordinateurs	mexicain
	les appareils-photo	chinois
	les compacts	japonais
	les restaurants	italien

Prononciation

Les consonnes finales

/-/ /d/

blon**d** blon**de**

As you know, when the last letter of a word
is a consonant, that consonant is often silent.
But when a word ends in "**e**," the consonant
before it is pronounced. As you practice the
following adjectives, be sure to distinguish
between the masculine and the feminine forms.

	MASCULINE ADJECTIVE (no final consonant sound)		FEMININE ADJECTIVE (final consonant sound)
Répétez:	blon**d**	/d/	blon**de**
	gran**d**		gran**de**
	peti**t**	/t/	peti**te**
	amusan**t**		amusan**te**
	françai**s**	/z/	françai**se**
	anglai**s**		anglai**se**
	américai**n**	/n/	américai**ne**
	canadie**n**		canadie**nne**

Joli,
petit
et bon!

Bureau
45 euros

Table
60 euros

Jolie,
petite
et bonne!

IKEA *Miracle économique!*

Leçon 19 **167**

COMPREHENSION:
10 expressing preferences

■ **Language note:** Remind students that the plural of l'appareil-photo is **les appareils-photo.**

■ **Expansion** (dialogue format):
– Je préfère les voitures anglaises. Et toi?
– Moi, je préfère les voitures américaines.

  19.5 **Vignette culturelle:** La France et ses voisins (44:44–46:13 min.)

VIDEODISC Disc 3, Side 2 30270–32981

Prononciation

Leçon 19, Section 6

■ **Teaching strategy:** Be sure students end the masculine adjectives on a vowel sound. In contrast, have them exaggerate the final consonants on the feminine adjectives.

■ **Realia note:**
Ask students:
Comment est le bureau?
[Il est joli, petit et bon.]
Et la table?
[Elle est jolie, petite et bonne.]

Now you will learn to talk about what others
did last weekend. (First ask one pair what
they did. Then ask the class to reaffirm.)
▶ **W et X, est-ce que vous avez étudié le weekend dernier?**
Oui, nous avons étudié. (Turn to class:)
Est-ce que W et X ont étudié?
Oui, ils/elles ont étudié.

▶ **Y et Z, est-ce que vous avez étudié?**
Non, nous n'avons pas étudié.
(Then ask the class:)
Est-ce que Y et Z ont étudié?
Non, ils/elles n'ont pas étudié.

(Use the questions on the facing page.)

T167

1 COMPREHENSION

1-d	4-c
2-a	5-e
3-b	

Leçon 19, Section 7

1 Allô!

Valérie is phoning some friends. Match her questions on the left with her friends' answers on the right.

1 Ton frère aime jouer au foot?

2 Cécile et Sophie sont mignonnes, n'est-ce pas?

3 Pourquoi est-ce que tu invites Olivier?

4 Tu aimes la classe?

5 Tu as des cousins?

a Oui, et intelligentes aussi!

b Parce qu'il est amusant et sympathique.

c Oui, j'ai un professeur très intéressant.

d Oui, il est très sportif.

e Oui, mais ils ne sont pas très sympathiques.

2 GUIDED ORAL EXPRESSION

1. une voisine anglaise
2. un prof canadien
3. des copines suisses
4. un livre français
5. une voiture japonaise

Leçon 19, Section 8

■ **Teaching tip:** As a preliminary activity, have students identify the flags.
1. C'est un drapeau anglais.
2. C'est un drapeau canadien.
3. C'est un drapeau suisse.
4. C'est un drapeau français.
5. C'est un drapeau japonais.

2 Créa-dialogue

With your classmates, talk about the people of different nationalities you may know or objects you may own.

des cousins

mignon?

▸ —J'ai des <u>cousins mexicains</u>.
—<u>Ils sont mignons</u>?
—<u>Oui, ils sont très mignons</u>.

1. une voisine	2. un prof	3. des copines	4. un livre	5. une voiture
blond?	sympathique?	sportif?	intéressant?	grand?

168 Unité 5

À votre tour

Depending on your goals and objectives, you may or may not wish to assign all of the activities in the **À votre tour** section.

Cooperative practice

Act. 1 and 2 lend themselves to cooperative pair practice. They can also be done in trios, with two students performing and the third acting as monitor and following along in the Answer Key.

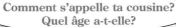
Comment s'appelle ta cousine?
Quel âge a-t-elle?

3 Une invitation

A French friend has invited you to go to a party with his/her cousin. You want to know as much as you can about this cousin. You may first ask your friend the cousin's name and age.

Then ask as many questions as you can about the cousin's physical appearance and personality traits. Act out your conversation with a classmate.

3 CONVERSATION

■ **Teaching strategy:** Have each student bring in a magazine picture of an imaginary "cousin" who will form the basis of the dialogue.

4 Avis de recherche

(Missing person's bulletin)

The two people in the pictures below have been reported missing. Describe each one as well as you can, using your imagination. Mention:

- the (approximate) age of the person
- the way he/she looks
- personality traits
- other features or characteristics

5 Composition: Descriptions

Describe one of the following well-known French people in a short paragraph, giving the person's name, profession, and approximate age. Also briefly describe the person's physical appearance.

Isabelle Adjani (actrice)

Surya Bonaly (athlète)

Jean-Jacques Goldman (chanteur)

Jacques Chirac (président)

4 WRITTEN EXPRESSION

5 WRITTEN EXPRESSION

■ **Cultural background:**
Isabelle Adjani, b.1955
Surya Bonaly, b.1973
Jean-Jacques Goldman, b.1951
Jacques Chirac, b.1932

6 WRITTEN SELF-EXPRESSION

Classroom Notes

6 Composition: Rencontres

Select two people whom you would like to meet (a man and a woman). These people may be famous singers, actors or actresses, sports figures, politicians, professional people, community leaders, etc. (You might even be able to contact them directly by e-mail!) Describe each person (physical traits and personality), using either affirmative or negative sentences.

```
Je voudrais
rencontrer X.
Il (Elle) est...
```

169

Portfolio assessment

You will probably select only one speaking activity and one writing activity to go into the students' portfolios for Unit 5.

In this lesson, Act. 3 is a good oral portfolio topic.

Act. 5 and 6 lend themselves well to written portfolio compositions.

Leçon 20

MAIN TOPIC:

Describing objects by color and size

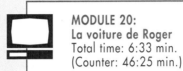

MODULE 20:
La voiture de Roger
Total time: 6:33 min.
(Counter: 46:25 min.)

VIDEODISC Disc 3, Side 2
33386–45220

20.4 Dialogue: La
voiture de Roger
(50:24–51:27 min.)

VIDEODISC Disc 3, Side 2
40518–42423

Leçon 20, Section 1

■ Photo culture note
Saint-Germain-des-Prés
The neighborhood around Saint-Germain-des-Prés (**le quartier Saint-Germain**) is one of the oldest areas of Paris.
Because of its numerous shops and movie theaters, **le boulevard Saint-Germain** is a favorite strolling place for Parisians. There are also many cafés, including the famous **Café des Deux Magots**.

La voiture de Roger

Dans la <u>rue</u>, il y a une voiture <u>rouge</u>. *street / red*
C'est une petite voiture. C'est une voiture de sport.
Dans la rue, il y a aussi un café. Au café, il y a un jeune homme.
Il s'appelle Roger.
C'est le <u>propriétaire</u> de la voiture rouge. *owner*

Une jeune fille <u>entre dans</u> le café. *enters*
Elle s'appelle Véronique.
C'est <u>l'amie de Roger</u>. *Roger's*
Véronique parle à Roger. *friend*

VÉRONIQUE: Tu as une <u>nouvelle</u> voiture, *new*
n'est-ce pas?
ROGER: Oui, j'ai une nouvelle voiture.
VÉRONIQUE: Est-ce qu'elle est grande ou petite?
ROGER: C'est une petite voiture.
VÉRONIQUE: De quelle couleur est-elle?
ROGER: C'est une voiture rouge.
VÉRONIQUE: Est-ce que c'est une voiture italienne?
ROGER: Oui, c'est une voiture italienne. Mais <u>dis donc</u>, *hey there*
Véronique, tu es <u>vraiment</u> *really*
très curieuse!
VÉRONIQUE: Et toi, tu n'es pas <u>assez</u> *curious*
<u>curieux</u>! *enough*
ROGER: Ah bon? Pourquoi?
VÉRONIQUE: Pourquoi?! . . . Regarde
la <u>contractuelle</u> là-bas! *meter maid*
ROGER: Ah, zut alors!

Setting the scene
Video Module 20 prepares students for the introductory dialogue by first teaching the colors.

The scene with Roger and his car constitutes Segment 4 of the video. (Section 1 of the audiocassette contains the video soundtrack.)

The *Vignette culturelle* develops the *Note culturelle* on the facing page about the French and their cars.

Compréhension

1. Qu'est-ce qu'il y a dans la rue?
2. Est-ce que la voiture est grande?
3. Comment s'appelle le jeune homme?
4. Où est-il?
5. Comment s'appelle la jeune fille?
6. De quelle couleur est la voiture?

COMPREHENSION

1. une voiture rouge
2. Non, elle est petite.
3. Roger
4. dans un café
5. Véronique
6. rouge

■ NOTE ■
CULTURELLE

Les Français et l'auto

France is one of the leading producers of automobiles in the world. The two automakers, **Renault** and **Peugeot-Citroën**, manufacture a variety of models ranging from sports cars to mini-vans and buses.

To obtain a driver's license in France, you must be eighteen years old and pass a very difficult driving test. French teenagers can, however, begin to drive at the age of sixteen, as long as they take lessons at an accredited driving school (**auto-école**) and are accompanied by an adult.

On the whole, because cars (even used cars) are expensive to buy and maintain, few French teenagers have cars. Instead, many get around on two-wheelers: motorcycles, scooters, and mopeds.

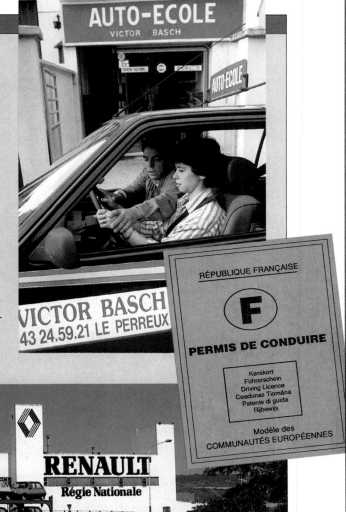

Note culturelle

20.5 Vignette culturelle: Les Français et l'auto (51:28–52:55 min.)

VIDEODISC Disc 3, Side 2
42440–45220

■ Cultural background
• Gasoline costs over 1 euro a liter, which comes to about 4 dollars a gallon.

■ Photo culture note
Renault
With a production of nearly 2 million vehicles per year, Renault is one of the leading European automobile manufacturers. It is owned partly by the French government (**régie nationale** = government enterprise).

■ **Language note:** In Québec, a driving school is **une école de conduite.**

Leçon 20 171

Talking about past events

Let's talk about what you did last weekend. Note that the past participle of **faire** is **fait**.

▶ **Est-ce que tu as fait une promenade le weekend dernier?**
Oui, j'ai fait une promenade.
(Non, je n'ai pas fait de promenade.)

• **Est-ce que tu as fait un match de tennis?**
• **Est-ce que tu as fait un match de basket?**
• **Est-ce que tu as fait un match de foot?**
• **Est-ce que tu as fait un pique-nique?**
(Remember to use **pas de** in the negative.)

Section A

COMMUNICATIVE FUNCTION:
Describing colors

20.1 Introduction: Les couleurs
20.2 Mini-scenes: De quelle couleur?
20.3 Mini-scenes: Qu'est-ce que tu préfères? (46:36–50:23 min.)

VIDEODISC Disc 3, Side 2
33544–40499

Leçon 20, Sections 2, 3, 4

Transparency 28
Les couleurs

■ **Language notes**
• When colors are used as nouns they are always masculine. J'aime **le noir.** Je déteste **le rose.**
• Another word for *brown* is **brun(e)**, which is used to describe hair and eyes

■ **Teaching strategy:** To activate colors, use names of articles of clothing, especially **tee-shirt** which is a cognate.
De quelle couleur est le tee-shirt de Jim? Il est bleu et jaune.

■ **Looking ahead:** In conjunction with colors, you may want to pre-teach selected items of clothing:
un pantalon   une chemise
un tee-shirt   une robe
un sweater   une jupe
un polo   des chaussures
(Clothes are taught in Lesson 25.)

① COMMUNICATION: asking about colors

② EXCHANGES: describing colors

1. une voiture rouge
2. un scooter jaune
3. un vélo noir
4. une guitare orange
5. un chien blanc
6. un chat jaune

T172

A. Les couleurs

Note the form and position of the color words in the following sentences:

Alice a un vélo **bleu.**   *Alice has a **blue** bicycle.*
Nous avons des chemises **bleues.**   *We have **blue** shirts.*

Names of colors are ADJECTIVES and take adjective ENDINGS. Like most descriptive adjectives, they come *after* the noun.

Vocabulaire: Les couleurs

De quelle couleur . . . ?   *What color . . . ?*   —**De quelle couleur** est la moto?
—Elle est rouge.

blanc (blanche)   noir (noire)   bleu (bleue)   rouge (rouge)   jaune (jaune)   vert (verte)   gris (grise)   marron (marron)   orange (orange)   rose (rose)

➡ The colors **orange** and **marron** are INVARIABLE. They do not take any endings.
un sac **orange**   des sacs **orange**
un tee-shirt **marron**   une chemise **marron**

① De quelle couleur?

Ask your classmates to name the colors of things they own. (They may invent answers.)

▶ ta chambre?

De quelle couleur est ta chambre?
Elle est blanche et bleue.

1. ta bicyclette?
2. ton tee-shirt?
3. ton appareil-photo?
4. ta montre?
5. ta raquette de tennis?
6. ton livre de français?
7. ton livre d'anglais?
8. ton chien (chat)?

172 Unité 5

② Possessions

Ask what objects or pets the following people own. A classmate will answer, giving the color.

▶ —**Est-ce que Monsieur Thomas a une voiture?**
—**Oui, il a une voiture bleue.**

▶ M. Thomas

1. Mme Mercier

2. Mar

3. Delphine

4. Sophie

5. Éric

6. Stéphanie

TPR Colors

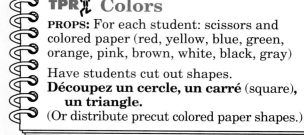

PROPS: For each student: scissors and colored paper (red, yellow, blue, green, orange, pink, brown, white, black, gray)

Have students cut out shapes.
Découpez un cercle, un carré (square), **un triangle.**
(Or distribute precut colored paper shapes.)

Have students hold up a shape.
Montrez-moi un cercle.
Take one student's circle and name its color.
Voici un cercle vert.
Si vous avez un cercle vert, levez la main.
Continue, teaching other colors and shapes.
X a un carré noir. Qui a un carré blanc?
Y a un triangle gris. Qui a un cercle gris?

3 **L'arche de Noé**

Noah's ark has just landed. Give the colors
of the animals as they get off the ship.

▶ le chien   **Le chien est blanc.**

1. le chat
2. l'éléphant *(m.)*
3. la panthère
4. le zèbre
5. le flamant
6. le cardinal
7. le lion
8. le perroquet

B. La place des adjectifs avant le nom

Compare the position of the adjectives in the following sentences.

Voici une voiture **française.**   Voici une **petite** voiture.
Paul est un garçon **intelligent.**   Pierre est un **beau** garçon.

▪ A few adjectives like **petit** and **beau** come BEFORE the noun they modify.

➡ The article **des** often becomes **de** before an adjective. Compare:
    des voitures → **de** petites voitures

Vocabulaire: Les adjectifs qui précèdent le nom

beau (belle)	*beautiful, handsome*	Regarde la **belle** voiture!
joli	*pretty*	Qui est la **jolie** fille avec André?
grand	*big, large, tall*	Nous habitons dans un **grand** appartement.
petit	*little, small, short*	Ma soeur a un **petit** ordinateur.
bon (bonne)	*good*	Tu es un **bon** copain.
mauvais	*bad*	Patrick est un **mauvais** élève.

➡ There is a LIAISON after the above adjectives when the noun which follows begins with a
    vowel sound. Note that in liaison:
    • the "**d**" of **grand** is pronounced /t/: **un grand appartement**
    • **bon** is pronounced like **bonne: un bon élève**

Leçon 20 **173**

3 DESCRIPTION: describing colors of animals

1. Le chat est orange.
2. L'éléphant est gris.
3. La panthère est noire.
4. Le zèbre est [noir et blanc].
5. Le flamant est rose.
6. Le cardinal est rouge.
7. Le lion est jaune.
8. Le perroquet est vert.

▪ **Teaching strategy:** Model the pronunciation of the animal names for students.

Section B

COMMUNICATIVE FUNCTION:
Describing objects

▪ **Language notes**
• In current French, it is becoming more and more common to use **des** before the adjective. Therefore, students should be able to recognize the **de** construction when they encounter it, but should not be penalized for failing to produce it.
• **Jeune** comes before the noun in expressions like **un jeune homme** and **une jeune fille.**

🔊 Leçon 20, Section 5

Transparency 21
Objects
Expansion Activities,
pp. A75, A76

Cooperative pair practice
Activities 1, 2

T173

4 Opinions personnelles

Give your opinion about the following people and things, using the adjectives **bon** or **mauvais**.

▶ Meryl Streep est (une) actrice *(actress)*.
Meryl Streep est une bonne actrice (une mauvaise actrice).

1. *La Menace fantôme* est un film.
2. «Star Trek» est un programme de télé.
3. Whitney Houston est (une) chanteuse.
4. Will Smith est (un) acteur.
5. Cameron Diaz est (une) actrice.
6. Dracula est une personne.
7. McDonald's est un restaurant.
8. Les Yankees sont une équipe *(team)* de baseball.
9. Les Lakers sont une équipe de basket.
10. Je suis [un(e)] élève.

■ **Language note:** If students ask, the **plural** forms are **Dites!** and **Dites donc!**

Expressions pour la conversation

How to get someone's attention:

| **Dis!** | *Say! Hey!* | **Dis,** Éric, est-ce que tu as une voiture? |
| **Dis donc!** | *Hey there!* | **Dis donc,** est-ce que tu veux faire une promenade avec moi? |

---

5 **ROLE PLAY:** discussing and describing possessions

■ **Expansion:** Have students use adjectives and write three original sentences about their possessions and friends.
J'ai une bicyclette rouge.
J'ai un bon copain.
J'ai une montre suisse.

5 Dialogue

Christine asks her cousin Thomas if he has certain things. He responds affirmatively, describing each one. Play both roles.

▶ un ordinateur (petit)

▶ une voiture (anglaise)

Dis, Thomas, tu as un ordinateur?

Oui, j'ai un petit ordinateur.

Dis, Thomas, tu as une voiture?

Oui, j'ai une voiture anglaise.

1. une télé (petite)
2. une guitare (espagnole)
3. un vélo (rouge)
4. une calculatrice (petite)
5. un sac (grand)
6. des livres (intéressants)
7. une copine (amusante)
8. une mobylette (bleue)
9. une montre (belle)
10. un copain (bon)
11. une cousine (jolie)
12. une radio (japonaise)

Cooperative pair practice
Activity 5

T174

Teaching strategy: Using chants

Certain grammatical constructions, such as the use of **c'est** vs. **il est,** can be internalized through the use of chants.

For example, the phrase **c'est un** can be chanted to the Mexican Hat Dance tune.

C'est un, c'est un, c'est un...
C'est un ami mexicain.
C'est une, c'est une, c'est une...
C'est une amie mexicaine.
C'est un, c'est un, c'est un...
C'est un vélo italien.
C'est une, c'est une, c'est une...
C'est une voiture italienne.

C. *Il est* ou *c'est?*

When describing a person or thing, French speakers use two different constructions, **il est (elle est)** and **c'est.**

		Il est + ADJECTIVE **Elle est** + ADJECTIVE	**C'est** + ARTICLE + NOUN (+ ADJECTIVE)
**Roger**	*He is . . .*	**Il est** amusant.	**C'est** un copain. **C'est** un copain amusant.
Véronique	*She is . . .*	**Elle est** sportive.	**C'est** une amie. **C'est** une bonne amie.
un scooter	*It is . . .*	**Il est** joli.	**C'est** un scooter français. **C'est** un bon scooter.
une voiture	*It is . . .*	**Elle est** petite.	**C'est** une voiture anglaise. **C'est** une petite voiture.

→ Note the corresponding plural forms:

| (Pierre et Marc) | *They are . . .* | **Ils sont** amusants. | **Ce sont** des copains. |
| (Claire et Anne) | *They are . . .* | **Elles sont** timides. | **Ce sont** des copines. |

→ In negative sentences, **c'est** becomes **ce n'est pas.**

Ce n'est pas un mauvais élève.   ***He's not*** *a bad student.*
Ce n'est pas une Peugeot.   ***It's not*** *a Peugeot.*

→ **C'est** is also used with names of people

C'est Véronique.   **C'est** Madame Lamblet.

SCOOTERS PEUGEOT

6 Descriptions

Complete the following descriptions with **Il est, Elle est,** or **C'est,** as appropriate.

A. Roger
1. _____ grand.
2. _____ brun.
3. _____ un garçon sympathique.
4. _____ un mauvais élève.

B. Véronique
5. _____ une fille brune.
6. _____ une amie sympathique.
7. _____ très amusante.
8. _____ assez grande.

C. La voiture de Roger
9. _____ une voiture moderne.
10. _____ une petite voiture.
11. _____ rouge.
12. _____ très rapide.

D. Le scooter de Véronique
13. _____ bleu et blanc.
14. _____ très économique.
15. _____ un joli scooter.
16. _____ assez confortable.

Leçon 20   175

Section C

COMMUNICATIVE FUNCTION:
Describing people and things

■ **Language notes**
• The adjective may either follow or precede the noun.
• **C'est** is also used when a possessive adjective introduces the noun:
  C'est mon frère.
  He's my brother.
• In *negative* sentences with **être,** the articles **un, une,** and **des** remain unchanged. Compare:
  Ce **n'est pas un** copain.
  Je **n'ai pas de** copain.
  Ce **ne sont pas des** motos japonaises.
  Nous **n'avons pas de** motos japonaises.

🔲 Leçon 20, Section 6

DESCRIPTION: pointing out people and things

1. Il est	9. C'est
2. Il est	10. C'est
3. C'est	11. Elle est
4. C'est	12. Elle est
5. C'est	13. Il est
6. C'est	14. Il est
7. Elle est	15. C'est
8. Elle est	16. Il est

Speaking activity: Show and tell

Have students bring an object to class and describe it using **il/elle est...,** **c'est...** and appropriate adjectives.
J'ai une montre.
Ce n'est pas une Timex. C'est une Swatch.
C'est une montre suisse.
Elle est rouge et noire.

C'est une jolie montre; elle marche très bien. J'aime beaucoup ma montre!
VARIATION: This can also be done as a written activity with students illustrating their objects.
NOTE: This works particularly well after the holiday season when students have gifts to talk about.

COMMUNICATIVE FUNCTION:
Expressing opinions

■ **Language note:** This construction is not used to describe specific people and things.
Paul? Il est amusant.
Les livres? Ils sont intéressants.

■ **Casual speech:** It is very common to drop the **ne** in negative expressions:
C'est pas amusant.
C'est pas vrai.

■ **Language notes**
• The French often tend to use negative constructions in a positive sense:
Ce (n')est pas mal. *That's not bad. = That's very good.*
Ce (n')est pas bête. *That's not stupid = That's a smart idea.*
• A current popular anglicism is:
C'est cool.
• **Super** may be used in combination with other expressions:
C'est super-chouette.
C'est super-difficile.
• **Extra** is the short form of **extraordinaire.**

7 COMPREHENSION:
geographic locations

1. faux (en France)
2. vrai
3. faux (en Suisse)
4. vrai
5. faux (à la Martinique)
6. faux (au Canada)

■ **Additional cues**
Montréal est au Canada. (vrai)
Casablanca est en Afrique. (vrai)
Rome est en France (faux: en Italie)
Vancouver est en France. (faux: au Canada)
Strasbourg est en France. (vrai)
Bordeaux est en Italie. (faux: en France)

D. Les expressions impersonnelles avec *c'est*

Note the use of **c'est** in the following sentences.

J'aime parler français. **C'est** intéressant. *It's interesting.*
Je n'aime pas travailler le weekend. **Ce n'est pas** amusant. *It's no(t) fun.*

To express an opinion on a general topic, the French use the construction:

> **C'est**
> **Ce n'est pas** } + MASCULINE ADJECTIVE

Vocabulaire: Opinions

C'est . . .		It's . . . , That's . . .	
Ce n'est pas . . .		It's not . . . , That's not . . .	
vrai	true	**chouette**	neat
faux	false	**super**	great
		extra	terrific
facile	easy	**pénible**	a pain, annoying
difficile	hard, difficult	**drôle**	funny

➡ To express an opinion, the French also use adverbs like **bien** and **mal.**

C'est bien. *That's good.* Tu étudies? **C'est bien.**
C'est mal. *That's bad.* Alain n'étudie pas. **C'est mal.**

7 **Vrai ou faux?**

Imagine that your little sister is talking about where certain cities are located. Tell her whether her statements are right or wrong.

1. Paris est en Italie.
2. Los Angeles est en Californie.
3. Genève est en Italie.
4. Dakar est en Afrique
5. Fort-de-France est au Canada.
6. Québec est en Franc

Talking about past events

► V, qu'est-ce que tu as fait hier soir?
J'ai étudié (regardé la télé, travaillé...).
► W et X, qu'est-ce que vous avez fait?
Nous avons joué au Nintendo (...).
Ask individuals what they did. Have others report back. Ask if they did the same thing.

• V, qu'est-ce que tu as fait hier soir?
• Y, qu'est-ce que V a fait hier soir?
Est-ce que tu as fait la même chose?
• W et X, qu'est-ce que vous avez fait?
• Z, qu'est-ce que W et X ont fait hier soir?
Est-ce que tu as fait la même chose?

8 Opinion personnelle

Ask your classmates if they like to do the following things. They will answer, using an expression from the **Vocabulaire.**

▶ parler français

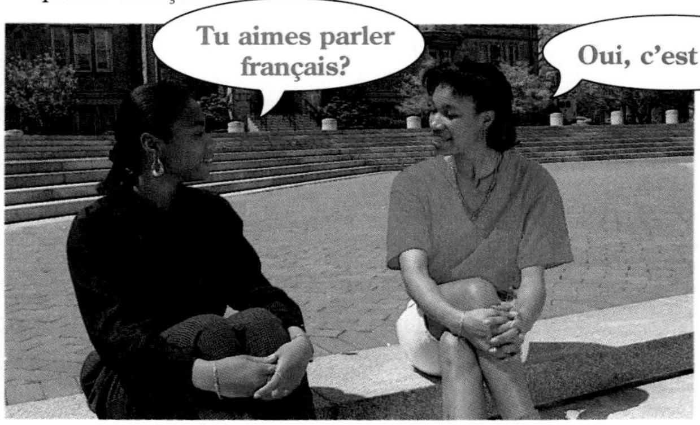
Tu aimes parler français?
Oui, c'est extra!

(Non, c'est difficile!)

1. téléphoner
2. parler en public
3. nager
4. danser
5. voyager
6. dîner en ville
7. regarder «Star Trek»
8. étudier le weekend
9. écouter la musique classique

Prononciation

ch /ʃ/

Les lettres «ch»

The letters "**ch**" are usually pronounced like the English "*sh.*"

Répétez: **chien chat chose marche**
chouette chocolat affiche
Michèle a un chat et deux chiens.

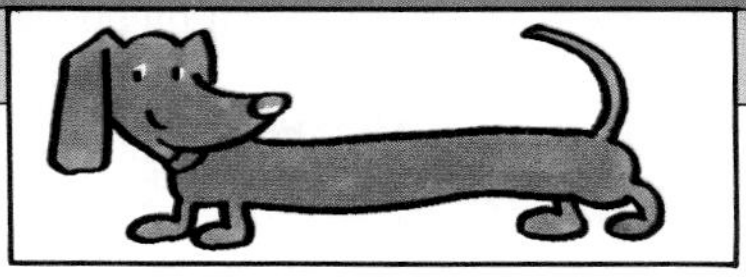

chien

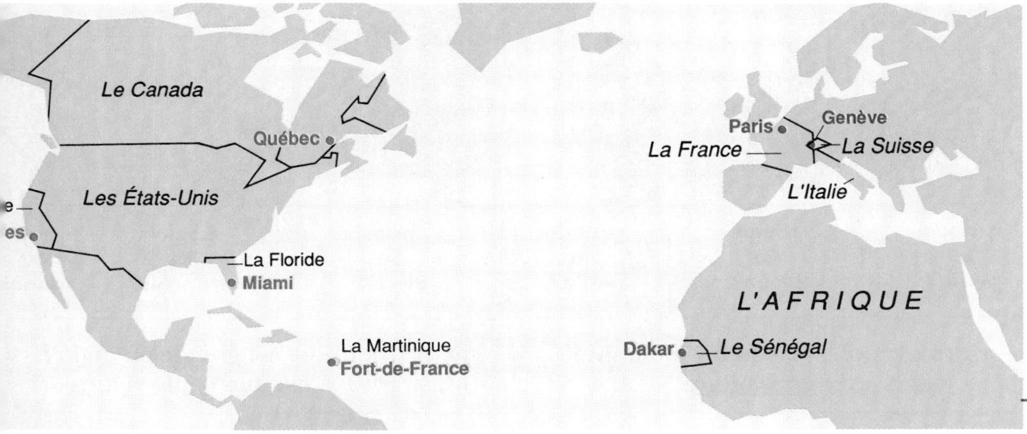
Le Canada
Québec
Les États-Unis
La Floride
Miami
La Martinique
Fort-de-France
Paris
Genève
La France
La Suisse
L'Italie
L'AFRIQUE
Dakar
Le Sénégal

8 COMMUNICATION: talking about what one likes to do

Re-entry and review: Verbs from Unit 4.

Challenge: The second student asks the same question of the first student, who must respond using another adjective.
– Tu aimes parler français?
– Oui, c'est extra! Et toi, tu aimes parler français?
– Non, c'est difficile.

Prononciation

Leçon 20, Section 7

Pronunciation notes

- Although "ch" is usually pronounced /tʃ/ in English, as in *march* and *chocolate,* the letters do represent the sound /ʃ/ in words and names that came directly from French: **Chevrolet, chef, chauffeur, chic, touché,** etc.
- Sometimes the letters "ch" are pronounced /k/ in French, just as they are in the corresponding English cognates: **orchestre, Christine, écho.**

Cooperative pair practice
Activity 8

1 COMPREHENSION

1-e	4-a
2-c	5-b
3-d	

🔊 **Leçon 20, Section 8**

2 GUIDED ORAL EXPRESSION

1. devant la pharmacie / une moto rouge
2. devant la librairie / une petite fille
3. devant le restaurant / un homme blond
4. devant le cinéma / un garçon anglais
5. devant la fontaine / un chien jaune

🔊 **Leçon 20, Section 9**

À votre tour!

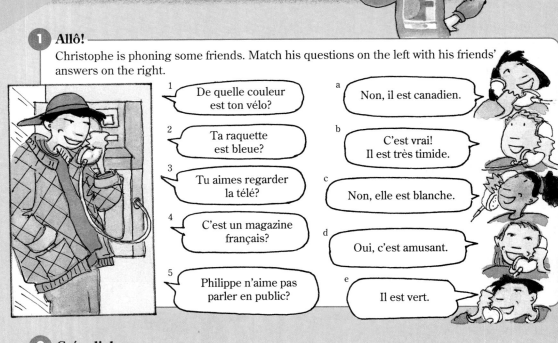

1 Allô!

Christophe is phoning some friends. Match his questions on the left with his friends' answers on the right.

1. De quelle couleur est ton vélo?
2. Ta raquette est bleue?
3. Tu aimes regarder la télé?
4. C'est un magazine français?
5. Philippe n'aime pas parler en public?

a. Non, il est canadien.
b. C'est vrai! Il est très timide.
c. Non, elle est blanche.
d. Oui, c'est amusant.
e. Il est vert.

2 Créa-dialogue

There has been a burglary in the rue Saint-Pierre. By walkie-talkie, two detectives are describing what they see. Play both roles.

(le)	1. (la)	2. (la)	3. (le)	4. (le)	5. (la)
grande ou petite?	rouge ou bleue?	grande ou petite?	brun ou blond?	anglais ou français?	noir ou jaune?

▶ DÉTECTIVE 1: **Qu'est-ce qu'il y a devant <u>le café</u>?**   DÉTECTIVE 1: **<u>Elle est grande</u> ou <u>petite</u>?**
DÉTECTIVE 2: **Il y a <u>une voiture</u>.**   DÉTECTIVE 2: **C'est <u>une petite voiture</u>.**

178 **Unité 5**

À votre tour

Depending on your goals and objectives, you may or may not wish to assign all of the activities in the **À votre tour** section.

👥 Cooperative practice

Act. 1, 2, and 3 lend themselves to cooperative pair practice.

3 Faisons connaissance!

Try to find out which students have the same interests you do. Select two activities you enjoy from Column A and ask a classmate if he/she likes to do them. Your classmate will answer yes or no, using an appropriate expression from Column B.

Tu aimes voyager?

Oui, c'est amusant.

A	B
chanter	chouette
danser	super
nager	extra
téléphoner	amusant
voyager	intéressant
jouer au foot	pénible
jouer au volley	drôle
organiser des boums	difficile
parler avec les voisins	facile
parler français en classe	
dîner au restaurant	

Tu aimes parler français en classe?

Non, c'est difficile.

4 Composition: La chambre de Véronique

Look at the picture of Véronique's room. Write a short paragraph in which you describe five of the following items. You may want to mention color or size **(grand? petit?)**, and perhaps give your opinion **(joli? beau? drôle? bon?,** etc.)

la chambre
la porte
le lit
la table
la chaise
la radiocassette
la guitare
l'affiche

▶ **La chambre de Véronique est bleue et blanche. Elle a un grand lit. . . .**

5 Composition: Ma chambre

Write a short description of your own room: real or imaginary. Use only vocabulary that you know. You may use the suggestions about Véronique's room as a guide.

---

3 CONVERSATION

4 GUIDED WRITTEN EXPRESSION

5 WRITTEN SELF-EXPRESSION

■ **Teaching strategy:** You may wish to have your students include a drawing of their room with their composition. They should label all furniture and items in French.

Classroom Notes

 Portfolio assessment

You will probably select only one speaking activity and one writing activity to go into the students' portfolios for Unit 5.

In this lesson, Act. 5 is a good written portfolio topic.

Vive la différence!

Le monde personnel

Parlons° de votre monde° personnel. Répondez aux questions suivantes.° D'après° vous, quelles sont les réponses des jeunes Français en général à ces° questions?

OBJECTIVES:
- Reading skills development
- Re-entry of materials in the unit
- Development of cultural awareness

Le monde personnel

OBJECTIVES:
- Rapid reading at the sentence level
- Reading for cultural information about personal possessions and attitudes of French people

1 Combien de télés est-ce qu'il y a chez vous?°

- zéro
- une
- deux
- trois ou plus°

Et dans une maison française typique, combien est-ce qu'il y a de télés?

2 Combien de livres est-ce qu'il y a chez vous?

- dix
- cinquante
- cent
- plus de° cent cinquante

Et dans une maison française typique, combien de livres est-ce qu'il y a?

3 Dans la classe de français, quel est le pourcentage d'élèves qui ont un walkman?

- moins de° 25% (vingt-cinq pour cent)
- entre° 26% et 50%
- entre 51% et 75%
- entre 76% et 100% (cent pour cent)

Selon° vous, quel est le pourcentage de jeunes Français qui ont un walkman?

4 En général, comment sont vos relations avec vos parents?

- très bonnes
- bonnes
- assez bonnes
- mauvaises

Et en France, comment sont les relations entre parents et enfants?°

5 Quand vous avez une ch[ose] importante à discuter° (p[ar] exemple, un problème personnel), à qui est-ce [que] vous préférez parler?

- à votre frère ou à votre s[œur]
- à votre père ou à votre m[ère]
- à un copain ou à une co[pine]
- à un professeur

Et les jeunes Français, à [qui] est-ce qu'ils préfèrent pa[rler] de leurs° problèmes?

6 En général, qu'est-ce qu[e] vous pensez° de vos professeurs?

- Ils sont «cool».
- Ils sont compréhensifs.°
- Ils sont sévères.°
- Ils sont sympathiques.

Et les élèves français, qu'est-ce qu'ils pensent [de] leurs professeurs?

7 Quelle est la chose la pl[us] importante dans votre v[ie]?

- l'argent°
- l'amitié°
- l'indépen[dance]
- les étude[s]

Et pour les jeunes Franç[ais,] quelle est la chose la plu[s] importante?

Et les Français?

1. La majorité des familles françaises ont seulement *(only)* une télé. 2. Les Français aiment lire *(to read)*. Ils ont en moyenne *(on the average)* plus de cent livres par famille. 3. 41% (quarante et un pour cent) 4. La majorité des jeunes Français ont de très bonnes relations avec leurs parents. 5. En général, ils préfèrent parler à un copain ou à une copine. 6. En général, ils pensent que leurs professeurs sont sympathiques. 7. C'est l'amitié.

Parlons *Let's talk* **monde** *world* **suivantes** *following* **D'après** *According to* **ces** *these* **chez vous** *in your home* **plus** *more* **plus de** *more than* **moins de** *less than* **entre** *between* **Selon** *According to* **enfants** *children* **discuter** *to discuss* **leurs** *their* **pensez** *think* **compréhensifs** *understanding* **sévères** *strict* **la plus** *the most* **vie** *life* **argent** *money* **amitié** *friendship* **études** *studies*

👥👥 Cooperative reading practice

Divide the class into groups of 4 or 5, each with a **secrétaire.**

For each question, have the students give their own opinions and then vote on what they imagine French responses to be. (Keep answers covered.)

Then have the recorders announce their results to the entire class. For example:

1. Nous avons deux télés chez nous. Selon nous, dans une maison française typique il y a deux télés.

When all results have been announced, let the students look at the answers.

La mobylette

Because mopeds or cyclomoteurs are easy and fun to drive, they are very popular with French teenagers. During the week, many students go to school on their mopeds. On weekends, they take their mopeds to go downtown or to go for a ride in the country with their friends.

Although the term mobylette is a trade name, students tend to use the term (or its shortened form mob) to refer to any type of moped. In France, you can drive a mobylette at age 14, and the only restrictions are that you must wear a helmet and cannot exceed 45 kilometers per hour.

Look at the ads on the right. Which moped would you like to have? Describe it using words that you know. (What color is it? What country is it from? Is it big or small?)

MOTOBÉCANE

Siège social: 16 rue Lesault, 93502 Pantin

PEUGEOT
concessionnaire
Ets SOUHART

scooters • cyclos • motos
métro Bir Hakeim   5, bd. de Grenelle   75015 PARIS
01 45 79 33 01

boulmich'
MOTO
129, bd St-Michel Paris 5
01 43 29 53 10

LA MOTO VERTE
Concessionnaire Exclusif
Yamaha
85 r Chardon Lagache
75016 Paris **01 42 24 56 56**

Entracte 5 (181)

LECTURE ET CULTURE

La mobylette

OBJECTIVES:
• Reading for information
• Understanding authentic documents

 18.5 Vignette culturelle: La mobylette
(51:28–52:55 min.)

VIDEODISC Disc 3, Side 2
21324–23676

■ As an introduction, play the *Vignette culturelle* about the **mobylette** from Video Module 18.

■ **Sample response:**
Je voudrais avoir la Motobécane. Elle est verte et noire. Elle est française. Elle n'est pas très grande.

■ **Pronunciation: mob** /mɔb/

■ **Realia notes**
• Motobécane:
  siège social *main office, company headquarters*
• Peugeot:
  un concessionnaire *dealership*
  un cyclo = cyclomoteur *motor bike*
• **Boulmich'** = Boulevard Saint Michel

📖 **Pre-reading**

Ask students what kinds of two-wheelers they have.
  Qui a un vélo?
  Qui a un VTT (vélo tout terrain: mountain bike)?
  Qui a une mobylette?

OBJECTIVES:
- Reading a complete text
- Building reading skills

■ Questions sur le texte
1. Quel âge a Brigitte?
2. Comment est-elle physiquement?
3. Quels sports est-ce qu'elle aime?
4. Où est-ce qu'elle habite?
5. Où travaille son père? Qu'est-ce qu'il fait?
6. Où travaille sa mère? Qu'est-ce qu'elle fait?
7. Comment s'appelle la soeur de Brigitte? Quel âge a-t-elle? Comment est-elle?
8. Comment s'appelle le frère de Brigitte? Quel âge a-t-il? Comment est-il?
9. Est-ce que Brigitte a des animaux?
10. Quelles choses est-ce qu'elle a?
11. Est-ce qu'elle a un petit copain?

■ Questions personnelles
1. Quel âge as-tu?
2. Est-ce que tu es grand(e), petit(e) ou de taille moyenne?
3. Est-ce que tu as les yeux bleus ou marron (brown) ou noirs?
4. Est-ce que tu as des frères ou des soeurs?
5. (Pour chaque frère ou chaque soeur):
   Comment est-ce qu'il/elle s'appelle?
   Quel âge est-ce qu'il/elle a?
   Comment est-il/elle?
6. Est-ce que tu as un chien? un chat? un poisson rouge?
   Comment est-ce qu'il s'appelle?
7. Est-ce que tu as un vélo?
   Est-ce que tu aimes faire des promenades à vélo?
8. Quels autres (other) objets est-ce que tu as?

𝓔𝓷𝓽𝓻𝓮 𝓪𝓶𝓲𝓼: Bonjour, Brigitte!

Chers copains américains,

Je m'appelle Brigitte Lavie. J'ai quatorze ans. Voici ma photo. Je ne suis pas très grande, mais je ne suis pas petite. Je suis de taille° moyenne.° Je suis brune mais j'ai les yeux° verts. Je suis sportive. J'aime le ski, le jogging et la danse moderne.

J'habite à Toulouse avec ma famille. Mon père travaille dans l'industrie aéronautique. Il est ingénieur.° Ma mère travaille dans une banque. Elle est directrice° du personnel.

J'ai une soeur et un frère. Ma petite soeur s'appelle Ariane. Elle a cinq ans. Elle est très mignonne. Mon frère s'appelle Jérôme. Il a treize ans. Il est pénible. J'ai un chien. Il s'appelle Attila mais il est très gentil. (Il est plus gentil que° mon frère!) J'ai aussi deux poissons rouges.° Ils n'ont pas de nom.°

J'ai une chaîne stéréo et des quantités de compacts. J'ai aussi une mobylette. Le weekend, j'adore faire des promena à mobylette avec mes copains. J'ai beaucoup de copains, mais je n'ai pas de « petit copain ».° Ça n'a pas d'importance!° Je suis heureuse° comme ça!

Amitiés,
Brigitte

Chers *Dear*   **taille** *size*   **moyenne** *average*   **yeux** *eyes*   **ingénieur** *engineer*   **directrice** *director*
plus gentil que *nicer than*   **poissons rouges** *goldfish*   **nom** *name*   **faire des promenades** *go for rides*
petit copain *boyfriend*   **Ça n'a pas d'importance!** *It doesn't matter!*   **heureuse** *happy*   **comme ça** *like that*

■ NOTE ■
CULTURELLE

★ Paris
Toulouse

Toulouse

Toulouse, with a population of over half a million people, is the center of the French aeronautic and space industry. It is in Toulouse that the Airbus planes and the Ariane rockets are being built in cooperation with other European countries.

 Pre-reading

Ask if students know in which American city NASA (National Aeronautic and Space Agency) is headquartered. [Houston]

Then ask if they know where the French space center is located. [Toulouse]
Tell them they will be reading a letter from Toulouse.

Comment lire
GUESSING FROM CONTEXT

* As you read French, try to guess the meanings of unfamiliar words before you look
  at the English equivalents. Often the context provides good hints. For example,
  Brigitte writes:

  Je ne suis pas très grande, mais je ne suis pas petite.
  Je suis <u>de taille moyenne</u>.

  She is neither tall nor short. She must be about average:

  de taille moyenne = *of medium height or size*

* Sometimes you know what individual words in an expression mean, but the phrase
  does not seem to make sense. Then you have to guess at the real meaning. For
  example, Brigitte writes that she has:

  deux poissons rouges *??red fish??*

  If you guessed that these are most likely *goldfish,* you are right!

Enrichissez votre vocabulaire
MORE ON COGNATES

* Some words are PARTIAL COGNATES. The English word may help you remember the
  regular meaning. For example:

gentil	looks like	*gentle*	but means	*nice*
grand	looks like	*grand*	but means	*tall, big*
j'adore	looks like	*I adore*	but means	*I love*

* Some cognates are spelled differently in the two languages. Knowing cognate
  patterns makes it easier to identify new words. For example:

FRENCH	ENGLISH	FRENCH	ENGLISH
-ique	*-ic*	**aéronautique**	*aeronautic, aeronautical*
-ique	*-ical*	**typique**	*typical*
-té	*-ty*	**quantité**	*quantity*

Activité

Can you identify the English equivalents of the following French words?

  la musique classique, une personne dynamique, un film comique,
  une guitare électrique, une société, une activité, une possibilité,
  la curiosité, la beauté

Activité: Une lettre à Brigitte

Write a letter to Brigitte in which you describe
yourself and your family. You may tell her:

* your name and how old you are
* if you are tall or short
* if you like sports
* if you have brothers and sisters (If so,
  give their names and ages.)

* if you have pets (If so, say what type
  and give their names.)
* a few things you own
* a few things you like to do with your friends

Comment écrire *(to write)* **une lettre**

Begin with: (to a boy) **Cher**   **Cher Patrick,**
           (to a girl) **Chère**   **Chère Brigitte,**

End with: **Amicalement,** *(In friendship,)*
          Amitiés, *(Best regards,)*

Entracte 5 183

Post-reading activity

Maybe your class would like to exchange
letters with a French class in another
school in your area. (The advantage of
cross-city exchanges is that letters can be
exchanged easily.)

Have your students each write letters
introducing themselves.

Place these in a large envelope and
exchange packets with a French teacher
in another school. The first set of correspondence will be distributed randomly.
From then on, however, students will
have a specific penpal to correspond with
during the year.

Classroom Notes

Variétés

OBJECTIVE:
• Reading for fun and vocabulary enrichment

■ **Casual speech:**
For **sensationnel(le)** one can also say **sensas** /sãsas/

Variétés

Petit catalogue des compliments et des insultes

 Pre-reading
Have students suggest English sayings about personality traits that mention animals. E.g.,
Blind as a bat. Sly as a fox.
An elephant never forgets.
More fun than a barrel of monkeys.
Stubborn as a mule.

Post-reading
Which of the French sayings are similar to American sayings? Which are different?

LES ANIMAUX ET LE LANGAGE

Selon° toi, est-ce que les animaux ont une personnalité? Pour les Français, les animaux ont des qualités et des défauts,° comme° nous. Devine° comment on° complète les phrases suivantes° en français.

1 Philippe n'aime pas étudier. Il préfère dormir.° Il est paresseux° comme° . . .

un tigre

un chat

un lézard

2 Charlotte adore parler. Elle est bavarde° comme . . .

une poule

une pie

un lion

3 Isabelle est une excellente élève. Elle a une mémoire extraordinaire. Elle a une mémoire d' . . .

un éléphant

un hippopotame

un kangourou

4 Le petit frère de Christine est jeune, mais il est très intelligent. Il est malin° comme . . .

un cheval

un singe

une girafe

5 Où est Jacques? Il n'est pas prêt!° Oh là là! Il est lent° comme . . .

une tortue

un poisson

un rhinocéros

6 Nicole a très, très faim. Elle a une faim de (d') . . .

lion

ours

loup

Voici les réponses:
1. un lézard 2. une pie 3. un éléphant 4. un singe 5. une tortue 6. loup

---

Selon *According to* **défauts** *shortcomings* **comme** *like* **Devine** *Guess* **on** *one* **phrases suivantes** *following sentences* **dormir** *to sleep* **paresseux** *lazy* **comme** *as* **bavarde** *talkative* **malin** *clever* **prêt** *ready* **lent** *slow*

Entracte 5 185

LECTURE ET CULTURE

UNITÉ 5 INTERNET PROJECT

Students may use the Internet to find out about the hobbies, interests, and **le monde personnel** of French-speaking teenagers from all over the world. They can start with the link available below, or use the alternate given. To expand this activity, have students generate new links by using the search engine of their choice and the keywords **loisirs (culture; musique; danse; folklore; voyage)** + *(name of French-speaking country)*.

Music: AfroPop Worldwide
http://www.afropop.org/

ALTERNATE
Répertoire de sites touristiques de l'Afrique du Nord
http://www.francomedia.qc.ca/~pberland/afrique.htm

Game: Cooperative pair reading

Be sure all students cover the answers at the bottom of the page. (If you prefer, you can make a transparency of the questions and project it on the overhead.)

Divide the class into pairs. How many groups can complete the six expressions correctly?

UNITÉ

6 En ville

186

Unit overview

COMMUNICATION GOALS: Students will be able to ask and give directions, and to describe their city and their home. They will also learn to talk about future plans.
LINGUISTIC GOALS: Students will learn to use the verbs **aller** and **venir**, and the possessive adjectives.

CRITICAL THINKING GOALS: Students will observe both linguistic similarities (use of **aller** to express future time) and differences (use of possessive adjectives) between French and English.
CULTURAL GOALS: This unit introduces students to two French cities: Paris (in the student text) and Tours (in the video).

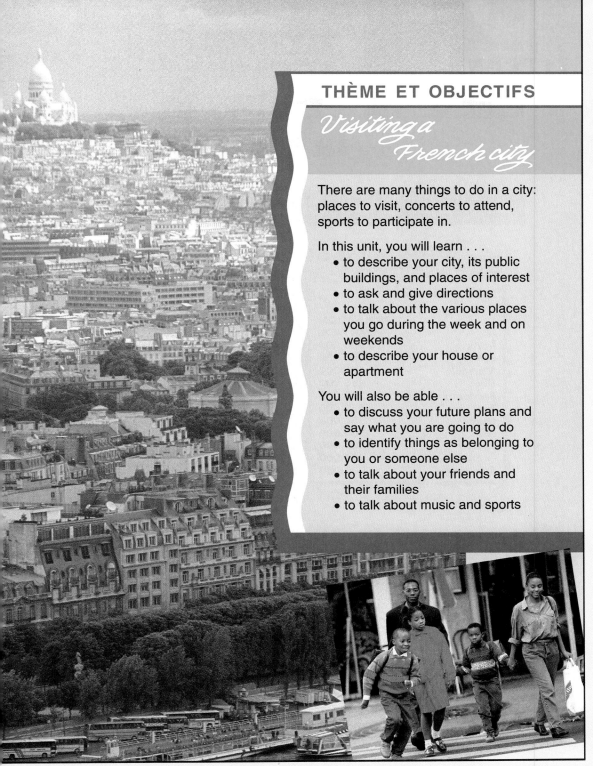

THÈME ET OBJECTIFS

Visiting a French city

There are many things to do in a city: places to visit, concerts to attend, sports to participate in.

In this unit, you will learn . . .
- to describe your city, its public buildings, and places of interest
- to ask and give directions
- to talk about the various places you go during the week and on weekends
- to describe your house or apartment

You will also be able . . .
- to discuss your future plans and say what you are going to do
- to identify things as belonging to you or someone else
- to talk about your friends and their families
- to talk about music and sports

Classroom Notes

➤ **Assessment Options**

ACHIEVEMENT TESTS

Lesson Quizzes 21-24 pp. 83-90
  Test Cassette B, Side 1

Unit Test 6
  Portfolio Assessment
  pp. T196-197, Activities
  1-5; pp. T208-209,
  Activities 1-5; pp.
  T218-219, Activities
  1-5; pp. T228-229,
  Activities 1-5

PROFICIENCY TESTS

 Listening Comprehension
  Performance Test, p. 37
  Test Cassette D, Side 1

 **Speaking Performance Test, p. 29**

 Reading Comprehension
  Performance Test, p. 28

 Writing Performance Test, p. 49

 Test Bank, Unit 6
  Version A or B

 CD-ROM DFi B,
  Exploration 6
  Cahier, Créa-dialogue

MODULE 21:
Le français pratique:
La ville et la maison
Total time: 7:17 min.
(Counter 00:40 min.)

21.1 Introduction: Listening — Les villes de France (00:50–1:57 min.)

21.2 Dialogue: La ville de Tours (1:58–5:02 min.)

21.3 Mini-scenes: Speaking — Qu'est-ce que c'est? (5:03–6:05 min.)

21.4 Mini-scenes: Listening — Pardon! Excusez-moi! (6:06–6:58 min.)

21.5 Vignette culturelle: La maison d'Olivier (6:59–7:55 min.)

VIDEODISC Disc 4, Side1
1536–14604

■ **Comprehension practice:** Play the entire module through as an introduction to the lesson.

  21.1 Introduction: Les villes de France
21.2 Dialogue: La ville de Tours (00:50–5:02 min.)

VIDEODISC Disc 4, Side1
1849–9386

■ **Cultural note:** Marseille was founded by the Phoenicians in 600 B.C. Paris and Lyon were founded by the Romans at the time of Julius Caesar around 43 B.C.

La ville et la maison

Accent sur ... Les villes françaises

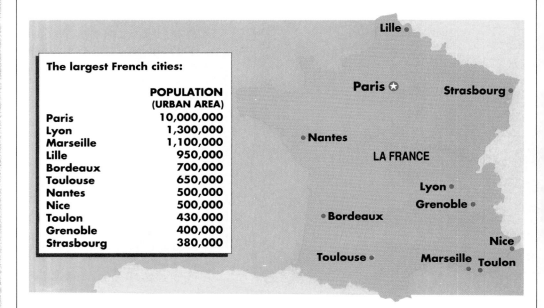

The largest French cities:	
	POPULATION (URBAN AREA)
Paris	10,000,000
Lyon	1,300,000
Marseille	1,100,000
Lille	950,000
Bordeaux	700,000
Toulouse	650,000
Nantes	500,000
Nice	500,000
Toulon	430,000
Grenoble	400,000
Strasbourg	380,000

- Today 80% of the French population lives in cities and their surrounding suburbs.

- French cities have a long history. Paris, Lyon, and Marseille, the three largest French cities, were founded well over two thousand years ago! Many cities have a historical district with houses and monuments dating back several centuries. At the same time, French cities also appear very modern, with growing numbers of new houses and modern office buildings.

- French cities differ in architectural style from region to region because of their geographical location and their historical background. However, they also share many common features.

188 Unité 6

Setting the scene

PROPS: Worksheets with a map of France and 11 dots representing the above cities + Tours. Names of the 11 cities are listed at bottom.

Have students keep their books closed. Divide the class into teams of 4 or 5. Have the teams try to locate the cities on the map.

Have the teams open their books to correct their maps.
- How many cities did they find correctly?
- Have they heard about any of these cities?

Tell students that in the video they will visit the city of Tours, in the Loire valley.

Here are some of the places you may see when you visit a French city:

- ### La gare

  For the French, trains are a rapid and inexpensive way to travel. Stations are usually near the center of town. The station **(la gare)** offers useful services, such as an information desk, a car/bicycle rental agency, luggage lockers, restaurants, shops and a travel agency.

- ### La poste

  There are many things you can do in a French post office **(la poste)** besides buying stamps. You can make long-distance phone calls and buy a phone card. You can deposit and withdraw money with special postal checking accounts. In many post offices you can use the **Minitel.**

- ### Les magasins

  Although supermarkets and grocery chain stores now exist all over France, most French people still love to shop at the local bakery **(la boulangerie),** the pastry shop **(la pâtisserie),** the butcher shop **(la boucherie),** the grocery store **(l'épicerie),** etc.

- ### Le parc

  The city park **(le parc public)** or public garden **(le jardin public)** is the place where French young people come at noon or after class to walk around or to sit on chairs and talk. The colorful flower beds and shrubbery of the public parks reflect the French love of nature and beauty. This is the Jardin du Luxembourg in Paris.

- ### Le château

  Many French cities were built around a medieval castle **(un château),** which offered protection against enemy attack. This is the castle of Angers built in the XIIIth century.

Leçon 21 **189**

■ Photo culture note

La gare
This picture shows the main hall in the **Gare de Lyon** in Paris. The train waiting on the track is a **TGV (un train à grande vitesse).**

La poste
Formerly known as the **PTT (Poste, Téléphone, Télégraphe)** and then as the **P et T (Poste et Télécommunications),** the French post office has now changed its official name to **La Poste.** Note that French post offices often have mail drops **(une boîte à lettres)** on the outside wall so pedestrians can mail letters at any time of day.

Les magasins
This photograph shows a combined bakery and pastry shop **(une boulangerie-pâtisserie).** There one can buy French bread **(une baguette)** as well as croissants, eclairs **(un éclair),** cakes **(un gâteau),** and pies **(une tarte).**

Angers
The city of Angers is the capital of the province of **Anjou,** located in the western part of France. This province was the home of the Angevin kings of England, the most famous of whom was Richard the Lion-Hearted **(Richard Coeur de Lion:** 1157–1199).

⟲ Le Minitel
To review information on the **Minitel,** see p. 132.

Talking about past events

Let's talk about what time you did certain things. (Review times, if needed.)

▶ **À quelle heure est-ce que tu as dîné hier?**
  J'ai dîné à sept heures et quart.

- **X, à quelle heure est-ce que tu as étudié?**

- **À quelle heure est-ce que tu as téléphoné à des amis?**
- **Y et Z, à quelle heure est-ce que vous avez dîné samedi soir?**
- **À quelle heure est-ce que vous avez regardé la télé?**

T189

■ **Vocabulary note:** Point out that **adresse** is feminine.

Supplementary vocabulary

au centre-ville *downtown*
dans la banlieue *in the suburbs*
à la campagne *in the country*
dans un immeuble *in an apartment house*

■ **Photo culture note**
Le "Vieux Tours"
In the background you see the **Place Plumereau** with its houses dating back to the 16th and 17th centuries. The exposed wooden beams and the steep slate roofs are typical of the period. Since its renovation in the 1960s, this area of Tours with its cafés and outdoor concerts has become very popular with young people.

1 COMMUNICATION: describing where you live

■ **Language note:** In item 4, help students with numbers.
In France, *P.O. Box* = **B.P. (Boîte postale).**
In Canada, *P.O. Box* = **C.P. (Case postale).**

2 ROLE PLAY: asking where people live

■ **Expansion:** Ask students questions about the person they were interviewing.
X, où est-ce que Y habite?

Cooperative pair practice
Activity 2

A. Où habites-tu?

How to talk about where one lives:

Où habites-tu?
J'habite | à Tours.
| à Villeneuve
| dans **une grande ville** (*city, town*)
| dans **un petit village**
| dans **un joli quartier** (*neighborhood*)
| dans **une rue** (*street*) intéressante

J'habite à Tours.

Quelle est **ton adresse?**
J'habite | 32, **avenue** Victor Hugo.
| 14, **rue** La Fayette
| 50, **boulevard** Wilson

■ NOTE ■
CULTURELLE

Le nom des rues

In France, streets are often named after famous people, especially writers, artists, and politicians.

16ᵉ Arr!
AVENUE VICTOR HUGO
(1802 · 1885)
ECRIVAIN POETE
ET HOMME POLITIQUE

9ᵉ Arr!
RUE LA FAYETTE
1757 · 1834
HEROS DE LA GUERRE D'INDEPENDANCE
AMERICAINE DE 1777 A 1782

• Victor Hugo (1802–1885), novelist and poet, is best known for his monumental novel *Les Misérables*.
• La Fayette (1757–1834) played an important role in the American and French Revolutions.
• Woodrow Wilson (1856–1924) is remembered as the United States President who sent American troops to help French forces fight against Germany during World War I (1914–1918).

1 **Expression personnelle**
Describe where you live by completing the following sentences.

1. J'habite à . . .
2. Ma ville est (n'est pas) . . . (grande? petite? moderne? jolie?)
   Mon village est (n'est pas) . . . (grand? petit? joli?)
3. Mon quartier est (n'est pas) . . . (intéressant? joli? moderne?)
4. Mon adresse est . . .
5. Ma ville favorite est . . .
6. Un jour, je voudrais visiter . . . (*name of city*)

2 **Interview**
You are a French journalist writing an article about living conditions in the United States. Interview a classmate and find out the following information.

1. Where does he/she live?
2. Is his/her city large or small?
3. Is his/her city pretty?
4. What is his/her address?

190 Unité 6

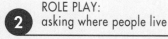

TPR **Places**

PROPS: Vocabulary cards of the places on p. 191: blue borders on masculine nouns, red borders on feminine nouns.

Model nouns as you place them on chalk-tray.
    Voici un théâtre. Voici une église. …

Hold up a picture. [museum card]
    Est-ce un café? [non]
    Est-ce un musée? [oui]
Ask students to pass cards to classmates.
    X, prends le parc et donne-le à Y. …
    Qui a le parc? [Y] …
Have all students with cards hold them up.
    Montrez-nous vos cartes.

B. Ma ville

▶ *How to talk about one's hometown:*

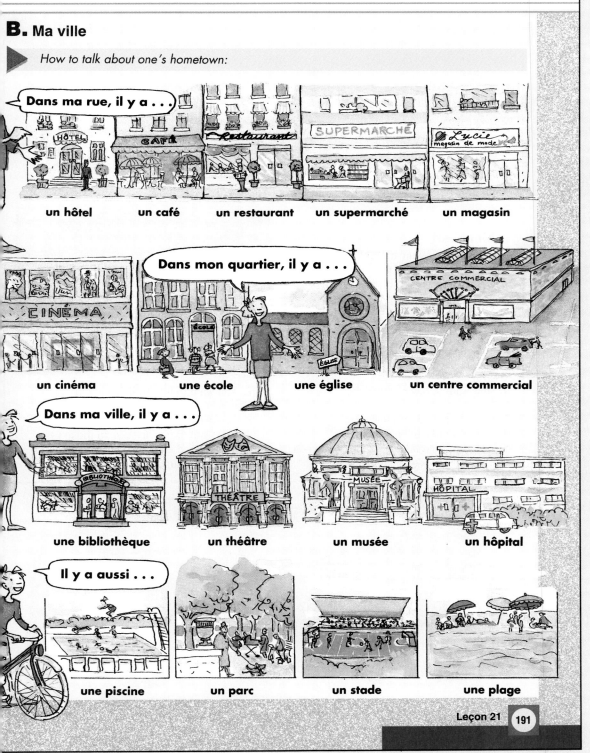

Dans ma rue, il y a . . .

un hôtel   un café   un restaurant   un supermarché   un magasin

Dans mon quartier, il y a . . .

un cinéma   une école   une église   un centre commercial

Dans ma ville, il y a . . .

une bibliothèque   un théâtre   un musée   un hôpital

Il y a aussi . . .

une piscine   un parc   un stade   une plage

Leçon 21   191

Section B

COMMUNICATIVE FUNCTION:
Identifying places in one's
hometown

21.3 Mini-scenes:
Qu'est-ce que c'est?
(5:03–6:05 min.)

VIDEODISC Disc 4, Side 1
9405–11287

Leçon 21, Sections 1, 2, 3

Transparency 30
Ma ville

Language note: Compare:
une église *Catholic church*
un temple (protestant) *Protestant*
church
une synagogue *Jewish temple or*
synagogue

Supplementary vocabulary

un aéroport *airport*
un collège *junior high school*
un fast-food *fast-food restaurant*
un lycée *senior high school*
un terrain de sport *athletic fields*

une banque *bank*
une boutique *shop*
une gare *(train) station*
une mairie *city hall*
une Maison des jeunes *youth*
center
une pharmacie *drugstore*
la poste *post office*
une station-service *gas station*
une université *university*

Note two cards on either side of the room.
Qui a l'hôtel? [X] **Qui a la piscine?** [Z]
Oh là là! L'hôtel est loin de la
piscine! [gesture distance]
Note two cards that are close together.
Où est le stade?   Où est le parc?
Est-ce que le stade est loin du parc?
[non]
Non, le stade est près du parc. ...

If time allows, have students pass around
the cards. For example, have X give the
hotel card to a student who is near Z.
X, lève-toi et donne l'hôtel à Y.
Et maintenant, est-ce que l'hôtel est
loin de la piscine? [non]
L'hôtel est près de la piscine.

3 Ton quartier

Say whether the following places are located in the area where you live. If so, you may want to give the name of the place.

▶ école   **Il y a une école. Elle s'appelle «Washington School».**
      (Il n'y a pas d'école.)

1. restaurant
2. cinéma
3. église
4. centre commercial
5. bibliothèque
6. café
7. plage
8. supermarché
9. hôpital
10. parc
11. stade
12. musée
13. hôtel
14. piscine
15. théâtre

■ **Teaching strategy:** Be sure students use expressions they have learned in the lesson.

▭ **Leçon 21, Section 3**

4 À Montréal

You are visiting your friend Pauline in Montreal. For each of the situations below, decide where you would like to go. Ask Pauline if there is such a place in her neighborhood.

▶ You are hungry.

Pauline, est-ce qu'il y a un restaurant dans ton quartier?

1. You want to have a soft drink.
2. You want to see a movie.
3. You want to swim a few laps.
4. You want to run on a track.
5. You want to read a book about Canada.
6. You want to see a French play.
7. You want to buy some fruit and crackers.
8. You want to see an art exhibit.
9. You want to play frisbee on the grass.
10. You slipped and you're afraid you sprained your ankle.

■ **Realia note**
Aux Anciens Canadiens is a traditional restaurant in Quebec City. **Le Grill** is located in Montréal. Have students note that prices are given in Canadian dollars (**un dollar canadien**).

LE GRILL 183 ST-PAUL EST 397-1044
LE BISTROT DU GRILL   LE RESTAURANT
                       CUISINE FRANÇAISE
• Steak frites
  Salade
  $5.95
• Poulet rôti
  frites, salade
  $5.95
CHANSON FRANÇAISE
jeu., ven. et sam.
dès 21h.
AMBIANCE GARANTIE
Atmosphère chaleureuse
Vieille maison du 17e siècle
LA PLUS BELLE TERRASSE DU VIEUX MONTRÉAL

aux Anciens Canadiens
RESTAURANT

Cooperative pair practice
Activities 4, 5

Teaching note: Sounding French

An aim of Act. 3 is to get students to sound French as they use the new words.

Warm-up: First, have students imagine that they live in a large city. Ask the class:
   Est-ce qu'il y a une école?
   Oui, il y a une école. ...
Be sure to correct pronunciation problems.

Then ask them to imagine they live in the desert, and have them answer negatively.
   Est-ce qu'il y a une école?
   Non, il n'y a pas d'école. ...
When they can handle the place names fluently, have students describe the area where they actually live.

C. Pour demander un renseignement (information)

▶ *How to ask for directions:*

| Pardon,
Excusez-moi, | monsieur.
madame
mademoiselle | Où est l'hôtel Normandie? |

Il est dans la rue Jean Moulin.

Où est-ce qu'il y a un café?

| Il y a un café | **rue** Saint Paul.
boulevard Masséna
avenue de Lyon | **une rue**
un boulevard
une avenue |

Où est-ce? *(Where is it?)*
Est-ce que c'est **loin** *(far)?*

Non, ce n'est pas loin.
C'est **près** *(nearby).*

| C'est | **à gauche** *(to the left).*
à droite *(to the right)*
tout droit *(straight ahead)* | **Tournez**
Continuez | à gauche.
à droite
tout droit. |

Merci beaucoup!

Pardon, monsieur.
Où est l'hôtel Normandie?

Il est dans
la rue Jean Moulin.

Où est-ce? Est-ce
que c'est loin?

Non, ce n'est pas loin.
C'est près.

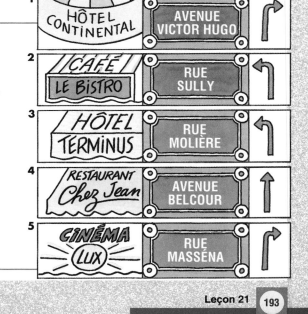

5 En ville

A tourist who is visiting a French city asks a local resident how to get to the following places. Act out the dialogues.

▶ — Pardon, mademoiselle (monsieur).
  Où est le Café de la Poste?
— Le Café de la Poste? Il est dans la
  rue Pascal.
— Où est-ce?
— Continuez tout droit!
— Merci, mademoiselle
  (monsieur).

1	HÔTEL CONTINENTAL	AVENUE VICTOR HUGO	↱
2	CAFÉ LE BISTRO	RUE SULLY	↰
3	HÔTEL TERMINUS	RUE MOLIÈRE	↰
4	RESTAURANT Chez Jean	AVENUE BELCOUR	↑
5	CINÉMA LUX	RUE MASSÉNA	↱

Section C

COMMUNICATIVE FUNCTION:
Asking for directions

📺 **21.4 Mini-scenes: Pardon!**
   Excusez-moi!
   (6:06–6:58 min.)

DEODISC   Disc 4, Side 1
   11292–12860

‖‖‖‖‖‖‖‖‖‖‖‖‖‖‖‖‖‖‖

🔲 **Leçon 21, Section 4**
   Cultural notes

- Jean Moulin (1899–1943) was a
  hero of the French resistance
  against the Nazi occupation in
  World War II.
- Masséna (1758–1817) was one
  of Napoléon's marshals.

Supplementary vocabulary

C'est près d'ici.   C'est à côté.
C'est tout près.   C'est en face.
C'est loin d'ici.

⑤ ROLE PLAY:
   asking and giving directions

1. l'hôtel Continental / dans
   l'avenue Victor Hugo / à droite
2. le café «Le Bistro» / dans la
   rue Sully / à gauche
3. l'hôtel Terminus / dans la rue
   Molière / à gauche
4. le restaurant «Chez Jean» /
   dans l'avenue Belcour / tout
   droit
5. le cinéma Lux / dans la rue
   Masséna / à droite

   Cultural notes
- Blaise Pascal (1623–1662),
  mathematician and philosopher.
- Duc de Sully (1559–1641),
  finance minister of Henri IV.
- Molière (1622–1673), classical
  author, writer of comedies.

 👥👥 **Class project**
Have students prepare a map of their city
or neighborhood, marking the various
place names in French.
    Let them use this map for role-play
activities in which they show visitors how
to get around.

**21.5 Vignette culturelle:
La maison d'Olivier**
(6:59–7:55 min.)

VIDEODISC Disc 4, Side 1
12876-14604

Leçon 21, Section 5

Transparency 31
La maison

Pronunciation: Be sure students do NOT pronounce an "n" in **en haut**: /ã o/. The word **haut** begins with an *aspirate h.* There is never liaison or elision before an *aspirate h.*

Language notes
• **Les toilettes:** also **les WC** (called **double vécé** or simply **vécé**); or **les cabinets**.
• **Une chambre** is a *room,* in the sense of *bedroom.*
• **Une pièce** is the more general word for *room of a house.*

Cultural notes
• Traditionally in a French home the toilet is in a small room separate from the bathroom.
• **Un salon** is a traditional formal living room. In modern, less formal homes, one may find **un séjour** (**une salle de séjour**), also referred to as **un living** (**un living-room**).
• In French homes, the shutters (**les volets**) are usually closed every night.

Supplementary vocabulary

une entrée
un escalier *staircase*
un ascenseur *elevator*
le toit *roof*
le grenier *attic*
le sous-sol *basement*
la cave *cellar*

T194

D. Ma maison

J'habite dans une maison.

How to describe one's home:

J'habite dans | **une maison** *(house).*
| **un appartement**
| **un immeuble** *(apartment building)*

Ma maison / mon appartement est | **moderne.**
| **confortable**

Ma chambre est | **en haut** *(upstairs).*
| **en bas** *(downstairs)*

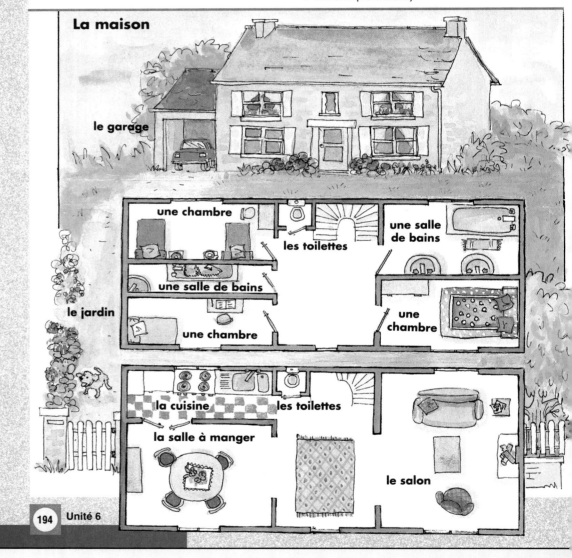

La maison

le garage
une chambre
les toilettes
une salle de bains
une salle de bains
le jardin
une chambre
une chambre
la cuisine
les toilettes
la salle à manger
le salon

194 Unité 6

TPR **The house**

PROPS: Transparency 31; magazine pictures of various rooms

Identify the new words on the transparency.
Voici le salon. Voilà la cuisine. …
X, viens ici et montre-nous le jardin. …

Place the magazine pictures on the desk. Have students pick up specific pictures and place themselves around the room.
X, prends le salon et mets-toi près de la porte.
Y, prends la salle à manger et mets-toi devant le tableau noir.

6 Ma maison

Describe your home by completing the following sentences.

1. J'habite dans . . . (une maison? un appartement?)
2. Mon appartement est . . . (grand? petit? confortable? joli?)
   Ma maison est . . . (grande? petite? confortable? jolie?)
3. La cuisine est . . . (grande? petite? moderne?)
4. La cuisine est peinte *(painted)* en . . . (jaune? vert? gris? blanc?   ??)
5. Ma chambre est peinte en . . . (bleu? rose?   ??)
6. Dans le salon, il y a . . . (une télé? un sofa? des plantes vertes?   ??)
7. En général, nous dînons dans . . . (la cuisine? la salle à manger?)
8. Ma maison / mon appartement a . . . (un jardin? un garage?   ??)

APPARTEMENTS PARIS

VUE SUR PARIS
Beau studio avec séj.,
cuis., s. de b., w-c,
cave. 80 000 euros

M° ST-PAUL
Exceptionnel dans imm.
historique, refaits neufs.
2 p. 75 m²

7 En haut ou en bas?

Imagine you live in a two-story house. Indicate where the following rooms are located.

▶ ma chambre

Ma chambre est en haut.

Ma chambre est en bas.

1. la cuisine
2. la salle à manger
3. les toilettes
4. la salle de bains
5. la chambre de mes *(my)* parents
6. le salon

8 Où sont-ils?

From what the following people are doing, guess where they are — in or around the house.

▶ Madame Martin répare *(is repairing)* la voiture.
  Elle est dans le garage.

1. Nous dînons.
2. Tu regardes la télé.
3. Antoine et Juliette jouent au frisbee.
4. J'étudie le français.
5. Monsieur Martin prépare le dîner.
6. Henri se lave *(is washing up)*.
7. Ma soeur téléphone à son copain.

CHAMBRE 2
408 x 290

CHAMBRE 1
419 x 311

PL.

S. de B.
300 x 170

PL.

SÉJOUR
467 x 436

ENTRÉE

W.-C.

PL.

CUISINE
601 x 170

COMMUNICATION:
describing your home

6

■ **Realia note:** Help students read the ads.
séj. = un séjour *(living room)*
cuis. = une cuisine
s. de b. = salle de bains
w-c *(pronounced /vese/: toilet)*
cave = une cave *(cellar storage area)*
imm. = un immeuble
refaits neufs *(completely remodeled)*
2 p. = 2 pièces *(two rooms)*
75 m² = 75 mètres carrés *(75 square meters or 810 square feet)*

DESCRIPTION:
indicating where rooms are located

7

■ **Language note:** Be sure students use the plural in item 3: Les toilettes **sont...**

COMPREHENSION:
describing where people are

8

■ **Realia note:** Ask questions about the floor plan:
Trouvez l'entrée, le séjour, les deux chambres, la cuisine, la salle de bains, les toilettes (les W-C).
Est-ce qu'il y a aussi des toilettes dans la salle de bains?
Combien de placards *(closets)* **y a-t-il?**

Once the layout of the house has been set, have other students go to various rooms.
Z, tu as faim. Va à la cuisine.
Qui est dans la cuisine? [Z]
W, tu veux regarder la télé. Va au salon.
V, tu dois te laver les mains [gesture].
Va dans la salle de bains. ...

Cooperative pair practice
Activity 7

COMPREHENSION

1-e   4-a
2-c   5-b
3-d

🔊 **Leçon 21, Section 6**

② GUIDED ORAL EXPRESSION

1. Il y a un café avenue de Bordeaux. / C'est près.
2. Il y a un restaurant boulevard de la République. / C'est près (c'est loin).
3. Il y a une église rue Saint-Louis. / C'est près.
4. Il y a un supermarché rue Pascal. / C'est près (c'est loin).
5. Il y a une bibliothèque avenue de Bordeaux. / C'est très près.
6. Il y a un stade avenue de Bordeaux. / C'est loin.
7. Il y a une piscine rue Jean Moulin. / C'est loin.
8. Il y a un cinéma rue Danton. / C'est près.
9. Il y a un hôpital avenue de Bordeaux. / C'est loin.

🔊 **Leçon 21, Section 7**

③ GUIDED ORAL EXPRESSION

🔊 **Leçon 21, Section 8**

À votre tour!

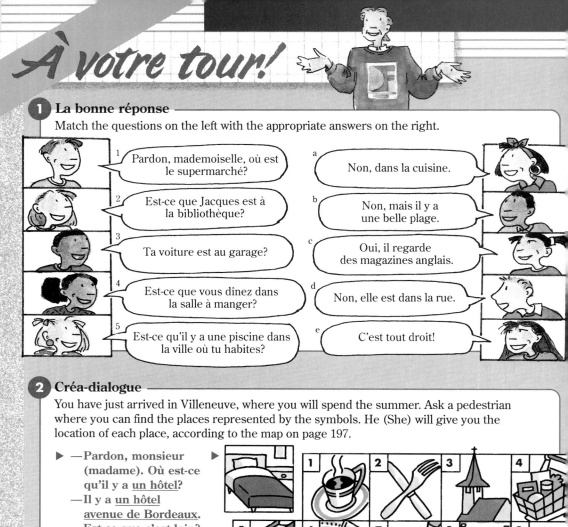

① La bonne réponse

Match the questions on the left with the appropriate answers on the right.

1. Pardon, mademoiselle, où est le supermarché?
2. Est-ce que Jacques est à la bibliothèque?
3. Ta voiture est au garage?
4. Est-ce que vous dînez dans la salle à manger?
5. Est-ce qu'il y a une piscine dans la ville où tu habites?

a. Non, dans la cuisine.
b. Non, mais il y a une belle plage.
c. Oui, il regarde des magazines anglais.
d. Non, elle est dans la rue.
e. C'est tout droit!

② Créa-dialogue

You have just arrived in Villeneuve, where you will spend the summer. Ask a pedestrian where you can find the places represented by the symbols. He (She) will give you the location of each place, according to the map on page 197.

▶ —Pardon, monsieur (madame). Où est-ce qu'il y a <u>un hôtel</u>?
—Il y a <u>un hôtel</u> <u>avenue de Bordeaux</u>.
—Est-ce que c'est loin?
—<u>Non, c'est près</u>.
—Merci beaucoup!

③ Où est-ce?

Now you have been in Villeneuve for several weeks and are familiar with the city. You meet a tourist on the avenue de Bordeaux at the place indicated on the map. The tourist asks you where certain places are and you indicate how to get there.

▶ l'hôpital Sainte Anne

Pardon, monsieur. Où est l'hôpital Sainte Anne?

C'est tout droit, mademoiselle.

Merci bien, monsieur.

À votre tour

Select those activities which are most appropriate for your students.

🎧 Cooperative practice
In Act. 2 and 3, you may want to have students work cooperatively in trios, with two performing and one consulting the Answer Key and acting as monitor.

■ Portfolio assessment

You will probably select only one speaking activity and one writing activity to go into the students' portfolios for Unit 6.

In this lesson, Act. 5 offers an excellent writing portfolio topic.

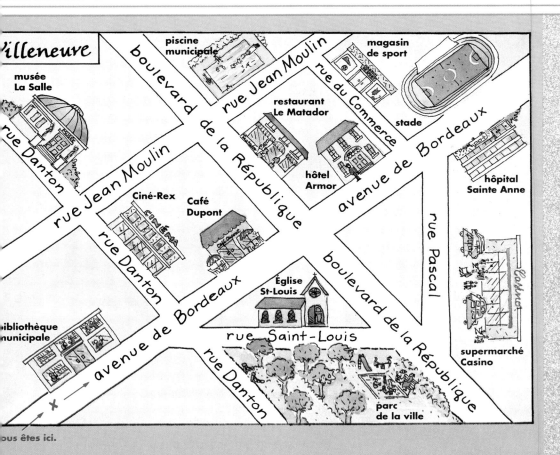

ous êtes ici.

Classroom Notes

4 WRITTEN SELF-EXPRESSION

5 WRITTEN SELF-EXPRESSION

■ **Realia notes**
• **Une villa** is a newer house built in the suburbs of the larger cities. It usually has a small yard or garden.
• **Le R.E.R. (Réseau Express Régional** or Regional Express Network) is a rapid train system that connects Paris and its suburbs.
• Vocabulary:
à partir de 200.000 euros *prices begin at 200,000 euros*
commerces *shops*
à 10 mn. *10 minutes away*

4 Mon quartier

Describe your neighborhood, listing five places and giving their names.

▶ **Dans mon quartier, il y a un supermarché. C'est le supermarché Casino.**

1. le musée La Salle
2. le supermarché Casino
3. l'hôtel Armor
4. le restaurant Le Matador
5. l'église Saint Louis

5 Composition: La maison idéale

Briefly describe your dream house. You may use the following adjectives to describe the various rooms: **grand, petit, moderne, confortable, joli,** as well as colors. If you wish, sketch and label a floor plan.

Modernes et confortables . . .
SUPERBES VILLAS
à partir de 200 000 euros
Près toutes commodités
Écoles, lycées, commerces, R.E.R. à 10 mn.

Leçon 21 **197**

Challenge activities: Villeneuve

If appropriate, you can introduce additional challenge activities using the map of Villeneuve.

Have students give more complex directions, using **continuez tout droit, tournez à gauche dans la rue Pascal, ...**

Getting around: Have students give directions from one place to the next, e.g., from **l'hôtel Armor** to **le musée La Salle**, from **le musée** to **le supermarché**, etc.

Mystery destination: Tell students that they are at place "x" on the map. Give them instructions in French to get to a new location. **Maintenant, où êtes-vous?**

MODULE 22:
Une promenade en ville
Total time: 6:35 min.
(Counter: 8:04 min.)

22.1 Mini-scenes: Listening — Où allez-vous? (8:34–9:04 min.)

22.2 Mini-scenes: Listening — Où est-ce que tu vas? (9:05–9:30 min.)

22.3 Mini-scenes: Speaking — Où vont-ils? (9:31–10:25 min.)

22.4 Mini-scenes: Listening — Qu'est-ce que vous allez faire? (10:26–11:34 min.)

22.5 Mini-scenes: Speaking — Tu vas nager? (11:35–12:22 min.)

22.6 Dialogue: Julien travaille (12:23–13:13 min.)

22.7 Vignette culturelle: Le métro (13:14–14:36 min.)

VIDEODISC Disc 4, Side1
14844–26635

Leçon 22, Section 1

LEÇON 22 Weekend à Paris

Aujourd'hui c'est samedi.
Les élèves <u>ne vont pas</u> en classe.   *are not going*
Où est-ce qu'ils vont alors?
Ça dépend!

Thomas <u>va</u> au café.   *is going*
Il a un <u>rendez-vous</u> avec une copine.   *date*

Florence et Karine vont aux
Champs-Élysées.
Elles vont regarder les magasins
de <u>mode</u>.   *fashion*
<u>Après</u>, elles vont <u>aller</u> au cinéma.   *Afterward / to go*

Daniel va <u>chez son</u> copain Laurent.   *to the house of /*
Les garçons vont jouer au ping-pong.
Après, ils vont aller au musée des
sciences de la Villette.
Ils vont jouer avec les machines
électroniques.

Béatrice a un grand sac et des
<u>lunettes de soleil</u>.   *sunglasses*
Est-ce qu'elle va à un rendez-vous
secret?
Non! Elle va au Centre Pompidou.
Elle va regarder les acrobates.
Et après, elle va écouter un concert.

Et Jean-François? Qu'est-ce qu'il va
faire aujourd'hui?
Est-ce qu'il va visiter le Centre Pompidou?
Est-ce qu'il va regarder les acrobates?
Est-ce qu'il va écouter un concert?
<u>Hélas</u>, non!   *Alas (Unfortuna*
Il va <u>rester</u> à la maison.   *to stay*
Pourquoi? Parce qu'il est <u>malade</u>.   *sick*
<u>Pauvre</u> Jean-François!   *Poor*
Il fait <u>si</u> beau <u>dehors</u>!   *so / outside*

198   Unité 6

Talking about past events

Let's talk about where you have been recently. Note that the past participle of **être** is **été**.

▶ **Est-ce que tu as été en ville le weekend dernier?**
Oui, j'ai été en ville.
(Non, je n'ai pas été en ville.)

- **Est-ce que tu as été à la piscine samedi?**
- **Est-ce que tu as été à la bibliothèque?**
- **Est-ce que tu as été au centre commercial? au musée? au parc?**
- **Est-ce que tu as été au théâtre samedi soir?**
- **Est-ce que tu as été à l'hôpital?**
- **Où est-ce que tu as été dimanche dernier?**

Compréhension

1. Quel jour est-ce aujourd'hui?
2. Pourquoi est-ce que Thomas va au café?
3. Avec qui est-ce que Florence va au cinéma?
4. Où va Daniel?
5. Qu'est-ce que Daniel et Laurent font d'abord *(first)*?
6. Où va Béatrice?
7. Pourquoi est-ce que Jean-François ne va pas en ville?
8. Quel temps fait-il aujourd'hui?

■ NOTE ■
CULTURELLE

À Paris

Paris offers many attractions for people of all ages. Here are some places particularly popular with young people.

Le parc de la Villette

This spacious park on the outskirts of Paris is home to a new modern science museum with its hundreds of hands-on exhibits. Also located on the grounds is Le Zénith, a large music hall that frequently features rock concerts.

Le Centre Pompidou

This immense cultural center, also known as Beaubourg, is dedicated to modern art. It has a large media library where young people have access to all types of audio-visual equipment. On the large plaza in front of the building, one can listen to reggae and jazz bands or watch mimes, jugglers, and acrobats.

Les Champs-Élysées

The Champs-Élysées is a wide avenue with elegant shops, movie theaters, and popular cafés.

199

COMPREHENSION

1. samedi
2. Il a un rendez-vous avec une copine.
3. avec Karine
4. chez son copain Laurent
5. Ils jouent au ping-pong.
6. au Centre Pompidou
7. Il est malade.
8. Il fait très beau.

💡 **Critical thinking activity**
Write on the chalkboard:
Elles vont aux Champs-Élysées.
Elles vont regarder les magasins.
Ask: How would you express these sentences in English?
In which sentence does **vont** mean that the girls are actually going to *a place?* Is the place mentioned?
In which sentence does **vont** mean that the girls are going to *do something?* Is the activity mentioned?
Read the opening text and look for examples of **va** and **vont**.
Which ones refer to movement?
Which ones refer to future activities?

Note culturelle

- **La Cité des Sciences** in the **parc de la Villette**. In the background you see a large steel sphere, **La Géode**, which houses the Omni theater and its circular panoramic screen.
- **Le Centre Pompidou** was named in honor of Georges Pompidou who was President of France (1969-1974).
The **Fontaine Igor Stravinski** contains colorful sculptures which Niki de Saint-Phalle designed to evoke Stravinsky's music such as "The Firebird" (**L'Oiseau de feu**).
- The Champs-Élysées is also the scene of the **Défilé** *(parade)* **du Quatorze Juillet** and the **Arrivée** *(finish)* **du Tour de France** bicycle race.

■ **Teaching strategy**
- Have students read the cultural notes and look at the photos.
- Play the cassette of the opening text (books closed).
- On the board, write words and phrases students remember.

■ **Language note:** Remind students of the elision (with **ne**) in the negative forms:
nous n'allons pas
vous n'allez pas

■ **Language usage:** The verb **aller** is usually accompanied by a word or phrase indicating a place. (After the verb *to go* in English, the place is often left out.) Compare:
Quand est-ce que tu vas à Paris?
When are you going to Paris?
Je vais à Paris en mai.
I am going (to Paris) in May.

■ **Pronunciation:** Be sure that students use liaison in **vas-y** and **allons-y.**

■ **Vocabulary expansion**
When speaking to several people:
Allez-y!
Allez-vous-en!

Note also:
On y va! *Let's go!*

A. Le verbe *aller* ———————————————

Aller *(to go)* is the only IRREGULAR verb that ends in **-er**. Note the forms of **aller** in the present tense.

aller	to go	J'aime **aller** au cinéma.
je **vais** tu **vas** il/elle **va**	*I go, I am going* *you go, you are going* *he/she goes, he/she is going*	Je **vais** à un concert. **Vas**-tu à la boum? Paul **va** à l'école.
nous **allons** vous **allez** ils/elles **vont**	*we go, we are going* *you go, you are going* *they go, they are going*	Nous **allons** au café. Est-ce que vous **allez** là-bas? Ils ne **vont** pas en classe.

➡ Remember that **aller** is used in asking people how they feel.

Ça **va**? Oui, ça **va**.
Comment **vas**-tu? Je **vais** bien, merci.
Comment **allez**-vous? Très bien.

➡ **Aller** is used in many common expressions.

To encourage someone to do something: To tell someone to go away:
Vas-y! *Come on! Go ahead! Do it!* **Va-t'en!** *Go away!*

To tell friends to start doing something:
Allons-y! *Let's go!*

Teaching note: Listening activities

A. Review gestures for the subject pronouns (see Lesson 15, TPR activity, p. 110). Make statements about where people are going; have students identify the subject.
 Il va au stade.
 [signal **il/elle**]
 Elles vont au cinéma.
 [signal **ils/elles**] ...

B. On the board, write **aller/avoir/être/faire.** Make statements using the four verbs. Students say which one they heard.
 Mes amis sont à Tours. [être]
 Ils ont des vélos. [avoir]
 Ils font une promenade. [faire]
 Ils vont à la piscine. [aller]
 Ils vont nager. [aller] ...

1 Les vacances

The following students at a boarding school in Nice are going home for vacation. Indicate to which of the cities they are going, according to the luggage tags shown below.

▶ Jean-Michel est canadien.

n-Michel va à Québec.

1. Je suis suisse.
2. Charlotte est américaine.
3. Nous sommes italiens.
4. Tu es français.
5. Vous êtes espagnols.
6. Michiko est japonaise.
7. Mike et Shelley sont anglais.
8. Ana et Carlos sont mexicains.

2 Jamais le dimanche!
(Never on Sunday!)

On Sundays, French students do not go to class. They all go somewhere else. Express this according to the model.

▶ Philippe/au cinéma
Le dimanche, Philippe ne va pas en classe.
Il va au cinéma.

1. nous / au café
2. vous / en ville
3. Céline et Michèle / à un concert
4. Jérôme / au restaurant
5. je / à un match de foot
6. tu / à la piscine

Leçon 22 201

COMPREHENSION: telling people what cities to go to

1. Genève   5. Madrid
2. Chicago 6. Tokyo
3. Rome   7. Londres
4. Lyon   8. Acapulco

↺ **Re-entry and review:** Adjectives of nationality (from Lesson 19).

■ **Challenge:** Let students name another city in the appropriate country.
Jean-Michel va à Montréal.

PRACTICE: describing where people are going/not going

Classroom Notes

☀ Warm-up: Cities and nationalities

Review nationalities, with books closed.
Indicate where people live, and have students give their nationalities. First use masculine singular subjects.
Henri habite à Paris. [Il est français.]
Bill habite à Boston. [Il est américain.]
Practice with the cities of Act. 1.

Then continue with feminine singular subjects.
Marie habite à Genève. [Elle est suisse.]
Finally practice with plural subjects.
Tatsuo et Michiko habitent à Kyoto. [Ils sont japonais.]
Sally et Susie habitent à Liverpool. [Elles sont anglaises.]

 **22.1** Mini-scenes: Où allez-vous?
22.2 Mini-scenes: Où est-ce que tu vas?
(8:34–9:30 min.)

VIDEODISC Disc 4, Side1
15065–17397

▭▭▭ Leçon 22, Sections 2, 3

■ **Teaching note:** Be sure students realize that the words in heavy print in the three columns on the right correspond to *the*, *at the*, and *to the*.

■ **Teaching note:** You may want to point out the use of **à** with certain verbs.
téléphoner à:
  Je téléphone à Pierre.
  Je téléphone au professeur.
jouer à:
  Je joue au tennis.
  Nous jouons à la balle.

3 EXCHANGES: asking where people are going

1. au stade/à la piscine
2. au cinéma/au théâtre
3. à l'hôtel/au supermarché
4. à la bibliothèque/au musée
5. à l'école/au parc

B. La préposition *à*; *à* + l'article défini

The preposition **à** has several meanings:

in	Patrick habite **à** Paris.	*Patrick lives **in** Paris.*
at	Nous sommes **à** la piscine.	*We are **at** the pool.*
to	Est-ce que tu vas **à** Toulouse?	*Are you going **to** Toulouse?*

CONTRACTIONS

Note the forms of **à** + DEFINITE ARTICLE in the sentences below.

Voici **le** café.	Marc est **au** café.	Corinne va **au** café.
Voici **les** Champs-Élysées.	Tu es **aux** Champs-Élysées.	Je vais **aux** Champs-Élysées.
Voici **la** piscine.	Anne est **à la** piscine.	Éric va **à la** piscine.
Voici **l'**hôtel.	Je suis **à l'**hôtel.	Vous allez **à l'**hôtel.

The preposition **à** contracts with **le** and **les,** but not with **la** and **l'.**

CONTRACTION	NO CONTRACTION		
à + le → **au**	à + la = **à la**	**au** cinéma	**à la** piscine
à + les → **aux**	à + l' = **à l'**	**aux** Champs-Élysées	**à l'**école

➡ There is liaison after **aux** when the next word begins with a vowel sound.
  Le professeur parle **aux élèves.** Je téléphone **aux amis** de Claire.

3 **Dans la rue**
Two friends meet in the street and talk about where they are going.

▶ Tu vas au café?

Non, je vais à la plage.

202 Unité 6

Teaching note: Additional practice

Although contractions are not hard to learn, students often fail to use them in conversation. Sometimes extra drill practice helps them internalize the patterns.

Je suis au café.
(le cinéma) **Je suis au cinéma.**

(la piscine)	**Je suis à la piscine.**
(l'hôpital)	**Je suis à l'hôpital.**
(le stade)	**Je suis au stade.**
(l'appartement)	**Je suis à l'appartement.**
(le musée)	**Je suis au musée.**
(la maison)	**Je suis à la maison.**
(le restaurant)	**Je suis au restaurant.**

4 Préférences

Ask your classmates about their preferences. Be sure to use contractions when needed.

▶ aller à (le concert ou le théâtre?)

1. dîner à (la maison ou le restaurant)?
2. étudier à (la bibliothèque ou la maison)?
3. nager à (la piscine ou la plage)?
4. regarder un match de foot à (la télé ou le stade)?
5. aller à (le cinéma ou le musée)?

Tu préfères aller au concert ou au théâtre?

Je préfère aller au concert.

(Je préfère aller au théâtre.)

5 À Paris

You are living in Paris. A friend asks you where you are going and why. Act out the dialogues with a classmate.

▶ —Où vas-tu?
—Je vais à l'Opéra.
—Pourquoi?
—Parce que j'aime le ballet classique.

OÙ?	POURQUOI?
▶ l'Opéra	J'aime le ballet classique.
1. l'Alliance Française	J'ai une classe de français.
2. le Centre Pompidou	J'aime l'art moderne.
3. le musée d'Orsay	C'est un musée intéressant.
4. les Champs-Élysées	J'ai un rendez-vous là-bas.
5. la tour Eiffel	Il y a une belle vue (view) sur Paris.
6. le Zénith	Il y a un concert de rock.
7. la Villette	Il y a une exposition (exhibit) intéressante.
8. le stade de Bercy	Il y a un match de foot.

6 Où vont-ils?

Read what the following people like to do. Then say where each one is going by choosing the appropriate place from the list.

▶ Daniel aime danser.
Il va à la discothèque.

1. Corinne aime l'art moderne.
2. Jean-François aime manger.
3. Delphine aime les westerns.
4. Marina aime nager.
5. Éric aime regarder les magazines.
6. Denise aime faire des promenades.
7. Philippe aime la musique.
8. Alice aime le football.
9. Cécile aime le shopping.

le stade
la bibliothèque
le cinéma
le centre commercial
la discothèque
le musée
le parc
le restaurant
la plage
le concert

LOUVRE droit d'entrée

Leçon 22 **203**

COMMUNICATION: expressing preferences

■ Expansion: Additional cues: aller à (le musée ou la bibliothèque)? aller à (le café ou le restaurant)? aller à (l'école ou le parc)?

EXCHANGES: explaining why one goes somewhere

■ Teaching note: Have students find these places on the map of Paris in the photo essay on p. 237.

■ Cultural background: L'Opéra There are two opera buildings in Paris:
L'Opéra Garnier, the old opera house, now home of the Paris ballet.
L'Opéra de la Bastille, concert hall built in 1989, home of the Paris opera. (See ticket on p. 204.)

COMPREHENSION: concluding where people are going

22.3 Mini-scenes: Où vont-ils? (9:31–10:35 min.)

VIDEODISC Disc 4, Side 1 17419-19066

Leçon 22, Section 4

T203

▷ Vocabulaire

Language note: The word **rendez-vous** includes all types of appointments with friends, teachers, doctors, dentists, etc. The term means that people have arranged to meet somewhere.

Supplementary vocabulary

une exposition *exhibit*

22.7 Vignette culturelle: Le métro (13:14–14:36 min.)

VIDEODISC Disc 4, Side 1
24099–26635

Transparency 33
Means of transportation

Language notes
• Un bus (un autobus) is a city bus that follows a regular route.
• An intercity or tour bus is **un car** or **un autocar**.
• A school bus is **un car scolaire**.

Realia note
Have the students look at the Opera ticket (**le billet**).
Quelle est la date du concert?
[le 19 mai]
Quel jour de la semaine est-ce?
[samedi]
À quelle heure est le concert?
[20 heures = 8 heures du soir]
Qui chante? [Montserrat Caballé]
Combien coûte le billet? [30 euros]

Vocabulaire:
la porte *door*   **le rang** *row*
l'allée *aisle*   **la place** *seat*
le parterre *orchestra (seating)*

COMMUNICATION:
answering personal questions

7

■ **Photo culture note**
Le Lycée Corot
The students are at the entrance to the lycée. (For more on this school, see pages 76–81.)

Vocabulaire: En ville

Quelques endroits où aller

un endroit	*place*	**une boum,**	
un concert	*concert*	**une fête,**	
un film	*movie*	**une soirée**	*party*
un pique-nique	*picnic*		
un rendez-vous	*date, appointment*		

OPERA BASTILL
DE PARIS
MONTSERRAT CABALLE (CONCERT)
19/05 Porte **08** Allée E
SAMEDI 20H00 RANG PLACE
30 € PA **10 . 36**
0215 8121 0028 PARTERRE

VERBES

arriver	*to arrive, come*	**J'arrive** à l'école à 9 heures.
rentrer	*to go back, come back*	À quelle heure **rentres**-tu à la maison?
rester	*to stay*	Les touristes **restent** à l'hôtel.

EXPRESSIONS

à pied	*on foot*	**en voiture**	*by car*	**en métro**	*by subway*
à vélo	*by bicycle*	**en bus**	*by bus*	**en taxi**	*by taxi*
		en train	*by train*		

faire une promenade à pied	*to go for a walk*
faire une promenade à vélo	*to go for a ride (by bike)*
faire une promenade en voiture	*to go for a drive*

7 Questions personnelles

1. En général, à quelle heure est-ce que tu arrives à l'école?
2. À quelle heure est-ce que tu rentres à la maison? Qu'est-ce que tu fais quand tu rentres à la maison?
3. Comment vas-tu à l'école? à pied, à vélo, en voiture ou en bus?
4. Le weekend, est-ce que tu restes à la maison? Où vas-tu?
5. Comment vas-tu à la piscine? à la plage? au cinéma?
6. Est-ce que tu aimes faire des promenades à pied? Où vas-tu? avec qui?
7. Est-ce que tu aimes faire des promenades à vélo? Où vas-tu?
8. En général, est-ce que tu aimes regarder les films à la télé? Quels films est-ce que tu préfères? (films d'action? films de science-fiction? comédies?)
9. Quand tu as un rendez-vous avec un copain ou une copine, où allez-vous?
10. Est-ce que tu fais *(go on)* des pique-niques? où?

Talking about past events

Let's talk about where you went yesterday. We will use the passé composé of **aller**:

present of **être** + **allé(e)**

(Note: since the focus is on spoken French, there is no need to introduce the agreement of the past participle at this time.)

▶ **Est-ce que tu es allé(e) en ville hier? Oui, je suis allé(e) en ville. (Non, je ne suis pas allé(e) en ville.)**

• **X, est-ce que tu es allé(e) au cinéma hier? à l'école? au supermarché?**

C. La préposition *chez*

Note the use of **chez** in the following sentences.

Paul est **chez Céline.**	*Paul is **at Céline's** (house).*
Je dîne **chez un copain.**	*I am having dinner **at a friend's** (home).*
Nathalie va **chez Juliette.**	*Nathalie is going **to Juliette's** (apartment).*
Tu vas **chez ta cousine.**	*You are going **to your cousin's** (place).*

The French equivalent of *to* or *at someone's (house, home)* is the construction:

chez + PERSON	**chez** Béatrice	**chez** ma cousine

➡ Note the interrogative expression: **chez qui?**

Chez qui vas-tu? *To whose house are you going?*

8 En vacances

When we are on vacation, we often like to visit friends and relatives. Say where the following people are going.

▶ Claire / Marc
Claire va chez Marc.

1. Hélène / Jérôme
2. Jean-Paul / Lucie
3. tu / un copain
4. Corinne / une cousine
5. vous / des copines à Québec
6. nous / un cousin à Paris

Chez nous...
l'argent va
plus loin
avec le train!

SNCF

9 Weekend

On weekends, we often like to visit friends and do things together. Say how the following people are spending Sunday afternoon.

▶ Cécile / jouer au ping-pong / Robert

Cécile joue au ping-pong chez Robert.

1. Nathalie / aller / Béatrice
2. Claire / dîner / des cousins
3. Éric / jouer au croquet / Sylvie
4. Marc / écouter des disques / un copain
5. Jean-Pierre / regarder la télé / une copine
6. Catherine / jouer au Monopoly / François

Leçon 22 205

Section C

COMMUNICATIVE FUNCTION: Talking about going to someone's house

◼ **Language notes**
• **Chez** also means *at the office of:* **Je vais chez le docteur.**
• Be sure students see that the word **chez** means *to* or *at someone's place.*
The preposition **à** is NEVER used with **chez**.

◼ **Looking ahead:** **Chez** + stress pronouns is presented in Lesson 23.

◼ **Pronunciation:** There is no liaison between **chez** and the name of a person:
chez Alice, chez Éric
However there is liaison with **un/une**:
chez un(e) ami(e)

8 PRACTICE: saying whom people are visiting

◼ **Realia note:** This ad has been placed by the French railroad company **SNCF (Société Nationale des Chemins de fer Français)** and features the rapid **TGV (le train à grande vitesse).**
Note the slogan: "At our house, money goes farther with the train." (That is, we save money when we take the train.)

9 DESCRIPTION: stating at whose home people do certain activities

• **Y, est-ce que tu es allé(e) chez des amis? chez des cousins?**
• **Est-ce que tu es allé(e) à un pique-nique? à la bibliothèque?**
• **Z, où est-ce que tu es allé(e) hier matin? hier après-midi? hier soir?**

Follow-up: Ask students what others did.
• **Est-ce que X est allé(e) au cinéma hier?**
• **Est-ce que Y est allé(e) chez des amis hier?**
• **Où est-ce que Z est allé(e) hier matin?**

22.4 Mini-scenes: Qu'est-ce que vous allez faire?

22.5 Mini-scenes: Tu vas nager?
(10:26–12:22 min.)

VIDEODISC Disc 4, Side 1
19095–22575

Leçon 22, Sections 5, 6

Casual speech: One can also say: **Vous allez rentrer quand?** Note that **Tu vas faire quoi?** is less common than **Qu'est-ce que tu vas faire?**

DESCRIPTION: describing destinations and plans

Cultural notes
- The coliseum (**le Colisée**) is a large stadium built by the Romans.
- The **Vieux Carré** is the part of the French Quarter known for its jazz clubs and its picturesque old buildings with wrought iron balconies.
- Historically, Kyoto was the capital of Japan; one can still visit the many Buddhist temples there as well as the Emperor's palace.

Realia note: These are two folding brochures (**un dépliant**), one for **le Louvre** (the famous Paris art museum), and the other for the Mediterranean village of **Sanary.**

Cooperative
pair practice
Activity 11

T206

D. La construction *aller* + l'infinitif

The following sentences describe what people are *going to do.* Note how the verb **aller** is used to describe these FUTURE events.

Nathalie **va nager.**	*Nathalie **is going to swim.***
Paul et Marc **vont jouer** au tennis.	*Paul and Marc **are going to play** tennis.*
Nous **allons rester** à la maison.	*We **are going to stay** home.*
Je **vais aller** en ville.	*I **am going to go** downtown.*

To express the NEAR FUTURE, the French use the construction:

PRESENT of **aller** + INFINITIVE

→ In negative sentences, the construction is:

SUBJECT	+	**ne**	+ PRESENT of **aller**	+	**pas**	+	INFINITIVE . . .
Sylvie		**ne**	va		**pas**		écouter le concert avec nous.

→ Note the interrogative forms:

Qu'est-ce que tu vas faire?	***What are you going** to do?*
Quand est-ce que vous allez rentrer?	***When are you going** to come back?*

Learning about language

To talk about FUTURE plans and intentions, French and English frequently use similar verbs: **aller** *(to be going to).*

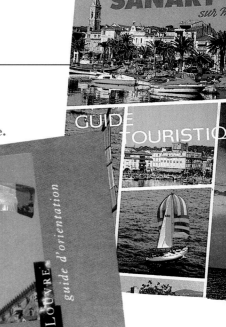

10 Tourisme

Say where the following people are going this summer and what they are going to visit.

▶ Monique (à Paris / le Louvre)
  Monique va à Paris. Elle va visiter le Louvre.

1. Alice (à New York / la statue de la Liberté)
2. nous (en Égypte / les pyramides)
3. vous (à Rome / le Colisée)
4. tu (à La Nouvelle Orléans / le Vieux Carré)
5. je (à San Francisco / Chinatown)
6. les élèves (à San Antonio / l'Alamo)
7. Madame Lambert (à Beijing / la Cité interdite *[Forbidden City]*)
8. les touristes (à Kyoto / les temples)

11 Qu'est-ce que tu vas faire?

Ask your classmates if they are going to do the following things this weekend.

► étudier

1. travailler
2. écouter la radio
3. regarder la télé
4. nager
5. inviter des amis
6. aller à une boum
7. jouer au tennis
8. rester à la maison
9. faire une promenade à vélo

Est-ce que tu vas étudier?

Oui, je vais étudier.

(Non, je ne vais pas étudier.)

12 Un jeu: Descriptions

Choose a person from Column A and say where the person is, what he or she has, and what he or she is going to do. Use the verbs **être, avoir,** and **aller** with the phrases in columns B, C, and D. How many logical descriptions can you make?

A	B (être)	C (avoir)	D (aller)
tu	sur le court	des livres	chanter
Monique	à la bibliothèque	un vélo	manger un sandwich
je	au salon	20 euros	étudier
les amis	en vacances	une télé	faire une promenade
nous	à la boum	une chaîne stéréo	regarder un film
vous	à la maison	une guitare	faire un match
	au café	une raquette	écouter des cassettes

► **Monique est en vacances. Elle a un vélo. Elle va faire une promenade.**

Prononciation /w/ /j/

Les semi-voyelles /w/ et /j/

In French, the semi-vowels /w/ and /j/ are pronounced very quickly, almost like consonants.

Répétez:

/w/ **oui chouette Louise**

/wa/, /wɛ̃/ **moi toi pourquoi voiture loin**
Chouette! La voiture de Louise n'est pas loin.

/j/ **bien chien radio piano Pierre Daniel violon pied étudiant**
Pierre écoute la radio avec Daniel.

oui

très bien

Leçon 22 **207**

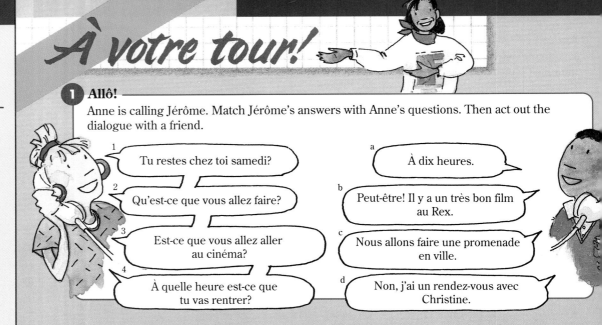

À votre tour!

1 COMPREHENSION

1-d	3-b
2-c	4-a

🔲 **Leçon 22, Section 9**

1 Allô!

Anne is calling Jérôme. Match Jérôme's answers with Anne's questions. Then act out the dialogue with a friend.

1. Tu restes chez toi samedi?

2. Qu'est-ce que vous allez faire?

3. Est-ce que vous allez aller au cinéma?

4. À quelle heure est-ce que tu vas rentrer?

a. À dix heures.

b. Peut-être! Il y a un très bon film au Rex.

c. Nous allons faire une promenade en ville.

d. Non, j'ai un rendez-vous avec Christine.

2 GUIDED ORAL EXPRESSION

1. au café / manger une pizza
2. au parc / faire une promenade
3. au stade / jouer au foot
4. à la piscine / nager
5. à la plage / jouer au volley
6. au supermarché / travailler
7. au centre commercial / (answers will vary)

■ **Teaching strategy:** If students have difficulty with item 7, you may wish to suggest possible activities: **rencontrer des amis, aller dans les magasins, manger un hot-dog,** etc.
(The verb **acheter** is introduced in Lesson 25.)

🔲 **Leçon 22, Section 10**

2 Créa-dialogue

As you are going for a walk in town, you meet several friends. Ask them where they are going and what they are going to do there.

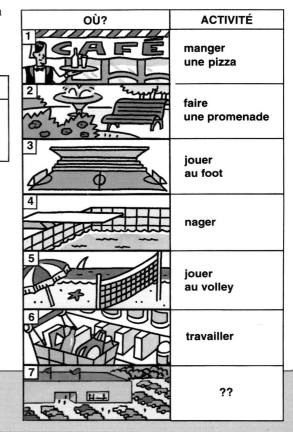

OÙ?	ACTIVITÉ
	dîner avec un copain

▶ —Salut, <u>Alison</u>. Ça va?
—Oui, ça va!
—Où vas-tu?
—Je vais au <u>restaurant</u>.
—Ah bon? Qu'est-ce que tu vas faire là-bas?
—Je vais <u>dîner avec un copain</u>.
—Avec qui?
—Avec <u>Chris</u>.

OÙ?	ACTIVITÉ
1 CAFÉ	manger une pizza
2	faire une promenade
3	jouer au foot
4	nager
5	jouer au volley
6	travailler
7	??

T208

À votre tour

Select those activities which are most appropriate for your students.

🔲 Cooperative practice

Act. 1–3 lend themselves well to cooperative pair practice. For preparation, have the class listen to the corresponding cassette recordings.

📁 Portfolio assessment

You will probably select only one speaking activity and one writing activity to go into the students' portfolios for Unit 6.

In this lesson, Act. 2 can be the basis for an oral portfolio dialogue. Act. 5 can be used as a writing portfolio topic.

3 Conversation libre

Have a conversation with a classmate. Ask your classmate questions about what he / she plans to do on the weekend. Try to find out as much as possible, using yes / no questions.

▶ Est-ce que tu vas rester à la maison?

Non, je ne vais pas rester à la maison.

Est-ce que tu vas aller en ville?

Oui, je vais aller en ville.

Est-ce que tu vas au cinéma?

Oui, je vais au cinéma.

(Non, je ne vais pas au cinéma.)

4 Qu'est-ce que vous allez faire?

Leave a note for your friend Jean-Marc, telling him three things that you and your friends are going to do tonight and three things that you are going to do this weekend.

Jean-Marc
Ce soir (Tonight)
1. Nous allons...
2.
3.
Ce weekend
1.
2.
3.

5 Bonnes résolutions

Imagine that it is January 1 and you are making up New Year's resolutions. On a separate sheet of paper, describe six of your resolutions by saying what you are going to do and what you are not going to do in the coming year.

1 JANVIER
1. Je vais toujours parler français en classe.
2. Je ne vais pas être pénible avec mes copains...

Leçon 22 **209**

3 CONVERSATION

4 WRITTEN SELF-EXPRESSION

5 WRITTEN SELF-EXPRESSION

Classroom Notes

Cooperative reading and writing practice

Have all students prepare Act. 5 as homework. Then, divide the class into groups of 4.

Ask students to share their lists of resolutions with those in their group. Then have each group compare the 4 lists and vote on the 6 best resolutions.

The recorder (**le/la secrétaire**) rewrites the 6 resolutions in the **nous**-form.
1. **Nous allons toujours parler français en classe.**
2. **Nous n'allons pas être pénibles avec nos copains.** etc.
The reporter (**le reporter**) will read the group's list to the rest of the class.

VIDEODISC Disc 4, Side 1
26963–36211

■ **Comprehension practice:** Play the entire module through as an introduction to the lesson.

Leçon 23, Section 1

LEÇON 23 Au Café de l'Univers

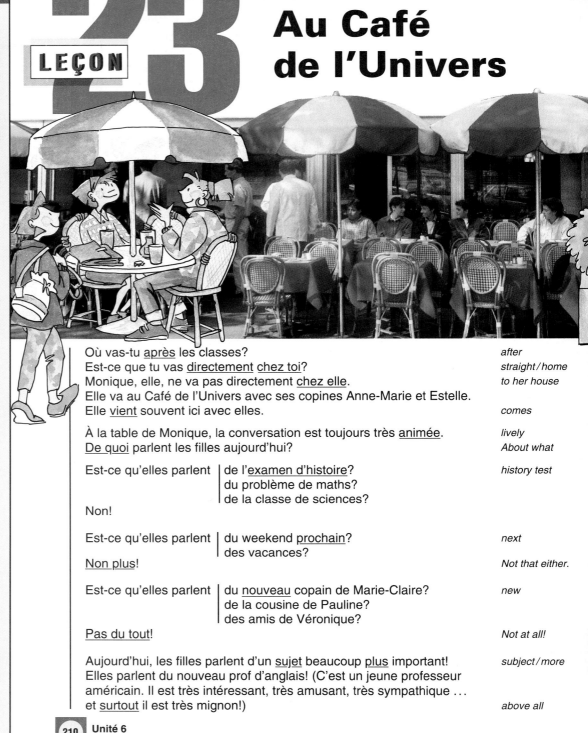

Où vas-tu <u>après</u> les classes?	*after*
Est-ce que tu vas <u>directement</u> <u>chez toi</u>?	*straight / home*
Monique, elle, ne va pas directement <u>chez elle</u>.	*to her house*
Elle va au Café de l'Univers avec ses copines Anne-Marie et Estelle.	
Elle <u>vient</u> souvent ici avec elles.	*comes*
À la table de Monique, la conversation est toujours très <u>animée</u>.	*lively*
<u>De quoi</u> parlent les filles aujourd'hui?	*About what*

Est-ce qu'elles parlent	de l'<u>examen d'histoire</u>?	*history test*
	du problème de maths?	
	de la classe de sciences?	
Non!		

Est-ce qu'elles parlent	du weekend <u>prochain</u>?	*next*
	des vacances?	
<u>Non plus</u>!		*Not that either.*

Est-ce qu'elles parlent	du <u>nouveau</u> copain de Marie-Claire?	*new*
	de la cousine de Pauline?	
	des amis de Véronique?	
<u>Pas du tout</u>!		*Not at all!*

Aujourd'hui, les filles parlent d'un <u>sujet</u> beaucoup <u>plus</u> important!	*subject / more*
Elles parlent du nouveau prof d'anglais! (C'est un jeune professeur américain. Il est très intéressant, très amusant, très sympathique ...	
et <u>surtout</u> il est très mignon!)	*above all*

210 Unité 6

Setting the stage

With books closed, ask students what they talk about when they get together. List the topics (in English) on the board.

Then play the cassette recording of the above text. Have students listen to see what topics of conversation are mentioned in the text.

Which of the topics on the students' list are the same as those mentioned by the speaker? Which are new?

Play the cassette again, and ask them to try to get additional information.

Finally have them open their books and follow along as you play the cassette once more.

Compréhension

1. Où va Monique après les classes?
2. Avec qui est-ce qu'elle va au café?
3. Qu'est-ce que les filles font au café?
4. Est-ce qu'elles parlent de l'école?
5. Est-ce qu'elles parlent des activités du weekend?
6. De quelle *(which)* personne parlent-elles aujourd'hui?
7. De quelle nationalité est le professeur d'anglais?
8. Comment est-il?

Et toi?

Describe what you do by completing the following sentences.

1. En général, après les classes,
   je vais . . .
   je ne vais pas . . .

   - à la bibliothèque
   - chez mes *(my)* copains
   - au café
   - directement chez moi

2. Avec mes copains,
   je parle . . .
   je ne parle pas . . .

   - de la classe de français
   - du prof de français
   - des examens
   - du weekend

3. Avec mes parents,
   je parle . . .
   je ne parle pas . . .

   - de l'école
   - de la classe de français
   - de mes notes *(grades)*
   - de mes copains

4. Avec mon frère ou ma soeur,
   je parle . . .
   je ne parle pas . . .

   - de mes copains
   - du weekend
   - de mes problèmes
   - des vacances

■ NOTE ■ CULTURELLE

Au café

For French teenagers, the café is much more than just a place to have a soft drink or a sandwich. Some go there to study, others go to listen to music, to play electronic games **(le flipper),** or to make a phone call. Most students, however, go to their favorite café after class or on weekends to meet their friends and simply talk.

A French café usually consists of two parts: **l'intérieur** (the indoor section) and **la terrasse** (the outdoor section which often occupies part of the sidewalk). In spring and summer, **la terrasse** is the ideal spot to enjoy the sun and to watch the people passing by.

Leçon 23 **211**

Talking about past events

Let's talk about where you went Saturday.

▶ **X et Y, est-ce que vous êtes allé(e)s au cinéma samedi soir?**
   Oui, nous sommes allé(e)s au cinéma.
   (Non, nous ne sommes pas allé(e)s au cinéma.)

- **Est-ce que vous êtes allé(e)s en ville? chez des amis? à un concert?**

- **Où êtes-vous allé(e)s samedi matin? samedi après-midi?**

Let's say where others went last weekend.

▶ **Est-ce que X et Y sont allé(e)s au cinéma samedi soir?**
   Oui, ils/elles sont allé(e)s au cinéma.
   (Non, ils/elles ne sont pas allé(e)s au cinéma.)

■ **Pronunciation note:** Be sure that students pronounce the third person plural form correctly: **viennent** /vjɛn/.

■ **Language note:** If someone is waiting for you and calls out: **Tu viens?** the usual French response is: **J'arrive** (which means *I'm just about ready and I'm coming*). However, if the person is simply asking if you are planning to join them, the French response is: **Oui, je viens** (which means, *Yes I'm coming along with you*).

① EXCHANGES: inviting friends to come along

■ **Challenge:** For negative answers, explain why you cannot come.
Non, je ne viens pas.
Je dois dîner avec Michelle.

② PRACTICE: saying who is coming to an event

A. Le verbe *venir*

The verb **venir** *(to come)* is irregular. Note the forms of **venir** in the present tense.

venir	Nous allons **venir** avec des amis.
je **viens** tu **viens** il / elle **vient**	Je **viens** avec toi. Est-ce que tu **viens** au cinéma? Monique ne **vient** pas avec nous.
nous **venons** vous **venez** ils / elles **viennent**	Nous **venons** à cinq heures. À quelle heure **venez**-vous à la boum? Ils **viennent** de Paris, n'est-ce pas?

➡ **Revenir** *(to come back)* is conjugated like **venir**.
—À quelle heure **revenez**-vous?
—Nous **revenons** à dix heures.

➡ Note the interrogative expression: **d'où?** *(from where?)*
D'où viens-tu?   ***Where* do you come *from?***

① Tu viens?

Tell a friend where you are going and ask him or her to come along.

▶ au restaurant

Je vais au restaurant. Tu viens avec moi?

D'accord, je viens.

(Non, je ne viens pas.)

1. au café
2. à la bibliothèque
3. à la piscine
4. au supermarché
5. au centre commercial
6. au magasin de disques
7. au stade
8. en classe

② Le pique-nique de Monique

Monique has invited friends to a picnic. Say who is coming and who is not.

▶ Philippe (non)
  Philippe ne vient pas.

1. Alice (oui)
2. Jean-Pierre (non)
3. Paul et Caroline (oui)
4. vous (non)
5. je (oui)
6. nous (non)
7. tu (non)
8. les copines d'Alice (oui)
9. le prof d'anglais (oui)

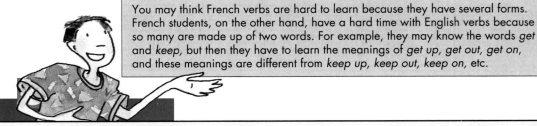

You may think French verbs are hard to learn because they have several forms. French students, on the other hand, have a hard time with English verbs because so many are made up of two words. For example, they may know the words *get* and *keep*, but then they have to learn the meanings of *get up, get out, get on,* and these meanings are different from *keep up, keep out, keep on,* etc.

Cooperative pair practice
Activity 1

Touring Paris

PROPS: Paper and pencils or crayons

Name and sketch on the board four Paris sites:
1. **le Louvre**
2. **la tour Eiffel**
3. **les Champs-Élysées**
4. **l'Arc de Triomphe**

Have the class count off by four's. Then have each student draw and label a site.
Si vous avez le numéro 1, dessinez le Louvre.
Si vous avez le numéro 2, dessinez...
Ask about tourist plans.
Qui va visiter la tour Eiffel aujourd'hui?
Levez le dessin.

B. La préposition *de; de* + l'article défini

The preposition **de** has several meanings:

from   Nous venons **de** la bibliothèque.   *We are coming **from** the library.*
of   Quelle est l'adresse **de** l'école?   *What is the address **of** the school?*
about   Je parle **de** mon copain.   *I am talking **about** my friend.*

CONTRACTIONS

Note the forms of **de** + DEFINITE ARTICLE in the sentences below.

Voici **le** café.   Marc vient **du** café.
Voici **les** Champs-Élysées.   Nous venons **des** Champs-Élysées.

Voici **la** piscine.   Tu reviens **de la** piscine.
Voici **l'**hôtel.   Les touristes arrivent **de l'**hôtel.

The preposition **de** contracts with **le** and **les,** but not with **la** and **l'.**

CONTRACTION	NO CONTRACTION			
de + le → **du**	de + la = **de la**	**du** café		**de la** plage
de + les → **des**	de + l' = **de l'**	**des** magasins		**de l'**école

➡ There is liaison after **des** when the next word begins with a vowel sound.
    Où sont les livres **des étudiants?**

3 Rendez-vous

The following students live in Paris. On a Saturday afternoon they are meeting in a café. Say where each one is coming from.

▶ Jacques: le musée d'Orsay

1. Sylvie: le Louvre
2. Isabelle: le parc de la Villette
3. Jean-Paul: le Centre Pompidou
4. François: le Quartier latin
5. Cécile: l'avenue de l'Opéra
6. Nicole: la tour Eiffel
7. Marc: le jardin du Luxembourg
8. André: les Champs-Élysées
9. Pierre: les Galeries Lafayette
10. Corinne: la rue Bonaparte

Jacques vient du musée d'Orsay.

Leçon 23 **213**

Section B

COMMUNICATIVE FUNCTION:
Talking about where people are coming from

■ **Teaching strategy:** Be sure students realize that the words in heavy print in the sentences on the left correspond to *the* and that those in the sentences on the right correspond to *from the.*

3   PRACTICE: saying where people are coming from

■ **Cultural background:** The **Quartier latin** is the historical students' quarter on the Left Bank. One of the streets is **la rue Bonaparte**, named in honor of Napoleon.
Le jardin du Luxembourg is also in that part of Paris.
Les Galeries Lafayette is a well-known Paris department store.

■ **Teaching strategy:** This exercise should be done quickly with the rhythm of a practice drill. Be sure to read the cues aloud, carefully modeling the pronunciation of the new place names.

■ **Variation:** Repeat the drill, changing the subjects orally.
nous: le musée d'Orsay
Nous venons du musée d'Orsay.

↩ **Re-entry and review:** Say that the people are going to these places.
Jacques va au musée d'Orsay.

Review **aller** and contractions with **à.** Ask each group where they are going.
  Qui va au Louvre?
  [Nous, nous allons au Louvre.]
  Vous allez à l'Arc de Triomphe?
  [Non, nous allons au Louvre!]...
On the board write: **au Louvre, aux Champs-Élysées, à la tour Eiffel, à l'Arc de Triomphe.**

Practice **venir** and contractions with **de.**
  Qui vient des Champs-Élysées?
  [Moi, je viens des Champs-Élysées.]
  Et X, est-ce qu'il vient des Champs-Élysées?
  [Non, il vient de la tour Eiffel.] ...
On the board write: **du Louvre, des Champs-Élysées, de la tour Eiffel, de l'Arc de Triomphe.**

4 **D'où viens-tu?**

During vacation, Philippe goes out every day. When he gets home, his sister Cécile asks him where he is coming from.

▶ mardi

D'où viens-tu?

Je viens du théâtre.

1. lundi
2. mercredi ▶
3. vendredi
4. dimanche
5. samedi
6. jeudi

LUNDI	le restaurant
MARDI	le théâtre
MERCREDI	la bibliothèque
JEUDI	l'opéra
VENDREDI	le concert
SAMEDI	le pique-nique de Moni
DIMANCHE	la boum de Christine

Vocabulaire: Les sports, les jeux et la musique

Les sports		**Les instruments de musique**	
le foot(ball)	le volley(ball)	le piano	la flûte
le basket(ball)	le tennis	le violon	la guitare
le ping-pong	le baseball	le saxo(phone)	la clarinette
		le clavier *(keyboard)*	la batterie *(drums)*

Les jeux *(games)*

les échecs *(chess)*	les dames *(checkers)*
le Monopoly	les cartes *(cards)*

VERBES

jouer à + **le, la, les** + SPORT or GAME	*to play*	Nous **jouons au** tennis.
jouer de + **le, la, les** + INSTRUMENT	*to play*	Alice **joue du** piano.

5 **Activités**

Ask your classmates if they play the following instruments and games.

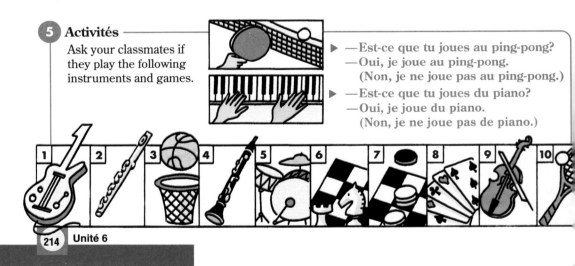

▶ —Est-ce que tu joues au ping-pong?
—Oui, je joue au ping-pong.
(Non, je ne joue pas au ping-pong.)

▶ —Est-ce que tu joues du piano?
—Oui, je joue du piano.
(Non, je ne joue pas de piano.)

214 **Unité 6**

⟨□⟩ **Using the video**

The entire video module for this lesson develops the themes of sports and music, and utilizes the expressions **jouer à** and **jouer de.**

If you do not want to present the whole module at once, you can show some of the segments at the end of the lesson for review.

C. Les pronoms accentués

In the answers to the questions below, the nouns in heavy print are replaced by pronouns. These pronouns are called STRESS PRONOUNS. Note their forms.

—François dîne avec **Florence?**   *Is François having dinner with **Florence?***
—Oui, il dîne avec **elle.**   *Yes, he is having dinner with **her.***

—Tu parles de **Jean-Paul?**   *Are you talking about **Jean-Paul?***
—Non, je ne parle pas de **lui.**   *No, I'm not talking about **him.***

FORMS

(SUBJECT PRONOUNS)	STRESS PRONOUNS	(SUBJECT PRONOUNS)	STRESS PRONOUNS
(je)	**moi**	(nous)	**nous**
(tu)	**toi**	(vous)	**vous**
(il)	**lui**	(ils)	**eux**
(elle)	**elle**	(elles)	**elles**

USES

Stress pronouns are used:

• to reinforce a subject pronoun
  Moi, je parle français.   *I speak French.*
  Vous, vous parlez anglais.   *You speak English.*

• after **c'est** and **ce n'est pas**
  —C'est Paul là-bas?
  —Non ce n'est pas **lui.**   *No, it's not **him.***

• in short sentences where there is no verb
  —Qui parle français ici?
  —**Moi!**   *I do!*

• before and after **et** and **ou**
  Lui et moi, nous sommes copains.   *He and I, (we) are friends.*

• After prepositions such as **de, avec, pour, chez**
  Voici Marc et Paul. Je parle souvent **d'eux.**   *I often talk **about them.***
  Voici Isabelle. Je vais au cinéma **avec elle.**   *I go to the movies **with her.***
  Voici M. Mercier. Nous travaillons **pour lui.**   *We work **for him.***

➡ Note the meaning of **chez** + STRESS PRONOUN:
  Je vais **chez moi.**   *I am going **home.***
  Paul étudie **chez lui.**   *Paul is studying **at home.***

  Tu viens **chez nous?**   *Are you coming **to our house?***
  Je suis chez Alice. Je dîne **chez elle.**   *I am having dinner **at her place.***

C'EST MOI
QUI POSE
LES QUESTIONS!

TF1
VENDREDI 29 MARS
20.50

Leçon 23 215

Section C

COMMUNICATIVE FUNCTION:
Referring to people

■ **Language notes**
• One can also reinforce the subject as follows:
  Je parle français, moi.
  Vous parlez anglais, vous.
• The stress form of **que** *(what)* is **quoi.**
It is used:
– alone: **Quoi?**
– after a preposition:
  De quoi est-ce que tu parles?
– in casual questions:
  Tu fais **quoi?**

⌐ **Transparency 16**
  Subject pronouns

■ **Teaching strategy**
• Use Transparency 16 to introduce stress pronouns, writing the corresponding pronoun in the box below each drawing.
• Erase the words from the transparency. As you make statements, have a student volunteer point to the corresponding pronouns.
  Qui vient? Lui! Toi! Nous!
  Qui joue au tennis? Eux! Vous! etc.
• Then point to the pronouns and let the students respond.
  Qui parle français?
  [point to "je"] **Moi.**
  Qui parle anglais?
  [point to "il"] **Lui.** etc.

■ **Photo culture note**
Une chambre
In the photograph of Act. 4 on the left page, note the position of the bed above the bookcase.
Because city apartments are often small, it is important to use space as efficiently as possible.

Talking about past events

Let's talk about what sports and games you and your friends played last weekend.

▶ **X et Y, est-ce que vous avez joué au tennis le weekend dernier?**
  Oui, nous avons joué au tennis.
  (Non, nous n'avons pas joué au tennis.)

• **Est-ce que vous avez joué au football? au baseball? au ping-pong? au volley? aux échecs? aux cartes? aux dames? au Monopoly?**
Additional challenge questions:
• **Où est-ce que vous avez joué?**
• **Avec qui est-ce que vous avez joué?**
• **Qui a gagné?** *(Who won?)*

Expression pour la conversation

How to contradict someone:

Pas du tout! *Not at all!* —Vous êtes français?
  Definitely not! —**Pas du tout!** Nous sommes italiens!

6 **Mais pas du tout!**

You are not good at guessing the identi-
ties of the following people. A classmate
will indicate that you are wrong.

Tarzan?

▶ —C'est Tarzan?
—Mais pas du tout!
Ce n'est pas lui!

1. Batman? 2. Superman? 3. Wonder Woman?

4. Big Bird? 5. Denzel Washington 6. Cameron Diaz

7 **Samedi soir** *(Saturday night)*

On Saturday night, some people stay
home and others do not. Read what the
following people are doing and say
whether or not they are at home.

▶ Alice étudie.
Elle est chez elle.

▶ Paul va au cinéma.
Il n'est pas chez lui.

1. François regarde la télé.
2. Jacqueline va au café.
3. Marc et Pierre dînent au restaurant.
4. Hélène et Pauline écoutent des disques.
5. Les voisins font une promenade.
6. Je travaille avec mon père.
7. Tu vas au théâtre.
8. Nous allons à la bibliothèque.
9. Tu prépares le dîner.

Expression pour la conversation

How to express surprise:

Vraiment?! *Really?!* —C'est Batman.
  —**Vraiment?**

C'EST BATMAN! VRAIME[...]

8 **Commérage** *(Gossip)*

Thomas likes to gossip. Act out the dialogues between him and his friend Sandrine.

▶ Marina dîne avec Jean-Pierre.

Marina dîne avec Jean-Pierre.

Vraiment?

Mais oui! Elle dîne avec lui!

1. Éric dîne avec Alice.
2. Thérèse va chez Paul.
3. Jérôme est au cinéma avec Delphine.
4. Monsieur Mercier travaille pour Mademoiselle Duval.
5. Philippe travaille pour le voisin.
6. Marc et Vincent dansent avec Mélanie et Juliette.

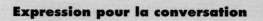

9 **Questions personnelles**

Use stress pronouns in your answers.

1. Est-ce que tu étudies souvent avec tes *(your)* copains?
2. Est-ce que tu vas souvent chez ta cousine?
3. Est-ce que tu travailles pour les voisins?
4. Est-ce que tu parles français avec ton père?
5. Est-ce que tu vas souvent au cinéma avec tes copines?
6. Est-ce que tu restes chez toi le weekend?
7. Est-ce que tu restes chez toi pendant *(during)* les vacances?

D. La construction: nom + *de* + nom

Compare the word order in French and English.

J'ai une raquette. C'est une **raquette de tennis.** *It's a **tennis racket.***
Paul a une voiture. C'est une **voiture de sport.** *It's a **sports car.***

When one noun is used to modify another noun, the French construction is:

MAIN NOUN + **de** + MODIFYING NOUN	**une classe de français**
↓ **d'** (+ VOWEL SOUND)	**une classe d'espagnol**

→ In French, the main noun comes *first*. In English, the main noun comes second.
→ There is no article after **de.**

10 **Précisions**

Complete the following sentences with an expression consisting of **de** + underlined noun.

▶ J'aime le <u>sport</u>. J'ai une voiture . . .

J'ai une voiture de sport!

1. Claire aime le <u>ping-pong</u>. Elle a une raquette . . .
2. Nous adorons le <u>jazz</u>. Nous écoutons un concert . . .
3. Jacques aime la <u>musique classique</u>. Il écoute un programme . . .
4. Vous étudiez l'<u>anglais</u>. Vous avez un livre . . .
5. Tu étudies le <u>piano</u>. Aujourd'hui, tu as une leçon . . .
6. Thomas et Paul aiment l'<u>espagnol</u>. Ils ont une bonne prof . . .
7. Je regarde mes <u>photos</u>. J'ai un album . . .

▶▶▶▶▶▶▶▶▶▶▶▶▶▶▶▶▶▶▶▶▶▶▶▶▶▶▶

Prononciation

Les voyelles /ø/ et /œ/

/ø/	/œ/
2	**9**
d**eu**x	n**eu**f

The letters "**eu**" and "**oeu**" represent vowel sounds that do not exist in English but that are not very hard to pronounce.

Répétez:
/ø/   d**eu**x   **eu**x   je v**eu**x
     je p**eu**x   un p**eu**   j**eu**x
     il pl**eu**t   un **eu**ro
     Tu p**eu**x aller chez **eu**x.
/œ/   n**eu**f   s**oeu**r   h**eu**re
     profess**eu**r   j**eu**ne
     Ma s**oeu**r arrive à n**eu**f h**eu**res.

---

9 COMMUNICATION: answering personal questions

Section D

COMMUNICATIVE FUNCTION: Describing objects and people

 Critical thinking: Point out that in English, the main noun comes second: *tennis <u>racket</u>, sports <u>car</u>.* In French, the main noun comes first: **une <u>raquette</u> de tennis, une <u>voiture</u> de sport.**
How do the French say:
orange juice [**un jus d'orange**]
tomato salad [**une salade de tomates**]
bathroom [**une salle de bains**]

 PRACTICE: describing **10** objects using **de** + noun

■ **Pronunciation:**
Item 7: **album** /albɔm/

Prononciation

 Leçon 23, Section 7

T217

À votre tour!

1 COMPREHENSION

1-b	3-d
2-c	4-a

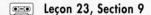 **Leçon 23, Section 8**

2 GUIDED ORAL EXPRESSION

1. chez Françoise / regarder la télé
2. chez Corinne et Claire / dîner
3. chez Nicolas et Patrick / jouer aux cartes
4. chez mon cousin / jouer aux échecs
5. chez ma cousine / jouer du piano
6. chez des copains / écouter de la musique

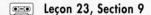 **Leçon 23, Section 9**

3 COMPREHENSION

1. de l'école
2. de la bibliothèque
3. du parc
4. du supermarché
5. du stade
6. de la piscine

1 Conversation

Saturday afternoon, Henri meets Stéphanie downtown. Match Henri's questions with Stéphanie's answers. Then act out the conversation with a classmate.

1. Salut, Stéphanie! D'où viens-tu?
2. Et où vas-tu maintenant?
3. Tu ne veux pas venir au cinéma avec moi?
4. Ah bon? Pourquoi?

a. J'ai un examen d'anglais lundi.
b. Du supermarché.
c. Je rentre chez moi.
d. Je ne peux pas. Je dois étudier.

2 Créa-dialogue

Ask your classmates whom they are going to visit and what they are going to do. Then decide if you are going to come along.

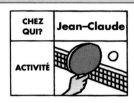

CHEZ QUI? Jean-Claude
ACTIVITÉ

▶ — Où vas-tu?
— Je vais chez <u>Jean-Claude</u>. Tu viens?
— Ça dépend! Qu'est-ce que tu vas faire chez <u>lui</u>?
— Nous allons <u>jouer au ping-pong</u>.
— D'accord, je viens!
  (Non, je ne viens pas.)

CHEZ QUI?	1. Françoise	2. Corinne et Claire	3. Nicolas et Patrick	4. mon cousin	5. ma cousine	6. des copains
ACTIVITÉ						

3 Retour à la maison

This afternoon, the following people went downtown. Say which places they are coming from.

▶ **Nous venons de l'école.**

nous

1 tu	2 vous	3 Madame Si...
4 Monsieur Dupont	5 Claire et Diane	6 Daniel et Ph...

218 Unité 6

À votre tour

Depending on your goals and objectives, you may or may not wish to assign all of the activities in the **À votre tour** section.

👤👤 Cooperative practice

Act. 1–4 lend themselves to cooperative pair practice.

For Act. 2 and 4, you may have students work in trios, with two performing while the other holds the Answer Key and acts as monitor.

Message illustré

Frédéric likes to use illustrations in his diary. Transcribe what he has written about himself and others, replacing the pictures with the corresponding missing words.

Une lettre à Sandrine

In a recent letter, Sandrine, your French pen pal, mentioned various hobbies she enjoys. In a short letter, tell her ...

- which sports you play
- which musical instruments you play
- which games you play

parc	**supermarché**	**stade**
école	**bibliothèque**	**piscine**

Leçon 23 **219**

4 READING COMPREHENSION

au volleyball
à la piscine
au tennis
de la clarinette
du violon
aux cartes
du stade
au foot[ball]

■ **Challenge:** You may wish to have the students prepare their own "messages illustrés."
(See *Challenge: De nouveaux messages*, p. T117.)

5 WRITTEN SELF-EXPRESSION

Classroom Notes

Portfolio assessment

You will probably select only one speaking activity and one writing activity to go into the students' portfolios for Unit 6.

In this lesson, Act. 2 lends itself well to an oral portfolio recording.

Act. 5 offers an excellent writing portfolio topic.

MODULE 24:
Où habitez-vous?
Total time: 5:09 min.
(Counter: 20:07 min.)

24.1 Presentation: Listening — C'est ma maison
(20:57–22:05 min.)

24.2 Mini-scenes: Listening — C'est ta voiture?
(22:06–22:55 min.)

24.3 Dialogue: C'est ta famille?
(22:56–23:55 min.)

24.4 Vignette culturelle: Un immeuble à Paris
(23:56–25:12 min.)

VIDEODISC   Disc 4, Side 1
36490–45688

■ **Comprehension practice:** Play the entire module through as an introduction to the lesson.

 Leçon 24, Section 1

 Transparency 34
Apartment building

Mes voisins

Bonjour!
Je m'appelle Frédéric Mallet.
J'habite à Versailles avec ma famille.
Nous habitons dans un <u>immeuble</u> de   *building*
six <u>étages</u>.   *floors*
Voici mon immeuble et voici <u>mes</u>   *my*
voisins.

Monsieur Lacroche habite au <u>sixième</u>   *sixth*
étage avec sa femme. Ils sont
musiciens. Lui, il joue du piano et elle,
elle chante. Oh là là, <u>quelle</u> musique!   *what*

Mademoiselle Jolivet habite au
<u>cinquième</u> étage avec <u>son</u> oncle et   *fifth / her*
<u>sa</u> tante.   *her*

Paul, mon <u>meilleur</u> ami, habite au   *best*
<u>quatrième</u> étage avec <u>sa</u> soeur et   *fourth / his*
<u>ses</u> parents.   *his*

Mademoiselle Ménard habite au
<u>troisième</u> étage avec son chien   *third*
Pomme, ses deux chats Fritz et Arthur,
son <u>perroquet</u> Coco et son canari   *parrot*
Froufrou. (Je <u>pense que</u> c'est une   *think / that*
personne très intéressante, mais mon
père pense qu'elle est un peu bizarre.)

Monsieur et Madame Boutin habitent
au <u>deuxième</u> étage avec <u>leur</u> <u>fils</u> et   *second / their*
leurs deux <u>filles</u>.   *son*
     daughters

Et qui habite au premier étage?
C'est un garçon super-intelligent,
super-cool et très sympathique! Et ce
garçon . . . c'est moi!

Setting the stage

PROP: Transparency 34

(Have students keep their books closed.)
Describe the building on the transparency.
   Voici un immeuble.
   Voici le rez-de-chaussée.
   **Voici le premier étage, le deuxième
   étage, . . .**

On the chalkboard, write the following list:
   Paul
   Frédéric Mallet
   Mademoiselle Jolivet
   Mademoiselle Ménard
   Monsieur et Madame Boutin
   Monsieur et Madame Lacroche

Compréhension

1. Où habite Frédéric?
2. Combien *(How many)* d'étages est-ce qu'il y a dans l'immeuble où il habite?
3. Quelle est la profession des Lacroche?
4. Comment s'appelle le meilleur ami de Frédéric?
5. Combien d'animaux a Mademoiselle Ménard?
6. Qui est Pomme?
7. Qui sont Fritz et Arthur?
8. Selon toi *(In your opinion)*, est-ce que Mademoiselle Ménard est une personne bizarre ou intéressante?
9. Quel est le numéro *(number)* de l'étage où habite Frédéric?
10. Est-ce que Frédéric habite en haut ou en bas de l'immeuble?

■ NOTES ■ CULTURELLES

1 Versailles

Versailles is a city of about 100,000 inhabitants, located about 8 miles (14 km) southwest of Paris. Its famous **château,** built for King Louis XIV (1638–1715), welcomes four million visitors every year. It is the third most visited monument in France (after the Pompidou Center and the Eiffel Tower).

2 La vie en appartement

Most French people in urban areas live in apartments. Newer high-rise apartment buildings have been built in the suburbs. In the cities, however, apartment houses are traditionally no more than six or seven stories high. (This is because, historically, there were no elevators.) The ground floor, which often houses stores and shops, is known as **le rez-de-chaussée** (literally, "level with the street"). The next floor, **le premier étage** (or "first" floor above the street), corresponds to the American second floor. Similarly, **le deuxième étage** corresponds to our third floor, etc. The top floor of older buildings used to consist of individual rooms, one per apartment. These original maid's rooms often became student rooms. In recent years, as elevators were installed in these buildings, the top-floor rooms frequently have been combined to form new apartments.

Leçon 24 **221**

COMPREHENSION

1. à Versailles
2. six
3. Ils sont musiciens.
4. Paul
5. cinq animaux
6. C'est un chien.
7. Ce sont des chats.
8. *(answers will vary)*
9. le numéro un
10. en bas

Notes culturelles

 24.4 Vignette culturelle: Un immeuble à Paris (23:56–25:12 min.)

VIDEODISC Disc 4, Side 1
43317–45688

■ Photo culture note
Versailles
Visitors to Versailles may visit not only the **château** itself with its magnificent Hall of Mirrors (**la Salle des Glaces**), but they can also walk through the park with its formal gardens and sculptured fountains.

Tell students to listen carefully to the cassette and to determine who lives on which floor. You may want to play the cassette recording more than once.

Then have students open their books and follow along as you play the recording once more.

Answers:
Paul (4e)
Frédéric Mallet (1er)
Mademoiselle Jolivet (5e)
Mademoiselle Ménard (3e)
Monsieur et Madame Boutin (2e)
Monsieur et Madame Lacroche (6e)

Teaching strategy: To help students remember the word order, have them think of **de** as meaning *of* or *which belongs to*.

PRACTICE: expressing relationships

DESCRIPTION: describing ownership

- Marc a la guitare d'Alice et la radio d'Éric.
- Alice a le vélo de Laure et le walkman de Marc.
- Éric a la raquette de Marc et l'appareil-photo de Laure.
- Laure a le scooter d'Alice et les compacts d'Éric.

A. La possession avec *de*

Note the words in heavy print:

Voici une moto.   C'est la moto **de Frédéric.**   It's **Frédéric's** *motorcycle.*
Voici un vélo.   C'est le vélo **de Sophie.**   It's **Sophie's** *bike.*

To express POSSESSION, French speakers use the construction:

le/la/les + NOUN + **de** + OWNER	la radio **de** Thomas
↓	les disques **de** Claire
d' (+ VOWEL SOUND)	la maison **d'**Émilie

⟹ The same construction is used to express RELATIONSHIP:

C'est **le copain de Daniel.**   That's **Daniel's friend.**
C'est **la mère de Paul.**   That's **Paul's mother.**

⟹ Remember that **de** contracts with **le** and **les**:

Pomme est le chien **du voisin.**   Pomme is **the neighbor's** *dog.*
Voici la chambre **des enfants.**   Here is **the children's** *room.*

⟹ While English often indicates possession with *s*, French always uses **de**.

la copine **de Monique**   **Monique's** *friend (the friend **of Monique**)*

1 Présentations *(Introductions)*

Imagine that you are hosting a party in France. Introduce the following people.

▶ Marc (cousin / Sylvie)

Marc est le cousin de Sylvie.

1. Carole (cousine / Jacques)
2. Michel (copain / Caroline)
3. Philippe (camarade / Charles)
4. Robert (frère / Guillaume)
5. Marina (copine / Paul)
6. Pauline (amie / Éric)
7. Thomas (frère / Christine)
8. Alice (soeur / Karine)

2 Échanges

The following friends have decided to trade a few of their possessions. On a separate sheet of paper, write out what each person has, once the exchange has been completed.

Marc   **Alice**   **Éric**   **Laure**

Talking about past events

Let's talk about what you and your friends did last weekend.

(Reminder: If the question contains **tu as...**, students should answer with **j'ai...** or **je n'ai pas...** If it contains **tu es...**, they should answer with **je suis...** or **je ne suis pas...**)

▶ Est-ce que tu es allé(e) à la plage?
Oui, je suis allé(e) à la plage.
(Non, je ne suis pas allé(e) à la plage.)
▶ Est-ce que tu as nagé?
Oui, j'ai nagé.
(Non, je n'ai pas nagé.)

Vocabulaire: La famille

la famille *(family)*

les grands-parents
   le grand-père   **la grand-mère**

les parents *(parents)*   **les parents** *(relatives)*
   le père   **la mère**   **l'oncle**   **la tante** *(aunt)*
   le mari *(husband)* **la femme** *(wife)*

les enfants *(children)*
   un enfant   **une enfant**
   le frère   **la soeur**   **le cousin**   **la cousine**
   le fils *(son)*   **la fille** *(daughter)*

3 La famille de Frédéric

Frédéric has drawn his family tree. Study it and explain the relationships between the people below.

▶ Éric/Isabelle Vidal
   Éric est le fils d'Isabelle Vidal.

1. Véronique/Frédéric
2. Martine Mallet/Véronique
3. Albert et Suzanne Mallet/Frédéric
4. Isabelle Vidal/Frédéric Mallet
5. François Mallet/Martine Mallet
6. Isabelle Vidal/Maurice Vidal
7. François Mallet/Suzanne Mallet
8. Catherine/Maurice Vidal
9. Véronique/Éric
10. Frédéric/Catherine

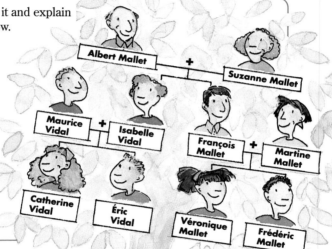

▶ Marc a la guitare d'Alice et . . .

Marc   Alice   Éric   Laure

Leçon 24 **223**

- Est-ce que tu es allé(e) à la plage?
- Est-ce que tu as nagé?
- Est-ce que tu es allé(e) au restaurant?
- Est-ce que tu as mangé une pizza?
- Est-ce que tu es allé(e) en ville?
- Est-ce que tu as acheté des vêtements?

- Est-ce que tu es allé(e) au parc?
- Est-ce que tu as joué au frisbee?
- Où est-ce que tu es allé(e)?
- Qu'est-ce que tu as fait?

▷ **Vocabulaire**

 Leçon 24, Section 2

↩ **Re-entry and review:**
The following words were taught in Lesson 7: père, mère, frère, soeur, cousin, cousine.

▪ **Pronunciation:** Make sure that students pronounce the following nouns correctly:
femme /fam/
fils /fis/
cousin /kuzɛ̃/
cousine /kuzin/

Supplementary vocabulary

les petits-enfants *grandchildren*
le petit-fils / la petite-fille
les jumeaux *twins*
un jumeau / une jumelle
un frère aîné / une soeur aînée
  older brother / sister
un frère cadet / une soeur cadette
  younger brother / sister
un(e) enfant unique *only child*
le neveu *nephew* **/ la nièce**
le beau-père / la belle-mère
  stepfather, father-in-law /
  stepmother, mother-in-law
le beau-frère / la belle-soeur
  stepbrother, brother-in-law /
  stepsister, sister-in-law
le demi-frère / la demi-soeur
  half-brother / half-sister
le parrain / la marraine
  godfather / godmother

 COMPREHENSION: describing family relationships
3

1. la soeur
2. la mère
3. les grands-parents
4. la tante
5. le mari
6. la femme
7. le fils
8. la fille
9. la cousine
10. le cousin

▭ **Transparency 8**
Family tree

 Leçon 24, Section 3

↩ **Review and expansion:**
Mon/ma and **ton/ta** were introduced in Lesson 7.

💡 **Critical thinking:** Point out that just as **ma** becomes **mon** before a vowel sound in French, the article *a* in English also changes form.
Contrast: *a* pear, *an* apple.

Classroom Notes

B. Les adjectifs possessifs:
mon, ton, son

Note the forms of the possessive adjectives in the chart below:

Learning about language
French, like English, shows possession and relationship with POSSESSIVE ADJECTIVES:
   ma voiture (**my** car), **mon** père (**my** father)
In French, possessive adjectives AGREE with the nouns they introduce.

(POSSESSOR)		SINGULAR		PLURAL			
		MASCULINE	FEMININE				
(je)	my	**mon**	**ma**	**mes**	**mon** frère	**ma** soeur	**mes** copains
(tu)	your	**ton**	**ta**	**tes**	**ton** oncle	**ta** tante	**tes** cousins
(il)	his	**son**	**sa**	**ses**	**son** père	**sa** mère	**ses** parents
(elle)	her	**son**	**sa**	**ses**	**son** père	**sa** mère	**ses** parents

➡ The feminine singular forms **ma, ta, sa** become **mon, ton, son** before a vowel sound.

| **une** amie | **mon** amie | **ton** amie | **son** amie |
| **une** auto | **mon** auto | **ton** auto | **son** auto |

➡ There is liaison after **mon, ton, son, mes, tes, ses** when the next word begins with a vowel sound.

   mon oncle   **mes** amis

➡ The choice between **son, sa,** and **ses** depends on the gender (masculine or feminine) and the number (singular or plural) of the noun that *follows*. It does NOT depend on the gender of the possessor (that is, whether the owner is male or female). Compare:

	un vélo	une radio	des cassettes
Voici Frédéric.	Voici son vélo. (his bike)	Voici sa radio. (his radio)	Voici ses cassett... (his cassettes)
Voici Sophie.	Voici son vélo. (her bike)	Voici sa radio. (her radio)	Voici ses cassett... (her cassettes)

TPR 🏃 **Possessions**

PROPS: Books, watches, etc.

Hold up your own textbook, saying:
   Voici un livre de français.
   C'est mon livre.
   X, montre-nous ton livre de français.
Continue with **ma/ta montre.**

Walk around holding up students' items.
   C'est le livre de X [boy]?
   Oui, c'est son livre.
   C'est le livre de Y [girl]?
   Oui, c'est son livre.
   C'est la montre de Z?
   Oui, c'est sa montre.
Follow-up (pointing out items):
   Comment dit-on: *his book? her book?*

4 Marc et Hélène

Marc Pertout never knows where his things are. Fortunately, his friend Hélène Sétout knows. Play both roles.

▶ le vélo / dans le garage

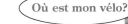

Où est mon vélo?

Ton vélo? Il est dans le garage.

1. les cassettes / ici
2. la raquette / là-bas
3. la montre / sur toi
4. les livres / dans le sac
5. la radio / sur le bureau
6. les tee-shirts / sous le lit
7. le chien / derrière la porte
8. l'appareil-photo / dans la chambre

5 Invitations

Each of the following people is bringing a friend or relative to the school party. Say whom each person is inviting, using the appropriate possessive adjectives.

▶ Michel / la copine
   Michel invite sa copine.

1. André / la cousine
2. Jean-Claude / la soeur
3. Marie-Noëlle / les frères
4. Pascal / l'amie Sophie
5. Monique / les cousins
6. Nathalie / l'ami Marc
7. Georges / l'amie Cécile
8. Paul / l'amie Thérèse
9. Isabelle / les copains

6 Chez Marie et Christophe Boutin

Items 1 to 8 belong to Marie. Items 9 to 16 belong to Christophe. Point these things out.

Marie		Christophe	
▶ le vélo **C'est son vélo.**		▶ les disques **Ce sont ses disques.**	
1. le walkman	5. la radiocassette	9. la guitare	13. les livres
2. le sac	6. la guitare	10. la chaîne stéréo	14. la montre
3. le chien	7. les disques	11. le chat	15. les photos
4. l'album	8. les cassettes	12. la mobylette	16. les skis

Expression pour la conversation

C'EST MON PANTALON !

TU ES SÛR?

How to question a statement or express a doubt:

Tu es sûr(e)? *Are you sure?* —C'est mon pantalon *(pants)*!
                                    —**Tu es sûr?**

---

7 Après la soirée

Last night Frédéric and Paul gave a party. They realize that their friends left certain things behind. Frédéric thinks he knows what belongs to whom.

▶ le sac / Claire   FRÉDÉRIC: **Voici le sac de Claire.**
                          PAUL: **Tu es sûr?**
                       FRÉDÉRIC: **Mais oui, c'est son sac!**

1. le sac / Jean-Pierre
2. la guitare / Antoine
3. l'appareil-photo / Cécile
4. le walkman / Stéphanie
5. les livres / Philippe
6. le chapeau *(hat)* / Thomas
7. la cassette / Roger
8. les compacts / Corinne

Leçon 24 **225**

---

4 ROLE PLAY: finding one's things

■ **Language note:** Be sure students use plural forms in items 1, 4, and 6.
1. Où sont...? Elles sont...
4. Où sont...? Ils sont ...
6. Où sont...? Ils sont...

5 PRACTICE: identifying friends and relatives

6 PRACTICE: identifying possessions

7 ROLE PLAY: identifying ownership

■ **Language note:** Be sure students use the plural **Ce sont** in items 5 and 8.

Talking about past events

Let's talk about a recent party.
Imaginez que vous avez organisé une boum le weekend dernier avec des amis.

▶ **Est-ce que tu as organisé une boum le weekend dernier?**
   Oui, j'ai organisé une boum.

• **Avec qui est-ce que tu as organisé la boum?**
• **À qui est-ce que vous avez téléphoné?**
• **Qui est-ce que vous avez invité?**
• **Est-ce que vous avez dansé?**
• **Est-ce que vous avez chanté?**
• **Qu'est-ce que vous avez mangé?**

Cooperative pair practice
Activities 4, 7

24.1 Mini-scenes:
C'est ma maison
24.2 Mini-scenes:
C'est ta voiture?
24.3 Dialogue: C'est ta
famille?
(20:57–23:55 min.)

DEODISC Disc 4, Side 1
37939–43300

 Leçon 24, Sections 4–6

■ **Language note:** Be sure students note that **notre**, **votre**, and **leur** are used with singular nouns and that **nos**, **vos**, and **leurs** are used with plural nouns. Contrast:
leur frère *their brother*
leurs frères *their brothers*

8 ROLE PLAY: asking for items in a store

9 PRACTICE: pointing out possessions

■ **Challenge:** To practice adjectives, have students make a comment on each thing they are pointing out.
Voici leur maison.
Elle est belle (grande, super, extra, etc.), n'est-ce pas?

COMPREHENSION: indicating family relationships

10

1. son   6. leurs
2. ses   7. leur
3. leur   8. ses
4. son   9. sa
5. sa

C. Les adjectifs possessifs: *notre, votre, leur*

Note the forms of the possessive adjectives in the chart below:

(POSSESSOR)		SINGULAR	PLURAL		
(nous)	*our*	**notre**	**nos**	**notre** prof	**nos** livres
(vous)	*your*	**votre**	**vos**	**votre** ami	**vos** copains
(ils / elles)	*their*	**leur**	**leurs**	**leur** radio	**leurs** disques

➡ There is liaison after **nos, vos, leurs** when the next word begins with a vowel sound.
nos amis   **vos** amies   **leurs** ordinateurs

C'est son vélo.

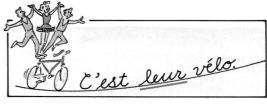

C'est leur vélo.

8 **Aux Galeries Lafayette**

At the Galeries Lafayette department store, a customer is looking for various things. The person at the information desk indicates where they can be found. Play both roles.

▶ les disques / là-bas

1. les livres / à gauche
2. les affiches / à droite
3. le restaurant / en haut
4. le garage / en bas
5. les ordinateurs / ici
6. la cafétéria / tout droit

S'il vous plaît, où sont vos disques?

Nos disques sont là-bas.

9 **Les millionnaires**

Imagine you are showing a millionaire's estate to French visitors.

▶ la maison
Voici leur maison.

1. la piscine
2. la Cadillac
3. les chiens
4. le parc
5. l'hélicoptère
6. les courts de tennis

10 **En famille**

We often do things with our family. Complete each sentence with a possessive adjective: **son, sa, ses, leur,** or **leurs.**

▶ Pascal joue au tennis avec <u>sa</u> cousine.
▶ Éric et Paul jouent au Monopoly avec <u>leurs</u> cousins.

1. Frédéric dîne chez … oncle.
2. André dîne chez … grands-parents.
3. Caroline et Paul vont chez … grand-mère.
4. Mlle Vénard fait une promenade avec … chien.
5. Antoine va à la piscine avec … soeur.
6. Stéphanie et Céline vont au cinéma avec … parents.
7. M. et Mme Boutin voyagent avec … fille.
8. Mme Denis visite Paris avec … fils, Marc et Frédéric.
9. M. Mallet est à Québec avec … femme.

226 Unité 6

Cooperative pair practice
Activities 8, 9

Game: Possessions

PREPARATION: Prepare 2 bags.
Bag A contains 12 sentence cards.
(6 cards with names of single people)
Voici Pierre. Voici Michelle. Voici…
(6 cards with names of two people)
Voici Anne et Paul. Voici Éric et Sylvie. …

Bag B contains 12 sentence cards.
(6 cards with singular nouns)
Voici son crayon, …son stylo, sa montre.
Voici leur crayon, …leur stylo, leur montre
(6 cards with plural nouns)
Voici ses crayons, …ses stylos, ses montres
Voici leurs crayons, …leurs stylos, leurs montres.

D. Les nombres ordinaux

Learning about language

Numbers like *first, second, third, fourth, fifth* are used to rank persons or things—to put them in a given order.

They are called ORDINAL NUMBERS.

In English, most ordinal numbers end in *-th*.

Compare the following regular numbers and the ordinal numbers in French:

(2)	deux	**deuxième**	Février est le **deuxième** mois de l'année.
(3)	trois	**troisième**	Mercredi est le **troisième** jour de la semaine.
(4)	quatre	**quatrième**	J'habite au **quatrième** étage *(floor)*.
(12)	douze	**douzième**	Qui habite au **douzième** étage?

To form ordinal numbers, the French use the following pattern:

NUMBER (minus final **-e**, if any) + **-ième**
(6) six : **six** + **-ième** → **sixième**
(11) onze : **onz-** + **-ième** → **onzième**

⇒ EXCEPTIONS:
un (une) → premier (première)
cinq → cinquième
neuf → neuvième

⇒ Ordinal numbers are adjectives and come BEFORE the noun.

Quatrième . . .

et pourtant premier.

La course *(The race)*

Frédéric and his friends are participating in a five-kilometer race. Announce the order of arrival of the following runners.

▶ Paul (6)   **Paul est sixième.**

1. Frédéric (4)
2. Jérôme (7)
3. Christophe (8)
4. Sophie (2)
5. Christine (1)
6. Claire (10)
7. Karine (11)
8. Olivier (12)

Prononciation

Les voyelles /o/ et /ɔ/

/o/   /ɔ/

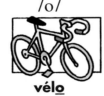   

vélo   **téléphone**

The French vowel /o/ is pronounced with more tension than in English. It is usually the last sound in a word.

Répétez: /o/ **vélo radio nos vos eau
château chaud
Nos vélos sont au château.**

The French vowel /ɔ/ occurs in the middle of a word. Imitate the model carefully.

Répétez: /ɔ/ **téléphone école Nicole notre
votre copain prof dommage
Comment s'appelle votre prof?**

Section D

COMMUNICATIVE FUNCTION: Indicating sequence

■ **Language notes:**
• For **deuxième**, one can also say **second(e)**, pronounced /səgɔ̃(d)/
• 21st = **vingt et unième**
  31st = **trente et unième**, etc. Note that the "u" of **unième** is pronounced /y/.

■ **Extra practice:** Write the numbers 1 to 20 on the board. Point to a number and have students give the corresponding ordinal number.
For example:
15 [quinzième], etc.

11 PRACTICE: ranking people

Prononciation

 Leçon 24, Section 7

■ **Pronunciation notes**
• Have students pronounce the /o/ with tension and clip off the ending before the glide /oᵘ/ of the English *go*.
• Be sure students do not pronounce these words with the vowel /o/. The French /ɔ/ is close to the "o" sound of the English *orange*.

PROCEDURE: Divide the class into two teams: **logique** and **illogique**. Each team names a scorekeeper.

Two players (one from each team) come to the front. One reads a card from Bag A, the other reads a card from Bag B.

If the sentences fit logically, the **logique** team earns a point. If not, a point goes to the **illogique** team. For example:
Voici Marc. Voici leur stylo. = illogique

Have students at their seats decide if the sentences are logical or not.

1 COMPREHENSION

1-c   3-b
2-a   4-d

🔲 Leçon 24, Section 8

2 GUIDED ORAL EXPRESSION

1. la guitare d'Alice / orange
2. le scooter de Paul et Anne / vert
3. le chien de tes cousins / noir
4. la mobylette d'Isabelle / rouge
5. la maison de M. et Mme Lavoie / blanche
6. la voiture de ton oncle / jaune

🔲 Leçon 24, Section 9

Classroom Notes

À votre tour!

1 Allô!

Émilie is on the phone with Bernard. Match Émilie's questions with Bernard's answers. Then act out the dialogue with a classmate.

1. Avec qui est-ce que tu vas au cinéma?
2. C'est le cousin de Monique?
3. Tu connais leurs parents?
4. Ils sont canadiens, n'est-ce pas?

a. Non, c'est son frère.
b. Bien sûr, ils sont très sympathiques.
c. Avec mon copain Marc.
d. Non, mais leurs voisins sont de Québec.

2 Créa-dialogue

We often identify objects by their color. Create conversations with your classmates according to the model.

le vélo / Paul?

▶ —C'est le vélo de Paul?
—Non, ce n'est pas son vélo.
—Tu es sûr?
—Mais oui. Son vélo est bleu.

1. la guitare / Alice?
2. le scooter / Paul et Anne?
3. le chien / tes cousins?
4. la mobylette / Isabelle?
5. la maison / M. et Mme Lavoie?
6. la voiture / ton oncle?

228 Unité 6

À votre tour

Depending on your goals and objectives, you may or may not wish to assign all of the activities in the **À votre tour** section.

👥 Cooperative practice

Act. 1–3 lend themselves to cooperative pair practice.

3 Faisons connaissance

You want to know more about certain relatives and acquaintances (friends, neighbors, teachers, etc.) of your classmates. Ask a classmate three questions: each question will be about a different person. You may want to use some of the following suggestions:

OUI/NON	INFORMATION
parler français?	où/habiter?
avoir une voiture?	quel âge/avoir?
aimer les sports?	où/travailler?
travailler beaucoup?	à quelle école/étudier?
voyager souvent?	quand/venir chez toi?

Où est-ce que tes grands-parents habitent?

4 Composition: Ma famille

Select five people in your family and write one to three sentences about each person.

Ma cousine s'appelle Barbara. Elle habite à San Francisco. Elle a treize ans.

5 Arbre généalogique *(Family tree)*

On a separate sheet of paper, draw your own (real or imaginary) family tree. Label the people and indicate their relationships to you.

Leçon 24 **229**

3 GUIDED ORAL EXPRESSION

■ **Expansion:** You may wish to have students record their partners' responses in the third person. For example:
Les grands-parents de Sylvie habitent à Miami.
Son père travaille beaucoup.
Ses cousins viennent chez elle en été. etc.

4 WRITTEN SELF-EXPRESSION

5 WRITTEN SELF-EXPRESSION

■ **Teaching strategy:** Some students may prefer preparing the family tree of a TV family or a family in the public eye.

■ **Photo culture note**
French people of African ancestry come principally from the French Caribbean islands of **Martinique** and **Guadeloupe**, and from countries of western Africa, especially **Mali, Sénégal, Cameroun, Congo,** and **Côte d'Ivoire**.

Portfolio assessment

You will probably select only one speaking activity and one writing activity to go into the students' portfolios for Unit 6.

In this lesson, Act. 3 lends itself well to an oral portfolio recording.

Act. 4 and 5 are appropriate writing portfolio topics.

T229

Entracte 6

OBJECTIVES:
- Reading skills development
- Re-entry of material in the unit
- Development of cultural awarenesss

Les loisirs

OBJECTIVES:
- Rapid reading at the sentence level
- Reading for cultural information about leisure time activities

---

ENTRACTE 6

Vive la différence!
Les loisirs

Parlons° de vos loisirs.° Répondez aux questions suivantes.° Selon° vous, quelles sont les réponses des jeunes Français en général à ces questions?

1 Qu'est-ce que vous préférez faire quand vous n'étudiez pas?
- aller au cinéma
- aller dans les magasins
- pratiquer un sport
- jouer avec les jeux vidéo

Selon vous, qu'est-ce que les jeunes Français préfèrent faire?

2 Quand vous allez au cinéma, quels films est-ce que vous préférez voir?°
- les films de science-fiction
- les films d'aventures
- les comédies
- les films d'horreur

Selon vous, quels sont les films préférés des jeunes Français?

3 Combien de fois° par an° est-ce que vous allez au concert?
- jamais°
- une fois ou deux
- de trois à six fois
- sept fois ou plus°

Et les jeunes Français, combien de fois vont-ils au concert en moyenne° par an?

4 Voici quatre acteurs américains très célèbres° en France. Quel est votre acteur préféré?
- Tom Cruise
- Jack Nicholson
- Robert Redford
- Dustin Hoffman

Selon vous, qui est l'acteur américain préféré des Français?

5 Quelle musique est-ce que vous préférez écouter?
- les chansons folkloriques°
- le rock
- le jazz
- la musique classique

Selon vous, quelle est la musique préférée des jeunes Français?

6 Quels livres est-ce que vous préférez lire?°
- les biographies
- les livres de science-fiction
- les livres d'aventures
- les albums de bandes dessinées°

Selon vous, quels sont les livres préférés des jeunes Français?

7 Quelle est votre dépense° principale?
- Je vais au concert.
- Je vais au cinéma ou au restaurant.
- J'achète° des cassettes ou des compacts.
- J'achète des vêtements.°

Et pour les jeunes Français, quelle est leur dépense principale?

Et les jeunes Français?

1. Ils préfèrent aller au cinéma.   2. Ils préfèrent les comédies.   3. Ils vont au concert en moyenne six fois par an.
4. Leur acteur américain préféré est Dustin Hoffman.   5. Ils préfèrent le rock.   6. Ils préfèrent les albums de bandes dessinées.   7. Ça dépend. Les garçons vont au cinéma ou au restaurant. Les filles achètent des vêtements.

Parlons *Let's talk*   **loisirs** *leisure activities*   **suivantes** *following*   **Selon** *According to*   **voir** *to see*   **fois** *times*
par an *per year*   **jamais** *never*   **plus** *more*   **en moyenne** *on the average*   **célèbres** *famous*   **chansons**
folkloriques *folksongs*   **lire** *to read*   **bandes dessinées** *comics, cartoons*   **dépense** *expense*   **achète** *buy*
vêtements *clothes*

 ## Cooperative reading practice

Divide the class into groups of 4 or 5, each with a recorder (**secrétaire**).

For each question, have the groups first vote on their own preferences and then on what they imagine the preferences of French young people to be. (Keep answers at the bottom of the page covered.)

Then have the recorders announce their results to the entire class. For example:
1. Quand nous n'étudions pas, nous préférons aller au cinéma.
Selon nous, les jeunes Français préfèrent aller au cinéma aussi.

EN FRANCE

Vive la musique!

Est-ce que vous préférez écouter votre groupe favori à la radio ou dans une salle de concert? Regardez bien ces documents.

Rolling Stones Story à partir du 25 décembre

1ᵉ diffusion le mardi à 21h 30 - 2ᵉ diffusion le vendredi à 23 h sur

EUROPE 1 RADIO 2

♪ Quel groupe est-ce qu'on peut écouter à la radio? Quels jours et à quelle heure?

♪ Est-ce que vous connaissez° ce groupe? Est-ce que vous avez leurs disques? Aimez-vous leur musique?

LE PLUS GRAND DES GRANDS CONCERTS

AVEC
avec RTL

Ricky MARTIN
Will SMITH
Dave MATTHEWS Band
Mariah CAREY
Lauryn HILL

Liberty Show
SAMEDI 24 JUIN
DE 12 À 24 HEURES

FRÉDÉRICK PARTOUCHE PRÉSENTE

HIPPODROME DE VINCENNES
PARIS
RÉSERVATIONS: 01 48 05 10 10

Pour la première fois dans
tous les CARREFOUR de France

Carrefour

Goo Goo Dolls
Backstreet Boys
TLC
Chris ISAAK
Alanis MORRISSETTE
Jewel

Quand a lieu° le concert? Où?

À quelle heure est-ce que le concert commence?°
À quelle heure est-ce qu'il finit?°

♪ Quel est le numéro de téléphone pour réserver les billets?°

♪ Qui sont les «stars» de ce concert? Quelles stars est-ce que vous connaissez? Qui est votre star préférée?

♪ Est-ce que vous aimeriez° aller à ce concert? Pourquoi ou pourquoi pas?

connaissez *know*   **a lieu** *does ... take place*   **commence** *does ... begin*   **finit** *does ... end*   **billets** *tickets*
aimeriez *would like*

Entracte 6 231

Vive la musique!

OBJECTIVES:
• Reading for information
• Understanding authentic documents

■ **Realia notes**
Le rock en France
French young people enjoy all kinds of popular music, especially British and American rock groups. When French teens form their own rock bands, they often give them English names like "The Chelsea Five."

■ **Answers**
• Les Rolling Stones; le mardi à 21h 30 et le vendredi à 23 h.
• *(Answers will vary.)*
• le samedi 24 juin
• à 12 h; à 24 h
• 01.48.05.10.10
• *(See names on poster.)*

📖 **Pre-reading**
Ask pairs of students to name their favorite music groups.
 **Quel est votre groupe favori?
Notre groupe favori est [Hootie and the Blowfish].**

Post-reading
OPTIONAL: Prepare a poster in French announcing a school event.

OBJECTIVES:
- Reading a longer text
- Building reading skills

■ **Questions sur le texte**
1. Est-ce que Karine habite très loin de l'école?
2. À quelle heure est-ce qu'elle arrive à l'école le matin?
3. Est-ce qu'elle rentre chez elle à midi?
4. Quels sports est-ce qu'elle pratique?
5. Combien de fois par mois est-ce qu'elle va au cinéma?
6. Qui est son acteur américain préféré?
7. Quels groupes est-ce qu'elle aime?
8. En général, est-ce qu'elle aime les Américains? Pourquoi?
9. Qu'est-ce qu'elle n'aime pas aux États-Unis?

■ **Questions personnelles**
1. Comment vas-tu à l'école?
2. Est-ce que tu rentres chez toi à midi?
3. À quelle heure rentres-tu chez toi l'après-midi?
4. Quels sports est-ce que tu pratiques à l'école?
5. Combien de fois par mois vas-tu au cinéma?
6. Qui est ton acteur favori?
7. Qui est ton actrice favorite?
8. Est-ce que tu joues d'un instrument? De quel instrument?

Entre amis: Interview avec Karine Legoff

Karine Legoff est élève dans un lycée° français. En mars, elle a passé° deux semaines aux États-Unis avec un programme d'échange.° Nous avons interviewé° Karine pendant° son séjour.° Voici les réponses de Karine à nos questions.

École
En France, comment vas-tu à l'école? — À pied, généralement.°
À quelle heure arrives-tu le matin? — À huit heures.
À quelle heure rentres-tu chez toi le soir? — Ça dépend des° jours. En général, à 5 heures 30 ou à 6 heures.
Où déjeunes-tu?° — Je déjeune à la cantine° du lycée.

Sports
Quels sports pratiques-tu à l'école? — Je joue au volley.
Et en dehors de° l'école? — Je joue au tennis.
Où? — Au club de la ville.

Loisirs
Est-ce que tu vas au cinéma? — Oui, de temps en temps.°
Combien de fois par mois?° — Une ou deux fois.
Qui sont tes acteurs préférés? — Christophe Lambert, Gérard Depardieu. Aussi Ben Affleck.
Et tes actrices préférées? — Isabelle Adjani, Emmanuelle Béart.
Est-ce que tu vas au concert? — Oui, mais pas très souvent.
Où vas-tu? — Ça dépend! Au Zénith, au parc des Princes.
Qui sont tes groupes ou tes chanteurs° préférés? — Dave Matthews Band, U2, Lauryn Hill.
Est-ce que tu joues d'un instrument? — Non.
Est-ce que tu vas à des boums? — Oui, de temps en temps.
Où et quand? — Chez des amis. Généralement le samedi soir.

Les États-Unis
Quelles sont tes impressions des États-Unis? — J'aime le pays° et les gens.
Pourquoi? — C'est un pays très dynamique et très ouvert.° Les gens sont francs, communicatifs et honnêtes avec eux-mêmes.° Les Américains sont très coo
Qu'est-ce que tu n'aimes pas? — La nourriture.°

lycée *high school* **a passé** *spent* **échange** *exchange* **avons interviewé** *interviewed* **pendant** *during*
séjour *stay* **généralement** *generally* **Ça dépend des** *It depends on the* **déjeunes-tu** *do you have lunch*
cantine *cafeteria* **en dehors de** *outside of* **de temps en temps** *from time to time* **fois par mois** *times a month*
chanteurs *singers* **pays** *country* **ouvert** *open* **eux-mêmes** *themselves* **nourriture** *food*

232 Unité 6

📖 **Pre-reading**
Ask the class if they have ever hosted French exchange students in their homes.
   If your school has an exchange program, have they met some of the students?
   Have they ever spent a week or two in a French-speaking country?

Post-reading
Which of Karine's answers, if any, do they find surprising?
   Do they agree with her impressions of the United States?

Comment lire
SOUNDING FRENCH

As you read the interview over, try to think how the new words sound in French.

- Remember to put the accent on the LAST syllable of a word or phrase.

  pro<u>gramme</u>   **acteur préfé<u>ré</u>**   **communi<u>catif</u>**

- Remember that many final consonants are silent.

  spor~~t~~   Zéni~~th~~   math~~s~~   instrumen~~t~~

If you think of the right French pronunciation as you read, you will be prepared to recognize these words when you hear them spoken.

Enrichissez votre vocabulaire
SUFFIXES

You can expand your reading vocabulary easily by learning to recognize common suffixes (or endings).

	FRENCH	ENGLISH		
(ADJECTIVE +)	**-ment**	*-ly*	**généralement**	*generally*
(VERB STEM +)	**-ant**	*-ing*	**amusant**	*amusing*
(VERB STEM +)	**-é**	*-ed*	**préféré**	*preferred*

Activité

Can you identify the English equivalents of the following French words?

- **normalement   finalement   rarement   rapidement   sûrement**
- **intéressant   alarmant   terrifiant   charmant**
- **importé   occupé   limité   marié**

Activité: Une interview
Interview a classmate about his / her school life and leisure activities. Use Karine's interview as a point of departure.

Activité: Une lettre à Karine
Write Karine a letter about yourself. Using her responses to the interview as a model, tell her about your school, the sports you play, your leisure-time activities, as well as your impressions of France and the French people.

Quelques stars du cinéma français

Gérard Depardieu   Christophe Lambert   Julie Delpy   Juliette Binoche

Entracte 6   233

■ **Teaching strategy (Une lettre à Karine):** Since most, if not all, of your students will not yet have had the opportunity to visit France, have them base their impressions on the video.

■ **Les stars du cinéma français**
Some other French movie stars:

actrices	Sabine Azéma
	Nathalie Baye
	Sandrine Bonnaire
	Catherine Deneuve
	Isabelle Huppert
	Sophie Marceau
	Miou-Miou
acteurs	Jean-Paul Belmondo
	Alain Delon
	Philippe Noiret
	Michel Serrault

Quatre stars

NOM	NÉ(E)	FILMS CONNUS
G. Depardieu	1948	Le Dernier Métro, Jean de Florette, Camille Claudel, Cyrano de Bergerac, The Man in the Iron Mask
C. Lambert	1957	LeSicilien, Le Retour, Nirvana, Beowulf
Julie Delpy	1969	An American Werewolf in Paris, Les mille merveilles de l'univers, Los Angeles Without a Map
Juliette Binoche	1964	Bleu, Le Hussard sur le toit, The English Patient

LECTURE ET CULTURE

Variétés

Les jeunes Français et le cinéma américain

En général, les jeunes Français aiment beaucoup les films américains. (Quand ils parlent anglais, ils peuvent° voir° ces films en «version originale».) Voici une liste de films qui ont eu° beaucoup de succès en France. Est-ce que vous pouvez° identifier ces films? Lisez° le titre° français de chaque° film. Faites correspondre° le titre de ce film avec le titre américain.

TITRES FRANÇAIS

1. *Blanche-Neige*
2. *Hommes en noir*
3. *Le Cochon dans la ville*
4. *Vous avez un mess@ge*
5. *E.T. l'extra-terrestre*
6. *Le mariage de mon meilleur ami*
7. *Le Prince d'Égypte*
8. *Il faut sauver le soldat Ryan*
9. *Les dents de la mer*
10. *Danse avec les loups*
11. *La Menace fantôme*
12. *Indiana Jones et la dernière croisade*
13. *1001 Pattes*
14. *Menteur Menteur*

TITRES AMÉRICAINS

A. *Jaws*
B. *The Phantom Menace*
C. *E.T. The Extra Terrestrial*
D. *Saving Private Ryan*
E. *Indiana Jones and the Last Crusade*
F. *Dances with Wolves*
G. *Babe II, Pig in the City*
H. *Men in Black*
I. *The Prince of Egypt*
J. *My Best Friend's Wedding*
K. *You've Got Mail*
L. *Liar Liar*
M. *A Bug's Life*
N. *Snow White and the Seven Dwarfs*

peuvent *can* **voir** *see* **ont eu** *had* **pouvez** *can* **Lisez** *Read* **titre** *title* **chaque** *each* **Faites correspondre** *Match*

234

UN FILM D'AVENTURES
américain

20.30

...LM AMÉRICAIN DE GEORGE LUCAS

DURÉE: 2h12

...TAR WARS: ÉPISODE 1 LA MENACE FANTÔME

MUSIQUE DE JOHN WILLIAMS

...ui-Gon Jinn ....Liam Neeson
...bi-Wan Kenobi..........Ewan McGregor
...oung Queen.................Natalie Portman

Anakin Skywalker ....Jake Lloyd
Palpatine.....................Ian McDiarmid
Mace Windu.................Samuel L. Jackson

Ce film américain a eu° beaucoup de succès en France.

- Est-ce que vous avez vu° ce film? Où? à la télévision? au cinéma? sur vidéocassette?
- Quel est le titre anglais du film?
- Qui est le réalisateur° du film?
- Qui sont les acteurs?
- Qui est le compositeur de la musique?
- Combien de temps dure° le film?

■ NOTE ■
CULTURELLE

Au cinéma

Le samedi, les jeunes Français adorent aller au cinéma. C'est pour eux l'occasion de voir° un bon film et aussi d'être avec leurs copains. En général, ils vont au cinéma pour voir des films récents. Leurs films préférés sont les films comiques. Ils aiment aussi les films d'aventures, les films de science-fiction et les films policiers.°

Beaucoup de jeunes vont aussi au ciné-club de leur école ou de la ville où ils habitent. Là ils peuvent° voir les «grands classiques» du cinéma. Ces grands classiques sont des films anciens° réalisés° par des cinéastes° français ou étrangers.°

UNITÉ 6
INTERNET PROJECT

FEATURE: Le Louvre
There are many stops on the Internet that feature **le Louvre.** Students can generate links by using the search engine of their choice and the keywords **"le Louvre"; "tourisme à Paris"; "monuments historiques."** Students can share links they find with other students.

a eu *had* **Est-ce que vous avez vu** *Did you see* **réalisateur** *director* **dure** *does...last* **de voir** *to see* **films policiers** *detective movies* **peuvent** *can* **anciens** *old* **réalisés** *made, directed* **cinéastes** *filmmakers* **étrangers** *foreign*

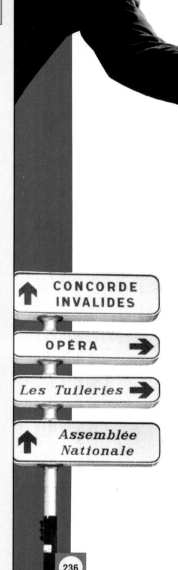

À PARIS

Bonjour, Paris!

À Paris

CULTURAL THEME:

Paris

VIDEO ESSAY:
À Paris
Total time: 8:12 min.
(Counter: 25:23 min.)

C.1 **Introduction à Paris**
(25:23–26:36 min.)

C.2 **Interview avec Jean-Marc Lacoste**
(26:37–27:32 min.)

C.3 **Visite de Paris**
(27:33–31:40 min.)

C.4 **Promenade en bateau-mouche**
(31:41–33:30 min.)

VIDEODISC Disc 1, Side 1
24710–39415

■ **Photo culture notes**
Street signs
• **Concorde:** The **Place de la Concorde**, at the end of the Champs-Élysées, is one of the largest squares in the world. At the center stands **l'obélisque**, a gift to the king of France (Charles X) from the viceroy of Egypt.

• **Invalides: Les Invalides** is a former French military hospital (hence its name). Tourists come to **Les Invalides** to see Napoleon's tomb and visit the military museum.

• **Opéra:** This sign shows the way to the "old" **Opéra Garnier** in the center of Paris. The "new" **Opéra de la Bastille** is also shown on the map at the right.

• **Les Tuileries:** Le jardin des **Tuileries** is a large public park which extends from the **Place de la Concorde** to the **Louvre**.

• **Assemblée nationale:** The French legislature has two houses, **l'Assemblée nationale** (similar to the U.S. House of Representatives) and **le Sénat**.

QUELQUES FAITS

■ Paris est la capitale de la France.

■ Paris est une très grande ville. La ville de Paris a deux millions d'habitants. La région parisienne a dix millions d'habitants. Quinze pour cent (15%) des Français habitent dans la région parisienne.

■ Paris est situé° sur la Seine. Ce fleuve° divise° la ville en deux parties: la rive° droite (au nord) et la rive gauche (au sud).

■ Administrativement, Paris est divisé en vingt arrondissements.°

■ Paris est une ville très ancienne.° Elle a plus de° deux mille° ans.

■ Paris est aussi une ville moderne et dynamique. C'est le centre économique, industriel et commercial de la France.

■ Avec ses musées, ses théâtres, ses bibliothèques, ses écoles d'art, Paris est un centre culturel et artistique très important.

■ Avec ses nombreux° monuments et ses larges avenues, Paris est une très belle ville. Pour beaucoup de gens, c'est la plus° belle ville du monde.° Chaque année,° des millions de touristes visitent Paris.

situé *located* **fleuve** *river* **divise** *divides*
rive *(river)bank* **arrondissements** *districts* **ancienne** *old*
plus de *more than* **mille** *thousand* **nombreux** *many*
la plus *the most* **monde** *world* **Chaque année** *Each year*

Using the video

In this Video Essay, **À Paris,** Jean-Marc Lacoste (see p. 243) takes the students around Paris. Play the entire module as an introduction to the photo essay.

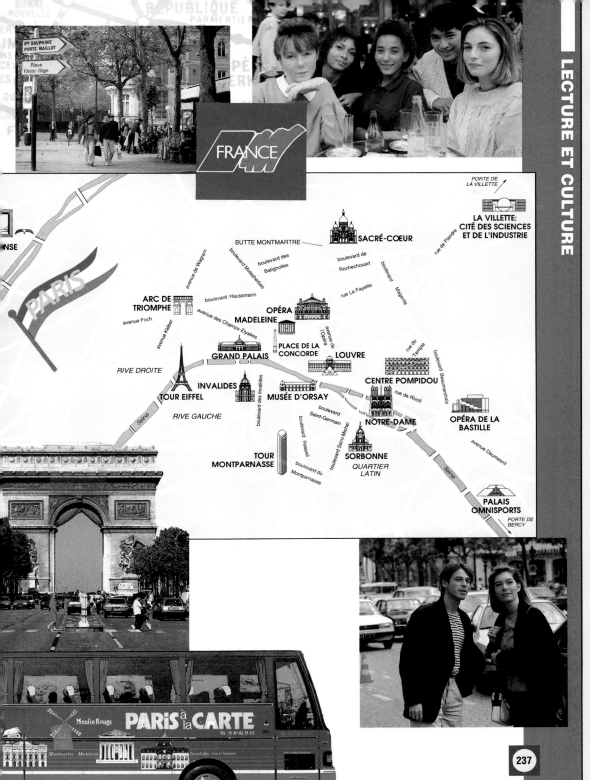

■ **Photo culture notes**
(clockwise)
• **La tour Eiffel**
• **La Place du Trocadéro**
• **Café Kléber** at the **Place du Trocadéro**
• **Les Champs-Élysées**
• **L'arc de Triomphe**

The tourist bus is decorated with pictures of various places in Paris. From left to right:
• **un bateau-mouche**
• **la tour Eiffel**
• **l'arc de Triomphe**
• **les Galeries Lafayette** (department store)
• **Notre Dame**
• **l'Opéra Garnier**
• **le Moulin Rouge** (in Montmartre)
• **la Madeleine** (near Place de la Concorde)
• **les Invalides**

237

T237

■ **Cultural background**

• The Eiffel Tower was built to commemorate the 100th anniversary of the French Revolution which began July 14, 1789 and lasted ten years.

• Napoleon came to power after the French Revolution. He declared himself Emperor in 1804 and was defeated at Waterloo in 1815. In France he is remembered as a military genius and an efficient administrator.

Le PARIS *traditionnel*

1 Notre-Dame

Notre-Dame est la cathédrale de Paris. Elle est située au centre de Paris sur une île,° l'île de la Cité. Notre-Dame a été construite° aux douzième et treizième siècles.°

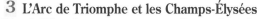

2 La tour Eiffel

Pour beaucoup de gens, la tour Eiffel est le symbole de Paris. Cette° immense tour de fer° a trois cent mètres de haut.° Elle a été inaugurée en 1889 (dix-huit cent quatre-vingt-neuf) par l'ingénieur Gustave Eiffel. Du sommet de la tour Eiffel, on° a une très belle vue sur Paris.

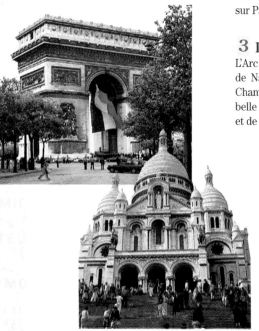

3 L'Arc de Triomphe et les Champs-Élysées

L'Arc de Triomphe est un monument qui° commémore les victoires de Napoléon (1769–1821). Ce monument est situé en haut° des Champs-Élysées. Les Champs-Élysées sont une très grande et très belle avenue avec beaucoup de cinémas, de cafés, de magasins et de boutiques élégantes.

4 Le Sacré-Coeur

Le Sacré-Coeur est une église de pierre° blanche qui domine Paris. Cette église est située sur la butte° Montmartre. Montmartre est un quartier pittoresque. Les artistes viennent ici pour peindre° et les touristes viennent pour regarder les artistes. Si vous voulez° avoir un souvenir personnel de Paris, allez à Montmartre et demandez à° un artiste de faire votre portrait.

île *island*	**a été construite** *was built*	**siècles** *centuries*	**Cette** *This*	**fer** *iron*
a trois cent mètres de haut *is 300 meters high*		**on** *one*	**qui** *which*	**en haut** *at the top*
pierre *stone*	**butte** *hill*	**peindre** *to paint*	**voulez** *want*	**demandez à** *ask*

238

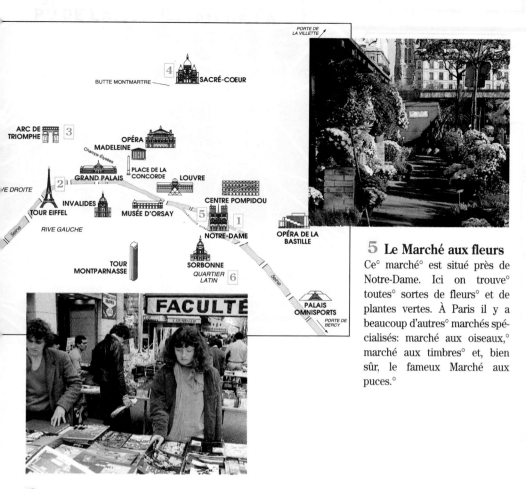

5 Le Marché aux fleurs

Ce° marché° est situé près de Notre-Dame. Ici on trouve° toutes° sortes de fleurs° et de plantes vertes. À Paris il y a beaucoup d'autres° marchés spécialisés: marché aux oiseaux,° marché aux timbres° et, bien sûr, le fameux Marché aux puces.°

6 Le Quartier latin

Le Quartier latin est le quartier des étudiants. C'est un quartier très animé avec des cafés, des cinémas, des librairies et des restaurants exotiques et bon marché.° Pourquoi est-ce que ce quartier s'appelle «Quartier latin»? Parce qu'autrefois° les étudiants parlaient° latin ici.

ACTIVITÉ CULTURELLE

Imaginez que vous passez une journée° à Paris. Où allez-vous aller le matin? Où allez-vous aller l'après-midi? Choisissez deux endroits à visiter et expliquez° votre choix.°

Ce *This*   **marché** *market*   **trouve** *finds*   **toutes** *all*   **fleurs** *flowers*   **d'autres** *other*   **oiseaux** *birds*
timbres *stamps*   **Marché aux puces** *flea market*   **bon marché** *inexpensive*   **autrefois** *in the past*
parlaient *used to speak*   **passez une journée** *are spending the day*   **expliquez** *explain*   **choix** *choice*

Le nouveau PARIS

■ **Cultural background**
- Mona Lisa (also known as "la Joconde") was painted by Léonard de Vinci (1452–1519).
- Le Centre Pompidou was named after Georges Pompidou (1911–1974), President of France (1969–1974).
- Claude Monet (1840–1926) and Auguste Renoir (1841–1919), Impressionist painters; Henri de Toulouse-Lautrec (1864–1901).

❶ Le Louvre et la pyramide du Louvre

Le Louvre est une ancienne° résidence royale transformée en musée. C'est dans ce° musée que se trouve° la fameuse «Mona Lisa». On entre dans le Louvre par° une pyramide de verre.° Cette pyramide moderne a été construite° par l'architecte américain I.M. Pei. Avec sa pyramide, le Louvre est le symbole du nouveau° Paris, à la fois° moderne et traditionnel.

❷ Le Centre Pompidou

Le Centre Pompidou est le monument le plus° visité de Paris. C'est un musée d'art moderne. C'est aussi une bibliothèque, une cinémathèque et un centre audio-visuel. À l'extérieur,° sur l'esplanade, il y a des musiciens, des mimes, des acrobates, des jongleurs° . . . Un peu plus loin,° il y a une place° avec des fontaines, un bassin° et des sculptures mobiles.

❸ Le musée d'Orsay

Autrefois,° c'était° une gare.° Aujourd'hui, c'est un musée. On vient ici admirer les chefs-d'oeuvre° des grands peintres° et sculpteurs français du dix-neuvième siècle.° On peut,° par exemple, admirer les oeuvres° de Monet, de Renoir et de Toulouse-Lautrec. À l'extérieur, il y a des sculptures qui représentent les cinq continents.

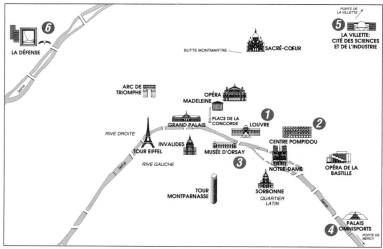

ancienne *former*   ce *this*   se trouve *is located*   par *by*   verre *glass*   a été construite *was built*   nouveau *new*   à la fois *at the same time*   le plus *the most*   À l'extérieur *Outside*   jongleurs *jugglers*   plus loin *farther away*   place *square*   bassin *ornamental pool*   Autrefois *Formerly*   c'était *it used to be*   gare *train station*   chefs-d'oeuvre *masterpieces*   peintres *painters*   siècle *century*   peut *can*   oeuvres *works*

240

⑤ Le parc de la Villette

Le parc de la Villette est un lieu° de récréation pour les jeunes de tout âge.° On trouve ici des parcs pour enfants,° des terrains de jeu° et différentes° constructions ultra-modernes.

- Le Zénith est une salle de concert où viennent les vedettes du monde° entier.
- La Géode est un cinéma omnimax avec un écran° circulaire géant.
- La Cité des sciences et de l'industrie est un grand musée scientifique où les jeunes peuvent° faire leurs propres° expériences° et jouer avec toutes sortes de gadgets électroniques.

④ Le Palais Omnisports de Bercy

Sport ou musique? Bercy est le nouveau stade de Paris. C'est aussi une immense salle° de concert. On vient ici écouter et applaudir les vedettes° de la chanson° française . . . et de la chanson américaine.

⑥ La Défense et son arche

La Défense est le nouveau centre d'affaires° situé à l'ouest de Paris. Chaque° jour, des milliers° de Parisiens viennent travailler dans ses gratte-ciel° de verre. Il y a aussi des magasins, des cinémas, des restaurants et une patinoire.° Récemment,° une immense arche a été construite pour commémorer le deux centième anniversaire de la Révolution française.

ACTIVITÉ CULTURELLE

Vous êtes à Paris pour une semaine. Pendant votre séjour, vous voulez faire les choses suivantes. Dites où vous allez pour cela.

Quand?	Pourquoi?	Où?
lundi	voir *(to see)* une exposition d'art moderne	??
mardi	voir une exposition sur les lasers	??
mercredi	voir la «Mona Lisa»	??
jeudi	voir un match de basket	??
vendredi	voir une exposition sur Toulouse-Lautrec	??
samedi	aller dans les magasins et faire du shopping	??

▶ Lundi, je veux voir une exposition d'art moderne. Je vais au Centre Pompidou.

salle *hall* **vedettes** *stars* **chanson** *song* **lieu** *place* **de tout âge** *of all ages* **parcs pour enfants** *playgrounds* **terrains de jeu** *playing fields* **différentes** *several* **monde** *world* **écran** *screen* **peuvent** *can* **propres** *own* **expériences** *experiments* **affaires** *business* **Chaque** *Each* **des milliers** *thousands* **gratte-ciel** *skyscrapers* **patinoire** *skating rink* **Récemment** *Recently*

241

■ **If students ask: Un gratte-ciel** is a "sky-scratcher." Which term do they find more appropriate: the French word or the English word?

■ **Activité culturelle**
Answers:
lundi: au Centre Pompidou
mardi: au parc de la Villette
mercredi: au Louvre
jeudi: au palais Omnisports de Bercy
vendredi: au musée d'Orsay
samedi: à la Défense

C.1 Introduction à Paris
C.2 Interview avec
Jean-Marc Lacoste
C.3 Visite de Paris
(25:30–31:40 min.)

VIDEODISC Disc 1, Side1
24710–35956

Salut, *les amis!*

Je m'appelle Jean-Marc Lacoste. Je suis parisien. J'habite rue Racine. C'est une petite rue du Quartier latin. Notre appartement est situé au quatrième étage° d'un vieil° immeuble. L'immeuble est très ancien (il n'y a pas d'ascenseur°), mais notre appartement est moderne et confortable.

Je vais à l'École Alsacienne où je suis élève de seconde. En général, je vais là-bas en bus. Quand il fait beau, je prends° ma mob,° ou bien° je vais à pied. C'est assez loin, mais j'adore marcher.

En semaine, j'ai beaucoup de travail et je n'ai pas le temps° de sortir.° Le weekend, c'est différent. Qu'est-ce que je fais? Ça dépend! Quand j'ai de l'argent,° je vais au concert. Le weekend prochain,° j'espère aller au Zénith écouter le groupe Indochine. Quand je n'ai pas d'argent, je vais au Centre Pompidou. Là, au moins,° le spectacle° est gratuit.°

J'aime aussi me promener° dans mon quartier avec mes copains. Il y a toujours quelque chose° à faire au Quartier latin. On° va au cinéma. On va dans les magasins de disques pour écouter les nouveaux albums. On va dans les librairies° pour regarder les vieux livres et les bandes dessinées.° On va au café. Là, on regarde les gens qui passent dans la rue. Parfois,° on rencontre° des filles...

Et vous, quand est-ce que vous allez venir à Paris? Bientôt,° j'espère. Je vous attends!°

Amitiés,°
Jean-Marc

étage *floor* vieil *old* ascenseur *elevator* prends *take* mob *moped* ou bien *or else* temps *time*
sortir *go out* argent *money* prochain *next* au moins *at least* spectacle *show* gratuit *free*
me promener *to go for walks* quelque chose *something* On *We* librairies *bookstores*
bandes dessinées *comics* Parfois *Sometimes* rencontre *meet* Bientôt *Soon*
Je vous attends! *I'm expecting you!* Amitiés *In friendship*

Pre-reading
Replay parts 2 and 3 of the video, so that students get to know Jean-Marc.
Then have them read his letter.

Post-reading
Have students make a list of the places that Jean-Marc mentions in his letter and then locate them on the map of Paris.
Which place or places they would like to visit with him?

PARIS en BATEAU-MOUCHE

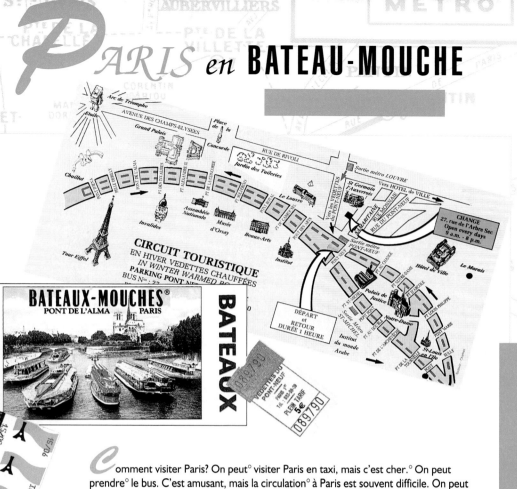

Paris en bateau-mouche

C.4 Promenade en
bateau-mouche
(31:41–33:20 min.)

 VIDEODISC   Disc 1, Side 1
36000–39415

■ **Activité culturelle**
Answers:
• 5 euros
• la tour Eiffel
  les Invalides
  l'Assemblée Nationale
  le musée d'Orsay
  l'École Nationale des Beaux-Arts
  l'Institut de France
  le Palais de Justice
  Notre Dame
  St-Louis-en-l'Île
  l'Hôtel de Ville
  le Louvre
  le jardin des Tuileries
  le Grand Palais

*C*omment visiter Paris? On peut° visiter Paris en taxi, mais c'est cher.° On peut prendre° le bus. C'est amusant, mais la circulation° à Paris est souvent difficile. On peut prendre le métro. C'est pratique, rapide et bon marché,° mais on ne voit rien.°

Pourquoi ne pas faire une promenade° en bateau-mouche?° Les bateaux-mouches sont des bateaux modernes et confortables qui circulent sur la Seine. Pendant° la promenade, on peut prendre des photos et admirer les monuments le long de° la Seine. Le soir, on peut voir les monuments illuminés!

ACTIVITÉ CULTURELLE

Vous faites une promenade en bateau-mouche.
• Combien coûte le billet?
• Quels° monuments est-ce que vous pouvez° voir?

On peut *One can*   **cher** *expensive*   **prendre** *take*   **circulation** *traffic*   **bon marché** *inexpensive*
ne voit rien *sees nothing*   **Pourquoi ne pas faire une promenade** *Why not take a ride*
bateau-mouche *sight-seeing boat*   **Pendant** *During*   **le long de** *along*   **Quels** *Which*   **pouvez** *can*

243

📺 **Using the video**
Play Part 4 of the video, in which students are taken on a bateau-mouche ride. Students may look for **Notre Dame, la tour Eiffel,** and the many beautiful bridges and **quais** along the Seine.

Unité 7

MAIN THEME:

Buying clothes

➤ **Teaching Resources**

Technology/Audio Visual

 VIDEO/VIDEODISC

Unité 7, Modules 25-28
25. Le français pratique: L'achat des vêtements
26. Rien n'est parfait!
27. Un choix difficile
28. Alice a un job

 DFi B, Modules 25-28 Exploration 7

 Writing Template Unité 7

 Unité 7, Leçons 25, 26, 27, 28

 35, 36, 37, 38, 39, 40, 41 Situational S15, S16

Print

Answer Key, Cassette Script, Video Script, Overhead Visuals Copymasters

Activity Book, pp. 203-241
Activity Book TAE

Video Activity Book pp. 103-122

Communipak, pp. 119-140

Teacher's Resource Package

 Teacher-to-Teacher: Games, Additional Activities

 Interdisciplinary Connections: Projects Book

 Teaching to Multiple Intelligences in the Modern Language Classroom

Internet Connections www.mcdougallittell.com

UNITÉ 7

Le shopping

244

Unit overview

COMMUNICATION GOALS: Students will be able to shop for clothing, describe what people are wearing, and make comparisons.

LINGUISTIC GOALS: Students will learn the present tense of **-ir** and **-re** verbs, the imperative, and comparative forms of adjectives.

CRITICAL THINKING GOALS: Students will observe similarities and differences in the ways French and English make commands and express comparisons.

CULTURAL GOALS: Students will become aware of the French concept of style and the ways in which young people earn and spend their money.

THÈME ET OBJECTIFS

Buying clothes

Are you interested in clothes? When you visit France, you will enjoy going window shopping. In fact, you will probably want to try on a few items and buy something special to bring home.

In this unit, you will learn . . .
- to name and describe the clothes you wear
- to discuss style
- to shop for clothes and other items
- to talk about money

You will also be able . . .
- to point out certain people or objects to your friends
- to make comparisons
- to make suggestions and tell others what to do

Classroom Notes

➤ Assessment Options

MODULE 25:
Le français pratique:
L'achat des vêtements
Total time: 7:52 min.
(Counter: 33:43 min.)

25.1 Introduction: Listening — Le shopping
(33:55–35:11 min.)

25.2 Dialogue: Aux Galeries Lafayette
(35:12–36:41 min.)

25.3 Mini-scenes: Listening — Qu'est-ce que vous cherchez?
(36:42–37:39 min.)

25.4 Mini-scenes: Speaking — Vous désirez?
(37:40–38:37 min.)

25.5 Mini-scenes: Speaking — Combien coûte la veste?
(38:39–39:22 min.)

25.6 Mini-scenes: Listening — Comment trouves-tu ma robe?
(39:23–39:59 min.)

25.7 Vignette culturelle: Où acheter les vêtements?
(40:00–41:31 min.)

VIDEODISC Disc 4, Side 2
1551–15645

■ **Comprehension practice:** Play the entire module through as an introduction to the lesson.

T246

LEÇON 25

LE FRANÇAIS PRATIQUE

L'achat des vêtements

Accent sur ... L'élégance française

French people like to look good. Young people are generally well-informed about fashions and trends. They like to be in style, even if their clothes are casual and not too expensive. Many well-known fashion design houses started in Paris: Christian Dior, Chanel, Yves Saint Laurent, Pierre Cardin, Sonia Rykiel, Lacroix, Gaultier.

Depending on their budgets, French young people may buy their clothes at:

- **une boutique de soldes** *(discount shop)*
- **un grand magasin** *(department store)*
- **une boutique de vêtements** *(clothing store)*
- **le Marché aux puces** *(flea market)*

- **Un grand magasin**
  A large Parisian department store, the **Galeries Lafayette** has branches in other French cities. It offers a wide variety of clothing, from modestly priced items to more expensive designer labels.

246 Unité 7

Setting the stage

Ask your students if they like to shop for clothes and where they go.

Est-ce que vous aimez faire du shopping? Où allez-vous?

Allez-vous dans un grand magasin? Comment s'appelle-t-il?

Allez-vous dans une boutique de vêtements? Comment s'appelle-t-elle?

Allez-vous dans une boutique de soldes? Comment s'appelle-t-elle?

Est-ce qu'il y a un marché aux puces dans votre ville?

Tell students that in the video they will observe French young people shopping for clothes. In the *Vignette culturelle*, they will see various types of clothing stores.

- **Une boutique de vêtements**
  There are several **Céline** shops in Paris. They sell relatively expensive designer clothes.

- **Une boutique de soldes**
  At a discount store called the **Mouton à cinq pattes,** you can find jeans and casual clothes at good prices.

- **Une maison de couture**
  One of the most famous French fashion design houses is that of **Christian Dior.** Every season it presents a new collection which influences fashion trends all over the world. Christian Dior sells original designer dresses at very high prices, but also markets a more affordable line of clothes under its ready-to-wear label.

- **Le Marché aux puces**
  At the **Marché aux puces,** you can find all types of used clothes, from hats of the 1930's to old military uniforms.

25.7 **Vignette culturelle: Où acheter les vêtements?**
(40:00–41:31 min.)

VIDEODISC   Disc 4, Side 2
12800–15645

■ **Language notes**
un mouton = sheep
une patte = foot (of an animal)

■ **Photo culture note**
Kookaï is a popular designer for girls; **Celio** for boys.

Classroom Notes

💡 Critical thinking skills

English has borrowed many words pertaining to clothing and fashion: **boutique, eau de cologne, haute couture.**

Ask students to list other borrowed French words relating to fashion and clothes.

For example:

chemise	**crêpe**
culottes	**maillot**
chic	

Section A

COMMUNICATIVE FUNCTION:
Talking about clothing

**25.1 Mini-scenes: Qu'est-
ce que vous cherchez?**
(36:42–37:39 min.)

VIDEODISC Disc 4, Side 2
1551–4200

 Leçon 25, Section 1

Transparency 35
Les vêtements

■ **Looking ahead:** Students will
learn the forms of **acheter** in
Lesson 26.

■ **Extra activity**
To review **euros,** ask the price of
each item.
Combien coûte le blouson?

■ **Language notes**
• **Un pull** is a shortened form of **un
pull-over,** which is a borrowed
word from English. It is used for
any sweater which is pulled over
the head. French has also borrowed the word **un sweater**
/swεtεr/.
• In Quebec, **un chandail** /ʃɑ̃daj/
is used for **un pull.**

■ **Pronunciation:** Be sure students
say **pull** /pyl/ with the /y/ of **tu.**

Supplementary vocabulary

faire les magasins *to go shopping
(browsing from store to store)*
un anorak *ski jacket*
un costume *man's suit*
un tailleur *woman's suit*

A. Les vêtements

Je vais
dans un magasin.

How to talk about shopping for clothes:

Où vas-tu?
    Je vais | dans **une boutique** *(shop).*
            | dans **un magasin** *(store)*
            | dans **un grand magasin** *(department store)*
Qu'est-ce que tu vas **acheter** *(to buy)*?
    Je vais acheter **des vêtements** *(clothes).*

Les vêtements

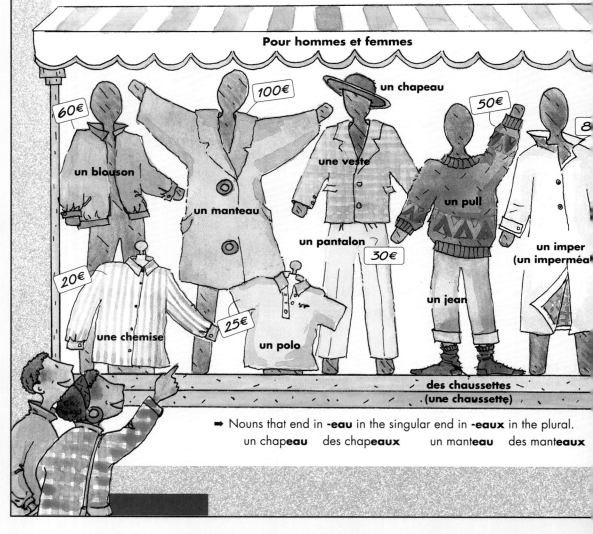

Pour hommes et femmes

60€ un blouson
100€ un manteau
un chapeau
une veste
50€
un pull
un pantalon 30€
8
un imper
(un imperméa
20€ une chemise
25€ un polo
un jean
des chaussettes
(une chaussette)

➡ Nouns that end in **-eau** in the singular end in **-eaux** in the plural.
    un chap**eau**   des chap**eaux**   un mant**eau**   des mant**eaux**

TPR Clothes

PROPS: A bag of old clothes in large sizes

Give students various items of clothing.
    X, montre-nous le pull.
    Y, montre-nous la cravate. …
    Qui a le pull? [X]…
If appropriate, have students try items on.

Z, mets le chapeau. Ah, c'est très joli!
Qui porte le chapeau? [Z]
Have students move the clothing around.
    X, mets le pull sur la chaise de Z.
    Où est le pull? [sur la chaise de Z]
    Z, donne le pull à W.
    Qui a le pull maintenant? [W]

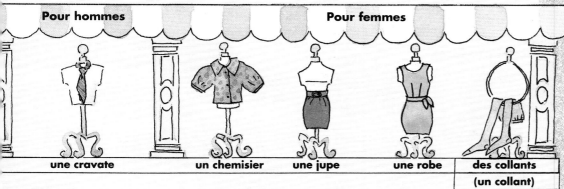

Pour hommes		Pour femmes		
une cravate	un chemisier	une jupe	une robe	des collants (un collant)

acheter	*to buy*	Je vais **acheter** une cravate.
porter	*to wear*	Qu'est-ce que tu vas **porter** demain?
mettre	*to put on, wear*	Oh là là, il fait froid. Je vais **mettre** un pull.

➡ **Mettre** is irregular. (Its forms are presented in Leçon 26.)

1 Shopping

Below are the names of several Paris stores. Using the illustrations as a guide, talk to a classmate about where you are going shopping and what you plan to buy.

▶ —Où vas-tu?
—Je vais au Monoprix.
—Qu'est-ce que tu vas acheter?
—Je vais acheter une chemise.

2. (au) BON MARCHÉ
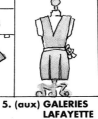

(au) MONOPRIX

1. (au) PRINTEMPS
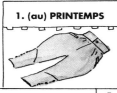

3. (au) PRISUNIC

4. (chez) CÉLINE

5. (aux) GALERIES LAFAYETTE

6. (chez) BURBERRY

7. (chez) DIOR

8. (à) LA SAMARITAINE

2 Quels vêtements?

What we wear often depends on the circumstances: where we are, what we will be doing, what the weather is like. Complete the following sentences with the appropriate items of clothing.

1. Aujourd'hui, je porte…
2. Le professeur porte…
3. L'élève à ma gauche porte…
4. L'élève à ma droite porte…
5. Quand je vais à une boum, je porte…
6. Quand je vais dans un restaurant élégant, je porte…
7. S'il pleut *(If it rains)* demain, je vais mettre…
8. S'il fait chaud demain, je vais mettre…
9. Si *(If)* je vais en ville samedi, je vais mettre…
10. Si je vais à un concert dimanche, je vais mettre…

Leçon 25 **249**

Supplementary listening practice

You can build listening comprehension skills by talking about the clothing that students are wearing. Students respond with gestures or one-word answers. Repeat each item of clothing in several different questions and responses.

For example:
Qui porte un polo aujourd'hui?
W et X portent un polo.
Y ne porte pas de polo.
Et toi, Z, tu portes un polo? [oui]
De quelle couleur est le polo de Z? [bleu]
Mais oui, il est bleu…

Cooperative pair practice
Activity 1

Section B

COMMUNICATIVE FUNCTION:
Talking about clothing
and accessories

25.4 Mini-scenes: Vous désirez?
(37:40–38:37 min.)

VIDEODISC Disc 4, Side 2
8650–10390

Leçon 25, Section 2

Transparency 36
Vêtements et accessoires

■ **Pronunciation: Un sweat** is pronounced /swit/.

■ **Casual speech: Un maillot de bain** is called **un maillot**.

■ **Language note:** Point out that **des lunettes (de soleil)** is feminine.

Supplementary vocabulary

LES ACCESSOIRES
des gants (m.) *gloves*
un foulard *(silk) scarf*
un mouchoir *handkerchief*
une casquette *cap*
des verres (m.) **de contact**
contact lenses
une écharpe *(winter) scarf*

LES BIJOUX
un bijou *piece of jewelry*
un collier *necklace*
un bracelet
une bague *ring*
une chaîne *chain*
des boucles (f.) **d'oreilles** *earrings*

3 DESCRIPTION: indicating what people are wearing

1. des lunettes de soleil, un polo, un short, des sandales
2. un maillot de bain, des tennis
3. un survêtement, des baskets
4. un sweat, un short, des lunettes de soleil
5. *(answers will vary)*

■ **Challenge:** Students say what each person is NOT wearing, using **pas de**.
Paul ne porte pas de tee-shirt.

B. D'autres vêtements et accessoires

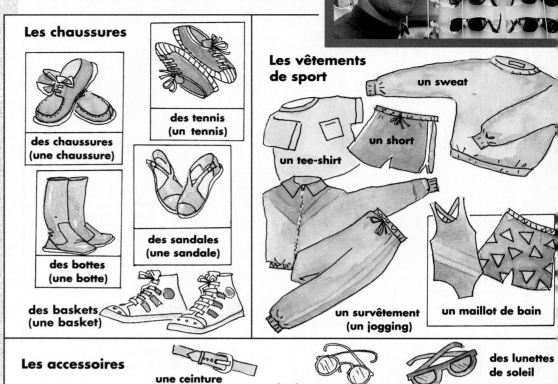

Les chaussures

des chaussures
(une chaussure)

des tennis
(un tennis)

des bottes
(une botte)

des sandales
(une sandale)

des baskets
(une basket)

Les vêtements de sport

un sweat

un short

un tee-shirt

un survêtement
(un jogging)

un maillot de bain

Les accessoires

une ceinture

des lunettes (f.)

des lunettes
de soleil

3 À la plage de Deauville

You are spending the summer vacation in Deauville, a popular ocean resort in Normandy.
Describe what you and your friends are wearing.

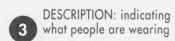

▶ **Paul**   1. **Anne**   2. **Sophie**   3. **Michel**   4. **Catherine**   5. **moi**

▶ Paul porte un maillot de bain...

Talking about past events

Let's talk about what you wore yesterday. Remember to use **pas de** in negative answers.

▶ Est-ce que tu as porté un manteau hier?
Oui, j'ai porté un manteau.
(Non, je n'ai pas porté de manteau.)

- Est-ce que tu as porté un chapeau hier?
- Est-ce que tu as porté un survêtement?
- Est-ce que tu as porté des lunettes de soleil?
- Est-ce que tu as porté des tennis?
- Est-ce que tu as porté une cravate?
- Est-ce que tu as porté une robe?

4 Qu'est-ce que tu portes?

Ask your classmates what they wear in the following circumstances. Let them use their imagination.

▶ jouer au tennis

1. aller à la piscine
2. aller à la plage
3. jouer au basket
4. travailler dans le jardin
5. aller au gymnase *(gym)*
6. faire une promenade dans la forêt *(forest)*
7. faire une promenade dans la neige *(snow)*

Qu'est-ce que tu portes quand tu joues au tennis?

Je porte un tee-shirt, un short et des tennis.

4 COMMUNICATION: talking about what one wears when

■ **Challenge:** Have students ask questions using **si** *(if)* and **mettre.**
– Qu'est-ce que tu vas mettre si tu vas à la plage samedi?
– Je vais mettre...

5 Un jeu

When you see what people are wearing, you can often tell what they are going to do. How many different logical sentences can you make in five minutes? Follow the model below.

A	B	C
André	un maillot de bain	nager
Sylvie	des lunettes de soleil	aller à la plage
Paul et Éric	un short	aller à un concert
Michèle et Anne	des chaussettes blanches	jouer au tennis
	un sweat	jouer au volley
	un pantalon très chic	jouer au football
	des chaussures noires	aller à la campagne *(country)*
	des bottes	faire du jogging *(to jog)*
	un costume *(suit)*	dîner en ville
	une robe	

Sylvie porte un short. Elle va jouer au football.

5 COMPREHENSION: describing clothes and related activities

■ **Variation** (conversation format): Student 1 states what someone is wearing. Student 2 asks why. Student 3 gives the reason.
– Sylvie porte un short.
– Pourquoi?
– Elle va jouer au football.

■ **Variation:** Have students reverse columns B and C, using **mettre.**
André va nager.
Il va mettre un maillot de bain.

6 Joyeux anniversaire!

The following people are celebrating their birthdays. Find a present for each person by choosing an item of clothing from pages 248, 249, or 250.

1. Pour mon père (ma mère), je vais acheter, ...
2. Pour ma grand-mère (mon grand-père), ...
3. Pour ma petite cousine Chantal (10 ans), ...
4. Pour mon grand frère Guillaume (18 ans), ...
5. Pour le professeur, ...
6. Pour mon meilleur *(best)* ami, ...
7. Pour ma meilleure amie, ...

6 COMMUNICATION: selecting gifts

- **Qu'est-ce que tu as porté hier?**
- **Qu'est-ce que tu as porté vendredi soir? samedi après-midi? dimanche matin?**

Follow-up:
- **Qu'est-ce que X a porté hier?**
- **Qu'est-ce que Y a porté vendredi soir?**
- **Qu'est-ce que Z a porté dimanche matin?**

Cooperative pair practice
Activity 4

25.1 **Introduction: Le shopping**
25.2 **Dialogue: Aux Galeries Lafayette** (33:55–36:41 min.)
25.6 **Mini-scenes: Comment trouves-tu ma robe?** (39:23–39:59 min.)

VIDEODISC Disc 4, Side 2
1551–12800

Classroom Notes

C. Dans un magasin

▶ *How to get help from a salesperson:*

Pardon, monsieur (madame).

Vous désirez (May I help you), | **monsieur?**
| **madame**
| **mademoiselle**

Pardon, madame.

Vous désirez, mademoiselle?

Je cherche un pantalon.

Je cherche (I'm looking for) . . .
un pantalon.

Quel est le prix (What is the price) du pantalon?
Combien (How much) **coûte** le pantalon?
Combien est-ce qu'il coûte?
Il coûte 40 euros.

Je cherche . . .
une veste.

Quel est le prix de la veste?
Combien coûte la veste?
Combien est-ce qu'elle coûte?
Elle coûte 65 euros.

▶ *How to discuss clothes with a friend:*

Qu'est-ce que tu penses du pantalon vert?
(What do you think of . . . ?)
Comment trouves-tu le pantalon vert?
(What do you think of . . . ?)

Qu'est-ce que tu penses de
la veste verte?
Comment trouves-tu
la veste verte?

Comment trouves-tu le pantalon vert?

Il est trop petit.

Il est	**joli.**		Elle est	**jolie.**
	élégant			élégante
	super			super
	chouette (terrific)			chouette
	à la mode (in style)			à la mode

| Il est | **moche** (plain, ugly). | | Elle est | **moche.** |
| | démodé (out of style) | | | démodée |

Il est **trop** (too)	**petit.**		Elle est **trop**	**petite.**
	grand (big)			grande
	court (short)			courte
	long (long)			longue

| Il est | **cher** (expensive). | | Elle est | **chère.** |
| | bon marché (cheap) | | | bon marché |

➡ **Super** and **bon marché** are INVARIABLE. They do not take adjective endings.
La robe rouge est **super**.   Les chaussures blanches sont **bon marché**.

VERBES

chercher	to look for	Je **cherche** un jean.
coûter	to cost	Les chaussures **coûtent** 300 francs.
penser	to think	Qu'est-ce que tu **penses** de cette (this) robe?
penser que	to think (that)	Je **pense qu'**elle est super!
trouver	to find	Je ne **trouve** pas ma veste.
	to think of	Comment **trouves**-tu mes lunettes de soleil?

➡ The verb **penser** is often used alone.
Tu **penses?**   Do you think so?   Je **ne pense pas**.   I don't think so.

 Game: Prices

PROP: Transparency 12

Using the menu on the transparency, have each student write an addition problem with an answer that is under 40 euros. For example:

Combien coûtent 2 steak-frites et 2 thés? [22 euros]

Place the problems into a hat. Divide the class into two teams. Draw a problem from the hat and read it aloud. Player A-1 plays against player B-1. The first player from either team to stand and answer correctly wins a point. If the response is incorrect, the other player tries to answer. Continue with players A-2 and B-2, etc.

Les nombres de 100 à 1000

100	**cent**	200	**deux cents**	500	**cinq cents**	800	**huit cents**
101	**cent un**	300	**trois cents**	600	**six cents**	900	**neuf cents**
102	**cent deux**	400	**quatre cents**	700	**sept cents**	1000	**mille**

7 Au Marché aux puces

You are at the Paris flea market looking for clothes with a French friend. Explain why you are not buying the following items. Use your imagination … and expressions from the **Vocabulaire.**

▸ — **Tu vas acheter le blouson?**
  — **Non, je ne pense pas.**
  — **Pourquoi pas?**
  — **Il est trop grand.**

▸

8 C'est combien?

You are at the Printemps, a department store in Paris. Ask a salesperson how much the various items cost.

▸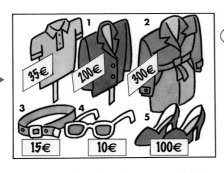

> Pardon, mademoiselle, combien coûte le polo?

> Il coûte 35 euros.

> Merci.

▷ **Les nombres de 100 à 1000**

🔲 **Leçon 25, Section 4**

▪ **Language notes**
• The word **mille** never takes an "s": **deux mille**, **trois mille**, etc. Note: at this level, students are not expected to spell the numbers.

7 EXCHANGES: explaining why one is not buying certain items

1. une cravate
2. un pull
3. un jean
4. un chapeau
5. une veste
6. un imper[méable]
7. des bottes (Elles sont …)

8 ROLE PLAY: asking about prices

1. la veste
2. l'imper[méable]
3. la ceinture
4. les lunettes de soleil
5. les chaussures

🖥 **25.5 Mini-scenes: Combien coûte la veste?**
(38:39–39:22 min.)

VIDEODISC Disc 4, Side 2
10390–11725

Challenge activity: Une idole

Une idole is a music superstar. Have students bring in a picture of an American **idole** and describe what he/she is wearing. They can give the approximate prices and comment on the style. For example:

Mon idole est Will Smith. Ici il porte un blouson qui (which) **coûte $150 et un pantalon qui coûte $75. Le blouson est trop grand mais le pantalon est très élégant. Il porte aussi des lunettes de soleil. Elles sont chouettes mais chères: elles coûtent $200!**

Cooperative pair practice
Activities 7, 8

T253

À votre tour!

1 La bonne réponse

You are in a French department store. Match the questions on the left with the appropriate answers on the right.

1. Vous désirez, monsieur?	a. Mon pantalon gris et ma veste bleue.
2. Est-ce que tu vas acheter le survêtement bleu?	b. 200 euros.
3. Comment trouves-tu les lunettes de soleil?	c. Je cherche une cravate.
4. Combien coûte l'imper?	d. Non, il est trop cher.
5. Qu'est-ce que tu vas mettre pour aller au restaurant?	e. Elles sont chouettes.

2 Créa-dialogue

You are at Place Bonaventure in Montreal looking at clothes in various shops. You like what the salesperson shows you and ask how much each item costs. React to the price.

joli/$60

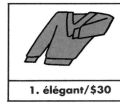
1. élégant/$30

2. joli/$150

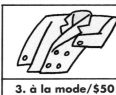
3. à la mode/$50

4. super/$15

5. chouette/$10

6. ??/??

▶ —**Vous désirez, monsieur (mademoiselle)?**
—**Je cherche _un pantalon_.**
—**Comment trouvez-vous _le pantalon gris_?**
—**Il est _joli_. Combien est-ce qu'_il_ coûte?**
—**_Soixante_ dollars.**
—**Oh là là, _il_ est cher!**
   (Il est bon marché.)

254 **Unité 7**

À votre tour

Depending on your goals and objectives, you may or may not wish to assign all of the activities in the **À votre tour** section.

Cooperative practice

Act. 1–4 lend themselves to cooperative pair practice.

3 Conversation dirigée

Sophie and Christophe are shopping in a department store. Act out their conversation in French.

Sophie				Christophe
	asks Christophe what he is looking for	→ ←	answers that he is looking for a tie	
	asks him what he thinks of the yellow tie	→ ←	says that it is pretty but adds that he is going to buy the blue tie	
	asks how much it costs	⇄	answers 5 euros	
	says that it is inexpensive but adds that the tie is out of style			

4 Qu'est-ce qui ne va pas? *(What's wrong?)*

The people in the pictures below are not very good shoppers. Describe what is wrong with each of the items they bought.

Monsieur Dupont **Édouard**

▶ Le chapeau de Monsieur Dupont est trop grand.

5 Les valises

Imagine that you are spending a year in Paris. On two different weekends, you have been invited by families of your classmates to visit their homes. On the first weekend, you will visit Nice and go sailing in the Mediterranean. For the second weekend, you have been invited to go skiing at Chamonix in the French Alps. Prepare your suitcases for the two trips, listing the items you will take with you.

un maillot de bain
deux shorts

un jean
un pull

6 À l'aéroport

Next week you are going to Paris for the first time on an exchange program. At the airport, you will be met by your host family. They do not have a picture of you. Describe yourself in a short note, telling what you look like and what you are going to wear.

▶

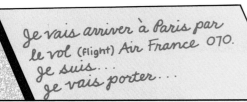

Je vais arriver à Paris par le vol (Flight) Air France 070.
Je suis...
Je vais porter...

---

3 GUIDED ORAL EXPRESSION

S: Qu'est-ce que tu cherches?
C: Je cherche une cravate.
S: Comment trouves-tu la cravate jaune?
C: Elle est jolie, mais je vais acheter la cravate bleue.
S: Combien est-ce qu'elle coûte?
C: Elle coûte 5 euros.
S: Elle est bon marché (elle n'est pas chère), mais elle est démodée.

🔊 Leçon 25, Section 9

4 COMPREHENSION

Monsieur Dupont:
La veste est trop grande.
Le pantalon est trop court.
Édouard:
La chemise est trop petite.
La cravate est trop longue (grande).
Le pantalon est trop long (grand).

5 WRITTEN SELF-EXPRESSION

6 WRITTEN SELF-EXPRESSION

📁 Portfolio assessment

You will probably select only one speaking activity and one writing activity to go into the students' portfolios for Unit 7.

In this lesson, Act. 2 lends itself well to an oral portfolio recording.

Act. 6 offers a good writing portfolio topic.

MODULE 26:
Rien n'est parfait!
Total time: 5:22 min.
(Counter: 41:41 min.)

26.1 Dialogue: Rien n'est parfait!
(42:08–43:11 min.)
**26.2 Mini-scenes: Listening
— Comment trouves-tu ce pull?**
(43:12–44:26 min.)
**26.3 Mini-scenes: Listening
— Quel café?**
(44:27–44:54 min.)
**26.4 Mini-scenes: Speaking
— Quelle veste désirez-vous?**
(44:55–45:38 min.)
26.5 Vignette culturelle: Un grand magasin
(45:39–46:59 min.)

VIDEODISC Disc 4, Side 2
15850–25450

■ **Comprehension practice:** Play the entire module through as an introduction to the lesson.

 26.1 Dialogue: Rien n'est parfait!
(42:08–43:11 min.)

VIDEODISC Disc 4, Side 2
16100–18550

 Leçon 26, Section 1

 Transparency 38
Dans un grand magasin

T256

Cet après-midi, Frédéric et Jean-Claude vont acheter des vêtements. Ils vont acheter ces vêtements dans un grand magasin. Ce magasin s'appelle Le Bon Marché.

This

these / This

Scène 1.
Frédéric et Jean-Claude regardent les pulls.

FRÉDÉRIC:	Regarde! Comment trouves-tu ce pull?
JEAN-CLAUDE:	Quel pull?	*Which*
FRÉDÉRIC:	Ce pull bleu.
JEAN-CLAUDE:	Il est chouette.
FRÉDÉRIC:	C'est vrai, il est très chouette.
JEAN-CLAUDE:	*(qui regarde le prix)* Il est aussi très cher.
FRÉDÉRIC:	Combien est-ce qu'il coûte?
JEAN-CLAUDE:	Deux cents euros.
FRÉDÉRIC:	Deux cents euros! Quelle horreur!	*What a scene*

■ NOTE ■
CULTURELLE

Le grand magasin

Many people consider the department store **(le grand magasin)** to be a typically American institution. However, it is a Frenchman, Aristide Boucicaut (1810–1877), who is generally credited with its creation. Monsieur Boucicaut's idea was to satisfy his Paris customers by offering them a large selection of good quality items at inexpensive prices. When he opened his new store in 1852, he appropriately named it Au Bon Marché. His success was soon imitated, leading to the creation in Paris of more department stores: Printemps, Galeries Lafayette, Samaritaine. These well-known stores still exist today and have branches in cities across France.

 ☀ Warm-up and review
PROP: Transparency 38

Using a transparency marker, fill in prices up to 300 euros in the price tags on the transparency. Then ask questions about the items of clothing and their prices.

Qu'est-ce que c'est?
C'est un pantalon noir.
Combien coûte le pantalon?
Il coûte [cent trente] euros.
C'est cher?
Mais oui, c'est très cher.

Scène 2.

Maintenant Frédéric et Jean-Claude regardent les vestes.

FRÉDÉRIC: Quelle veste est-ce que tu préfères?
JEAN-CLAUDE: Je préfère cette veste jaune. Elle est très élégante et elle n'est pas très chère.
FRÉDÉRIC: Oui, mais elle est trop grande pour toi!
JEAN-CLAUDE: Dommage!

Scène 3.

Frédéric est au <u>rayon</u> des chaussures. Quelles chaussures est-ce qu'il va acheter?

department

JEAN-CLAUDE: Alors, quelles chaussures est-ce que tu achètes?
FRÉDÉRIC: J'achète ces chaussures noires. Elles sont très confortables ... et elles ne sont pas chères. Regarde, elles sont <u>en solde</u>.

on sale

JEAN-CLAUDE: C'est vrai, elles sont en solde ... mais elles <u>ne sont plus</u> à la mode.

are no longer

FRÉDÉRIC: <u>Hélas, rien n'est parfait</u>!

too bad/nothing is perfect

Compréhension

1. Où vont Frédéric et Jean-Claude cet après-midi?
2. Qu'est-ce qu'ils vont faire?
3. Qu'est-ce qu'ils regardent d'abord *(first)*?
4. Combien coûte le pull bleu?
5. Quelle *(What)* est la réaction de Frédéric?
6. Qu'est-ce que Jean-Claude pense de la veste jaune?
7. Pourquoi est-ce qu'il n'achète pas la veste?
8. Qu'est-ce que Frédéric pense des chaussures noires?
9. Pourquoi est-ce qu'il n'achète pas les chaussures?

26.5 Vignette culturelle: Un grand magasin (45:39–46:59 min.)

 VIDEODISC Disc 4, Side 2
22990–25450

COMPREHENSION

1. dans un grand magasin (au Bon Marché)
2. acheter des vêtements
3. les pulls
4. 200 euros
5. Il pense que le pull est trop cher.
   (Il ne va pas acheter le pull.)
6. Elle est élégante. Elle n'est pas chère.
7. Elle est trop grande.
8. Elles sont confortables.
   (Elles ne sont pas chères.)
9. Elles ne sont pas à la mode.

Note culturelle

■ In 1989, **Au Bon Marché** changed its name to **Le Bon Marché.**

■ **Photo culture note**
La Samaritaine
The Samaritaine department store in Paris faces the Seine River. On the top floor is a restaurant which is especially popular because of its panoramic view of the city.

COMMUNICATIVE FUNCTION:
Indicating what people
prefer and what people
are buying

 Leçon 26, Section 2

■ Teaching strategies
• Point out that the stem changes
occur only in those forms of the
verb where the ending is not
pronounced. There is no stem
change before -ons and -ez.
• For your visually-minded students you can present stem-
changing verbs as "boot verbs."
Within the "boot" the verb endings are not pronounced and
there is the same change in the
stem. Outside the boot, the endings are pronounced, and there
is no stem change.

j'achète	nous achetons
tu achètes	vous achetez
il achète	ils achètent

COMPREHENSION:
describing purchases

A. Les verbes *acheter* et *préférer*

Verbs like **acheter** *(to buy)* end in: **e** + CONSONANT + **-er.**
Verbs like **préférer** *(to prefer)* end in: **é** + CONSONANT + **-er.**

Note the forms of these two verbs in the chart, paying attention to:
• the **e** of the stem of **acheter**
• the **é** of the stem of **préférer**

INFINITIVE	**acheter**	**préférer**
PRESENT	J' ach**è**te une veste.	Je préf**è**re la veste bleue.
	Tu ach**è**tes une cravate.	Tu préf**è**res la cravate jaune.
	Il/Elle ach**è**te un imper.	Il/Elle préf**è**re l'imper gris.
	Nous achetons un jean.	Nous préférons le jean noir.
	Vous achetez un short.	Vous préférez le short blanc.
	Ils/Elles ach**è**tent un pull.	Ils/Elles préf**è**rent le pull rouge.

➡ Verbs like **acheter** and **préférer** take regular endings and have the following changes in the stem:

acheter e → è	}	in the **je, tu, il,** and **ils**
préférer é → è		forms of the present

① Achats *(Purchases)*

What we buy depends on how much
money we have. Complete the sentences
below with **acheter** and one or more of
the items from the list.

1. Avec dix dollars, tu …
2. Avec quinze dollars, j' …
3. Avec trente dollars, nous …
4. Avec cinquante dollars, Jean-Claude …
5. Avec cent dollars, vous …
6. Avec quinze mille dollars, mes parents …
7. Avec ?? dollars, mon cousin …
8. Avec ?? dollars, j' …

une voiture

des chaussure

une cravate

un survêtement

des lunettes de soleil **un polo** **une veste**

un compact

un jean

??

Talking about past events

Let's talk about what clothes you bought
last summer.
▶ **Est-ce que tu as acheté un jean
l'été dernier?**
Oui, j'ai acheté un jean.
(Non, je n'ai pas acheté de jean.)
• **Est-ce que tu as acheté un polo?**

• **Est-ce que tu as acheté des sandales?**
• **Est-ce que tu as acheté un maillot de
bain?**
• **Est-ce que tu as acheté une veste?**
• **Qu'est-ce que tu as acheté?**
Follow-up:
Est-ce que X a acheté un jean?

Vocabulaire: Verbes comme *(like)* *acheter et préférer*

acheter	*to buy*	Qu'est-ce que tu **achètes?**
amener	*to bring (a person)*	François **amène** sa copine à la boum.
préférer	*to prefer*	**Préfères**-tu le manteau ou l'imper?
espérer	*to hope*	J'**espère** visiter Paris en été.

➡ In French, there are two verbs that correspond to the English *to bring:*
amener + PEOPLE   J'**amène** une copine au pique-nique.
apporter + THINGS   J'**apporte** des sandwichs au pique-nique.

2 Pique-nique

Everyone is bringing someone or something to the picnic. Complete the sentences below with the appropriate forms of **amener** or **apporter.**

▶ **Nous** <u>amenons</u> **un copain.   Marc** <u>apporte</u> **des sandwichs.**

1. Tu . . . ta guitare.
2. Philippe . . . sa soeur.
3. Nous . . . nos voisins.
4. Vous . . . un dessert.
5. Michèle . . . des sodas.
6. Antoine et Vincent . . . leur cousine.
7. Raphaël . . . ses cassettes.
8. Mon cousin . . . sa copine.
9. J' . . . ma radiocassette.

3 Expression personnelle

Complete the sentences below with one of the suggested options or an expression of your choice. Note: You may wish to make some of the sentences negative.

Quand je vais à un pique-nique, j'amène mon chat.

Et moi, j'amène mon chien.

1. Quand je vais à un pique-nique, j'amène . . . (ma petite soeur, mes voisins, mon chien, ??) J'apporte . . . (mon walkman, mon livre de français, des sandwichs, ??)
2. Quand je vais à une fête, j'amène . . . (des copains, une copine, ma grand-mère, ??) J'apporte . . . (des sandwichs, ma guitare, mes cassettes, ??)
3. Le weekend, je préfère . . . (étudier, aller au cinéma, rester à la maison, ??) Ce *(This)* weekend, j'espère . . . (travailler, avoir un rendez-vous avec un copain ou une copine, jouer au volley, ??)
4. Pendant *(During)* les vacances, j'espère . . . (rester à la maison, trouver un job, voyager, ??) Un jour, j'espère . . . (visiter la France, parler français, aller à l'université, être millionnaire, ??)

Leçon 26   **259**

Talking about past events

Let's talk about what things you brought to a recent party.
▶ **Tu es allé(e) à une boum récemment. Est-ce que tu as apporté des cassettes? Oui, j'ai apporté des cassettes. (Non, je n'ai pas apporté de cassettes.)**

- **Est-ce que tu as apporté des compacts?**
- **Est-ce que tu as apporté des disques?**
- **Est-ce que tu as apporté une guitare?**
- **Est-ce que tu as apporté des pizzas?**
- **Est-ce que tu as apporté des sodas?**
- **Qu'est-ce que tu as apporté?**

**26.2 Mini-scenes:
Comment trouves-tu
ce pull?**
(43:12–44:26 min.)

VIDEODISC Disc 4, Side 2
18570–20815

Leçon 26, Section 3

■ **Teaching strategies**
• Point out that **ces** (like **les, des, mes**) is used with both masculine and feminine plural nouns. (There is no **cettes.**)
• Tell students that the masculine singular form **cet** is derived from the feminine singular form **cette** minus **-te: cette → cet.**

■ **Language note:** The tag **-ci** is related to **ici** (here) and **-là** means *there.* The expression **voici** has evolved from **vois ici** (see here) and **voilà** from **vois là** (see there).

4 ROLE PLAY: commenting on items in a store

■ **Expansion:** Now Nathalie is with Jérôme who is critical of everything. Have students use an expression of their choice in Jérôme's responses.
N: **Regarde cette robe!
Elle est jolie!**
J: **Cette robe-là?
Elle est moche.**
(**Elle n'est pas à la mode.** etc.)

5 ROLE PLAY: discussing preferences

**Cooperative
pair practice**
Activities 4, 5, 6

T260

B. L'adjectif démonstratif *ce*

Note the forms of the demonstrative adjective **ce** in the chart below.

	SINGULAR *(this, that)*	PLURAL *(these, those)*		
MASCULINE	**ce** ↓ **cet** (+ VOWEL SOUND)	**ces**	**ce** blouson **cet** homme	**ces** blousons **ces** hommes
FEMININE	**cette**	**ces**	**cette** veste **cette** amie	**ces** vestes **ces** amies

➡ There is liaison after **cet** and **ces** when the next word begins with a vowel sound.

➡ To distinguish between a person or an object that is close by and one that is further away, the French sometimes use **-ci** or **-là** after the noun.

Philippe achète **cette chemise-ci.** — *Philippe is buying **this shirt** (over here).*
François achète **cette chemise-là.** — *François is buying **that shirt** (over there).*

4 **À la Samaritaine**

Marc and Nathalie are at the Samaritaine department store. Marc likes everything that Nathalie shows him. Play both roles.

▶ une robe (jolie)   NATHALIE: **Regarde cette robe!**
                      MARC: **Elle est jolie!**

1. un imper (élégant)
2. des bottes (à la mode)
3. une cravate (chouette)
4. un survêtement (super)
5. des livres (amusants)
6. un ordinateur (super)
7. une télé (moderne)
8. une ceinture (jolie)
9. des sandales (jolies)

Expression pour la conversation

How to emphasize a question or remark:

Eh bien!   *Well!*   —**Eh bien,** est-ce que tu viens en ville avec nous?
                           —**Eh bien,** non!

---

5 **Différences d'opinion**

Whenever they go shopping together, Éric and Brigitte cannot agree on what they like. Play both roles.

▶ un short

1. une chemise
2. un blouson
3. des chaussures
4. des lunettes
5. des disques
6. une affiche
7. un stylo
8. un ordinateur

J'aime ce short-ci.

Eh bien, moi, je préfère ce short-là.

C. L'adjectif interrogatif *quel?*

The interrogative adjective **quel** *(what? which?)* is used in questions. It agrees with the noun it introduces and has the following forms:

	SINGULAR	PLURAL		
MASCULINE	quel	quels	**Quel** garçon?	**Quels** cousins?
FEMININE	quelle	quelles	**Quelle** fille?	**Quelles** copines?

→ Note the liaison after **quels** and **quelles** when the next word begins with a vowel sound.
Quelles affiches est-ce que tu préfères?

J'achète une jupe.

Cette jupe jaune.

Quelle jupe est-ce que tu achètes?

6 Vêtements d'été

You are shopping for the following items before going on a summer trip to France. A friend is asking you which ones you are buying. Identify each item by color.

une jupe/ jaune

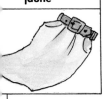

1. un maillot de bain/bleu

2. des chaussettes/ vertes

3. un pantalon/ noir

4. une veste/ bleue

5. des chaussures/ blanches

6. des sandales/ brunes

7. un sweat/ gris

8. une chemise/ orange

9. un pull/ rouge

7 Questions personnelles

1. À quelle école vas-tu?
2. Dans quel magasin achètes-tu tes vêtements?
3. Dans quel magasin achètes-tu tes chaussures?
4. Quels disques aimes-tu écouter?
5. Quels programmes aimes-tu regarder à la télé?
6. Quel est ton restaurant préféré?

Section C

COMMUNICATIVE FUNCTION: Asking for clarification

　26.3 Mini-scenes: Quel café?
26.4 Mini-scenes: Quelle veste désirez-vous? (44:27–45:38 min.)

VIDEODISC Disc 4, Side 2
20815–22970

　Leçon 26, Sections 4, 5

■ **Language notes**
• Point out that all four forms of **quel** sound the same.
• **Quel** may be separated from its noun by **être**.
Quelle est la date?

■ **Teaching strategy:** Ask students if they can remember any questions they learned that use **quel**.
Quelle est la date?
Quelle heure est-il?
Quel temps fait-il?
Quel jour est-ce?
De quelle couleur est...?

　ROLE PLAY: discussing
6 purchases

↩ **Re-entry and review:** This activity reviews colors from Lesson 20.

COMMUNICATION: answering personal
7 questions

Listening activity: Préférences

PROPS: One red and one blue index card for each student

On the board, write **QUEL(S)** in blue chalk and **QUELLE(S)** in red chalk. Then read aloud questions containing forms of **quel**. If the form is spelled **quel(s)**, students hold up the blue card. If it is spelled **quelle(s)**, they hold up the red card.

1. **Quel sweat préfères-tu?** [B]
2. **Quels appareils...?** [B]
3. **Quelle jupe...?** [R]
4. **Quel blouson...?** [B]
5. **Quelles affiches...?** [R]
6. **Quelles chaussettes...?** [R]
7. **Quel pull...?** [B]
8. **Quelle école...?** [R]

COMPREHENSION:
describing where people
put things

8

■ **Variation:** Have students give
illogical answers.
**Mme Arnaud met la voiture dans
le salon.**

■ **Realia note**
Ask students:
**Comment s'appelle le grand
   magasin?** [les Galeries
   Lafayette]
**À quel étage sont les meubles et
   les lampes?** [au 4ème étage]
**Quelles choses est-ce qu'on peut
   mettre dans ce meuble?** [des
   vêtements, des livres et des
   cartes]

T262

D. Le verbe *mettre*

The verb **mettre** *(to put, place)* is irregular. Note its forms in the chart below.

INFINITIVE	**mettre**	
PRESENT	je **mets**	nous **mettons**
	tu **mets**	vous **mettez**
	il / elle **met**	ils / elles **mettent**

➡ In the singular forms, the "**t**" of the stem is silent. The "**t**" is pronounced in the plural forms.

➡ The verb **mettre** has several English equivalents:

to put, place	Je **mets** mes livres sur la table.
to put on, wear	Caroline **met** une robe rouge.
to turn on	Nous **mettons** la télé.

8 Où?

Say where the people of Column A put the ▶
objects of Column B, by choosing a place from
Column C. Be logical!

> Madame Arnaud met la voiture
> dans le garage.

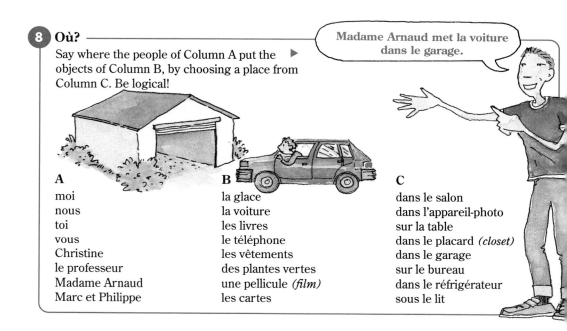

A	**B**	**C**
moi	la glace	dans le salon
nous	la voiture	dans l'appareil-photo
toi	les livres	sur la table
vous	le téléphone	dans le placard *(closet)*
Christine	les vêtements	dans le garage
le professeur	des plantes vertes	sur le bureau
Madame Arnaud	une pellicule *(film)*	dans le réfrigérateur
Marc et Philippe	les cartes	sous le lit

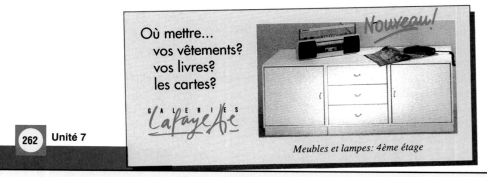

Où mettre...
   vos vêtements?
   vos livres?
   les cartes?

G A L E R I E S
Lafayette

Nouveau!

Meubles et lampes: 4ème étage

✕▢ **Teaching note: Un jeu**

Divide the students into pairs. Have each
student take a sheet of paper. At a given
signal, students write a phrase using elements from columns A and B (e.g., **Je
mets la glace...**). As soon as they finish,
they exchange papers and complete their
partner's sentence using an element from
column C (**...dans le réfrigérateur**).

Then, they write another phrase using
columns A and B, exchange papers, and
again complete their partner's sentence
using column C.

After you have called time, have the
pairs exchange papers for peer correction.
The winner is the pair with the most
correct sentences.

9 **Questions personnelles**

1. Est-ce que tu mets la radio quand tu étudies?
2. Chez vous, est-ce que vous mettez la télé quand vous dînez?
3. Est-ce que tu mets des lunettes de soleil quand tu vas à la plage?
4. Où est-ce que tes parents mettent leur voiture? (dans le garage? dans la rue?)
5. Quels programmes de télé est-ce que tu mets le dimanche? le samedi?
6. Quels disques (ou quelles cassettes) est-ce que tu mets quand tu vas à une boum?
7. Quels vêtements est-ce que tu mets quand il fait froid?
8. Quels vêtements est-ce que tu mets quand tu joues au basket?

COMMUNICATION: answering personal questions **9**

Prononciation

Les lettres «e» et «è»

e = /ə/	e = /ɛ/	è = /ɛ/
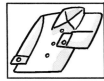		
chemise	**chaussette**	**chère**

Practice pronouncing "**e**" within a word:

- /ə/ (as in **je**)   [. . . "e" + _one_ CONSONANT + VOWEL]

  Répétez: **chemise   regarder   Denise   Renée   petit   venir**

  Note that in the middle of a word the /ə/ is sometimes silent.

  acheter   achetons   amener   samedi   rarement   avenue

- /ɛ/ (as in **elle**)   [. . . "e" + _two_ CONSONANTS + VOWEL]

  Répétez: **chaussette   veste   quelle   cette   rester   professeur   raquette**

Now practice pronouncing "**è**" within a word:

- /ɛ/ (as in **elle**)   [. . . "è" + _one_ CONSONANT + VOWEL]

  Répétez: **chère   père   mère   achète   amènent   espère   deuxième**

NOS CHEMISES

MONOPRIX UNIPRIX

25€

Leçon 26   **263**

Prononciation

🔲 Leçon 26, Section 6

■ **Pronunciation notes**
- The sound /ə/ is called a *mute e* because it is sometimes mute or silent.
- The sound /ɛ/ is called an *open e* because when you say it your mouth is more open than when you say /e/ as in **café**.

■ **Realia note**
Monoprix
Monoprix is a moderately priced chain store that sells clothing, cosmetics, stationery supplies, toys, and housewares. Many of the stores also have a supermarket section.
Ask: **Combien coûtent les chemises au Monoprix?**

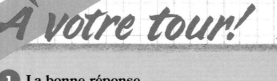

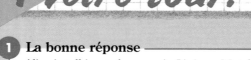

1 COMPREHENSION

1-d   3-c
2-a   4-b

 Leçon 26, Section 7

2 GUIDED ORAL EXPRESSION

1. ces livres
2. ce monsieur (cet homme)
3. cette jupe
4. cette cravate
5. ces chaussures
6. ces lunettes de soleil
7. ce manteau

 Leçon 26, Section 8

1 La bonne réponse

Alice is talking to her cousin Jérôme. Match Alice's questions with Jérôme's answers. Act out the dialogue with a classmate.

Alice

Jérôme

1   Je vais à la soirée de Delphine. Et toi?

2   Tu amènes une copine?

3   Qu'est-ce que vous allez apporter?

4   Qu'est-ce que tu vas mettre?

a   Oui, Christine.

b   Mon pull jaune et mon blouson marron.

c   Nous allons acheter des pizzas.

d   Moi aussi.

2 Créa-dialogue

Ask your classmates what they think about the following. They will answer affirmatively or negatively.

▶   — Comment trouves-tu <u>cette fille</u>?
    — <u>Quelle fille</u>?
    — <u>Cette fille-là</u>!
    — Eh bien, je pense qu'<u>elle</u> est <u>jolie</u>.
    (<u>Elle</u> n'est pas <u>jolie</u>.)

jolie?

1. intéressants?

2. sympathique?

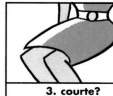
3. courte?

4. moche?

5. bon marché?

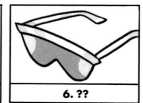
6. ??

7. ??

264   **Unité 7**

À votre tour

Depending on your goals and objectives, you may or may not wish to assign all of the activities in the **À votre tour** section.

👥 Cooperative practice

Act. 1–3 lend themselves to cooperative pair practice.

3 Shopping

You and a friend are shopping by catalog. Choose an object and tell your friend what you are buying. Identify it by color and explain why you like it.

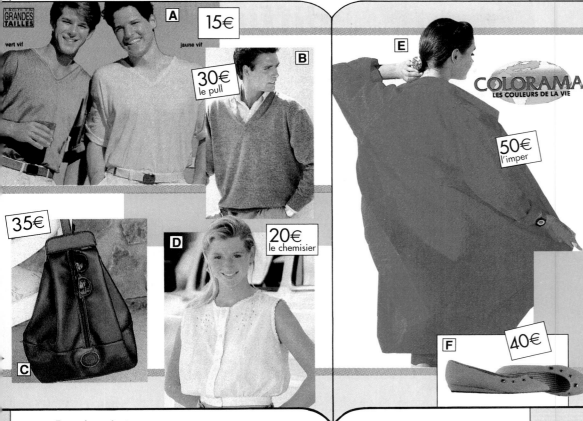

GRANDES TAILLES

vert vif · jaune vif

A 15€

B 30€ le pull

E

COLORAMA
LES COULEURS DE LA VIE

50€ l'imper

35€

D 20€ le chemisier

C

F 40€

▶ —Je vais acheter un sac.
—Quel sac?
—Ce sac noir.
—Pourquoi?
—Parce qu'il est joli.

4 Composition: La soirée

You have been invited to a party by a French friend. In a short paragraph, describe ...

- what clothes you are going to wear
- whom you are going to bring along
- what things (food? records? cassettes?) you are going to bring

Leçon 26 265

MODULE 27:
Un choix difficile
Total time: 5:56 min.
(Counter: 47:10 min.)

27.1 Dialogue: Un choix difficile
(47:45–48:55 min.)
27.2 Mini-scenes: Listening — Comparaisons
(48:56–50:27 min.)
27.3 Mini-scenes: Speaking — Comparaisons
(50:28–51:24 min.)
27.4 Vignette culturelle: Dans un centre commercial
(51:25–53:00 min.)

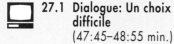 **VIDEODISC** Disc 4, Side 2
25680–36300

■ **Comprehension practice:** Play the entire module through as an introduction to the lesson.

27.1 Dialogue: Un choix difficile
(47:45–48:55 min.)

VIDEODISC Disc 4, Side 2
25900–28870

 Leçon 27, Section 1

T266

LEÇON 27 Un choix difficile

Dans un mois, Delphine va aller au mariage de sa cousine. Elle va acheter une <u>nouvelle</u> robe pour cette occasion. Pour cela, elle va dans une boutique de mode avec sa copine Véronique. Il y a beaucoup de jolies robes dans cette boutique.
   Delphine <u>hésite entre</u> une robe jaune et une robe rouge. Quelle robe est-ce que Delphine va <u>choisir</u>? Ah là là, le <u>choix</u> n'est pas facile.

new

is hesitating / between
to choose / choice

Scène 1.

VÉRONIQUE: Alors, quelle robe est-ce que tu choisis?
DELPHINE: Eh bien, <u>finalement</u> je choisis la robe rouge. Elle est <u>plus jolie que</u> la robe jaune.
VÉRONIQUE: C'est vrai, elle est plus jolie . . . mais la robe jaune est <u>moins</u> chère et elle est <u>plus grande</u>. Regarde. La robe rouge est trop petite pour toi.
DELPHINE: Mais non, elle n'est pas trop petite.
VÉRONIQUE: Bon, écoute, <u>essaie-la</u>!

finally
prettier than

less / larger

try it!

■ NOTE ■ CULTURELLE

Le choix de vêtements

Since clothes are more expensive in France than in the United States and because budgets are limited, French teenagers are very careful when buying clothes. They spend a lot of time window shopping, comparing (brands, labels, and prices), and discussing with their friends what is in or out of fashion, before finally deciding what to buy. In general, French teenagers would rather buy one item of good quality than several of lesser quality. Of course, this item has to be the right one!

266 Unité 7

Setting the scene

Have the class imagine they have all been invited to a wedding. What will they wear?
Imaginez que nous sommes invités à un mariage ce weekend.
Moi, je vais mettre ... [describe the outfit you would plan to wear]

Have various students describe what they are going to wear.
Et toi, X, qu'est-ce que tu vas mettre?
Y, est-ce que tu vas mettre [...] aussi?
Introduce Section 27.1 of the video:
Ce weekend Delphine va à un mariage.
Qu'est-ce qu'elle va mettre?

Scène 2.

Delphine <u>sort</u> de la <u>cabine d'essayage</u>.

DELPHINE: C'est vrai, la robe rouge est <u>plus petite</u> mais ce n'est pas un problème.

VÉRONIQUE: Pourquoi?

DELPHINE: Parce que j'ai un mois pour <u>maigrir</u>.

VÉRONIQUE: Et <u>si</u> tu <u>grossis</u>?

DELPHINE: Toi, <u>tais-toi</u>!

comes out / fitting room
smaller

to lose weight
if / gain weight
be quiet

● **Compréhension**

1. Où vont Delphine et Véronique?
2. Qu'est-ce que Delphine va acheter?
3. Pourquoi?
4. Delphine hésite entre deux robes. De quelle couleur sont-elles?
5. Quelle robe est-ce qu'elle choisit?
6. Pourquoi est-ce qu'elle préfère la robe rouge?
7. Selon (*According to*) Véronique, quel est le problème avec la robe rouge?
8. Qu'est-ce que Delphine doit (*must*) faire pour porter la robe?

Note culturelle

■ **Cultural note:** In France, window displays almost always include the prices of the items shown. Only the most expensive designer boutiques do not indicate prices.

 27.4 Vignette culturelle: Dans un centre commercial (51:25–53:00 min.)

VIDEODISC Disc 4, Side 2
33340–36300

 COMPREHENSION

1. dans une boutique de mode
2. une nouvelle robe
3. parce qu'elle va aller au mariage de sa cousine
4. jaune et rouge
5. la robe rouge
6. parce qu'elle est plus jolie que la robe jaune
7. Elle est trop petite.
8. Elle doit maigrir.

Talking about past events

Let's talk about where you went yesterday and what you wore. Note that the past participle of **mettre** is **mis.**

▶ **Imagine que tu es allé(e) à la plage hier. Qu'est-ce que tu as mis?**
J'ai mis un maillot de bain et des sandales.

• **Imagine que tu es allé(e) à une boum hier. Qu'est-ce que tu as mis?**
• **Imagine que tu es allé(e) en ville hier. Qu'est-ce que tu as mis?**
• **Imagine que tu es allé(e) au stade hier. Qu'est-ce que tu as mis?**
• **Imagine que tu es allé(e) à un pique-nique hier. Qu'est-ce que tu as mis?**

Section A

COMMUNICATIVE FUNCTION:
Describing actions

Transparency 39
-ir verbs

 Leçon 27, Section 2

■ **Teaching strategy:** Using subject pronoun cue cards, have students conjugate other -ir verbs orally and in writing (e.g., **choisir, réussir**).

1 PRACTICE: saying who finishes a race

Supplementary vocabulary

a) Some -ir verbs correspond to English verbs in **-ish**
finir to finish
établir to establish
abolir to abolish

b) Verbs derived from adjectives often end in **-ir**
COLORS:
(rouge) rougir to blush, to turn red
(blanc, blanche) blanchir
  to blanche, to turn white
(jaune) jaunir to turn yellow
(brun) brunir to turn brown, to tan

SIZE:
(grand) grandir to grow tall
Note:
(gros, grosse–fat) grossir
(maigre–thin) maigrir

2 COMPREHENSION: indicating who is gaining or losing weight

Many French verbs end in *-ir*. Most of these verbs are conjugated like **finir** *(to finish)*. Note the forms of this verb in the present tense, paying special attention to the endings.

INFINITIVE	finir	STEM (infinitive minus **-ir**)	ENDINGS
PRESENT	Je **finis** à deux heures. Tu **finis** à une heure. Il/Elle **finit** à cinq heures. Nous **finissons** à midi. Vous **finissez** à une heure. Ils/Elles **finissent** à minuit.	fin-	-is -is -it -issons -issez -issent

⇒ Note that all final consonants are silent.

1 **Le marathon de Paris**

Not everyone who enters the Paris marathon finishes. Say which of the following runners finish the marathon and which do not.

▶ Philippe (non) **Philippe ne finit pas.**

1. moi (oui)   3. nous (oui)   5. Éric (oui)   7. Frédéric et Marc (non)
2. toi (non)   4. vous (non)   6. Stéphanie (non)   8. Anne et Cécile (oui)

Vocabulaire: Verbes réguliers en *-ir*

choisir	to choose	Quelle veste **choisis**-tu?
finir	to finish	Les classes **finissent** à midi.
grossir	to gain weight, get fat	Marc **grossit** parce qu'il mange beaucoup.
maigrir	to lose weight, get thin	Je **maigris** parce que je ne mange pas beaucoup.
réussir	to succeed	Tu vas **réussir** parce que tu travailles!
réussir à un examen	to pass an exam	Nous **réussissons à nos examens.**

2 **Le régime** *(Diet)*

Read about the following people. Then say whether they are gaining weight or losing weight. Use the verbs **grossir** and **maigrir**.

▶ Philippe mange beaucoup de pizzas.
  Il grossit.

1. Vous faites des exercices.
2. Nous allons souvent au gymnase.
3. Vous êtes inactifs.
4. Je mange des carottes.
5. Monsieur Moreau adore la bonne cuisine.
6. Vous n'êtes pas très sportifs.
7. Ces personnes mangent trop *(too much)*.
8. Je nage, je joue au volley et je fais des promenades.

☀ Warm-up and review: Telling time

PROPS: Clock with movable hands or Transparency 6

Review times by changing the hands on the clock.
Quelle heure est-il?
Il est deux heures vingt-cinq. ...

Have students practice forms of the verb **finir** together with clock times.
[moi: 1h30] **Je finis à une heure et demie.**
[vous: 8h45] **Vous finissez à neuf heures moins le quart.**
[X: 3h10] **X finit à trois heures dix.**

3 **Questions personnelles**

1. À quelle heure finissent les classes aujourd'hui?
2. À quelle heure finit la classe de français?
3. Quand finit l'école cette année *(year)*?
4. Tu es invité(e) au restaurant ou au cinéma. Où choisis-tu d'aller?
5. Quand tu vas au cinéma avec ta famille, qui choisit le film?
6. En général, est-ce que tu réussis à tes examens? Est-ce que tu vas réussir à l'examen de français?
7. Est-ce que tes copains réussissent aussi?

3 COMMUNICATION: answering personal questions

B. Les adjectifs *beau, nouveau* et *vieux*

The adjectives **beau** *(beautiful, good-looking)*, **nouveau** *(new)*, and **vieux** *(old)* are irregular. Note their forms and their position.

		beau	**nouveau**	**vieux**
SINGULAR	MASC.	le **beau** manteau (le **bel** imper)	le **nouveau** manteau (le **nouvel** imper)	le **vieux** manteau (le **vieil** imper)
	FEM.	la **belle** veste	la **nouvelle** veste	la **vieille** veste
PLURAL	MASC.	les **beaux** manteaux	les **nouveaux** manteaux	les **vieux** manteaux
	FEM.	les **belles** vestes	les **nouvelles** vestes	les **vieilles** vestes

➡ The adjectives **beau, nouveau,** and **vieux** usually come BEFORE the noun. If the noun begins with a vowel sound, there is liaison between the adjective and the noun.

   les **nouveaux**‿ordinateurs   les **belles**‿affiches   les **vieux**‿impers

➡ In the masculine singular, the liaison forms **bel, nouvel,** and **vieil** are used before a vowel sound. Note that **vieil** is pronounced like **vieille:**

   un **vieil**‿imper   une **vieille** robe

Section B

COMMUNICATIVE FUNCTION: Describing people and things (new, beautiful, old)

🔲 **Transparency 40** Beau, nouveau, vieux

■ **Pronunciation notes**
• Remind students that in liaison "x" is pronounced /z/; the "il" of **vieil** is pronounced /j/.
• Point out that all three masculine singular liaison forms sound like the corresponding feminine singular forms.

4 **La collection de printemps**

Mod Boutique is presenting its spring collection. You are impressed by the new clothes and accessories. Point them out to a French friend, using the appropriate forms of **beau.**

▶ une chemise
   Regarde la belle chemise!

1. une robe	5. un imper
2. un pantalon	6. des sandales
3. des jeans	7. un manteau
4. des blousons	8. un chapeau

5 **Différences d'opinion**

François is showing the new things he bought to his sister Valérie. She prefers his old things. Play both roles.

▶ des chaussures

1. un polo
2. des lunettes de soleil
3. un imper
4. des affiches
5. une veste
6. une montre
7. un ordinateur
8. des baskets
9. un survêtement

> **Tu aimes mes nouvelles chaussures?**

> **Eh bien, non, je préfère tes vieilles chaussures.**

4 PRACTICE: saying things are beautiful

■ **Expansion** (dialogue format):
– **Regarde la belle chemise!**
– **C'est vrai. Elle est belle.**

5 ROLE PLAY: discussing preferences between old and new items

Talking about past events

Let's talk about what you ordered when you ate out the last time. Note that the past participle of **-ir** verbs ends in **-i.**

▶ **Est-ce que tu as choisi une pizza?**
   Oui, j'ai choisi une pizza.
   (Non, je n'ai pas choisi de pizza.)
• **Est-ce que tu as choisi une salade?**
• **Est-ce que tu as choisi un steak?**
• **Est-ce que tu as choisi une glace?**
• **Est-ce que tu as choisi un soda?**
• **Est-ce que tu as choisi un café?**
• **Qu'est-ce que tu as choisi?**
Follow-up:
• **Est-ce que X a choisi une pizza? ...**

Cooperative pair practice Activity 5

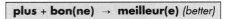

Section C

COMMUNICATIVE FUNCTION:
Expressing comparisons

27.2 Mini-scenes:
Comparaisons
27.3 Mini-scenes:
Comparaisons
(48:56–51:24 min.)

VIDEODISC Disc 4, Side 2
28870–3330

Leçon 27, Sections 3, 4

■ **Language notes**
• In French as in English, the second part of the comparison may be left out:
Cette robe est plus chère.
• The comparative form of **bon marché** is **meilleur marché.** This form is not actively presented at this time

COMMUNICATION:

expressing one's opinion about relative prices

6

C. La comparaison avec les adjectifs

Note how COMPARISONS are expressed in French.

Cet imper est **plus cher que** ce manteau.	*… more expensive than …*
Cette jupe est **plus jolie que** cette robe.	*… prettier than …*
Paul est **moins sportif que** Patrick.	*… less athletic than …*
Il est **moins amusant que** lui.	*… less amusing than …*
Je suis **aussi grand que** toi.	*… as tall as …*
Tu **n'es pas aussi timide que** moi.	*… not as timid as …*

To make comparisons with adjectives, the French use the following constructions:

+	**plus**		**plus cher (que)**	*more expensive (than)*
–	**moins**	+ ADJECTIVE (+ **que** …)	**moins cher (que)**	*less expensive (than)*
=	**aussi**		**aussi cher (que)**	*as expensive (as)*

➡ Note the irregular **plus**-form of **bon** *(good):*

plus + bon(ne) → **meilleur(e)** *(better)*

   Ta cassette est **bonne,** mais ma cassette est **meilleure.**
   But: Cette cassette est **moins bonne que** ce disque.
           Est-ce que les Red Sox sont **aussi bons que** les Yankees?

➡ There is liaison after **plus** and **moins** when the next word begins with a vowel sound.
   Cette robe-ci est **plus_élégante.**   Ce livre-là est **moins_intéressant.**

➡ In comparisons, the adjective always agrees with the noun (or pronoun) it describes.

   La jupe est plus **chère** que le chemisier.

   Les vestes sont moins **chères** que les manteaux.

➡ In comparisons with people, STRESS PRONOUNS are used after **que.**
   Paul est plus petit **que moi.**   Je suis plus grand **que lui.**

6 **Comparaisons**

How much do you think the following pairs of items cost? Give your opinion, saying whether the first one is more expensive, less expensive, or as expensive as the second one.

▶ une guitare/une raquette   **Une guitare est plus (moins, aussi) chère qu'une raquette.**

1. un vélo/un scooter
2. une mobylette/une moto
3. une pizza/un sandwich
4. une télé/un ordinateur
5. des chaussures/des sandales
6. un pantalon/une robe

7. des bottes/des tennis
8. un sweat/un maillot de bain
9. des chaussettes/des collants
10. des lunettes de soleil/une montre

Cooperative
pair practice
Activity 8

TPR **Comparisons**

PROPS: Plastic bag with 30 "money cards" (labelled with amounts from $50–$1000)

Have students come up and draw a "prize."
   Vous êtes tous riches.
   Vous avez gagné à la loterie hier.
   Venez chercher vos prix!

Review numbers by asking what they drew.
   X, montre-nous ton prix. [holds up $100]
   Combien d'argent as-tu? [cent dollars]
   Est-ce que X est riche aujourd'hui? [oui!]
   Y, montre-nous ton prix. …
Call up two students with different "prizes."
   X et Y, venez ici.
   Combien d'argent a X? [$100] **Et Y?** [$500

Expression pour la conversation

How to introduce a personal opinion:

à mon avis ...   *in my opinion ...*   **À mon avis,** le français est facile.

7 Expression personnelle

Compare the following by using the adjectives suggested. Give your personal opinion.

▶ le tennis/intéressant/le ping-pong

À mon avis, le tennis est plus intéressant que le ping-pong.

(moins, aussi)

1. le basket/intéressant/le foot
2. l'anglais/facile/le français
3. la classe de français/amusant/ la classe d'anglais
4. la ville de New York/beau/ la ville de Chicago
5. la Floride/beau/la Californie
6. les Yankees/bon/les Red Sox
7. les Celtics/bon/les Lakers
8. les Cowboys/bon/les Saints
9. la cuisine américaine/bon/ la cuisine française
10. les voitures japonaises/bon/ les voitures américaines
11. les filles/intelligent/les garçons
12. les Américains/intelligent/ les Français

▶▶▶▶▶▶▶▶▶▶▶▶▶▶▶▶▶▶▶▶▶

8 Et toi?

Use the appropriate stress pronouns in answering the questions below.

▶ —Es-tu plus grand(e) que ton copain?
—Oui, je suis plus grand(e) que lui.
(Non, je suis moins grand(e) que lui.)
(Je suis aussi grand(e) que lui.)

1. Es-tu plus grand(e) que ta mère?
2. Es-tu aussi riche que Donald Trump?
3. Es-tu plus sportif (sportive) que tes cousins?
4. Es-tu plus intelligent(e) qu'Einstein?

Prononciation

Les lettres «ill»   ill /j/

In the middle of a word, the letters "**ill**" almost always represent the semi-vowel /j/ which is like the "**y**" of *yes*.

ma<u>ill</u>ot

Répétez: **ma<u>ill</u>ot trava<u>ill</u>ez ore<u>ill</u>e vie<u>ill</u>e
f<u>ill</u>e fam<u>ill</u>e ju<u>ill</u>et
En ju<u>ill</u>et, Mire<u>ill</u>e va trava<u>ill</u>er pour sa vie<u>ill</u>e tante.**

At the end of a word, the sound /j/ is sometimes spelled **il.**

Répétez: **appare<u>il</u>-photo vie<u>il</u> trava<u>il</u>** *(job)*
Mon oncle a un vie<u>il</u> appare<u>il</u>-photo.

EXCEPTION: The letters **ill** are pronounced /il/ in the following words:

Répétez: **v<u>ill</u>e v<u>ill</u>age m<u>ill</u>e L<u>ill</u>e**

Leçon 27 **271**

COMMUNICATION:
comparing people and things

7

■ **Teaching strategies**
• Remind students that the adjective must agree with the subject.
• For items 6–10, remind students that **plus + bon(ne) → meilleur(e)**; as in English, there is no change for **moins bon(ne)** and **aussi bon(ne)**.

COMMUNICATION:
comparing oneself to others

8

Prononciation

▣ **Leçon 27, Section 5**

■ **Pronunciation:** Note that **tranquille** *(quiet)* also contains the sound /il/: /trãkil/

Place Y next to the chalkboard to the left, and place X to the right.
Mais Y est plus riche que X.
Between the two, write: **plus riche que.**
Call on other students to demonstrate the other comparisons, also writing them.
Z est moins riche que B. [$300 < $650]
A est aussi riche que C. [$400 = $400]

Ask all students to hold up their cards.
Montrez-nous vos prix. Qui a $200? [M]
Qui est plus riche que M? Qui est moins riche que lui/elle? Qui est aussi riche?
Have students hand around their "prizes."
En ce moment, Z est moins riche que M. S'il te plaît, D, va donner tes $1000 à Z. Maintenant Z est plus riche que B., etc.

1 COMPREHENSION

1-c   3-d
2-a   4-b

🔘 **Leçon 27, Section 6**

2 GUIDED ORAL EXPRESSION

1. la chaîne stéréo :: le walkman
2. les bottes :: les chaussures
3. le chien jaune :: le chien blanc
4. Alice :: Anne
5. Paul :: Philippe

🔘 **Leçon 27, Section 7**

À votre tour!

1 La bonne réponse

François and Stéphanie are shopping. Match François's questions with Stéphanie's answers. You may act out the dialogue with a friend.

François

1. Tu aimes cette veste verte?
2. Combien est-ce qu'elle coûte?
3. Alors, qu'est-ce que tu vas choisir?
4. Et qu'est-ce que tu penses de cette veste rouge?

Stéphanie

a. 300 euros.
b. À mon avis, elle est moins jolie.
c. Oui, mais elle est très chère.
d. La veste bleue. Elle est meilleur marché et elle est aussi élégante.

2 Créa-dialogue

With a classmate, prepare a dialogue comparing the items in one of the following pictures. Use the suggested verb and some of the suggested adjectives.

▶ —Tu <u>choisis</u> <u>la voiture rouge</u> ou <u>la voiture noire</u>?
   —Je <u>choisis</u> <u>la voiture rouge</u>.
   —Pourquoi?
   —Parce qu'<u>elle</u> est <u>plus petite</u> et <u>moins chère</u>.

▶ **choisir**

petit/grand/confortable/
rapide/cher

1. acheter

petit/grand/cher/bon

2. préférer

joli/confortable/cher/bon

3. choisir

petit/grand/mignon/joli

4. amener

ALICE   ANNE

mignon/amusant/intelligent
intéressant/sympathique

5. inviter

PAUL   PHILIPPE

??

272 Unité 7

À votre tour

Depending on your goals and objectives, you may or may not wish to assign all of the activities in the **À votre tour** section.

👥 Cooperative practice

Act. 1–3 lend themselves to cooperative pair practice.

3 Choix personnels

Select two people or two items in each of the following categories and ask a classmate to indicate which one he / she prefers. You may ask your classmate to explain why.

▶ *2 actors*

préfères
Hanks ou
rad Pitt?

Je préfère Brad Pitt.

urquoi?

Parce que Brad Pitt est plus mignon que Tom Hanks.

(plus beau, plus jeune . . .)

CATEGORIES:
- ▶ *2 actors*
- *2 actresses*
- *2 singers (male)*
- *2 singers (female)*
- *2 baseball teams*
- *2 cities*
- *2 restaurants in your town*
- *2 stores in your town*

4 Composition: Portrait comparatif

Write a description of yourself, comparing yourself to six other people (your friends, your family, well-known personalities, etc.) You may use some of the following adjectives:

grand petit jeune vieux amusant
intelligent bête sportif sympathique
timide élégant beau joli mignon

▶ Je suis moins sportif (sportive) que Sammy Sosa (Martina Hingis).

5 Composition: Comparaisons personnelles

Choose a friend or relative about your age. Give this person's name and age. Then, in a short paragraph, compare yourself to that person in terms of physical appearance and personality traits.

▶ Mon cousin s'appelle Patrick. Il a quinze ans. Je suis plus jeune que lui, mais il est moins grand que moi...

3 GUIDED ORAL EXPRESSION

4 WRITTEN SELF-EXPRESSION

5 WRITTEN SELF-EXPRESSION

Classroom Notes

📁 Portfolio assessment

You will probably select only one speaking activity and one writing activity to go into the students' portfolios for Unit 7.

In this lesson, Act. 2 lends itself well to an oral portfolio recording.

Act. 4 and 5 are good writing portfolio topics.

MODULE 28:
Alice a un job
Total time: 5:53 min.
(Counter 53:11 min.)

28.1 Dialogue: Alice a un job
(53:54–54:26 min.)
28.2 Mini-scenes: Listening — Qu'est-ce qu'on vend?
(54:27–55:13 min.)
28.3 Mini-scenes: Speaking — Qu'est-ce qu'on vend ici?
(55:14–55:56 min.)
28.4 Mini-scenes: Listening — On dîne?
(55:57–56:33 min.)
28.5 Mini-scenes: Speaking — On joue au tennis?
(56:34–57:31 min.)
28.6 Vignette culturelle: Au magasin hifi
(57:32–59:02 min.)

VIDEODISC Disc 4, Side 2
36560–47104

■ **Comprehension practice:** Play the entire module through as an introduction to the lesson.

28.1 Dialogue: Alice a un job
(53:54–54:26 min.)

VIDEODISC Disc 4, Side 2
36784–38783

■ **Language note:** Un emploi and un travail are also used for "a job."

LEÇON 28 Alice a un job

Alice a un nouveau job. Elle travaille dans un magasin hifi. Dans ce magasin, <u>on</u> <u>vend</u> <u>toutes</u> sortes de choses: des chaînes stéréo, des <u>mini-chaînes</u>, des radiocassettes . . . On vend aussi des cassettes et des compacts.

one, they / sell(s) / all
compact stereos

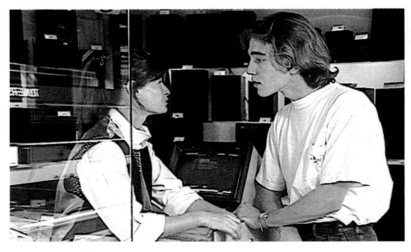

Un jour, son cousin Jérôme <u>lui rend visite.</u>

comes to visit her

JÉRÔME: Salut, ça va?
ALICE: Oui, ça va.
JÉRÔME: Et ce nouveau job?
ALICE: C'est super.
JÉRÔME: Qu'est-ce qu'on vend dans ton magasin?
ALICE: Eh bien, tu <u>vois</u>, on vend toutes sortes de matériel hifi. . .
Moi, je vends des mini-chaînes.   *see*
JÉRÔME: Tu es bien <u>payée</u>?   *paid*
ALICE: Non, on n'est pas très bien payé, mais on a des réductions sur l'équipement stéréo et sur les compacts.
JÉRÔME: Qu'est-ce que tu vas faire avec ton <u>argent</u>?   *money*
ALICE: Je ne sais pas . . . J'<u>ai envie de</u> voyager cet été.   *feel like*
JÉRÔME: Tu <u>as de la chance.</u> Moi aussi, j'ai envie de voyager, mais je n'ai pas d'argent.   *are lucky*
ALICE: Écoute, Jérôme, si tu as <u>besoin</u> d'argent, <u>fais comme moi.</u>   *need / do as I do*
JÉRÔME: <u>Comment</u>?   *What?*
ALICE: <u>Cherche</u> un job!   *Find*

274 Unité 7

Compréhension

1. Où travaille Alice?
2. Qu'est-ce qu'elle vend?
3. Qu'est-ce qu'elle espère faire cet été?
4. Pourquoi est-ce que Jérôme ne va pas voyager?
5. Qu'est-ce que Jérôme doit *(must)* faire pour avoir de l'argent?

NOTE CULTURELLE

L'argent des jeunes

Do you have a job? Do you have an older brother or sister who works in a supermarket or a restaurant? In the United States, many teenagers work to earn money. Because French labor laws restrict the type of work that young people can do, few French teenagers have regular jobs. (In addition, during the school year most families expect their children to concentrate on their studies.)

It is, however, more and more common for young people in France to earn money by babysitting or doing odd jobs in the neighborhood, such as washing cars or walking dogs. Some (lucky ones) work a few hours a week in stores owned by a relative or a friend of the family.

On the whole, most French teenagers must rely on the generosity of their parents for their spending money. How much they receive depends on particular circumstances, such as how well they do in school, how much they help at home, and obviously, how much their parents can afford. On the average, the allowance of a fifteen-year-old is about 40 euros per month.

COMPREHENSION

1. dans un magasin hifi /ifi/
2. des mini-chaînes
3. voyager
4. Il n'a pas d'argent.
5. Il doit chercher un job.

■ **Photo culture note**
Ask students how many ice cream flavors (**un parfum**) they recognize. Note also:
menthe *mint*
noix *hazelnut*
cassis *black currant*
fraise de bois *wild strawberry*
goyave *guava*

Talking about past events

Let's about what you and your family did during a recent vacation.

▶ **Toi et ta famille, est-ce que vous avez voyagé pendant les vacances? Oui, nous avons voyagé. (Non, nous n'avons pas voyagé.)**
• **Où êtes-vous allés?**
• **Est-ce que vous êtes allés à Disneyland?**
• **Est-ce que vous avez trouvé un bon hôtel?**
• **Est-ce que vous avez dîné au restaurant?**
• **Qu'est-ce que vous avez visité?**

▦ **Language notes**
- Point out that **payer** is also a "boot" verb (see p. 258).
- Some students may understand the **avoir** idioms better if they think of them as *I have need of...* and *I have desire of...*

▦ **Casual speech:**
One can also say:
Ce disque coûte combien?
Tu as combien d'argent?
Tu as combien de disques?

Supplementary vocabulary

un euro
un centime
un eurocentime
l'argent de poche   *allowance, pocket money*
la monnaie   *change*
un job   *(part-time) job*
économiser   *to save money*
par jour   *per day, a day*
par semaine   *per week, a week*
par heure   *per hour, an hour*

---

1 EXCHANGES: asking how many things people have

▬▬▬

■ **Pronunciation:** Be sure students pronounce the **de** of **combien de** correctly with a mute "e" so that it does not sound like **des**.

■ **Language note:** There is no elision before **un** when it represents the number *one:*
un billet de un dollar. (cf. item 7)

■ **Variation** (using casual speech):
Tu as combien de disques?

Cooperative pair practice
Activities 1, 2

T276

Vocabulaire: L'argent

NOMS

l'argent *(m.)*	money	une pièce	coin
un billet	bill, paper money		

ADJECTIFS

riche ≠ pauvre   *rich ≠ poor*

VERBES

dépenser	to spend	Je n'aime pas **dépenser** mon argent.
gagner	to earn, to win	Je **gagne** 10 dollars par *(per)* jour. Tu joues bien. Tu vas **gagner** le match.
payer	to pay, pay for	Qui va **payer** aujourd'hui?

EXPRESSIONS

combien + VERB		how much	**Combien** coûte ce disque?
combien de + NOUN		how much / how many	**Combien d'**argent as-tu? **Combien de** disques as-tu?
avoir besoin de + NOUN / + INFINITIVE		to need / to need to, have to	J'**ai besoin de** 5 dollars. J'**ai besoin d'**étudier.
avoir envie de + NOUN / + INFINITIVE		to want / to feel like, want to	J'**ai envie d'**une pizza. J'**ai envie de** manger.

➡ Verbs like **payer** that end in **-yer,** have the following stem change:

y → i in the **je, tu, il, ils** forms of the verb

je **paie**   tu **paies**   il / elle **paie**   ils / elles **paient**

But: nous payons   vous payez

L'ARGENT NE FAIT PAS LE BONHEUR

Money does not buy happiness.

1 **Combien?**

Ask your classmates how many of the following they have.

▶ des disques   —Combien de disques as-tu?
                  —J'ai vingt disques.
                    (Je n'ai pas de disques.)

1. des frères	3. des compacts	5. des tee-shirts	7. des billets de un dollar
2. des soeurs	4. des affiches	6. des jeans	8. des pièces de dix cents

Qu'est-ce que tu as envie de faire?

Ask your classmates if they feel like doing the following things.

▶ aller au cinéma

1. aller au restaurant
2. manger une pizza
3. aller à la piscine
4. parler français
5. étudier
6. visiter Paris
7. jouer au Frisbee
8. acheter une moto
9. faire une promenade
10. aller à la bibliothèque

Au restaurant

The following students are in a restaurant in Quebec. Say what they feel like buying and estimate how much money they need.

▶ Hélène / une pizza
Hélène a envie d'une pizza. Elle a besoin de cinq dollars.

1. Marc / un sandwich
2. nous / une glace
3. moi / un soda
4. toi / un jus d'orange
5. vous / une salade
6. mes copains / un steak

Questions personnelles

1. Est-ce que tu as un job? Où est-ce que tu travailles? Combien est-ce que tu gagnes par *(per)* heure? par semaine?
2. Quand tu vas au cinéma, qui paie? toi ou ton copain (ta copine)?
3. Combien est-ce que tu paies quand tu achètes un hamburger? une pizza? une glace?
4. Est-ce que tu as des pièces dans ta poche *(pocket)?* quelles pièces?
5. Qui est représenté sur le billet d'un dollar? sur le billet de cinq dollars? sur le billet de dix dollars?
6. Est-ce que tu préfères dépenser ou économiser *(to save)* ton argent? Pourquoi?
7. Est-ce que tu espères être riche un jour? Pourquoi?

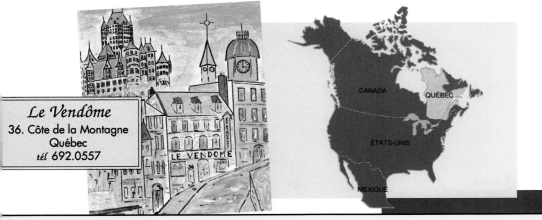

Le Vendôme
36. Côte de la Montagne
Québec
tél 692.0557

CANADA
QUÉBEC
ÉTATS-UNIS
MEXIQUE

28.2 Mini-scenes: Qu'est-ce qu'on vend?

28.3 Mini-scenes: Qu'est-ce qu'on vend ici?

28.4 Mini-scenes: On dîne?

28.5 Mini-scenes: On joue au tennis?
(54:27–57:31 min.)

VIDEODISC Disc 4, Side 2
38802–44318

Leçon 28, Sections 3, 4, 5, 6

■ **Looking ahead:** The forms of **vendre** are presented in section B of this lesson.

COMPREHENSION: discussing what languages are spoken in certain cities

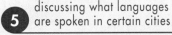

1. français (ou anglais)
2. anglais
3. espagnol
4. français
5. français
6. japonais
7. espagnol
8. anglais
9. italien
10. chinois

■ **Variation** (using the negative in many responses):
– Est-ce qu'on parle français à Acapulco?
– Non, on ne parle pas français.

■ **Challenge:** Have students turn to the world map on pp. R2–R3. They can ask additional questions: **Est-ce qu'on parle français à Dakar?** etc.

Cooperative pair practice
Activities 6, 7

A. Le pronom *on*

Note the use of the subject pronoun **on** in the sentences below.

Qu'est-ce qu'**on** vend ici?	*What do **they** (do **you**) sell here?*
Où est-ce qu'**on** achète ce magazine?	*Where does **one** (do **people**) buy that magazine?*
En France, **on** parle français.	*In France, **people** (**you**, **they**) speak French.*

The pronoun **on** is used in GENERAL statements, according to the construction:

on + **il/elle-** form of verb	**On** travaille beaucoup.	**One** works a lot. **They** work a lot. **You** work a lot. **People** work a lot.

⇒ There is liaison after **on** when the next word begins with a vowel sound.
Est-ce qu'**on** invite Stéphanie à la boum?

⇒ In conversation, **on** is often used instead of **nous:**
—Est-ce qu'**on** dîne à la maison?   *Are **we** having dinner at home?*
Non, **on** va au restaurant.   *No, **we** are going to the restaurant.*

5 **Ici on parle . . .**

Imagine you have won a grand prize of a world tour. Say which of the following languages is spoken in each of the cities that you will be visiting.

▶ Acapulco

À Acapulco, on parle espagnol.

1. Québec
2. Boston
3. Madrid
4. Bruxelles
5. Genève
6. Tokyo
7. Buenos Aires
8. Londres *(London)*
9. Rome
10. Beijing

anglais   français   espagnol   italien   japonais   chinois

Did you know that more and more French companies are investing in the United States? There may be places where you can use French right in your home state!

278   **Unité 7**

Expression pour la conversation

How to indicate approval:
C'est une bonne idée!   *That's a good idea!*

6 Projets de weekend

Suggest possible weekend activities to your classmates. They will let you know whether they think each idea is a good one or not.

▶ jouer au baseball?

1. étudier?
2. aller à la bibliothèque?
3. aller à la plage?
4. téléphoner au professeur?
5. faire une promenade à vélo?
6. aller dans les magasins?
7. acheter des vêtements?
8. écouter des disques?

On joue au baseball?

Oui, c'est une bonne idée!

Non, ce n'est pas une bonne idée.

7 En Amérique et en France

A French student and an American student are comparing certain aspects of life in their own countries. Play both roles.

▶ jouer au baseball (au foot)

En Amérique, on joue au baseball.

En France, on joue au foot.

1. parler anglais (français)
2. étudier le français (l'anglais)
3. dîner à six heures (à huit heures)
4. manger des hamburgers (des omelettes)
5. voyager souvent en avion *(by plane)* (en train)
6. skier dans le Colorado (dans les Alpes)
7. aller à l'école le mercredi après-midi (le samedi matin)
8. chanter «la Bannière étoilée» *("The Star-Spangled Banner")* («la Marseillaise»)

8 Expression personnelle

Describe what you, your friends, and your relatives generally do. Complete the following sentences according to your personal routine.

1. À la maison, on dîne . . . (à quelle heure?)
2. À la télé, on regarde . . . (quel programme?)
3. À la cafétéria de l'école, on mange . . . (quoi?)
4. En été, on va . . . (où?)
5. Le weekend, avec mes copains, on va . . . (où?)
6. Avec mes copains, on joue . . . (à quel sport?)
7. On a une classe de français . . . (quels jours?)
8. On a un examen de français . . . (quel jour?)

Supplementary vocabulary

C'est une mauvaise idée.

6 EXCHANGES: suggesting weekend activities and indicating one's approval

7 ROLE PLAY: describing cultural differences

8 COMMUNICATION: describing one's usual activities

■ **Language note:** Be sure that students realize that in this activity **on** means *we*.

Classroom Notes

Section B

COMMUNICATIVE FUNCTION:
Describing actions

Transparency 41
-re verbs

Leçon 28, Section 7

■ **Teaching strategy:** Point out that the plural endings of **-re** verbs are the same as those of **-er** verbs: **nous vend<u>ons</u>, vous vend<u>ez</u>,** and **ils vend<u>ent</u>.**

■ **Language note:** You may indicate that **vendre** is a REGULAR verb since many verbs follow the same pattern. However, **mettre** is IRREGULAR since the pattern applies only to verbs that have **mettre** as a root: **permettre, promettre,** etc.

↩ **Re-entry and review:** The verb chart reviews possessive adjectives (Lesson 24).

■ **Realia note**
Ask students:
How do you say *whale* in French?
[**la baleine**]
In which river can one go whale watching? [the Saint-Lawrence: **le Saint-Laurent**]

■ **Cultural note:** Observing the seasonal migration of whales up and down the St. Lawrence River is a major tourist attraction. One of the favorite tours in Quebec is **la route des baleines.**

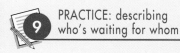
PRACTICE: describing
who's waiting for whom
9

B. Les verbes réguliers en *-re*

Many French verbs end in **-re**. Most of these are conjugated like **vendre** *(to sell)*. Note the forms of this verb in the present tense, paying special attention to the endings.

INFINITIVE	vendre	STEM (infinitive minus **-re**)	ENDINGS
PRESENT	Je **vends** ma raquette. Tu **vends** ton scooter. Il/Elle/On **vend** son ordinateur. Nous **vendons** nos disques. Vous **vendez** vos cassettes. Ils/Elles **vendent** leur voiture.	vend-	-s -s — -ons -ez -ent

⟹ The "**d**" of the stem is silent in the singular forms, but it is pronounced in the plural forms.

Vocabulaire: Verbes réguliers en *-re*

attendre	*to wait, wait for*	Pierre **attend** Michèle au café.
entendre	*to hear*	Est-ce que tu **entends** la radio?
perdre	*to lose, waste*	Jean-Claude **perd** le match.
rendre visite à	*to visit (a person)*	Je **rends visite à** mon oncle.
répondre à	*to answer*	Nous **répondons à** la question du prof.
vendre	*to sell*	À qui **vends**-tu ton vélo?

➡ There are two French verbs that correspond to the English verb *to visit*.

visiter (+ PLACES)   Nous **visitons** Québec.
rendre visite à (+ PEOPLE)   Nous **rendons visite à** nos cousins canadiens.

Visitez Québec ...
et la route des baleines.

Société écologique
des baleines
du Saint-Laurent

9 **Rendez-vous**

The following people have been shopping and are now waiting for their friends at a café. Express this, using the appropriate forms of the verb **attendre**.

▶ Jérôme (Michèle)   **Jérôme attend Michèle.**

1. nous (nos copains)
2. vous (vos cousines)
3. moi (Christophe)
4. toi (Anne)
5. Olivier et Éric (Claire et Sophie)

6. les étudiants (les étudiantes)
7. Jacques et moi, nous (Pauline et Hélène)
8. Annette et toi, vous (Jean-Marc)
9. on (notre copine)

Talking about past events

Let's talk about whom you visited last summer. (Note that the past participle of -re verbs ends in **-u**.)

▶ **Est-ce que tu as rendu visite à ta tante l'été dernier?**
Oui, j'ai rendu visite à ma tante.
(**Je n'ai pas rendu visite à ma tante.**)

• **Est-ce que tu as rendu visite à ton oncle l'été dernier?**
• **As-tu rendu visite à tes cousins?**
• **As-tu rendu visite à tes grands-parents**
• **Et le weekend dernier, à qui est-ce que tu as rendu visite?**

10 Qui

Who is doing what? Answer the following questions, using the suggested subjects.

1. Qui perd le match? (toi, vous, Alice)
2. Qui rend visite à Pierre? (Patrick, Corinne et Hélène, toi)
3. Qui entend l'avion *(plane)*? (moi, vous, les voisins)
4. Qui vend des disques? (on, ce magasin, ces boutiques, moi)
5. Qui attend le bus? (les élèves, le professeur, on, vous)
6. Qui répond au professeur? (toi, nous, les élèves)

11 Qu'est-ce qu'ils font?

Read about the following people. Then complete each sentence with the appropriate form of one of the verbs from the list. Be logical!

1. Guillaume est patient. Il ... ses amis.
2. Vous êtes à Paris. Vous ... à vos cousins français.
3. Tu joues mal. Tu ... le match.
4. Je suis dans ma chambre. J' ... un bruit *(noise)* curieux.
5. Les élèves sont en classe. Ils ... aux questions du professeur.
6. Jacqueline travaille dans une boutique. Elle ... des robes.
7. On est au café. On ... nos copains.

attendre   entendre   perdre   rendre visite   **répondre**   vendre

C. L'impératif

Compare the French and English forms of the imperative in the sentences below.

Écoute ce disque!   **Listen** to this record!
Ne vendez pas votre voiture!   **Don't sell** your car!
Allons au cinéma!   **Let's go** to the movies!

> **Learning about language**
> The IMPERATIVE is used to make suggestions and to give orders and advice. The commands or suggestions may be affirmative or negative.

Note the forms of the imperative in the chart below.

INFINITIVE	parler	finir	vendre	aller
IMPERATIVE (tu) (vous) (nous)	parle parlez parlons	finis finissez finissons	vends vendez vendons	va allez allons

For regular verbs and most irregular verbs, the forms of the imperative are the same as the corresponding forms of the present tense.

➡ EXCEPTION: For all -er verbs, including **aller,** the -s of the **tu-** form is dropped in the imperative. Compare.

Tu **parles** anglais.   **Parle** français, s'il te plaît!
Tu **vas** au café.   **Va** à la bibliothèque!

➡ The negative imperative is formed as follows:

ne + VERB + **pas** ...	**Ne choisis pas** ce blouson.

Leçon 28   **281**

12 ROLE PLAY: offering and accepting assistance

■ **Challenge:** Have students invent suggestions that are turned down. They can use the same verb and change the rest of the sentence.
J'amène mes parents?
Mais non, n'amène pas tes parents!
Remind students to use **pas de** where needed.

13 ROLE PLAY: giving good and bad advice

■ **Teaching strategy:** Have the girls respond as the demons and the boys as the angels; then change roles.

■ **Realia note**
Ask students:
To whom is this advertisement addressed? [to students and their parents]
What does **Réussissez au bac!** mean? [pass the "bac"!]

■ **Cultural note:** The **bac (le baccalauréat)** is the final comprehensive exam that lycée students must pass before continuing on to the university.

14 COMPREHENSION: giving logical advice

■ **Variation** (using the **nous** form):
N'étudions pas! Voyageons!

■ **Challenge:** For each situation, have students invent additional advice. Encourage them to be creative.
Visitez Québec!
Faites "la route des baleines".
Dînez au Vendôme!

12 **Mais oui!**

You have organized a party at your home. Juliette offers to do the following. You accept.

▶ apporter une pizza?

1. faire une salade?
2. inviter nos copains?
3. acheter des croissants?
4. apporter des cassettes?
5. choisir des disques de danse?
6. venir à huit heures?

13 **L'ange et le démon**

(The angel and the devil)

Véronique is wondering whether she should do certain things. The angel gives her good advice. The devil gives her bad advice. Play both roles.

▶ étudier les verbes
  Étudie les verbes.
  N'étudie pas les verbes.

1. téléphoner à ta tante
2. attendre tes copains
3. faire attention en classe
4. aller à l'école
5. finir la leçon
6. écouter tes professeurs
7. mettre *(set)* la table
8. inviter tes amis
9. rendre visite à ta grand-mère
10. choisir des copains sympathiques
11. acheter un cadeau *(gift)* pour ton frère
12. réussir à l'examen

ÉTUDIANTS
ET
PARENTS D'ÉTUDIANTS

Réussissez au bac!

14 **Oui ou non?**

For each of the following situations, give your classmates advice as to what to do and what not to do. Be logical.

▶ Nous sommes en vacances. (étudier? voyager?)
  N'étudiez pas! Voyagez!

1. Nous sommes à Paris. (parler anglais? parler français?)
2. C'est dimanche. (aller à la bibliothèque? aller au cinéma?)
3. Il fait beau. (rester à la maison? faire une promenade?)
4. Il fait froid. (mettre un pull? mettre un tee-shirt?)
5. Il est onze heures du soir. (rester au café? rentrer à la maison?)
6. Il fait très chaud. (aller à la piscine? regarder la télé?)

Cooperative pair practice
Activities 12, 13, 15

 Game: Drilling with dice

PROPS: Dice (one for every pair of students); transparency with the verb list at right

INSTRUCTIONS (students play in pairs):
Student A rolls the die. For example, 5 spots = **vous**. Student B writes the corresponding form of the first verb: **vous cherchez.**

Then Student B rolls the die and Student A writes the corresponding form of the next verb: 2 spots + **gagner** → **tu gagnes**.
Keep track of pairs as they finish. Then have teams exchange their papers for peer correction. The first pair with the most correct answers is the winning team.

5 L'esprit de contradiction (Disagreement)

Make suggestions to your friends about things to do. Your friends will not agree and will suggest something else.

▶ aller au cinéma (à la plage)

Allons au cinéma!

Non, n'allons pas au cinéma!
Allons à la plage!

1. jouer au tennis (au volley)
2. écouter la radio (des disques)
3. regarder la télé (un film vidéo)
4. dîner au restaurant (à la maison)
5. inviter Michèle (Sophie)
6. organiser un pique-nique (une boum)
7. faire des sandwichs (une pizza)
8. aller au musée (à la bibliothèque)
9. faire une promenade à pied (en voiture)
10. rendre visite à nos voisins (à nos copains)

15 EXCHANGES: making plans

■ **Challenge:** Expand the conversation to include three people. The third one does not like the second suggestion and has another idea.
– Allons au cinéma!
– Non, n'allons pas au cinéma! Allons à la plage.
– Mais non, n'allons pas à la plage. Restons à la maison!

Prononciation

🔊 Leçon 28, Section 8

■ **Pronunciation notes**
• Exception: the "**en**" in **examen** represents the sound /ɛ̃/ as in **pain**: examen /egzamɛ̃/
• In the combination **ien**, the letters "**en**" also represent the sound /ɛ̃/: **italien** /italjɛ̃/

Prononciation   an, en /ã/

Les lettres «an» et «en»

The letters "**an**" and "**en**" represent the nasal vowel /ã/ Be sure not to pronounce the sound "**n**" after the vowel.

enfant

Répétez:

/ã/ en**fant** **an** m**an**teau coll**an**ts gr**an**d élég**an**t
André m**an**ge un gr**an**d s**an**dwich.

/ã/ en**fant** **en** arg**en**t dép**en**ser att**en**ds ent**en**d
v**en**d **en**vie
Vinc**en**t dép**en**se rarem**en**t son arg**en**t.

**André mange
un grand sandwich.**

Classroom Notes

Drilling with dice
1. chercher
2. gagner
3. acheter
4. amener
5. finir
6. grossir
7. maigrir
8. réussir
9. attendre
10. entendre
11. perdre
12. répondre
13. aller
14. avoir
15. être
16. faire
17. mettre
18. permettre (permit)
19. revenir
20. venir

| 1 = je |
| 2 = tu |
| 3 = elle |
| 4 = nous |
| 5 = vous |
| 6 = ils |

1 COMPREHENSION

1-d	3-b
2-c	4-a

🔲 Leçon 28, Section 9

2 GUIDED ORAL EXPRESSION

🔲 Leçon 28, Section 10

1 La bonne réponse

Anne is talking to Jean-François. Match Anne's questions with Jean-François's answers. You may act out the conversation with a classmate.

Anne

1. Est-ce que tu rends visite à tes cousins ce weekend?
2. Tu veux aller dans les boutiques avec moi?
3. Est-ce que tu as envie d'aller au cinéma?
4. Et après *(afterwards)* qu'est-ce qu'on fait?

Jean-François

a. Eh bien, allons au restaurant!
b. Bonne idée! Il y a un nouveau film au «Majestic».
c. Écoute! Je n'ai pas besoin de vêtements.
d. Non, je reste ici.

2 Créa-dialogue

When we are with our friends, it is not always easy to agree on what to do. With your classmates, discuss the following possibilities.

Qu'est-ce qu'on fait **samedi**?

Allons au cinéma.

Je n'ai pas envie d'aller au cinéma.

Eh bien, **rendons visite à nos amis. D'accord?**

Oui, c'est bonne i[…]

Quand?	Première suggestion	Deuxième suggestion
▶ samedi	aller au cinéma	rendre visite à nos amis
1. ce soir *(tonight)*	étudier	regarder la télé
2. dimanche	aller au café	dîner au restaurant
3. après *(after)* les classes	jouer au basket	faire une promenade
4. cet été	trouver un job	voyager
5. ce weekend	faire un pique-nique	??
6. demain	aller à la bibliothèque	??

À votre tour

Depending upon your goals and objectives, you may or may not wish to assign all of the activities in the **À votre tour** section.

👥 Cooperative practice

Act. 1–4 lend themselves to cooperative pair practice.

3 GUIDED ORAL EXPRESSION

4 COMPREHENSION

5 WRITTEN SELF-EXPRESSION

3 **Conseils**

Your friends tell you what they would like to do. Give them appropriate advice, either positive or negative. Use your imagination.

▶ Je voudrais maigrir. **Alors, mange moins.**
(Alors, ne mange pas de pizza.)

1. Je voudrais avoir un «A» en français.
2. Je voudrais gagner beaucoup d'argent.
3. Je voudrais organiser une boum.
4. Je voudrais préparer un pique-nique.

4 **Que faire?**

Give a classmate advice about what to do or not to do in the following circumstances.

Pendant *(During)* **la classe**	**Après** *(After)* **la classe**	**Ce weekend**	**Pendant les vacances**

écouter le prof
parler à tes copains
regarder les bandes
  dessinées *(comics)*
manger un sandwich
répondre en français
??
	étudier
	aller au cinéma
	préparer tes leçons
	rentrer chez toi
	regarder la télé
	??
		rester à la maison
		aller en ville
		dépenser ton argent
		organiser une boum
		faire une promenade
		  à pied
		??
			voyager
			travailler
			grossir
			oublier *(forget)*
			  ton français
			??

▶ **Pendant la classe, écoute le prof.**
Ne parle pas à tes copains.

5 **Bon voyage!**

Your French friend Ariane is going to visit the United States next summer with her cousin. They are traveling on a low budget and are asking you for advice as to how to save money. Make a list of suggestions, including five things they could do and five things they should not do. You may want to use some of the following ideas:

- voyager (comment?)
- rester (dans quels hôtels?)
- dîner (dans quels restaurants?)
- visiter (quelles villes?)
- aller (où?)
- acheter (quelles choses?)
- apporter (quelles choses?)

▶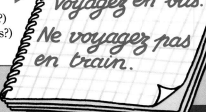
Voyagez en bus.
Ne voyagez pas en train.

Classroom Notes

📁 Portfolio assessment

You will probably select only one speaking activity and one writing activity to go into the students' portfolios for Unit 7.

In this lesson, Act. 2 lends itself well to an oral portfolio recording.

Act. 5 offers a good writing portfolio topic.

Entracte 7

La mode et les vêtements

Petit test culturel
La mode et les vêtements

Aujourd'hui la mode° est internationale. Les jeunes Français adoptent le «look» américain ou anglais. Les Américains achètent des vêtements de style français ou italien.

Imaginez que vous habitez en France. Est-ce que vous pouvez° répondre aux questions suivantes?° Vérifiez° vos réponses au bas° de la page.

1 Vincent va en ville pour acheter des «tennis». Qu'est-ce qu'il va acheter?
a. une raquette
b. un short
c. des chaussures
d. des chemises

2 Monique habite à Paris. Elle a envie d'acheter un blouson. Où va-t-elle?
a. à la Villette
b. aux Galeries Lafayette
c. au Zénith
d. au Centre Pompidou

3 Dans ce magasin on vend des vêtements de marques° différentes. Voici quatre marques. Quelle est la marque qui n'est *pas* française?
a. Benetton
b. Christian Dior
c. Pierre Cardin
d. Yves Saint-Laurent

4 René Lacoste est un champion français de tennis. Aujourd'hui son nom° est associé° avec une marque de . . .
a. vêtements de sport
b. chaussures de ski
c. chocolats
d. vitamines

5 Jean Vuarnet est un champion olympique de ski. À quels produits° est-ce que son nom est associé?
a. des skis
b. des chaussures
c. des vêtements de sport
d. des lunettes de soleil

6 Coco Chanel est le nom d'une couturière° française très célèbre.° Son nom est aussi associé avec . . .
a. un parfum
b. un festival de cinéma
c. une compétition sportive
d. une eau minérale°

7 Les jeans sont faits° avec un coton spécial appelé° «denim». Ce mot vient du français «de Nîmes». Nîmes est le nom . . .
a. d'un textile
b. d'un vêtement
c. d'un couturier° français
d. d'une ville française

RÉPONSES:
1. c; 2. b; 3. a; 4. a; 5. d; 6. a; 7. d

mode *fashion* **pouvez** *can* **suivantes** *following* **Vérifiez** *Check*
au bas *at the bottom* **marques** *designer labels* **nom** *name* **associé** *associated*
produits *products* **couturière** *fashion designer* **célèbre** *famous*
eau minérale *mineral water* **faits** *made* **appelé** *called* **couturier** *fashion designe*

286 Unité 7

 Cooperative reading practice

Divide the class into groups of 4 or 5, each with a **secrétaire.**

For each question, have the groups first vote on the correct answer (keeping the box at the bottom of the page covered).

Then have the recorders check the right answers and announce their group score to the entire class.
Nous avons six réponses correctes.

EN FRANCE

Les Trois Suisses

La compagnie Les Trois Suisses vend des vêtements par correspondance. Voici une page de son catalogue.

Sur cette page, trois articles sont en «promo».° Quels sont ces trois articles?

Combien coûte le pantalon jogging?

Combien coûtent les tennis en euros? et en dollars? Est-ce que c'est cher? Quelles couleurs est-ce qu'on peut choisir? Quelle couleur préférez-vous?

Combien coûte le sweat? Quelles couleurs est-ce qu'on peut° choisir? Quelle couleur préférez-vous?

promo = promotion *special sale*
peut *can*

Entracte 7 287

Pre-reading

Ask students if they sometimes order clothes from catalogues.
   Which catalogues do they like best?

Post-reading

Have students each select an item they plan to buy (for themselves or as a gift for a friend). In pairs, have students describe their intended purchases to one another.
– **Moi, je vais acheter un sweat.**
– **Ah bon? Pour qui? ...**

Les jeunes Français et la mode

OBJECTIVES:
- Reading at the paragraph level
- Building reading skills

■ **Pronunciation:** Chloé /kloe/

■ **Cultural note:** The literal translation of **l'habit ne fait pas le moine** is *the habit (monk's attire) does not make the monk.* Compare to the English: *Clothes do not make the man.*

■ **Questions sur le texte**
1. Comment est-ce que Florence gagne son argent?
2. Où est-ce qu'elle achète ses vêtements?
3. Est-ce que Jean-Marc aime être bien habillé?
4. Est-ce qu'il achète beaucoup de vêtements?
5. Est-ce que Chloé achète beaucoup de vêtements?
6. Qu'est-ce qu'elle fait pour être à la mode?
7. Qui achète les vêtements d'Antoine?
8. Où est-ce que la mère d'Antoine achète les vêtements de son fils?
9. Est-ce que Julien aime être à la mode?
10. Qu'est-ce qu'il fait avec son argent?

■ **Cultural note (Les grandes surfaces):** Larger stores of this type (a combination supermarket plus discount chain store) are also called **hypermarchés**.

Entre amis: ## Les jeunes Français et la mode

Est-ce que vous aimez être à la mode?° Où est-ce que vous achetez vos vêtements? Et qu'est-ce qui compte° le plus° pour vous? le style? la qualité? le prix? Nous avons posé° ces questions à cinq jeunes Français. Voilà leurs réponses.

Florence (16 ans)
J'aime être à la mode. Malheureusement,° mon budget est limité. La solution? Le samedi après-midi je travaille dans une boutique de mode. Là, je peux acheter mes jupes et mes pulls à des prix très avantageux.° Pour le reste, je compte sur la générosité de mes parents.

Jean-Marc (15 ans)
Aujourd'hui la présentation extérieure° est très importante. Mais il n'est pas nécessaire d'être à la mode pour être bien habillé.° Pour moi, la qualité d[es] vêtements est aussi importan[te] que leur style. En général, j'attends les soldes.° J'achète peu de° vêtements mais je fai[s] attention à la qualité.

Chloé (15 ans)
Pour moi, le style, c'est tout.° Hélas, la mode n'est pas bon marché. Heureusement° j'ai une cousine qui a une machine à coudre° et qui est très très adroite.° Alors, nous faisons nos propres° robes! Nous choisissons le tissu,° la couleur, le style … Ainsi, nous sommes toujours à la mode. C'est chouette, non?

Antoine (12 ans)
Moi, je n'ai pas le choix!° C'es[t] ma mère qui choisit mes vêtements. En ce qui concern[e] la mode, elle n'est pas dans le coup.° Elle achète tout dan[s] les grandes surfaces. C'est pas° drôle!

Julien (14 ans)
Vous connaissez° le proverbe: «L'habit ne fait pas le moine».° Eh bien, pour moi les vêtements n'ont aucune° importance. Avec mon argent je préfère acheter des compacts. Quand j'ai besoin de jeans ou de tee-shirts, je vais aux Puces.* C'est pas cher et c'est marrant!°

*****Marché aux puces** *flea market*

à la mode *in style*   **compte** *counts*   **le plus** *the most*
avons posé *asked*   **Malheureusement** *Unfortunately*
avantageux *reasonable*
présentation extérieure *outward appearance*   **habillé** *dressed*
soldes *sales*   **peu de** *few*   **tout** *everything*
Heureusement *Fortunately*   **machine à coudre** *sewing machine*
adroite *skillful*   **propres** *own*   **tissu** *fabric*   **choix** *choice*
En ce qui concerne *As for*   **dans le coup** *"with it"*
C'est pas = Ce n'est pas   **connaissez** *know*   **moine** *monk*
aucune *no*   **marrant** *fun*

■ **NOTES** ■
CULTURELLES

1 **Les grandes surfaces**

Les grandes surfaces sont des magasins [en] libre-service° où on peut acheter toutes° les marchandises nécessaires à la vie quotidienne.° En général les prix ne sont [pas] très élevés,° mais la qualité est moyenne.

Pre-reading
Have students glance over the reading quickly. What are the questions that were asked in the interview?

Post-reading
Ask each student to decide which of the five people he/she would most want to be introduced to and why.
Imaginez que vous pouvez faire la connaissance d'un de ces jeunes Français. Qui voulez-vous rencontrer? Pourquoi?

Comment lire

DIFFERENCES IN SPOKEN AND WRITTEN LANGUAGE

The interviews you read were conducted orally. Notice how casual speech is different from standard written language.

- Spoken language often contains slang expressions.

    Elle n'est pas dans le coup!   **C'est marrant!**   **C'est chouette!**

- Spoken French sometimes drops the **ne** in **ne . . . pas.**

    C'est pas cher. = Ce n'est pas cher.

Enrichissez votre vocabulaire

MORE COGNATE PATTERNS

Here are a few common cognate patterns to help you recognize new words more easily.

FRENCH	ENGLISH		FRENCH	ENGLISH
-x	*-ce*		**le prix**	*price*
-eux	*-ous*		**avantageux**	*advantageous, reasonable*
-eur	*-or*		**la couleur**	*color*
-aire	*-ary*		**nécessaire**	*necessary*

Activité

Can you identify the English equivalents of the following French words?

- **le choix   la voix**
- **courageux   sérieux   dangereux   curieux**
- **un acteur   une odeur   un docteur   supérieur   une erreur**
- **un salaire   le vocabulaire   un commentaire   un anniversaire**

Activité: Et toi?

Voici ce que disent les jeunes Français. Est-ce que c'est vrai pour vous aussi?

Oui, c'est vrai pour moi.

Non, ce n'est pas vrai pour moi.

OUI OU NON?
- ▶ ☐ 1. J'aime être à la mode.
- ☐ 2. Mon budget est limité.
- ☐ 3. J'attends les soldes.
- ☐ 4. Je fais attention à la qualité.

OUI OU NON?
- ☐ 5. J'achète le tissu et je fais mes vêtements.
- ☐ 6. Ma mère choisit mes vêtements.
- ☐ 7. Je préfère acheter des compacts.
- ☐ 8. J'achète mes vêtements aux Puces.

2 Les soldes

En général, les boutiques de vêtements ont des soldes° deux ou trois fois° par an. On peut alors acheter des vêtements de bonne qualité à des prix avantageux. Certaines boutiques ont des soldes toute l'année.°

libre-service *self-service*   **toutes** *all*   **quotidienne** *daily*   **élevés** *high*
moyenne *average*   **soldes** *sales*   **fois** *times*   **toute l'année** *all year long*

■ Questions personnelles

1. Comment est-ce que tu gagnes ton argent?
2. Est-ce que tu travailles? Où?
3. Où est-ce que tu achètes tes vêtements?
4. Est-ce que tu attends les soldes pour acheter tes vêtements?
5. Qu'est-ce que tu achètes dans les grandes surfaces?
6. Jean-Marc dit: "La présentation extérieure est très importante." Est-ce que tu es d'accord avec cette opinion?
7. Julien dit: "L'habit ne fait pas le moine." Est-ce que tu es d'accord avec ce proverbe?

Classroom Notes

OBJECTIVES:
- Reading for fun
- Taking a French self-test

Variétés

L'argent et vous

Nous avons tous° besoin d'argent. L'argent est nécessaire, mais l'argent crée° aussi des problèmes. Quelle est votre attitude envers° l'argent? Répondez aux questions suivantes.°

1 Que représente l'argent pour vous?

   a. l'indépendance
   b. la possibilité d'acheter beaucoup de choses
   c. la possibilité d'aider vos amis

2 Selon vous, quel est le rapport° entre l'argent et le bonheur?°

   a. L'argent est nécessaire.
   b. L'argent est utile.°
   c. Il n'y a pas de rapport.

3 Vous avez trois possibilités de job ce weekend. Qu'est-ce que vous choisissez?

   a. faire du baby-sitting (3 dollars par heure pour 4 heures)
   b. laver° la voiture des voisins (5 dollars au total)
   c. vendre des hot dogs à un match de football (un pourcentage de 10% sur les ventes°)

4 C'est votre anniversaire. Vos grands-parents vous donnent° cinquante dollars. Qu'est-ce que vous faites?

   a. J'invite mes copains à un concert.
   b. J'achète des vêtements.
   c. Je mets mon argent à la banque.°

5 Pendant les vacances vous avez le choix entre les trois possibilités suivantes. Qu'est-ce que vous choisissez?

   a. faire un grand voyage avec la famille
   b. travailler comme volontaire° dans un hôpital
   c. travailler dans un supermarché

6 Selon vous, quel est l'aspect le plus° important quand on cherche un travail?°

   a. avoir un bon salaire
   b. avoir un travail intéressant
   c. avoir la possibilité de travailler avec des gens sympathiques

tous *all*   **crée** *creates*   **envers** *toward*   **suivantes** *following*
rapport *relationship*   **bonheur** *happiness*   **utile** *useful*
laver *wash*   **ventes** *sales*   **vous donnent** *give you*   **banque** *bank*
comme volontaire *as a volunteer*   **le plus** *the most*   **travail** *job*

■ **Photo culture note**
Banking
The **Crédit Lyonnais**, one of the largest French banks, has branches throughout the country. Note the line of customers waiting their turn at the automatic teller (**le guichet automatique** or **le distributeur de billets automatique**).

Pre-reading
Ask students to look at these two pages and decide what type of reading it is. [a personality quiz]

Post-reading
Once students have read the questions and selected their answers, have them get together in pairs to analyze their scores. Do they agree with the interpretation? **Êtes-vous d'accord avec l'interprétation?**

INTERPRÉTATION

Comptez° vos points en utilisant° la grille° suivante.

Questions		1	2	3	4	5	6
Options	a	3	3	2	1	1	3
	b	2	2	1	2	2	1
	c	1	1	3	3	3	2

Combien de points avez-vous?

15 points ou plus:

Vous avez beaucoup d'énergie. Pour vous, l'argent est important et vous êtes prêt(e)° à travailler dur° pour gagner votre argent.

entre 9 et 14 points:

Vous êtes réaliste. Pour vous l'argent est un moyen° et pas un but.°

8 points ou moins:

Vous êtes idéaliste et généreux (généreuse). Entre l'amitié° et l'argent, vous préférez l'amitié.

Comptez Count   **en utilisant** by using
grille grid   **prêt(e)** ready   **dur** hard   **moyen** means
but end   **amitié** friendship

 **UNITÉ 7
INTERNET PROJECT**

Students may use the Internet to find out more about French fashion. What kinds of styles do they like? Do they see any clothing that they would like to buy if they could afford it? Students can start with the link available below, or use the alternate given. To expand this activity, have students generate new links by using the search engine of their choice and the keyword **"la mode."**

La Mode française
http://www.lamodefrancaise.
tm.fr/

ALTERNATE
KIABI: les produits quatre étoiles
http://www.kiabi.fr/fr/
etoile.htm

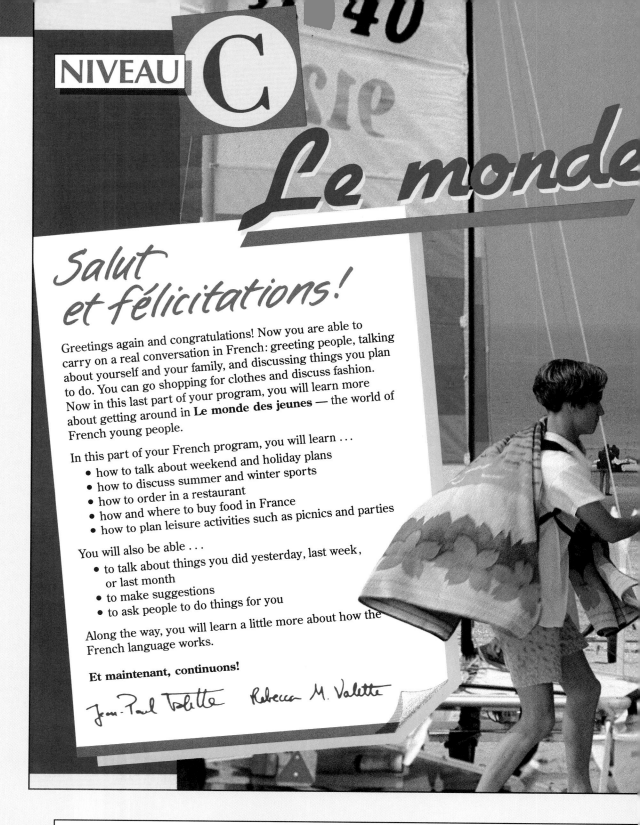

NIVEAU C
Le monde

Salut et félicitations!

Greetings again and congratulations! Now you are able to carry on a real conversation in French: greeting people, talking about yourself and your family, and discussing things you plan to do. You can go shopping for clothes and discuss fashion. Now in this last part of your program, you will learn more about getting around in **Le monde des jeunes** — the world of French young people.

In this part of your French program, you will learn . . .
- how to talk about weekend and holiday plans
- how to discuss summer and winter sports
- how to order in a restaurant
- how and where to buy food in France
- how to plan leisure activities such as picnics and parties

You will also be able . . .
- to talk about things you did yesterday, last week, or last month
- to make suggestions
- to ask people to do things for you

Along the way, you will learn a little more about how the French language works.

Et maintenant, continuons!

Jean-Paul Valette   *Rebecca M. Valette*

Overview of Niveau C

Niveau C takes students beyond the core of Niveau B, and introduces them to somewhat more complex language structures: object pronouns, the partitive, and a formal presentation of the **passé composé** (which they have been using informally).

Although it is desirable to present these units, it is not critical to finish them, since the material is re-entered and expanded in the first part of **Discovering French–Blanc.**

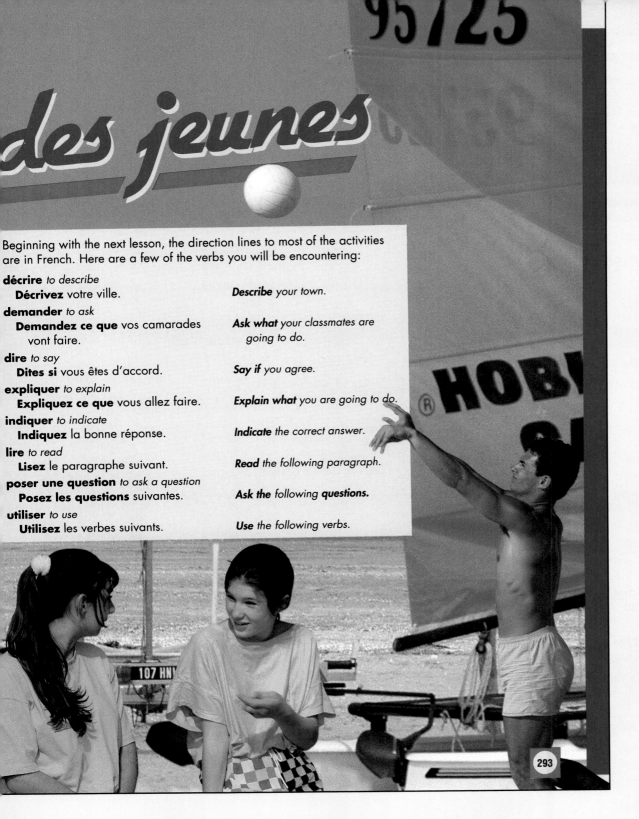

des jeunes

Beginning with the next lesson, the direction lines to most of the activities are in French. Here are a few of the verbs you will be encountering:

décrire *to describe*
 Décrivez votre ville.

Describe *your town.*

demander *to ask*
 Demandez ce que vos camarades vont faire.

Ask what *your classmates are going to do.*

dire *to say*
 Dites si vous êtes d'accord.

Say if *you agree.*

expliquer *to explain*
 Expliquez ce que vous allez faire.

Explain what *you are going to do.*

indiquer *to indicate*
 Indiquez la bonne réponse.

Indicate *the correct answer.*

lire *to read*
 Lisez le paragraphe suivant.

Read *the following paragraph.*

poser une question *to ask a question*
 Posez les questions suivantes.

Ask the *following* **questions.**

utiliser *to use*
 Utilisez les verbes suivants.

Use *the following verbs.*

293

In format, Niveau C is similar to Niveau B, with an emphasis on a four-skills approach and a focus on communicative interaction, as well as activities designed for Cooperative Practice.

➤ Teaching Resources

Technology/Audio Visual

 VIDEO/VIDEODISC

Unité 8, Modules 29-32
29. Le français pratique: Le weekend et les vacances
30. Mercredi après-midi
31. Pas de chance!
32. Samedi/Weekend

 CD-ROM **DFi C,**
Modules 29-32
Exploration 8

 Writing Template
Unité 8

CD Unité 8, Leçons 29, 30, 31, 32

42, 43, 44
Situational S17, S18

Print

Answer Key, Cassette Script, Video Script, Overhead Visuals Copymasters

Activity Book, pp. 243-276
Activity Book TAE

Video Activity Book pp. 123-146

Communipak, pp. 141-166

Teacher's Resource Package

 Teacher-to-Teacher:
Games, Additional Activities

 Interdisciplinary Connections:
Projects Book

 Teaching to Multiple Intelligences in the Modern Language Classroom

 Internet Connections
www.mcdougallittell.com

T294

UNITÉ

8

Le temps libre

294

Unit overview

COMMUNICATION GOALS: Students will be able to talk about individual sports, helping out at home, and what they did over the weekend or during vacation.
LINGUISTIC GOALS: Students will learn to describe and narrate past events using the passé composé.

CRITICAL THINKING GOALS: Students will observe the similarities and differences between the passé composé in French and the past tense in English.
CULTURAL GOALS: Students will learn about weekend and sports activities popular in France and the importance of leisure time to the French people.

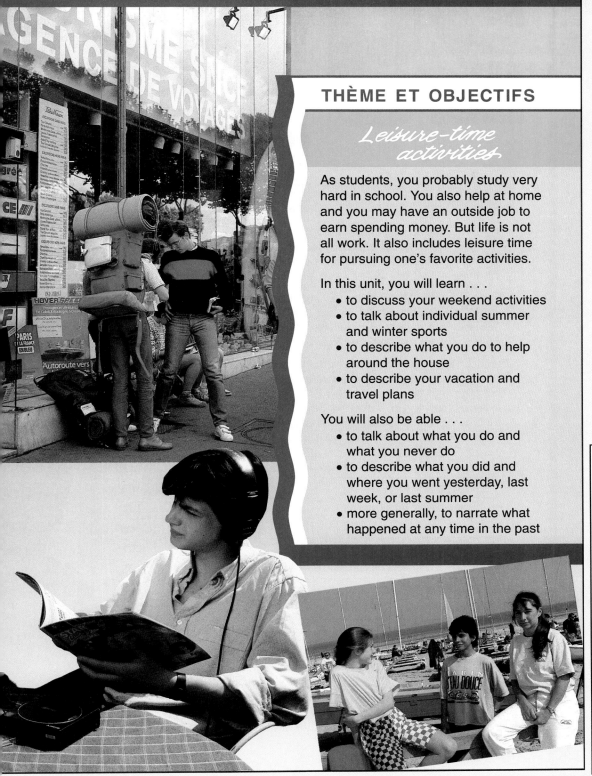

THÈME ET OBJECTIFS

Leisure-time activities

As students, you probably study very hard in school. You also help at home and you may have an outside job to earn spending money. But life is not all work. It also includes leisure time for pursuing one's favorite activities.

In this unit, you will learn . . .
• to discuss your weekend activities
• to talk about individual summer and winter sports
• to describe what you do to help around the house
• to describe your vacation and travel plans

You will also be able . . .
• to talk about what you do and what you never do
• to describe what you did and where you went yesterday, last week, or last summer
• more generally, to narrate what happened at any time in the past

Pacing

Your pacing of Units 8 and 9 depends on what point in the academic year you begin Niveau C.

Since this material is reintroduced in **Discovering French—blanc,** you may wish to present the material of Units 8 and 9 primarily for student recognition. Or you may wish to focus on Unit 8 so that the students have a solid introduction to the passé composé.

For further suggestions on pacing, see the general discussion in the Front Matter.

> ## ➤ Assessment Options

ACHIEVEMENT TESTS

Lesson Quizzes 29-32 pp. 99-106
   Test Cassette B, Side 2

Unit Test 8
   Portfolio Assessment
   pp. T304-305, Activities
   1-4; pp. T316-317,
   Activities 1-6;
   pp. T326-327,
   Activities 1-6; pp.
   T336-337, Activities 1-5

PROFICIENCY TESTS

 Listening Comprehension
   Performance Test, p. 41
   Test Cassette D, Side 2

 Speaking Performance Test, p. 37

 Reading Comprehension
   Performance Test, p. 34

Writing Performance Test, p. 55

 Test Bank, Unit 8
   Version A or B

 DFi C,
CD-ROM   Exploration 8
   Cahier, Créa-dialogue

MODULE 29:
Le français pratique:
Le weekend et les vacances
Total time: 6:11 min.
(Counter: 00:40 min.)

VIDEODISC Disc 5, Side 1
1558–12621

**LE FRANÇAIS
PRATIQUE**

LEÇON 29
Le weekend et les vacances

Accent sur ... Les loisirs

If you had to decide between earning more money or having more free time, what would you choose? When asked this question on a survey, French people indicated their overwhelming preference for more leisure time.

For the French, leisure plays an important role in what they call **la qualité de la vie** (quality of life). In fact, they consider leisure time to be not only a necessity but a right. By law, French workers are entitled to five weeks of paid vacation, as compared to two weeks for the average American.

French teenagers also place great value on their leisure time. Because they have so much homework and need to study so hard for their exams, they have no real time — and also little opportunity — to take an outside job. Instead, they try to make the most of their leisure hours. What are their favorite activities? Here is how French young people answered the question "What do you do when you have a free evening?"

Qu'est-ce que tu aimes faire le soir?	GARÇONS	FILLES
Je regarde la télé.	24%	18%
Je sors° avec mes copains.	20%	18%
Je vais au cinéma.	16%	14%
Je lis.°	14%	20%
Je vais au concert ou au théâtre.	10%	12%
Je vais danser.	8%	12%
Je fais du sport.	6%	4%
Je bricole.°	2%	2%

sors *go out*   **lis** *read*
bricole *do things around the house*

 Je regarde la télé.

■ **Comprehension practice:** Play the entire module through as an introduction to the lesson.

🖵 **Using the video**

The main focus of Video Module 29 is on what French people do in their leisure time, both on weekends and on vacation. As students watch, have them look for similarities and differences in the ways the French and Americans spend their leisure time.

The *Vignette culturelle* introduces students to the sport of windsurfing (**la planche à voile),** which is very popular throughout metropolitan France, as well as in the overseas departments of Martinique and Guadeloupe.

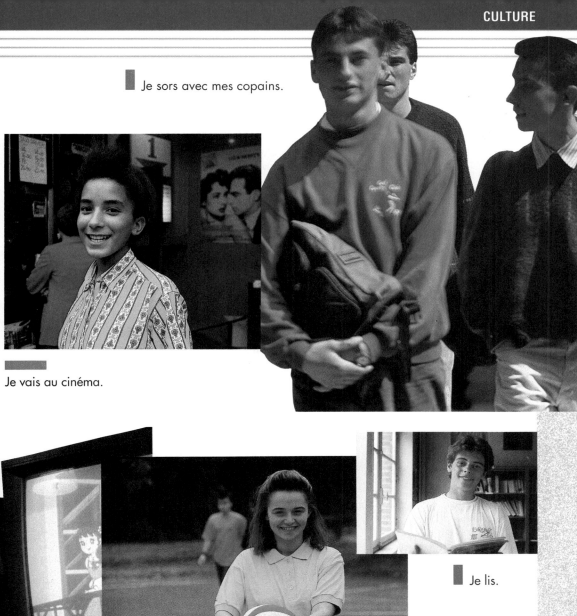

Je sors avec mes copains.

Je vais au cinéma.

Je lis.

Je fais du sport.

■ Cultural notes

Les vacances

You may want to point out that for French people from all walks of life, vacation time is sacred. Often they enjoy a week of winter sports or travel, plus a longer vacation in July or August.

Les examens

French students are concerned about doing well on their final **baccalauréat** exams in the last two years at the **lycée.** Younger students work hard to score well on the **entrée en sixième** (to enter the right secondary school sequence) and the **entrée en seconde** (to enter the right **lycée** sequence). (See chart on p.81.)

🌐 Cross-cultural comparisons

Ask your students what they like to do when they have a free evening, using the suggestions in the **sondage** on p. 296. Then analyze your results and compare them to those in the reading.

You can review numbers by tallying the results in French, using a calculator.

Dans la classe, il y a [12] garçons et [16] filles.

[4] garçons regardent la télé.

Ça fait [25% – vingt-cinq pour cent].

[4] filles regardent la télé.

Ça fait [33 % – trente-trois pour cent].

Section A

COMMUNICATIVE FUNCTION:
Discussing weekend
activities

29.1 Introduction: Le
weekend
29.2 Mini-scenes: Que
faites-vous le week-
end?
29.3 Dialogue: Le
weekend
(00:52–2:38 min.)

VIDEODISC Disc 5, Side 1
1910–5066

Leçon 29, Sections 1, 2

Transparency 42
Weekend activities

■ **Language note:** Expressions
used in Quebec:
un centre d'achats (a shopping
center)
un mail /maj/ (a mall)
magasiner/faire du magasinage
(to go shopping)

■ **Looking ahead:** The present
tense forms of **voir** are presented
in Lesson 31.

Supplementary vocabulary

ranger (sa chambre) to clean
(one's room)
Compare:
ranger to straighten up,
to pick up
nettoyer to dust and vacuum

retrouver (des amis) to meet
(friends)
Compare:
retrouver to meet as arranged
rencontrer to run into (by chance)

■ **Teaching strategy:** Like **payer**,
nettoyer is also a "boot" verb.
Have students draw a boot and
write the appropriate forms of
nettoyer inside and outside their
drawing.

A. Le weekend

▶ *How to plan your weekend activities:*

Qu'est-ce que
tu vas faire samedi?

Je vais rester chez moi
pour réparer mon vélo.

Qu'est-ce que tu vas faire | samedi?
samedi **matin**
dimanche **après-midi**
demain **soir**
ce **weekend**
le weekend **prochain** (next)

le matin morning
l'après-midi afternoon
le soir evening

Je vais rester chez moi **pour** (in order to) | faire mes **devoirs** (homework).
réparer (to fix) mon vélo
préparer le dîner
aider (to help) mes parents
laver (to wash) ma mobylette
nettoyer (to clean) ma chambre

Je vais aller ...
en ville
dans les magasins
au **centre commercial** (mall)

pour ...
faire des achats
(go shopping).

Moi, je vais aller en ville
pour faire des achats.

au cinéma
au café
au stade

voir (to see) un film
rencontrer (to meet) mes copains
assister à (to go to, attend)
un match de foot

à la campagne (countryside) | **faire un pique-nique** (to have a picnic)

Je vais aller à une boum.
Avant (Before) la boum, je vais faire des achats.
Pendant (During) la boum, je vais écouter des cassettes.
Après (After) la boum, je vais faire mes devoirs.

➡ The verb **nettoyer** is conjugated like **payer**:
je **nettoie**   tu **nettoies**   il / elle / on **nettoie**   ils / elles **nettoient**
but: nous nettoyons   vous nettoyez

☀ **Warm-up and review**
Review the TPR gestures for the subject
pronouns (page 110). Have students iden-
tify the forms **of faire.**
C'est le weekend.
Je fais une promenade. [gesture **je**]
Vous faites une promenade. [**vous**]
Ils font une promenade aussi. etc.

Review times and possessive adjectives,
asking when students do their homework.
**X, à quelle heure est-ce que tu fais tes
devoirs?**
[Je fais mes devoirs à sept heures et demie.]
**Y, à quelle heure est-ce que X fait ses
devoirs?**
[Il fait ses devoirs à sept heures et demie.]

1 Et toi?

Décris tes activités. Pour cela, complète les phrases suivantes.

1. En général, je vais
   au cinéma . . .
   - le vendredi soir
   - le samedi soir
   - le dimanche après-midi
   - . . . ?

2. En général, je rencontre
   mes copains . . .
   - chez moi
   - chez eux
   - dans un café
   - . . . ?

3. En général, je fais
   mes devoirs . . .
   - avant le dîner
   - après le dîner
   - pendant la classe
   - . . . ?

4. Je préfère assister à . . .
   - un match de foot
   - un match de baseball
   - un concert de rock
   - . . . ?

5. En général, je préfère faire
   mes achats . . .
   - seul(e) *(by myself)*
   - avec mes copains
   - avec mes frères et mes soeurs
   - . . . ?

6. En général, quand je rentre
   chez moi après les classes, . . .
   - je fais mes devoirs
   - je regarde la télé
   - j'aide ma mère ou mon père
   - . . . ?

7. En été, je préfère faire
   un pique-nique . . .
   - dans mon jardin
   - à la campagne
   - à la plage
   - . . . ?

8. Si *(If)* je dois aider mes
   parents à la maison et si j'ai
   le choix *(choice)*, je préfère . . .
   - nettoyer le salon
   - laver la voiture
   - faire la vaisselle *(dishes)*
   - . . . ?

2 Qu'est-ce qu'ils font?

Informez-vous sur les personnes suivantes. Décrivez
ce qu'elles font ou ce qu'elles vont faire. Pour cela,
complétez les phrases avec une expression du
vocabulaire à la page 298.

▶ Sandrine est au garage.
   Elle <u>répare son vélo</u> (<u>sa mobylette</u>).

1. Mme Jolivet est dans la cuisine. Elle . . .
2. Vincent Jolivet est aussi dans la cuisine. Il . . .
3. Anne et Sylvie sont au Bon Marché. Elles . . .
4. Je suis dans ma chambre et je regarde mon livre
   de français. Je . . .
5. Olivier et ses copains achètent des billets *(tickets)*
   de cinéma. Ils vont . . .
6. Mes amis vont à Yankee Stadium. Ils vont . . .
7. Tu vas au café. Tu vas . . .
8. Vous faites des sandwichs. Vous allez . . . à la campagne.

3 Mon calendrier personnel

Décrivez ce que vous allez
faire.

MERCREDI

1. Après la classe, je vais . . .
2. Avant le dîner, . . .
3. Après le dîner, . . .
4. Demain soir, . . .
5. Vendredi soir, . . .
6. Samedi après-midi, . . .
7. Samedi soir, . . .
8. Dimanche après-midi, . . .
9. Pendant les vacances, . . .

299

---

1 COMMUNICATION:
describing leisure activities

■ **Variations**
- In pairs:
  Have students work in pairs,
  sharing their answers.
- In small groups:
  (See suggested activity on
  p.T91.)

2 COMPREHENSION: describing what people are doing

3 COMMUNICATION:
describing future plans

**29.4 Mini-scenes:
Samedi**
(2:39–3:41 min.

VIDEODISC   Disc 5, Side 1
5087–6926

▣ Leçon 29, Section 3

Teaching note: Directions to activities

From now on, direction lines for the
activities are given in French. You may
want to present the key verbs listed on
p. 293. Encourage your students to guess
the meanings of other new words and
expressions from context.

With more challenging activities, you may
wish to have a volunteer paraphrase the
instructions in English.

29.5 Introduction: Les
vacances
29.6 Dialogues: Les
vacances
29.7 Mini-scenes: Qu'est-
ce qu'il fait?
(3:42–5:27 min.)

 **VIDEODISC** Disc 5, Side 1
6978–10160

 Leçon 29, Sections 4, 5

Supplementary vocabulary

HOLIDAYS
la Hanoukka
la Pâque (Passover)

SPORTS AND ACTIVITIES
faire du ballet
faire du bateau
faire du deltaplane (hang gliding)
faire du motocross
faire du ski alpin
faire du ski de fond (cross
country)
faire du vélo

faire de la danse moderne
faire de la gymnastique
faire de la marche (fast walking)
faire de la moto
faire de la natation (swimming)
faire de la planche à roulettes
(skateboard)

■ **Looking ahead:** The negative
construction (**Je ne fais pas de ski**)
will be presented in Unit 9 when
students learn the partitive.
However, you may introduce the
negative construction at this time,
if students need it for self-expression.

■ **Realia note**
La Plagne is a popular high
altitude ski resort in the French
Alps. In 1992, La Plagne was
selected to host the bobsled
competition for the Winter
Olympic Games at Albertville.

T300

B. Les vacances

▶ *How to plan your vacation activities:*

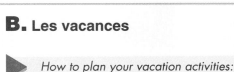

Qu'est-ce que tu vas faire
cet été?

Je vais aller à la mer.

Qu'est-ce que tu vas faire	à **Noël?**	**Noël** Christmas
	à **Pâques**	**Pâques** Easter
	pendant les vacances de printemps	**les vacances** vacation
	pendant **les grandes vacances**	**les grandes vacances**
	cet été	summer vacation

| Je vais aller | à **la mer** (ocean, shore). |
| | à **la montagne** (mountains) |

Je vais voyager	en avion.	**un avion** plane
	en train	**un train** train
	en autocar	**un autocar, un car** touring bus
	en bateau	**un bateau** boat, ship
	en voiture	

Je vais voyager en avion.

| Je vais voyager | **seul(e)** (alone). |
| | avec ma famille |

Je vais **passer** (to spend)	dix jours	là-bas.	**un jour** day
	six semaines		**une semaine** week
	deux mois		**un mois** month

| J'aime | **le ski** (skiing). | En hiver, je vais à la montagne pour **faire du ski** (to ski). |
| | **le ski nautique** (waterskiing) | En été, je vais à la mer pour **faire du ski nautique** (to waterski). |

J'aime le ski!

Moi,
à La Plagne
je fais vraiment
du ski

La Plagne
l'amour fou du

Réservations:
votre agence de voyag
Maison de la Plag
Point - Show Voy
66, Champs-Élys
75008 Paris

300 **Unité 8**

TPR Sports

PROPS: Blue cards with logos for jogging,
skiing, waterskiing, mountain climbing;
red cards with logos for sailing,
swimming, and windsurfing
Identify the cards: **Ces cartes représentent des sports différents. Voici
l'alpinisme.**

Hand out the sports cards.
Moi, j'aime le ski. Qui aime le ski ici?
X et Y, vous aimez le ski? [Oui.]
Give them "skiing" card.
Talk about who does what sport.
X et Y, vous faites du ski en hiver?
[oui]
Ils font du ski.

Activités sportives

le sport	sport(s)	Je **fais du sport.**	I practice sports.
le jogging	jogging	Nous **faisons du jogging.**	We jog.
le ski	skiing	Tu **fais du ski?**	Do you ski?
le ski nautique	waterskiing	Anne **fait du ski nautique.**	Anne waterskis.
la voile	sailing	Paul **fait de la voile.**	Paul sails.
la planche à voile	windsurfing	Vous **faites de la planche à voile?**	Do you windsurf?
la natation	swimming	Tu **fais de la natation** en été?	Do you go swimming in (the) summer?
l'alpinisme (m.)	mountain climbing	J'aime **faire de l'alpinisme.**	I like to go mountain climbing.

➡ To describe participation in individual sports or other activities, the French use the construction:

$$\text{faire} \begin{Bmatrix} \textbf{du} \\ \textbf{de la} \\ \textbf{de l'} \end{Bmatrix} + \begin{array}{l} \text{SPORT} \\ \text{or} \\ \text{ACTIVITY} \end{array}$$

le camping	→	**faire du camping**
la voile	→	**faire de la voile**
l'alpinisme	→	**faire de l'alpinisme**

■ NOTE CULTURELLE

Le calendrier des fêtes françaises

Voici les principales fêtes *(holidays)* en France:

le jour de l'an	*New Year's Day*
Mardi Gras	*Shrove Tuesday*
Pâques	*Easter*
le premier mai	*Labor Day*
la Pentecôte	*Pentecost*
le 14 juillet	*Bastille Day* *(French National Holiday)*
la Toussaint	*All Saints' Day (November 1)*
le 11 novembre	*Armistice Day*
Noël	*Christmas (December 25)*

Mardi Gras

Le 14 juillet

Leçon 29 301

COMMUNICATION:
describing one's vacation
preferences

4

■ **Expansion** (question 2):
**Pendant les fêtes de Hanoukka,
je préfère ...**

■ **Variation:** See variation for
Act. 1, p. T299.

■ **Challenge:** Have students give
an original completion for each
sentence. For example:
1. Mes vacances préférées sont
[les vacances de "Thanks-
giving".]

COMPREHENSION:
describing people's
activities

5

 **29.8 Vignette culturelle:
La planche à voile**
(5:28–6:47 min.)

VIDEODISC Disc 5, Side 1
10177–12621

■ **Photo culture note**
La planche à voile
The sport of windsurfing (**la
planche à voile**) originated in
California and was introduced in
France in the the early 1970s. It
has become one of the favorite
sports of French young people.
In international competition, the
French windsurfers (**un véliplan-
chiste**) are among the world's
best.

4 **Et toi?**

Indique tes préférences personnelles en complétant les phrases suivantes.

1. Mes vacances
   préférées sont . . .
   - les vacances de Noël
   - les vacances de printemps
   - les grandes vacances
   - . . . ?

2. Pendant les vacances
   de Noël, je préfère . . .
   - rester avec ma famille
   - rendre visite à mes grands-parents
   - faire du ski
   - . . . ?

3. Pendant les grandes
   vacances, je préfère . . .
   - aller à la mer
   - aller à la montagne
   - aller à la campagne
   - . . . ?

4. Quand je voyage pendant
   les vacances, je préfère
   voyager . . .
   - seul(e)
   - avec mes copains
   - avec ma famille
   - . . . ?

5. Quand je vais loin, je
   préfère voyager . . .
   - en train
   - en avion
   - en car
   - . . . ?

5 **Leurs activités favorites**

Les personnes suivantes ont certaines activités favorites.
Lisez où elles sont et dites ce qu'elles font. Pour cela
choisissez une activité appropriée de la liste à droite.

▶ Je suis à la plage.

1. Jean-Pierre est au stade.
2. Anne et Marie sont dans un studio de danse.
3. En juillet, nous allons dans le Colorado.
4. Tu passes les vacances de Noël en Suisse.
5. Mes copains passent les vacances à la campagne.
6. Pauline est à la salle *(room)* de gymnastique.
7. Vous êtes à la mer.
8. Nous sommes à Tahiti.
9. Avant le dîner, nous allons au parc municipal.
10. Je suis à la Martinique.

Je fais de la planche à vo[...]

  **Cooperative group practice**

For Act. 4, divide the class into groups of
4 or 5 students. Name one person as
recorder (**secrétaire**).

For each question, members of the
group each state their preferences, by
selecting one of the completions.

The **secrétaires** tally the responses of
their groups and report back to the entire
class or hand results to the teacher.
**La majorité préfère les grandes
vacances.**
**Pendant les vacances de Noël, la
majorité préfère rester avec la
famille. ...**

6. En été, je vais à la plage spécialement *(especially)* pour . . .
   - nager
   - faire du ski nautique
   - bronzer *(to get a tan)*
   - . . . ?

7. Je voudrais être un champion (une championne) de . . .
   - ski
   - ski nautique
   - planche à voile
   - . . . ?

8. Je voudrais aller à la Guadeloupe principalement *(mainly)* pour . . .
   - nager
   - parler français
   - faire de la planche à voile
   - . . . ?

9. Je voudrais aller dans le Colorado pour . . .
   - faire du ski
   - faire des promenades à pied
   - faire de l'alpinisme
   - . . . ?

10. Je voudrais aller à Paris et rester là-bas pendant . . .
    - dix jours
    - trois semaines
    - six mois
    - . . . ?

🎽	la gymnastique
🤸	la danse moderne
⚽	le sport
🏃	le jogging
⛺	le camping
⛵	la voile
🏄	la planche à voile
🎿	le ski
🏄	le ski nautique
🧗	l'alpinisme

6 Questions personnelles

1. En général, qu'est-ce que tu fais pendant les vacances de Noël?
2. Est-ce que tu vas voyager pendant les grandes vacances? Où vas-tu aller? Combien de temps *(How long)* est-ce que tu vas rester là-bas?
3. Qu'est-ce que tu aimes faire quand tu es à la plage?
4. Est-ce que tu voyages souvent? Comment voyages-tu?

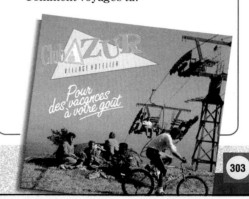

303

■ **Cultural note:** Remind students that Guadeloupe is a French island in the Caribbean.

COMMUNICATION: answering personal questions
6

Classroom Notes

Cooperative pair practice Activity 6

1 COMPREHENSION

1. à la campagne / faire une promenade à vélo
2. à la campagne / faire un pique-nique
3. à Aspen / faire du ski
4. à la Floride / faire du ski nautique
5. à la mer (plage) / faire de la voile
6. à la montagne / faire de l'alpinisme
7. (answers will vary) / faire du jogging
8. (answers will vary)
9. (answers will vary)

🔲 Leçon 29, Section 6

2 GUIDED ORAL EXPRESSION

JP: Où vas-tu cet été?
H: Je vais à la mer avec des amis.
JP: Est-ce que vous allez voyager en voiture?
H: (Non,) nous allons voyager en train parce que nous n'avons pas de voiture.
JP: Est-ce que tu vas faire de la voile?
H: Oui, et je vais faire de la planche à voile aussi.
JP: Au revoir, Hélène. Bonnes vacances!
H: Au revoir!

🔲 Leçon 29, Section 7

À votre tour!

1 Créa-dialogue

Des amis parlent de leurs projets. Avec un(e) camarade de classe, choisissez une scène et composez le dialogue correspondant.

▶ —Où vas-tu vendredi?
—Je vais en ville.
—Qu'est-ce que tu vas faire là-bas?
—Je vais faire des achats.

▶ **vendredi** | **en ville** | [image]

1. samedi matin	[image]	2. samedi après-midi	[image]	3. à Noël	à Aspen	[image]
4. pendant les vacances de printemps	en Floride	5. en juillet	[image]	6. en août	[image]	
7. demain matin	[image]	8. dimanche après-midi	[image]	9. cet été	[image]	

2 Conversation dirigée

Avec un(e) camarade, composez un dialogue basé sur les instructions suivantes. Jean-Pierre demande à Hélène si elle a des projets de vacances.

Jean-Pierre			Hélène
asks Hélène where she is going this summer	→ ↙	says that she is going to the ocean with friends	
asks her if they are going to travel by car	→ ↗	answers that they are going to travel by train because they do not have a car	
asks her if she is going to go sailing	→ ↙	answers yes and says that she is also going to windsurf	
says good-bye to Hélène and wishes her a good vacation (**Bonnes vacances!**)	→	answers good-bye	

304 Unité 8

À votre tour

Depending on your goals and objectives, you may or may not wish to assign all of the activities in the **À votre tour** section.

👥👥 Cooperative practice

In Act. 1 and 2, you may want to have students work cooperatively in trios, with two performing and one consulting the Answer Key and acting as monitor.

3 Composition: Le weekend prochain

Make plans for next weekend. Prepare a list of activities describing ...

- four things that you are going to do at home
- four things that you are going to do outside

4 Au club de vacances

Avec qui passez-vous vos vacances? On peut passer ses vacances avec sa famille ou avec des copains. On peut aussi aller dans un club de vacances. Là on peut faire du sport et rencontrer d'autres jeunes.

Lisez le document suivant.

Ce club de vacances offre la possibilité d'aller dans différents «villages de mer». Choisissez un des villages de mer proposés par le club.

- Dans quel pays est situé ce village?
- Quels sports est-ce qu'on peut pratiquer *(participate in)* dans ce village?
- Pourquoi est-ce que vous choisissez ce village?
- En général, quels sports pratiquez-vous?

VILLAGES DE MER

	AGADIR MAROC	LES ALMADIES SÉNÉGAL	ASSINIE CÔTE D'IVOIRE	BORA-BORA TAHITI-POLYNÉSIE FR.SE	LES BOUCANIERS MARTINIQUE	CANCÚN MEXIQUE	CAP SKIRRING SÉNÉGAL	LA CARAVELLE GUADELOUPE	LES CORAUX EILAT-ISRAËL	DJERBA LA DOUCE TUNISIE
Village-hôtel, bungalow										
Ski nautique, planche à voile										
Voile										
Plongée libre										
Plongée scaphandre										
Piscine										
Équitation										
Tennis										
Tir à l'arc										
Promenades en mer			PIROGUE						PÊCHE À LA TRAÎNE	
Pêche en haute mer										
Arts appliqués										

Portfolio assessment

You will probably select only one speaking activity and one writing activity to go into the students' portfolios for Unit 8.

In this lesson, you might suggest that students do their own variations of Act. 2 as an oral portfolio recording.

You may also want to use the Challenge activities in the margin, above.

---

3 WRITTEN SELF-EXPRESSION

■ **Follow-up activity:** Have students in pairs compare their compositions. How many similar activities did they choose?

4 READING COMPREHENSION

■ **Challenge**
Conversational role play: At the challenge level, students might want to prepare one of the following conversations.

1. Curious Thomas is trying to find out what Nathalie is going to do this weekend. Nathalie, who is a quiet person, knows what she plans to do but answers only with oui or non.
   (Roles: Thomas and Nathalie)

2. Two close friends are arguing about what they are going to do this weekend. One wants to go out and the other wants to stay in.
   (Roles: two friends)

3. Shortly before vacation, Carole calls her cousin Olivier. They discuss their summer plans. Carole is going to go to the ocean with her family. Olivier is going to spend some time in the mountains with a friend.
   (Roles: Carole and Olivier)

■ **Realia note**
Students may be able to guess these terms from the icons:
la plongée libre *snorkeling*
la plongée scaphandre *scuba diving*
   (**un scaphandre** *diving suit*)
l'équitation *horseback riding*
le tir à l'arc *archery*
une promenade en mer *ocean cruise*
une pirogue *pirogue (native boat hollowed out from the trunk of a tree)*
la pêche en haute mer *deep-sea fishing*
les arts appliqués *arts and crafts*

MODULE 30:
Mercredi après-midi
Total time: 5:57 min.
(Counter: 6:59 min.)

30.1 Introduction: Listening — Mercredi après-midi (7:06–8:16 min.)
30.2 Dialogue: L'examen de maths (8:17–8:51 min.)
30.3 Mini-scenes: Listening — Qu'est-ce que vous avez fait hier? (8:52–10:02 min.)
30.4 Mini-scenes: Listening — Est-ce que tu as joué au tennis? (10:03–10:55 min.)
30.5 Mini-scenes: Speaking — Est-ce que tu as joué au tennis? (10:56–11:55 min.)
30.6 Vignette culturelle: Le cinéma (11:56–12:52 min.)

VIDEODISC Disc 5, Side 1
12899–23594

◼ **Comprehension practice:** Play the entire module through as an introduction to the lesson.

▭ Leçon 30, Section 1

LEÇON 30 Vive le weekend!

Le weekend, nous avons nos occupations préférées. Certaines personnes aiment aller en ville et rencontrer leurs amis.
<u>D'autres</u> préfèrent rester à la maison et <u>bricoler</u>. Qu'est-ce que les personnes suivantes <u>ont fait</u> le weekend <u>dernier</u>?

Others / do things around the house
did . . . do / last

Le weekend

J'aime acheter des vêtements.

Tu aimes réparer ton vélo.

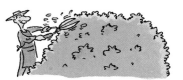

M. Lambert aime travailler dans le jardin.

Nous aimons organiser des boums.

Le weekend dernier

J'<u>ai acheté</u> des vêtements.   *bo*

Tu <u>as réparé</u> ton vélo.   *fixe*

Il <u>a travaillé</u> dans le jardin.   *wo*

Nous <u>avons organisé</u> une boum.   *or*

306 Unité 8

Setting the scene

In this lesson, the video module is independent of the opening text. However, the opening scenes are narrated in Section 1 of the audiocassette.

The video first shows how Jean-Claude and Nathalie spent the day on Wednesday. Then it shows them talking on Thursday morning when Jean-Claude realizes that he has forgotten about his math test.

To set the scene, ask students if they have ever forgotten about a test (**oublier la date d'un examen**). If so, how did they perform on the exam?

Le weekend

Vous aimez jouer au foot.

Pluton et Philibert aiment rencontrer leurs amis.

Le weekend dernier

Vous <u>avez joué</u> au foot.   *played*

Ils <u>ont rencontré</u> leurs amis.   *met*

Et toi?

Indique si oui ou non tu as fait les choses suivantes le weekend dernier. Pour cela complète les phrases suivantes.

1. (J'ai/Je n'ai pas) . . . acheté des vêtements.
2. (J'ai/Je n'ai pas) . . . réparé mon vélo.
3. (J'ai/Je n'ai pas) . . . travaillé dans le jardin.
4. (J'ai/Je n'ai pas) . . . organisé une fête.
5. (J'ai/Je n'ai pas) . . . joué au foot.
6. (J'ai/Je n'ai pas) . . . rencontré mes amis.

▪ NOTE ▪ CULTURELLE

Le weekend

Le weekend ne commence pas° le vendredi soir pour tout le monde.° Dans beaucoup d'écoles françaises, les élèves ont classe le samedi matin. Pour eux, le weekend commence seulement° le samedi à midi.

Que font les jeunes Français le samedi? Ça dépend. Beaucoup° vont en ville. Ils vont dans des magasins pour écouter les nouveaux disques ou pour regarder, essayer° et parfois° acheter des vêtements. Ils vont au café ou au cinéma avec leurs copains. Certains° préfèrent rester chez eux ou aller chez des copains. Parfois ils vont à une soirée. Là on écoute de la musique, on mange des sandwichs et on danse . . .

En général, le dimanche est réservé aux activités familiales.° Un weekend, on invite des cousins. Un autre° weekend, on rend visite aux grands-parents . . . Le dimanche, on déjeune° et on dîne en famille.° Le soir, on regarde la télé et souvent on fait ses devoirs pour les classes du lundi matin.

ne commence pas *does not begin* **tout le monde** *everyone* **seulement** *only* **Beaucoup** *Many* **essayer** *try on* **parfois** *sometimes* **Certains** *Some of them* **activités familiales** *family activities* **Un autre** *Another* **déjeune** *has lunch* **en famille** *at home (with the family)*

COMMUNICATION: describing what one did last weekend.

▪ **Expansion:** Ask for more information. Have students give only short answers unless they have been practicing the passé composé.
1. où? quels vêtements?
2. quand?
3. quel jour? avec qui?
4. quand? où?
5. où?
6. où?

Note culturelle

 30.6 Vignette culturelle: Le cinéma (11:56–12:52 min.)

VIDEODISC Disc 5, Side 1
21793–23594

🌐 Cross-cultural observation

The *Vignette culturelle* of the video presents one of the favorite pastimes of French young people: going to the movies.

Have students watch to see whether they have the same taste in films as the students who were interviewed in Paris.

The *Vignette* shows two short interviews, the first with two young boys and the second with a girl. The boys like going to see "L'Ours." The first boy likes **les films d'aventures;** his friend's favorite actress is Kim Basinger in "Batman." The girl's favorite actress is Marilyn Monroe.

Note the use of **avoir** in the following sentences:

J'**ai faim**.   *I am hungry.*
Brigitte **a soif**.   *Brigitte is thirsty.*

French speakers use **avoir** in many expressions where English speakers use the verb *to be*.

Vocabulaire: Expressions avec *avoir*

avoir chaud	*to be (feel) warm*	Quand j'**ai chaud** en été, je vais à la plage.
avoir froid	*to be (feel) cold*	Est-ce que tu **as froid**? Voici ton pull.
avoir faim	*to be hungry*	Tu **as faim**? Est-ce que tu veux une pizza?
avoir soif	*to be thirsty*	J'**ai soif**. Je voudrais une limonade.
avoir raison	*to be right*	Est-ce que les profs **ont** toujours **raison**?
avoir tort	*to be wrong*	Marc n'étudie pas. Il **a tort**!
avoir de la chance	*to be lucky*	J'**ai de la chance**. J'ai des amis sympathiques.

1 Tort ou raison?

Informez-vous sur les personnes suivantes et dites si, à votre avis, elles ont tort ou raison.

▶ Les élèves n'étudient pas.
  Ils ont tort!

▶ Tu écoutes le prof.
  Tu as raison!

1. Catherine est généreuse avec ses copines.
2. Nous aidons nos parents.
3. Tu fais tes devoirs.
4. Vous êtes très impatients avec vos amis.
5. Mes copains étudient le français.
6. Jean-François dépense son argent inutilement *(uselessly)*.
7. M. Legros mange trop *(too much)*.
8. Alain et Nicolas sont impolis *(impolite)*.
9. Vous nettoyez votre chambre.

2 De bonnes questions

Étudiez ce que font les personnes suivantes. Ensuite, posez une question logique sur chaque personne. Pour cela, utilisez l'une des expressions suivantes:

avoir faim	avoir soif	avoir chaud
avoir froid	avoir de la chance	

▶ Philippe va au restaurant.
  Est-ce que Philippe a faim?

1. Tu veux un soda.
2. Jean-Pierre mange une pizza.
3. Cécile porte un manteau.
4. Vous gagnez à la loterie.
5. Vous faites des sandwichs.
6. Tu mets ton blouson.
7. Mes copains vont aller à la piscine.
8. Ces élèves n'étudient pas beaucoup, mais ils réussissent toujours à leurs examens.
9. Tu as des grands-parents très généreux.

Section A

COMMUNICATIVE FUNCTION: Expressing thirst, hunger, and other feelings

 Transparency 44
Expressions with **avoir**

 Leçon 30, Section 2

↩ **Re-entry and review:** The purpose of this section is to have students review **avoir** before practicing the passé composé. Students have already learned **avoir faim/soif** (Lesson 18).

■ **Teaching strategy:** Introduce the **avoir** expressions using appropriate gestures. For example:
avoir chaud (fanning self)
avoir froid (shivering)
avoir faim (pointing to stomach)
avoir soif (pointing to throat)
avoir tort (wagging index finger back and forth)
avoir de la chance (extending arms in a "youpie!" manner)
See TPR activity, p. T90.

Supplementary vocabulary

avoir sommeil *to be (feel) sleepy*
avoir peur *to be scared, afraid*

 COMPREHENSION: evaluating actions of others

 COMPREHENSION: asking logical questions

 Warm-up: Quel âge as-tu?

Quickly review the forms of **avoir** by asking students how old they are.

Quel âge as-tu, X? [J'ai [treize] ans.]
Dis, Y, quel âge a X? [X a treize ans.]
Et Z, quel âge as-tu? [J'ai treize ans.]
Comme X! Alors, Z et X, quel âge avez-vous? [Nous avons treize ans.]

Eh bien, tout le monde, quel âge ont X et Z? [Ils ont treize ans.]

EXPANSION: Hold up magazine ads and have the class estimate the people's ages.

T308

B. Le passé composé des verbes en *-er*

The sentences below describe past events. In the French sentences, the verbs are in the PASSÉ COMPOSÉ. Note the forms of the passé composé and its English equivalents.

Hier j'**ai réparé** mon vélo.
Le weekend dernier, Marc **a organisé** une boum.
Pendant les vacances, nous **avons visité** Paris.

Yesterday I **fixed** *my bicycle.*
Last weekend, Marc **organized** *a party.*
During vacation, we **visited** *Paris.*

FORMS

The PASSÉ COMPOSÉ is composed of two words. For most verbs, it is formed as follows:

> PRESENT of **avoir** + PAST PARTICIPLE

Note the forms of the passé composé for **visiter.**

PASSÉ COMPOSÉ	PRESENT of **avoir** + PAST PARTICIPLE	
J'**ai visité** Québec.	j' **ai**	
Tu **as visité** Paris.	tu **as**	
Il/Elle/On **a visité** Montréal.	il/elle/on **a**	**visité**
Nous **avons visité** Genève.	nous **avons**	
Vous **avez visité** Strasbourg.	vous **avez**	
Ils/Elles **ont visité** Fort-de-France.	ils/elles **ont**	

➡ For all **-er** verbs, the past participle is formed by replacing the `-er` of the infinitive by `-é`.

jou`er` → jou`é`   Nous **avons joué** au tennis.
parl`er` → parl`é`   Éric **a parlé** à Nathalie.
téléphon`er` → téléphon`é`   Vous **avez téléphoné** à Cécile.

Learning about language

The PASSÉ COMPOSÉ, as its name indicates, is a "past" tense "composed" of two parts. It is formed like the present perfect tense in English.

AUXILIARY VERB + PAST PARTICIPLE of the main verb
Nous **avons** **travaillé.**
We have *worked.*

USES

The passé composé is used to describe past actions and events. It has several English equivalents.

J'ai visité Montréal.
    { *I* **visited** *Montreal.*
      I **have visited** *Montreal.*
      I **did visit** *Montreal.*

Leçon 30 309

Section B

COMMUNICATIVE FUNCTION:
Talking about what happened in the past

■ **Language note/Looking ahead:**
In English, the auxiliary verb is always *to have.* In French, the auxiliary verb is usually, but not always, **avoir.**
The passé composé with **être** is presented in Lesson 32.

■ **Teaching strategy:** If you have been practicing the passé composé orally, this material will be familiar to the students.
You will want to focus particularly on the written forms.

■ **Photo culture note**
Montréal
With a population of over two million people, Montreal is a bustling commercial and industrial center as well as the artistic and intellectual capital of Quebec. Its inland port, located on an island in the St. Lawrence river, ranks among the busiest in North America.
Below the skyscrapers of downtown Montreal is a honeycomb of shopping malls connected to one another and to the various subway stations by underground pedestrian tunnels. This way, in the ice and cold of the Canadian winter, shoppers have easy access to their favorite stores.

TPR **Past activities**

Review the gestures your class developed for the verbs on pp. 108–109.
    Tout le monde: dansez.
    Chantez. Téléphonez. Nagez.
Have an individual act out an activity.
    X, joue au tennis. C'est bien. Merci.
Then describe what the student did.

Qu'est-ce que X a fait?
Il a joué au tennis.
Then have two students act out an activity.
    Y et Z, dansez. Voilà, c'est très bien.
Describe what the students did.
    Qu'est-ce que Y et Z ont fait?
    Ils ont dansé.

1. un jean
2. une montre
3. une guitare
4. des chemises
5. une chaîne stéréo
6. des chaussures
7. des livres
8. une voiture

■ **Variation:** Have students ask and answer questions in the plural.
– **Vous avez acheté des sodas?**
– **Mais oui, nous avons acheté des sodas.**

■ **Realia note**
Le Jazz en France
The poster reads **"Nice, l'arène du jazz"** (Nice, the arena of jazz). When said aloud, it could be interpreted as **"Nice, la reine du jazz"** (Nice, the queen of jazz).
Jazz has always been popular in France, especially after the creation of the **Hot Club de France** in 1932. Festivals are regularly organized in many cities, attracting both French and American musicians.

3 Achats

Samedi dernier *(Last Saturday)*, les personnes suivantes ont fait des achats. Dites ce que chaque personne a acheté.

▶ Philippe (des compacts)
  Philippe a acheté des compacts.

Philippe | 1. Pauline | 2. moi

4 Vive la différence!

Caroline et Jean-Pierre sont des copains, mais ils aiment faire des choses différentes. Ils parlent de ce qu'ils ont fait ce weekend.

▶ jouer au volley (au tennis)

J'ai joué au volley.

Eh bien, moi, j'ai joué au tennis.

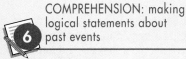

1. acheter des cassettes (des magazines)
2. dîner au restaurant (chez moi)
3. inviter mon cousin (un ami)
4. téléphoner à ma tante (à mon grand-père)
5. aider ma mère (mon père)
6. nettoyer ma chambre (le garage)
7. réparer ma mobylette (mon vélo)
8. assister à un match de foot (à un concert de rock)
9. laver mes tee-shirts (mes jeans)

5 La boum

Anne et Éric organisent une boum ce weekend. Florence demande à Philippe s'il a fait les choses suivantes. Il répond oui.

▶ acheter des sodas?

Tu as acheté des sodas?

Mais oui, j'ai ach[eté] des sodas.

1. acheter des jus de fruit
2. préparer les sandwichs
3. nettoyer le salon
4. réparer la chaîne stéréo
5. apporter des CD
6. inviter nos copains

6 Un jeu

Décrivez ce que certaines personnes ont fait samedi dernier. Pour cela, faites des phrases logiques en utilisant les éléments des Colonnes A, B et C. Combien de phrases est-ce que vous pouvez *(can)* faire en cinq minutes?

▶ **Vous avez assisté à un concert de jazz.**

A	B	C
nous	acheter	une boum
vous	assister	un musée
Marc	dîner	des vêtements
Hélène et Juliette	jouer	un film à la télé
Éric et Stéphanie	organiser	au Monopoly
mes copains	regarder	dans le jardin
les voisins	travailler	dans un restaurant vietnamien
	visiter	à un concert de jazz

NICE, L'ARÈNE DU JAZZ

Cooperative pair practice
Activities 4, 5

Game: Samedi dernier

You can treat Act. 6 as a team game. Divide the class into teams of three. Each team picks a person from column A and decides what that subject did last Saturday. All three team members must then write the same sentence down correctly.

Then the team formulates another sentence using elements of columns A, B, and C, and again all three members write it down.

The game is played against the clock. The team whose three members have written the greatest number of correct sentences in five minutes is the winner.

3. toi	4. vous	5. nous	6. Stéphanie et Isabelle	7. Patrick et Jean-Paul	8. M. et Mme Dupont

Expressions pour la conversation

How to indicate the order in which actions take place:

d'abord	*first*	**D'abord,** nous avons invité nos copains à la boum.
après	*after, afterwards*	**Après,** tu as préparé des sandwichs.
ensuite	*then, after that*	**Ensuite,** Jacques a acheté des jus de fruit.
enfin	*at last*	**Enfin,** vous avez décoré le salon.
finalement	*finally*	**Finalement,** j'ai apporté mes cassettes.

7 **Dans quel ordre?**

Décrivez ce que les personnes suivantes ont fait dans l'ordre logique.

▶ nous (manger / préparer la salade / acheter des pizzas)
D'abord, nous avons acheté des pizzas.
Après, nous avons préparé la salade.
Ensuite, nous avons mangé.

1. Alice (travailler / trouver un job / acheter une moto)
2. les touristes canadiens (voyager en avion / visiter Paris / réserver les billets [*tickets*])
3. tu (assister au concert / acheter un billet / acheter le programme)
4. vous (danser / apporter des disques / inviter des copains)
5. nous (payer l'addition [*check*] / dîner / trouver un restaurant)

D'abord, la protection des ressources naturelles . . .

Ensuite, la jouissance des générations futures . . .

 Parcs Canada

Leçon 30 **311**

COMPREHENSION: narrating past events in logical sequence

7

■ **Teaching strategy:** Note that several logical sequences are sometimes possible.

■ **Realia note**
Like the United States, Canada has developed a park system (**Parcs Canada**) to protect natural resources for the enjoyment of future generations.

Section C

COMMUNICATIVE FUNCTION:
Talking about what did not happen in the past

30.1 **Introduction:**
Mercredi après-midi
30.2 **Dialogue: L'examen**
de maths
(7:06–8:51 min.)

DEODISC   Disc 5, Side 1
13047–16185

▭ꞏ▭ **Leçon 30, Section 6**

▪ **Teaching strategy:** Point out to students that if the English sentence contains *did not* or *didn't*, the equivalent French sentence will use the negative passé composé.

8   ROLE PLAY: talking about what one did not do

▪ **Teaching strategy:** Be sure that students are able to quickly produce the form: **je n'ai pas...**

▪ **Cultural note:** *Paris-Match* is a French magazine.

T312

C. Le passé composé: forme négative

Compare the affirmative and negative forms of the passé composé in the sentences below.

AFFIRMATIVE

Alice **a travaillé**.

NEGATIVE

Éric **n'a pas travaillé**.

*Éric **has not worked**.*
*Éric **did not work**.*

Nous **avons visité** Paris.

Nous **n'avons pas visité** Lyon.

*We **have not visited** Lyon.*
*We **did not visit** Lyon.*

In the negative, the passé composé follows the pattern:

> negative form of **avoir** + PAST PARTICIPLE

Note the negative forms of the passé composé of **travailler.**

PASSÉ COMPOSÉ (NEGATIVE)	PRESENT of **avoir** (NEGATIVE) + PAST PARTICIPLE	
Je **n'ai pas travaillé.**	je **n'ai pas**	
Tu **n'as pas travaillé.**	tu **n'as pas**	
Il/Elle/On **n'a pas travaillé.**	il/elle/on **n'a pas**	**travaillé**
Nous **n'avons pas travaillé.**	nous **n'avons pas**	
Vous **n'avez pas travaillé.**	vous **n'avez pas**	
Ils/Elles **n'ont pas travaillé.**	ils/elles **n'ont pas**	

8 **Oublis** *(Things forgotten)*

Éric a décidé de faire certaines choses, mais il a oublié *(forgot)*. Sabine demande s'il a fait les choses suivantes.

▶ nettoyer ta chambre?

1. réparer ta chaîne stéréo?
2. apporter tes livres?
3. étudier?
4. téléphoner à ta tante?
5. inviter tes copains?
6. acheter *Paris-Match*?
7. laver tes chemises?

Tu as nettoyé ta chambre?

Euh, non . . .
Je n'ai pas nettoyé
ma chambre.

9 Quel mauvais temps!

Le weekend, il a fait mauvais et les personnes suivantes sont restées *(stayed)* chez elles. Dites qu'elles n'ont pas fait les choses suivantes.

▶ nous / nager
Nous n'avons pas nagé.

1. vous / jouer au tennis
2. Philippe / rencontrer ses copains à la plage
3. Nathalie / dîner en ville
4. les voisins / travailler dans le jardin
5. Mlle Lacaze / laver sa voiture
6. mes copains / organiser un pique-nique
7. nous / assister au match de foot
8. toi / visiter le musée

LA MÉTÉO au Québec / dimanche / PLUIE

10 Une question d'argent

Les personnes suivantes n'ont pas beaucoup d'argent. Décrivez leur choix. Pour cela, dites ce qu'elles ont fait et ce qu'elles n'ont pas fait.

▶ nous / dîner au restaurant ou chez nous?
Nous avons dîné chez nous. Nous n'avons pas dîné au restaurant.

1. Philippe / acheter un tee-shirt ou une chemise?
2. vous / manger un steak ou un sandwich?
3. nous / assister au concert ou au match de foot?
4. les touristes / voyager en car ou en avion?
5. mes voisins / acheter une Mercedes ou une Ford?
6. Marc / passer dix jours ou trois semaines à Paris?

11 Impossibilités

Sans *(Without)* certaines choses il n'est pas possible de faire certaines activités. Expliquez cela logiquement en choisissant une personne de la Colonne A, un objet de la Colonne B et une activité de la Colonne C.

▶ **Je n'ai pas d'aspirateur. Je n'ai pas nettoyé le salon.**

A	B	C
je	une raquette	écouter les disques
vous	un billet *(ticket)*	voyager en Europe
nous	un passeport	nettoyer le salon
Frédéric	une chaîne stéréo	regarder la comédie
Éric et Olivier	une télé	assister au concert
Claire et Caroline	un aspirateur *(vacuum cleaner)*	jouer au tennis

TORNADO *Nettoie tout dans la maison.*

TORNADO
Aspirateur "Las'Air", variateur électronique linéaire, accessoires intégrés, dépression 3 000 mm, 1300 W*, 210 €

9 PRACTICE: describing what people didn't do

■ **Teaching note:** Be sure students use **pas de** in item 6.

■ **Realia note**
La météo (short for **météorologie**) is the French word for weather report.

10 COMPREHENSION: describing what did and did not happen

■ **Teaching note:** Be sure students use **pas de** in items 1, 2, and 5.

11 COMPREHENSION: drawing conclusions about what did not happen

■ **Teaching note:** Remind students to use **pas de** with the items in Column B.

■ **Variation** (game format): See how many logical sentences teams of students can construct within a given time limit.
See **Game: Samedi dernier** on p. T310.

■ **Realia note**
Comment s'appelle cet aspirateur? [Tornado]
Combien coûte-t-il? [deux cent dix (210) euros]

T313

■ **Teaching strategy:** Remind students that in French, unlike English, interrogative expressions cannot be separated. Compare:
Pour qui as-tu travaillé?
For <u>whom</u> did you work?
<u>Who(m)</u> did you work <u>for</u>?

■ **Expansion:** You may want to present inversion with **il/elle/on** for recognition.
A-t-il téléphoné?
A-t-elle téléphoné?
A-t-on téléphoné?

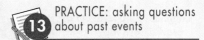

EXCHANGES: discussing
12 past activities
_____

■ **Teaching note:** Remind students to use **pas de** in items 3, 5, and 8.

■ **Variation:** Have students ask and answer the questions in the plural.
– **Est-ce que vous avez visité Paris?**
– **Oui, nous avons visité Paris. (Non, nous n'avons pas visité Paris.)**

PRACTICE: asking questions
13 about past events
_____

D. Les questions au passé composé

Compare the statements and questions in the passé composé.

STATEMENT	QUESTION	
Tu as travaillé.	Tu as travaillé?	*Did you work?*
	Est-ce que tu as travaillé?	
Philippe a voyagé cet été.	**Quand est-ce que** Philippe a voyagé?	*When did Philippe travel?*
	Où est-ce qu'il a voyagé?	*Where did he travel?*

For most verbs, questions in the passé composé are formed as follows:

> PRESENT of **avoir** (interrogative form) + PAST PARTICIPLE

	YES/NO QUESTIONS	INFORMATION QUESTIONS
WITH INTONATION	Tu as voyagé? Paul a téléphoné?	— —
WITH est-ce que	**Est-ce que** tu as voyagé? **Est-ce qu'**Alice a téléphoné?	**Avec qui est-ce que** tu as voyagé? **À qui est-ce qu'**Alice a téléphoné?

→ When the subject is a pronoun, questions in the passé composé can also be formed by inversion.
As-tu assisté au match de foot? *Did you go to the soccer game?*
Avec qui **avez-vous joué** au foot? *With whom did you play soccer?*
Who(m) did you play soccer with?

12 **Expériences personnelles**
Demandez à vos camarades s'ils ont déjà *(already)* fait les choses suivantes.

▶ visiter Paris?

Est-ce que tu as visité Paris?

Oui, j'ai visité Paris.

(Non, je n'ai pas visité Paris.)

1. visiter le Tibet?
2. voyager en Alaska?
3. piloter un avion?
4. dîner dans un restaurant vietnamien?
5. manger des escargots *(snails)*?
6. gagner à la loterie?
7. assister à un match de catch *(wrestling)*?
8. rencontrer un fantôme *(ghost)*?

13 **Curiosité**
Lisez ce que les personnes suivantes ont fait et posez des questions sur leurs activités.

▶ Paul a joué au tennis. (avec qui?)
Avec qui est-ce qu'il a joué au tennis?

1. Thomas a visité Québec. (quand?)
2. Corinne a téléphoné. (à quelle heure?)
3. Nathalie a voyagé en Italie. (comment?)
4. Marthe a acheté une robe. (où?)
5. Michèle a visité Genève. (avec qui?)
6. Philippe a trouvé un job. (où?)
7. Éric et Véronique ont dîné en ville. (dans quel restaurant?)
8. Les voisins ont téléphoné. (quand?)

314 Unité 8

Cooperative
pair practice
Activities 12, 14, 15

Casual French

Information questions using intonation may be formed by placing the interrogative expression in the same position in the sentence as the corresponding answer. Usually, but not always, this is at the end.

Paul a voyagé <u>avec qui</u>?
  Paul a voyagé <u>avec ses parents</u>.
Vous avez téléphoné <u>quand</u>?
  J'ai téléphoné à <u>cinq heures</u>.
Claire a amené <u>qui</u> à la boum?
  Elle a amené <u>Bruno</u> à la boum.

14 Jérôme et Valérie

Jérôme est très curieux. Il veut toujours savoir ce que Valérie a fait. Valérie répond à ses questions.

▶ où/ dîner? (dans un restaurant italien)
JÉRÔME: **Où est-ce que tu as dîné?**
VALÉRIE: **J'ai dîné dans un restaurant italien.**

1. avec qui / jouer au tennis? (avec Marc)
2. quand / assister au concert? (samedi après-midi)
3. qui / inviter au café? (ma copine Nathalie)
4. où / rencontrer Pierre? (dans la rue)
5. où / acheter ta veste? (au Bon Marché)
6. combien / payer ce disque? (10 euros)
7. à qui / téléphoner? (à ma grand-mère)
8. chez qui / passer le weekend? (chez une amie)

15 Conversation

Demandez à vos camarades ce qu'ils ont fait hier.

▶ à quelle heure/ dîner?

J'ai dîné à six heures.

Dis, Hélène, à quelle heure est-ce que tu as dîné?

1. avec qui / dîner?
2. à qui / téléphoner?
3. quel programme / regarder à la télé?
4. quel programme / écouter à la radio?
5. qui / rencontrer après les classes?
6. quand / étudier?

ROLE PLAY: asking and answering questions about **14** past events

■ **Variation** (with inversion): **Où as-tu dîné?**

EXCHANGES: talking about **15** yesterday

■ **Teaching strategy:** Encourage students to give only affirmative answers, since they have not yet learned the negative forms **ne...rien, ne...personne.** These forms will be introduced in Lesson 32.

Prononciation

Les lettres «ain» et «in»

ain /ɛ̃/   **aine** /ɛn/   **in** /ɛ̃/   **ine** /in/

sa main

semaine

magasin

magazine

When the letters "**ain**," "**aim**," "**in**," "**im**" are at the end of a word or are followed by a *consonant*, they represent the nasal vowel / ɛ̃ /.

REMEMBER: Do not pronounce an /n/ after the nasal vowel /ɛ̃/.

Répétez: /ɛ̃/ **demain faim train main voisin cousin jardin magasin maintenant intelligent intéressant important**

When the letters "**ain**," "**aim**," "**in(n)**," "**im**" are followed by a *vowel*, they do NOT represent a nasal sound.

Répétez: /ɛn/ **semaine américaine**
/ɛm/ **j'aime**

/in/ **voisine cousine cuisine magazine cinéma Corinne finir**
/im/ **timide dimanche Mimi centime**

Alain Minime a un rendez-vous important demain matin, avenue du Maine.

Prononciation

🔊 Leçon 30, Section 7

■ **Teaching strategy:** Before doing the **prononciation** section, have students practice minimal pairs containing /ɛ̃/, /ɛn/ and /ɛ̃/, /in/.

/ɛ̃/	/ɛn/
certain	**certaine**
américain	**américaine**
musicien	**musicienne**

/ɛ̃/	/in/
cousin	**cousine**
voisin	**voisine**
Martin	**Martine**

■ **Pronunciation:** Point out that **maintenant, intelligent,** etc. all end in the sound /ɛ̃/. Be sure students do not pronounce the final "n" or "t."

À votre tour!

1 Allô!

Reconstituez la conversation entre Alain et Christine. Pour cela, faites correspondre les réponses de Christine avec les questions d'Alain.

1. À quelle heure est-ce que tu as dîné hier soir?

2. Et après, tu as regardé la télé?

3. Qu'est-ce que tu as regardé après?

4. Qui a gagné?

5. Dis, tu as préparé la leçon pour demain?

a. Le match Marseille–Nice.

b. Nice. Par un score de trois à un.

c. Mais oui! J'ai étudié avant le dîner.

d. Oui, mais d'abord j'ai aidé ma mère.

e. À sept heures et demie.

2 Dis-moi . . .

I will tell you a few things that I did yesterday after school and a few things that I did not do, then you will tell me what you did and did not do.

• J'ai étudié.
• J'ai dîné avec mes parents.
• J'ai téléphoné à une copine.

• Je n'ai pas nettoyé ma chambre.
• Je n'ai pas rencontré mes copains.
• Je n'ai pas regardé la télé.

Et maintenant, dis-moi . . .

3 Créa-dialogue

Demandez à vos camarades s'ils ont fait les choses suivantes le weekend dernier. En cas de réponse affirmative, continuez la conversation.

▸ — Est-ce que tu as <u>dîné au restaurant</u>?
— Oui, j'ai <u>dîné au restaurant</u>.
— <u>Avec qui</u>?
— <u>Avec mes cousins</u>.
— <u>Où est-ce que vous avez dîné</u>?
— <u>Nous avons dîné Chez Tante Lucie</u>
(<u>à McDonald's</u>, etc.).

MENU
avec qui?
où?

1
avec qui?
quand?

2
quand?
où?

3
quand?
pourquoi?

4
quand?
où?

5
quand?
avec qui?

À votre tour

Depending on your goals and objectives, you may or may not want to assign all of the activities in the **À votre tour** section.

👥 Cooperative practice

In Act. 1 and 3, you may want to have students work cooperatively in trios, with two performing and one consulting the Answer Key and acting as monitor.

4 Situation

Avec un(e) camarade, composez un dialogue correspondant à la situation suivante. Jouez ce dialogue en classe.

You are spending a week in Paris with your best friend. Up to now you have been touring the city together, but today you both decided to go out on your own. At the end of the day, you both meet back at your hotel room. Discuss . . .

• what monuments you visited
• what things you bought
• whom you met
• what you ate at noon
• where you had dinner

5 Conversation libre *(free)*

Avec un(e) camarade analysez la situation suivante. Composez un dialogue original basé sur cette situation. Jouez le dialogue en classe.

Last weekend, you stayed home and your friend went into town. Now you are both trying to find out what the other one did. Ask each other questions, using the passé composé of **-er** verbs that you know. (Do not use **aller** or **rester,** since they have special passé composé forms that you have not learned yet.)

▶ — **Moi, j'ai nettoyé ma chambre. Et toi?**
— **J'ai assisté à un concert, mais d'abord j'ai dîné avec des copains.**

6 Composition: Vive les vacances!

Vacations are for fun, not for work. Write a brief composition in the passé composé about what you did on a recent vacation, describing . . .

• four things that you did   • four things that you did not do

You may want to use some of the verbs in the box. (Do not use **aller** or **rester.**)

jouer	inviter	nager	parler	travailler	voyager	visiter
téléphoner	rencontrer	acheter	trouver	dépenser	gagner	

Comment dit-on . . . ?

How to wish somebody a nice time:

Bon weekend! *(Have a nice weekend!)*

Bonnes vacances! *(Have a good vacation!)*

Bonne journée! *(Have a nice day!)*

Bon voyage! *(Have a good trip!)*

317

4 GUIDED ORAL EXPRESSION

■ **Challenge:**
Conversational role play
1. Your friend Corinne went shopping. She meets you at your favorite café, loaded down with packages. You want to know...
• what she bought
• where she bought each item
• how much she spent

2. Yesterday your French friend Sylvie went out for dinner. You phone Sylvie to find out...
• with whom she had dinner
• where they had dinner
• what they ate
• who paid
• if they spoke English or French

5 CONVERSATION

6 WRITTEN SELF-EXPRESSION

Supplementary vocabulary

Amuse-toi bien! *Have a good time*
Amusez-vous bien!

■ **Language note:** In Quebec, the traditional term for *weekend* is **fin de semaine: Bonne fin de semaine!** *(Have a nice weekend!)*

■ **Portfolio assessment**

You will probably select only one speaking activity and one writing activity to go into the students' portfolios for Unit 8.

In this lesson, Act. 6 offers an excellent writing portfolio topic. Act. 4 and 5 are good oral portfolio conversation topics.

At the challenge level, students might want to prepare one of the conversational role plays suggested to the right.

MODULE 31:
Pas de chance!
Total time: 5:10 min.
(Counter: 13:06 min

31.1 Dialogue: Pas de chance!
(13:20–14:43min.)

31.2 Mini-scenes: Listening — Qu'est-ce que vous avez fait?
(14:44–15:23 min.)

31.3 Mini-scenes: Speaking — Est-ce qu'ils ont perdu?
(15:24–16:33 min.)

31.4 Vignette culturelle: La télé
(16:34–18:04 min.)

 Disc 5, Side 1
23891–32863

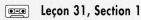

■ **Comprehension practice:** Play the entire module through as an introduction to the lesson.

Leçon 31, Section 1

■ **Challenge activity:** Have students consult a French-English dictionary and try to find out the meanings of the suspects' last names.
filou *(dishonest person, thief)*
la roulette *(roulette wheel)*
l'escroc *(crook)*
malin *(shrewd, cunning)*

LEÇON 31

L'alibi

l'inspecteur Lefl█

Êtes-vous bon (bonne) détective? <u>Pouvez</u>-vous trouver la solution du mystère <u>suivant</u>?

Samedi dernier à deux heures de l'après-midi, <u>il y a eu</u> une <u>panne d'électricité</u> dans la petite ville de Marcillac-le-Château. La panne <u>a duré</u> une heure. <u>Pendant</u> la panne, un <u>cambrioleur a pénétré</u> dans la Banque Populaire de Marcillac-le-Château. Bien sûr, l'alarme n'a pas fonctionné et c'est <u>seulement</u> lundi matin que le directeur de la banque <u>a remarqué</u> le <u>cambriolage</u>: un million d'euros.

Lundi après-midi, l'<u>inspecteur</u> Leflic a interrogé quatre suspects, mais <u>chacun</u> a un alibi.

Can
following

there was / p█
failure
lasted / Durin█
burglar / ent█
only
noticed / burg█
police detecti█
each one

Sophie Filou

Euh, ... excusez-moi, Monsieur l'Inspecteur.
Ma mémoire n'est pas très bonne.
<u>Voyons</u>, qu'est-ce que <u>j'ai fait</u> samedi après-midi?
Ah oui, <u>j'ai fini</u> un livre.
Le <u>titre</u> du livre? *Le crime ne paie pas!*

Let's see / di█
I finished
title

Marc Laroulette

Qu'est-ce que j'ai fait samedi?
J'<u>ai rendu visite</u> à mes copains.
Nous avons joué aux cartes.
C'est moi qui ai gagné!

visited

Patrick Lescrot

Voyons, samedi dernier ...
Ah oui ... J'ai invité des amis chez moi.
Nous avons regardé la télé.
Nous <u>avons vu</u> le match de foot France-<u>Allemagne</u>.
Quel match! <u>Malheureusement</u>, c'est la France qui <u>a perdu</u>!
Dommage!

saw / German█
Unfortunately

Pauline Malin

Ce n'est pas moi, Monsieur l'Inspecteur!
Samedi j'ai fait un pique-nique à la campagne avec une copine.
Nous <u>avons choisi</u> un <u>coin</u> près d'une rivière.
Ensuite, nous avons fait une promenade à vélo.
Nous <u>avons eu de la chance</u>!
<u>Il a fait un temps extraordinaire</u>!

chose / spot

were lucky
The weather █ great!

Lisez <u>attentivement</u> les quatre déclarations. À votre avis, qui est le cambrioleur ou la cambrioleuse? Pourquoi? (Vous pouvez comparer votre réponse avec la réponse de l'inspecteur à la page 325.)

carefully

 **Cooperative reading**

Since this is a longer story, you may want to use it as a recapitulation at the end of the lesson.

Divide the class into groups of three or four. Have each group read the story, without turning to p. 325 to see the solution.

The recorder (**secrétaire**) of each group writes down the solution: who is the guilty one and why. **Qui est le coupable et pourquoi?**

After all the recorders have given their reports to the class, the students may read the solution in the text.

Compréhension

Certains événements ont eu lieu *(took place)* samedi dernier. Indiquez si oui ou non les événements suivants ont eu lieu.

1. Le directeur de la banque a vu *(saw)* le cambrioleur.
2. Un cambriolage a eu lieu *(took place)* à Marcillac-le-Château.
3. L'inspecteur Leflic a arrêté *(arrested)* quatre personnes.
4. Sophie Filou a vu le film *Le crime ne paie pas* à la télé.
5. Marc Laroulette a perdu un million d'euros.
6. L'Allemagne a gagné un match de foot.
7. Pauline Malin a fait une promenade à vélo à la campagne.
8. Il a fait beau.

Et toi?

Dis si oui ou non tu as fait les choses suivantes le weekend dernier.

1. (J'ai / Je n'ai pas) ... rendu visite à mes copains.
2. (J'ai / Je n'ai pas) ... vu un match de foot à la télé.
3. (J'ai / Je n'ai pas) ... fini un livre.
4. (J'ai / Je n'ai pas) ... fait une promenade à vélo.
5. (J'ai / Je n'ai pas) ... fait un pique-nique.

■ NOTE ■ CULTURELLE

Les jeunes Français et la télé

Combien d'heures par° jour est-ce que tu regardes la télé? Une heure? deux heures? trois heures? plus? moins? En général, les jeunes Français regardent la télé moins souvent et moins longtemps° que les jeunes Américains: en moyenne° 1 heure 15 les jours d'école et 2 heures 15 les autres° jours (mercredi, samedi et dimanche). Dans beaucoup de familles, les parents contrôlent l'usage° de la télé. Souvent ils exigent° que leurs enfants finissent leurs devoirs avant de regarder la télé. Ainsi,° beaucoup de jeunes regardent la télé seulement° après le dîner.

Quels sont leurs programmes favoris? Les jeunes Français aiment surtout° les films, les programmes de sport, les variétés et les jeux télévisés,° comme «La roue° de la fortune» et «Le prix est juste».° Les séries américaines (comme «Les Simpson» et «Chicago Hope») sont aussi très populaires.

par *per* **moins longtemps** *for a shorter time* **en moyenne** *on an average of* **autres** *other* **usage** *use* **exigent** *insist* **Ainsi** *Thus* **seulement** *only* **surtout** *especially* **jeux télévisés** *TV games* **roue** *wheel* **juste** *right*

Leçon 31 **319**

Setting the scene

Video Module 31 opens with **Pas de chance** *(out of luck)*, a humorous series of dialogues. Philippe has had a bad day, and in these conversations he explains what happened.

The *Vignette culturelle* focuses on French television and expands on the cultural note in the student text.

Leçon 31, Section 2

■ **Pronunciation:** Be sure students maintain the sound /vwa/ in all forms of the verb, especially in:
nous voyons /vwajɔ̃/
vous voyez /vwaje/

PRACTICE: seeing sights in Paris

■ **Teaching strategy:** Tell students that **voir** is another "boot" verb.

je vois	nous voyons
tu vois	vous voyez
il voit	ils voient

COMMUNICATION: answering personal questions

A. Le verbe *voir*

The verb **voir** *(to see)* is irregular. Note the forms of **voir** in the present tense.

INFINITIVE	**voir**	
PRESENT	Je **vois** Marc. Tu **vois** ton copain. Il/Elle/On **voit** un accident.	Nous **voyons** un film. Vous **voyez** un match de baseball. Ils/Elles **voient** le professeur.

1 Weekend à Paris

Les personnes suivantes passent le weekend à Paris. Décrivez ce que chacun voit.

▶ Olivier   **Olivier voit Notre-Dame.**

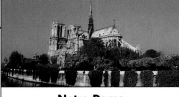
▶ **Notre-Dame**

1. le musée d'Orsay

2. l'Arc de Triomphe

3. le Centre Pompidou

4. le Quartier latin

5. la pyramide du Louvre

6. le musée Picasso

1. nous	3. moi	5. vous
2. toi	4. Sophie	6. les touristes japonais

2 Questions personnelles

1. Est-ce que tu vois bien? Est-ce que tu portes des lunettes?
2. Est-ce que tu vois tes amis pendant les vacances? Est-ce que tu vois tes professeurs?
3. Est-ce que tu vois souvent tes cousins? Est-ce que tu vois tes cousins pendant les vacances? à Noël?
4. Qu'est-ce que tu préfères voir à la télé? un match de football ou un match de baseball?
5. Quand tu vas au cinéma, quels films aimes-tu voir? les comédies? les films d'aventures? les films policiers *(detective movies)*?

B. Le passé composé des verbes réguliers en *-ir* et *-re*

Note the passé composé of the verbs below, paying special attention to the ending of the past participle.

choisir	J'**ai choisi** ce disque.	Je **n'ai pas choisi** cette cassette.
finir	Nous **avons fini** le magazine.	Nous **n'avons pas fini** le livre.
vendre	Tu **as vendu** ton vélo.	Tu **n'as pas vendu** ta moto.
attendre	Jacques **a attendu** Paul.	Il **n'a pas attendu** François.
répondre	J'**ai répondu** au professeur.	Tu **n'as pas répondu** à la question.

The past participle of regular **-ir** and **-re** verbs is formed as follows:

-ir → -i	-re → -u
chois|ir| → chois|i|	vend|re| → vend|u|
fin|ir| → fin|i|	attend|re| → attend|u|

3 **Besoins d'argent** *(Money needs)*

Parce qu'elles ont besoin d'argent, les personnes suivantes ont vendu certains objets. Dites ce que chaque personne a vendu.

▶ Philippe/sa guitare
Philippe a vendu sa guitare.

1. M. Roche/sa voiture
2. mes copains/leur chaîne stéréo
3. moi/mon appareil-photo
4. toi/ton vélo
5. les voisins/leur piano
6. nous/nos livres
7. vous/votre ordinateur
8. François et Victor/leurs disques

4 **Bravo!**

Les personnes suivantes méritent *(deserve)* des félicitations *(congratulations)*. Expliquez pourquoi.

▶ les élèves/réussir à l'examen
Les élèves ont réussi à l'examen.

1. M. Bedon/maigrir
2. Mlle Legros/perdre dix kilos
3. Florence/gagner le match de tennis
4. ces enfants/finir leur soupe
5. nous/choisir une classe difficile
6. toi/finir les exercices
7. Marc/rendre visite à un copain à l'hôpital
8. vous/attendre vos copains
9. les élèves/répondre en français

À vendre
INSTRUMENTS DE MUSIQUE

Section B

COMMUNICATIVE FUNCTION:
Talking about the past

■ **Teaching strategy:** Point out that like **-er** verbs, most **-ir** and **-re** verbs form the passé composé with **avoir**. Note the endings of the past participle.

 PRACTICE: describing what people sold

■ **Variation** (in the negative):
Philippe n'a pas vendu sa guitare.

 PRACTICE: describing people's accomplishments

■ **Variation** (in the negative):
Les élèves n'ont pas réussi à l'examen.

■ **Realia note**
à vendre *for sale*

T321

5 Non!

Jean-Louis répond négativement aux questions de Béatrice. Jouez les deux rôles.

▶ gagner le match / perdre

Tu as gagné le match?

Non! J'ai perdu.

1. étudier ce weekend / rendre visite à un copain
2. acheter une cassette / choisir un compact
3. finir ce livre / regarder la télé
4. vendre ta guitare / vendre mon appareil-photo
5. téléphoner à Marc / rendre visite à son cousin
6. maigrir / grossir
7. répondre à la lettre / téléphoner

6 Aujourd'hui et hier

Dites ce que les personnes suivantes font aujourd'hui et ce qu'elles ont fait hier.

▶ Paul / acheter un blouson / un pantalon
Aujourd'hui, Paul achète un blouson.
Hier, il a acheté un pantalon.

1. moi / téléphoner à mon cousin / à mes copains
2. toi / finir ce livre / ce magazine
3. nous / manger des sandwichs / une pizza
4. Mélanie / choisir une jupe / un chemisier
5. les élèves / réussir à l'examen de français / à l'examen d'anglais
6. Philippe / vendre sa chaîne stéréo / ses disques
7. Philippe et Jean-Pierre / rendre visite à leurs cousins / à leur grand-mère
8. les touristes / attendre le train / le car

7 Excuses

Quand Olivier ne fait pas une chose, il a toujours une excuse. Jouez le dialogue entre Olivier et sa soeur Caroline.

▶ étudier / perdre mon livre

Tu as étudié?

Pourquoi est-ce que tu n'as pas étudié?

Non, je n'ai pas étudié.

Parce que j'ai perdu mon livre.

1. jouer au tennis / perdre ma raquette
2. acheter une veste / choisir un blouson
3. finir le livre / regarder la télé
4. rendre visite à Marc / étudier
5. réussir à l'examen / perdre mes notes
6. écouter tes disques / vendre ma chaîne stéréo

Classroom Notes

Cooperative pair practice
Activities 5, 7, 8, 9

TPR Past and present

Teach students gestures for present and past.
Montrez-moi le présent. [index finger pointing to floor]
Montrez-moi le passé. [thumb pointing back over shoulder]
Now read sentences aloud containing the present or the passé composé and have students identify the tense by using the appropriate gesture.
Est-ce que c'est le présent ou le passé?
• **Tu finis la leçon de natation.** [P]
• **J'ai fini la leçon de ski nautique.** [PC]
• **Paul a eu un accident de ski.** [PC]

C. Le passé composé des verbes *être*, *avoir*, *faire*, *mettre* et *voir*

The verbs **être**, **avoir**, **faire**, **mettre**, and **voir** have irregular past participles.

être	→	été	Nous **avons été** à Paris.
avoir	→	eu	M. Lambert **a eu** un accident.
faire	→	fait	Qu'est-ce que tu **as fait** hier?
mettre	→	mis	Nous **avons mis** des jeans.
voir	→	vu	J'**ai vu** un bon film.

"On n'a jamais fait quelque chose d'aussi appétissant avec des petits pois."

MONOPRIX UNIPRIX

➡ In the passé composé, the verb **être** has two different meanings:

Mme Lebrun **a été** malade.   *Mme Lebrun **has been** sick.*
Elle **a été** à l'hôpital.   *She **was** in the hospital.*

8 Dialogue

Demandez à vos camarades s'ils ont fait les choses suivantes récemment *(recently)*.

▶ faire une promenade?
—Est-ce que tu as fait une promenade récemment?
—Oui, j'ai fait une promenade. (Non, je n'ai pas fait de promenade.)

1. faire un pique-nique?
2. faire une promenade en voiture?
3. être malade *(sick)*?
4. avoir la grippe *(flu)*?
5. avoir une dispute *(fight)* avec ton copain?
6. avoir une bonne surprise?
7. avoir un «A» en français?
8. voir un film?
9. voir tes cousins?
10. mettre des affiches dans ta chambre?

9 Pourquoi?

Avec vos camarades de classe, parlez des personnes suivantes.

▶ Éric est content.
(avoir un «A» à l'examen)

Éric est content.

Il a eu un «A» à l'examen.

Ah, bon? Pourquoi?

1. Mes copains sont furieux.
(avoir un «F» à l'examen)
2. Pauline est très contente. (voir son copain)
3. Mon père n'est pas content. (avoir une dispute avec son chef [*boss*])
4. Philippe est pâle. (voir un accident)
5. Juliette est fatiguée *(tired)*. (faire du jogging)
6. Alice et Laure sont bronzées *(tanned)*. (être à la mer)
7. Mon frère est fatigué. (faire des exercices de gymnastique)
8. Patrick et Marc sont contents. (voir un bon film)
9. Isabelle est très élégante. (mettre une jolie robe)

Leçon 31   **323**

Section C

COMMUNICATIVE FUNCTION:
Talking about the past

 31.2 Mini-scenes:
Qu'est-ce que vous avez fait?
31.3 Mini-scenes:
Est-ce qu'ils ont perdu?
(14:44–16:33 min.)

VIDEODISC   Disc 5, Side 1
26834–30092

 Leçon 31, Sections 3, 4

■ **Language note:** Point out that the passé composé of most irregular verbs is formed with **avoir**.

■ **Pronunciation:** Be sure students pronounce the past participle **eu** /y/, as in **tu**.

8 COMMUNICATION: asking about past activities

■ **Pronunciation:**
récemment /resamã/

■ **Teaching note:** Remind students to use **pas de** in items 1, 2, 5, 6, 7, and 8 if they choose to answer in the negative.

9 EXCHANGES: explaining people's looks and moods

■ **Cultural note:** The French grading system is often based on a scale of **10** for primary school and **20** for **collège** or **lycée**.
Ex: **Il a eu une très bonne note–il a eu 18/20.**

- **Nous sommes à la mer.** [P]
- **Sophie fait de l'alpinisme.** [P]
- **Marc a fait de la planche à voile.** [PC]
- **Vous avez acheté un vélo.** [PC]
- **J'ai grossi cet été.** [PC]
- **Nous passons les vacances à la mer.** [P]
- **Mes cousins ont vu un match de tennis.** [PC]
- **Stéphanie met son maillot de bain.** [P]

COMPREHENSION: describing what people did and did not do

■ **Realia note**
Villages vacances
Most French employees get at least five weeks of paid vacation. One popular option is to go to a "vacation village" (**un village vacances**).
In this ad, the Viva group announces that they have a network (**un réseau**) of such "villages" and that, in addition to room and board, they offer sports instruction and numerous social events (**les villages sont "animés"**).

Supplementary vocabulary

cette année   *this year*
l'année dernière
l'année prochaine
en deux mille un
en deux mille dix
etc.

 COMMUNICATION: finding out when past events took place

---

10 Vive les vacances!

Dites où les personnes suivantes ont été pendant les vacances. Dites aussi si oui ou non elles ont fait les choses entre parenthèses. Soyez logique *(Be logical)*.

▶ Christophe: à la piscine (étudier / nager)
Christophe a été à la piscine. Il n'a pas étudié. Il a nagé.

1. Sylvie: à la montagne (nager / faire de l'alpinisme)
2. nous: à la campagne (visiter des monuments / faire du camping)
3. vous: à Paris (parler italien / voir la tour Eiffel)
4. moi: à la mer (faire de la planche à voile / travailler)
5. mes parents: en Égypte (voir les pyramides / visiter Paris)
6. vous: dans un club de sport (faire de la gymnastique / grossir)
7. Christine: à la plage (mettre des lunettes de soleil / jouer au tennis)

VIVE LES VACANCES
viva
RÉSEAU DE VILLAGES
VACANCES ANIMÉS

Vocabulaire: *Quand?*

		maintenant	avant	après
	le jour	**aujourd'hui**	**hier**	**demain**
	le matin	**ce matin**	**hier matin**	**demain matin**
	l'après-midi	**cet après-midi**	**hier après-midi**	**demain après-midi**
	le soir	**ce soir**	**hier soir**	**demain soir**
	le jour	**samedi**	**samedi dernier** *(last)*	**samedi prochain** *(next)*
	le weekend	**ce weekend**	**le weekend dernier**	**le weekend prochain**
	la semaine	**cette semaine**	**la semaine dernière**	**la semaine prochaine**
	le mois	**ce mois-ci**	**le mois dernier**	**le mois prochain**

---

11 Quand?

Demandez à vos camarades quand ils ont fait les choses suivantes. Ils vont répondre en utilisant une expression du **Vocabulaire.**

▶ faire tes devoirs?

1. faire des achats?
2. nettoyer ta chambre?
3. rencontrer tes voisins?
4. voir ton copain?
5. voir un film?
6. avoir un examen?
7. faire une promenade à pied?
8. être en ville?
9. mettre *(set)* la table?

Quand est-ce que tu as fait tes devoirs?

J'ai fait mes devoirs hier après-midi.

(vendredi soir, le weekend dernier, . . .)

 Cooperative pair practice
Activity 11

 Game: Moi aussi
For homework, have students write out their answers to Act. 12.

In class, students share their responses with one another. The object of the game is to find ten classmates who wrote the same answers.

One student reads the first statement, without showing the text to his/her partner.

The partner then reads his/her first statement.

X: Ce matin, j'ai regardé la télé. Et toi?
Y: Moi aussi. Ce matin, j'ai regardé la télé.

12 Le passé et le futur

Décrivez ce que vous avez fait (phrases 1 à 5) et ce que vous allez faire (phrases 6 à 10). Dites la vérité ... ou utilisez votre imagination!

1. Ce matin, j'ai ... ✓
2. Hier matin, j'ai ... ✓
3. Samedi après-midi, j'ai ... ✓
4. La semaine dernière, j'ai ... ✓
5. Le mois dernier, j'ai ... ✓

6. Ce soir, je vais ... _____
7. Demain soir, je vais ... _____
8. Vendredi soir, je vais ... _____
9. Le weekend prochain, je vais ... _____
10. La semaine prochaine, je vais ... _____

13 Questions personnelles

1. En général, est-ce que tu étudies avant ou après le dîner?
2. En général, est-ce que tu regardes la télé avant ou après le dîner?
3. À quelle heure est-ce que tu as dîné hier soir?
4. Quel programme de télé est-ce que tu as regardé hier après-midi?
5. Qu'est-ce que tu vas faire le weekend prochain?
6. Où vas-tu aller le weekend prochain?

COMMUNICATION:
describing past events and future plans **12**

COMMUNICATION:
answering personal questions **13**

Prononciation

 Leçon 31, Section 6

Prononciation

Les lettres «gn»

gn /ɲ/

The letters "**gn**" represent a sound similar to the "**ny**" in *canyon*. First, practice with words you know.

Répétez: **espagnol   gagner   mignon
la montagne   la campagne
un magnétophone**

Now try saying some new words. Make them sound French!

Répétez: **Champagne   Espagne** *(Spain)* **un signe
la vigne** *(vineyard)* **la ligne** *(line)* **un signal
la dignité   ignorer   magnétique   magnifique   Agnès**

Agnès Mignard a gagné son match. C'est magnifique!

espagnol

(L'alibi, p. 318)

La réponse de l'inspecteur:

C'est Patrick Lescrot le cambrioleur. Samedi après-midi, il y a eu une panne d'électricité. Patrick Lescrot n'a pas pu *(was not able to)* regarder la télé. Son alibi n'est pas valable *(valid)*.

Leçon 31 **325**

The answers match, so each one writes the other's name next to #1. Then they both read their responses to the next item.

Often the answers will not be the same:

X: Hier matin, j'ai étudié. Et toi?
Y: Hier matin, j'ai joué au tennis.

Here the answers do not match, so they continue with #3. If time remains when they have shared the ten responses with one another, they may talk to another partner to try to find the missing matches.

At the end of the time limit, the student who has found the most matches wins.

À votre tour!

1 COMPREHENSION

1-b   4-c
2-d   5-e
3-a

📟 Leçon 31, Section 7

1 Allô!

Reconstituez la conversation entre Robert et Julien. Pour cela, faites correspondre les réponses de Julien avec les questions de Robert.

1. Tu as fini tes devoirs de français?
2. Qu'est-ce que tu as fait alors?
3. Tu as gagné?
4. Mais d'habitude *(usually)* tu joues bien?
5. Peut-être que Caroline a joué mieux *(better)* que toi?

a. Non, j'ai perdu!
b. Non, je n'ai pas étudié cet après-midi.
c. C'est vrai, mais aujourd'hui, je n'ai pas eu de chance . . .
d. J'ai joué au tennis avec Caroline.
e. Tu as raison. Elle a joué comme une championne.

2 GUIDED ORAL EXPRESSION

2 Dis-moi . . .

I will tell you about some nice things that happened to me recently; then you will tell me about three nice things that happened to you.

- J'ai réussi à mon examen d'anglais. (J'ai eu un «A».)
- J'ai eu un rendez-vous avec une personne très intéressante.
- J'ai vu un très bon film.

Et maintenant, dis-moi . . .

3 GUIDED ORAL EXPRESSION

📟 Leçon 31, Section 8

■ **Realia note**
Le tennis
The French not only love to play tennis, they are avid tennis fans. It was a national event when France won the Davis Cup in 1991.
Roland Garros is the tennis stadium near Paris which hosts the annual French Open (**Les Internationaux de France**). The stadium was named in memory of Roland Garros (1888–1918), a World War I fighter pilot and the first aviator to cross the Mediterranean (1913).

3 Créa-dialogue

Avec vos camarades, discutez de ce que vous avez fait récemment *(recently)*. Vous pouvez utiliser les expressions et les activités suggérées. Continuez la conversation avec des questions supplémentaires.

Quand?

dimanche après-midi	lundi dernier
hier soir	la semaine dernière
samedi soir	le mois dernier
le weekend dernier	

Quoi?

jouer au tennis	dîner au restaurant
faire des achats	voir un film
faire une promenade à la campagne	avoir un rendez-vous
voir mes cousins	rendre visite à un copain

▶ —Qu'est-ce que tu as fait <u>dimanche après-midi</u>?
—J'ai <u>joué au tennis</u> avec ma soeur.
—Est-ce que tu as gagné?
—Non, j'ai perdu.
—Dommage!

À votre tour

Depending on your goals and objectives, you may or may not wish to assign all of the activities in the **À votre tour** section.

👥 Cooperative practice

In Act. 1 and 3, you may want to have students work cooperatively in trios, with two performing and one consulting the Answer Key and acting as monitor.

4 Situation

Avec un(e) camarade, composez un dialogue original correspondant à la situation suivante. Jouez ce dialogue en classe.

Your friend Michèle (played by a classmate) went to Canada for spring vacation.

Ask Michèle . . .
- how she traveled (by plane? by car?)
- if she visited Montreal
- whom she visited **(rendre visite à)**
- if she saw Quebec City **(Québec)**
- if she went skiing and with whom
- if she went shopping and what she bought

5 Conversation libre

Avec un(e) camarade, composez un dialogue basé sur la situation suivante. Jouez ce dialogue en classe.

Philippe spent spring vacation in Nice, on the French Riviera **(la Côte d'Azur).** Juliette spent her vacation in a small village high in the Alps **(les Alpes).** They meet and compare what they did. (In your dialogue, try to use several expressions with **faire.**)

▶ PHILIPPE: J'ai été à Nice. J'ai fait de la voile.
  JULIETTE: Moi, j'ai été dans les Alpes. J'ai fait du ski.

4 GUIDED ORAL EXPRESSION

■ **Challenge activity**
Have students prepare an original dialogue on this model where they talk about a real or imaginary trip to a destination of their choice.

5 CONVERSATION

6 WRITTEN SELF-EXPRESSION

6 Composition: Quand?

Describe two things that you or people you know have done at each of the times indicated below:

La semaine dernière,... | *Le mois dernier,...* | *L'an dernier (Last year),...*

▶ La semaine dernière, mon père a vendu sa voiture.
  La semaine dernière, mes cousins ont acheté une moto.

Comment dit-on . . . ?

How to wish someone good luck or give encouragement:

Bonne chance!

Bon courage!

Leçon 31 **327**

Classroom Notes

Portfolio assessment

You will probably select only one speaking activity and one writing activity to go into the students' portfolios for Unit 8.

In this lesson, Act. 4 and 5 lend themselves well to oral portfolio recordings.

MODULE 32:
Samedi / Weekend
Total Time: 6:36 min.
(Counter: 18:15 min.)

32.1 Dialogue: Un bon weekend (18:22–20:00 min.)

32.2 Mini-scenes: Listening — Où êtes-vous allé? Et qu'est-ce que vous avez fait? (20:01–21:48 min.)

32.3 Mini-scenes: Speaking — Où est-ce qu'ils sont allés? (21:49–23:00 min.)

32.4 Vignette culturelle: La musique (23:01–24:47 min.)

VIDEODISC Disc 5, Side 1
33175–44985

■ **Comprehension practice:** Play the entire module through as an introduction to the lesson.

Leçon 32, Section 1

■ **Photo culture note**
Le métro
Valérie and Anne are standing in front of an entrance to the Paris subway (**le métro**, or **métropolitain** as it was originally called). The architecture is typical of the **Art Nouveau** style.

LEÇON 32

Qui a de la chance?

Vendredi après-midi

Anne et Valérie parlent de leurs projets pour le weekend.

ANNE: Qu'est-ce que tu vas faire samedi soir?
VALÉRIE: Je vais aller au cinéma avec Jean-Pierre.
ANNE: Tu as de la chance! Moi, je dois rester à la maison.
VALÉRIE: Mais pourquoi?
ANNE: Les amis de mes parents viennent chez nous ce weekend. Mon père insiste <u>pour que</u> je reste pour le dîner. <u>Quelle barbe!</u>   *that / What a pain!*
VALÉRIE: C'est vrai! Tu n'as pas de chance!

Lundi matin

Anne et Valérie parlent de leur weekend.

ANNE: Alors, tu as passé un bon weekend?
VALÉRIE: Euh non, pas très bon.
ANNE: Mais tu <u>es sortie</u> avec Jean-Pierre!   *went out*
VALÉRIE: C'est vrai. Je <u>suis allée</u> au cinéma avec lui . . .   *went*
Nous avons vu un très, très mauvais film! Après le film, j'ai eu une <u>dispute</u> avec Jean-Pierre. Et, <u>en plus</u>, j'ai perdu mon <u>porte-monnaie</u> . . . et je <u>suis rentrée</u> chez moi à pied! Et toi, tu <u>es restée</u> chez toi?   *quarrel / in addition / wallet / went back / stayed*
ANNE: Non.
VALÉRIE: Comment? Les amis de tes parents <u>ne sont pas venus</u>?   *didn't come*
ANNE: Si, si, ils sont venus . . . avec leur fils!
VALÉRIE: Et alors?
ANNE: Eh bien, c'est un garçon très <u>sympa</u> et très amusant . . .   *sympa = sympathique*
Après le dîner, nous <u>sommes allés</u> au Zénith.* Nous avons assisté à un concert de rock absolument extraordinaire. Après, nous sommes allés dans un café et nous avons fait des projets pour le weekend prochain.   *went*
VALÉRIE: Qu'est-ce que vous allez faire?
ANNE: Nous allons faire une promenade à la campagne dans la nouvelle voiture de sport de Thomas. (C'est le nom de mon nouveau copain!)
VALÉRIE: Toi, vraiment, tu as de la chance!

* Une salle *(hall)* de concert à Paris, parc de la Villette.

328   **Unité 8**

👥 Cooperative reading

Since this is a longer story, you may want to use it as a recapitulation at the end of the lesson.

Have students read the title. Then, in pairs, have them read the story and write out brief answers to the following questions:

Qui a de la chance? Pourquoi?
Qui n'a pas de chance? Pourquoi?

Compréhension

1. Qu'est-ce que Valérie va faire samedi soir?
2. Pourquoi est-ce qu'Anne doit *(must)* rester à la maison?
3. Est-ce que Valérie a aimé le film?
4. Qu'est-ce qu'elle a perdu?
5. Comment est-ce qu'elle est rentrée chez elle?
6. Où et avec qui est-ce qu'Anne a dîné?
7. Où est-ce qu'elle est allée après le dîner?
8. Qu'est-ce qu'elle va faire le weekend prochain?
9. Comment s'appelle son nouveau copain?

Et toi?

Dis si oui ou non tu as fait les choses suivantes samedi dernier.

1. (Je suis / Je ne suis pas) ... allé(e) en ville.
2. (Je suis / Je ne suis pas) ... allé(e) au cinéma.
3. (Je suis / Je ne suis pas) ... allé(e) à un concert.
4. (Je suis / Je ne suis pas) ... rentré(e) chez moi pour le dîner.
5. (Je suis / Je ne suis pas) ... resté(e) chez moi le soir.

■ NOTE ■ CULTURELLE

Les jeunes Français et la musique

«Pour moi, la musique c'est tout!»° déclare Anne, une jeune Française de quinze ans. Sa copine Hélène est d'accord:° «Aujourd'hui, on ne peut pas° vivre° sans° musique.»

Comme les jeunes Américains, les jeunes Français sont des «fanas»° de musique. Quel type de musique est-ce qu'ils préfèrent? D'abord le rock. Ils aiment aussi la chanson° française et la chanson étrangère,° la musique classique, la musique folk et le jazz.

Les jeunes Français ont l'équipement nécessaire pour écouter leur musique favorite: 70% ont une radio, 58% une chaîne stéréo, 42% un lecteur CD et 39% un walkman. Dans les grandes villes, les jeunes vont au concert. A Paris, ils vont à Bercy ou au Zénith écouter les grandes vedettes° de la chanson française et de la musique anglaise et américaine.

Les jeunes Français ne se contentent pas° d'écouter la musique. Beaucoup jouent d'un instrument. Ils jouent du piano, de la flûte, de la guitare et du synthétiseur° . . . Et toi, est-ce que tu peux vivre sans musique? Est-ce que tu joues d'un instrument? De quel instrument joues-tu?

tout *everything* **est d'accord** *agrees* **ne peut pas** *cannot*
vivre *live* **sans** *without* **fanas** = *fanatiques*
chanson *song* **étrangère** *foreign* **vedettes** *stars*
ne se contentent pas *do not limit themselves*
synthétiseur *keyboard*

PARIS BERCY

Leçon 32 **329**

COMPREHENSION

1. Elle va aller au cinéma avec Jean-Pierre.
2. Des amis de ses parents viennent chez eux.
3. non
4. son porte-monnaie
5. à pied
6. à la maison avec ses parents
7. au Zénith (à un concert de rock) et dans un café
8. Elle va faire une promenade à la campagne.
9. Thomas.

COMMUNICATION: describing what one did last weekend

Note culturelle

32.4 Vignette culturelle: La musique (23:01–24:47 min.)

VIDEODISC Disc 5, Side 1 41719–44985

Leçon 32, Section 5

■ **Realia note**
Bercy is a large modern sports complex at the edge of Paris along the Seine. It is also used for rock concerts and other large-scale events.

Setting the scene

The opening scene of Video Module 32 presents two girls who are at a café talking about where they went last Saturday. At the end, the conversation takes an unexpected twist.

The *Vignette culturelle* of the video expands on the culture note in the text. French young people are interviewed about their tastes in music.

32.2 Mini-scenes:
  Où êtes-vous allé?
  Et qu'est-ce que
  vous avez fait?
32.3 Où est-ce qu'ils
  sont allés?
  (20:01–23:00 min.)

VIDEODISC Disc 5, Side 1
36285–41700

Leçon 32, Sections 2, 3

Pronunciation: In spoken French, the four forms of **allé** sound the same.

Classroom Notes

A. Le passé composé avec *être*

Note the forms of the passé composé of **aller** in the sentences below, paying attention to the endings of the past participle **(allé).**

Jean-Paul **est allé** au cinéma.	*Jean-Paul went to the movies.*
Mélanie **est allée** à la plage.	*Mélanie went to the beach.*
Éric et Patrick **sont allés** en ville.	*Éric and Patrick went downtown.*
Mes copines **sont allées** à la campagne.	*My friends went to the country.*

The passé composé of **aller** and certain verbs of motion is formed with **être** according to the pattern:

> PRESENT **of être** + PAST PARTICIPLE

➡ When the passé composé of a verb is conjugated with **être** (and not with **avoir**), the PAST PARTICIPLE *agrees* with the SUBJECT in gender and number.

INFINITIVE	aller	
PASSÉ COMPOSÉ	je **suis allé** tu **es allé** il **est allé** nous **sommes allé**s vous **êtes allé**s ils **sont allé**s	je **suis allé**e tu **es allé**e elle **est allé**e nous **sommes allé**es vous **êtes allé**es elles **sont allé**es
NEGATIVE	je **ne suis pas allé**	je **ne suis pas allé**e
INTERROGATIVE	est-ce que tu **es allé**? tu **es allé**? (**es**-tu **allé?**)	est-ce que tu **es allé**e? tu **es allé**e? (**es**-tu **allé**e**?**)

➡ When **vous** refers to a single person, the past participle is in the singular:
  Mme Mercier, est-ce que vous êtes **allée** au concert hier soir?

☀ Warm-up and review

As a preparation for the passé composé of **aller,** have students review the forms of **être,** together with the expression **chez.**

You will indicate what people are doing, and the students will let you know whether those people are at home or not.

Paul joue au foot. [Il n'est pas chez lui.]
Je regarde la télé. [Je suis chez moi.]
Nous étudions. [Nous sommes chez nous.]
Mes copains dînent. [Ils sont chez eux.]
Tu fais de la voile. [Tu n'es pas chez toi.]

1 À Paris

Des amis sont allés à Paris samedi dernier. Chacun est allé à un endroit différent. Dites qui est allé aux endroits suivants. Complétez chaque phrase avec le sujet approprié et la forme correspondante du verbe **aller.**

Olivier   Claire   Éric et Jacques   Anne et Monique

▶ <u>Anne et Monique</u> sont allées au Louvre.

1. ... allée à la tour Eiffel.
2. ... allé au Centre Pompidou.
3. ... allés à l'Opéra.
4. ... allées aux Galeries Lafayette.
5. ... allé à la Villette.
6. ... allés au Zénith.
7. ... allé au musée d'Orsay.
8. ... allées au Quartier latin.

Musée
d'Orsay
petit
guide

2 Conversation

Demandez à vos camarades s'ils sont allés aux endroits suivants.

▶ ce matin / à la bibliothèque?

Ce matin, est-ce que tu es allé à la bibliothèque?

Oui, je suis allé à la bibliothèque.

(Non, je ne suis pas allé à la bibliothèque.)

1. hier matin/à l'école?
2. hier soir/au cinéma?
3. dimanche dernier/au restaurant?
4. samedi dernier/dans les magasins?
5. l'été dernier/chez tes cousins?
6. le weekend dernier/à la campagne?
7. le mois dernier/à un concert?
8. la semaine dernière/chez le coiffeur *(barber, hairdresser)*?
9. les vacances dernières/à la mer?

3 Le weekend dernier

Dites ce que les personnes de la Colonne A ont fait en choisissant une activité de la Colonne B. Puis dites où ces personnes sont allées en choisissant un endroit de la Colonne C. Soyez logiques!

A	B	C
je	voir des clowns	à la campagne
tu	nager	au zoo
nous	dîner en ville	dans un magasin de chaussures
Catherine	regarder les éléphants	à la bibliothèque
vous	choisir des livres	à la plage
mon petit frère	faire une promenade	au restaurant
André et Thomas	acheter des sandales	au cirque *(circus)*
les filles		

▶ J'ai nagé. Je suis allé(e) à la plage.

PRACTICE: describing who went where

1. Claire est
2. Olivier est
3. Éric et Jacques sont
4. Anne et Monique sont
5. Olivier est
6. Éric et Jacques sont
7. Olivier est
8. Anne et Monique sont

COMMUNICATION: finding out where people went

COMPREHENSION: describing where people went to do certain things

■ **Pronunciation**
clown /klun/
zoo /zo/ or /zoo/

■ **Teaching note:** This activity may be done in a game format. See **Teaching note,** p. T262.

Sophie nettoie sa chambre. [Elle est chez elle.]
Elles font du ski. [Elles ne sont pas chez elles.]
Vous voyagez. [Vous n'êtes pas chez vous.]

Cooperative pair practice
Activity 2

ROLE PLAY: talking about last weekend

4

▷ **Vocabulaire**

Looking ahead: If you wish to present the other verbs conjugated with **être**, you can have students refer to the Appendix, page R11. These verbs will be formally introduced in Book Two.

Extra practice: Use Transparency 16 to do rapid substitution drills. Give the model sentence and then point to various subject pronouns.
▶ **Je suis venu(e) hier.**
  [tu] **Tu es venu(e) hier.**
Je suis arrivé(e) à midi.
Je suis rentré(e) à minuit.

COMPREHENSION: concluding who stayed home and who did not

5

Variation: Have students respond using **chez** plus stress pronouns.
Paul est resté chez lui.
Mélanie n'est pas restée chez elle.

Realia note
This is an ad for **Sport Magazine.** The word **infos** is a shortened form of **informations**, meaning news and background information.

4 **Weekend**

Des amis parlent de leur weekend.
Jouez ces dialogues.

▶ en ville / acheter des vêtements

1. au stade / regarder un match de foot
2. à la plage / jouer au volley
3. à une boum / danser
4. à la campagne / faire une promenade à pied
5. au Bon Marché / acheter des cassettes
6. dans un restaurant italien / manger des spaghetti

> Où est-ce que tu es allée?
>
> Je suis allée en ville.
>
> Ah bon! Qu'est-ce que tu as fait?
>
> J'ai acheté des vêtements.

Vocabulaire: Quelques verbes conjugués avec *être* au passé composé

INFINITIVE	PAST PARTICIPLE		
aller	**allé**	to go	Nous **sommes allés** en ville.
arriver	**arrivé**	to arrive	Vous **êtes arrivés** à midi.
rentrer	**rentré**	to return, go back, come back	Nous **sommes rentrés** à la maison à onze heures.
rester	**resté**	to stay	Les touristes **sont restés** à l'hôtel Ibis.
venir	**venu**	to come	Qui **est venu** hier?

---

5 **Qui est resté à la maison?**

Samedi après-midi, les personnes suivantes ont fait certaines choses. Dites si oui ou non elles sont restées à la maison.

▶ Paul a regardé la télé. **Il est resté à la maison.**
▶ Mélanie a fait des achats. **Elle n'est pas restée à la maison.**

1. Mlle Joly a lavé sa voiture.
2. Nous avons fait une promenade à vélo.
3. Tu as nettoyé le garage.
4. Éric et Olivier ont joué au volley.
5. Christine et Isabelle ont travaillé dans le jardin.
6. Vous avez fait une promenade en voiture.
7. Mes cousins ont fait de la voile.
8. J'ai fait du jogging.

JOGGING

INFOS *Sport* magazine

TPR **Destinations and arrival times**

PROPS: Map (or transparency) of France, clock with movable hands
Imagine that the class is visiting France.
Je suis allé(e) à Nice. [point to Nice]
Je suis arrivé(e) à midi. [move clock to 12]

Have pairs of students come up to show where they went and when they arrived.
X et Y, vous êtes allé(e)s à Lyon.
Vous êtes arrivé(e)s à 1h20.
Venez nous montrer la ville et l'heure.

6 La journée de Nathalie

Pendant les vacances, Nathalie travaille dans une agence de tourisme. Le soir, elle raconte *(tells about)* sa journée à son père.

Je suis allée au bureau.

▶ aller au bureau *(office)*

1. arriver à neuf heures
2. téléphoner à un client anglais
3. parler avec des touristes japonais
4. aller au restaurant à midi et demi
5. rentrer au bureau à deux heures
6. copier des documents
7. préparer des billets *(tickets)* d'avion
8. rester jusqu'à *(until)* six heures
9. dîner en ville
10. rentrer à la maison à neuf heures

7 Une question de circonstances *(A matter of circumstances)*

Nos activités dépendent souvent des circonstances. Dites si oui ou non les personnes suivantes ont fait les choses indiquées.

▶ On est mardi aujourd'hui.
  - les élèves / rester à la maison?
  Les élèves ne sont pas restés à la maison.

1. On est dimanche.
   - M. Boulot / travailler?
   - nous / aller à l'école?
   - vous / dîner à la cantine *(school cafeteria)*?

2. Il fait très beau aujourd'hui.
   - moi / aller à la campagne?
   - mes copines / regarder la télé?
   - toi / venir à la piscine avec nous?

3. Il fait très mauvais!
   - Marc / faire un pique-nique?
   - Hélène et Juliette / rester à la maison?
   - ma mère / rentrer à la maison à pied?

4. Mes copains et moi, nous n'avons pas beaucoup d'argent.
   - toi / aller dans un restaurant cher?
   - mes copains / venir chez moi en taxi?
   - moi / acheter des vêtements?

Leçon 32 333

ROLE PLAY: narrating the day's events

6

■ **Variation** (using other subjects):
[elle] **Elle est allée au bureau.**
[nous] **Nous sommes allés au bureau.**
[Élisabeth et sa soeur Alice (elles)] **Elles sont allées au bureau.**

COMPREHENSION: drawing conclusions about past actions

7

■ **Teaching note:** Remind students to use **pas de** in items 3 and 4:
3. **Marc n'a pas fait de pique-nique.**
4. **Je n'ai pas acheté de vêtements.**

■ **Expansion:** Have students write an original affirmative and negative sentence for each item.
▶ **Nous avons eu un examen de français.**
Je n'ai pas regardé la télé ce matin.

Follow-up questions:
Où est-ce que X et Y sont allé(e)s?
À quelle heure sont-ils(elles) arrivé(e)s?

■ **Teaching strategy:** Point out that the pattern with **ne... jamais** in the passé composé is the same as with **ne... pas.**

8 PRACTICE: talking about what one never does

9 COMMUNICATION: answering personal questions

Cooperative pair practice
Activity 10

T334

B. La construction négative *ne . . . jamais*

Compare the following negative constructions.

Éric **ne** parle **pas** à Paul.	*Éric does **not** speak to Paul.*
Éric **ne** parle **jamais** à Paul.	*Éric **never** speaks to Paul.*
Nous **n'**étudions **pas** le dimanche.	*We do **not** study on Sundays.*
Nous **n'**étudions **jamais** le dimanche.	*We **never** study on Sundays.*

To say that one NEVER does something, French speakers use the construction **ne . . . jamais,** as follows:

SUBJECT	+	**ne**	+	VERB	+	**jamais** . . .
Nous		**ne**		regardons		**jamais** la télé.

➡ **Ne** becomes **n'** before a vowel sound.
   Nous **n'**allons **jamais** à l'opéra.

➡ Note the use of **ne . . . jamais** in the passé composé:
   Nous **n'**avons **jamais** visité Québec. *We **never** visited Quebec.*
   Je **ne** suis **jamais** allé à Genève. *I **never** went to Geneva.*

8 **Jamais le dimanche**

Le dimanche les personnes suivantes ne font jamais ce qu'elles font pendant la semaine. Exprimez cette situation.

▶ François va à l'école.
   Le dimanche, il ne va jamais à l'école.

1. Anne étudie.
2. Marc travaille.
3. Nous parlons français.
4. Vous allez à la bibliothèque.
5. M. Bernard va en ville.
6. Les élèves mangent à la cantine.
7. Tu rends visite à tes copains.
8. Vous dînez chez vous.
9. Je nettoie ma chambre.
10. Je lave la voiture.

9 **Questions personnelles**

Dans tes réponses, utilise les expressions **souvent, rarement** ou **ne . . . jamais.**

▶ Est-ce que tu vas souvent au zoo?
   Oui, je vais souvent au zoo.
   (Non, je vais rarement au zoo.)
   (Non, je ne vais jamais au zoo.)

1. Est-ce que tu parles souvent français à la maison?
2. Est-ce que tu mets *(set)* la table?
3. Est-ce que tu fais souvent ton lit?
4. Est-ce que tu téléphones souvent au professeur?
5. Est-ce que tu nages souvent en hiver?
6. Est-ce que tu vas souvent à l'opéra?
7. Est-ce que tu vois souvent des matchs de boxe?
8. Est-ce que tu voyages souvent en limousine?

Do you like cars? Then you must know about Michelin radial tires. But did you know that Michelin employs over 16,000 people in its North American plants in South Carolina, Alabama, and Nova Scotia?

C. Les expressions *quelqu'un, quelque chose* et leurs contraires

Compare the affirmative and negative constructions in heavy print.

—Tu attends **quelqu'un?**   *Are you waiting for **someone (anyone)?***
—Non, je **n'**attends **personne.**   *No, I'm **not** waiting for **anyone.***

—Vous faites **quelque chose** ce soir?   *Are you doing **something (anything)** tonight?*
—Non, nous **ne** faisons **rien.**   *No, we're **not** doing **anything.***
     *No, we're doing **nothing.***

To refer to unspecified people or things, French speakers use the following expressions:

quelqu'un	*someone, anyone* *somebody, anybody*	**ne ... personne**	*no one, not anyone* *nobody, not anybody*
quelque chose	*something, anything*	**ne ... rien**	*nothing, not anything*

➡ Like all negative expressions, **personne** and **rien** require **ne** before the verb. Remember that **ne** becomes **n'** before a vowel sound.

➡ In short answers, **personne** and **rien** may be used alone.

     Qui est là? **Personne.**
     Qu'est-ce que tu fais? **Rien.**

10 **Florence est malade**

Florence est malade *(sick)* aujourd'hui. Elle répond négativement aux questions de Paul.

▶ dîner avec quelqu'un?

Tu dînes avec quelqu'un?

Non, je ne dîne avec personne.

1. inviter quelqu'un?
2. faire quelque chose ce soir?
3. manger quelque chose à midi?
4. regarder quelque chose à la télé?
5. attendre quelqu'un ce matin?
6. voir quelqu'un cet après-midi?
7. préparer quelque chose pour le dîner?
8. rencontrer quelqu'un après le dîner?

Prononciation   qu /k/

Les lettres «qu»

The letters "**qu**" represent the sound /k/. First, practice with words you know.

un bouquet

Répétez: **qui   quand   quelque chose   quelqu'un   quatre   quatorze   Québec   Monique   Véronique   sympathique   un pique-nique   le ski nautique**

Now try reading some new words. Make them sound French!

Répétez: **un bouquet   un banquet   la qualité   la quantité   la conséquence   une équipe** *(team)* ** l'équipement   fréquent   la séquence**

     Véronique pense que Monique aime la musique classique.

Section C

COMMUNICATIVE FUNCTION: Identifying people and things

32.1 Dialogue: Un bon weekend
(18:22–20:00 min.)

 IDEODISC   Disc 5, Side 1
33323–36270

🔊 Leçon 32, Section 1

▪ **Language note:** Word order with **ne... personne** and **ne... rien** is presented in Book Two. In general, **personne** and **rien** have the same position in the sentence as **quelqu'un** and **quelque chose**:
Quelqu'un a téléphoné?
Non, personne n'a téléphoné.
EXCEPTION: In the passé composé **rien** comes between the auxiliary and the past participle:
Tu as acheté quelque chose?
Non, je n'ai rien acheté.

▪ **Teaching strategy:** Point out that **pas** is never used together with **personne** or **rien**.

10 ROLE PLAY: giving negative responses

Prononciation

🔊 Leçon 32, Section 6

1 COMPREHENSION

1-e   4-a
2-c   5-b
3-d

🔊 Leçon 32, Section 7

2 GUIDED ORAL EXPRESSION

■ **Expansion:** I did not see you last weekend. Please answer my questions in French. Tell me:
• Did you stay home Saturday morning?
• What did you do?
• Where did you go Saturday afternoon?
• What did you do there?
• Did you meet your friends?
• If so, what did you do together?

3 GUIDED ORAL EXPRESSION

🔊 Leçon 32, section 8

À votre tour!

1 Allô!

Reconstituez la conversation entre Sophie et Charlotte. Pour cela, faites correspondre les réponses de Charlotte avec les questions de Sophie.

1 Tu es restée chez toi samedi soir?

2 Qu'est-ce que vous avez vu?

3 Qu'est-ce que vous avez fait ensuite?

4 Vous avez mangé quelque chose?

5 À quelle heure es-tu rentrée chez toi?

a Oui, des sandwichs.

b À onze heures et demie.

c Un vieux western avec Gary Cooper.

d Nous sommes allées dans un café sur le boulevard Saint Michel.

e Non! J'ai téléphoné à une copine et nous sommes allées au cinéma.

2 Dis-moi ...

I will tell you a few things that I did Saturday; then you will tell me where you went on Saturday and what you did.

• Le matin, je suis resté(e) à la maison. J'ai nettoyé ma cham
• L'après-midi, je suis allé(e) au cinéma avec mon copain Jean-Claude. Nous avons vu une comédie. Après, je suis rentré(e) chez moi.
• Le soir, j'ai dîné avec mes parents. Après, je suis resté(e) dans ma chambre et j'ai écouté mes cassettes.

Et maintenant, dis-moi ...

3 Créa-dialogue

Avec vos copains, discutez de ce que vous avez fait récemment *(recently)*. Utilisez les suggestions suivantes.

▶ —**Tu es resté(e) chez toi hier matin?**
   —**Oui, je suis resté(e) chez moi.**
   —**Qu'est-ce que tu as fait?**
   —**J'ai nettoyé ma chambre.**

▶ —**Tu es resté(e) chez toi hier matin?**
   —**Non, je ne suis pas resté(e) chez moi.**
   —**Qu'est-ce que tu as fait?**
   —**Je suis allé(e) à l'école.**

hier matin	1. samedi après-midi	2. vendredi soir	3. s
rester chez toi	aller en ville	rentrer chez toi	r
??	??	??	n

336 Unité 8

À votre tour

Depending on your goals and objectives, you may or may not wish to assign all of the activities in the **À votre tour** section.

👥👥 Cooperative practice

In Act. 1 and 3, you may want to have students work cooperatively in trios, with two performing and one consulting the Answer Key and acting as monitor.

4 Situation

Avec un(e) camarade, composez un dialogue correspondant à la situation suivante. Jouez ce dialogue en classe.

Your French friend Marie-Hélène (played by your classmate) has just come back from a vacation with a great suntan. Try to find out . . .
- where she went
- how long **(combien de temps)** she stayed there
- what she did
- when she came back

5 Conversation libre

Avec un(e) camarade, composez un dialogue original basé sur la situation suivante.

You and your cousin Valérie have not seen each other for a while. Talk about what you did either . . .
- last night **(hier soir),** or
- during spring vacation **(pendant les vacances de printemps),** or
- during summer vacation **(pendant les vacances d'été)**

You will each ask the other at least three different questions to find out where your cousin went and what she saw or did, etc.

6 Composition: Un voyage

Write a short paragraph describing a trip you took — real or imaginary! You may want to use some of the following suggestions.

aller (où?)	voir (quoi?)
voyager (comment?)	rencontrer (qui?)
arriver (quel jour?)	acheter (quoi?)
rester (où? combien de temps?)	faire (quoi?)
visiter (quoi?)	rentrer (quel jour?)

▶ **L'été dernier, je suis allé(e) à Montréal . . .**

Comment dit-on . . . ?

How to celebrate a happy occasion:

Bon anniversaire!

Bonne année!

	5. le weekend dernier	6. la semaine dernière	7. le mois dernier	8. l'été dernier
the				
a	aller à la campagne	aller à une boum	faire un voyage	travailler
	??	??	??	??

Leçon 32 | 337

4 GUIDED ORAL EXPRESSION

■ **Challenge: Conversational role play**
Your cousin Annette has just come back from two weeks in Paris. Ask her about her trip. You may want to find out:
- when she arrived in Paris
- where she stayed (in a hôtel? with friends?)
- if she visited a museum (which museum?)
- what she saw
- whom she met
- what she bought
- when she came back

5 CONVERSATION

6 WRITTEN SELF-EXPRESSION

■ Portfolio assessment

You will probably select only one speaking activity and one writing activity to go into the students' portfolios for Unit 8.

In this lesson, Act. 6 offers an excellent writing portfolio topic. Act. 4 and 5 lend themselves well to oral recordings.

Entracte 8

OBJECTIVES:
- Reading skills development
- Re-entry of materials in the unit
- Development of cultural awareness

Sports, vacances et tourisme

OBJECTIVES:
- Rapid reading at the sentence level
- Learning about the geography of France and the French-speaking world

■ Photo culture note
The photo is of Port-Camargue, a small resort town on the Mediterranean, near Montpellier and Nîmes.

Petit test culturel
Sports, vacances et tourisme

Quand on est en vacances, on aime voyager. Est-ce que vous pouvez répondre aux questions suivantes? Vérifiez vos réponses au bas° de la page.

1 Christèle habite à Paris. Elle va passer les vacances à Nice chez des cousins. Où est-ce qu'elle va passer les vacances?
- a. à la mer
- b. à la montagne
- c. à la campagne
- d. chez elle

2 Les Dupont adorent passer les vacances à la montagne. Cette année ils ont réservé une chambre d'hôtel. Dans quelle ville?
- a. à Bordeaux
- b. à Marseille
- c. à Grenoble
- d. à Tours

3 En hiver, beaucoup de touristes vont à la Martinique. Quel sport est-ce qu'on ne peut° pas pratiquer là-bas?
- a. le ski
- b. le ski nautique
- c. la voile
- d. la planche à voile

4 Nous sommes en février. Un copain revient de vacances bien bronzé.° Il dit:° «J'ai passé d'excellentes vacances dans une île° où on parle français.» Où est-il allé?
- a. aux Bermudes
- b. à Tahiti
- c. à Puerto Rico
- d. à la Jamaïque

5 Madame Gilbert travaille pour une agence de tourisme. Samedi dernier elle est allée de Paris à New York. Elle dit: «J'ai fait la traversée° de l'Atlantique en trois heures!» Quel avion est-ce qu'elle a pris?°
- a. un Boeing 747
- b. un DC-10
- c. un Airbus
- d. un Concorde

6 Quand il est rentré de vacances, Jean-François a dit:° «J'ai passé un mois magnifique chez mon oncle en Bretagne.» Dans quelle partie de la France est-ce qu'il est allé?
- a. à l'ouest°
- b. à l'est
- c. au sud
- d. au nord

nord

ouest

sud

au bas *at the bottom* **peut** *can* **bronzé** *tanned* **dit** *says* **île** *island* **traversée** *crossing* **a pris** *did . . . take*
a dit *said* **ouest** *west*

 338 Unité 8

🗣️🗣️ Cooperative reading practice

Divide the class into groups of 4 or 5, each with a **secrétaire.**

Keeping the box at the bottom of the page covered, have the groups vote on the correct answer for each question.

Then have the recorders check the right answers. If appropriate, have recorders announce their group score to the entire class.

Nous avons six réponses correctes.

Follow-up: Have the students find all the places mentioned on the maps in the Reference section, pp. R2–R3.

Vive le sport!

Quels sports pratiquez-vous pendant les vacances? Où allez-vous pour pratiquer votre sport favori? Voici plusieurs possibilités:

◗ Quels sports est-ce qu'on peut pratiquer dans ce club?

◗ En quelle saison?

◗ Quel est le numéro de téléphone du club?

TENNIS ACTION
DE MAI À SEPTEMBRE
STAGES CET ÉTÉ À PARIS!
GOLF ACTION
01 47 34 36 36

Vous aimez...
le SKI NAUTIQUE...
la PLANCHE À VOILE?

C'est maintenant à 10 min. du Centre-Ville !!!

SKI NAUTIQUE et PLANCHE À VOILE?

C'est, maintenant, sur la belle plage du PLM La Batelière les skis nautiques, les 8 Dufour et les 4 Windglider de

SPORTS LOISIRS

LOCATION OUVERTE TOUTE LA SEMAINE ET LE DIMANCHE de 9h à 17h sans interruption

 Comment s'appelle ce club?

 Quels sports est-ce qu'on peut pratiquer dans ce club?

◗ Comment s'appelle ce centre de loisirs?°

◗ Quels sports est-ce qu'on peut pratiquer?

◗ Quelles autres° activités sont offertes?

LE STADIUM CENTRE DE LOISIRS

VACANCES DE PÂQUES

PATINAGE
SKATE
NATATION

BOWLING
JUDO et
sports de combat
DANSE

SAMEDI SOIR - Animation SPÉCIALE AVEC L'ORCHESTRE SQUAD - 21 h à 24 h

66, AVENUE D'IVRY (M°PORTE D'IVRY) 05.45.83.11.00

Vous avez la possibilité d'aller dans un des endroits mentionnés plus haut.° Quel endroit est-ce que vous allez choisir? Pourquoi?

loisirs *leisure activities* **autres** *other* **plus haut** *above*

Vive le sport!

OBJECTIVES:
- Reading for information
- Understanding authentic documents

■ **Realia notes**

un stage *organized instruction or class*
PLM *a French hotel chain*
la location *rental*
le tarif *rates, price*
un abonnement *membership (subscription)*
une animation spéciale *special entertainment*
skate = le skateboard (la planche à roulettes)
M° = métro

■ **Answers to questions**

Tennis action
- le tennis et le golf
- en été
- 01.47.34.36.36

Sports loisirs
- Sports loisirs
- le ski nautique et la planche à voile

Le stadium
- Le stadium
- le patinage, le skate et la natation
- le bowling, le judo et les sports de combat, la danse

📖 Pre-reading

Ask students if they sometimes go to sports clubs or take sports lessons. Which sports do they prefer?

Quels sports préférez-vous?

Post-reading

As students answer the last questions about which club they prefer, tally their responses on the board.

La majorité préfère …
Ensuite, il y a [9] élèves qui préfèrent…
Il y a seulement [3] élèves qui préfèrent…

Entre amis: Le weekend

Qu'est-ce que vous faites le weekend? Qu'est ce que vous avez fait le weekend dernier? Voici les réponses de cinq jeunes du monde° francophone.°

Carole, 15 ans, France
Le weekend dernier, j'ai fait une promenade en mobylette avec une copine. Nous sommes allées à la campagne. À midi, on a fait un pique-nique. Après, on a visité un vieux château en ruines. Malheureusement,° j'ai eu une crevaison.° Je suis rentrée chez moi seulement° pour le dîner. Après le dîner, j'ai regardé la télé et j'ai fait mes devoirs pour lundi.

Pierre, 16 ans, la Martinique
Le samedi, je joue généralement au foot. Je fais partie de° l'équipe° junior de mon village. Le weekend dernier, nous avons fait un match. Nous avons bien joué, mais nous avons perdu! Après le match, je suis allé à la plage. Le soir, je suis allé chez des copains. Nous avons mis de la musique et nous avons dansé.

Yvan, 14 ans, Québec
Le matin, je suis allé à la patinoire° avec des copains, mais je ne suis pas resté très longtemps.° À midi, je suis rentré chez moi. L'après-midi, j'ai aidé mes parents à repeindre° la cuisine. Pour le dîner, nous sommes allés au restaurant.

Élisabeth, 15 ans, Belgique
Samedi matin, j'ai fait des achats. J'ai choisi un cadeau° pour l'anniversaire de mon père. (J'ai acheté une cravate en soie.°) L'après-midi, je suis allée au ciné-club avec un copain. Nous avons vu *Les Temps modernes*, un vieux film de Charlie Chaplin. Après, nous sommes allés dans un café et nous avons rencontré d'autres° copains. J'ai passé la soirée° en famille.

Djemila, 16 ans, Algérie
Samedi dernier, nous avons eu une grande réunion de famille chez mon oncle Karim. Une centaine° de personnes sont venues. Nous avons fait un «méchoui». (C'est un repas° où on rôtit° un mouton° entier à la broche.°) J'ai eu l'occasion° de voir tous° mes cousins et cousines. On s'est bien amusé!°

monde world   **francophone** *French-speaking*   **Malheureusement** *Unfortunately*   **crevaison** *flat tire*   **seulement** *just*   **cadeau** *present*   **soie** *silk*   **d'autres** *other*   **soirée** *evening*   **fais partie de** *am a member of*   **équipe** *team*   **Une centaine** *About a hundred*   **repas** *meal*   **rôtit** *roasts*   **mouton** *sheep*   **à la broche** *on the spit*   **occasion** *chance*   **tous** *all*   **On s'est bien amusé!** *We had a good time!*   **patinoire** *skating rink*   **très longtemps** *for a very long time*   **repeindre** *to repaint*

■ NOTES ■ CULTURELLES

Alger

1 L'Algérie

L'Algérie est un pays° d'Afrique du Nord. C'est une ancienne° colonie française. Aujourd'hui beaucoup de familles d'origine algérienne habitent en France. Dans ces familles, on parle généralement français et arabe.

Le weekend

OBJECTIVES:
• Reading at the paragraph level
• Building reading skills

■ **Pronunciation:**
Djemila /dʒemila/
Karim /karim/

■ **Questions sur le texte**

Carole: Qu'est-ce que Carole a fait le matin?
Qu'est-ce qu'elle a fait l'après-midi?
Pourquoi est-ce qu'elle est rentrée chez elle tard *(late)* pour le dîner?

Élisabeth: Pourquoi est-ce qu'Élisabeth a acheté un cadeau?
Où est-ce qu'elle est allée l'après-midi?
Quel film est-ce qu'elle a vu?
Est-ce qu'elle est restée chez elle après le dîner?

Pierre: Qu'est-ce que Pierre a fait l'après-midi?
Est-ce qu'il a gagné le match?
Qu'est-ce qu'il a fait le soir?

Djemila: Où est allée Djemila le weekend dernier?
Qui est-ce qu'elle a vu là-bas?

Yvan: Qu'est-ce qu'Yvan a fait le matin?
À quelle heure est-ce qu'il est rentré chez lui?
Où est-ce qu'il a dîné?

📖 Pre-reading

Have students glance over the reading quickly.
What are the questions that were asked in the interview?

Post-reading

Ask each student to decide which of the five people they would like to spend a weekend with and why.
Imaginez que vous avez la possibilité de passer un weekend avec un de ces jeunes. Qui allez-vous choisir? Pourquoi?

Comment lire
WORDS WITH SEVERAL MEANINGS

Sometimes a word may have several meanings. For example, the French word **temps** can mean:

weather	Quel beau **temps!**
time	Je n'ai pas le **temps** d'aller au cinéma.

Enrichissez votre vocabulaire
MORE COGNATE PATTERNS

Here are two important cognate patterns that will help you read French more easily.

- French verbs in **-er** sometimes correspond to English verbs in *-ate*.
  situer   *to situate*
  Note also how this pattern works in past participles:
  situé   *situated*

- The circumflex accent on a vowel often indicates that the English cognate contains an "*s.*"
  rôtir   *to roast*
  coûter   *to cost*

Activité

Can you identify the English equivalents of the following French words?

- **séparer   indiquer   associer   apprécier   opérer
  décoré   créé   libéré   illustré   agité   animé**

- **un hôpital   une forêt   honnête   en hâte   une hôtesse   une île**

■ **Vocabulary note:** Other words with several meanings:
passer *to pass [by], to spend*
gagner *to earn, to win*
l'anniversaire *anniversary, birthday*

■ **Vocabulary note:** Other cognates with a circumflex accent:
un mât, arrêter, un hôte, la pâte

Notes culturelles

■ **Les Algériens en France**
The Algerians represent the largest group of foreigners living in France. Young French people of Algerian origin often refer to themselves as **Beurs.**

■ **Bruxelles**
Brussels is an important center for the 15-member European Union (**l'Union européenne**). It is the seat of the Council of Ministers and houses the working committees of the European Parliament.

2 La Belgique

La Belgique est un petit pays situé au nord-est° de la France. Sa capitale, Bruxelles, est un centre européen important. La Belgique est un pays trilingue. Les langues officielles sont le français, le néerlandais *(dutch)* et l'allemand.

pays *country* **ancienne** *former*
nord-est *northeast*

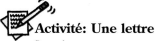 **Activité: Une lettre**

Imaginez que vous avez passé le weekend avec l'une des cinq personnes. Choisissez cette personne (Carole, Élisabeth, Pierre, Djemila ou Yvan). Dans une lettre, décrivez ce weekend de votre point de vue personnel.

▶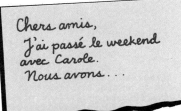

*Chers amis,
J'ai passé le weekend
avec Carole.
Nous avons . . .*

Entracte 8   **341**

Variétés

OBJECTIVES:
• Reading for fun
• Logical thinking: finding errors of fact

■ **Photo culture notes**
Paris
This postcard shows a **bateau-mouche** passing in front of Notre Dame. These double-deckered boats offer tourists a spectacular view of Paris, especially in the evening when the monuments are illuminated.
(For more information, see p. 243.)

Normandie
This postcard shows a section of Omaha Beach. On June 6, 1944, D-Day, allied troups landed on the beaches in Normandy (code-named Omaha, Utah, Juno and Sword). In the ensuing months, the Allies liberated France and the rest of Europe from German occupation. The American military cemetery at Omaha Beach is maintained by the U.S. Government and is considered as part of U.S. territory.

■ **Cultural note: Une marmite** is a covered stewing pot with small handles on each side. It is a symbol of home-cooked food.

Les quatre erreurs d'Hélène

Pendant les vacances, Hélène Ladoucette, une jeune étudiante québécoise, est allée en France. Là, elle a voyagé et elle a visité beaucoup d'endroits différents. Pendant son voyage, elle a écrit des cartes postales à ses copains. Dans chaque° carte postale, Hélène a fait une erreur.° (Les erreurs d'Hélène concernent l'histoire ou la géographie.) Pouvez-vous° trouver ces erreurs? Lisez° attentivement chaque carte et découvrez° l'erreur qui s'y trouve.°

PARIS

Paris, le 2 juillet

Cher Alain,
Je suis arrivée à Paris samedi dernier. Avant-hier,° j'ai visité Notre-Dame et le musée d'Orsay. Hier, j'ai rendu visite à une copine parisienne. Nous avons fait une promenade sur la Saône en bateau-mouche.° Après, nous sommes allées dans un restaurant qui s'appelle la "Petite Marmite". J'ai mangé des escargots!°

Amitiés, Hélène

NORMANDIE

Deauville, le 8 j...

Ma chère Pauline,
Je suis maintenant en Norman...
Je suis venue ici avec Véronique, m...
copine parisienne. Il y a beaucou...
choses à faire ici. Hier, nous avons vis...
le Havre, un grand port sur l'Atlantiq...
Aujourd'hui, nous sommes allées sur...
les plages où les soldats° canadiens et...
américains ont débarqué° en 1844.
C'est très impressionnant!°

Amicalement, Hélène

chaque *each* **erreur** *mistake*
Pouvez-vous *Can you* **Lisez** *Read* **découvrez** *discover*
qui s'y trouve *that is there* **Avant hier** *The day before yesterday*
bateau-mouche *sight-seeing boat* **escargots** *snails*
soldats *soldiers* **ont débarqué** *landed* **impressionnant** *impressive*

(342) Unité 8

📖 **Pre-reading activity**
Have students look at each of the postcards and read the descriptions of the places pictured. Then have them locate the four cities on a map of France.

Post-reading activity
Have students imagine that they had been able to accompany Hélène on one part of her trip. Which part would they have chosen and why?

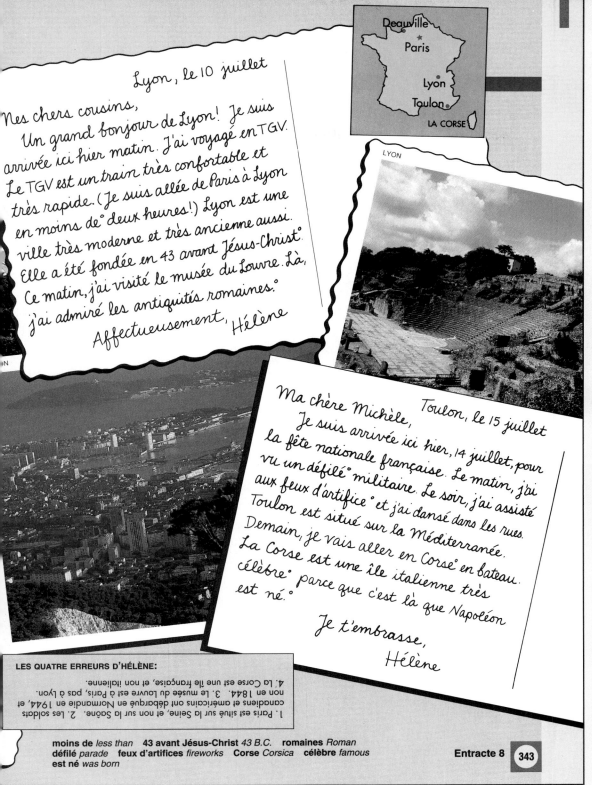

Lyon, le 10 juillet

Nes chers cousins,

Un grand bonjour de Lyon! Je suis arrivée ici hier matin. J'ai voyagé en TGV. Le TGV est un train très confortable et très rapide. (Je suis allée de Paris à Lyon en moins de° deux heures!) Lyon est une ville très moderne et très ancienne aussi. Elle a été fondée en 43 avant Jésus-Christ.° Ce matin, j'ai visité le musée du Louvre. Là, j'ai admiré les antiquités romaines.°

Affectueusement, Hélène

Toulon, le 15 juillet

Ma chère Michèle,

Je suis arrivée ici hier, 14 juillet, pour la fête nationale française. Le matin, j'ai vu un défilé° militaire. Le soir, j'ai assisté aux feux d'artifice° et j'ai dansé dans les rues. Toulon est situé sur la Méditerranée. Demain, je vais aller en Corse° en bateau. La Corse est une île italienne très célèbre° parce que c'est là que Napoléon est né.°

Je t'embrasse,
Hélène

LES QUATRE ERREURS D'HÉLÈNE:

1. Paris est situé sur la Seine, et non sur la Saône. 2. Les soldats canadiens et américains ont débarqué en Normandie en 1944, et non en 1844. 3. Le musée du Louvre est à Paris, pas à Lyon. 4. La Corse est une île française, et non italienne.

moins de *less than* **43 avant Jésus-Christ** *43 B.C.* **romaines** *Roman*
défilé *parade* **feux d'artifices** *fireworks* **Corse** *Corsica* **célèbre** *famous*
est né *was born*

Entracte 8 **343**

■ **Photo culture notes**
Lyon
This postcard shows **l'amphithéâtre des Trois Gaules** in Lyon. Lyon, which is the third largest city of France, is located at the junction of two rivers, **le Rhône** and **la Saône**. It was founded by the Romans in 43 B.C. Because of its strategic location, it became the capital of Gaul (**la Gaule**), as France was called in Roman times.

Toulon
This postcard shows the harbor of Toulon as viewed from the mountains to the north of the city. Toulon, with a population of 400,000, is an important French naval base and also a port of call for the U.S. fleet in the Mediterranean.

UNITÉ 8
INTERNET PROJECT

Scavenger Hunt: À Paris

Give students an Internet scavenger hunt. Make a list of things for them to find out or verify via the Internet. The student who correctly completes each item in the scavenger hunt wins!

Sample
What does SNCF stand for?
What kinds of things can you buy at a FNAC?
Where is the American Embassy in Paris located?
What is the weather typically like in Paris for the month of August?
What is the RER?
What is the name of the café located within the Musée d'Orsay?
etc.

Search Engines
Yahoo
http://www.yahoo.com
Mosaic
http://www.mckinley.com/
WebCrawler
http://webcrawler.com/

Cooperative writing practice

Ask students to bring in local postcards. Divide the class into small groups.

Each group of students writes a postcard in French. In the text, however, they introduce an error of history or geography.

Then let groups exchange cards and try to find the errors.

UNITÉ 9

Les repas

Unit overview

COMMUNICATION GOALS: Students will be able to buy food and order a meal.
LINGUISTIC GOALS: Students will learn to express quantities and use object pronouns.
CRITICAL THINKING GOALS: Students will begin to understand the concept of the partitive and to observe the differences between object pronouns in French and English.
CULTURAL GOALS: Students will learn about French meals, restaurants, and cafeterias as well as grocery shopping habits in France.

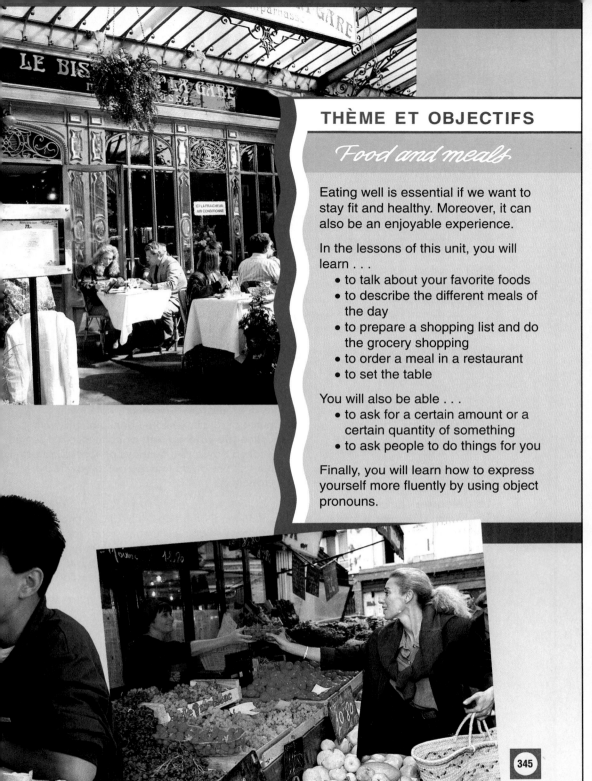

THÈME ET OBJECTIFS

Food and meals

Eating well is essential if we want to stay fit and healthy. Moreover, it can also be an enjoyable experience.

In the lessons of this unit, you will learn . . .
- to talk about your favorite foods
- to describe the different meals of the day
- to prepare a shopping list and do the grocery shopping
- to order a meal in a restaurant
- to set the table

You will also be able . . .
- to ask for a certain amount or a certain quantity of something
- to ask people to do things for you

Finally, you will learn how to express yourself more fluently by using object pronouns.

■ Photo culture notes
À la cantine
At the school cafeteria in Savigny-sur-Orge, food is served at the table, family style. Have students note how the French bread has been cut in pieces (**en morceaux**) and is served in a basket (**une corbeille**).

Déjeuner au café
In spring and summer, weather permitting, city cafés and restaurants often serve meals on the sidewalk (**la terrasse**). The sign on the door indicates that inside the café is air-conditioned (**la fraîcheur** = coolness). Note that the menu (**le menu**) is posted outside the café. This restaurant is called **Le bistrot de la gare**. The name **bistrot** is often given to small café-restaurants.

Le marché
French people prefer buying fruits and vegetables at outdoor markets (**le marché**). Many foodstores also have a sidewalk stand (**un étal**) where passersby can buy these products. Note that the shopper in the picture has her own shopping basket (**un sac à provisions**). This is important in France, because many merchants at open-air markets do not provide shopping bags.

Pacing

Your pacing of Unit 9 will depend on where you are in the academic year. Since this material is reintroduced in **DISCOVERING FRENCH— BLANC**, you may want to present the material primarily for student recognition. However, if you have the time, present all four lessons of Unit 9 so that students have a solid introduction to object pronouns.

For further suggestions on pacing, see the general discussion in the Front Matter.

345

VIDEODISC Disc 5, Side 2
1543–13331

■ **Comprehension practice:** Play the entire module through as an introduction to the lesson.

■ **Cultural note: Biscottes** are dried slices of toasted bread that have been baked in the oven. They don't get stale and can be stored easily.

LEÇON 33 Les repas et la nourriture

LE FRANÇAIS PRATIQUE

Accent sur ... Les repas français

For French people, a meal is more than just food served on a plate. It is a social occasion in which family and friends sit down together to enjoy one another's company. French meals are different from American meals not only in terms of the foods and beverages that are served, but also in the way these foods are presented and in the order in which they are served.

• **Le petit déjeuner** (*Breakfast*)
The French **petit déjeuner** is simpler and not as abundant as the American breakfast. Usually it consists of bread, warm toast **(du pain grillé)** or dry toast **(des biscottes),** eaten with butter and jam. Children drink hot milk with coffee **(du café au lait)** or hot chocolate served in deep bowls. On Sundays or special occasions, the first person up may go out to buy fresh croissants.

• **Le déjeuner** (*Lunch*)
The French **déjeuner** is traditionally the main meal of the day. It begins with one or several appetizers **(les hors-d'oeuvre),** such as salami, cucumber salad, radishes, and grated carrots. Next, comes the main course **(le plat principal),** which may be a meat or fish dish accompanied by vegetables. This is followed by a green salad, a cheese course, and a dessert. Children drink water, mineral water, apple cider, or carbonated fruit juices. Adults drink mineral water and sometimes may enjoy a glass of wine. When coffee is served, it always comes at the very end of the meal.

💻 Using the video

Ask students whether they prefer to eat in restaurants, cafés, or fast-food places. What do they usually order there? What kinds of foods do they eat at home? Where do their families shop for groceries?

Then show the Video Module 33 and have students look for similarities and differences in eating and grocery shopping habits in France and the U.S.

In the first part, French people are eating out in cafés and restaurants. Then diners express their preferences for various foods in an interview situation. The *Vignette culturelle* shows French shoppers purchasing fruits and vegetables at an open-air market.

- **Le goûter** (*Afternoon snack*)
  When children come back from school, they often have a light snack which traditionally consists of bread and a piece of chocolate. Some days they may stop at the pastry shop (**la pâtisserie**) for a **pain au chocolat** (a croissant-like pastry with chocolate inside).

- **Le dîner** (*Supper*)
  In France, supper is served between seven and eight o'clock. It is traditionally a simpler meal than lunch, consisting of soup, a light main course (such as a slice of ham, an omelet, pasta, or a light meat dish), and then a green salad and a simple dessert (yogurt or fruit).
    Supper is a sit-down meal, served once everyone is home. This is the occasion for parents and children to spend time together and talk about the events of the day. (In France, children are not allowed to go to the refrigerator and fix their own meals. They are expected to sit down at the table and are not excused until everyone is finished.)

Leçon 33 347

■ **Photo culture notes**
Le petit déjeuner
This French breakfast mixes traditional elements (**des biscottes, du pain, du beurre, de la confiture**) with modern foods (**des céréales**). Note that the coffee is served in deep bowls (**un bol**).
Note also the open cupboard (**le buffet**) in the back of the room. It is used to display decorative dishes.

Le déjeuner
In summer, lunches are lighter and may consist of cold cuts (**des viandes froides**), salad, and fruit. Note the bottle of mineral water which is almost always present on a French table.

Le goûter
Many department stores have snack counters where one can buy sandwiches, croissants, mini-pizzas, and light pastries.

Le dîner
Note the basket of fruit on the table. In France, it is typical to serve fruit at the end of the meal. Note also the wardrobe (**l'armoire**) against the wall.

■ **Cultural note:** Eating habits in Quebec are a blend between those in France and English-speaking Canada. Like other Canadians, the **Québécois** have bacon, eggs, toast, and cereal for breakfast. But, like the French, they enjoy wine, mineral water, and croissants at a sidewalk café. Ethnic food, particularly in Montreal, is also very popular. People eat out in cafés, restaurants, and fast-food places. **Le casse-croûte** (*snack bar*) is a favorite place for a quick lunch.

33.1 Introduction: Où allez-vous quand vous avez faim? (25:16–26:04 min.)

 VIDEODISC Disc 5, Side 2
1852–3449

Leçon 33, Section 1

Looking ahead: The verb **prendre** is formally presented in Lesson 34. Here students will be using only the **je** and **tu** forms.

Language note: Remind students that **la cuisine** is also *the kitchen*.

Language note: In Quebec, meals of the day are:
le déjeuner *(breakfast)*
le dîner *(lunch)*
le souper *(dinner)*

Transparency 45
Table setting

Cultural note: In setting the table in France, the spoon is usually placed above the plate.

Supplementary vocabulary

une nappe *tablecloth*
une soucoupe *saucer*
le couvert *place setting*
mettre le couvert *to set the table (putting out the dishes, glasses, silverware)*

A. Les repas et la table

How to talk about meals:

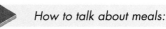

—En général, à quelle heure est-ce que tu **prends le petit déjeuner** *(have breakfast)*?
—Je prends le petit déjeuner à sept heures et demie.
—Où est-ce que tu vas **déjeuner** *(to have lunch)* aujourd'hui?
—Je vais déjeuner à **la cantine de l'école** *(school cafeteria)*.

Les repas et la nourriture

NOMS		VERBES	
un repas	meal		
le petit déjeuner	breakfast	**prendre le petit déjeuner**	to have breakfast
le déjeuner	lunch	**déjeuner**	to have lunch
le dîner	dinner	**dîner**	to have dinner
la nourriture	food		
la cuisine	cooking, cuisine		

—Tu peux **mettre** *(set)* la table?
—D'accord. Je vais mettre la table.

un verre · une tasse · une cuillère · une assiette · une serviette · une fourchette · un couteau

---

TPR Table setting

PROPS: Plastic dishes and place settings

Present the new vocabulary.
Voici une cuillère. Voici une assiette. …
X, viens ici. Montre-nous la serviette.

Have students pass around the items.
X, donne le verre à Y et la tasse à Z.

Have students manipulate the items.
X, mets la tasse sur l'assiette.
Puis, mets le couteau sur l'assiette et la cuillère dans la tasse.
Ouvre la serviette et mets-la sur la tasse. …

1 Et toi?

Exprime tes préférences. Pour cela complète les phrases suivantes.

1. Mon repas préféré est …
   - le petit déjeuner
   - le dîner
   - le déjeuner

2. Je préfère déjeuner …
   - chez moi
   - à la cantine de l'école
   - dans un fast food
   - … ?

3. En général, la nourriture de la cantine de l'école est …
   - excellente
   - bonne
   - mauvaise
   - … ?

4. Je préfère dîner …
   - chez moi
   - chez mes copains
   - au restaurant
   - … ?

5. Je préfère la nourriture …
   - mexicaine
   - italienne
   - chinoise
   - … ?

6. Quand je dois aider avec le dîner, je préfère …
   - préparer la salade
   - mettre la table
   - laver les assiettes
   - … ?

2 Questions personnelles

1. À quelle heure est-ce que tu prends ton petit déjeuner le lundi? Et le dimanche?
2. En général, à quelle heure est-ce que tu dînes?
3. Où est-ce que tu déjeunes pendant la semaine? le samedi? le dimanche?
4. Où est-ce que tu as déjeuné hier? Avec qui?
5. Où est-ce que tu vas dîner ce soir? Avec qui?
6. Est-ce que tu vas souvent au restaurant? Quand? Avec qui? Quel est ton restaurant préféré?
7. Est-ce que tu as jamais *(ever)* déjeuné dans un restaurant français? (dans un restaurant mexicain? dans un restaurant italien? dans un restaurant chinois? dans un restaurant vietnamien?) Quand et avec qui?
8. Est-ce que tu mets la table chez toi? Qui a mis la table pour le petit déjeuner? Et pour le dîner?

3 Au restaurant

Vous êtes dans un restaurant français. Vous avez commandé *(ordered)* les choses suivantes. Le serveur a oublié *(forgot)* d'apporter le nécessaire (les ustensiles, etc.).

▶ pour le jus d'orange

Monsieur, je voudrais un verre pour le jus d'orange.

Pardon. Voici un verre.

1. pour l'eau minérale *(mineral water)*
2. pour le thé
3. pour la soupe
4. pour les frites
5. pour le steak
6. pour le gâteau *(cake)*

COMMUNICATION: expressing opinions about food

■ **Language note: Un fast-food** (in official French, **un restaurant rapide**) is a restaurant that serves hamburgers, pizza, etc.

COMMUNICATION: answering personal questions

ROLE PLAY: asking for missing utensils

Cooperative pair practice Activity 3

T349

33.2 Mini-scenes:
Qu'est-ce que vous aimez manger?
33.3 Mini-scenes: Vous préférez les frites ou les spaghetti?
33.4 Mini scenes:
Qu'est-ce que vous préférez?
(26:05–28:22 min.)

VIDEODISC Disc 5, Side 2
3467–7581

Transparencies 46A, 46B
La nourriture et les boissons

Leçon 33, Sections 2, 3, 4

Pronunciation
• l'oeuf /lœf/
• les oeufs /lezø/

Supplementary vocabulary

LE PETIT DÉJEUNER
les oeufs brouillés *scrambled eggs*
les oeufs sur le plat *fried eggs*
le beurre de cacahuète *peanut butter*

LA VIANDE
le rôti *roast*
l'agneau *lamb*
le boeuf *beef*
le porc *pork*
une côtelette *chop, cutlet*

LE POISSON
le saumon *salmon*
la morue *cod*
la perche *perch*

B. La nourriture et les boissons

How to express food preferences:

— Est-ce que tu aimes **le poisson** (fish)?
— Oui, j'aime le poisson mais je préfère **la viande** (meat).
— Quelle viande est-ce que tu aimes?
— J'aime **le rosbif** (roast beef) et **le poulet** (chicken).

> Quelle viande est-ce que tu aimes?

Les plats (m.)
(Dishes)

Les Plats

Pour le déjeuner et le dîner

Les hors-d'oeuvre (m.)
(appetizers)

la soupe

le jambon
(ham)

le saucisson
(salami)

la sole

Le poisson
(fish)

le thon
(tuna)

La viande
(meat)

le veau
(veal)

le rosbif

Pour le petit déjeuner

le pain

la confiture

le poulet

le beurre

un oeuf

les céréales (f.)

Les autres plats
(other dishes)

les frites (f.)
(French fries)

le riz
(rice)

les spaghetti (m.)

350 Unité 9

Teaching strategy: Foods and beverages

Use Transparencies 46A and B to present the various foods and beverages. Since the partitive will not be introduced until Lesson 34, ask questions about students' likes and dislikes using the definite article.

X, est-ce que tu préfères le poulet ou le jambon?
Y, est-ce que tu aimes les céréales?
Z, est-ce que W aime la confiture? etc.

J'aime le rosbif et le poulet.

aimer	to like	Alice **aime** le poulet.
préférer	to prefer	Philippe **préfère** le rosbif.
détester	to hate	Paul **déteste** le poisson.

Les Plats

Les ingrédients (m.)

la mayonnaise

le ketchup

le sucre *(sugar)*

le sel *(salt)*

La salade et le fromage

Le dessert

le gâteau *(cake)*

la glace *(ice cream)*

la tarte *(pie)*

le fromage *(cheese)*

le yaourt

la salade *(lettuce)*

Les boissons (une boisson) *(drink, beverage)*

l'eau *(f.)* *(water)*

le lait *(milk)*

l'eau minérale

le jus d'orange

le jus de pomme *(apple juice)*

le thé glacé *(iced tea)*

Leçon 33 **351**

■ **Photo culture note**
Le rayon de charcuterie
Many French supermarkets have a deli counter (**un rayon de charcuterie**) where one can buy salami (**du saucisson**), sausages (**des saucisses**), slices of ham (**des tranches de jambon**), and all types of **pâtés**.

■ **Looking ahead:** Vegetables and fruits are activated in the next section of this lesson.

■ **Pronunciation**
• le yaourt /jaurt/
• la mayonnaise /majɔnɛz/
• le ketchup /kɛtʃœp/

Supplementary vocabulary

LES INGRÉDIENTS
le poivre *pepper*
l'huile *oil*
le vinaigre *vinegar*
la moutarde *mustard*
la sauce tomate
la margarine

At your discretion, you may want to introduce some common adult beverages:
le vin *wine*
la bière *beer*
le cidre *cider*

■ **Cultural note:** Soft drinks are usually ordered by brand name. All are masculine: **un Orangina, un Coca-cola**, etc.

■ **Language note**
In Quebec:
le yogourt /yogurt/ *yogurt*
un breuvage *beverage*
la crème glacée *ice cream*

💡 Critical Thinking: The French connection

Ask students: Which of the above food names have English cognates?

dessert < **dessert**	juice < **jus**;
salad < **salade**	sole < **sole**;
poultry < **poulet**	soup < **soupe**;
tart < **tarte**	

Which food names has English borrowed from French? [hors d'oeuvre, mayonnaise]
Which food names has French borrowed from English? [**le rosbif, le ketchup**]

T351

4 COMMUNICATION: expressing food preferences

1. le poulet
2. les frites
3. l'eau minérale
4. les oeufs
5. le yaourt
6. les spaghetti
7. le jambon
8. le thon
9. le gâteau
10. le thé glacé
11. le poisson/la sole
12. le riz
13. les céréales
14. le veau/le rosbif

Reentry and review: You may wish to review the use of the definite article in the general sense; see page 156.

5 ROLE PLAY: asking a friend to pass you food

1. le sel
2. le sucre
3. le beurre
4. le lait
5. le fromage
6. la confiture
7. l'eau

6 ROLE PLAY: choosing food

Cooperative pair practice
Activities 5, 6, 7

Je n'aime pas le fromage.
J'aime le fromage.

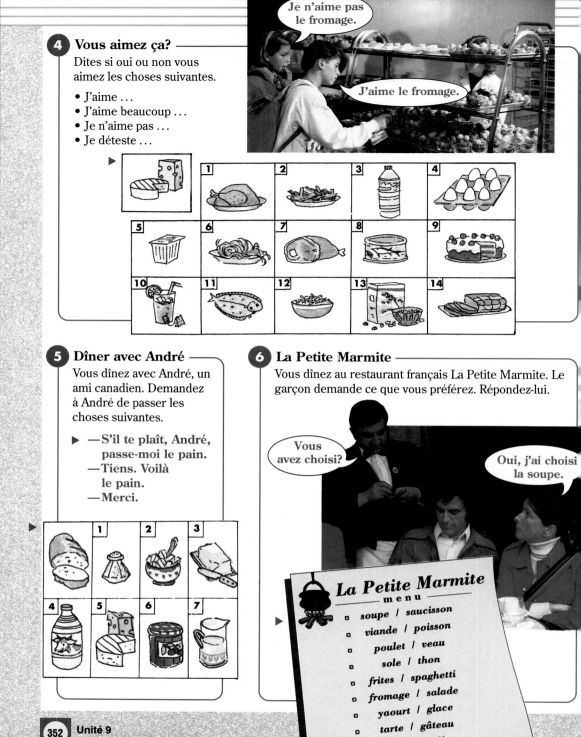

4 Vous aimez ça?

Dites si oui ou non vous aimez les choses suivantes.

- J'aime ...
- J'aime beaucoup ...
- Je n'aime pas ...
- Je déteste ...

▶

5 Dîner avec André

Vous dînez avec André, un ami canadien. Demandez à André de passer les choses suivantes.

▶ **—S'il te plaît, André, passe-moi le pain.**
—Tiens. Voilà le pain.
—Merci.

▶

6 La Petite Marmite

Vous dînez au restaurant français La Petite Marmite. Le garçon demande ce que vous préférez. Répondez-lui.

▶

Vous avez choisi?
Oui, j'ai choisi la soupe.
La Petite Marmite
menu
soupe / saucisson
viande / poisson
poulet / veau
sole / thon
frites / spaghetti
fromage / salade
yaourt / glace
tarte / gâteau
thé / café

7 **Dans le réfrigérateur ou sur la table?**

Choisissez un produit et demandez à vos camarades où est le produit. Ils vont dire
si le produit est dans le réfrigérateur ou sur la table.

▶ Où est la confiture?

Elle est sur la table.

7 EXCHANGES: asking where certain foods are

- **Dans le réfrigérateur:**
  les oeufs
  le yaourt
  le beurre
  le jambon
  la mayonnaise
  le gâteau
  le lait
- **Sur la table:**
  le poulet
  l'eau minérale
  les céréales
  le sel
  le riz
  le pain
  le ketchup
  la confiture

■ **Language note:** In France, a
refrigerator is often referred to as
un frigo or **un frigidaire**.

8 **Les préférences**

Indiquez les préférences
culinaires des personnes
suivantes en complétant
les phrases.

1. J'aime . . .
2. Je déteste . . .
3. Ma mère aime . . .
4. Mon petit frère (ma
   petite soeur) déteste . . .
5. Mon copain aime . . .
6. Ma copine déteste . . .
7. Les enfants aiment . . .
8. En général, les Italiens
   aiment . . .
9. En général, les Japonais
   aiment . . .

9 **Les courses** *(Food shopping)*

Vous passez les vacances en France avec votre famille.
Faites la liste des courses pour les repas suivants.

▶ un repas végétarien

▶
L I S T E

Un repas
végétarien:
– oeufs
– salade
– fromage
– pain
– yaourt
– eau minérale

1. un pique-nique à la
   campagne
2. un bon petit déjeuner
3. un repas d'anniversaire
4. le dîner de ce soir
5. le déjeuner de demain
6. un repas de régime *(diet)*

COMMUNICATION:
8 expressing preferences

COMMUNICATION: writing
9 shopping lists

 Cooperative group practice

Have groups of 3 or 4 students work
together to compose a shopping list for
one of the meals suggested in Act. 9.
    Each recorder (**secrétaire**) then reads
aloud the shopping list that the group has
prepared. The rest of the class tries to
guess the corresponding menu.

T353

C. Les fruits et les légumes *(Fruits and vegetables)*

▶ *How to shop for food:*

À la maison

— Où vas-tu?
— Je vais au **marché.**
Je vais **faire les courses** *(to do the food shopping).*
— Qu'est-ce que tu vas acheter?
— Je vais acheter des **tomates** et des **oranges.**

> Où vas-tu?

> Je vais au marché.

Au marché

— Pardon, madame. Combien coûtent les **pommes?**
— Elles coûtent trois euros le kilo.
— Donnez-moi deux **kilos de** pommes, s'il vous plaît.
— Voilà. Ça fait six euros.

> Pardon, madame. Combien coûtent les pommes?

> Elles coûtent trois euros le kilo.

10 **Qu'est-ce que vous préférez?**
Indiquez vos préférences.

▶ pour le petit déjeuner: un oeuf ou des céréales? **Je préfère des céréales.**

1. pour le petit déjeuner: un pamplemousse ou une banane?
2. après le déjeuner: une pomme ou une poire?
3. avec le poulet: des haricots verts ou des petits pois?
4. avec le steak: des pommes de terre ou des carottes?
5. comme *(as)* salade: une salade de tomates ou une salade de concombres *(cucumbers)*?
6. pour le dessert: une tarte aux cerises ou une tarte aux poires?
7. comme glace: une glace à la vanille ou une glace à la fraise?

11 **Les achats**
Vos copains reviennent du marché.
Demandez ce qu'ils ont acheté.

▶ —Qu'est-ce que tu as acheté au marché?
— J'ai acheté des carottes et des tomates.

TPR **Fruits and vegetables**
PROPS: Plastic fruits and vegetables

Place the items on a desk ("market stand").
Have students "buy" and distribute them.
**X, viens au marché et achète une
pomme.**
Maintenant, donne la pomme à Y.

Frequently ask who has what.
Qui a la pomme? [Y] **Qui a l'orange?** [Z]

Les fruits (un fruit)

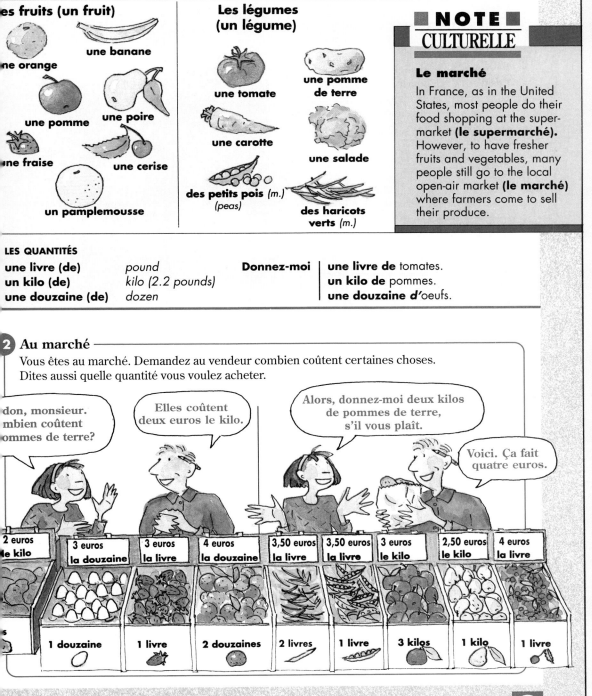

une orange
une banane
une pomme
une poire
une fraise
une cerise
un pamplemousse

Les légumes (un légume)

une tomate
une pomme de terre
une carotte
une salade
des petits pois (m.) (peas)
des haricots verts (m.)

■ NOTE ■
CULTURELLE

Le marché

In France, as in the United States, most people do their food shopping at the supermarket **(le supermarché).** However, to have fresher fruits and vegetables, many people still go to the local open-air market **(le marché)** where farmers come to sell their produce.

LES QUANTITÉS

une livre (de)	pound	Donnez-moi	une livre de tomates.
un kilo (de)	kilo (2.2 pounds)		un kilo de pommes.
une douzaine (de)	dozen		une douzaine d'oeufs.

2 **Au marché**

Vous êtes au marché. Demandez au vendeur combien coûtent certaines choses. Dites aussi quelle quantité vous voulez acheter.

…don, monsieur. …mbien coûtent …ommes de terre?

Elles coûtent deux euros le kilo.

Alors, donnez-moi deux kilos de pommes de terre, s'il vous plaît.

Voici. Ça fait quatre euros.

2 euros le kilo | 3 euros la douzaine | 3 euros la livre | 4 euros la douzaine | 3,50 euros la livre | 3,50 euros la livre | 3 euros le kilo | 2,50 euros le kilo | 4 euros la livre

1 douzaine | 1 livre | 2 douzaines | 2 livres | 1 livre | 3 kilos | 1 kilo | 1 livre

■ Cultural notes

- In general, farmers come to sell their produce on a given day of the week (**le jour du marché**). These open-air markets exist in large cities as well as in small villages.
- French people often buy food in speciality shops, such as:
  la boulangerie *(bakery)*
  la pâtisserie *(pastry shop)*
  la boucherie *(butcher shop)*
  la charcuterie *(delicatessen)*
  la crémerie *(dairy shop)*
  l'épicerie *(grocery store)*
- In the metric system, a pound (**une livre**) equals 500 grams or 1.1 U.S. pounds.

Supplementary vocabulary

LES FRUITS
un ananas /anana/ or /ananas/
un citron
un melon
le raisin *grapes*
une cerise
une pastèque *watermelon*
une pêche

LES LÉGUMES
un champignon *mushroom*
un chou-fleur *cauliflower*
un concombre
des épinards (m.) *spinach*
un oignon *onion*
un poivron *pepper*
une aubergine *eggplant*
une laitue
une salade

12 ROLE PLAY: Purchasing food at the market

■ **Teaching note:** The cues for this activity are written on the ends of the "boxes" at the bottom of the illustration.
- les oeufs / ça fait 3 euros
- les fraises / ça fait 3 euros
- les oranges / ça fait 8 euros
- les haricots verts / ça fait 7 euros
- les petits pois / ça fait 3 euros 50
- les pommes / ça fait 9 euros
- les poires / ça fait 2 euros 50
- les cerises / ça fait 4 euros

Transparency 47, 48
Fruits and vegetables
Expansion Activities, pp. A121, A122, A123

OPTIONAL: If the fruits and vegetables are light in weight and if the class is well behaved, manipulate the props as follows:
Y, donne-moi la pomme, s'il te plaît.
Attention, je vais lancer la pomme à X.
[Toss the apple to X.]

Qui a l'orange? X? Bien, lance l'orange à Y.

À votre tour!

1 Créa-dialogue

Vous êtes à Deauville avec un(e) ami(e). Essayez de découvrir *(try to discover)* ce que votre ami(e) aime manger. Proposez à votre ami(e) de déjeuner dans le restaurant correspondant à ses préférences.

▶ —Tu aimes <u>la viande</u>?
—Non, je n'aime pas <u>la viande</u>.
—Tu aimes <u>les légumes</u>?
—Non, je n'aime pas <u>les légumes</u>.
—Tu aimes <u>le poisson</u>?
—Oui, j'aime beaucoup <u>le poisson</u>.
—On déjeune <u>à La Marine</u>?
—D'accord.

la marine spécialités de la mer

1 CHEZ RIGOLETTO — spécialités italiennes

2 AU PALAIS DES GLACES — spécialités de glaces

3 À la Normandie — spécialités de fromages

4 À LA CAMPAGNE — Restaurant végétarien

5 L'Auvergnat — spécialités de jambon

6 CHEZ OBÉLIX — spécialités de bonnes viandes

7 Au petit gourmand — ses glaces et ses gâtea[ux]

2 Conversation dirigée

Avec un(e) camarade, composez un dialogue basé sur les instructions suivantes. C'est samedi aujourd'hui. Ce matin Marc et Juliette ont fait des achats en ville. Il est midi et demi maintenant.

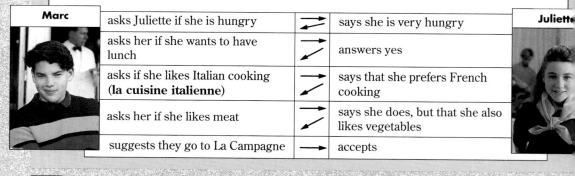

Marc			Juliette
asks Juliette if she is hungry	⤢	says she is very hungry	
asks her if she wants to have lunch	↗ ↙	answers yes	
asks if she likes Italian cooking (**la cuisine italienne**)	→ ↙	says that she prefers French cooking	
asks her if she likes meat	↗ ↙	says she does, but that she also likes vegetables	
suggests they go to La Campagne	→	accepts	

3 Composition: À la pension

This summer you are going to spend two weeks in France with your family. There are five people in your family and you are going to stay in a **pension** *(an inn offering a room and all meals)*. Write a letter to the owner saying what each family member likes or does not like to eat. Use your imagination.

▶

le 18 mai

Chère Madame,
J'aime . . .
Je n'aime pas . . .
Mon père aime . . .
Il n'aime pas . . .
Ma mère . . .
Mon frère . . .
Ma sœur . . .

3 WRITTEN SELF-EXPRESSION

4 Au «Départ»

Vous êtes à Paris avec des copains. Il est une heure et vous avez faim. Vous allez déjeuner dans le café suivant.

Regardez bien les illustrations.
• Comment s'appelle le café?
• Où est-il situé?

Regardez le menu et choisissez un sandwich ou une salade et un dessert (crêpe ou pâtisserie).
• Qu'est-ce que vous avez choisi?
• Combien coûte le sandwich ou la salade? le dessert?
• Quel est le prix total de votre repas?

Le DÉPART

1, Place Saint-Michel
75005 PARIS

4 READING COMPREHENSION

■ **Realia notes**
Le Départ
"Le Départ" is a small Parisian café-restaurant on the Left Bank (**la rive gauche**). The name of the restaurant recalls the nineteenth century when there used to be a train station across the street (**la gare Saint Michel**).
Note that in addition to mixed salads, sandwiches and pastries, one can also order **crêpes**.

Tarte Tatin
Tarte Tatin is an upside-down apple tart which is usually served warm.

Salades Composées

SALADE NIÇOISE ....7€
Salade, thon, olives, tomates, oeuf dur, anchois, poivron
Lettuce, tuna, olives, tomatoes, hard-boiled egg, anchovies, sweet pepper

SALADE 4 SAISONS ....6€
Crudités de saison
Vegetables in season

SALADE SAINT-MICHEL ....6€
Salade, jambon épaule, comté, pomme fruit
Lettuce, ham, Comté cheese, apples

SALADE MIXTE ....5€
Salade, tomates, oeuf dur
Lettuce, tomatoes, hard-boiled egg

SALADE DE POULET ....7€
Salade, poulet, comté, mayonnaise
Lettuce, chicken, Comté cheese, mayonnaise

SALADE CAMPAGNARDE ....7€
Salade, pommes de terre l'huile, cantal, jambon cru
Lettuce, potato salad, Cantal cheese, country ham

SALADE VERTE ....4€
Green salad

Sandwichs

Rillettes paysannes ....3€
Country minced potted pork

Paté du Quercy ....3€
Quercy style meat pie

Jambon de Paris ....3€
Paris ham

Saucisson d'Auvergne ....3€
Dry sausage from Auvergne

Le Végétarien ....5€
Salade tomate, oeuf dur
Lettuce, tomato, hard-boiled egg

Fromage ....3€
Cheese

Mixte (jambon et gruyére) ....5€
Combination (ham and Gruyère cheese)

Club Sandwich ....6€
Poulet, tomate, oeuf dur, salade, mayonnaise
Chicken, tomato, hard-boiled egg, lettuce, mayonnaise

Saucisses chaudes ....5€
Hot sausages

Crêpes Maison

Crêpe au sucre ....3€
Pancake sprinkled with sugar

Crêpe à la confiture ....4€
Groseille, abricot, fraise
Pancake with red currant, apricot, or strawberry jam

Crêpe aux noix et crème de cassis ....6€
Pancake with nuts and black currant cream

Crêpe aux marrons et Chantilly ....6€
Pancake with chestnuts and whipped cream

Crêpe au miel ....5€
Pancake with honey

Crêpe au Grand-Marnier .....6€
Pancake with Grand-Marnier

Crêpe Belle-Époque ....7€
Banane fruit, glace vanille, noisettes, Chantilly
Pancake with bananas, vanilla ice cream, hazelnuts, whipped cream

Crêpe au chocolat ....5€
Pancake with chocolate sauce

Pâtisseries

Tarte du jour ....5€
Tart of the day

Tarte aux pommes ....5€
Apple tart

Tarte aux fraises (selon saison) ....6€
Strawberry tart (in season)

Salade de fruits rafraîchis ....5€
Cold fruit salad

Gâteau du jour ....5€
Cake of the day

Tarte Tatin chaude ....6€
Hot Tatin tart

Tarte Tatin chaude, crème fraîche ....7€
Hot Tatin tart with cream

PRIX SERVICE COMPRIS (15%)

 ## Portfolio assessment

You will probably select only one speaking activity and one writing activity to go into the students' portfolios for Unit 9.
In this lesson, Act. 1 can be used as an oral portfolio recording. Act. 3 is an excellent topic for a written portfolio piece.

MODULE 34:
Les courses
Total time: 7:02 min.
(Counter: 31:40 min.)

34.1 Dialogue: Le pique-nique
(31:49–34:17 min.)
34.2 Mini-scenes: Listening — Voici du pain
(34:18–35:40 min.)
34.3 Mini-scenes: Listening — Je prends du beurre?
(35:41–36:07 min.)
34.4 Mini-scenes: Speaking — Tu veux du pain?
(36:08–37:33 min.)
34.5 Vignette culturelle: Le petit déjeuner
(37:34–38:39 min.)

Disc 5, Side 2
13537–26116

■ **Comprehension practice:** Play the entire module through as an introduction to the lesson.

 Leçon 34, Section 1

COMPREHENSION

1. à midi et demi
2. Jean-Paul
3. non
4. Il aime le gâteau et la glace.
5. Oui. Il aime les desserts au menu (le gâteau et la glace).

À la cantine

Il est midi et demi. Sophie va à la cantine. Elle rencontre Jean-Paul.

SOPHIE: Est-ce que tu veux déjeuner avec moi?
JEAN-PAUL: Ça dépend. Qu'est-ce qu'il y a aujourd'hui?
SOPHIE: Il y a du poisson!
JEAN-PAUL: Du poisson?
SOPHIE: Oui, du poisson.
JEAN-PAUL: <u>Quelle horreur</u>! Bon, aujourd'hui, je ne veux pas déjeuner.   *How disgusting!*
SOPHIE: Il y a aussi du gâteau.
JEAN-PAUL: Du gâteau! Hm . . .
SOPHIE: Et de la glace!
JEAN-PAUL: Une minute . . . je vais <u>prendre</u> un <u>plateau</u>.   *to take/tray*

● **Compréhension**

1. À quelle heure est-ce que Sophie va déjeuner?
2. Qui est-ce qu'elle rencontre?
3. Est-ce que Jean-Paul aime le poisson?
4. Qu'est-ce qu'il aime?
5. Est-ce qu'il va déjeuner avec Sophie? Pourquoi?

Setting the scene

Ask questions about the school cafeteria.
Est-ce que vous déjeunez à la cantine de l'école? Si oui, levez la main.
Est-ce que vous aimez la nourriture?
Qu'est-ce que vous aimez particulièrement?
Qu'est-ce que vous détestez?

Then have students read the opening text and the *Note culturelle* to find out what foods and beverages French students are served at school and what their reactions are.

Et toi?

1. En général, où est-ce que tu déjeunes?
2. À quelle heure est-ce que tu déjeunes?
3. En général, est-ce que tu aimes la nourriture de la cantine?
4. Qu'est-ce que tu fais quand tu n'aimes pas la nourriture de la cantine?

COMMUNICATION:
talking about lunch habits

■ NOTE ■
CULTURELLE

À la cantine

Où est-ce que tu déjeunes pendant la semaine? Quand on habite près de l'école, on peut° rentrer à la maison. Quand on habite loin, on déjeune à la cantine. À midi, beaucoup de jeunes Français déjeunent à la cantine de leur école.

À la cantine, chacun° prend° un plateau et va chercher° sa nourriture. Cette nourriture est généralement bonne, abondante° et variée. Le menu change chaque° jour de la semaine. Un repas typique inclut° les plats suivants:

- **un hors-d'oeuvre**
  salade de concombres,
  salade de pommes de terre,
  carottes râpées,° jambon . . .

- **un plat principal° chaud**
  poulet, steak, côtelette de porc°

- **une garniture°**
  spaghetti, frites, petits pois,
  purée de pommes de terre°

- **une salade verte**

- **du fromage**

- **un dessert**
  glace ou fruit

- **une boisson**
  eau minérale, limonade, jus de fruit

Où est-ce que tu préférerais° déjeuner?
À ton école ou dans une école française?

peut *can* **chacun** *each one* **prend** *takes* **chercher** *to get* **abondante** *plentiful* **chaque** *each*
inclut *includes* **râpées** *grated* **principal** *main* **côtelette de porc** *pork chop* **garniture** *side dish*
purée de pommes de terre *mashed potatoes* **est-ce que tu préférerais** *would you prefer*

Note culturelle

■ **Cultural notes**
- **une salade de concombres:** thinly sliced cucumbers served with an oil and vinegar dressing
- **une salade verte:** lettuce and vinaigrette, served after the main course
- **du fromage:** cheese is served as a separate course, after the salad

■ **Photo cultural note**
À la cantine
In school cafeterias in France, there are two ways of serving meals:
- family style (as shown in the top photo): the cafeteria personnel brings the dishes to the table and students serve themselves. There is no choice of menu.
- cafeteria style (as shown on the bottom photo): students take a tray (**un plateau**) and select what they want to eat.

🖥 Using the video

In the opening segment of Video Module 34, a father and son are sent to the super-market to get food for a picnic. Students will see what a French supermarket looks like.

In the middle segments, people talk about various foods, often in contexts where they naturally use the partitive article.

The *Vignette culturelle* is filmed at Nathalie Aubin's house. The family members each explain what they usually have for breakfast.

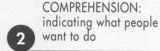

A. Le verbe *vouloir*

Note the forms of the irregular verb **vouloir** *(to want)*.

INFINITIVE	**vouloir**	
PRESENT	Je **veux** aller au café. Tu **veux** déjeuner. Il/Elle/On **veut** dîner.	Nous **voulons** une glace. Vous **voulez** des spaghetti. Ils/Elles **veulent** des frites.
PASSÉ COMPOSÉ	J'**ai voulu** dîner chez Maxim's.	

➡ When making a request, French people often use
je voudrais *(I would like)*, which is more polite than **je veux** *(I want)*.

    Je voudrais un café.   ***I would like*** *a cup of coffee.*
    Je voudrais dîner.   ***I would like*** *to have dinner.*

➡ When accepting an offer, the French often use the expression **je veux bien.**

    — Est-ce que tu veux déjeuner avec moi?   *Do you want to have lunch with me?*
    — Oui, **je veux bien.**   *Yes, **I do.** (Yes, I want to.)*

1 Vive la différence!

Nous sommes samedi. Des amis
vont en ville. Pour le déjeuner,
chacun veut faire des choses
différentes.

▶ Cécile/aller dans un café
  Cécile veut aller dans un café.

1. nous/manger des frites
2. toi/manger une pizza
3. vous/aller dans un restaurant
   italien
4. moi/aller dans un restaurant
   chinois
5. Patrick et Alain/déjeuner à midi
6. Isabelle/déjeuner à une heure

2 Oui ou non?

Dites si oui ou non les personnes entre
parenthèses veulent faire les choses indiquées.

▶ Il est midi. (nous/déjeuner?)
  Oui, nous voulons déjeuner.

▶ C'est samedi. (les élèves/étudier?)
  Non, les élèves ne veulent pas étudier.

1. Il fait froid. (Éric/jouer au foot?)
2. Il fait beau. (mes copains/aller à la plage?)
3. La nourriture est mauvaise. (vous/déjeuner
   à la cantine?)
4. Il y a des spaghetti. (moi/dîner?)
5. Il y a une excellente comédie. (toi/regarder
   la télé?)
6. C'est dimanche. (nous/travailler)

3 Expression personnelle

Complétez les phrases suivantes avec une expression personnelle.

1. Ce weekend, je voudrais ...
   Je ne veux pas ...
2. Cet été, je voudrais ...
   Je ne veux pas ...
3. Après l'école, je voudrais ...
   Je ne veux pas ...
4. Dans la vie *(life)*, je voudrais ...
   Je ne veux pas ...

B. Le verbe *prendre*

Note the forms of the irregular verb **prendre** *(to take)*.

INFINITIVE	prendre	
PRESENT	Je **prends** une pizza.	Nous **prenons** le train.
	Tu **prends** un sandwich.	Vous **prenez** l'avion.
	Il / Elle / On **prend** une salade.	Ils / Elles **prennent** des photos.
PASSÉ COMPOSÉ	J'**ai pris** un steak.	

➡ The singular forms of **prendre** follow the pattern of regular **-re** verbs. The plural forms are irregular.

Vocabulaire: Verbes comme *prendre*

prendre	*to take*	Nous **prenons** le métro.
	to have (food)	Est-ce que tu **prends** un café?
apprendre	*to learn*	Nous **apprenons** le français.
apprendre à + *inf.*	*to learn how to*	Sophie **apprend à** jouer de la guitare.
comprendre	*to understand*	Est-ce que vous **comprenez** quand le professeur parle français?

---

4 Qu'est-ce qu'ils prennent?

Dites ce que les personnes suivantes prennent. Pour cela, choisissez une expression logique de la liste.

▶ Philippe a faim.
Il prend un steak et des frites.

1. J'ai très soif.
2. Vous n'avez pas très faim.
3. Hélène a un nouvel appareil-photo.
4. Tu vas à l'aéroport.
5. Nous allons à l'école.
6. Les touristes vont à la Statue de la Liberté.

un bateau	une salade
un taxi	une limonade
le bus	un steak et des frites
des photos	

5 Questions personnelles

1. À quelle heure est-ce que tu prends le petit déjeuner le lundi? Et le dimanche?
2. Est-ce que tu prends le bus pour aller à l'école? Et tes copains?
3. Est-ce que tu prends des photos? Avec quel appareil?
4. Quand tu fais un grand voyage, est-ce que tu prends l'autocar? le train? l'avion?
5. Est-ce que tu apprends le français? l'italien? l'espagnol? Et ton copain?
6. Est-ce que tu apprends à jouer du piano? à jouer de la guitare? à faire du ski? à faire de la planche à voile?
7. Où est-ce que tu as appris à nager? À quel âge?
8. Est-ce que tu comprends bien quand le professeur parle français? Et les autres *(other)* élèves?
9. À ton avis, est-ce que les adultes comprennent les jeunes? Est-ce que les jeunes comprennent les adultes?

Leçon 34 **361**

■ **Pronunciation:** You may point out that **prendre** has three stems, all pronounced differently:
prend- /prã/
    je prends, tu prends, il prend
pren- /prən/
    nous prenons, vous prenez
prenn- /prɛn/
    ils prennent
Note: The "d" is silent in all the singular forms, and is dropped in the plural forms.

■ **Language note:** Remind students that *to take* a person somewhere is **amener**. (Also: *to take* a test is **passer** un examen.)

COMPREHENSION:
describing what people are doing
4

1. Je prends une limonade.
2. Vous prenez une salade.
3. Elle prend des photos.
4. Tu prends un taxi.
5. Nous prenons le bus.
6. Ils prennent un bateau.

COMMUNICATION:
answering personal questions
5

■ **Teaching strategy:** Help students with answer for item 7: à l'âge de [huit] ans

34.1 Dialogue: Le pique-nique
34.2 Mini-scenes:
Listening — Voici du pain
34.3 Mini-scenes:
Listening — Je prends du beurre?
34.4 Mini-scenes:
Speaking — Tu veux du pain?
(31:49–37:33 min.)

VIDEODISC Disc 5, Side 2
13786–24110

 Leçon 34, Section 3–6

 Transparency 49
Le partitif

■ **Looking ahead:** This section introduces the forms and basic uses of the partitive article. This concept is further developed in Book Two.

C. L'article partitif: *du, de la*

Learning about language

The pictures on the left represent *whole* items: a whole chicken, a whole cake, a whole head of lettuce, a whole fish. The nouns are introduced by INDEFINITE ARTICLES: **un, une.**

The pictures on the right represent a *part* or *some quantity* of these items: a serving of chicken, a slice of cake, some leaves of lettuce, a piece of fish. The nouns are introduced by PARTITIVE ARTICLES: **du, de la.**

Voici . . .

un poulet

un gâteau

une salade

une sole

Voilà . . .

du poulet

du gâteau

de la salade

de la sole

FORMS

The PARTITIVE ARTICLE is used to refer to A CERTAIN QUANTITY or A CERTAIN AMOUNT OF SOMETHING and corresponds to the English *some* or *any.* It has the following forms:

| MASCULINE | **du** | *some* | **du** fromage, **du** pain |
| FEMININE | **de la** | *some* | **de la** salade, **de la** limonade |

➡ Note that **du** and **de la** become **de l'** before a vowel sound.
de l'eau minérale

Mangez chaque jour...
du fromage, de la viande, des fruits et du pain.
🍁 Santé et Bien-être social   Health and Welfare
Canada   Canada

Teaching strategy

PROP: Transparency 49

Use Transparency 49 to present the differences between the indefinite article and the partitive article.

Help students notice the difference between *a whole item* (**un/une**) and *a part or amount of something* (**du/de la**).

Voici un poulet. [pointing to transparency]
Voici du poulet. [pointing to transparency]

Then have various students come up and point to the corresponding items as you mention them randomly in sentences. Meanwhile, students at their desks point to the illustrations in their books. Begin slowly, and then speak more rapidly.

USES

Note how the partitive article is used in the sentences below.

Philippe mange **du** fromage.   *Philippe is eating (some) cheese.*
Nous prenons **de la** salade.   *We are having (some) salad.*

—Est-ce que tu veux **du** lait?   *Do you want (any, some) milk?*
—Non, mais je voudrais **de l'**eau.   *No, but I would like some water.*

➡ While the words *some* or *any* are often omitted in English, the articles **du** and **de la** must be used in French.

➡ Partitive articles may also be used with nouns designating things other than foods and beverages. For example:

Tu as **de l'argent?**   *Do you have (any) money?*

Partitive articles are often, but not always, used after the following expressions and verbs.

voici	**Voici du** pain.	*Here is (some) bread.*
voilà	**Voilà de la** mayonnaise.	*Here is (some) mayonnaise.*
il y a	Est-ce qu'**il y a de la** salade?	*Is there (any) salad?*
acheter	Nous **achetons du** fromage.	*We are buying (some) cheese.*
avoir	Est-ce que tu **as de la** limonade?	*Do you have (any) lemon soda?*
manger	Marc **mange du** rosbif.	*Marc is eating (some) roast beef.*
prendre	Est-ce que vous **prenez du** café?	*Are you having (any) coffee?*
vouloir	Est-ce que tu **veux de la** glace?	*Do you want (any) ice cream?*

Voici un gâteau.

Voici du gâteau.

6 Le menu

Vous avez préparé un dîner pour le Club Français. Dites à un(e) camarade ce qu'il y a au menu.

▶ la viande   **Il y a de la viande.**

1. le rosbif	3. la salade	5. la glace	7. l'eau minérale
2. le poulet	4. le fromage	6. la tarte	8. le jus d'orange

Voici un poulet.
Je voudrais du gâteau.
Nous achetons du poulet.
Voilà une sole.

Tu prends de la sole?
Il y a une salade sur la table.
Je vais prendre de la salade.
Maman va faire un gâteau.

If students ask: The plural partitive article **des** is used with plural "mass nouns":
des spaghetti
des épinards (spinach)
des oeufs brouillés (scrambled eggs)
des carottes râpées (grated carrots)

Language notes

• Depending on the context, these expressions (**voici, voilà, il y a,** etc.) can also be followed by definite and indefinite articles:
Voici **le gâteau**.
Voici **un gâteau**.
Voici **du gâteau**.
Since these distinctions sometimes tend to be confusing, they are not developed until Book Two. At this point, the important thing is that students become familiar with the partitive and its uses.

• The partitive article is also used with **boire**, which is taught in section E of this lesson.

6 PRACTICE: describing a menu

Cooperative pair practice
Activity 6

T363

7 Au choix

Vous déjeunez avec votre famille. Offrez aux membres de votre famille le choix entre les choses suivantes. Ils vont indiquer leurs préférences.

▶ le lait ou l'eau minérale?

> Tu veux du lait ou de l'eau minérale?

> Je voudrais de l'eau minérale.

1. la soupe ou la salade?
2. le poisson ou la viande?
3. le rosbif ou le poulet?
4. le ketchup ou la mayonnaise?
5. le fromage ou le yaourt?
6. le beurre ou la margarine?
7. le gâteau ou la tarte?
8. le jus d'orange ou le jus de pomme?

8 Qu'est-ce qu'on met?

Dites quels produits de la liste on met dans ou sur les choses suivantes.

▶ On met <u>du beurre</u> (<u>de la confiture</u>) sur le pain.

1. On met … dans le café.
2. On met … dans le thé.
3. On met … dans la soupe.
4. On met … dans un sandwich.
5. On met … sur un hamburger.
6. On met … sur un hot dog.
7. On met … dans les céréales.
8. On met … sur un toast.

le fromage
le jambon
le beurre
la confiture
le ketchup
la mayonnaise
le sel
la crème
le sucre
la moutarde (mustard)
le lait

9 Les courses

M. Simon a fait les courses. Dites ce qu'il a acheté.

▶ **Il a acheté de la viande.**

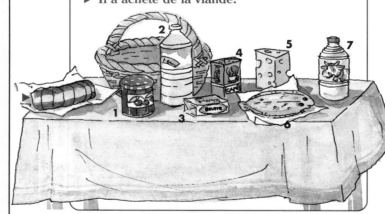

10 Le cochon d'or

Jacqueline est allée au restaurant. Voici l'addition. Dites ce qu'elle a pris.

▶ **Jacqueline a pris de la salade de tomates.**

RESTAURANT
Le Cochon d'Or

salade de tomates	3
jambon	4
poulet	
salade	3
fromage	
glace	3 €
eau minérale	2 €
café	2

Teaching project: Les repas

PROPS: One large paper plate per student
Have students illustrate their paper plates with drawings or pictures of at least five food items for one meal of the day. (They should write their names on the back of the plate.) Then in small groups, students take turns telling what they have for the particular meal.

As a follow-up activity, collect the plates and redistribute them so that each student has another student's plate. Then have them write what this person is having. For example:
Pierre prend un hot dog, des frites avec du ketchup et de la salade.
Comme dessert, il prend du gâteau et de la glace.

11 Au café

Au café, une cliente demande les choses suivantes. Le serveur apporte ces choses.

S'il vous plaît, monsieur, je voudrais du café.

Voici du café, mademoiselle.

11 ROLE PLAY: asking for things in a restaurant

1. du pain
2. du sucre
3. du beurre
4. du yaourt
5. du thé
6. de l'eau
7. du jus d'orange
8. du sel
9. de la glace

2 Menus

Préparez des menus pour les personnes suivantes. Dites ce que vous allez acheter pour chaque personne.

▶ une personne qui aime manger
Je vais acheter du rosbif, du fromage, de la glace …

1. une personne malade *(sick)*
2. un(e) athlète
3. un petit enfant
4. un végétarien (une végétarienne)
5. une personne qui veut maigrir
6. un invité *(guest)* japonais
7. une invitée française

12 COMPREHENSION: preparing special menus

D. L'article partitif dans les phrases négatives

Note the forms of the partitive articles in the negative sentences below.

AFFIRMATIVE	NEGATIVE	
Tu manges **du jambon?**	Non, je **ne** mange **pas de jambon.**	*No, I don't eat ham.*
Tu veux **de la salade?**	Non, merci, je **ne** veux **pas de salade.**	*Thanks, I don't want any salad.*
Est-ce qu'il y a **de l'eau minérale?**	Non, il **n'**y a **pas d'eau minérale.**	*No, there is no mineral water.*

In negative sentences, the PARTITIVE ARTICLE follows the pattern:

du, de la (de l')	→	ne … pas de (d')
Marc prend **du** café.		Éric **ne** prend **pas de** café.
Sophie prend **de la** limonade.		Alain **ne** prend **pas de** limonade.
Anne prend **de l'**eau.		Nicole ne prend **pas d'**eau.

Section D

COMMUNICATIVE FUNCTION: Making negative statements

■ **Language note:** The same pattern occurs with **ne… jamais.** Je **ne** prends **jamais de** sucre avec le café.

Leçon 34 **365**

Game: Menus

Prepare slips of paper numbered 1 to 7. Divide the class into seven groups, and distribute the numbered slips.

Each group prepares a menu for the corresponding guest in Act. 11 (e.g., group 2 sets up a menu for **un(e) athlète**).

The recorder (**secrétaire**) of each group then reads the menu: **Nous allons servir du rosbif, …** The rest of the class tries to identify the guest.

13 Un mauvais restaurant

Une cliente demande au serveur s'il y a certaines choses au menu. Le serveur répond négativement.

▶ le rosbif

Est-ce que vous avez du rosbif?

Je regrette mademoiselle, mais nous n'avons pas de rosbif.

1. le jambon
2. le melon
3. le thon
4. la sole
5. le veau
6. le yaourt
7. le jus de pamplemousse
8. l'eau minérale
9. le champagne

14 Au régime *(On a diet)*

Les personnes suivantes sont au régime parce qu'elles veulent maigrir. Répondez négativement aux questions suivantes.

▶ —Est-ce qu'Anne mange du pain?
  —Non, elle ne mange pas de pain.

1. Est-ce que Marc prend de la mayonnaise?
2. Est-ce que Pauline veut du gâteau?
3. Est-ce que Jean-Pierre mange de la glace?
4. Est-ce qu'Alice prend du beurre?
5. Est-ce que Monsieur Ledodu veut de la tarte?
6. Est-ce que Mademoiselle Poix met de la crème dans son café?

15 EXCHANGES: talking about what one does and does not eat

■ Photo culture note
À la cantine
In the cafeteria, French students eat directly from the tray. On the table you will note a pitcher of water (**un pichet**).

15 Conversation

Demandez à vos camarades s'ils mangent souvent les choses suivantes.

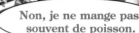

Est-ce que vous mangez souvent du poisson?

Oui, je man... souvent du poi...

Non, je ne mange pas souvent de poisson.

▶ du poisson

1. de la glace
2. du veau
3. du pain français
4. du fromage français
5. de la tarte aux fraises
6. de la soupe
7. du rosbif
8. du poulet
9. du thon

16 EXCHANGES: describing which foods are available- and which are not

1. oui   6. non
2. non   7. oui
3. oui   8. non
4. non   9. non
5. oui   10. non

■ Variation: Ask students whether these items are in their refrigerators at home.
– Et chez toi, est-ce qu'il y a du lait dans le réfrigérateur?
– Oui, il y a du lait. (Non, il n'y a pas de lait.)

16 Dans le réfrigérateur

Vous préparez le dîner. Demandez à un(e) camarade s'il y a les choses suivantes dans le réfrigérateur.

▶ le lait   —Est-ce qu'il y a du lait?
            —Non, il n'y a pas de lait.

1. le jus d'orange?
2. le pain?
3. la glace?
4. le beurre?
5. le jambon?
6. l'eau minérale?
7. le jus de pomme?
8. le fromage?
9. la mayonnaise?
10. le ketchup?

Cooperative pair practice
Activities 13, 14, 15, 16

Game: Qu'est-ce qu'il y a?

PROPS: Vocabulary cards of food items

Divide the class in half—Team A and Team B. Place 5 cards backwards on the chalkledge so that students cannot see the pictures. Player A-1 guesses a food item:
Est-ce qu'il y a du pain?
[Oui, il y a du pain. (Non, ...)]

If A-1 guesses correctly, his/her team wins a point. The teacher replaces the appropriate card with another one and the student guesses again. If not, player B-1 gets a chance to guess, etc. The team with the most points at the end of the game wins. NOTE: It is easier to remember the position of the cards if you alphabetize them as you place them on the chalkledge.

E. Le verbe *boire*

Note the forms of the irregular verb **boire** *(to drink)*.

INFINITIVE	**boire**	
PRESENT	Je **bois** du lait.	Nous **buvons** du café.
	Tu **bois** de l'eau.	Vous **buvez** du thé glacé.
	Il/Elle/On **boit** du soda.	Ils/Elles **boivent** du jus d'orange.
PASSÉ COMPOSÉ	J'**ai bu** du jus de tomate.	

17 Pique-nique

Philippe a organisé un pique-nique avec ses amis. Chacun *(Each person)* boit quelque chose de différent.

▶ Philippe boit de l'eau.

Philippe	1. nous	2. toi	3. vous	4. Cécile	5. mes copains	6. moi

18 Expression personnelle

Complétez les phrases suivantes avec la forme appropriée du verbe **boire** et une expression de votre choix. Attention: utilisez le passé composé dans les phrases 6 à 8.

1. Au petit déjeuner, je …
2. Au petit déjeuner, mes parents …
3. À la cantine de l'école, nous …
4. Quand il fait chaud, on …
5. Quand il fait froid, on …
6. Hier soir au dîner, j' …
7. Hier matin, au petit déjeuner, ma mère …
8. À la dernière boum, nous …

Prononciation   ou /u/   u /y/

Les lettres «ou» et «u»

la p**ou**le   le p**u**ll

The letters "**ou**" always represent the sound /u/.

Répétez: /u/   v**ou**s   n**ou**s   p**ou**let   s**ou**pe
            f**ou**rchette   c**ou**teau   d**ou**zaine

The letter "**u**" always represents the sound /y/.

Répétez: /y/   t**u**   d**u**   **u**ne   lég**u**me   j**u**s
            s**u**cre   bien s**û**r   aven**u**e   m**u**sée

Now distinguish between the two vowel sounds:

Répétez: /u/ – /y/   p**ou**le *(hen)* – p**u**ll
               r**ou**e *(wheel)* – r**u**e   v**ou**s – v**u**e *(view)*
               je j**ou**e – le j**u**s

Vou**s b**u**vez d**u** j**u**s de pamplem**ou**sse.**
Je vou**drais de la s**ou**pe, d**u** p**ou**let et d**u** j**u**s de raisin.**

▶▶▶▶▶▶▶▶▶▶▶▶▶▶▶▶▶

Leçon 34 367

Section E

COMMUNICATIVE FUNCTION: Talking about what one is drinking

17 PRACTICE: describing what people are drinking

1. du jus de raisin
2. de la limonade
3. du thé glacé
4. de l'eau minérale
5. du jus de pomme
6. du soda (de l'Orangina)

■ **Variation:** Have students give sentences in the negative.
Philippe ne boit pas d'eau.

18 COMMUNICATION: describing beverage choices

Prononciation

🔊 **Leçon 34, Section 8**

■ **Teaching strategy:** If your students still have trouble pronouncing /y/, be sure they pronounce the vowel as /i/. Then have them repeat the word, rounding their lips as if to whistle. For example, to pronounce **du**, first say **di**. Then repeat **di** with rounded lips. The resulting word will be quite close to **du**.

 TPR Drinking beverages

PROPS: Vocabulary cards of beverages

Hold up the beverages and pick one.
   J'ai soif. Qu'est-ce que je vais boire? [gesture "drinking" milk]
   Normalement je bois du lait.
Have individual students select beverages.
   X, viens ici. Qu'est-ce que tu bois?

[X picks water] **Ah, X boit de l'eau.**
Similarly present plural forms of **boire**.
   Y et Z, qu'est-ce que vous buvez?
[coffee]
   Tiens, Y et Z boivent du café.
   Moi aussi, je vais boire du café.
   Nous trois, nous buvons du café.

À votre tour!

1 COMPREHENSION

1-d   4-e
2-a   5-c
3-b

[cassette icon] Leçon 34, Section 9

1 Allô!

Reconstituez la conversation entre Frédéric et Sandrine. Pour cela, faites correspondre les réponses de Sandrine avec les questions de Frédéric.

1. Tu dînes au restaurant ce soir?

2. Tu as fait les courses?

3. Qu'est-ce que tu as acheté?

4. Tu n'as pas acheté de viande?

5. C'est vrai. Et pour le dessert, tu as acheté de la glace?

a. Oui, je suis allée au supermarc[hé] ce matin.
b. Du riz, des oeufs, de la salade [et] du fromage.
c. Non, j'ai pris un gâteau au cho[colat]
d. Non, j'ai invité mon copain Fab[ien] à dîner chez moi.
e. Mais non, tu sais *(know)* bien que Fabien est végétarien.

2 GUIDED ORAL EXPRESSION

[monitor icon] **34.5 Vignette culturelle:
Le petit déjeuner**
(37:34–38:39 min.)

VIDEODISC Disc 5, Side 2
24125–26116

[barcode]

[cassette icon] Leçon 34, Section 7

2 Dis-moi . . .

I will tell you about my breakfast this morning.

- J'ai pris le petit déjeuner à sept heures.
- J'ai mangé du pain avec du beurre et de la confiture.
- J'ai bu du café noir.

Now choose one of the meals you had yesterday and tell me . . .
- *at what time you had that meal*
- *what you ate*
- *what you drank*

3 GUIDED ORAL EXPRESSION

1. du rosbif, de la salade et de la glace
2. du poulet, du fromage et du yaourt
3. du fromage, du lait et du thon
4. de l'eau minérale et du jus de raisin
5. de la glace et du jus d'orange
6. *(answers will vary)*
7. *(answers will vary)*

[cassette icon] Leçon 34, Section 10

3 Créa-dialogue

Avec vos camarades, décrivez où vous êtes allé(e)s et ce que vous avez fait aux endroits suivants.

au supermarché
acheter

Où es-tu allée?

Qu'est-ce que tu as acheté?

Je suis allée au supermarc[hé]

J'ai acheté du pain, du lait et de la confiture.

368   **Unité 9**

À votre tour

Depending on your goals and objectives, you may or may not wish to assign all of the activities in the **À votre tour** section.

[faces icon] Cooperative practice

Act. 1 and 3 lend themselves to cooperative pair practice. Act. 3 can also be done in trios, with two students performing and the third acting as monitor and following along in the Answer Key.

4 Situation

Avec un(e) camarade, composez un dialogue correspondant à la situation suivante et jouez ce dialogue en classe.

You are talking to Florence, a French friend (played by your classmate). You have just invited her for dinner, but you understand she is on a special diet. Try to find out:

- what she eats
- what she does not eat
- what she drinks
- what she does not drink

5 Conversation libre

Avec un(e) camarade, composez un dialogue original basé sur la situation suivante.

You and your friend Caroline are in charge of the French Club picnic. Now you are walking up and down the aisles of a supermarket, discussing what things to buy or not to buy. For example:

▶ —Est-ce qu'on achète du pain?
—Oui, achetons du pain.
(Non, n'achetons pas de pain. J'ai du pain à la maison.)

6 Composition: Un bon repas

Think of a nice meal you had not too long ago — perhaps for a birthday or special holiday. Using the passé composé, write a short paragraph in which you describe . . .

- when, where, and with whom you had that meal
- what you ate and drank

Comment dit-on . . . ?

How to show your appreciation for good food:

Hm. . . C'est délicieux!   **C'est exquis!**   **C'est fameux!**

1. à la cantine manger	2. au restaurant manger	3. au marché acheter	4. à la boum boire

5. à la cuisine prendre	6. au café boire	7. dans un restaurant chinois ??

■ **Teaching strategy:** You may suggest supplementary vocabulary, such as:
la dinde *(turkey)*
le maïs /mais/ *(corn)*
le homard *(lobster)*
le rôti *(roast)*

Classroom Notes

■ Portfolio assessment

You will probably select only one speaking activity and one writing activity to go into the students' portfolios for Unit 9.

In this lesson, Act. 2 and 3 can be adapted as oral portfolio recordings.

Act. 6 is an excellent topic for a written portfolio piece.

MODULE 35:
Un client difficile
Total time: 7:40 min.
(Counter: 34:48 min.)

35.1 Dialogue: Un client difficile
(39:09–41:25 min.)

35.2 Mini-scenes: Listening — Apportez-moi du poulet
(41:26–42:54 min.)

35.3 Mini-scenes: Speaking — Qu'est-ce que tu veux?
(42:55–43:47 min.)

35.4 Vignette culturelle: La recette des crêpes
(43:48–46:21 min.)

VIDEODISC Disc 5, Side 2
26355–39987

■ **Comprehension practice:** Play the entire module through as an introduction to the lesson.

35.1 Dialogue: Un client difficile
(39:09–41:25 min.)

VIDEODISC Disc 5, Side 2
26501–31060

 Leçon 35, Section 1

■ **Language note** Tell students the meaning of **un ronchon** *(grouch).*

LEÇON 35 Un client difficile

M. Ronchon a beaucoup d'appétit . . . mais pas beaucoup de patience. <u>En fait</u>, M. Ronchon est rarement <u>de bonne humeur</u>. Et quand il est de mauvaise humeur, c'est un client difficile. Aujourd'hui, <u>par exemple</u>, au restaurant . . .

As a matter of
a good mood

for instance

—<u>Garçon!</u>
—J'arrive!
— Qu'est-ce que vous avez <u>comme</u> hors-d'oeuvre?
— Nous avons du jambon et du saucisson.
— Apportez-moi <u>tout ça</u> . . . avec du pain et du beurre!
— Bien, monsieur.

Waiter!
I'm coming!
as, for

all of that

—Et comme boisson, qu'est-ce que je vous apporte?
—Donnez-moi de l'eau minérale . . . <u>Dépêchez-vous!</u> J'ai soif!

Hurry up!

—Apportez-moi du poulet et des frites. . . <u>Vite!</u> J'ai très faim!
—Je vous apporte ça <u>tout de suite</u>.

Fast!

right away

—Et apportez-moi aussi du fromage, de la glace, de la tarte aux pommes et de la tarte aux <u>abricots</u>. . . Mais, qu'est-ce que vous attendez?
—Tout de suite, monsieur, tout de suite.

apricots

—Mais qu'est-ce que vous m'apportez?
—Je vous apporte l'<u>addition</u>!

check

370

Setting the scene

This comic scene is much more effective if presented by video. If this is not possible, play the corresponding cassette segment which has been taken from the video soundtrack.

Making crêpes

The *Vignette culturelle*, Part 4 of Video Module 35, shows how to make **crêpes**. If students ask, a **crêpe** recipe can be found at the end of Entracte 9, pp. 396–397.

Compréhension

1. En général, est-ce que M. Ronchon est de bonne humeur ou de mauvaise humeur?
2. Qu'est-ce qu'il va prendre comme hors-d'oeuvre?
3. Qu'est-ce qu'il va prendre comme plat principal *(main course)*?
4. Qu'est-ce qu'il va boire?
5. Qu'est-ce qu'il va manger comme dessert?
6. Qu'est-ce que le garçon apporte après le dessert?
7. Quelle est la réaction de M. Ronchon? Est-ce qu'il est de bonne humeur ou de mauvaise humeur?

Et toi?

1. En général, est-ce que tu es de bonne humeur?
2. Et aujourd'hui, est-ce que tu es de bonne humeur ou de mauvaise humeur?
3. En général, est-ce que tu as beaucoup d'appétit?
4. Est-ce que tu es une personne patiente?
5. Quand tu vas au restaurant avec un copain (une copine), qui paie l'addition?

■ NOTE ■ CULTURELLE

Les restaurants français et la cuisine française

Les Français aiment manger chez eux, mais ils aiment aussi aller au restaurant. Pour les gens pressés,° il y a les «self-service», les «fast foods» et les pizzerias.

Pour les gens qui veulent faire un bon repas, il y a toutes° sortes de restaurants spécialisés: auberges,° restaurants régionaux, restaurants de poisson, . . . Il y a aussi les «grands restaurants» où la cuisine est extraordinaire . . . et très chère!

La cuisine française a une réputation internationale. Pour beaucoup de personnes, c'est la meilleure° cuisine du monde.°

Les Américains ont emprunté° un grand nombre de mots° au vocabulaire de la cuisine française. Est-ce que tu connais les mots suivants: **soupe, sauce, mayonnaise, omelette, filet mignon, tarte, purée, soufflé?** Est-ce que tu aimes **les croissants? les crêpes? la mousse au chocolat?**

pressés *in a hurry* toutes *all* auberges *country inns*
meilleure *best* du monde *in the world*
ont emprunté *have borrowed* mots *words*

Leçon 35 **371**

COMPREHENSION

1. Il est de mauvaise humeur.
2. du jambon, du saucisson, du pain et du beurre
3. du poulet et des frites
4. de l'eau minérale
5. du fromage, de la glace, de la tarte aux pommes et de la tarte aux abricots
6. l'addition
7. Il est de mauvaise humeur.

COMMUNICATION: describing one's personality

Note culturelle

■ **Teaching strategy:** First, have the students pronounce the borrowed French words in boldface type as we do in English. Then have them try to pronounce the words "sounding French."

■ **Photo culture notes**
Le Procope
This photo was taken in the **Café Procope** which was founded in 1689 and is the oldest café in Paris. Its walls are decorated with portraits of some of its most famous patrons: Voltaire, Robespierre, Napoléon Bonaparte, Musset, etc.

La cuisine française
Most people who appreciate fine cooking consider French cuisine to be the best in the world. French chefs (**un chef**) like to create new dishes that will enhance their reputations. In France the top chefs enjoy the status of superstars.

Section A

COMMUNICATIVE FUNCTION:
Referring to oneself and to
those one is addressing

A. Les pronoms compléments *me, te, nous, vous*

In the sentences below, the pronouns in heavy print are called OBJECT PRONOUNS. Note the form and the position of these pronouns in the sentences below.

Anne **me** parle.	Elle **m'**invite.	*Anne talks to me.*	*She invites me.*
Mes amis **te** parlent.	Ils **t'**invitent.	*My friends talk to you.*	*They invite you.*
Tu **nous** parles.	Tu **nous** invites.	*You talk to us.*	*You invite us.*
Je **vous** parle.	Je **vous** invite.	*I am talking to you.*	*I invite you.*

FORMS

The OBJECT PRONOUNS that correspond to the subject pronouns **je, tu, nous, vous** are:

me ↓ **m'** (+ VOWEL SOUND)	*me, to me*	**nous**	*us, to us*
te ↓ **t'** (+ VOWEL SOUND)	*you, to you*	**vous**	*you, to you*

Cette carte **vous** donne l'accès à 60 musées.

CARTE
MUSÉES ET MONUMENTS

POSITION

In French, object pronouns usually come *before* the verb, according to the following patterns:

AFFIRMATIVE			NEGATIVE				
SUBJECT + OBJECT PRONOUN + VERB …			SUBJECT + **ne** + OBJECT PRONOUN + VERB + **pas** …				
Paul	**nous**	invite.	Éric	**ne**	**nous**	invite	**pas.**

1 **D'accord!**

Demandez à vos camarades de faire les choses suivantes pour vous.
Ils sont d'accord pour faire ces choses.

▶téléphoner ce soir?

1. téléphoner demain?
2. attendre après la classe?
3. inviter à ta fête/soirée?
4. inviter à dîner?
5. rendre visite ce weekend?
6. rendre visite cet été?
7. acheter une glace?
8. apporter un sandwich?
9. vendre ta raquette?
10. écouter?

Tu me téléphones ce soir?

D'accord, je te téléphone ce soir.

EXCHANGES: asking
friends to do things for you

■ **Variation** (response in the negative):
Non, je ne te téléphone pas.

■ **Variation** (in the plural):
– **Tu nous téléphones?**
– **Oui, je vous téléphone.**

■ **Photo culture note**
Les vélos
Note the different types of cycles used by students:
• mountain bikes (**un VTT** or **un vélo tout terrain**)
• racing bicycles (**un vélo de course**)
• mopeds (**une mobylette**)

Cooperative pair practice
Activities 1, 2

Teaching strategy: Object pronouns

The introduction of **me, te, nous, vous** before **le, la, les, lui, leur** serves two purposes:
• These pronouns are very useful in conversation.
• Students can practice sentence word order with these pronouns without

having to make the distinction between direct and indirect objects.
The third person pronouns are presented in Lesson 36.

2 Pauvre Nathalie!

Stéphanie a de la chance. Sa copine Nathalie n'a pas de chance. Jouez les deux rôles.

▶ mon copain/inviter

1. ma tante / inviter au restaurant
2. mes cousins / téléphoner souvent
3. mon frère / écouter
4. mes parents / comprendre
5. mes voisins / inviter à dîner
6. ma copine / aider avec mes devoirs
7. mon grand-père / acheter des cadeaux *(gifts)*
8. mes amis / attendre après la classe

Mon copain m'invite.

Tu as de la chance. Mon copain ne m'invite pas.

Vocabulaire: Les services personnels

aider quelqu'un	to help	J'**aide** mes copains avec les devoirs.
amener quelqu'un	to bring	Le taxi **amène** les touristes à la gare *(train station)*.
apporter quelque chose à quelqu'un	to bring	Le serveur **apporte** le menu **aux** clients.
donner quelque chose à quelqu'un	to give	Mme Marin **donne** 10 euros **à** sa fille.
montrer quelque chose à quelqu'un	to show	Est-ce que tu **montres** tes photos **à** ton copain?
prêter quelque chose à quelqu'un	to lend, loan	Est-ce que tu **prêtes** tes disques **à** tes amis?

3 Questions personnelles

Réponds affirmativement ou négativement aux questions suivantes.

1. Est-ce que tes copains t'aident avec tes devoirs?
2. Est-ce que ta mère ou ton père t'aide avec les devoirs de français?
3. Est-ce que ton père ou ta mère te prête sa voiture?
4. Est-ce que ton frère ou ta soeur te prête ses disques?
5. Est-ce que tes profs te donnent des conseils *(advice)*?
6. Est-ce que ton copain te montre ses photos?
7. Est-ce que tes cousins t'apportent des cadeaux *(gifts)* quand ils viennent chez toi?
8. Est-ce que tes parents t'amènent au restaurant pour ton anniversaire?

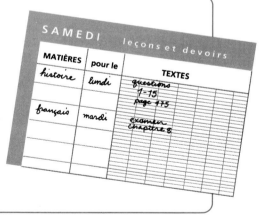

Leçon 35 **373**

ROLE PLAY: describing others' actions

■ **Teaching note:** Remind students to use **pas de** in item 7.

■ **Variation** (with **ne... jamais**): Mon copain ne m'invite jamais.

▷ **Vocabulaire**

■ **Language note:** The verbs **donner**, **montrer**, and **prêter** are new.

↻ **Re-entry and review:** You may want to review the conjugation of **amener**:
j'**amène**, nous **amenons**, etc. Remind students of the distinction between **amener** *(to bring people)* and **apporter** *(to bring things)*.

▭ Leçon 35, Section 2

COMMUNICATION: answering personal questions

■ **Realia note**
Le cahier de texte
French students are often required to buy special notebooks of the type pictured here (**un cahier de texte**) in which they write down their daily homework assignments.

PRACTICE: describing what people do for others

4

1. nous
2. t'
3. vous
4. me
5. te
6. nous
7. vous
8. nous
9. m'

■ **Realia note:** This is an advertisement for a paging device (beeper). Have students translate the caption **Quand on me cherche, on me trouve.** ["When one looks for me, one finds me."] Tell students that the caption is a takeoff from the French proverb **Qui cherche, trouve.** ("He who seeks, finds.")

Section B

COMMUNICATIVE FUNCTION:
Giving orders

35.2 Mini-scenes: Apportez-moi du poulet
35.3 Mini-scenes: Qu'est-ce que tu veux? (41:26–43:47 min.)

 VIDEODISC Disc 5, Side 2
31086–35311

 Leçon 35, Sections 3, 4

■ **Language note:** The <u>only</u> time the pronoun follows the verb is the affirmative imperative: **Téléphone-moi.**

5 EXCHANGES: borrowing things from friends

1. ton appareil-photo
2. ta veste
3. ton ordinateur
4. tes disques
5. ton vélo
6. ton walkman

Cooperative pair practice
Activities 5, 8

T374

---

4 **Bons services**

Informez-vous sur les personnes suivantes. Dites ce que leurs amis ou leurs parents font pour eux. Pour cela, complétez les phrases avec les pronoms **me (m'), te (t'), nous** ou **vous.**

▶ J'organise une boum.   **Ma soeur <u>me</u> prête ses cassettes.**
▶ Nous avons faim.   **Cécile <u>nous</u> apporte des sandwichs.**

1. Nous organisons un pique-nique. Nos copains … aident.
2. Tu as soif. Je … apporte un soda.
3. Vous préparez l'examen. Le prof … donne des conseils *(advice).*
4. J'ai besoin d'argent. Mon cousin … prête cent francs.
5. Tu es chez les voisins. Ils … montrent leur appartement.
6. Nous sommes à l'hôpital. Nos amis … rendent visite.
7. Vous êtes sympathiques. Je … invite chez moi.
8. Nous allons prendre l'avion. Le taxi … amène à l'aéroport.
9. Je nettoie le garage. Mon frère … aide.

"QUAND ON ME CHERCHE, ON ME TROUVE."
EUROSIGNAL
TELECOMMUNICATIONS

B. Les pronoms compléments à l'impératif

Compare the position and the form of the object pronouns when the verb is in the imperative.

AFFIRMATIVE	NEGATIVE
Téléphone-**moi** ce soir!	Ne **me** téléphone pas demain!
Invite-**moi** samedi!	Ne **m'**invite pas dimanche!
Apporte-**nous** du thé!	Ne **nous** apporte pas de café!

■ When the IMPERATIVE verb is AFFIRMATIVE, the object pronouns come *after* the verb.
⇒ **me** becomes **moi**

■ When the imperative verb is negative, the object pronouns come *before* the verb.

5 **Prêts** *(Loans)*
Demandez à vos copains de vous prêter les choses suivantes. Ils vont accepter.

Prête-moi ta raquette!

Tiens, voilà ma raquette.

Merci.

374 Unité 9

TPR 🏃 **Showing and distributing things**

PROPS: Miscellaneous objects from Lesson 33 (plastic fruits and vegetables; picnicware)

Place the objects on a table. Show and give the class certain items but not others.
Je vous montre une tasse. [hold up cup]
Je ne vous montre pas le verre. [hide glass]

Then call on students.
X, viens ici. Montre-nous la pomme.
Ne nous montre pas l'orange.
Y, viens ici et donne-moi le couteau.
Ne me donne pas la fourchette.
Donne la fourchette à Z.
Z, ne me montre pas la fourchette.
Passe la fourchette à W. …

6 À Paris

Vous visitez Paris. Demandez certains services aux personnes suivantes.

▶ au garçon de café *(waiter)*
  • apporter un sandwich
  S'il vous plaît, apportez-moi un sandwich.

1. au garçon de café
  • apporter de l'eau
  • apporter une limonade
  • donner un croissant

2. à la serveuse *(waitress)* du restaurant
  • montrer le menu
  • donner du pain
  • apporter l'addition *(check)*
3. au chauffeur de taxi *(cab driver)*
  • amener au musée d'Orsay
  • montrer Notre-Dame
  • aider avec les bagages
4. à un copain parisien
  • téléphoner ce soir
  • donner ton adresse
  • prêter ton plan *(map)* de Paris

7 Quel service?

Demandez à vos camarades certains services. Pour cela complétez les phrases en utilisant ces verbes.

aider	amener	apporter
donner	montrer	prêter

▶ J'ai soif. ... de la limonade.
  S'il te plaît, apporte-moi (donne-moi) de la limonade.

1. Je ne comprends pas les devoirs de maths.
2. Je voudrais téléphoner à ta cousine.
3. Je n'ai pas d'argent pour aller au cinéma.
4. Je voudrais voir tes photos.
5. J'ai soif.
6. J'organise une boum.
7. Je vais peindre *(to paint)* ma chambre.
8. Je vais à l'aéroport.
9. Je ne sais pas où tu habites.

▶ J'ai faim. ... un sandwich
  S'il te plaît, apporte-moi (donne-moi) un sandwich.

... avec le problème.
... son numéro de téléphone.
... six dollars.
... tes photos.
... de l'eau minérale.
... tes disques.
... avec ce projet.
... là-bas avec ta voiture.
... ton adresse.

8 Non!

Proposez à vos camarades de faire les choses suivantes pour eux. Ils vont refuser et donner une explication.

▶ téléphoner ce soir (Je ne suis pas chez moi.)

1. téléphoner demain soir (Je dois faire mes devoirs.)
2. inviter ce weekend (Je vais à la campagne.)
3. inviter dimanche (Je dîne chez mes cousins.)
4. attendre après la classe (Je dois rentrer chez moi.)
5. prêter mes disques (Je n'ai pas de chaîne stéréo.)
6. acheter un sandwich (Je n'ai pas faim.)
7. rendre visite ce soir (Je vais au cinéma.)

Je te téléphone ce soir?

Non, ne me téléphone pas. Je ne suis pas chez moi.

■ **Teaching note:** Have students use the **vous** form in items 1, 2, and 3; and the **tu** form in item 4.

■ **Expansion:** Have students make original requests to the people in items 1–4. Sample answers:
1. S'il vous plaît, apportez-moi le menu.
2. S'il vous plaît, apportez-moi (donnez-moi) du beurre.
3. S'il vous plaît, amenez-moi au musée du Louvre.
4. S'il te plaît, montre-moi la tour Eiffel.

7 COMPREHENSION: asking for appropriate services

1. Aide-moi...
2. Donne-moi (Montre-moi)...
3. Prête-moi...
4. Montre-moi...
5. Donne-moi (Apporte-moi)...
6. Prête-moi...
7. Aide-moi...
8. Amène-moi...
9. Donne-moi...

8 EXCHANGES: asking friends not to do things

■ **Teaching note:** Remind students to use **pas de** in item 6.

Leçon 35, Section 5

⟳ **Review and expansion:** The
je form of **devoir** and the **je** and **tu**
forms of **pouvoir** were introduced
in Lesson 13.

■ **Teaching strategy:** Have
students note how the forms of
pouvoir are similar to those of
vouloir.

■ **Language notes:**
• In writing, the accent circonflexe
appears on the past participle
dû to distinguish it from the
partitive article **du**.
• **Devoir** + noun means *to owe.*
Je dois dix euros à Hélène.

9 COMPREHENSION:
determining shopping options

1. Ils peuvent acheter un disque.
2. Je peux acheter une veste.
3. Tu peux acheter des chaussures.
4. Vous pouvez acheter un
   appareil-photo.
5. Elle peut acheter un pantalon.
6. Nous pouvons acheter une
   raquette.
7. Il peut acheter des livres.

C. Les verbes *pouvoir* et *devoir*

FORMS

Note the forms of the irregular verbs **pouvoir** *(can, may, be able)* and **devoir** *(must, have to).*

INFINITIVE	pouvoir	devoir
PRESENT	Je **peux** venir. Tu **peux** travailler. Il / Elle / On **peut** voyager. Nous **pouvons** dîner ici. Vous **pouvez** rester. Ils / Elles **peuvent** aider.	Je **dois** rentrer avant midi. Tu **dois** gagner de l'argent. Il / Elle / On **doit** visiter Paris. Nous **devons** regarder le menu. Vous **devez** finir vos devoirs. Ils / Elles **doivent** mettre la table.
PASSÉ COMPOSÉ	J'**ai pu** étudier.	J'**ai dû** faire mes devoirs.

USES

• **Pouvoir** has several English equivalents.

can	Est-ce que tu **peux** venir au pique-nique?	*Can you come to the picnic?*
may	Est-ce que je **peux** prendre la voiture?	*May I take the car?*
to be able	Jacques ne **peut** pas réparer sa mobylette.	*Jacques **is not able** to fix his moped.*

• **Devoir** is used to express an OBLIGATION.

| must | Vous **devez** faire vos devoirs. | *You **must** do your homework.* |
| to have to | Est-ce que je **dois** nettoyer ma chambre? | *Do I **have to** clean my room?* |

→ **Devoir** is usually followed by an infinitive. It cannot stand alone.

Est-ce que tu **dois étudier** ce soir?   *Do you **have to study** tonight?*
Oui, je **dois étudier.**   *Yes, I **have to** (study).*
Non, je **ne dois pas étudier.**   *No, I **don't have to** (study).*

9 **Le coût de la vie** *(The cost of living)*

Décrivez ce que les personnes suivantes
peuvent acheter avec leur argent.

▶ Philippe a quinze euros.
  Il peut acheter des lunettes de soleil.

1. Alice et Françoise ont cinq euros.
2. J'ai cent euros.
3. Tu as soixante euros.
4. Vous avez quatre-vingts euros.
5. Ma copine a soixante-cinq euros.
6. Nous avons cinquante euros.
7. Mon frère a vingt-cinq euros.

Cooperative
pair practice
Activity 10

10 Obligations?

Demandez à vos camarades s'ils doivent faire les choses suivantes.

▶ étudier?

1. étudier ce soir?
2. nettoyer ta chambre?
3. mettre la table?
4. réussir à l'examen?
5. aller chez le dentiste cette semaine?
6. parler au professeur après la classe?

> Est-ce que tu dois étudier?

> Oui, je dois étudier.

(Non, je ne dois pas étudier.)

7. être poli(e) *(polite)* avec tes voisins?
8. rentrer chez toi après la classe?

10 EXCHANGES: finding out what friends have to do and don't have to do

11 Excuses

Thomas demande à ses amis de repeindre *(to repaint)* sa chambre avec lui, mais chacun a une excuse. Dites que les personnes suivantes ne peuvent pas aider Thomas. Dites aussi ce qu'elles doivent faire.

▶ Hélène (étudier)
Hélène ne peut pas aider Thomas. Elle doit étudier.

1. nous (faire les courses)
2. Lise et Rose (acheter des vêtements)
3. moi (aider ma mère)
4. toi (nettoyer le garage)
5. Alice (rendre visite à sa grand-mère)
6. vous (déjeuner avec vos cousins)
7. mon frère et moi (laver la voiture)
8. Nathalie et toi (préparer l'examen)

12 Expression personnelle

Complétez les phrases suivantes avec vos idées personnelles.

1. Chez moi, je peux …
   Je ne peux pas …
2. À l'école, nous devons …
   Nous ne devons pas …
3. À la maison, je dois …
   Mes frères (Mes sœurs) doivent …
4. Quand on est riche, on peut …
   On doit …
5. Quand on est malade *(sick),* on doit …
   On ne doit pas …
6. Quand on veut maigrir, on doit …
   On ne peut pas …

11 PRACTICE: making excuses

■ **Teaching note:** Help students choose correct pronouns for items 7 and 8:
nous lavons…, vous préparez…

12 COMMUNICATION: talking about what one can and should do

Prononciation   s /z/   ss /s/

Les lettres «s» et «ss»

Be sure to distinguish between "**s**" and "**ss**" in the middle of a word.

poison   **poisson**

Répétez: /z/   **mauvaise cuisine fraise mayonnaise quelque chose magasin**

/s/   **poisson saucisson dessert boisson assiette pamplemousse**

/z/ – /s/   **poison – poisson   désert** *(desert)* **– dessert**

Comme dessert nous choisissons une tarte aux fraises.

Prononciation

🎧 Leçon 35, Section 6

Leçon 35   **377**

1 COMPREHENSION

1-e	4-c
2-d	5-a
3-b	

▣—▣ **Leçon 35, Section 7**

2 GUIDED ORAL EXPRESSION

3 GUIDED ORAL EXPRESSION

1. ta raquette
2. tes cassettes
3. ton appareil-photo
4. un dollar
5. cinq dollars

▣—▣ **Leçon 35, Section 8**

À votre tour!

1 Allô!

Reconstituez la conversation entre Corinne et Philippe. Pour cela, faites correspondre les réponses de Philippe avec ce que dit Corinne.

Corinne

Phi

1. Dis, Philippe, j'ai besoin d'un petit service.

a. C'est vrai . . . Bon, je t'achète tout ça *(all that)*.

2. Prête-moi ta mobylette, s'il te plaît.

b. D'accord! Je vais aller à la librairie *(bookstore)* Duchemin.

3. Dans ce cas, apporte-moi *Paris-Match*.

c. Écoute, je n'ai pas assez d'argent.

4. Alors, achète-moi aussi le nouvel album d'Astérix.

d. Ah, je ne peux pas. Je dois aller en ville cet après-midi.

5. Je t'ai prêté vingt euros hier!

e. Qu'est-ce que je peux faire pour toi?

2 Dis-moi . . .

I am going to spend a month living in your city and studying at your school. Since you are my friend, I will ask you a few favors, for instance:

- Prête-moi ton livre d'anglais.
- Montre-moi où est la cantine.
- Amène-moi à la bibliothèque.
- Invite-moi à ton club.
- Donne-moi le plan *(map)* de la ville.
- Téléphone-moi ce weekend.

Now imagine that you are visiting me in France. I am ready to help you. Ask me three or four favors.

3 Créa-dialogue

Demandez certains services à vos camarades. Ils vont vous demander pourquoi. Répondez à leurs questions. Ils vont accepter le service.

▶ —S'il te plaît, <u>prête-moi ton vélo</u>!
—Pourquoi?
—Parce que je voudrais <u>faire une promenade à la campagne</u>.
—D'accord, je te <u>prête mon vélo</u>.

	▶ prêter	1. prêter	2. prêter	3. apporter	4. prêter	5. donner	6. donner
QUEL SERVICE?							
POURQUOI?	faire une promenade à la campagne	jouer au tennis	organiser une boum	prendre des photos	acheter une glace	??	??

À votre tour

Depending on your goals and objectives, you may or may not wish to assign all of the activities in the **À votre tour** section.

Cooperative practice

Act. 1 and 3 lend themselves to cooperative pair practice. They can also be done in trios, with two students performing and the third acting as monitor and following along in the Answer Key.

4 Situation

Avec un(e) camarade, préparez un dialogue original correspondant à la situation suivante.

You are having dinner at a French restaurant called Sans-Souci. You have a friendly but inexperienced waiter/waitress (played by your classmate) who forgets to bring you what you need. Whenever you mention something however, he/she agrees to bring it right away **(tout de suite).** Tell your waiter/waitress . . .

- to please show you the menu **(le menu)**
- to please give you some water
- to bring you a napkin
- to give you a beverage (of your choice)
- to bring you a dessert (of your choice)
- to bring you the silverware that you need for eating the dessert

6 Composition: Bonnes relations

Select a person you like (a friend, a neighbor, a relative, a teacher) and write a short paragraph mentioning at least four things this person does for you. You may want to use some of the following verbs:

**acheter   amener   aider   donner   inviter
montrer   prêter   rendre visite   téléphoner**

> J'ai une bonne copine. Elle s'appelle Stéphanie. Elle est très sympathique. Elle me téléphone souvent et le weekend, elle m'invite chez elle. Elle est très intelligente et quand je ne comprends pas, elle m'aide avec mes devoirs de français. Elle me donne toujours des conseils (advice) excellents.

Now tell me about a friend of yours and let me know some of the things this friend does for you.

5 Conversation libre

Avec un(e) camarade, composez une conversation basée sur la situation suivante.

Imagine you are looking for someone to help you out. Ask a classmate to do you five favors. He/she will accept or refuse. In case of refusal, he/she will give you a reason. You may want to use some of the following verbs:

aider, amener, apporter, inviter, donner, montrer, prêter, vendre, acheter

For example, your conversation might begin like this:

▶ —S'il te plaît, invite-moi chez toi samedi après-midi.
—Je regrette, mais je ne peux pas.
—Pourquoi?
—Je dois faire les courses.

Comment dit-on . . . ?

How to show your reaction to bad food:

**Pouah! . . . C'est infect!   C'est dégoûtant!
C'est infâme!**

Leçon 35   379

4   GUIDED ORAL EXPRESSION

- Montrez-moi le menu, s'il vous plaît.
- Donnez-moi (Apportez-moi) de l'eau (minérale), s'il vous plaît.
- Apportez-moi une serviette, s'il vous plaît.
- Apportez-moi [du jus de pomme], s'il vous plaît.
- Apportez-moi [du gâteau].
- Donnez-moi (Apportez-moi) [une fourchette] pour le dessert, s'il vous plaît.

5   CONVERSATION

6   WRITTEN SELF-EXPRESSION

Classroom Notes

 ### Portfolio assessment

You will probably select only one speaking activity and one writing activity to go into the students' portfolios for Unit 9.

In this lesson, Act. 4 and 5 can be used as the basis for oral portfolio recordings. Act. 6 could be used as written portfolio topic.

MODULE 36:
Sur la plage
Total time: 5:35 min.
(Counter: 46:34 min.)

36.1 Dialogue: Sur la plage
(47:42–48:55 min.)

36.2 Mini-scenes: Listening — Tu le connais?
(48:57–50:00 min.)

36.3 Mini-scenes: Listening — On va lui parler?
(50:01–50:50 min.)

36.4 Vignette culturelle: À la plage de Deauville
(50:51–52:06 min.)

VIDEODISC Disc 5, Side 2
40310–50329

■ **Comprehension practice:** Play the entire module through as an introduction to the lesson.

▭ Leçon 36, Section 1

■ **Photo culture notes**
Deauville
On the coast of Normandy, **Deauville** is one of the oldest and most fashionable ocean resorts of France.
This photo shows the boardwalk (**la promenade des planches**).

Un pique-nique
On the left, French youngsters are having a picnic on the grass (**un pique-nique sur l'herbe**) in a park. On the right, French teenagers are having a picnic at the beach. Note that they have simply spread a tablecloth (**une nappe**) on the ground.

In France, public picnic grounds with tables are mainly found at the rest areas along the super-highways (**les autoroutes**).

LEÇON 36 Pique-nique

Florence et Jérôme organisent un pique-nique ce weekend. Ils préparent la liste des <u>invités</u>. *guests*
Qui vont-ils inviter?

FLORENCE: Tu connais Stéphanie?
JÉRÔME: Oui, je la connais. C'est une copine.
FLORENCE: Je l'invite au pique-nique?
JÉRÔME: Bien sûr. Invite-la.
FLORENCE: Et son cousin Frédéric, tu le connais?
JÉRÔME: Oui, je le connais un peu.
FLORENCE: Je l'invite aussi?
JÉRÔME: Non, ne l'invite pas. Il est trop snob.

■ NOTE ■ CULTURELLE

Un pique-nique français

Quand ils vont à la campagne, les Français adorent faire des pique-niques. Un pique-nique est un repas froid assez simple. Il y a généralement du poulet froid et des oeufs durs° et aussi du jambon, du saucisson ou du pâté* pour les sandwichs. Quand on a l'équipement nécessaire, on peut aussi faire des grillades° sur un barbecue. Comme dessert, il y a des fruits (bananes, oranges, pommes, poires, raisin°). Comme boisson, il y a de l'eau minérale, du cidre, des jus de fruit.

* The French have created dozens of varieties of **pâté,** ranging from the expensive and refined **foie gras** (made from the livers of fattened geese) to the everyday **pâté de campagne** (a type of cold meat loaf served in thin slices with bread).

durs *hard-boiled* **grillades** *grilled meat* **raisin** *grapes*

380 Unité 9

Setting the scene

1. Ask students if they go on picnics with family or friends.

2. Where do they go? What do they do?

3. And what do they eat and drink?

1. Est-ce que vous faites des pique-niques avec votre famille/vos copains?

2. Où allez-vous? Qu'est-ce que vous faites?

3. Qu'est-ce que vous mangez? Qu'est-ce que vous buvez?

 **36.4 Vignette culturelle:
À la plage de
Deauville**
(50:51–52:06 min.)

VIDEODISC Disc 5, Side 2
48003–50329

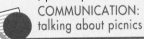

■ **Photo culture note**
La plage à Deauville

• sailboats (**un bateau à voile**)
• beach cabanas (**une cabine**)
• beach umbrellas (**un parasol**)
• beach chairs (**un transat**)
(The word **transat** /trãzat/ is a
shortened form of **transatlantique**,
deck chairs used on ocean crossings.)

 COMPREHENSION

1. C'est une copine de Jérôme.
2. C'est le cousin de Stéphanie.
3. Il a une mauvaise opinion de
   Frédéric. Il pense qu'il est trop
   snob.
4. Elle le trouve intelligent et
   sympathique.
5. Oui, parce qu'il a une voiture.

COMMUNICATION:
talking about picnics

■ **Pronunciation:**
un barbecue /barb kju/
borrowed from English, refers to
the meal and the grill.

Supplementary vocabulary

du poulet frit *fried chicken*
du poulet rôti *roast chicken*
des chips (m.) /ʃip/ or /ʃips/
des côtes (f.) **de porc** *spare ribs*
de la salade de pommes de terre
  potato salad
de la salade de chou *cole slaw*

FLORENCE: <u>Comment</u>? Tu le trouves snob? Moi, je le trouve intelligent
et sympathique. Et <u>puis</u>, il a une voiture et nous avons
besoin d'une voiture pour transporter <u>tout le monde</u>. . .

JÉRÔME: Florence, tu es <u>géniale</u> . . . C'est vrai, Frédéric n'est pas
<u>aussi snob que ça</u> . . . <u>Téléphonons-lui</u> <u>tout de suite</u> et
invitons-le au pique-nique!

What?
also
everyone
brilliant
*that snobbish / right
  away*

Compréhension
1. Qui est Stéphanie?
2. Qui est Frédéric?
3. Est-ce que Jérôme a une bonne ou une mauvaise
   opinion de Frédéric? Pourquoi?
4. Et Florence, comment est-ce qu'elle trouve Frédéric?
5. Finalement, est-ce que Jérôme va inviter Frédéric
   au pique-nique? Pourquoi?

Et toi?
1. Est-ce que tu aimes faire des pique-niques?
2. Quand tu fais un pique-nique avec des copains, où
   allez-vous?
3. Qui invites-tu?
4. En général, qu'est-ce qu'on mange à un pique-nique
   américain?
5. Qu'est-ce qu'on boit?
6. Dans ta famille, est-ce qu'on fait des barbecues?
   Où? Qui est le «chef»? Qu'est-ce qu'on mange et
   qu'est-ce qu'on boit?

 ## Using the video

Video Module 36 was filmed in Normandy
at the resort town of Deauville. In the dialogue scenes, two boys on vacation are
trying to figure out how to introduce
themselves to a girl at the beach.

In the *Vignette culturelle,* other young
people are interviewed about their vacation activities. The theme of the module
provides an appropriate point for wishing
your students a relaxing summer vacation.

COMMUNICATIVE FUNCTION:
Talking about whom one
knows

 Leçon 36, Section 2

■ **Spelling hint:** The circumflex
appears on the "î" of **connaître**
<u>only</u> when the next letter is a "t."

■ **Supplementary vocabulary:**
The verb **reconnaître** *(to recognize)* is conjugated like **connaître**.

■ **Teaching strategies**
• This is a simplified explanation
of the distinction between
connaître and **savoir**. The more
complex differences are presented formally in Book Two, e.g.,
Je connais la leçon *(I know
which one it is)* vs. **Je sais la
leçon** *(I know it because I have
studied it)*.
• You may wish to present the
complete conjugation of **savoir**.
See Appendix, p. R10.

PRACTICE: describing
whom or what people know

COMMUNICATION:
answering personal
questions

■ **Language note:** In item 5,
connaître means to know in the
sense of *to know of* or *to know by
reputation.* Students should be
able to name one person in each
category.

A. Le verbe *connaître*

Note the forms of the irregular verb **connaître** *(to know).*

INFINITIVE	**connaître**	
PRESENT	Je **connais** Stéphanie.	Nous **connaissons** Paris.
	Tu **connais** son cousin?	Vous **connaissez** Montréal?
	Il/Elle/On **connaît** ces garçons.	Ils/Elles **connaissent** ce café.
PASSÉ COMPOSÉ	J'**ai connu** ton frère pendant les vacances.	

➡ In the passé composé, **connaître** means *to meet for the first time.*

➡ The French use **connaître** to say that they *know* or *are acquainted with people or places.*
To say that they *know information,* they use **je sais, tu sais.** Compare:

PEOPLE/PLACES   INFORMATION

Je **connais** Éric.   Je **sais** où il habite.
Tu **connais** Frédéric.   Tu **sais** à quelle heure il vient?
Je **connais** un bon restaurant.   Je **sais** qu'il est près du théâtre.

Je connais Éric.

Je sais où il habite.

1 **On ne peut pas tout connaître**
Les personnes suivantes connaissent
la première personne ou la première
chose entre parenthèses. Elles ne
connaissent pas la deuxième.

▶ Philippe (Isabelle/sa soeur)
Philippe connaît Isabelle.
Il ne connaît pas sa soeur.

1. nous (Paul/ses copains)
2. vous (le prof d'anglais/le prof de
maths)
3. moi (les voisins/leurs amis)
4. toi (Paris/Bordeaux)
5. les touristes (le Louvre/le musée
d'Orsay)
6. mon copain (ce café/ce restaurant)

2 **Questions personnelles**
1. Est-ce que tu connais New York?
Chicago? San Francisco? Montréal?
Quelles villes est-ce que tu connais bien?
2. Dans ta ville est-ce que tu connais un bon
restaurant? Comment est-ce qu'il s'appelle?
Est-ce que tu connais un supermarché?
un centre commercial? un magasin de
disques? Comment est-ce qu'ils s'appellent?
3. Est-ce que tu connais des monuments
à Paris? Quels monuments?
4. Est-ce que tu connais bien tes voisins?
Est-ce qu'ils sont sympathiques?
Est-ce que tu connais personnellement
le directeur (la directrice) de ton école?
Est-ce qu'il (elle) est strict(e)?
5. Quels acteurs de cinéma est-ce que tu
connais? Quelles actrices? Quels
musiciens? Quels athlètes professionnels?

382 Unité 9

TPR 👤 **Direct object pronouns**

PROPS: 3 pictures of known personalities: a
man, a woman, a couple

Tape the 3 pictures on the chalkboard.
Point to the picture of the man:
Vous le connaissez? [write **le** on board]
Bien sûr, vous le connaissez. C'est …

Present the other 2 pictures (writing **la, les**).
Have students point to the right picture.
X, tu le connais? [X points to man]
Tu ne la connais pas? [X points to woman]
Tu les connais? [X points to couple]

Vary the verbs (beginning with consonants).
Y, tu la vois souvent? [Y points to woman]
Tu les trouves intéressants? [points to couple]

B. Les pronoms compléments: *le, la, les*

In the questions below, the nouns in heavy type follow the verb directly. They are the DIRECT OBJECTS of the verb. Note the forms and position of the DIRECT OBJECT PRONOUNS which are used to replace those nouns in the answers.

Tu connais **Éric?**	Oui, je **le** connais.	*Yes, I know **him.***
	Je **l'**invite souvent.	*I invite **him** often.*
Tu connais **Stéphanie?**	Oui, je **la** connais.	*Yes, I know **her.***
	Je **l'**invite aussi.	*I invite **her** also.*
Tu connais **mes copains?**	Je **les** connais bien.	*I know **them** well.*
	Je **les** invite.	*I invite **them.***
Tu connais **mes amies?**	Je **les** connais aussi.	*I know **them** too.*
	Je **les** invite souvent.	*I invite **them** often.*

FORMS AND USES

Direct object pronouns have the following forms:

	SINGULAR	PLURAL
MASCULINE	**le** ↓ *him, it* **l'** (+ VOWEL SOUND)	**les** *them*
FEMININE	**la** ↓ *her, it* **l'** (+ VOWEL SOUND)	

Qui le vend?
Qui le répare?

On le trouve
dans les pages
jaunes!

TELECOMMUNICATIONS

→ The direct object pronouns **le, la, l', les** can refer to either people or things.

Tu vois **Nicole?**	Oui, je **la** vois.	*Yes, I see **her.***
Tu vois **ma voiture?**	Oui, je **la** vois.	*Yes, I see **it.***
Tu comprends **le professeur?**	Oui, je **le** comprends.	*Yes, I understand **him.***
Tu comprends **ce mot** *(word)?*	Oui, je **le** comprends.	*Yes, I understand **it.***

POSITION

Direct object pronouns generally come *before* the verb according to the following patterns:

	AFFIRMATIVE		NEGATIVE			
	SUBJECT + **le/la/les** + VERB ...		SUBJECT + **ne** + **le/la/les** + VERB + **pas** ...			
Éric?	Je	**le** connais bien.	Tu	**ne**	**le**	connais **pas.**
Ces filles?	Nous	**les** invitons.	Vous	**ne**	**les**	invitez **pas.**

Leçon 36 — 383

Once students are comfortable with **le, la, les**, you may wish to introduce verbs beginning with vowels.
Z, tu les admires? [Z points to couple]
Tu l'admires aussi? [Z is confused]

Point to the man, addressing the entire class:
Cet homme, est-ce que vous l'admirez?
Write **l'** under the man's picture.

Et cette femme, vous l'admirez? Oui?
Write **l'** under the woman's picture.

Section B

COMMUNICATIVE FUNCTION: Talking about people and things

36.2 Mini-scenes: Tu le connais?
(48:57–50:50 min.)

VIDEODISC Disc 5, Side 2
44556–46439

Leçon 36, Sections 3, 4

■ **Pronunciation:** Be sure students make the liaison when the next word begins with a vowel sound.

■ **Language notes**
• Point out that direct object pronouns, in French as in English, replace the entire noun group: article (possessive, demonstrative, number), noun, adjective.
• Direct object pronouns are NOT used to replace nouns introduced by **un**, **une**, **des**, **du**, **de la.**
• The pronoun **en** is introduced in Book Two.

■ **Teaching strategy:** The following common verbs take direct objects in French. You may want to write them on the board.
WITH PEOPLE:
  aider
  inviter
  rencontrer
WITH THINGS:
  acheter
  avoir
  laver
  nettoyer
  prendre
  vendre
WITH PEOPLE OR THINGS:
  aimer
  connaître
  trouver
  voir
Point out that while **attendre**, **écouter**, and **regarder** take direct objects in French, the English equivalents have prepositions: *to wait <u>for</u>, to listen <u>to</u>, to look <u>at</u>.*

3 ROLE PLAY: indicating whether one knows people

4 EXCHANGES: answering questions using pronouns

5 ROLE PLAY/ COMPREHENSION: asking about activities

■ **Photo culture note**
Fontaine Igor Stravinski
The students in the photo are seated along the **Fontaine Igor Stravinski** which is behind the **Centre Pompidou** in Paris. (See TE note, page T199.)

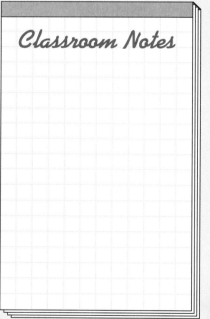

Classroom Notes

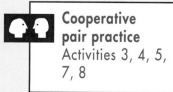
Cooperative pair practice
Activities 3, 4, 5, 7, 8

---

3 À la boum de Delphine

Pierre connaît tous les invités *(all the guests)* à la boum de Delphine, mais Lise ne les connaît pas. Jouez les trois rôles.

▶ ces garçons?

Tu connais ces garçons?

Et toi, Lise?

Oui, je les connais.

Non, je ne les connais pas.

1. Christophe?
2. Jacqueline?
3. Anne et Valérie?
4. Jérôme et Jean-François?
5. la fille là-bas?
6. cette étudiante?
7. ma cousine?
8. les cousins de Véronique?
9. la copine de Jacques?
10. ses frères?

4 Un choix difficile

Vous allez passer le mois de juillet en France. Vous êtes limité(e) à 20 kilos de bagages. Un(e) camarade demande si vous allez prendre les choses suivantes. Répondez affirmativement ou négativement.

▶ ta raquette?
—Tu prends ta raquette?
— Oui, je la prends.
(Non, je ne la prends pas.)

1. tes cassettes?
2. ton livre de français?
3. ta guitare?
4. ton walkman?
5. ta chaîne stéréo?
6. ton maillot de bain?
7. ton vélo?
8. tes tee-shirts?
9. tes sandales?

5 Questions et réponses

Michèle pose des questions à Jérôme en utilisant les éléments des Colonnes A et B. Jérôme répond logiquement en utilisant les éléments des Colonnes B et C et un pronom complément. Avec un(e) camarade, jouez les deux rôles.

A	B	C
où	rencontrer tes copains	le samedi matin
quand	voir ta cousine	à 8 heures du matin
à quelle heure	regarder la télé	à 9 heures du soir
	nettoyer ta chambre	à la Boîte à Musique
	faire les courses	à Mod' Shop
	acheter tes disques	au café Le Pont Neuf
	acheter tes vêtements	dans un supermarché
	prendre le petit déjeuner	le weekend
		pendant les vacances
		dans la cuisine
		dans le salon

Où est-ce que tu rencontres tes copains?

Je les rencontre au café Le Pont Neuf.

Quand est-ce que tu rencontres tes copains?

Je les rencontre le weekend.

C. La place des pronoms à l'impératif

Note the position of the object pronoun when the verb is in the imperative.

	AFFIRMATIVE COMMAND	NEGATIVE COMMAND
J'invite **Frédéric?**	Oui, invite-**le!**	Non, ne **l'**invite pas!
Je prends **la guitare?**	Oui, prends-**la!**	Non, ne **la** prends pas!
J'achète **les cassettes?**	Oui, achète-**les!**	Non, ne **les** achète pas!

In AFFIRMATIVE COMMANDS, the object pronoun comes *after* the verb and is joined to it by a hyphen.

In NEGATIVE COMMANDS, the object pronoun comes *before* the verb.

Section C

COMMUNICATIVE FUNCTION:
Giving orders

COMPREHENSION: making
suggestions about whom to
6 invite

6 Invitations

Vous préparez une liste de personnes à inviter à une boum. Vous êtes limité(e)s à quatre *(4)* des personnes suivantes. Faites vos suggestions d'après les modèles.

▶ Caroline est sympathique.
Invitons-la!

▶ Jean-Louis est pénible.
Ne l'invitons pas!

1. Sylvie est très sympathique.
2. Cécile et Anne aiment danser.
3. Jacques est stupide.
4. Robert joue bien de la guitare.
5. Ces filles sont intelligentes.
6. Martin et Thomas sont snobs.
7. Nicolas n'est pas mon ami.
8. Ces garçons sont pénibles.
9. Cette fille est gentille.
10. Tes copains sont méchants.

7 Le pique-nique

Olivier demande à Claire s'il doit prendre certaines choses pour le pique-nique.

▶ ma guitare (oui)

Est-ce que je prends ma guitare?

Oui, prends-la!

1. la limonade (oui)
2. les sandwichs (non)
3. la salade (oui)
4. le lait (non)
5. le gâteau (non)
6. mon appareil-photo (oui)
7. mes lunettes de soleil (oui)
8. les impers (non)

Variation (dialogue format):
With a classmate, decide if you
will invite the following people.
▶ Caroline est sympathique.
– J'invite Caroline?
– Oui, invite-la.
▶ Jean-Louis est pénible.
– J'invite Jean-Louis?
– Non, ne l'invite pas.

ROLE PLAY: offering and
accepting or refusing
7 services

ROLE PLAY: telling a friend
8 what to do and not to do

8 Oui ou non?

Votre petit cousin de Québec passe deux semaines chez vous. Il vous demande s'il doit ou peut faire les choses suivantes. Répondez affirmativement ou négativement.

1. Je fais les courses?
2. Je regarde tes photos?
3. Je nettoie ma chambre?
4. J'achète le journal *(newspaper)?*
5. J'invite les voisins à déjeuner?
6. Je prépare le dîner?
7. Je prends ton vélo?
8. J'écoute tes disques?

9. J'aide ta mère?
10. Je mets la télé?

Je fais les devoirs?

Oui, fais-les.

(Non, ne les fais pas.)

36.4 Mini-scenes: On va lui parler?
(50:01–50:50 min.)

VIDEODISC Disc 5, Side 2
46455–47970

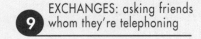

Leçon 36, Section 5

■ **Realia note**
This is a French **télécarte** or telephone "smart card." Most public telephones in the larger cities now take **télécartes** rather than coins. At the end of your phone conversation, the cost of the call is automatically deducted from the card. You can buy a **télécarte** at any post office or tobacco shop (**bureau de tabac**).

9 EXCHANGES: asking friends whom they're telephoning

■ **Variation** (in the plural):
– Vous téléphonez à votre copine?
– Oui, nous lui téléphonons. (Non, nous ne lui téléphonons pas.)

D. Les pronoms compléments lui, leur

In the questions below, the nouns in heavy type are INDIRECT OBJECTS. These nouns represent PEOPLE and are introduced by **à.**

Note the forms and position of the corresponding INDIRECT OBJECT PRONOUNS in the answers on the right.

Tu téléphones **à Philippe?**	Oui, je **lui** téléphone.
Tu parles **à Juliette?**	Non, je ne **lui** parle pas.
Tu téléphones **à tes amis?**	Oui, je **leur** téléphone.
Tu prêtes ton vélo **à tes cousines?**	Non, je ne **leur** prête pas mon vélo.

FORMS

INDIRECT OBJECT PRONOUNS replace **à** + <u>noun representing people</u>. They have the following forms:

	SINGULAR		PLURAL	
MASCULINE/FEMININE	**lui**	to him, to her	**leur**	to them

POSITION

Like other object pronouns, **lui** and **leur** come *before* the verb, *except* in affirmative commands.

Voici Henri.   Parle-**lui!**   Prête-**lui** ton vélo!

→ In negative sentences, **lui** and **leur,** like other object pronouns, come *between* **ne** and the verb.

Voici Éric.	Je ne **lui** téléphone pas.
Voici mes voisins.	Je ne **leur** parle pas.

9 **Au téléphone**

Demandez à vos camarades s'ils téléphonent aux personnes suivantes.

▶ ta copine

Tu téléphones à ta copine?

Oui, je lui téléphone.

(Non, je ne lui téléphone pas.)

1. ton copain
2. tes cousins
3. ta grand-mère
4. ton prof de français
5. tes voisins
6. ta tante favorite

Cooperative pair practice
Activity 9

T386

Vocabulaire: Verbes suivis *(followed)* **d'un complément indirect**

parler à	*to speak, talk (to)*	Je **parle à** mon copain.
rendre visite à	*to visit*	Nous **rendons visite à** nos voisins.
répondre à	*to answer*	Tu **réponds au** professeur.
téléphoner à	*to phone, call*	Jérôme **téléphone à** Juliette.
demander à	*to ask*	Je ne **demande** pas d'argent **à** mes frères.
donner à	*to give (to)*	Tu **donnes** ton adresse **à** ta copine.
montrer à	*to show (to)*	Nous **montrons** nos photos **à** nos amis.
prêter à	*to lend, loan (to)*	Je ne **prête** pas mon walkman **à** ma soeur.

➡ **Répondre** is a regular **-re** verb.

  Je réponds à François.   **J'ai répondu** à Catherine.

➡ The verbs **téléphoner, répondre,** and **demander** take indirect objects in French, but not in English. Compare:

téléphoner	Nous **téléphonons**	à	Paul.	Nous **lui téléphonons.**
	*We **are calling***	. . .	*Paul.*	*We **are calling him.***

répondre	Tu **réponds**	à	tes parents.	Tu **leur réponds.**
	*You **answer***	. . .	*your parents.*	*You **answer them.***

demander	Je **demande**	à	Sylvie	. . .	ses disques.	Je **lui demande** ses disques.
	*I **am asking***	. . .	*Sylvie*	*for*	*her records.*	*I **am asking her** for her records.*

---

10 **Les copains de Dominique**

Dominique a beaucoup de copains. Décrivez ce que chacun fait pour elle. Complétez les phrases avec **Dominique** ou **à Dominique**.

▶ Françoise invite <u>Dominique</u>.
  Patrick rend visite <u>à Dominique</u>.

1. Marc téléphone . . .
2. Jean-Paul voit . . . samedi prochain.
3. Sophie prête son vélo . . .
4. Corinne écoute . . .
5. François donne son adresse . . .
6. Philippe regarde . . . pendant la classe.
7. Delphine attend . . . après la classe.

8. Nathalie parle . . .
9. Pauline invite . . . au concert.
10. Pierre répond . . .
11. Isabelle montre ses photos . . .
12. Thomas demande . . . son numéro de téléphone.

▷ **Vocabulaire**

▨ **Language note:** Point out that **rendre visite** takes an indirect object because the expression literally means *render a visit <u>to</u> someone.*

▨ **Extra practice:** Have students reword the sample sentences using object pronouns.
Je lui parle.
Nous leur rendons visite. etc.

PRACTICE: distinguishing between direct and indirect objects

10

1. à Dominique
2. Dominique
3. à Dominique
4. Dominique
5. à Dominique
6. Dominique
7. Dominique
8. à Dominique
9. Dominique
10. à Dominique
11. à Dominique
12. à Dominique

■ **Expansion** (using object pronouns):
Dominique, C'est une fille!
Françoise l'invite.
Patrick lui rend visite.

11 **Joyeux anniversaire!**

Choisissez un cadeau d'anniversaire pour les personnes suivantes. Un(e) camarade va vous demander ce que vous donnez à chaque personne.

▶ à ton copain

> Qu'est-ce que tu donnes à ton copain?

> Je lui donne un livre.

Cadeaux
un pull
des compacts
une cravate
un livre
des billets (tickets) de théâtre
un magazine
ma photo
une boîte (box) de chocolats
un gâteau
??

1. à ton petit frère
2. à ta mère
3. à ta grand-mère
4. à ta copine
5. à tes cousins
6. à ton (ta) prof
7. à tes copains

12 **Questions personnelles**

Réponds aux questions suivantes. Utilise **lui** ou **leur** dans tes réponses.

1. Le weekend, est-ce que tu rends visite à tes copains? à ton oncle?
2. Est-ce que tu prêtes tes disques à ta soeur? à ton frère? à tes copains?
3. Est-ce que tu demandes de l'argent à ton père? à ta mère?
4. Est-ce que tu demandes des conseils *(advice)* à tes parents? à tes professeurs?
5. Est-ce que tu donnes de bons conseils à tes copains?
6. Est-ce que tu montres tes photos à ton frère? à ta soeur? à ta copine? à ton copain? à tes cousins?
7. En classe, est-ce que tu réponds en français à ton professeur?
8. Quand tu as un problème, est-ce que tu parles à tes copains? à ton professeur? à tes grands-parents? à tes parents?

Section E

COMMUNICATIVE FUNCTION: Describing what people say and write

↩ **Re-entry and review:** Ask students which two other verbs have **vous** forms ending in **-tes**: **vous êtes, vous faites.**

■ **Looking ahead:** The verb **lire** is not introduced until Book Two. If you wish to present the forms quickly for recognition, have students turn to the Appendix, page R9.

E. **Les verbes *dire* et *écrire***

Note the forms of the irregular verbs **dire** *(to say, tell)* and **écrire** *(to write)*.

INFINITIVE	**dire**	**écrire**
PRESENT	je **dis** tu **dis** il/elle/on **dit** nous **disons** vous **dites** ils/elles **disent**	j' **écris** tu **écris** il/elle/on **écrit** nous **écrivons** vous **écrivez** ils/elles **écrivent**
PASSÉ COMPOSÉ	j'**ai dit**	j'**ai écrit**

➡ Note the use of **que/qu'** *(that)* after **dire** and **écrire**.

Florence **dit que** Frédéric est sympathique.   *Florence **says (that)** Frédéric is nice.*
Alain **écrit qu'**il est allé à un pique-nique.   *Alain **writes (that)** he went on a picnic.*

➡ **Décrire** *(to describe)* follows the same pattern as **écrire**.

388 Unité 9

Cooperative pair practice
Activity 11

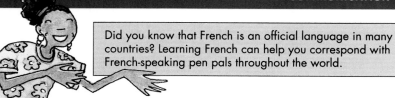

Did you know that French is an official language in many countries? Learning French can help you correspond with French-speaking pen pals throughout the world.

3 Correspondance

Pendant les vacances, on écrit beaucoup de lettres. Dites à qui les personnes suivantes écrivent.

▶ Juliette / à Marc
   Juliette écrit à Marc.

1. nous / à nos copains
2. toi / à ta cousine
3. moi / à ma grand-mère

4. Nicolas / à ses voisins
5. vous / à vos parents
6. les élèves / au professeur

4 La boum

Des amis sont à une boum. Décrivez ce que chacun dit.

▶ toi / la musique est super
   Tu dis que la musique est super.

1. Nicole / les sandwichs sont délicieux
2. nous / les invités *(guests)* sont sympathiques
3. Pauline / Jérôme danse bien
4. moi / ces garçons dansent mal
5. vous / vous n'aimez pas cette cassette
6. mes copains / ils vont organiser une soirée le weekend prochain

15 Questions personnelles

1. Est-ce que tu aimes écrire?
2. Pendant les vacances, est-ce que tu écris à tes copains? à tes voisins? à ton(ta) meilleur(e) *(best)* ami(e)?
3. À Noël, est-ce que tu écris des cartes *(cards)*? À qui?
4. À qui as-tu écrit récemment *(recently)*?
5. Est-ce que tu dis toujours la vérité *(truth)*?
6. À ton avis, est-ce que les journalistes disent toujours la vérité? Et les politiciens?

Prononciation

Les lettres «on» et «om»

Be sure to distinguish between the nasal and non-nasal vowel sounds.

REMEMBER: Do not pronounce an /n/ or /m/ after the nasal vowel /ɔ̃/.

on /ɔ̃/	on(n)e /ɔ/

lion	**lionne**

Répétez: /ɔ̃/ **mon ton son bon avion montrer répondre invitons blouson**

/ɔn/ **téléphone Simone donner connais mayonnaise personne bonne**

/ɔm/ **fromage promenade tomate pomme dommage comment**

/ɔ̃/–/ɔn/ **lion–lionne bon–bonne Simon–Simone Yvon–Yvonne**

Monique donne une pomme à Raymond.
Simone connaît mon oncle Léon.

---

13 PRACTICE: telling whom people are writing

■ **Variation** (dialogue format, reviewing **lui, leur**):
– Est-ce que Juliette écrit à Marc?
– Oui, elle lui écrit.

■ **Variation** (in the passé composé):
Juliette a écrit à Marc.

14 PRACTICE: describing what people are saying

15 COMMUNICATION: answering personal questions

Prononciation

 Leçon 36, Section 7

■ **Pronunciation:** Remind students that the letters "on" and "om" represent a nasal vowel when they occur at the end of a word or when they are followed by a consonant. When these letters are followed by a vowel, they do not represent a nasal sound.

■ **Additional practice**
/ɔ̃/	/ɔn/
champion	championne
mignon	mignonne

1 COMPREHENSION

1-d   4-f
2-c   5-b
3-e   6-a

📼 Leçon 36, Section 8

2 GUIDED ORAL EXPRESSION

3 GUIDED ORAL EXPRESSION

📼 Leçon 36, Section 9

1 Allô!

Reconstituez la conversation entre Jacques et Florence. Pour cela, faites correspondre les réponses de Florence avec les questions de Jacques.

1. Qu'est-ce que tu fais ce weekend?

2. Tu m'invites?

3. Et Catherine? Tu l'invites aussi?

4. C'est ma nouvelle copine.

5. Tu veux son numéro de téléphone?

6. C'est le 01.44.32.28.50

a. Je lui téléphone tout de suite *(right aw*
b. Oui, je ne l'ai pas.
c. Bien sûr, je t'invite.
d. J'organise une fête.
e. Catherine? Je ne la connais pas. Qui
f. Ah oui, je vois qui c'est maintenant. Eh bien, d'accord! Je l'invite.

2 Dis-moi ...

I met your cousin at a party last weekend. She is a very bright and pleasant person. I would like to see her again. Tell me ...

- Comment est-ce qu'elle s'appelle?
- Où est-ce qu'elle habite?
- Est-ce que tu la vois souvent?
- Est-ce que je lui téléphone? Quand?
- Est-ce que je l'invite au restaurant? À quel restaurant?

3 Créa-dialogue

Avec vos camarades, discutez de certaines choses que vous faites. Posez plusieurs questions sur chaque activité.

▶ regarder la télé?
à quelle heure?

Tu regardes la télé?

Oui je la regarde.

À quelle heure est-ce que tu la regardes?

À huit heures.

1. inviter tes amis?	2. voir tes cousins
quand? à quelle occasion?	quand? où?

5. faire tes devoirs?	6. télépho à tes copain
quand? où?	quand pourqu

À votre tour

Depending on your goals and objectives, you may or may not wish to assign all of the activities in the **À votre tour** section.

👥👥 Cooperative practice

Act. 1 and 3 lend themselves to cooperative pair practice. They can also be done in trios, with two students performing and the third acting as monitor and following along in the Answer Key.

4 Situation

Avec un(e) camarade, composez un dialogue original correspondant à la situation suivante. Jouez ce dialogue en classe.

You and another classmate know a very nice Canadian girl by the name of Catherine. Next weekend is her birthday and you want to do something special. With your friend discuss . . .

• whether to invite her to your house or to a restaurant
• what small gift *(petit cadeau)* you may buy for her
• what else you may do for her

5 Conversation libre

Avec un(e) camarade, composez un dialogue basé sur la situation suivante. Jouez ce dialogue en classe.

A group of French students are going to visit your town next week. As members of the Foreign Students Club, you and a classmate discuss what kinds of activities you will organize for them. You may want to use the following verbs:

inviter (où?), montrer (quels endroits?), amener (où?), donner (quels petits cadeaux [gifts]?)

4 GUIDED ORAL EXPRESSION

5 CONVERSATION

6 Composition: Les personnes dans ma vie *(life)*

Make a list of two or three people you know well. Give the name of each person and describe one thing you do for this person and one thing you don't do.

You may want to select:

• un cousin/une cousine
• un frère/une soeur
• un copain/une copine
• un voisin/une voisine
• un ami/une amie
• un professeur de français (d'anglais, de maths, d'histoire)

6 WRITTEN SELF-EXPRESSION

Ma cousine s'appelle Denise. Je la vois pendant les vacances de Noël. Je ne lui rends pas souvent visite.

. faire les courses?	4. aider ta mère?
quand? où?	quand? comment?
. rendre visite à ta grand-mère?	8. écrire à ton cousin?
quand? pourquoi?	pourquoi?

Comment dit-on . . . ?

How to tell someone to leave you alone:

Laisse-moi tranquille!

Fiche-moi la paix!

Leçon 36 — 391

Classroom Notes

Portfolio assessment

You will probably select only one speaking activity and one writing activity to go into the students' portfolios for Unit 9.

In this lesson, Act. 4 and 5 can be used as the basis for oral portfolio recordings.

Entracte 9

OBJECTIVES:
- Reading skills development
- Re-entry of material in the unit
- Development of cultural awareness

Bon appétit!

OBJECTIVES:
- Rapid reading at the sentence level
- Reading for cultural information about French foods and eating habits

■ **Photo culture note**
La Champagne
The photo shows the Champagne region in eastern France. This area is known around the world for its vineyards (**les vignobles**) and its famous sparkling wine (**le champagne**).

ENTRACTE 9

Petit test culturel
Bon appétit!

Répondez aux questions suivantes. Vérifiez vos réponses au bas° de la page.

1 Dans un repas français, quand est-ce qu'on mange la salade en général?
a. comme° premier plat
b. avec la viande
c. après le plat principal
d. après le dessert

2 En général, à quel repas est-ce qu'on mange des croissants en France?
a. au petit déjeuner
b. au déjeuner
c. au dîner
d. aux trois repas

3 Dans un restaurant français typique, qu'est-ce qu'on mange généralement avec un steak?
a. du riz
b. des spaghetti
c. des frites
d. des épinards°

4 Quand est-ce que les Français boivent le café?
a. avant le repas
b. pendant le repas
c. avec le fromage
d. à la fin° du repas

5 Le «camembert» est une spécialité qui vient originairement de Normandie. Qu'est-ce que c'est?
a. un gâteau
b. un fromage
c. une glace
d. un jus de fruit

6 La «bouillabaisse» est le plat traditionnel de Marseille, un grand port français sur la Méditerranée. Qu'est-ce que c'est?
a. une salade de fruits
b. une soupe de poisson
c. une tarte aux bananes
d. une omelette au jambon

7 Quelle province française a donné son nom à un vin° célèbre?°
a. la Savoie
b. la Champagne
c. la Bretagne
d. la Picardie

Réponses:
1. c; 2. a; 3. c; 4. d; 5. b;
6. b; 7. b.

au bas *at the bottom*   **comme** *as*
épinards *spinach*   **fin** *end*
vin *wine*   **célèbre** *famous*

392 **Unité 9**

 ## Cooperative reading practice

Divide the class into group of 4 or 5, each with a **secrétaire.**

For each question, have the groups first vote on the correct answer (keeping the box at the bottom of the page covered).

Then have the recorders check the right answers and announce their group score to the entire class.

Nous avons six réponses correctes.

Follow-up: Have students find all the places mentioned on the map in the reference section, page R4.

Petit déjeuner au Château Frontenac

Vous voyagez au Canada avec votre famille. Cette semaine vous êtes à Québec. Vous restez au Château Frontenac, un célèbre hôtel de la ville. Regardez bien le menu.

À quelle heure est servi° le petit déjeuner?

Vous avez le choix entre deux menus. Quel menu allez-vous choisir? Combien coûte-t-il?

Vous avez décidé de choisir le menu «Le Comte de Frontenac».

Quel jus de fruit allez-vous choisir?

Quelle boisson allez-vous choisir?

Quels oeufs allez-vous prendre?

Est-ce que vous allez prendre du jambon, du bacon ou des saucisses?

Est-ce que vous allez choisir des rôties, un croissant ou une danoise? Et qu'est-ce que vous allez prendre comme° confiture?

servi *served* **comme** *as, for*

Le Château Frontenac

(De 6h30 à midi)
PETIT DÉJEUNER CONTINENTAL
(From 6:30 to noon)
CONTINENTAL BREAKFAST
$7.75

☐ Jus d'orange ou
☐ Jus de tomate ou
☐ Jus de pamplemousse

☐ Orange juice or
☐ Tomato juice or
☐ Grapefruit juice

☐ Café ou
☐ Thé ou
☐ Lait

☐ Coffee or
☐ Tea or
☐ Milk

avec ☐ rôties, ou ☐ croissant, ou
☐ danoise, beurre et confitures

served with ☐ toast, or ☐ croissant, or
☐ sweet roll, butter and preserves

LE COMTE DE FRONTENAC
$11.25

☐ Jus d'orange ou
☐ Jus de tomate ou
☐ Jus de pamplemousse ou
☐ 1/2 pamplemousse ou
☐ Pruneaux

☐ Orange juice or
☐ Tomato juice or
☐ Grapefruit juice or
☐ 1/2 grapefruit or
☐ Stewed prunes

☐ Café ou
☐ Thé ou
☐ Lait

☐ Coffee or
☐ Tea or
☐ Milk

☐ Deux oeufs frits ou
☐ Oeufs brouillés ou
☐ Deux oeufs à la coque ou
☐ Crêpes canadiennes ou
☐ Crêpes françaises

☐ Two fried eggs or
☐ Scrambled eggs or
☐ Two boiled eggs or
☐ Canadian pancakes or
☐ French pancakes

☐ Jambon ou
☐ Bacon ou
☐ Saucisses

☐ Ham or
☐ Bacon or
☐ Sausages

avec
☐ rôties ou
☐ croissant ou
☐ danoise
beurre et confitures

☐ Fraises
☐ Framboises
☐ Orange
☐ Miel

served with
☐ toast or
☐ croissant or
☐ sweet roll
butter and preserves

☐ Strawberry
☐ Raspberry
☐ Orange
☐ Honey

LE CAFÉ CANADIEN
Pour un petit déjeuner léger ou complet service à la carte ou buffet de 07h00 à 11h00.

LE CAFÉ CANADIEN
Light and full course breakfast à la carte or buffet from 7 to 11:00 a.m.

Au Canada

OBJECTIVES:
• Reading authentic documents
• Vocabulary expansion

■ **Photo culture note**
Le Château Frontenac
The landmark hotel of Quebec City, **le Château Frontenac**, was named after Louis de Frontenac (1620-1698), Governor of **la Nouvelle France**, the former French territory which is now part of Canada.

■ **Language note:** In France, one would say:
des toasts (rather than **des rôties**)
une pâtisserie (rather than **une danoise**)

📖 Pre-reading
Have students look quickly at the menu and decide what meal is presented. How can they tell?

Post-reading
Have students pretend that they are on a student tour to Quebec City and are staying at the Château Frontenac. They have assembled in the reception area and are talking in pairs about what they each had for breakfast.
Moi, j'ai pris le Continental. J'ai choisi …

Le petit déjeuner

OBJECTIVES:
• Reading at the paragraph level
• Building reading skills

■ Questions sur le texte

1. Qu'est-ce que Fabrice met sur son pain?
2. Qu'est-ce qu'il boit?
3. Qu'est-ce que Sylvie boit au petit déjeuner?
4. Quel jour est-ce qu'elle mange des croissants?
5. Pourquoi est-ce que Daniel dit qu'il prend le petit déjeuner à l'américaine?
6. Pourquoi est-ce que Marie-Hélène ne mange pas beau coup au petit déjeuner?
7. Qu'est-ce qu'elle boit?
8. Où habite Chantal?
9. En général, qu'est-ce qu'elle mange au petit déjeuner?
10. Qu'est-ce qu'elle mange avec le blaff de poisson?

■ Questions personnelles

1. Est-ce que tu bois du jus de fruit le matin? Quel jus de fruit?
2. Est-ce que tes parents boivent du café? Sinon, qu'est-ce qu'ils boivent?
3. Est-ce que tu manges souvent des croissants? Quand?
4. Est-ce que tu aimes la confiture? Quelle est ta confiture préférée?
5. Est-ce que tu manges des céréales? De quelles sortes?
6. Est-ce que tu préfères le petit déjeuner français ou le petit déjeuner américain? Pourquoi?

■ Realia note

La Villa Créole is a small Martinique restaurant on the beach at Anse-Mitan (**anse** = bay) in the town of Trois Ilets (**îlet** = small island).

Entre amis: **Le petit déjeuner**

«Qu'est-ce que vous prenez au petit déjeuner?» Aux États-Unis, le petit déjeuner est généralement un repas abondant.° En France, c'est un repas simple.

Fabrice (13 ans)

Chez nous, nous sommes très traditionnels. Je mange du pain avec du beurre et de la confiture. Je bois un grand bol° de café au lait.

Sylvie (14 ans)

Je mange des tartines de pain grillé° et je bois du lait chaud ou du chocolat avec beaucoup de sucre. Le dimanche, il y a parfois° des croissants. (Ça dépend si quelqu'un veut faire les courses!)

Daniel (12 ans)

Chez nous, nous prenons le petit déjeuner «à l'américaine». Je mange des céréales et je bois du jus d'orange.

Marie-Hélène (16 ans)

Je ne veux pas grossir. Alors, je mange une ou deux biscottes.° Sans° beurre, bien sûr. Et je bois du thé.

Chantal (13 ans)

Je suis martiniquaise. En général, je mange du pain et de la confiture comme° tout le monde.° Parfois ma mère prépare un petit déjeuner martiniquais typique. On mange du blaff de poisson° et des bananes vertes cuites.° On mange aussi des ananas,° des papayes et de la gelée de goyave.° C'est délicieux!

abondant *copious, large* **bol** *deep bowl* **pain grillé** *buttered toast* **parfois** *sometimes* **biscottes** *dried toast* **Sans** *Without* **comme** *like* **tout le monde** *everybody* **blaff de poisson** *fish stew* **cuites** *cooked* **ananas** *pineapples* **gelée de goyave** *guava jelly*

■ **NOTE** ■
CULTURELLE

La cuisine créole

La cuisine créole est une cuisine régionale typique de la Martinique et de la Guadeloupe. C'est une cuisine assez épicée° qui utilise les produits locaux,° principalement les produits de la mer et les fruits exotiques.

épicée *hot (spiced)* **locaux** *local*

LA VILLA CRÉOLE
La Bonne Cuisine Française et
ANSE-MITAN TROIS-ILETS
☎ 66.05.53

📖 Pre-reading

Have students glance over the reading quickly.
   What is the question that was asked in the interview?

Post-reading

Ask each student to decide which of the five people they would like to have breakfast with and why.
Chez qui veux-tu prendre le petit déjeuner?
Pourquoi?

Comment lire
MORE GUESSING FROM CONTEXT

When you are reading, the context is not only the printed word. Sometimes there are illustrations to help you understand the text. As you read the recipe for **crêpes** on the next page, try guessing what the new words mean by studying the pictures. (You can check how well you are doing by looking at the English equivalents at the bottom of the page.)

Enrichissez votre vocabulaire
INCREASING YOUR ENGLISH VOCABULARY

Learning French will also help you increase your English vocabulary. Sometimes a French word you know will help you guess the meaning of an unfamiliar English word. For example:

a repast   looks like **un repas**   and is an old word for *meal*

Activité
Match these English words with their corresponding definitions.

1. to blanch   a. painfully difficult work
2. facile   b. easily done
3. travail   c. very hungry
4. famished   d. to whiten, to bleach

Activité: Mon petit déjeuner
Décrivez le petit déjeuner chez vous.
- pendant la semaine
- le dimanche matin

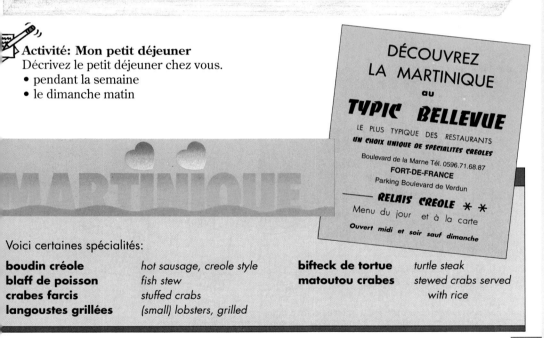

DÉCOUVREZ
LA MARTINIQUE
au
TYPIC BELLEVUE
LE PLUS TYPIQUE DES RESTAURANTS
UN CHOIX UNIQUE DE SPÉCIALITÉS CRÉOLES
Boulevard de la Marne Tél. 0596.71.68.87
FORT-DE-FRANCE
Parking Boulevard de Verdun
—— **RELAIS CRÉOLE** ✶✶ ——
Menu du jour et à la carte
Ouvert midi et soir sauf dimanche

Voici certaines spécialités:

boudin créole	*hot sausage, creole style*	**bifteck de tortue**	*turtle steak*
blaff de poisson	*fish stew*	**matoutou crabes**	*stewed crabs served*
crabes farcis	*stuffed crabs*		*with rice*
langoustes grillées	*(small) lobsters, grilled*		

Realia note
Le menu
At the **Typic Bellevue** one can either select the **prix fixe** menu (**le menu du jour**) or order dishes from the main menu (**à la carte**).

OBJECTIVES:
- Reading for information
- Understanding and following instructions

 35.4 Vignette culturelle: La recette des crêpes
(43:48–46:21 min.)

VIDEODISC Disc 5, Side 2
35328 to 50329

■ **Photo culture note**
Une cuisine française
French kitchens are smaller than American kitchens, but they are usually equipped in the same way. Note in the background:
- the counter (**le comptoir**)
- the cabinets (**les placards**)
- the sink (**l'évier**)
- pots and pans (**les casseroles**)
- the microwave oven (**le four à micro-ondes**)

■ **Realia note**
Crêpes bretonnes
The area of Brittany (**la Bretagne**) in western France is known for its **crêpes**. For festive occasions, the women of Brittany have traditionally won starched lace head-dresses (**une coiffe bretonne**).

LECTURE ET CULTURE

Variétés

Les crêpes

Les crêpes sont d'origine bretonne.° Aujourd'hui, on vend les crêpes dans les «crêperies». On peut aussi faire des crêpes à la maison. Voici une recette° très simple.

LES INGRÉDIENTS

3 oeufs
3 cuillères à soupe de sucre
une pincée° de sel
2 tasses de lait
1 tasse de farine°
1 cuillère à soupe d'huile°
du beurre

LES USTENSILES

 un petit bol

 un fouet

 un grand bol

une poêle

D'abord: Pour faire la pâte°

Mettez les oeufs dans le petit bol. Battez-les° bien avec le fouet.

Ajoutez° le sucre, le sel et un peu de lait.

Mettez la farine dans le grand bol. Versez° le contenu° du petit bol dans le grand bol.

Ajoutez l'huile et le reste du lait. Mélangez° bien la pâte. Attendez deux heures.

La Crêperie Québécoise
1775 St-Hubert, Montréal H2L 3Z1
(Métro Berri-de-Montigny)   Tél: 521-8362

---

bretonne *from Brittany*   **recette** *recipe*   **pincée** *pinch*   **farine** *flour*   **huile** *oil*   **pâte** *batter*
Battez-les *Beat them*   **Ajoutez** *Add*   **Versez** *Pour*   **contenu** *contents*   **Mélangez** *Mix, Stir*

396 Unité 9

Ensuite: Pour faire les crêpes

Chauffez° la poêle. Mettez du beurre dans la poêle.

Mettez une cuillère de pâte dans la poêle.

Agitez° la poêle pour étendre° la pâte.

Retournez° la crêpe quand elle est dorée.°

Si vous êtes adroit(e), faites sauter° la crêpe en l'air. Si vous n'êtes pas adroit(e), abstenez-vous!°

Enfin: Pour servir les crêpes

Mettez la crêpe sur une assiette chaude. Faites les autres° crêpes.

Mettez du sucre ou de la confiture sur chaque° crêpe.

Au choix, roulez-la° ou pliez-la° en quatre.

Chauffez *Heat* **Agitez** *Shake* **étendre** *spread*
Retournez *Turn over* **dorée** *golden brown* **faites sauter** *flip*
abstenez-vous *don't try* **autres** *other* **chaque** *each*
roulez-la *roll it* **pliez-la** *fold it*

Entracte 9 397

UNITÉ 9
INTERNET PROJECT

Students may use the Internet to find out more about outdoor recreation and national parks in Canada. If students could plan a picnic anywhere in North America, where would they go? Students can start with the link available below and look at the numerous parks listed there, or explore the alternate given. To expand this activity, have students generate new links by using the search engine of their choice and the keywords **"parcs nationaux"**; écotourisme.

Parcs nationaux
http://parkscanada.pch.gc.ca/NP/np_f.htm

ALTERNATE
Écotourisme et aventures
http://ecoroute.uqcn.qc.ca/ecot/index.htm

Teaching strategy: Les crêpes

You might want to cooperate with the home economics department and let the students learn to make **crêpes** in the school kitchen.

REFERENCE SECTION

CONTENTS

APPENDIX 1
Maps

The French-Speaking World

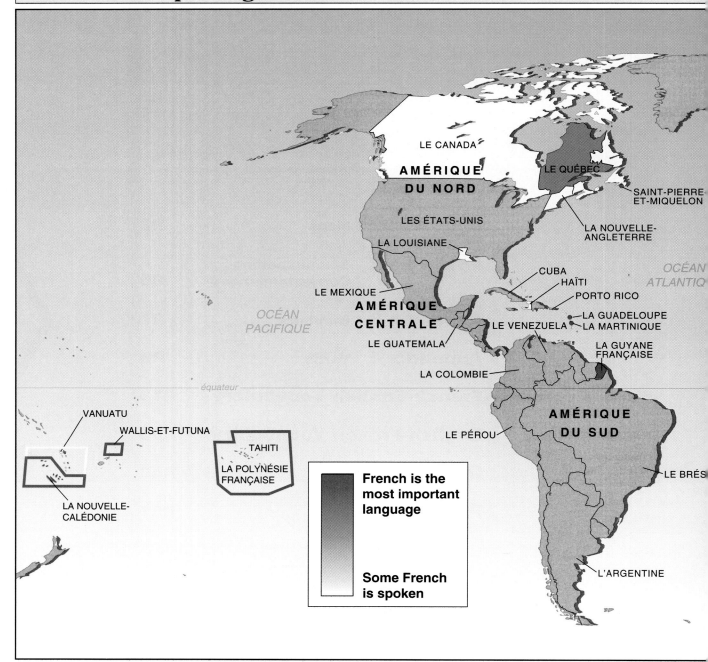

LE CANADA

AMÉRIQUE DU NORD

LE QUÉBEC

SAINT-PIERRE-ET-MIQUELON

LES ÉTATS-UNIS

LA NOUVELLE-ANGLETERRE

LA LOUISIANE

OCÉAN ATLANTIQ

CUBA

HAÏTI

PORTO RICO

LE MEXIQUE

OCÉAN PACIFIQUE

AMÉRIQUE CENTRALE

LA GUADELOUPE

LE VENEZUELA

LA MARTINIQUE

LE GUATEMALA

LA GUYANE FRANÇAISE

LA COLOMBIE

équateur

VANUATU

WALLIS-ET-FUTUNA

AMÉRIQUE DU SUD

LE PÉROU

TAHITI

LA POLYNÉSIE FRANÇAISE

LE BRÉS

LA NOUVELLE-CALÉDONIE

French is the most important language

Some French is spoken

L'ARGENTINE

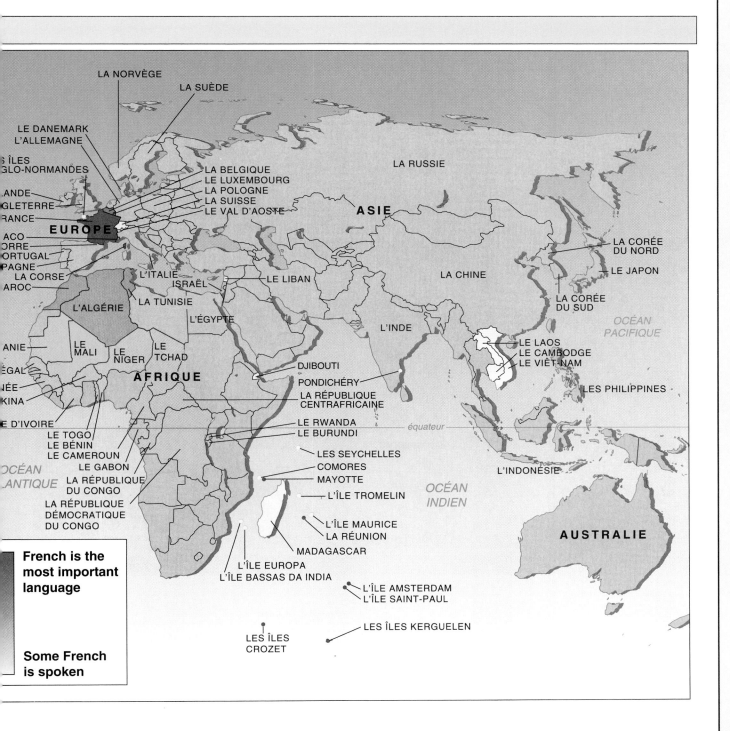

LA NORVÈGE
LA SUÈDE
LE DANEMARK
L'ALLEMAGNE
S ÎLES
GLO-NORMANDES
LANDE
GLETERRE
RANCE
LA BELGIQUE
LE LUXEMBOURG
LA POLOGNE
LA SUISSE
LE VAL D'AOSTE
ACO
ORRE
ORTUGAL
PAGNE
LA CORSE
AROC
L'ALGÉRIE
L'ITALIE
ISRAËL
LA TUNISIE
L'ÉGYPTE
EUROPE
ANIE
LE MALI
LE NIGER
LE TCHAD
ÉGAL
NÉE
KINA
E D'IVOIRE
AFRIQUE
LA RUSSIE
ASIE
LA CHINE
L'INDE
LE LIBAN
LA CORÉE
DU NORD
LE JAPON
LA CORÉE
DU SUD
OCÉAN
PACIFIQUE
LE LAOS
LE CAMBODGE
LE VIÊT-NAM
LES PHILIPPINES

DJIBOUTI
PONDICHÉRY
LA RÉPUBLIQUE
CENTRAFRICAINE
LE RWANDA
LE BURUNDI
équateur
LE TOGO
LE BÉNIN
LE CAMEROUN
LE GABON
LA RÉPUBLIQUE
DU CONGO
LA RÉPUBLIQUE
DÉMOCRATIQUE
DU CONGO

LES SEYCHELLES
COMORES
MAYOTTE
L'ÎLE TROMELIN
L'ÎLE MAURICE
LA RÉUNION
MADAGASCAR
L'ÎLE EUROPA
L'ÎLE BASSAS DA INDIA

L'INDONÉSIE

OCÉAN
INDIEN

AUSTRALIE

OCÉAN
LANTIQUE

**French is the
most important
language**

**Some French
is spoken**

L'ÎLE AMSTERDAM
L'ÎLE SAINT-PAUL
LES ÎLES KERGUELEN
LES ÎLES
CROZET

France

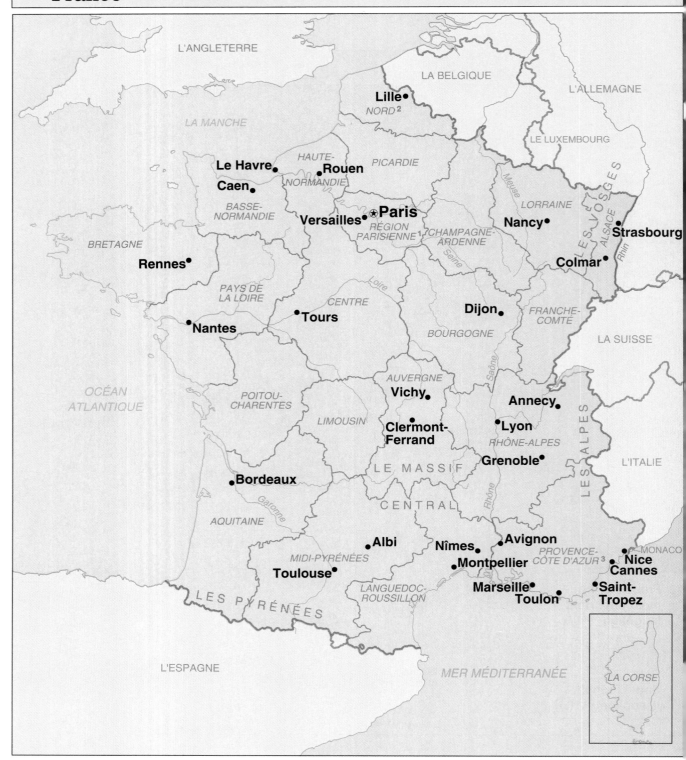

L'ANGLETERRE

LA BELGIQUE

L'ALLEMAGNE

Lille•
NORD [2]

LE LUXEMBOURG

LA MANCHE

HAUTE-
NORMANDIE

PICARDIE

Le Havre• •Rouen

Caen•

BASSE-
NORMANDIE

Versailles• ☆Paris
RÉGION
PARISIENNE [1]

CHAMPAGNE-
ARDENNE

LORRAINE

Nancy•

Strasbourg•

Colmar•

BRETAGNE

Rennes•

PAYS DE
LA LOIRE

CENTRE

Tours•

Dijon•

FRANCHE-
COMTÉ

BOURGOGNE

LA SUISSE

Nantes•

OCÉAN
ATLANTIQUE

POITOU-
CHARENTES

LIMOUSIN

AUVERGNE

Vichy•

Clermont-
Ferrand•

Annecy•

•Lyon

RHÔNE-ALPES

Grenoble•

L'ITALIE

Bordeaux•

LE MASSIF

C E N T R A L

AQUITAINE

Albi•

Nîmes•

Avignon•

PROVENCE-
CÔTE D'AZUR [3]

Nice•
Cannes

Montpellier•

MIDI-PYRÉNÉES

Toulouse•

LANGUEDOC-
ROUSSILLON

Marseille•

Saint-
Tropez•

Toulon•

LES PYRÉNÉES

L'ESPAGNE

MER MÉDITERRANÉE

LA CORSE

[1]Also known as Île-de-France
[2]Also known as Nord-Pas-de-Calais
[3]Also known as Provence-Alpes-Côte d'Azur *(Bottin 1989)*

Vowels

Sound	Spelling	Examples
/a/	**a, à, â**	Madame, là-bas, théâtre
/i/	**i, î**	visite, Nice, dîne
	y (initial, final, or between consonants)	Yves, Guy, style
/u/	**ou, où, oû**	Toulouse, où, août
/y/	**u, û**	tu, Luc, sûr
/o/	**o** (final or before silent consonant)	piano, idiot, Margot
	au, eau	jaune, Claude, beau
	ô	hôtel, drôle, Côte-d'Ivoire
/ɔ/	**o**	Monique, Noël, jolie
	au	Paul, restaurant, Laure
/e/	**é**	Dédé, Québec, télé
	e (before silent final **z, t, r**)	chez, et, Roger
	ai (final or before final silent consonant)	j'ai, mai, japonais
/ɛ/	**è**	Michèle, Ève, père
	ei	seize, neige, tour Eiffel
	ê	tête, être, Viêt-nam
	e (before two consonants)	elle, Pierre, Annette
	e (before pronounced final consonant)	Michel, avec, cher
	ai (before pronounced final consonant)	française, aime, Maine
/ə/	**e** (final or before single consonant)	je, Denise, venir
/ø/	**eu, oeu**	deux, Mathieu, euro, oeufs
	eu (before final **se**)	nerveuse, généreuse, sérieuse
/œ/	**eu** (before final pronounced consonant except /z/)	heure, neuf, Lesieur
	oeu	soeur, coeur, oeuf
	oe	oeil

Nasal vowels

Sound	Spelling	Examples
/ɑ̃/	**an, am**	France, quand, lampe
	en, em	Henri, pendant, décembre
/ɔ̃/	**on, om**	non, Simon, bombe
/ɛ̃/	**in, im**	Martin, invite, impossible
	yn, ym	syndicat, sympathique, Olympique
	ain, aim	Alain, américain, faim
	(o) + in	loin, moins, point
	(i) + en	bien, Julien, viens
/œ̃/	**un, um**	un, Lebrun, parfum

Sound	Spelling	Examples
/j/	**i, y** (before vowel sound)	bien, piano, Lyon
	-il, -ill (after vowel sound), **-ll**	oeil, travaille, Marseille, fille
/ɥ/	**u** (before vowel sound)	lui, Suisse, juillet
/w/	**ou** (before vowel sound)	oui, Louis, jouer
/wa/	**oi, oî**	voici, Benoît
	oy (before vowel)	voyage

Consonants

Sound	Spelling	Examples
/b/	**b**	Barbara, banane, Belgique
/k/	**c** (before **a, o, u,** or consonant)	Coca-Cola, cuisine, classe
	ch(**r**)	Christine, Christian, Christophe
	qu, q (final)	Québec, qu'est-ce que, cinq
	k	kilo, Kiki, ketchup
/ʃ/	**ch**	Charles, blanche, chez
/d/	**d**	Didier, dans, médecin
/f/	**f**	Félix, franc, neuf
	ph	Philippe, téléphone, photo
/g/	**g** (before **a, o, u,** or consonant)	Gabriel, gorge, légumes, gris
	gu (before **e, i, y**)	vague, Guillaume, Guy
/ɲ/	**gn**	mignon, champagne, Allemagne
/ʒ/	**j**	je, Jérôme, jaune
	g (before **e, i, y**)	rouge, Gigi, gymnastique
	ge (before **a, o, u**)	orangeade, Georges, nageur
/l/	**l**	Lise, elle, cheval
/m/	**m**	Maman, moi, tomate
/n/	**n**	banane, Nancy, nous
/p/	**p**	peu, Papa, Pierre
/r/	**r**	arrive, rentre, Paris
/s/	**c** (before **e, i, y**)	ce, Cécile, Nancy
	ç (before **a, o, u**)	ça, garçon, déçu
	s (initial or before consonant)	sac, Sophie, reste
	ss (between vowels)	boisson, dessert, Suisse
	t (before **i** + vowel)	attention, Nations Unies, natation
	x	dix, six, soixante
/t/	**t**	trop, télé, Tours
	th	Thérèse, thé, Marthe
/v/	**v**	Viviane, vous, nouveau
/gz/	**x**	examen, exemple, exact
/ks/	**x**	Max, Mexique, excellent
/z/	**s** (between vowels)	désert, Louise, télévision
	z	Suzanne, zut, zéro

A. Cardinal numbers

0	zéro	18	dix-huit	82	quatre-vingt-deux
1	un (une)	19	dix-neuf	90	quatre-vingt-dix
2	deux	20	vingt	91	quatre-vingt-onze
3	trois	21	vingt et un (une)	100	cent
4	quatre	22	vingt-deux	101	cent un (une)
5	cinq	23	vingt-trois	102	cent deux
6	six	30	trente	200	deux cents
7	sept	31	trente et un (une)	201	deux cent un
8	huit	32	trente-deux	300	trois cents
9	neuf	40	quarante	400	quatre cents
10	dix	41	quarante et un (une)	500	cinq cents
11	onze	50	cinquante	600	six cents
12	douze	60	soixante	700	sept cents
13	treize	70	soixante-dix	800	huit cents
14	quatorze	71	soixante et onze	900	neuf cents
15	quinze	72	soixante-douze	1.000	mille
16	seize	80	quatre-vingts	2.000	deux mille
17	dix-sept	81	quatre-vingt-un (une)	1.000.000	un million

Notes:
1. The word **et** occurs only in the numbers 21, 31, 41, 51, 61, and 71:   **vingt et un** / **soixante et onze**
2. **Un** becomes **une** before a feminine noun: **trente et une filles**
3. **Quatre-vingts** becomes **quatre-vingt** before another number: **quatre-vingt-cinq**
4. **Cents** becomes **cent** before another number: **trois cent vingt**
5. **Mille** never adds an **-s:**   **quatre mille**

B. Ordinal numbers

1$^{er\ (ère)}$	**premier (première)**	5^e	**cinquième**	9^e	**neuvième**
2^e	**deuxième**	6^e	**sixième**	10^e	**dixième**
3^e	**troisième**	7^e	**septième**	11^e	**onzième**
4^e	**quatrième**	8^e	**huitième**	12^e	**douzième**

Note: Premier becomes **première** before a feminine noun: **la première histoire**

C. Metric equivalents

1 gramme	= 0.035 ounces		1 ounce	= **28,349 grammes**
1 kilogramme	= 2.205 pounds		1 pound	= **0,453 kilogrammes**
1 litre	= 1.057 quarts		1 quart	= **0,946 litres**
1 mètre	= 39.37 inches		1 foot	= **30,480 centimètres**
1 kilomètre	= 0.62 miles		1 mile	= **1,609 kilomètres**

APPENDIX 4
Verbs

A. Regular verbs

Infinitive	Present		Passé composé	
parler *(to talk, speak)*	je **parle** tu **parles** il **parle**	nous **parlons** vous **parlez** ils **parlent**	j'ai **parlé** tu **as parlé** il **a parlé**	nous **avons parlé** vous **avez parlé** ils **ont parlé**
	IMPERATIVE: **parle, parlons, parlez**			
finir *(to finish)*	je **finis** tu **finis** il **finit**	nous **finissons** vous **finissez** ils **finissent**	j'ai **fini** tu **as fini** il **a fini**	nous **avons fini** vous **avez fini** ils **ont fini**
	IMPERATIVE: **finis, finissons, finissez**			
vendre *(to sell)*	je **vends** tu **vends** il **vend**	nous **vendons** vous **vendez** ils **vendent**	j'ai **vendu** tu **as vendu** il **a vendu**	nous **avons vendu** vous **avez vendu** ils **ont vendu**
	IMPERATIVE: **vends, vendons, vendez**			

B. *-er* verbs with spelling changes

Infinitive	Present		Passé composé
acheter *(to buy)*	j'**achète** tu **achètes** il **achète**	nous **achetons** vous **achetez** ils **achètent**	j'ai **acheté**
	Verb like **acheter**: amener *(to bring, take along)*		
espérer *(to hope)*	j'**espère** tu **espères** il **espère**	nous **espérons** vous **espérez** ils **espèrent**	j'ai **espéré**
	Verbs like **espérer**: célébrer *(to celebrate)*, préférer *(to prefer)*		
commencer *(to begin, start)*	je **commence** tu **commences** il **commence**	nous **commençons** vous **commencez** ils **commencent**	j'ai **commencé**
manger *(to eat)*	je **mange** tu **manges** il **mange**	nous **mangeons** vous **mangez** ils **mangent**	j'ai **mangé**
	Verbs like **manger**: nager *(to swim)*, voyager *(to travel)*		
payer *(to pay, pay for)*	je **paie** tu **paies** il **paie**	nous **payons** vous **payez** ils **paient**	j'ai **payé**
	Verbs like **payer**: nettoyer *(to clean)*		

Infinitive	Present		Passé composé
avoir *(to have, own)*	j'**ai** tu **as** il **a**	nous **avons** vous **avez** ils **ont**	j'ai **eu**
	IMPERATIVE: **aie, ayons, ayez**		
être *(to be)*	je **suis** tu **es** il **est**	nous **sommes** vous **êtes** ils **sont**	j'ai **été**
	IMPERATIVE: **sois, soyons, soyez**		
aller *(to go)*	je **vais** tu **vas** il **va**	nous **allons** vous **allez** ils **vont**	je **suis allé(e)**
	IMPERATIVE: **va, allons, allez**		
boire *(to drink)*	je **bois** tu **bois** il **boit**	nous **buvons** vous **buvez** ils **boivent**	j'ai **bu**
connaître *(to know)*	je **connais** tu **connais** il **connaît**	nous **connaissons** vous **connaissez** ils **connaissent**	j'ai **connu**
devoir *(to have to, should, must)*	je **dois** tu **dois** il **doit**	nous **devons** vous **devez** ils **doivent**	j'ai **dû**
dire *(to say, tell)*	je **dis** tu **dis** il **dit**	nous **disons** vous **dites** ils **disent**	j'ai **dit**
dormir *(to sleep)*	je **dors** tu **dors** il **dort**	nous **dormons** vous **dormez** ils **dorment**	j' ai **dormi**
écrire *(to write)*	j' **écris** tu **écris** il **écrit**	nous **écrivons** vous **écrivez** ils **écrivent**	j'ai **écrit**
	Verb like **écrire**: décrire *(to describe)*		
faire *(to make, do)*	je **fais** tu **fais** il **fait**	nous **faisons** vous **faites** ils **font**	j'ai **fait**
lire *(to read)*	je **lis** tu **lis** il **lit**	nous **lisons** vous **lisez** ils **lisent**	j'ai **lu**
mettre *(to put, place)*	je **mets** tu **mets** il **met**	nous **mettons** vous **mettez** ils **mettent**	j'ai **mis**
	Verb like **mettre**: promettre *(to promise)*		

Infinitive	Present		Passé composé
ouvrir *(to open)*	j'**ouvre** tu **ouvres** il **ouvre**	nous **ouvrons** vous **ouvrez** ils **ouvrent**	j'ai **ouvert**

Verbs like **ouvrir**: découvrir *(to discover)*, offrir *(to offer)*

partir *(to leave)*	je **pars** tu **pars** il **part**	nous **partons** vous **partez** ils **partent**	je **suis parti(e)**
pouvoir *(to be able, can)*	je **peux** tu **peux** il **peut**	nous **pouvons** vous **pouvez** ils **peuvent**	j'ai **pu**
prendre *(to take)*	je **prends** tu **prends** il **prend**	nous **prenons** vous **prenez** ils **prennent**	j'ai **pris**

Verbs like **prendre**: apprendre *(to learn)*, comprendre *(to understand)*

savoir *(to know)*	je **sais** tu **sais** il **sait**	nous **savons** vous **savez** ils **savent**	j'ai **su**
sortir *(to go out, get out)*	je **sors** tu **sors** il **sort**	nous **sortons** vous **sortez** ils **sortent**	je **suis sorti(e)**
venir *(to come)*	je **viens** tu **viens** il **vient**	nous **venons** vous **venez** ils **viennent**	je **suis venu(e)**

Verb like **venir**: revenir *(to come back)*

voir *(to see)*	je **vois** tu **vois** il **voit**	nous **voyons** vous **voyez** ils **voient**	j'ai **vu**
vouloir *(to want)*	je **veux** tu **veux** il **veut**	nous **voulons** vous **voulez** ils **veulent**	j'ai **voulu**

D. Verbs with *être* in the *passé composé*

aller *(to go)*	je **suis allé(e)**	**passer** *(to go by, through)*	je **suis passé(e)**
arriver *(to arrive, come)*	je **suis arrivé(e)**	**rentrer** *(to go home)*	je **suis rentré(e)**
descendre *(to go down)*	je **suis descendu(e)**	**rester** *(to stay)*	je **suis resté(e)**
entrer *(to enter, go in)*	je **suis entré(e)**	**revenir** *(to come back)*	je **suis revenu(e)**
monter *(to go up)*	je **suis monté(e)**	**sortir** *(to go out, get out)*	je **suis sorti(e)**
mourir *(to die)*	Il/elle **est mort(e)**	**tomber** *(to fall)*	je **suis tombé(e)**
naître *(to be born)*	je **suis né(e)**	**venir** *(to come)*	je **suis venu(e)**
partir *(to leave)*	je **suis parti(e)**		

FRENCH-ENGLISH VOCABULARY

VOCABULARY
French-English

The French-English vocabulary contains active and passive words from the text, as well as the important words of the illustrations used within the units. Obvious passive cognates have not been listed.

The numbers following an entry indicate the lesson in which the word or phrase is activated. (**B** stands for the photo essay that precedes **Niveau B; C** stands for the list of phrases and expressions that precedes **Niveau C;** and **E** stands for **Entracte.**)

Nouns: If the article of a noun does not indicate gender, the noun is followed by *m. (masculine)* or *f. (feminine)*. If the plural (*pl.*) is irregular, it is given in parentheses.

Adjectives: Adjectives are listed in the masculine form. If the feminine form is irregular, it is given in parentheses. Irregular plural forms (*pl.*) are also given in parentheses.

Verbs: Verbs are listed in the infinitive form. An asterisk (*) in front of an active verb means that it is irregular. (For forms, see the verb charts in Appendix 4C.) Irregular present tense forms are listed when they are used before the verb has been activated. Irregular past participle (*p.p.*) forms are listed separately.

Words beginning with an **h** are preceded by a bullet (•) if the **h** is aspirate; that is, if the word is treated as if it begins with a consonant sound.

A ━━━━━━━━━━━━

a: il y a there is, there are **17**
à at, in, to **14, 22**
  à côté next door; next to
  à demain see you tomorrow **8**
  à droite on (to) the right **21**
  à gauche on (to) the left **21**
  à la mode popular; in fashion; fashionable **25**
  à mon avis in my opinion **27**
  à partir de as of, beginning
  à pied on foot **22**
  à samedi! see you Saturday! **8**
  à vélo by bicycle **22**
abolir to abolish
abondant plentiful, copious, large
abord: d'abord (at) first **30**
un **abricot** apricot
absolument absolutely
un **accent** accent mark, stress
accepter to accept
des **accessoires** *m.* accessories **25**

un **accord** agreement
  d'accord okay, all right **13**
  être d'accord to agree **14**
un **achat** purchase
  faire des achats to go shopping **29**
acheter to buy **25, 26**
  acheter + du, de la (*partitive*) to buy (some) **34**
un **acteur, une actrice** actor, actress
une **activité** activity
l' **addition** *f.* check
adorer to love
une **adresse** address **21**
  quelle est ton adresse? what's your address? **21**
adroit skilled, skillful
un(e) **adulte** adult
  aéronautique aeronautic, aeronautical
un **aéroport** airport
affectueusement affectionately (*at the end of a letter*)
une **affiche** poster **17**
affirmativement affirmatively
l' **Afrique** *f.* Africa
l' **âge** *m.* age

  quel âge a-t-il/elle? how old is he/she? **17**
  quel âge as-tu? how old are you? **7**
  quel âge a ton père/ta mère? how old is your father/your mother? **7**
âgé old
une **agence** agency
  une agence de tourisme tourist office
  une agence de voyages travel agency
agiter to shake
agité agitated
ah! ah!, oh!
  ah bon? oh? really? **16**
  ah non! ah, no!
ai (*see* avoir): **j'ai** I have **17**
  j'ai... ans I'm ... (years old) **7**
aider to help **29, 35**
une **aile** wing
aimer to like **15, 33**
  est-ce que tu aimes...? do you like ...? **13**
  j'aime... I like ... **13**
  j'aimerais I would like
  je n'aime pas... I don't like ... **13**

ainsi thus

aîné older

  un frère aîné older brother

  une soeur aînée older sister

ajouter to add

l' **Algérie** *f.* Algeria *(country in North Africa)*

algérien (algérienne) Algerian

l' **Allemagne** *f.* Germany

allemand German

* **aller** to go **22**

  aller + *inf.* to be going to + *inf.* **22**

  allez *(see* **aller**): **allez-vous-en** go away!

  allez-y come on!, go ahead!, do it!

  comment allez-vous? how are you? **3**

  allô! hello! *(on the telephone)*

  allons *(see* **aller**): **allons-y** let's go! **22**

alors so, then **19**

une **alouette** lark

les **Alpes** *f.* (the) Alps

l' **alphabet** *m.* alphabet

l' **alpinisme** *m.* mountain climbing **29**

  faire de l'alpinisme to go mountain climbing **29**

l' **Alsace** *f.* Alsace *(province in eastern France)*

amener to bring *(a person)* **26, 35**

américain American **2, 19**

  à l'américaine American-style

un **Américain, une Américaine** American person

l' **Amérique** *f.* America

un **ami, une amie** (close) friend **5**

amicalement love *(at the end of a letter)*

l' **amitié** *f.* friendship

  amitiés best regards *(at the end of a letter)*

amusant funny, amusing **19**

amuser to amuse

  s'amuser to have fun

  on s'est bien amusé! we had a good time!

un **an** year

avoir... ans to be . . . (years old) **18**

  il/elle a... ans he/she is . . . (years old) **7**

  j'ai... ans I'm . . . (years old) **7**

  l'an dernier last year

  par an per year

un **ananas** pineapple

ancien (ancienne) former, old, ancient

un **âne** donkey

un **ange** angel

anglais English **2, 19**

un **Anglais, une Anglaise** English person

un **animal** (*pl.* **animaux**) animal

une **animation** live entertainment

animé animated, lively

une **année** year **8**

  bonne année! Happy New Year! **32**

  toute l'année all year long

un **anniversaire** birthday **8**

  bon anniversaire! happy birthday! **32**

  c'est quand, ton anniversaire? when is your birthday? **8**

  mon anniversaire est le (2 mars) my birthday is (March 2nd) **8**

un **annuaire** telephone directory

un **anorak** ski jacket

les **antiquités** *f.* antiquities, antiques

août *m.* August **8**

un **appareil-photo** (*pl.* **appareils-photo**) (still) camera **17**

un **appartement** apartment **21**

s' **appeler** to be named, called

  comment s'appelle...? what's . . .'s name? **6**

  comment s'appelle-t-il/elle? what's his/her name? **17**

  comment t'appelles-tu? what's your name? **1**

  il/elle s'appelle... his/her name is . . . **6**

  je m'appelle... my name is . . . **1**

apporter to bring *(things)* **26**

apporter quelque chose à quelqu'un to bring something to someone **35**

  apporte-moi (apportez-moi) bring me **B**

* **apprendre (à)** + *inf.* to learn (to) **34**

apprécier to appreciate

approprié appropriate

après after **29;** after, afterwards **30, 31**

  d'après according to

l' **après-midi** *m.* afternoon **29**

  cet après-midi this afternoon **31**

  de l'après-midi in the afternoon, P.M. **4**

  demain après-midi tomorrow afternoon **31**

  hier après-midi yesterday afternoon **31**

l' **arabe** *m.* Arabic *(language)*

un **arbre** tree

  un arbre généalogique family tree

l' **arche** *f.* **de Noé** Noah's Ark

l' **argent** *m.* money **28**

  l'argent de poche allowance, pocket money

arrêter to arrest; to stop

arriver to arrive, come **22**

  j'arrive! I'm coming!

une **arrivée** arrival

un **arrondissement** district

un **artifice: le feu d'artifice** fireworks

un **artiste, une artiste** artist

as *(see* **avoir**): **est-ce que tu as...?** do you have . . . ? **17**

un **ascenseur** elevator

un **aspirateur** vacuum cleaner

asseyez-vous! sit down! **B**

assez rather **19;** enough

assieds-toi! sit down! **B**

une **assiette** plate **33**

  assister à to go to, attend **29**

associer to associate

l' **Atlantique** *m.* Atlantic Ocean

attendre to wait, wait for **28**

attention *f.:* **faire attention** to be careful, pay attention **16**

attentivement carefully

au (à + le) to (the), at (the), in (the) **14, 22**

  au revoir! good-bye! **3**

une **auberge** inn

  une auberge de campagne country inn **35**

aucun: ne... aucun none, not any

aujourd'hui today **8, 31**

  aujourd'hui, c'est... today is . . . **8**

aussi also, too **2, 15**

  aussi... que as . . . as **27**

une **auto (automobile)** car, automobile **17**

  une auto-école driving school

un **autobus** bus

un **autocar** touring bus **29**

l' **automne** *m.* autumn, fall

  en automne in (the) autumn, fall **12**

autre other **33**

  d'autres others

  un(e) autre another

aux (à + les) to (the), at (the), in (the) **22**

avant before **29**

  avant hier the day before yesterday

  en avant let's begin

avantageux (avantageuse) reasonable, advantageous

avec with **14**

  avec moi, avec toi with me, with you **13**

  avec qui? with who(m)? **16**

une **avenue** avenue **21**

un **avion** airplane, plane **29**

  en avion by airplane **29**

un **avis** opinion

  avis de recherche missing person's bulletin

  à mon avis in my opinion **27**

  à votre avis in your opinion

* **avoir** to have **18**

  avoir... ans to be . . . (years old) **18**

  avoir besoin de to need **28**

  avoir chaud to be warm, hot **30**

avoir de la chance to be lucky **30**

avoir envie de to feel like, want **28**

avoir faim to be hungry **18**

avoir froid to be cold **30**

avoir lieu to take place

avoir raison to be right **30**

avoir soif to be thirsty **18, 30**

avoir tort to be wrong **30**

avril *m.* April **8**

B

le **babyfoot** tabletop soccer game

le **babysitting: faire du babysitting** to baby-sit

les **bagages** *m.* bags, baggage

bain: un maillot de bain bathing suit **25**

une **banane** banana **33**

une **bande dessinée** comic strip

  des bandes dessinées comics

la **Bannière étoilée** Star-Spangled Banner

une **banque** bank

une **barbe: quelle barbe!** what a pain! *(colloq.)*

bas: en bas downstairs **21**

  au bas at the bottom

le **baseball** baseball **23**

basé based

le **basket (basketball)** basketball **23**

  jouer au basket to play basketball **13**

des **baskets** *f.* hightops (sneakers) **25**

un **bateau** boat, ship **29**

  un bateau-mouche sightseeing boat

la **batterie** drums **23**

battre to beat

bavard talkative

beau (bel, belle; *m.pl.* **beaux)** handsome, good-looking, beautiful **17, 20, 27**

il est beau he is good-looking, handsome **17**

il fait beau it's beautiful (nice) out **12**

un **beau-frère** stepbrother, brother-in-law

un **beau-père** stepfather, father-in-law

beaucoup (de) much, very much, many, a lot **15**

la **beauté** beauty

un **bec** beak

bel (*see* **beau)** beautiful, handsome **27**

la **Belgique** Belgium

belle (*see* **beau)** beautiful **17, 20, 27**

  elle est belle she is beautiful **17**

une **belle-mère** stepmother, mother-in-law

une **belle-soeur** stepsister, sister-in-law

les **Bermudes** *f.* Bermuda

le **besoin** need

  avoir besoin de to need, to have to **28**

  des besoins d'argent money needs

bête dumb, silly **19**

le **beurre** butter **33**

une **bibliothèque** library **21**

une **bicyclette** bicycle **17**

bien well, very well, carefully **15**

  bien sûr of course **13**

  ça va bien everything's fine (going well) **3**

  ça va très bien I'm (everything's) very well **3**

  c'est bien that's good (fine) **20**

  eh bien! well! **26**

  je veux bien (...) I'd love to (. . .), I do, I want to **13, 34**

  oui, bien sûr... yes, of course . . . **13**

  très bien very well **15**

bientôt: à bientôt! see you soon!

bienvenue welcome

le **bifteck** steak

  un bifteck de tortue turtle steak

bilingue bilingual

un billet bill, paper money **28;** ticket

la biologie biology

une biscotte dry toast

blaff de poisson *(m.)* fish stew

blanc (blanche) white **20**

Blanche-Neige Snow White

blanchir to blanch, turn white

bleu blue **20**

blond blonde **17**

  il/elle est blond(e) he/she is blond **17**

un blouson jacket **25**

* **boire** to drink **34**

une boisson drink, beverage **10, 33**

une boîte box

un bol deep bowl

bon (bonne) good **20**

  bon marché *(inv.)* inexpensive **25**

  ah bon? oh, really? **16**

  de bonne humeur in a good mood

  il fait bon the weather's good (pleasant) **12**

le bonheur happiness

bonjour hello **1, 3**

une botte boot **25**

une bouche mouth **E3**

une boucherie butcher shop

le boudin sausage

une boulangerie bakery

un boulevard boulevard **21**

une boum party *(colloq.)* **22**

une boutique boutique, shop **25**

  boxe: un match de boxe boxing match

un bras arm **E3**

brésilien (brésilienne) Brazilian

la Bretagne Brittany *(province in northwestern France)*

bricoler to do things around the house

broche: à la broche on the spit

bronzé tan

un bruit noise

brun brown, dark-haired **17**

  il/elle est brun(e) he/she has dark hair **17**

brunir to turn brown

Bruxelles Brussels

le bulletin de notes report card

un bureau desk **B, 17;** office

un bus bus

  en bus by bus **22**

un but goal; end

C

ça that, it

  ça fait combien? ça fait... how much is that (it)? that (it) is . . . **11**

  ça, là-bas that (one), over there **17**

  ça va? how's everything? how are you? **3**

  ça va everything's fine, I'm OK **3**

  ça va (très) bien, ça va bien everything's going very well, everything's fine (going well) **3**

  ça va comme ci, comme ça everything's (going) so-so **3**

  ça va (très) mal things are going (very) badly **3**

  regarde ça look at that **17**

une cabine d'essayage fitting room

les cabinets *m.* toilet

un cadeau *(pl.* **cadeaux)** gift, present

cadet (cadette) younger

  un frère cadet (a) younger brother

  une soeur cadette (a) younger sister

le café coffee **10**

  un café au lait coffee with hot milk

un café café *(French coffee shop)* **14**

  au café to (at) the café **14**

un cahier notebook **B**

une calculatrice calculator **17**

un calendrier calendar

un camarade, une camarade classmate **17**

le Cambodge Cambodia *(country in Asia)*

un cambriolage burglary

un cambrioleur burglar

une caméra movie camera

la campagne countryside **29**

  à la campagne to (in) the countryside **29**

  une auberge de campagne country inn

  camping: faire du camping to go camping **29**

le Canada Canada

canadien (canadienne) Canadian **2, 19**

un Canadien, une Canadienne Canadian person

un canard duck

la cantine de l'école school cafeteria **33**

un car touring bus **29**

  un car scolaire school bus

une carotte carrot **33**

  des carottes râpées grated carrots

un carré square

  le Vieux Carré *the French Quarter in New Orleans*

une carte map **B;** card

  une carte postale postcard

  les cartes *f.* (playing) cards **23**

  jouer aux cartes to play cards **23**

un cas case

  en cas de in case of

une cassette cassette tape **B, 17**

le catch wrestling

une cathédrale cathedral

une cave cellar

un CD (un compact) (audio) compact disc **B**

  un CD vidéo laser disc **B**

ce (c') this, that, it

  ce n'est pas that's/it's not **20**

  ce que what **C**

  ce sont these are, those are, they are **20**

  c'est it's, that's **5, 17, 20**

  c'est + *day of the week* it's . . . **8**

  c'est + *name or noun* it's . . . **5**

  c'est bien/mal that's good/bad **20**

  c'est combien? how much is that/it? **11**

c'est le (12 octobre) it's (October 12) **8**

qu'est-ce que c'est? what is it? what's that? **17**

qui est-ce? who's that/this? **17**

ce (cet, cette; ces) this, that, these, those **26**

ce... -ci this . . . (over here) **26**

ce mois-ci this month **31**

ce n'est pas it's (that's) not **20**

ce soir this evening, tonight **31**

une **cédille** cedilla

une **ceinture** belt **25**

cela that

célèbre famous

cent one hundred **6, 25**

cent un, cent deux 101, 102 **25**

deux cents, trois cents, … neuf cents 200, 300, . . . 900 **25**

une **centaine** about a hundred

un **centime** centime *(1/100 of a euro)*

un **centre** center

un centre commercial shopping center **21**

les **céréales** *f.* cereal **33**

une **cerise** cherry **33**

certain certain

certains some of them

ces *(see* **ce**) these, those **26**

c'est *(see* **ce**)

cet *(see* **ce**) this, that **26**

cette *(see* **ce**) this, that **26**

chacun each one, each person

une **chaise** chair **B, 17**

une **chaîne** (TV) channel

une **chaîne stéréo** stereo set **17**

une mini-chaîne compact stereo

la **chaleur** heat, warmth

une **chambre** bedroom **17, 21**

un **champion, une championne** champion

la **chance** luck

avoir de la chance to be lucky **30**

bonne chance! good luck! **31**

une **chanson** song

chanter to sing **13, 15**

un **chanteur, une chanteuse** singer

un **chapeau** *(pl.* **chapeaux)** hat **25**

chaque each, every

charmant charming

un **chat** cat **7, E5**

un **château** *(pl.* **châteaux)** castle

chaud warm, hot

avoir chaud to be warm (hot) *(people)* **30**

il fait chaud it's warm (hot) *(weather)* **12**

chauffer to warm, heat up

un **chauffeur** driver

une **chaussette** sock **25**

une **chaussure** shoe **25**

un **chef** boss; chef

une **chemise** shirt **25**

un **chemisier** blouse **25**

cher (chère) expensive; dear **25**

chercher to look for, to get, to find **25**

je cherche... I'm looking for . . . **25**

un **cheval** *(pl.* **chevaux)** horse **E5**

les **cheveux** *m.* hair **E3**

chez + *person* at (to) someone's house **22**; at (to) the office of

chez moi (toi, lui...) (at) home **23**

chic *(inv.)* nice; elegant, in style

une chic fille a great girl

un **chien** dog **7**

la **chimie** chemistry

chinois Chinese **19**

le **chinois** Chinese *(language)*

le **chocolat** hot chocolate, cocoa **10**

une glace au chocolat chocolate ice cream

choisir to choose **27**

un **choix** choice

au choix choose one, your choice

une **chorale** choir

une **chose** thing **17**

quelque chose something **32**

chouette great, terrific **20, 25**

le **cidre** cider

un **cinéaste, une cinéaste** film maker

un **cinéma** movie theater **21**

le cinéma the movies

au cinéma to (at) the movies, movie theater **14**

cinq five **1**

cinquante fifty **3**

cinquième fifth **24**

une **circonstance** circumstance

cité: la Cité Interdite Forbidden City

une **clarinette** clarinet **23**

une **classe** class

en classe in class **14**

classique classical

un **clavier** keyboard **23**

un **client, une cliente** customer

un **clip** music video

un **cochon** pig

un **coiffeur, une coiffeuse** hairdresser

un **coin** spot

une **coïncidence** coincidence

le **Colisée** the Coliseum *(a large stadium built by the Romans)*

des **collants** *m.* (pair of) tights, pantyhose **25**

un **collège** junior high school

une **colonie** colony

une **colonne** column

combien how much **28**

combien coûte...? how much does . . . cost? **11, 25**

combien de how much, how many **28**

combien de temps? how long?

combien d'heures? how many hours?

ça fait combien? how much is this (it)? **11**

c'est combien? how much is this (it)? **11**

commander to order

comme like, as, for

comme ci, comme ça so-so

ça va comme ci, comme ça everything's so-so **3**

commencer to begin, start
comment? how? **16;** what?
  comment allez-vous?
    how are you? **3**
  comment est-il/elle?
    what's he/she like? what
    does he/she look like? **17**
  comment dit-on... en
    français? how do you
    say . . . in French? **B**
  comment lire reading
    hints
  comment s'appelle...?
    what's . . .'s name? **6**
  comment s'appelle-t-
    il/elle? what's his/her
    name? **17**
  comment t'appelles-tu?
    what's your name? **1**
  comment trouves-tu...?
    what do you think of . . .?
    25
  comment vas-tu? how are
    you? **3**
un **commentaire** comment,
  commentary
commercial: un centre
  commercial shopping
  center **21**
le **commérage** gossip
communiquer to
  communicate
un **compact** compact disc
  (CD) **17**
complément object
compléter to complete
* **comprendre** to understand **34**
  je (ne) comprends (pas)
    I (don't) understand **B**
compter to count (on); to
  expect, intend
concerne: en ce qui
  concerne as for
un **concert** concert **22**
un **concombre** cucumber
la **confiture** jam **33**
confortable comfortable **21**
une **connaissance** acquaintance
  faire connaissance
  (avec) to become
  acquainted (with)
* **connaître** to know, be
  acquainted with; *(in passé*
  composé) to meet for the
  first time **36**

tu connais...? do you
  know . . .? are you
  acquainted with . . .? **6**
connu (*p.p. of* **connaître**)
  knew, met **36**
un **conseil** piece of advice,
  counsel
  des conseils *m.* advice
un **conservatoire** conservatory
une **consonne** consonant
se **contenter** to limit oneself
le **contenu** contents
continuer to continue **21**
une **contradiction** disagreement
une **contravention** (traffic) ticket
cool cool, neat
un **copain, une copine** friend,
  pal **5**
  un petit copain, une
    petite copine boyfriend,
    girlfriend
copier to copy
une **copine** friend **5**
coréen (coréenne) Korean
un **corps** body
correspondant corresponding
correspondre to correspond,
  agree
la **Corse** Corsica *(French island*
  off the Italian coast)
un **costume** man's suit
la **Côte d'Azur** Riviera
  (southern coast of France
  on the Mediterranean)
la **Côte d'Ivoire** Ivory Coast
  (French-speaking country
  in West Africa)
côté: à côté (de) next door;
  next to
une **côtelette de porc** pork chop
le **cou** neck **E3**
une **couleur** color **20**
  de quelle couleur ...?
    what color . . .? **20**
un **couloir** hall, corridor
coup: dans le coup with it
courage: bon courage! good
  luck! **31**
courageux (courageuse)
  courageous
le **courrier électronique** e-mail,
  electronic mail
une **course** race
  faire les courses to go
    shopping *(for food)* **33**

court short **25**
un **cousin, une cousine** cousin
  7, 24
le **coût: le coût de la vie** cost
  of living
un **couteau** (*pl.* **couteaux**) knife
  33
coûter to cost
  combien coûte...? how
    much does . . . cost? **11,**
    25
  il (elle) coûte... it
    costs . . . **11**
un **couturier, une couturière**
  fashion designer
un **couvert** place setting **33**
un **crabe** crab
  des matoutou crabes
    stewed crabs with rice
la **craie** chalk
  un morceau de craie
    piece of chalk **B**
une **cravate** tie **25**
un **crayon** pencil **B, 17**
créer to create
un **crétin** idiot
une **crêpe** crepe (pancake) **9**
une **crêperie** crepe restaurant
une **crevaison** flat tire
une **croisade** crusade
un **croissant** crescent (roll) **9**
une **cuillère** spoon **33**
  une cuillère à soupe
    soup spoon
la **cuisine** cooking **33**
une **cuisine** kitchen **21**
cuit cooked
culturel (culturelle) cultural
curieux (curieuse) curious,
  strange
la **curiosité** curiosity
le **Cyberespace** information
  highway, cyberspace
les **cybernautes** people who like
  to use the Internet
un **cyclomoteur** moped

D ▬▬▬▬▬▬▬▬

d'abord (at) first **30**
d'accord okay, all right
  être d'accord to agree **14**
  oui, d'accord yes, okay **13**
une **dame** lady, woman *(polite*
  term) **5**
les **dames** *f.* checkers *(game)* **23**

dangereux (dangereuse) dangerous

dans in **17**

danser to dance **13, 15**

la **date** date **8**

    quelle est la date? what's the date? **8**

de (d') of, from, about **14, 23**

    de l'après-midi in the afternoon **4**

    de quelle couleur... ? what color . . .? **20**

    de qui? of whom? **16**

    de quoi? about what?

    de temps en temps from time to time

    pas de not any, no **18, 34**

débarquer to land

décembre *m.* December **8**

décider (de) to decide (to)

une **déclaration** statement

décoré decorated

* **découvrir** to discover

* **décrire** to describe **C**

    décrivez... describe. . . **C**

un **défaut** shortcoming

un **défilé** parade

dégoûtant: c'est dégoûtant! it's (that's) disgusting **35**

dehors outside

    en dehors de outside of

déjà already; ever

déjeuner to eat (have) lunch **33**

le **déjeuner** lunch **33**

    le petit déjeuner breakfast **33**

délicieux (délicieuse) delicious **34**

demain tomorrow **8**

    à demain! see you tomorrow! **8**

    demain, c'est... (jeudi) tomorrow is . . . (Thursday) **8**

demander (à) to ask **C, 36**

    demandez ... ask . . . **C**

un **demi-frère** half-brother

une **demi-soeur** half-sister

demi: ... heures et demie half past . . . **4**

    midi et demi half past noon **4**

minuit et demi half past midnight **4**

démodé out of style, unfashionable **25**

un **démon** devil

une **dent** tooth

un **départ** departure

se **dépêcher: dépêchez-vous!** hurry up!

dépend: ça dépend that depends

une **dépense** expense

dépenser to spend (money) **28**

dernier (dernière) last **31**

derrière behind, in back of **17**

des some, any **18;** of (the), from (the), about (the) **23**

le **désert** desert

désirer to wish, want

    vous désirez? what would you like? may I help you? **10, 25**

désolé sorry

le **dessert** dessert **33**

le **dessin** art, drawing

    un dessin animé cartoon

détester to hate, detest **3**

deux two **1**

deuxième second **24**

    le deuxième étage third floor

devant in front of **17**

développer to develop

deviner to guess

* **devoir** to have to, should, must **35**

un **devoir** homework assignment **B**

les **devoirs** *m.* homework

    faire mes devoirs to do my homework **29**

d'habitude usually

différemment differently

différent different

difficile hard, difficult **20**

la **dignité** dignity

dimanche *m.* Sunday **8**

dîner to have dinner **15, 33**

    dîner au restaurant to have dinner at a restaurant **13**

le **dîner** dinner, supper **33**

* **dire** to say, tell **C, 36**

que veut dire...? what does . . . mean? **B**

directement straight

un **directeur, une directrice** director, principal

dirigé directed, guided

dis! (*see* **dire**) say!, hey! **20**

    dis donc! say there!, hey there! **20**

discuter to discuss

une **dispute** quarrel, dispute

un **disque** record **17**

    un (disque) compact compact disc **17**

une **disquette** floppy disc **B**

dit (*p.p. of* **dire**) said

dit (*see* **dire**): **comment dit-on... en français?** how do you say . . . in French? **B**

dites... (*see* **dire**) say . . ., tell . . . **C**

dix ten **1, 2**

dix-huit eighteen **2**

dixième tenth **24**

dix-neuf nineteen **2**

dix-sept seventeen **2**

un **docteur** doctor

dois (*see* **devoir**): **je dois** I have to (must) **13**

domestique domestic

    les animaux *m.* **domestiques** pets **7**

dommage! too bad! **15**

donner (à) to give (to) **35, 36**

    donne-moi... give me . . . **9, B**

    donnez-moi... give me **10, B**

    s'il te plaît, donne-moi... please, give me . . . **10**

doré golden brown

* **dormir** to sleep

le **dos** back **E3**

une **douzaine** dozen **33**

douze twelve **2**

douzième twelfth **24**

droit: tout droit straight **21**

droite right

    à droite to (on) the right **21**

drôle funny **20**

du (de + le) of (the), from (the) **23;** some, any **34**

du matin in the morning, A.M. **4**

du soir in the evening, P.M. **4**

dû (*p.p. of* **devoir**) had to **35**

dur hard

des oeufs (*m.*) **durs** hard-boiled eggs

durer to last

dynamique dynamic

E ▬▬▬▬▬▬▬▬▬▬

e-mail e-mail, electronic mail

l' **eau** *f.* (*pl.* **eaux**) water **33**

l'eau minérale mineral water **33**

un **échange** exchange

les **échecs** *m.* chess **23**

une **éclosion** hatching

une **école** school **21**

économiser to save money

écouter to listen to **B, 15**

écouter la radio to listen to the radio **13**

écouter des cassettes to listen to cassettes **29**

l' **écran** *m.* screen (computer)

* **écrire** to write **36**

l' **éducation** *f.* education

l'éducation civique civics

l'éducation physique physical education

une **église** church **21**

égyptien (égyptienne) Egyptian

eh bien! well! **26**

électronique: une guitare électrique electric guitar

élégant elegant **25**

un **éléphant** elephant **E5**

un **élève, une élève** pupil, student **17**

élevé high

elle she, it **11, 14, 18;** her **23**

elle coûte... it costs . . . **11**

elle est (canadienne) she's (Canadian) **6**

elle s'appelle... her name is . . . **6**

embrasser: je t'embrasse love and kisses (*at the end of a letter*)

un **emploi du temps** time-table (*of work*)

emprunter à to borrow from

en in, on, to, by

en avion by airplane, plane **29**

en bas (haut) downstairs (upstairs) **21**

en bus (métro, taxi, train, voiture) by bus (subway, taxi, train, car) **22**

en ce qui concerne as for

en face opposite, across (the street)

en fait in fact

en famille at home

en plus in addition

en scène on stage

en solde on sale

va-t'en! go away! **22**

un **endroit** place **22**

un **enfant, une enfant** child **24**

enfin at last **30**

ensuite then, after that **30**

entendre to hear **28**

entier (entière) entire

l' **entracte** *m.* interlude

entre between

une **entrée** entry (*of a house*)

un **entretien** discussion

envers toward

l' **envie** *f.* envy; feeling

avoir envie de to want; to feel like, want to **28**

épicé hot (spicy)

une **épicerie** grocery store

les **épinards** *m.* spinach

une **équipe** team

une **erreur** error, mistake

es (*see* **être**)

tu es + *nationality* you are . . . **2**

tu es + *nationality*? are you . . .? **2**

tu es de... ? are you from . . .? **2**

un **escalier** staircase

un **escargot** snail

l' **Espagne** *f.* Spain

espagnol Spanish **19**

parler espagnol to speak Spanish **13**

espérer to hope **26**

un **esprit** spirit

essayer to try on, to try

l' **essentiel** *m.* the important thing

est (*see* **être**)

est-ce que (qu')...? *phrase used to introduce a question* **14**

c'est... it's . . ., that's . . . **5, 7, 20**

c'est le + *date* it's . . . **8**

il/elle est + *nationality* he/she is . . . **6**

n'est-ce pas...? isn't it? **14**

où est...? where is . . . ? **14**

quel jour est-ce? what day is it? **8**

qui est-ce? who's that (this)? **5, 17**

l' **est** *m.* east

et and **2, 14**

et demi(e), et quart half past, quarter past **4**

et toi? and you? **1**

établir to establish

un **étage** floor of a building, story

les **États-Unis** *m.* United States

été (*p.p. of* **être**) been, was **31**

l' **été** *m.* summer

en été in (the) summer **12**

l'heure d'été daylight savings time

étendre to spread

une **étoile** star

étrange strange

étranger (étrangère) foreign

* **être** to be **14**

être à to belong to

être d'accord to agree **14**

une **étude** study

un **étudiant, une étudiant(e)** (college) student **17**

étudier to study **13, 15**

eu (*p.p. of* **avoir**) had **31**

il y a eu there was

euh... er . . ., uh . . .

euh non... well, no

un **euro** euro; monetary unit of Europe

européen (européenne) European

eux they, them **23**

eux-mêmes themselves

un **événement** event

un **examen** exam, test

R21

réussir à un examen to pass an exam, a test
excusez-moi excuse me **21**
un **exemple** example
   par exemple for instance
un **exercice** exercise
   faire des exercices to exercise
exiger to insist
expliquer to explain **C**
   expliquez… explain . . . **C**
exprimer to express
exquis: c'est exquis! it's exquisite! **34**
extérieur: à l'extérieur outside
extra terrific **20**
extraordinaire extraordinary
   il a fait un temps extraordinaire! the weather was great!

F ━━━━━━━━━━━━━

face: en face (de) opposite, across (the street) from
facile easy **20**
faible weak
la **faim** hunger
   avoir faim to be hungry **30**
   j'ai faim I'm hungry **9**
   tu as faim? are you hungry? **9**
faire to do, make **16**
   faire attention to pay attention, be careful **16**
   faire de + *activity* to do, play, study, participate in **29**
   faire des achats to go shopping **29**
   faire les courses to go shopping **33**
   faire mes devoirs to do my homework **29**
   faire partie de to be a member of
   faire sauter to flip
   faire un match to play a game (match) **16**
   faire un pique-nique to have a picnic **29**
   faire un voyage to take a trip **16**

faire une promenade to take a walk **16**
faire une promenade à pied (à vélo, en voiture) to take a walk (a bicycle ride, a drive) **22**
fait *(p.p. of faire)* did, done, made **31**
fait: en fait in fact
fait *(see faire):* **ça fait combien?** how much is that (it)? **11**
   ça fait… francs that's (it's) . . . francs **11**
   il fait (beau, etc.) it's (beautiful, etc.) *(weather)* **12**
   quel temps fait-il? what (how) is the weather? **12**
fameux: c'est fameux! it's superb! **34**
familial with the family
une **famille** family **7, 24**
   en famille at home
un **fana, une fana** fan
un **fantôme** ghost
la **farine** flour
fatigué tired
faux (fausse) false **20**
favori (favorite) favorite
les **félicitations** *f.* congratulations
une **femme** woman **17;** wife **24**
une **fenêtre** window **B, 17**
fermer to close **B**
une **fête** party, holiday
le **feu d'artifice** fireworks
une **feuille** sheet, leaf **B**
   une feuille de papier sheet of paper **B**
un **feuilleton** series, serial story *(in newspaper)*
février *m.* February **8**
fiche-moi la paix! leave me alone! *(colloq.)* **36**
la **fièvre** fever
une **fille** girl **5;** daughter **24**
un **film** movie **22, 29**
   un film policier detective movie
un **fils** son **24**
la **fin** end
finalement finally **30**
fini *(p.p. of finir)* over, finished **31**
finir to finish **27**

flamand Flemish
un **flamant** flamingo
une **fleur** flower
un **fleuve** river
un **flic** cop *(colloq.)*
une **flûte** flute **23**
une **fois** time
   à la fois at the same time
la **folie: à la folie** madly
folklorique: une chanson folklorique folksong
fonctionner to work, function
fondé founded
le **foot (football)** soccer **23**
   le football américain football
   jouer au foot to play soccer **13**
une **forêt** forest
formidable great!
fort strong
   plus fort louder **B**
un **fouet** whisk
une **fourchette** fork **33**
la **fourrure** fur
   un manteau de fourrure fur coat
frais: il fait frais it's cool *(weather)* **12**
une **fraise** strawberry **33**
un **franc** franc *(former monetary unit of France)* **11**
   ça fait… francs that's (it's) . . . francs **11**
français French **2, 19**
   comment dit-on… en français? how do you say… in French? **B**
   parler français to speak French **13**
le **français** French *(language)*
un **Français, une Française** French person
la **France** France **14**
   en France in France **14**
francophone French-speaking
un **frère** brother **7, 24**
des **frites** *f.* French fries **33**
   un steak-frites steak and French fries **9**
froid cold
   avoir froid to be (feel) cold *(people)* **30**

il fait froid it's cold out *(weather)* **12**

le **fromage** cheese **33**

un sandwich au fromage cheese sandwich

un **fruit** fruit **33**

furieux (furieuse) furious

une **fusée** rocket

G

gagner to earn, to win **28**

un **garage** garage **21**

un **garçon** boy **5**; waiter

une **gare** train station

une **garniture** side dish

un **gâteau** *(pl.* **gâteaux)** cake **33**

gauche left

à gauche to (on) the left **21**

une **gelée** jelly

généralement generally

généreux (généreuse) generous

la **générosité** generosity

génial brilliant

des **gens** *m.* people **18**

gentil (gentille) nice, kind **19**; sweet

la **géographie** geography

une **girafe** giraffe **E5**

une **glace** ice cream **9, 33**; mirror, ice

glacé iced

un thé glacé iced tea **33**

un **goûter** afternoon snack

une **goyave** guava

grand tall **17**; big, large **20**; big *(size of clothing)* **25**

un grand magasin department store **25**

une grande surface big store, self-service store

grandir to get tall; to grow up

une **grand-mère** grandmother **7, 24**

un **grand-père** grandfather **7, 24**

les **grands-parents** *m.* grandparents **24**

grec (grecque) Greek

un **grenier** attic

une **grillade** grilled meat

une **grille** grid

grillé: le pain grillé toast

une tartine de pain grillé buttered toast

la **grippe** flu

gris gray **20**

gros (grosse) fat, big

grossir to gain weight, get fat **27**

la **Guadeloupe** Guadeloupe *(French island in the West Indies)*

une **guerre** war

une **guitare** guitar **17, 23**

un **gymnase** gym

H

habillé dressed

habiter to live **15**

Haïti Haiti *(French island in the West Indies)*

un **hamburger** hamburger **9**

les • **haricots** *m.* **verts** green beans **33**

la • **hâte** haste

en hâte quickly

• **haut** high

en haut upstairs **21**

plus haut above

• **hélas!** too bad!

hésiter to hesitate

l' **heure** *f.* time, hour; o'clock **4**

... heure(s) (dix) (ten) past ... **4**

... heure(s) et demie half past ... **4**

... heure(s) et quart quarter past ... **4**

... heure(s) moins (dix) (ten) of ... **4**

... heure(s) moins le quart quarter to ... **4**

à... heures at ... o'clock **14**

à quelle heure...? at what time ...? **16**

à quelle heure est...? at what time is ...? **4**

il est... heure(s) it's ... o'clock **4**

par heure per hour, an hour

quelle heure est-il? what time is it? **4**

heureux (heureuse) happy

hier yesterday **31**

avant-hier the day before yesterday

un **hippopotame** hippopotamus **E5**

une **histoire** story, history

l' **hiver** *m.* winter **12**

en hiver in (the) winter **12**

• **hollandais** Dutch

un **homme** man **17**

honnête honest

un **hôpital** *(pl.* **hôpitaux)** hospital **21**

une **horreur** horror

quelle horreur! what a scandal! how awful!

un • **hors-d'oeuvre** appetizer **33**

un • **hot dog** hot dog **9**

un **hôte,** une **hôtesse** host, hostess

un **hôtel** hotel **21**

un hôtel de police police department

l' **huile** *f.* oil

• **huit** eight **1**

huitième eighth **24**

l' **humeur** *f.* mood

de bonne humeur in a good mood

un **hypermarché** shopping center

I

ici here **14**

une **idée** idea

c'est une bonne idée! it's (that's) a good idea! **28**

ignorer to be unaware of

il he, it **11, 14, 18**

il est it is **20**

il/elle est + *nationality* he/she is ... **6**

il y a there is, there are **17**

il y a + **du, de la** *(partitive)* there is (some) **34**

il y a eu there was

il n'y a pas de... there is/are no ... **18**

est-ce qu'il y a...? is there, are there ...? **17**

qu'est-ce qu'il y a...? what is there ...? **17**

une **île** island

illustré illustrated

un **immeuble** apartment building **21**

un **imper (imperméable)** raincoat **25**

l' **impératif** *m.* imperative (command) mood

impoli impolite

l' **importance** *f.* importance

ça n'a pas d'importance it doesn't matter

importé imported

impressionnant impressive

l' **imprimante** *f.* printer

inactif (inactive) inactive

inclure to include

l' **indicatif** *m.* area code

indiquer to indicate, show **C**

indiquez... indicate . . . **C**

infâme: c'est infâme! that's (it's) awful! **35**

infect: c'est infect! that's revolting! *(colloq.)* **35**

les **informations** *f.* news

l' **informatique** *f.* computer science

s' **informer (de)** to find out about

un **ingénieur** engineer

un **ingrédient** ingredient **33**

un **inspecteur, une inspectrice** police detective

un **instrument** instrument **23**

intelligent intelligent **19**

intéressant interesting **19**

l' **intérieur** *m.* interior, inside

les **internautes** people who like to use the Internet

Internet the Internet

interroger to question

interviewer to interview

inutilement uselessly

un **inventaire** inventory

un **invité, une invitée** guest

inviter to invite **15**

israélien (israélienne) Israeli

italien (italienne) Italian **19**

un **Italien, une Italienne** Italian person

J

j' (*see* **je**)

jamais ever; never

jamais le dimanche! never on Sunday!

ne... jamais never **32**

la **Jamaïque** Jamaica

une **jambe** leg **E3**

un **jambon** ham **33**

janvier *m.* January **8**

japonais Japanese **19**

un **jardin** garden **21**

jaune yellow **20**

jaunir to turn yellow

je I **14**

un **jean** pair of jeans **23**

un **jeu** (*pl.* **jeux**) game **25**

les **jeux télévisés** TV game shows

les **jeux électroniques** computer games

jeudi *m.* Thursday **8**

jeune young **17**

les **jeunes** *m.* young people

un **job** (part-time) job

le **jogging** jogging **29**

faire du jogging to jog **29**

un **jogging** jogging suit **25**

joli pretty (*for girls, women*) **17**; (*for clothing*) **25**

plus joli(e) que prettier than

jouer to play **15**

jouer à + *game, sport* to play a game, sport **23**

jouer au tennis (volley, basket, foot) to play tennis (volleyball, basketball, soccer) **13**

jouer de + *instrument* to play a musical instrument **23**

un **jour** day **8, 29**

le **Jour de l'An** New Year's Day

par jour per week, a week

quel jour est-ce? what day is it? **8**

un **journal** (*pl.* **journaux**) newspaper

une **journée** day, whole day

bonne journée! have a nice day!

joyeux (joyeuse) happy

juillet *m.* July **8**

le **quatorze juillet** Bastille Day (*French national holiday*)

juin *m.* June **8**

un **jumeau** (*pl.* **jumeaux**), une

jumelle twin

une **jupe** skirt **25**

le **jus** juice

le **jus d'orange** orange juice **10, 33**

le **jus de pomme** apple juice **10, 33**

le **jus de raisin** grape juice **10**

le **jus de tomate** tomato juice **10**

jusqu'à until

juste right, fair

le **mot juste** the right word

K

un **kangourou** kangaroo **E5**

le **ketchup** ketchup **33**

un **kilo** kilogram

un kilo (de) a kilogram (of) **33**

L

l' (*see* **le, la**)

la the **6, 18**; her, it **36**

là here, there **14**

là-bas over there **14**

ça, là-bas that (one), over there **17**

ce... -là that . . . (over there) **26**

oh là là! uh, oh!; oh, dear!; wow!; oh, yes!

laid ugly

laisser: laisse-moi tranquille! leave me alone! **36**

le **lait** milk **33**

une **langue** language

large wide

laver to wash **29**

se laver to wash (oneself), wash up

le the **6, 18**; him, it **36**

le + *number* + *month* the . . . **8**

le (lundi) on (Mondays) **18**

une **leçon** lesson

un **lecteur** drive (computer), reader

un **lecteur optique interne/ de CD-ROM** internal CD-ROM drive **B**

un lecteur de CD vidéo laserdisc player

un **légume** vegetable **33**
lent slow
les the **18;** them **36**
une **lettre** letter
leur(s) their **24**
leur (to) them **36**
se **lever: lève-toi!** stand up! **B**
levez-vous! stand up! **B**
un **lézard** lizard **E5**
le **Liban** Lebanon *(country in the Middle East)*
libanais Lebanese
libéré liberated
une **librairie** bookstore
libre free
un **lieu** place, area
avoir lieu to take place
une **ligne** line
limité limited
la **limonade** lemon soda **10**
un **lion** lion **E5**
* **lire** to read **C**
comment lire reading hints
lisez... *(see* **lire***)* read ... **B, C**
une **liste** list
une liste des courses shopping list
un **lit** bed **17**
un **living** living room *(informal)*
un **livre** book **B, 17**
une **livre** metric pound **33**
local *(m.pl.* **locaux***)* local
une **location** rental
logique logical
logiquement logically
loin far **21**
loin d'ici far (from here)
le **loisir** leisure, free time
un **loisir** leisure-time activity
Londres London
long (longue) long **25**
longtemps (for) a long time
moins longtemps que for a shorter time
le **loto** lotto, lottery, bingo
un **loup** wolf **E5**
lui him **23;** (to) him/her **36**
lui-même: en lui-même to himself
lundi *m.* Monday **8**
des **lunettes** *f.* glasses **25**
des lunettes de soleil sunglasses **25**

le **Luxembourg** Luxembourg
un **lycée** high school

M

m' *(see* **me***)*
M. (monsieur) Mr. (Mister) **3**
ma my **7, 24**
et voici ma mère and this is my mother **7**
ma chambre my bedroom **17**
une **machine** machine
une machine à coudre sewing machine
Madagascar Madagascar *(French-speaking island off of East Africa)*
Madame (Mme) Mrs., ma'am **3**
Mademoiselle (Mlle) Miss **3**
un **magasin** store, shop **21, 25**
faire les magasins to go shopping (browsing from store to store)
un grand magasin department store **25**
magnétique magnetic
un **magnétophone** tape recorder **17**
un **magnétoscope** VCR (videocassette recorder) **B**
magnifique magnificent
mai *m.* May **8**
maigre thin, skinny
maigrir to lose weight, get thin **27**
un **maillot de bain** bathing suit **25**
une **main** hand **E3**
maintenant now **15, 31**
mais but **14**
j'aime..., mais je préfère... I like ..., but I prefer ... **13**
je regrette, mais je ne peux pas... I'm sorry, but I can't ... **13**
mais oui! sure! **14**
mais non! of course not! **14**
une **maison** house **21**
à la maison at home **14**
mal badly, poorly **3, 15**
ça va mal things are

going badly **3**
ça va très mal things are going very badly **3**
c'est mal that's bad **20**
malade sick
malheureusement unfortunately
malin clever
manger to eat **15**
j'aime manger I like to eat **13**
manger + du, de la *(partitive)* to eat (some) **34**
une salle à manger dining room **21**
un **manteau** *(pl.* **manteaux***)* overcoat **25**
un manteau de fourrure fur coat
un **marchand, une marchande** merchant, shopkeeper, dealer
marcher to work, to run *(for objects)* **17;** to walk *(for people)* **17**
il/elle (ne) marche (pas) bien it (doesn't) work(s) well **17**
est-ce que la radio marche? does the radio work? **17**
un **marché** open-air market **33**
un marché aux puces flea market
bon marché *(inv.)* inexpensive **25**
mardi *m.* Tuesday **8**
le Mardi gras Shrove Tuesday
un **mari** husband **24**
le **mariage** wedding, marriage
marié married
une **marmite** covered stew pot
le **Maroc** Morocco *(country in North Africa)*
une **marque** brand (name)
une **marraine** godmother
marrant fun
marron *(inv.)* brown **20**
mars *m.* March **8**
martiniquais from Martinique
la **Martinique** Martinique *(French island in the West Indies)*

un **match** game, (sports) match
faire un match to play a game, (sports) match **16**
les **maths** *f.* math
le **matin** morning **29**
ce matin this morning **31**
demain matin tomorrow morning **31**
du matin in the morning, A.M. **4**
hier matin yesterday morning **31**
le matin in the morning
des **matoutou crabes** *m.* stewed crabs with rice
mauvais bad **20**
c'est une mauvaise idée that's a bad idea
il fait mauvais it's bad *(weather)* **12**
la **mayonnaise** mayonnaise **33**
me (to) me **35**
méchant mean, nasty **19**
un **médecin** doctor
un médecin de nuit doctor on night duty
la **Méditerranée** Mediterranean Sea
meilleur(e) better, best **27**
mélanger to mix, stir
même same; even
eux-mêmes themselves
les mêmes choses the same things
une **mémoire** memory
mentionner to mention
la **mer** ocean, shore **29**
à la mer to (at) the sea **29**
merci thank you **3**
oui, merci yes, thank you **13**
mercredi *m.* Wednesday **8**
une **mère** mother **7, 24**
mériter to deserve
mes my **24**
la **messagerie vocale** voice mail
le **métro** subway
en métro by subway **22**
* **mettre** to put on, to wear **25**; to put, to place, to turn on **26**
mettre la table to set the table **33**
mexicain Mexican **19**
midi *m.* noon **4**

mieux better
mignon (mignonne) cute **19**
militaire military
mille one thousand **6, 25**
minérale: l'eau *f.* **minérale** mineral water **33**
une **mini-chaîne** compact stereo
minuit *m.* midnight **4**
mis *(p.p. of* **mettre***)* put, placed **31**
mixte mixed
Mlle Miss **3**
Mme Mrs. **3**
une **mob (mobylette)** motorbike, moped **17**
moche plain, ugly **25**
la **mode** fashion
à la mode popular; in fashion; fashionable **25**
moderne modern **21**
moi me **1, 23**; (to) me **35**
moi, je m'appelle (Marc) me, my name is (Marc) **1**
avec moi with me **13**
donne-moi give me **9**
donnez-moi give me **10**
excusez-moi... excuse me . . . **21**
prête-moi... lend me . . . **11**
s'il te plaît, donne-moi... please give me . . . **10**
un **moine** monk
moins less
moins de less than
moins... que less . . . than **27**
... heure(s) moins (dix) (ten) of . . . **4**
... heure(s) moins le quart quarter of . . . **4**
un **mois** month **8, 29**
ce mois-ci this month **31**
le mois dernier last month **31**
le mois prochain next month **31**
par mois per month, a month
mon (ma; mes) my **7, 24**
mon anniversaire est le... my birthday is the . . . **8**
voici mon père this is my father **7**
le **monde** world
du monde in the world

tout le monde everyone
la **monnaie** money; change
le **Monopoly** Monopoly **23**
Monsieur (M.) Mr., sir **3**
un **monsieur** *(pl.* **messieurs***)* gentleman, man *(polite term)* **5**
une **montagne** mountain **29**
à la montagne to (at) the mountains **29**
une **montre** watch **17**
montrer à to show . . . to **35, 36**
montre-moi (montrez-moi) show me **B**
un **morceau** piece
un morceau de craie piece of chalk **B**
un **mot** word
une **moto** motorcycle **17**
la **moutarde** mustard
un **mouton** sheep
moyen (moyenne) average, medium
en moyenne on the average
un **moyen** means
muet (muette) silent
le **multimédia** multimedia
un **musée** museum **21**
la **musique** music **23**

N ▬▬▬▬▬▬▬▬▬▬▬▬

n' *(see* **ne***)*
nager to swim **15**
j'aime nager I like to swim **13**
une **nationalité** nationality **2**
nautique: le ski nautique water-skiing **29**
ne (n')
ne... aucun none, not any
ne... jamais never **32**
ne... pas not **14**
ne... personne nobody **32**
ne... plus no longer
ne... rien nothing **32**
n'est-ce pas? right?, no?, isn't it (so)?, don't you?, aren't you? **14**
né born
nécessaire necessary
négatif (négative) negative
négativement negatively
la **neige** snow

neiger to snow

il neige it's snowing **12**

le **Net** the Internet

netsurfer/surfer sur le Net to "surf the Net"

nettoyer to clean **29**

neuf nine **1**

neuvième ninth **24**

un **neveu** (*pl.* **neveux**) nephew

un **nez** nose **E3**

une **nièce** niece

un **niveau** (*pl.* **niveaux**) level

Noël *m.* Christmas

à Noël at Christmas **29**

noir black **20**

un **nom** name; noun

un **nombre** number

nombreux (nombreuses) numerous

nommé named

non no **2, 14**

non plus neither

mais non! of course not! **14**

le **nord** north

le nord-est northeast

normalement normally

nos our **24**

une **note** grade

notre (*pl.* **nos**) our **24**

la **nourriture** food **33**

nous we **14**; us **23**; (to) us **35**

nouveau (nouvel, nouvelle; *m.pl.* nouveaux) new **27**

la **Nouvelle-Angleterre** New England

la **Nouvelle-Calédonie** New Caledonia (*French island in the South Pacific*)

novembre *m.* November **8**

le onze novembre Armistice Day

la **nuit** night

un **numéro** number

O

objectif (objective) objective

un **objet** object **17**

une **occasion** occasion; opportunity

occupé occupied

un **océan** ocean

octobre *m.* October **8**

une **odeur** odor

un **oeil** (*pl.* **yeux**) eye **E3**

un **oeuf** egg **33**

officiel (officielle) official

offert (*p.p. of* **offrir**) offered

* **offrir** to offer, to give

oh là là! uh,oh!, oh, dear!, wow!, oh, yes!

un **oiseau** (*pl.* **oiseaux**) bird

une **omelette** omelet **9**

on one, they, you, people **28**

on est... today is . . .

on va dans un café? shall we go to a café?

on y va let's go

comment dit-on... en français? how do you say . . . in French? **B**

un **oncle** uncle **7, 24**

onze eleven **2**

opérer to operate

l' **or** *m.* gold

orange (*inv.*) orange (*color*) **20**

une **orange** orange (*fruit*)

le jus d'orange orange juice **10, 33**

un **ordinateur** computer **B, 17**

une **oreille** ear **E3**

organiser to organize **15**

originairement originally

l' **origine** *f.* origin, beginning

d'origine bretonne from Brittany

orthographiques: les signes *m.* **orthographiques** spelling marks

ou or **2, 14**

où where **14, 16**

où est...? where is . . .? **14**

où est-ce? where is it? **21**

d'où? from where? **23**

oublier to forget

l' **ouest** *m.* west

oui yes **2, 14**

oui, bien sûr... yes, of course . . . **13**

oui, d'accord... yes, okay . . . **13**

oui, j'ai... yes, I have . . . **17**

oui, merci... yes, thank you . . . **13**

mais oui! sure! **14**

un **ouragan** hurricane

un **ours** bear **E5**

ouvert open

* **ouvrir** to open

ouvre... (ouvrez...) open . . . **B**

P

le **pain** bread **33**

pâle pale

un **pamplemousse** grapefruit **33**

une **panne** breakdown

une panne d'électricité power failure

un **pantalon** pants, trousers **25**

une **panthère** panther

une **papaye** papaya

le **papier** paper

une feuille de papier a sheet (piece) of paper **B**

Pâques *m.* Easter **29**

à Pâques at Easter **29**

par per

par exemple for example

par jour per day

un **parc** park **21**

un parc public city park

parce que (parce qu') because **16**

pardon excuse me **21, 25**

les **parents** *m.* parents, relatives **24**

paresseux (paresseuse) lazy

parfait perfect

rien n'est parfait nothing is perfect

parfois sometimes

parisien (parisienne) Parisian

parler to speak, talk **B, 15**

parler à to speak (talk) to **36**

parler (français, anglais, espagnol) to speak (French, English, Spanish) **13**

un **parrain** godfather

une **partie** part

* **partir** to leave

à partir de as of, beginning

partitif (partitive) partitive

pas not

ne... pas not **14**

pas de not a, no, not any **18, 34**

pas du tout not at all, definitely not **23**

pas possible not possible

pas toujours not always **13**

pas très bien not very well

le **passé composé** compound past tense

passer to spend (time) **29**; to pass by

passionnément passionately

une **pâte** dough

patient patient

le **patinage** ice skating, roller skating

une **patinoire** skating rink

une **pâtisserie** pastry, pastry shop

une **patte** foot, paw (of bird or animal)

pauvre poor **28**

payer to pay, pay for **28**

un **pays** country

la **peau** skin, hide

* **peindre** to paint

peint painted

une **pellicule** film (camera)

pendant during **29**

pénétrer to enter

pénible bothersome, a pain **20**

penser to think **25**

penser de to think of **25**

penser que to think that **25**

qu'est-ce que tu penses de...? what do you think of . . .? **25**

une **pension** inn, boarding house

Pentecôte f. Pentecost

perdre to lose, to waste **28**

perdu (p.p. of **perdre**) lost

un **père** father **7, 24**

* **permettre** to permit

un **perroquet** parrot

personne (de) nobody **32**

ne... personne nobody, not anybody, not anyone **32**

une **personne** person **5**

personnel (personnelle) personal

personnellement personally

péruvien (péruvienne) Peruvian

petit small, short **17, 20, 25**

il/elle est petit(e) he/she is short **17**

un **petit copain, une petite copine** boyfriend, girlfriend

plus petit(e) smaller

le **petit déjeuner** breakfast **33**

prendre le petit déjeuner to have breakfast **33**

le **petit-fils, la petite-fille** grandson, granddaughter

les **petits pois** m. peas **33**

peu little, not much

un peu a little, a little bit **15**

un peu de a few

peut (see **pouvoir**)

peut-être perhaps, maybe **14**

peux (see **pouvoir**)

est-ce que tu peux...? can you . . .? **13**

je regrette, mais je ne peux pas... I'm sorry, but I can't . . . **13**

la **photo** photography

une **phrase** sentence **B**

la **physique** physics

un **piano** piano **23**

une **pie** magpie **E5**

une **pièce** coin **28**; room

un **pied** foot **E3**

à pied on foot **22**

faire une promenade à pied to take a walk **22**

piloter to pilot (a plane)

une **pincée** pinch

le **ping-pong** Ping-Pong **23**

un **pique-nique** picnic **22**

faire un pique-nique to have a picnic **29**

une **piscine** swimming pool **21**

une **pizza** pizza **9**

un **placard** closet

une **plage** beach **21**

plaît: s'il te plaît please (informal) **9**; excuse me (please)

s'il te plaît, donne-moi... please, give me . . .**10**

s'il vous plaît please (formal) **10**; excuse me (please)

un **plan** map

la **planche à voile** windsurfing **29**

faire de la planche à voile to windsurf **29**

une **plante** plant

un **plat** dish, course (of a meal) **33**

le **plat principal** main course

un **plateau** tray

pleut: il pleut it's raining **12**

plier to fold

plumer to pluck

plus more

plus de more than

plus joli que prettier than

plus... que more . . . than, . . .-er than **27**

en plus in addition

le **plus** the most

ne... plus no longer, no more

non plus neither

plusieurs several

une **poche** pocket

l'argent m. **de poche** allowance, pocket money

une **poêle** frying pan

un **point de vue** point of view

une **poire** pear **33**

pois: les petits pois m. peas **33**

un **poisson** fish **E5, 33**

un poisson rouge goldfish

blaff de poisson fish stew

poli polite

un **politicien, une politicienne** politician

un **polo** polo shirt **25**

une **pomme** apple

le jus de pomme apple juice **10, 33**

une **pomme de terre** potato **33**

une purée de pommes de terre mashed potatoes

le **porc: une côtelette de porc** pork chop

une **porte** door **B, 17**

un **porte-monnaie** change purse, wallet

porter to wear **25**

portugais Portuguese

poser: poser une question to ask a question **C**

une **possibilité** possibility
la **poste** post office
pouah! yuck! yech!
une **poule** hen **E5**
le **poulet** chicken **33**
pour for **14**; in order to **29**
   pour que so that
   pour qui? for whom? **16**
le **pourcentage** percentage
pourquoi why **16**
* **pouvoir** to be able, can, may **35**
pratique practical
pratiquer to participate in
des **précisions** *f.* details
préféré favorite
préférer to prefer **26**; to like (in general)
   je préfère I prefer **13**
   tu préférerais? would you prefer?
premier (première) first **24**
   le premier de l'an New Year's Day
   le premier étage second floor
   le premier mai Labor Day *(in France)*
   c'est le premier juin it's June first **8**
* **prendre** to take, to have *(food)* **B, 34**
   prendre + du, de la *(partitive)* to have (some) **34**
   prendre le petit déjeuner to have breakfast **33**
un **prénom** first name
préparer to prepare; to prepare for **29**
près nearby **21**
   près d'ici nearby, near here
   tout près very close
une **présentation** appearance
   la présentation extérieure outward appearance
des **présentations** *f.* introductions
pressé in a hurry
prêt ready
un **prêt** loan
prêter à to lend to, to loan **35, 36**
   prête-moi... lend me ... **11**

principalement mainly
le **printemps** spring **12**
   au printemps in the spring **12**
pris *(p.p. of* **prendre***)* took **34**
un **prix** price
   quel est le prix ...? what's the price ...? **25**
un **problème** problem
prochain next **29, 31**
   le weekend prochain next weekend **29**
un **produit** product
un **prof, une prof** teacher *(informal)* **5, 17**
un **professeur** teacher **17**
professionnel (professionnelle) professional
un **programme** program
un **projet** plan
une **promenade** walk
   faire une promenade à pied to go for a walk **16, 22**
   faire une promenade à vélo to go for a ride (by bike) **22**
   faire une promenade en voiture to go for a drive (by car) **22**
* **promettre** to promise
une **promo** special sale
proposer to suggest
propre own
un **propriétaire, une propriétaire** landlord/landlady, owner
la **Provence** Provence *(province in southern France)*
pu *(p.p. of* **pouvoir***)* could, was able to **35**
   n'a pas pu was not able to
public: un parc public city park
   un jardin public public garden
la **publicité** commercials, advertising, publicity
une **puce** flea
   un marché aux puces flea market
puis then, also
puisque since
un **pull** sweater, pullover **25**

les **Pyrénées** (the) Pyrenees *(mountains between France and Spain)*

Q

qu' *(see* **que***)*
une **qualité** quality
quand when **16**
   c'est quand, ton anniversaire? when is your birthday? **8**
une **quantité** quantity **33**
quarante forty **3**
un **quart** one quarter
   ... heure(s) et quart quarter past ... **4**
   ... heure(s) moins le quart quarter of ... **4**
un **quartier** district, neighborhood **21**
   un joli quartier a nice neighborhood **21**
quatorze fourteen **2**
quatre four **1**
quatre-vingt-dix ninety **6**
quatre-vingts eighty **6**
quatrième fourth **24**
que that, which
   que veut dire...? what does ... mean? **B**
   qu'est-ce que (qu') what *(phrase used to introduce a question)* **16**
   qu'est-ce que c'est? what is it? what's that? **17**
   qu'est-ce que tu penses de...? what do you think of ...? **25**
   qu'est-ce que tu veux? what do you want? **9**
   qu'est-ce qu'il y a? what is there? **17**; what's the matter?
   qu'est-ce qui ne va pas? what's wrong?
un **Québécois, une Québécoise** person from Quebec
québécois from Quebec
quel (quelle) what, which, what a **26**
   quel (quelle)...! what a ...!
   quel âge a ta mère/ton père? how old is your

mother/your father? **7**

quel âge a-t-il/elle? how old is he/she? **17**

quel âge as-tu? how old are you? **7**

quel est le prix...? what is the price . . .? **25**

quel jour est-ce? what day is it? **8**

quel temps fait-il? what's (how's) the weather? **12**

quelle est la date? what's the date? **8**

quelle est ton adresse? what's your address? **21**

quelle heure est-il? what time is it? **4**

à quelle heure? at what time? **4**

à quelle heure est...? at what time is . . .? **4**

de quelle couleur...? what color is . . .? **20**

quelqu'un someone **32**

quelque chose something **32**

quelques some, a few **17**

une **question** question

une **queue** tail

qui who, whom **16**

qui est-ce? who's that (this)? **5, 17**

qui se ressemble... birds of a feather . . .

à qui? to whom? **16**

avec qui? with who(m)? **16**

c'est qui? who's that? *(casual speech)*

de qui? about who(m)? **16**

pour qui? for who(m)? **16**

quinze fifteen **2**

quoi? what? **17**

quotidien (quotidienne) daily

la vie quotidienne daily life

R

raconter to tell about

une **radio** radio **17**

écouter la radio to listen to the radio **13**

une **radiocassette** boom box **17**

raisin: le jus de raisin grape juice **10**

une **raison** reason

avoir raison to be right **30**

rapidement rapidly

un **rapport** relationship

une **raquette** racket **17**

une raquette de tennis tennis racket **23**

rarement rarely, seldom **15**

un **rayon** department *(in a store)*

réalisé made, directed

récemment recently

une **recette** recipe

recherche: un avis de recherche missing person's bulletin

un **récital** *(pl. récitals)* (musical) recital

reconstituer to reconstruct

un **réfrigérateur** refrigerator

refuser to refuse

regarder to look at, watch **B, 15**

regarde ça look at that **17**

regarder la télé to watch TV **13**

un **régime** diet

être au régime to be on a diet

régional *(m.pl. régionaux)* regional

regretter to be sorry

je regrette, mais... I'm sorry, but . . . **13**

régulier (régulière) regular

une **reine** queen

rencontrer to meet **29**

une **rencontre** meeting, encounter

un **rendez-vous** date, appointment **22**

j'ai un rendez-vous à... I have a date, appointment at . . . **4**

rendre visite à to visit, come to visit **28, 36**

la **rentrée** first day back at school in fall

rentrer to go back, come back **22;** to return, go back, come back **32**

réparer to fix, repair **29**

un **repas** meal **33**

* **repeindre** to repaint

répéter to repeat **B**

répondre (à) to answer, respond (to) **B, 36**

répondez-lui (moi) answer him (me)

répondre que oui to answer yes

une **réponse** answer

un **reportage** documentary

représenter to represent

réservé reserved

une **résolution** resolution

un **restaurant** restaurant **21**

au restaurant to (at) the restaurant **14**

dîner au restaurant to have dinner at a restaurant **13**

un restaurant trois étoiles three star restaurant

rester to stay **22, 32**

retard: un jour de retard one day behind

en retard late

retourner to return; to turn over

réussir to succeed **27**

réussir à un examen to pass an exam **27**

* **revenir** to come back **23**

revoir: au revoir! good-bye! **3**

le **rez-de-chaussée** ground floor

un **rhinocéros** rhinoceros **E5**

riche rich **28**

rien (de) nothing **32**

rien n'est parfait nothing is perfect

ne... rien nothing **32**

une **rive** (river)bank

une **rivière** river, stream

le **riz** rice **33**

une **robe** dress **25**

romain Roman

le **rosbif** roast beef **33**

rose pink **20**

rosse nasty *(colloq.)*

une **rôtie** toast *(Canadian)*
rôtir to roast
une **roue** wheel
rouge red **20**
rougir to turn red
rouler to roll
roux (rousse) red-head
une **rue** street **21**
dans la rue (Victor Hugo) on (Victor Hugo) street **21**
russe Russian

S

sa his, her **24**
un **sac** bag, handbag **17**
sais *(see* savoir*)*
je sais I know **B, 17, 36**
je ne sais pas I don't know **B, 17**
tu sais you know **36**
une **saison** season **12**
toute saison all year round (any season)
une **salade** salad **9, 33;** lettuce **33**
un **salaire** salary
une **salle** hall, large room
une salle à manger dining room **21**
une salle de bains bathroom **21**
une salle de séjour informal living room
un **salon** formal living room **21**
salut hi!, good-bye! **3**
une **salutation** greeting
samedi Saturday **8, 31**
samedi soir Saturday night
à samedi! see you Saturday! **8**
le samedi on Saturdays **18**
une **sandale** sandal **25**
un **sandwich** sandwich **9**
sans without
des **saucisses** *f.* sausages
le **saucisson** salami **33**
* **savoir** to know *(information)*
je sais I know **B, 17, 36**
je ne sais pas I don't know **B, 17**
tu sais you know **36**

un **saxo (saxophone)** saxophone **23**
une **scène** scene, stage
les **sciences** *f.* **économiques** economics
les **sciences** *f.* **naturelles** natural science
un **scooter** motorscooter **17**
second second
seize sixteen **2**
un **séjour** stay; informal living room
le **sel** salt **33**
selon according to
selon toi in your opinion
une **semaine** week **8, 29**
cette semaine this week **31**
la semaine dernière last week **31**
la semaine prochaine next week **31**
par semaine per week, a week
semblable similar
le **Sénégal** Senegal *(French-speaking country in Africa)*
sensationnel (sensationnelle) sensational
séparer to separate
sept seven **1**
septembre *m.* September **8**
septième seventh **24**
une **série** series
sérieux (sérieuse) serious
un **serveur, une serveuse** waiter, waitress
servi served
une **serviette** napkin **33**
ses his, her **24**
seul alone, only; by oneself **29**
seulement only, just
un **short** shorts **25**
si if, whether **C**
si! so, yes! *(to a negative question)* **18**
un **signal** *(pl.* **signaux***)* signal
un **signe** sign
un signe orthographique spelling mark
un **singe** monkey **E5**
situé situated
six six **1**

sixième sixth **24**
un **skate** skateboard
le **ski** skiing
le ski nautique waterskiing **29**
faire du ski to ski **29**
faire du ski nautique to go water-skiing **29**
skier to ski
snob snobbish
la **Société Nationale des Chemins de Fer (SNCF)** *French railroad system*
une **société** society
un **soda** soda **10**
une **soeur** sister **7, 24**
la **soie** silk
la **soif** thirst
avoir soif to be thirsty **30**
j'ai soif I'm thirsty **10**
tu as soif? are you thirsty? **10**
un **soir** evening **29**
ce soir this evening, tonight **31**
demain soir tomorrow night (evening) **29, 31**
du soir in the evening, P.M. **4**
hier soir last night **31**
le soir in the evening
une **soirée** (whole) evening; (evening) party
soixante sixty **3, 5**
soixante-dix seventy **5**
un **soldat** soldier
un **solde** (clearance) sale
en solde on sale
la **sole** sole (fish) **33**
le **soleil** sun
les lunettes *f.* **de soleil** sunglasses **25**
sommes *(see* être*)*
nous sommes... it is, today is ... *(date)*
son (sa; ses) his, her **24**
un **sondage** poll
une **sorte** sort, type, kind
* **sortir** to leave, come out
un **souhait** wish
la **soupe** soup **33**
une **souris** mouse (computer) **B**
sous under **17 B**
le **sous-sol** basement

souvent often **15**

soyez (*see* **être**): **soyez logique** be logical

les spaghetti *m.* spaghetti **33**

spécialement especially

spécialisé specialized

une spécialité specialty

le sport sports **23, 29**
  faire du sport to play sports **29**
  des vêtements *m.* **de sport** sports clothing **25**
  une voiture de sport sports car **23**

sportif (sportive) athletic **19**

un stade stadium **21**

un stage sports training camp; internship

une station-service gas station

un steak steak **9**

un steak-frites steak and French fries **9**

un stylo pen **B, 17**

le sucre sugar **33**

le sud south

suggérer to suggest

suis (*see* **être**)
  je suis + *nationality* I'm . . . **2**
  je suis de... I'm from . . . **2**

suisse Swiss **19**

la Suisse Switzerland

suivant following

suivi followed

un sujet subject, topic

super terrific **15**; great **20, 25**

un supermarché supermarket **21**

supersonique supersonic

supérieur superior

supplémentaire supplementary, extra

sur on **17**; about

sûr sure, certain
  bien sûr! of course! **14**
  oui, bien sûr... yes, of course . . .! **13**
  tu es sûr(e)? are you sure? **24**

sûrement surely

la surface: une grande surface big store, self-service store

surtout especially

un survêtement jogging or track suit **25**

un sweat sweatshirt **25**

une sweaterie shop specializing in sweatshirts and sportswear

sympa nice, pleasant *(colloq.)*

sympathique nice, pleasant **19**

une synagogue Jewish temple or synagogue

un synthétiseur electronic keyboard, synthesizer

T

t' (*see* **te**)

ta your **7, 24**

une table table **B, 17**
  mettre la table to set the table **33**

un tableau (*pl.* **tableaux**) chalkboard **B**

Tahiti Tahiti *(French island in the South Pacific)*

une taille size
  de taille moyenne of medium height or size

un tailleur woman's suit

se taire: tais-toi! be quiet!

une tante aunt **7, 24**

la tarte pie **33**

une tasse cup **33**

un taxi taxi
  en taxi by taxi **22**

te (to) you **35**

un tee-shirt T-shirt **25**

la télé TV **B, 17**
  à la télé on TV
  regarder la télé to watch TV **13**

un téléphone telephone **17**

téléphoner (à) to call, phone **13, 15, 36**

télévisé: des jeux *m.* **télévisés** TV game shows

un temple Protestant church

le temps time; weather
  combien de temps? how long?
  de temps en temps from time to time

quel temps fait-il? what's (how's) the weather? **12**

tout le temps all the time

le tennis tennis **23**
  jouer au tennis to play tennis **13**

des tennis *m.* tennis shoes, sneakers **25**

un terrain de sport (playing) field

une terrasse outdoor section of a café, terrace

la terre earth
  une pomme de terre potato **33**

terrifiant terrifying

tes your **24**

la tête head **E3**

le thé tea **10**
  un thé glacé iced tea **33**

un théâtre theater **21**

le thon tuna **33**

tiens! look!, hey! **5, 18**

un tigre tiger **E5**

timide timid, shy **19**

le tissu fabric

un titre title

toi you **23**
  avec toi with you **13**
  et toi? and you? **1**

les toilettes *f.* bathroom, toilet **21**

un toit roof

une tomate tomato **33**
  le jus de tomate tomato juice **10**

un tombeau tomb

ton (ta; tes) your **7, 24**
  c'est quand, ton anniversaire? when's your birthday? **8**

tort: avoir tort to be wrong **30**

une tortue turtle **E5**
  un bifteck de tortue turtle steak

toujours always **15**
  je n'aime pas toujours... I don't always like . . . **13**

un tour turn
  à votre tour it's your turn

la Touraine Touraine *(province in central France)*

tourner to turn **21**

la Toussaint All Saints' Day *(November 1)*

tout (toute; tous, toutes)
all, every, the whole
tous les jours every day
tout ça all that
tout le monde everyone
tout le temps all the time
toutes sortes all sorts,
kinds
tout completely, very
tout droit straight **21**
tout de suite right away
tout près very close
tout all, everything
pas du tout not at all **23**
un **train** train **29**
tranquille quiet
laisse-moi tranquille!
leave me alone! **36**
un **transistor** transistor radio
un **travail** (*pl.* **travaux**) job
travailler to work **13, 15**
une **traversée** crossing
treize thirteen **2**
trente thirty **3**
un **tréma** diaeresis
très very **19**
très bien very well **15**
ça va très bien things are
going very well **3**
ça va très mal things are
going very badly **3**
trois three **1**
troisième third **24**; *9th
grade in France*
trop too, too much **25**
trouver to find, to think of **25**
comment trouves-tu...?
what do you think of . . .?
how do you find . . .? **25**
s'y trouve is there
tu you **14**
la **Tunisie** Tunisia (*country in
North Africa*)

U ▬▬▬▬▬▬▬▬▬▬

un, une one **1**; a, an **5, 18**
unique only
uniquement only
une **université** university, college
l' **usage** *m.* use
un **ustensile** utensil
utile useful
utiliser to use **C**

en utilisant (by) using
utilisez... use . . . **C**

V ▬▬▬▬▬▬▬▬▬▬

va (*see* **aller**)
va-t'en! go away! **22**
ça va? how are you? how's
everything? **3**
ça va! everything's fine
(going well); fine, I'm OK **3**
on va dans un café? shall
we go to a café?
on y va let's go
les **vacances** *f.* vacation
bonnes vacances! have a
nice vacation!
en vacances on vacation
14
les grandes vacances
summer vacation **29**
une **vache** cow
vais (*see* **aller**): **je vais** I'm
going **22**
la **vaisselle** dishes
faire la vaisselle to do the
dishes
valable valid
une **valise** suitcase
vanille: une glace à la vanille
vanilla ice cream
varié varied
les **variétés** *f.* variety show
vas (*see* **aller**)
comment vas-tu? how are
you? **3**
vas-y! come on!, go ahead!,
do it! **22**
le **veau** veal **33**
une **vedette** star
un **vélo** bicycle **17**
à vélo by bicycle **22**
**faire une promenade à
vélo** to go for a bicycle
ride **22**
un **vendeur, une vendeuse**
salesperson
vendre to sell **28**
vendredi *m.* Friday **8**
vendu (*p.p. of* **vendre**) sold
31
* **venir** to come **23**
le **vent** wind
une **vente** sale
le **ventre** stomach **E3**

venu (*p.p. of* **venir**) came,
come **32**
vérifier to check
la **vérité** truth
un **verre** glass **33**
verser to pour
vert green **20**
les • haricots *m.* **verts**
green beans **33**
une **veste** jacket **25**
des **vêtements** *m.* clothing **25**
des vêtements de sport
sports clothing **25**
veut (*see* **vouloir**): **que veut
dire...?** what does . . .
mean? **B**
veux (*see* **vouloir**)
est-ce que tu veux...? do
you want . . .? **13**
je ne veux pas... I don't
want . . . **13**
je veux... I want . . . **13,
34**
je veux bien... I'd love to,
I do, I want to . . . **13, 34**
qu'est-ce que tu veux?
what do you want? **9**
tu veux...? do you
want . . .? **9**
la **viande** meat **33**
une **vidéocassette** videocassette **B**
un **vidéodisque** laserdisc,
videodisc **B**
la **vie** life
la vie quotidienne daily
life
viens (*see* **venir**)
viens... come . . . **B**
oui, je viens yes, I'm
coming along with you
vieux (vieil, vieille; *m.pl.*
vieux) old **27**
le Vieux Carré *the French
Quarter in New Orleans*
le **Viêt-nam** Vietnam (*country in
Southeast Asia*)
vietnamien (vietnamienne)
Vietnamese
une **vigne** vineyard
un **village** town, village **21**
un petit village small
town **21**
une **ville** city
en ville downtown, in
town, in the city **14**

une **grande ville** big city, town **21**
le **vin** wine
vingt twenty **2, 3**
un **violon** violin **23**
une **visite** visit
rendre visite à to visit *(a person)* **28, 36**
visiter to visit *(places)* **15, 28**
vite! fast!, quick!
vive: vive les vacances! three cheers for vacation!
* **vivre** to live
le **vocabulaire** vocabulary
voici... here is, this is..., here come(s) . . . **5**
voici + du, de la *(partitive)* here's some **34**
voici mon père/ma mère here's my father/my mother **7**
voilà... there is . . ., there come(s) . . . **5**
voilà + du, de la *(partitive)* there's some **34**
la **voile** sailing **29**
faire de la voile to sail **29**
la planche à voile windsurfing **29**
* **voir** to see **29, 31**
voir un film to see a movie **29**
un **voisin,** une **voisine** neighbor **17**
une **voiture** car **17**
une voiture de sport sports car **23**

en voiture by car **22**
faire une promenade en voiture to go for a drive by car **22**
une **voix** voice
le **volley (volleyball)** volleyball **23**
jouer au volley to play volleyball **13**
un **volontaire,** une **volontaire** volunteer
comme volontaire as a volunteer
vos your **24**
votre *(pl.* **vos***)* your **24**
voudrais *(see* **vouloir***):* je **voudrais** I'd like **9, 10, 13, 34**
* **vouloir** to want **34**
vouloir + du, de la *(partitive)* to want some (of something) **34**
vouloir dire to mean **34**
voulu *(p.p. of* **vouloir***)* wanted **34**
vous you **14;** (to) you **35**
vous désirez? what would you like? may I help you? **10, 25**
s'il vous plaît please **10**
un **voyage** trip
bon voyage! have a nice trip!
faire un voyage to take a trip **16**
voyager to travel **13, 15**
vrai true, right, real **20**
vraiment really **23**
vu *(p.p. of* **voir***)* saw, seen **31**

une **vue** view
un point de vue point of view

W ▬▬▬▬▬▬▬▬▬▬▬▬▬▬

un **walkman** walkman **17**
les **WC** *m.* toilet
le **Web ("la toile d'araignée")** the World Wide Web
un **weekend** weekend **29, 31**
bon weekend! have a nice weekend!
ce weekend this weekend **29, 31**
le **weekend** on weekends
le **weekend dernier** last weekend **31**
le **weekend prochain** next weekend **29, 31**

Y ▬▬▬▬▬▬▬▬▬▬▬▬▬▬

y there
il y a there is, there are **17**
est-ce qu'il y a...? is there . . .?, are there . . .? **17**
qu'est-ce qu'il y a? what is there? **17**
allons-y! let's go! **22**
vas-y! come on!, go ahead!, do it! **22**
le **yaourt** yogurt **33**
des **yeux** *m.* *(sg.* **oeil***)* eyes **E3**

Z ▬▬▬▬▬▬▬▬▬▬▬▬▬▬

un **zèbre** zebra
zéro zero **1**
zut! darn! **3**

French-English

ENGLISH-FRENCH VOCABULARY

VOCABULARY

English-French

The English-French vocabulary contains only active vocabulary.

The numbers following an entry indicate the lesson in which the word or phrase is activated. (**B** stands for the photo essay that precedes **Niveau B; C** stands for the list of phrases and expressions that precedes **Niveau C;** and **E** stands for **Entracte.**)

Nouns: If the article of a noun does not indicate gender, the noun is followed by *m.* (*masculine*) or *f.* (*feminine*). If the plural (*pl.*) is irregular, it is given in parentheses.

Verbs: Verbs are listed in the infinitive form. An asterisk (*) in front of an active verb means that it is irregular. (For forms, see the verb charts in Appendix 4C.)

Words beginning with an **h** are preceded by a bullet (•) if the **h** is aspirate; that is, if the word is treated as if it begins with a consonant sound.

A

a, an un, une **5, 18**
  a few quelques **17**
  a little (bit) un peu **15**
  a lot beaucoup **15**
able: to be able (to) *pouvoir **35**
about de **23**
  about whom? de qui? **16**
accessories des accessoires *m.* **25**
acquainted: to be acquainted with *connaître **36**
  are you acquainted with . . . ? tu connais...? **6**
address une adresse **21**
  what's your address? quelle est ton adresse? **21**
after après **29, 30**
  after that ensuite **30**
afternoon l'après-midi *m.* **29**
  in the afternoon de l'après-midi **4**
  this afternoon cet après-midi **31**
  tomorrow afternoon demain après-midi **31**
  yesterday afternoon hier après-midi **31**
afterwards après **30**
to **agree** *être d'accord **14**
airplane un avion **29**
  by airplane en avion **29**
all tout
  all right d'accord **13**
  not at all pas du tout **23**
alone seul **29**

leave me alone! laisse-moi tranquille! **36**
also aussi **2, 15**
always toujours **15**
  not always pas toujours **13**
A.M. du matin **4**
am (*see* **to be**)
  I am . . . je suis + *nationality* **2**
American américain **2, 19**
  I'm American je suis américain(e) **2**
amusing amusant **19**
an un, une **5, 18**
and et **2, 14**
  and you? et toi? **1**
annoying pénible **20**
another un(e) autre
to **answer** répondre (à) **36**
any des **18;** du, de la, de l', de **34**
  not any pas de **18, 34**
anybody: not anybody ne... personne **32**
anyone quelqu'un **32**
anything quelque chose **32**
  not anything ne... rien **32**
apartment un appartement **21**
  apartment building un immeuble **21**
appetizer un •hors-d'oeuvre **33**
apple une pomme
  apple juice le jus de pomme **10, 33**
appointment un rendez-vous **22**
  I have an appointment

at . . . j'ai un rendez-vous à... **4**
April avril *m.* **8**
are (*see* **to be**)
  are there? est-ce qu'il y a? **17**
  are you . . .? tu es + *nationality?* **2**
  there are il y a **17**
  these/those/they are ce sont **20**
arm un bras **E3**
to **arrive** arriver **22**
as . . . as aussi... que **27**
to **ask** demander (à) **36**
at à **14;** chez **22**
  at (the) au, à la, à l', aux **22**
  at . . .'s house chez... **22**
  at . . . o'clock à... heure(s) **14**
  at home à la maison **14**
  at last enfin **30**
  at the restaurant au restaurant **14**
  at what time? à quelle heure? **4, 16**
  at what time is . . .? à quelle heure est...? **4**
athletic sportif (sportive) **19**
to **attend** assister à **29**
attention: to pay attention *faire attention **16**
August août *m.* **8**
aunt une tante **7, 24**
automobile une auto, une voiture **17**
autumn l'automne *m.*

in (the) autumn en automne **12**

avenue une avenue **21**

away: go away! va-t'en! **22**

B

back le dos **E3**

back: to come back rentrer **22, 32**; *revenir **23**

to go back rentrer **22, 32**

in back of derrière **17**

bad mauvais **20**

I'm/everything's (very) bad ça va (très) mal **3**

it's bad (weather) il fait mauvais **12**

that's bad c'est mal **20**

too bad! dommage! **15**

badly mal **3**

things are going (very) badly ça va (très) mal **3**

bag un sac **17**

banana une banane **33**

banknote un billet **28**

baseball le baseball **23**

basketball le basket (basketball) **23**

bathing suit un maillot de bain **25**

bathroom une salle de bains **21**

to **be** *être **14**

to be . . . (years old) *avoir... ans **18**

to be able (to) *pouvoir **35**

to be acquainted with *connaître **36**

to be active in *faire de + *activity* **29**

to be careful *faire attention **16**

to be cold *(people)* *avoir froid **30**; *(weather)* il fait froid **12**

to be going to *(do something)* *aller + *inf.* **22**

to be hot *(people)* *avoir chaud **30**

to be hungry *avoir faim **18, 30**

to be lucky *avoir de la chance **30**

to be present at assister à **29**

to be right *avoir raison **30**

to be supposed to *devoir **35**

to be thirsty *avoir soif **18, 30**

to be warm *(people)* *avoir chaud **30, 31**

to be wrong *avoir tort **30**

beach une plage **21**

beans: green beans les • haricots *m.* verts **33**

beautiful beau (bel, belle; *m.pl.* beaux) **17**

it's beautiful (nice) weather il fait beau **12**

because parce que (qu') **16**

bed un lit **17**

bedroom une chambre **17, 21**

been été *(p.p. of* *être) **31**

before avant **29, 31**

behind derrière **17**

below en bas **21**

belt une ceinture **25**

best meilleur **27**

better meilleur **27**

beverage une boisson **10, 33**

bicycle un vélo, une bicyclette **17**

by bicycle à vélo **22**

take a bicycle ride *faire une promenade à vélo **22**

big grand **17, 20**

bill *(money)* un billet **28**

birthday un anniversaire **8**

my birthday is (March 2) mon anniversaire est le (2 mars) **8**

when is your birthday? c'est quand, ton anniversaire? **8**

bit: a little bit un peu **15**

black noir **20**

blond blond **17**

blouse un chemisier **25**

blue bleu **20**

boat un bateau *(pl.* bateaux) **29**

book un livre **B, 17**

boom box une radiocassette **17**

boots des bottes *f.* **25**

bothersome pénible **20**

boulevard un boulevard **21**

boutique une boutique **25**

boy le garçon **5, 6**

boyfriend un petit copain

bread le pain **33**

breakfast le petit déjeuner **33**

to have breakfast prendre le petit déjeuner **33**

to **bring** *(a person)* amener **26**; *(things)* apporter **35**

to bring something to someone apporter quelque chose à quelqu'un **35**

brother un frère **7, 24**

brown brun **17**; marron *(inv.)* **20**

building: apartment building un immeuble **21**

bus un bus

by bus en bus **22**

touring bus un autocar, un car **29**

but mais **13**

butter le beurre **33**

to **buy** acheter **25, 26**

to buy (some) acheter + du, de la *(partitive)* **34**

by: by airplane, plane en avion **29**

by bicycle à vélo **22**

by bus en bus **22**

by car en voiture **22**

by oneself seul(e) **29**

by subway en métro **22**

by taxi en taxi **22**

by train en train **22**

C

café un café **14**

at (to) the café au café **14**

cafeteria: school cafeteria la cantine de l'école **33**

cake un gâteau *(pl.* gâteaux) **33**

calculator une calculatrice **17**

to **call** téléphoner **15**

came venu *(p.p. of* *venir) **31**

camera un appareil-photo *(pl.* appareils-photo) **17**

camping le camping **29**

to go camping *faire du camping **29**

can *pouvoir **35**

can you . . .? est-ce que tu peux...? **13**

I can't je ne peux pas **13**

Canada le Canada

Canadian canadien (canadienne) **2, 19**

he's/she's (Canadian) il/elle est (canadien/ canadienne) **6**

cannot: I cannot je ne peux pas **13**

I'm sorry, but I cannot je regrette, mais je ne peux pas **13**

car une auto, une voiture **17**

by car en voiture **22**

R37

card une carte
  (playing) cards des cartes *f.* 23
careful: to be careful *faire attention 16
carrot une carotte 33
cassette tape une cassette **B, 17**
  cassette recorder un magnétophone 17
cat un chat 7
CD-ROM un disque optique B
cereal les céréales *f.* 33
chair une chaise **B, 17**
chalk la craie B
  piece of chalk un morceau de craie B
chalkboard un tableau (*pl.* tableaux) B
checkers les dames *f.* 23
cheese le fromage 33
cherry une cerise 33
chess les échecs *m.* 23
chicken le poulet 33
child un (une) enfant 24
  children des enfants *m.* 24
Chinese chinois 19
chocolate: hot chocolate un chocolat 10
to **choose** choisir 27
chose, chosen choisi (*p.p. of* choisir) 31
Christmas Noël 29
  at Christmas à Noël 29
church une église 21
cinema le cinéma 14
  to the cinema au cinéma 14
city une ville 21
  in the city en ville 14
clarinet une clarinette 23
class une classe 14
  in class en classe 14
classmate un (une) camarade 17
to **clean** nettoyer 29
clothing des vêtements *m.* 25
  sports clothing des vêtements *m.* de sport 25
coffee le café 10, 21
coin une pièce 28
cold le froid
  to be (feel) cold *avoir froid 30
  it's cold (*weather*) il fait froid 12
college student un étudiant, une étudiante 17

color une couleur 20
  what color? de quelle couleur? 20
to **come** arriver 22; *venir 23
  come on! vas-y! 22
  here comes . . . voici... 5
  to come back rentrer 22, 32; *revenir 23
  to come to visit rendre visite à 28, 36
comfortable comfortable 21
compact disc un (disque) compact (un CD) **B, 17**
computer un ordinateur **B, 17**
  computer games les jeux électroniques
concert un concert 22
to **continue** continuer 21
cooking la cuisine 33
cool: it's cool (*weather*) il fait frais 12
cost le coût 25
to **cost** coûter
  how much does . . . cost? combien coûte...? 11, 25
  it costs . . . il/elle coûte... 11
country(side) la campagne 29
  to (in) the country(side) à la campagne 29
course: of course! bien sûr! 13; mais oui! 14
  of course not! mais non! 14
cousin un cousin, une cousine 7, 24
crepe une crêpe 9
croissant un croissant 9
cuisine la cuisine 33
cup une tasse 33
cute mignon (mignonne) 19

D ■■■■■■

to **dance** danser 13, 15
dark-haired brun 17
darn! zut! 3
date la date 8; un rendez-vous 22
  I have a date at . . . j'ai un rendez-vous à... 4
  what's the date? quelle est la date? 8
daughter une fille 24
day un jour 8, 29
  what day is it? quel jour est-ce? 8

whole day une journée
dear cher (chère) 25
December décembre *m.* 8
department store un grand magasin 25
to **describe** *décrire C
  describe . . . décrivez... C
desk un bureau **B, 17**
dessert le dessert 33
to **detest** détester 33
did fait (*p.p. of* *faire) 31
difficult difficile 20
dining room une salle à manger 21
dinner le dîner 33
  to have (eat) dinner dîner 15, 33
  to have dinner at a restaurant dîner au restaurant 13
dish (*course of a meal*) un plat 33
to **do** *faire 16
  do it! vas-y! 22
  I do je veux bien 34
  to do + *activity* *faire de + *activity* 29
  to do my homework *faire mes devoirs 29
dog un chien 7
door une porte **B, 17**
done fait (*p.p. of* *faire) 31
downstairs en bas 21
downtown en ville 14
dozen une douzaine 33
dress une robe 25
drink une boisson 10, 33
to **drink** *boire 34
  drive: to take a drive *faire une promenade en voiture 22
drums une batterie 23
dumb bête 19
during pendant 29

E ■■■■■■

e-mail e-mail, le courrier électronique
ear une oreille E3
to **earn** gagner 28
Easter Pâques *m.* 29
  at Easter à Pâques 29
easy facile 20
to **eat** manger 15
  I like to eat j'aime manger 13

to eat breakfast *prendre le petit déjeuner **33**

to eat dinner dîner **15, 33**

to eat lunch déjeuner **33**

to eat (some) manger + du, de la (*partitive*) **34**

egg un oeuf **33**

eight •huit **1**

eighteen dix-huit **2**

eighth •huitième **24**

eighty quatre-vingts **6**

elegant élégant **25**

elephant un éléphant **E5**

eleven onze **2, 11**

eleventh onzième **24**

England l'Angleterre *f.*

English anglais(e) **2, 19**

errand: to run errands *faire les courses **33**

euro un euro

evening un soir **29**

in the evening du soir **4**

this evening ce soir **31**

tomorrow evening demain soir **29, 31**

everything tout

everything's going (very) well ça va (très) bien **3**

everything's (going) so-so ça va comme ci, comme ça **3**

how's everything? ça va? **3**

exam un examen

to pass an exam réussir à un examen **27**

excuse me excusez-moi **21**

expensive cher (chère) **25**

to explain expliquer **C**

eye un oeil (*pl.* yeux) **E3**

F ▬▬▬▬▬▬▬▬▬▬

fall l'automne **12**

in (the) fall en automne **12**

false faux (fausse) **20**

family une famille **7, 24**

far (from) loin (de) **21**

fashion la mode

in fashion (fashionable) à la mode **25**

fat: to get fat grossir **27**

father un père **24**

this is my father voici mon père **7**

February février *m.* **8**

to feel like *avoir envie de + *inf.* **28**

few: a few quelques **17**

fifteen quinze **2**

fifth cinquième **24**

fifty cinquante **3**

film un film **22, 29**

finally finalement **30**

to find trouver **25**

fine ça va **3**

fine! d'accord **13**

everything's fine ça va bien **3**

that's fine c'est bien **20**

to finish finir **27**

finished fini (*p.p. of* finir) **31**

first d'abord **30**; premier (première) **24**

it's (June) first c'est le premier (juin) **8**

fish un poisson **33**

five cinq **1**

to fix réparer **29**

floppy disk une disquette **B**

flute une flûte **23**

food la nourriture **33**

foot un pied **E3**

on foot à pied **22**

for pour **14**

for whom? pour qui? **16**

fork une fourchette **33**

forty quarante **3**

four quatre **1**

fourteen quatorze **2**

fourth quatrième **24**

franc (former monetary unit of France) un franc **11**

that's (it's) . . . francs ça fait...francs **11**

France la France **14**

in France en France **14**

French français(e) **2, 19**

how do you say . . . in French? comment dit-on... en français? **B**

French fries des frites *f.* **33**

steak and French fries un steak-frites **9**

Friday vendredi *m.* **8**

friend un ami, une amie **5**; un copain, une copine **5**

boyfriend, girlfriend un petit copain, une petite copine

school friend un (une) camarade **17**

from de **14**

from (the) du, de la, de l', des **23**

from where? d'où? **23**

are you from . . . ? tu es de...? **2**

I'm from . . . je suis de... **2**

front: in front of devant **17**

fruit(s) des fruits *m.* **33**

funny amusant **19**; drôle **20**

G ▬▬▬▬▬▬▬▬▬▬

to gain weight grossir **27**

game un jeu (*pl.* jeux) **23**; un match **16**

to play a game (match) *faire un match **16**

to play a game jouer à + *game* **23**

garage un garage **21**

garden un jardin **21**

gentleman un monsieur (*pl.* messieurs) **5**

to get: to get fat grossir **27**

to get thin maigrir **27**

girl une fille **5**

girlfriend une petite copine

to give (to) donner (à) **35, 36**

give me donne-moi, donnez-moi **9, 10**

please give me s'il te plaît donne-moi **10**

glass un verre **33**

glasses des lunettes *f.* **25**

sunglasses des lunettes *f.* de soleil **25**

to go *aller **22**

go ahead! vas-y! **22**

go away! va-t'en! **22**

to go (come) back rentrer **22, 32**; *revenir **23**

to go by bicycle *aller en vélo **22**

to go by car, by train . . . *aller en auto, en train... **22**

to go camping *faire du camping **29**

to go food shopping *faire les courses **33**

to go mountain climbing *faire de l'alpinisme **29**

to go shopping *faire des achats **29**

to go to assister à **29**

gone allé(e) (*p.p. of* *aller) **32**

good bon (bonne) **20**

good morning (afternoon) bonjour **1**

that's good c'est bien **20**
the weather's good (pleasant) il fait bon **12**
good-bye! au revoir!, salut! **3**
good-looking beau (bel, belle; *m.pl.* beaux) **17, 20, 27**
grandfather un grand-père **7, 24**
grandmother une grand-mère **7, 24**
grandparents les grands-parents *m.* **24**
grape juice le jus de raisin **10**
grapefruit un pamplemousse **33**
gray gris **20**
great chouette, super **20, 25**
green vert **20**
green beans les •haricots *m.* verts **33**
guitar une guitare **17, 23**

H

had eu (*p.p. of* *avoir) **31**
hair les cheveux *m.* **E3, 23**
he/she has dark hair il/elle est brun(e) **17**
half: half past . . . ... heure(s) et demie **4**
half past midnight minuit et demi **4**
half past noon midi et demi **4**
ham le jambon **33**
hamburger un hamburger **9**
hand une main **E3**
handbag un sac **17**
handsome beau (bel, belle; *m.pl.* beaux) **17, 20, 27**
hard difficile **20**
hat un chapeau (*pl.* chapeaux) **25**
to hate détester **33**
to have *avoir **18**; *(food)* *prendre **34**
do you have . . .? est-ce que tu as...? **17**
I have j'ai **17**
I have to (must) je dois **13**
to have (some) *avoir + du, de la *(partitive)*; *prendre + du, de la *(partitive)* **34**
to have a picnic *faire un pique-nique **29**

to have breakfast *prendre le petit déjeuner **33**
to have dinner dîner **33**
to have dinner at a restaurant dîner au restaurant **13**
to have to *avoir besoin de + *inf.* **28**; *devoir **35**
he il **11, 14, 18**; lui **23**
he/she is . . . il/elle est + *nationality* **6**
head la tête **E3**
to hear entendre **28**
hello bonjour **1, 3**
to help aider **29, 35**
may I help you? vous désirez? **10, 25**
her elle **23**; son, sa; ses **24**; la **36**
(to) her lui **36**
her name is . . . elle s'appelle... **6**
what's her name? comment s'appelle-t-elle? **17**
here ici **14**
here comes, here is voici **5**
here's my mother/father voici ma mère/mon père **7**
here's some voici + du, de la *(partitive)* **34**
this . . . (over here) ce...-ci **26**
hey! dis! **20**; tiens! **5, 18**
hey there! dis donc! **20**
hi! salut! **3**
high school student un (une) élève **17**
him lui **23**; le **36**
(to) him lui **36**
his son, sa; ses **24**
his name is . . . il s'appelle... **6**
what's his name? comment s'appelle-t-il? **17**
home, at home à la maison **14**; chez (moi, toi...) **23**
to go home rentrer **22, 32**
homework les devoirs *m.* **29**
homework assignment un devoir **B**
to do my homework *faire mes devoirs **29**
to hope espérer **26**
horse un cheval (*pl.* chevaux) **E5**

hospital un hôpital **21**
hot chaud **12, 31**
hot chocolate un chocolat **10**
hot dog un •hot dog **9**
to be hot *(people)* *avoir chaud **30**
it's hot *(weather)* il fait chaud **12**
hotel un hôtel **21**
house une maison **21**
at someone's house chez + *person* **22**
how? comment? **16**
how are you? comment allez-vous?, comment vas-tu?, ça va? **3**
how do you find . . .? comment trouves-tu...? **25**
how do you say . . . in French? comment dit-on... en français? **B**
how much? combien (de)? **28**
how much does . . . cost? combien coûte...? **11, 25**
how much is that/this/it? c'est combien?, ça fait combien? **11**
how old are you? quel âge as-tu? **7**
how old is he/she? quel âge a-t-il/elle? **17**
how old is your father/mother? quel âge a ton père/ta mère? **7**
how's everything? ça va? **3**
how's the weather? quel temps fait-il? **12**
to learn how to *apprendre à **34**
hundred cent **6, 25**
hungry avoir faim **9**
are you hungry? tu as faim? **9**
I'm hungry j'ai faim **9**
to be hungry avoir faim **18, 30**
husband un mari **24**

I

I je **14,** moi **23**
I don't know je ne sais pas **B, 17**

I have a date/appointment at . . . j'ai un rendez-vous à... **4**
I know je sais **B, 17, 36**
I'm fine/okay ça va **3**
I'm (very) well/so-so/(very) bad ça va (très) bien/comme ci, comme ça/(très) mal **3**
ice la glace **9, 33**
ice cream une glace **9, 33**
iced tea un thé glacé **33**
idea une idée **28**
it's (that's) a good idea c'est une bonne idée **28**
if si **C**
in à **14, 22;** dans **17**
in (Boston) à (Boston) **14**
in class en classe **14**
in front of devant **17**
in order to pour **29**
in the afternoon de l'après-midi **4**
in the morning/evening du matin/soir **4**
in town en ville **14**
in (the) au, à la, à l', aux **22**
to indicate indiquer **C**
inexpensive bon marché *(inv.)* **25**
information highway l'autoroute de l'information, l'Inforoute, le Cyberespace
ingredient un ingrédient **33**
instrument un instrument **23**
to play a musical instrument jouer de + *instrument* **23**
intelligent intelligent **33**
interesting intéressant **19**
to invite inviter **15**
is *(see* to be*)*
is there? est-ce qu'il y a? **17**
isn't it (so)? n'est-ce pas? **14**
there is il y a **17**
there is (some) il y a + du, de la *(partitive)* **34**
it il, elle **14, 18;** le, la **36**
it's . . . c'est... **5**
it's . . . (o'clock) il est... heure(s) **4**
it's . . . francs ça fait... francs **11**
it's fine/nice/hot/cool/

cold/bad *(weather)* il fait beau/bon/chaud/frais/ froid/mauvais **12**
it's (June) first c'est le premier (juin) **8**
it's not ce n'est pas **20**
it's raining il pleut **12**
it's snowing il neige **12**
what time is it? quelle heure est-il? **4**
who is it? qui est-ce? **5, 17**
its son, sa; ses **24**
Italian italien, italienne **19**

J

jacket un blouson, une veste **25**
jam la confiture **33**
January janvier *m.* **8**
Japanese japonais(e) **19**
jeans: pair of jeans un jean **25**
to jog *faire du jogging **29**
jogging le jogging **29**
jogging suit un jogging, un survêtement **25**
juice le jus
apple juice le jus de pomme **10, 33**
grape juice le jus de raisin **10**
orange juice le jus d'orange **10, 33**
tomato juice le jus de tomate **10**
July juillet *m.* **8**
June juin *m.* **8**

K

ketchup le ketchup **33**
keyboard un clavier **23**
kilogram un kilo (de) **33**
kind gentil (gentille) **19**
kitchen une cuisine **21**
knife un couteau **33**
to know *connaître **36**
do you know . . . ? tu connais...? **6**
I (don't) know je (ne) sais (pas) **B, 17, 36**
you know tu sais **36**

L

lady une dame **5**
large grand **17, 20**
laserdisc un CD vidéo, un vidéodisque **B**
last dernier (dernière) **31**

last month le mois dernier **31**
last night hier soir **31**
last Saturday samedi dernier **31**
at last enfin **30**
to learn (how to) *apprendre (à) + *inf.* **34**
left gauche
on (to) the left à gauche **21**
leg une jambe **E3**
lemon soda la limonade **10**
to lend prêter (à) **35, 36**
lend me prête-moi **11**
less . . . than moins... que **27**
let's go! allons-y! **22**
lettuce la salade **33**
library une bibliothèque **21**
like: what does he/she look like? comment est-il/elle? **17**
what's he/she like? comment est-il/elle? **17**
to like aimer **15**
do you like? est-ce que tu aimes? **13**
I also like j'aime aussi **13**
I don't always like je n'aime pas toujours **13**
I don't like je n'aime pas **13**
I like j'aime **13**
I like . . ., but I prefer . . . j'aime..., mais je préfère... **13**
I'd like je voudrais **9, 10, 13**
what would you like? vous désirez? **10, 25**
to listen écouter **15**
to listen to cassettes écouter des cassettes **29**
to listen to the radio écouter la radio **13**
little petit **17, 20, 25**
a little (bit) un peu **15**
to live habiter **15**
living room *(formal)* un salon **21**
to loan prêter (à) **35, 36**
long long (longue) **25**
to look (at) regarder **15**
look! tiens! **5, 18**
look at that regarde ça **17**
I'm looking for . . . je cherche... **25**
to look for chercher **25**

what does he/she look like? comment est-il/elle? **17**

to **lose** perdre **28**
  to lose weight maigrir **27**
lot: a lot beaucoup **15**
to **love: I'd love to** je veux bien **13**
  luck la chance **30**
  to be lucky *avoir de la chance **30**
  lunch le déjeuner **33**
  to have (eat) lunch déjeuner **33**

M

made fait (*p.p. of* *faire) **31**
to **make** *faire **16**
man un homme **17;** un monsieur *(polite term)* **5**
many beaucoup (de) **15**
  how many combien de **28**
map une carte **B**
March mars *m.* **8**
match un match **16**
  to play a match *faire un match **16**
May mai *m.* **8**
may *pouvoir **35**
maybe peut-être **14**
mayonnaise la mayonnaise **33**
me moi **1, 35**
  excuse me pardon **21, 25**
  (to) me me, moi **35**
meal un repas **33**
mean méchant **19**
to **mean** *vouloir dire **34**
  what does . . . mean? que veut dire...? **B**
meat la viande **33**
to **meet** rencontrer **29**
  to meet for the first time *connaître *(in passé composé)* **36**
Mexican mexicain(e) **19**
midnight minuit *m.* **4**
milk le lait **33**
mineral water l'eau *f.* minérale **33**
Miss Mademoiselle (Mlle) **3**
modern moderne **21**
Monday lundi *m.* **8**
money l'argent *m.* **29**
Monopoly le Monopoly **23**

month un mois **8, 27**
  last month le mois dernier **31**
  next month le mois prochain **31**
  this month ce mois-ci **31**
moped une mob (mobylette) **17**
more . . . than plus... que **27**
morning le matin **29**
  good morning bonjour **1**
  in the morning du matin **4**
  this morning ce matin **29**
  tomorrow morning demain matin **31**
  yesterday morning hier matin **31**
mother une mère **7, 24**
  this is my mother voici ma mère **7**
motorbike une mob (mobylette) **17**
motorcycle une moto **17**
motorscooter un scooter **17**
mountain une montagne **29**
  mountain climbing l'alpinisme *m.* **29**
  to (at/in) the mountain(s) à la montagne **29**
  to do mountain climbing *faire de l'alpinisme **29**
mouse une souris **B**
mouth une bouche **E3**
movie un film **22, 29**
  movie theater un cinéma **14**
movies le cinéma **21**
  at (to) the movies au cinéma **14**
Mr. Monsieur (M.) **3**
Mrs. Madame (Mme) **3**
much, very much beaucoup **15**
  how much? combien? **28**
  how much does . . . cost? combien coûte...? **11, 25**
  how much is it? ça fait combien?, c'est combien? **11**
  too much trop **25**
museum un musée **21**
music la musique **23**
must *devoir **35**
  I must je dois **13**
my mon, ma; mes **7, 24**
  my birthday is (March 2) mon anniversaire est le (2 mars) **8**

my name is . . . je m'appelle... **1**

N

name: his/her name is . . . il/elle s'appelle... **6**
  my name is . . . je m'appelle... **1**
  what's . . .'s name? comment s'appelle...? **6**
  what's his/her name? comment s'appelle-t-il/elle? **17**
  what's your name? comment t'appelles-tu? **1**
napkin une serviette **33**
nasty méchant **19**
nationality la nationalité **2**
nearby près **21**
neck le cou **E3**
to **need** *avoir besoin de **28**
  neighbor un voisin, une voisine **17**
neighborhood un quartier **21**
  a nice neighborhood un joli quartier **21**
never ne... jamais **32**
new nouveau (nouvel, nouvelle; *m.pl.* nouveaux) **27**
next prochain **29, 31**
  next week la semaine prochaine **31**
nice gentil (gentille), sympathique **19**
  it's nice (beautiful) weather il fait beau **12**
night: tomorrow night demain soir **4**
  last night hier soir **31**
nine neuf **1**
nineteen dix-neuf **2**
ninety quatre-vingt-dix **6**
ninth neuvième **24**
no non **2,14**
  no . . . pas de **18, 34**
  no? n'est-ce pas? **14**
nobody ne... personne, personne **32**
noon midi *m.* **4**
nose le nez **E3**
not ne... pas **14**
  not a, not any pas de **18, 34**
  not always pas toujours **13**

not anybody ne... personne **32**

not anything ne... rien **32**

not at all pas du tout **23**

it's (that's) not ce n'est pas **20**

of course not! mais non! **14**

notebook un cahier **B**

nothing ne... rien, rien **32**

November novembre *m.* **8**

now maintenant **15, 31**

O

o'clock heure(s)

   at . . . o'clock à... heures **4**

   it's . . . o'clock il est... heure(s) **4**

object un objet **17**

ocean la mer **29**; l'océan *m.*

   to (at) the oceanside à la mer **29**

October octobre *m.* **8**

of de **14**

   of (the) du, de la, de l', des **23**

   of course not! mais non! **14**

   of course! bien sûr **13**

   of whom de qui **16**

often souvent **15**

oh: oh, really? ah, bon? **16**

okay d'accord **13**

   I'm okay ça va **3**

old vieux (vieil, vieille; *m.pl.* vieux) **27**

   he/she is . . . (years old) il/elle a... ans **7**

   how old are you? quel âge as-tu? **7**

   how old is he/she? quel âge a-t-il/elle? **17**

   how old is your father/ mother? quel âge a ton père/ta mère? **7**

   I'm . . . (years old) j'ai... ans **7**

   to be . . . (years old) *avoir... ans **18**

omelet une omelette **9**

on sur **17**

   on foot à pied **22**

   on Monday lundi **18**

   on Mondays le lundi **18**

   on vacation en vacances **14**

one un, une **1**; *(we, they, people)* on **28**

oneself: by oneself seul **29**

only seul **29**

open *ouvrir

   open . . . ouvre... (ouvrez...) **B**

opinion: in my opinion à mon avis **27**

or ou **2, 14**

orange *(color)* orange *(inv.)* **20**

orange une orange **33**

   orange juice le jus d'orange **10, 33**

order: in order to pour **29**

to organize organiser **15**

other autre **33**

our notre; nos **24**

out of style démodé **25**

over: over (at) . . .'s house chez... **23**

   over there là-bas **14**

   that (one), over there ça, là-bas **17**

overcoat un manteau *(pl.* manteaux) **25**

to own *avoir **18**

P

P.M. du soir **4**

pain: a pain pénible **20**

pants un pantalon **25**

pantyhose des collants *m.* **25**

paper le papier **B**

   sheet of paper une feuille de papier **B**

parents les parents *m.* **24**

park un parc **21**

party *(informal)* une fête, une soirée, une boum **22**

to pass a test (an exam) réussir à un examen **27**

past: half past . . . ... heure(s) et demie **4**

   quarter past . . . ... heure(s) et quart **4**

to pay (for) payer **28**

   to pay attention *faire attention **16**

pear une poire **33**

peas les petits pois *m.* **33**

pen un stylo **B, 17**

pencil un crayon **B, 17**

people des gens *m.* **18**; on **28**

perhaps peut-être **14**

person une personne **5, 17**

pet un animal *(pl.* animaux)

domestique **7**

to phone téléphoner **15**

piano un piano **23**

picnic un pique-nique **22**

   to have a picnic *faire un pique-nique **29**

pie une tarte **33**

piece: piece of chalk un morceau de craie **B**

ping-pong le Ping-Pong **23**

pink rose **20**

pizza une pizza **9**

place un endroit **22**

   place setting un couvert **33**

to place *mettre **26**

placed mis *(p.p. of* *mettre) **31**

plain moche **25**

plane un avion **29**

   by plane en avion **29**

plate une assiette **33**

to play jouer **15**

   to play a game jouer à + *game* **23**

   to play a game (match) *faire un match **16**

   to play a musical instrument jouer de + *instrument* **23**

   to play basketball (soccer, tennis, volleyball) jouer au basket (au foot, au tennis, au volley) **13**

pleasant sympathique **19**

   it's pleasant (good) weather il fait bon **12**

please s'il vous plaît *(formal)* **10**; s'il te plaît *(informal)* **9**

   please give me . . . s'il te plaît, donne-moi... **10**

polo shirt un polo **25**

pool: swimming pool une piscine **21**

poor pauvre **28**

poorly mal **3**

popular à la mode **25**

poster une affiche **17**

potato une pomme de terre **33**

pound une livre (de) **33**

to prefer préférer **26, 33**

   I prefer je préfère + *inf.* **13**

   I like . . ., but I prefer . . . j'aime..., mais je préfère... **13**

to prepare préparer **29**

pretty joli **17, 25**

price un prix **25**

what's the price? quel est le prix? **25**
pullover un pull **25**
pupil un (une) élève **17**
to **purchase** acheter **29**
to **put** *mettre **26**
    to **put on** *mettre **26**

Q

quantity une quantité **33**
quarter un quart
    quarter of . . . ... heure(s) moins le quart **4**
    quarter past . . . ... heure(s) et quart **4**

R

racket une raquette **17**
radio une radio **17**
    to listen to the radio écouter la radio **13**
rain: it's raining il pleut **12**
raincoat un imper (imperméable) **25**
rarely rarement **15**
rather assez **19**
really: oh, really? ah, bon? **16**
    really?! vraiment?! **23**
record un disque **17**
red rouge **20**
relatives les parents *m.* **24**
to **repair** réparer **29**
to **respond** répondre **36**
restaurant un restaurant **21**
    at (to) the restaurant au restaurant **14**
    have dinner at a restaurant dîner au restaurant **13**
to **return** rentrer **32**; *revenir **23**
rice le riz **33**
rich riche **28**
ride: to take a bicycle ride *faire une promenade à vélo **22**
right vrai **20**; droite
    right? n'est-ce pas? **14**
    all right d'accord **13**
    to be right *avoir raison **30**
    to (on) the right à droite **21**
roast beef le rosbif **33**
room une chambre **17**; une salle **21**

bathroom une salle de bains **21**
dining room une salle à manger **21**
formal living room un salon **21**
to **run** *(referring to objects)* marcher **17**

S

sailing la voile **29**
salad une salade **9, 33**
salami le saucisson **33**
salt le sel **33**
sandal une sandale **25**
sandwich un sandwich **9**
Saturday samedi *m.* **8, 31**
    see you Saturday! à samedi! **8**
    last Saturday samedi dernier **31**
    next Saturday samedi prochain **31**
saw vu *(p.p. of *voir)* **31**
saxophone un saxo (saxophone) **23**
say *dire **36**
    say . . . dites... **C**
    say! dis (donc)! **20**
    how do you say . . . in French? comment dit-on... en français? **B**
school une école **21**
    school cafeteria une cantine de l'école **33**
    school friend un (une) camarade **17**
sea la mer **29**
    to (at) the sea à la mer **29**
season une saison **12**
second deuxième **24**
to **see** *voir **29**
    see you tomorrow! à demain! **8, 29**
seen vu *(p.p. of *voir)* **31**
seldom rarement **15**
to **sell** vendre **28**
September septembre *m.* **8**
to **set the table** *mettre la table **33**
seven sept **1**
seventeen dix-sept **2**
seventh septième **24**
seventy soixante-dix **5**

she elle **14, 18, 23**
sheet of paper une feuille de papier **B**
ship un bateau *(pl.* bateaux) **29**
shirt une chemise **25**
shoe une chaussure **5**
    tennis shoes des tennis *m.* **25**
shop une boutique **25**
shopping: shopping center un centre commercial **21**
    to go food shopping *faire les courses **33**
    to go shopping *faire des achats **29**
shore la mer **29**
short court **25**; petit **17, 20, 25**
    he/she is short il/elle est petit(e) **17**
shorts un short **25**
should *devoir **35**
to **show** indiquer **C**; montrer à **35, 36**
to **shut** fermer **B**
shy timide **19**
silly bête **19**
to **sing** chanter **13, 15**
sir Monsieur (M.) **3**
sister une soeur **7, 24**
six six **1**
sixteen seize **2**
sixth sixième **24**
sixty soixante **3, 5**
to **ski** *faire du ski **29**
    skiing le ski **29**
skirt une jupe **25**
small petit **17, 20, 25**
sneakers des tennis *m.* **25**
    hightop sneakers des baskets *f.* **25**
snow: it's snowing il neige **12**
so alors **19**
    so-so comme ci, comme ça **3**
    everything's (going) so-so ça va comme ci, comme ça **3**
soccer le foot (football) **23**
sock une chaussette **25**
soda un soda **10**
    lemon soda une limonade **10**
sold vendu *(p.p. of* vendre) **31**
sole *(fish)* la sole **33**
some des **18**; du, de la, de l' **34**; quelques **17**

somebody quelqu'un **32**
someone quelqu'un **32**
something quelque chose **32**
son un fils **24**
sorry: to be sorry regretter
   I'm sorry, but (I cannot) je
   regrette, mais (je ne peux
   pas) **13**
soup la soupe **33**
spaghetti les spaghetti *m.* **33**
Spanish espagnol(e) **19**
to **speak** parler **15**
   **to speak (French, English,
   Spanish)** parler (français,
   anglais, espagnol) **13**
   to speak to parler à **36**
to **spend** *(money)* dépenser **28**;
   (time) passer **29**
spoon une cuillère **33**
sports le sport **29**
   to play a sport *faire du
   sport **29**; jouer à + *sport* **23**
   sports clothing des
   vêtements *m.* de sport **25**
spring le printemps **12**
   in the spring au printemps
   12
stadium un stade **21**
to **stay** rester **22**
steak un steak **9**
   steak and French fries un
   steak-frites **9**
stereo set une chaîne stéréo **17**
stomach le ventre **E3**
store un magasin **21, 25**
   department store un grand
   magasin **25**
straight tout droit **21**
strawberry une fraise **33**
street une rue **21**
student *(high school)* un (une)
   élève **17**; *(college)* un
   étudiant, une étudiante **17**
to **study** étudier **13, 15**
stupid bête **19**
style: in style à la mode **25**
   out of style démodé **25**
subway le métro **22**
   by subway en métro **22**
to **succeed** réussir **27**
sugar le sucre **33**
summer l'été *m.* **12**
   summer vacation les
   grandes vacances **29**
   in the summer en été **12**

sun le soleil **25**
Sunday dimanche *m.* **8**
sunglasses des lunettes *f.* de
   soleil **25**
supermarket un supermarché
   21
supper le dîner **33**
   to have (eat) supper dîner
   15, 33
sure bien sûr **13**
   sure! mais oui! **14**
   are you sure? tu es sûr(e)?
   24
sweater un pull **25**
sweatshirt un sweat **25**
to **swim** nager **15**
   I like to swim j'aime nager
   13
swimming pool une piscine **21**
swimsuit un maillot de bain **25**
Swiss suisse **19**

T

table une table **B, 17**
   to set the table *mettre la
   table **33**
to **take** *prendre **B, 34**
   to take along amener **26,
   35**
   to take a bicycle ride *faire
   une promenade à vélo **22**
   to take a drive *faire une
   promenade en voiture **22**
   to take a trip *faire un
   voyage **16**
   to take a walk *faire une
   promenade à pied **22**
to **talk** parler **15**
   to talk to parler à **36**
tall grand **17, 20**
tape: tape recorder un
   magnétophone **17**
   cassette tape une cassette
   B, 17
taxi un taxi **22**
   by taxi en taxi **22**
tea le thé **10**
   iced tea un thé glacé **33**
teacher un (une) prof **5, 17**;
   un professeur **17**
telephone un téléphone **17**
to **telephone** téléphoner **15**
television la télé **B, 17**

   to watch television regarder
   la télé **13**
to **tell** *dire **36**
ten dix **1, 2**
tennis le tennis **23**
   tennis racket une raquette
   de tennis **23**
   tennis shoes des tennis *m.*
   25
   to play tennis jouer au
   tennis **13**
tenth dixième **24**
terrific chouette **20, 25**; extra
   20; super **20, 25**
test un examen
   to pass a test réussir à un
   examen **27**
than que **27**
thank you merci **3**
that que **25**; ce, cet, cette **26**
   that is . . . c'est... **17, 20**
   that (one), over there ça,
   là-bas **17**
   that's . . . c'est... **5, 17, 20**;
   voilà **5**
   that's . . . francs ça fait...
   francs **11**
   that's bad c'est mal **20**
   that's a good idea! c'est une
   bonne idée! **28**
   that's good (fine) c'est bien
   20
   that's not . . . ce n'est pas...
   20
   what's that? qu'est-ce que
   c'est? **17**
the le, la, l' **6, 18**; les **18**
theater un théâtre **21**
   movie theater un cinéma **21**
their leur, leurs **24**
them eux, elles **23**; les **36**
   (to) them leur **36**
   themselves eux-mêmes
then alors **19**; ensuite **30**
there là **14**
   there is (are) il y a **17**
   **there is (here comes
   someone)** voilà **5**
   there is (some) il y a + du,
   de la *(partitive)* **34**
   there's some voilà + du, de
   la *(partitive)* **34**
   over there là-bas **14**
   that (one), over there ça,
   là-bas **17**; ce...-là **26**

what is there? qu'est-ce qu'il y a? **17**

these ces **26**

  these are ce sont **20**

they ils, elles **14**; eux **23**; on **28**

  they are ce sont **20**

thin: to get thin maigrir **27**

thing une chose

  things are going (very) badly ça va (très) mal **3**

to **think** penser **25**

  to think of penser de, trouver **25**

  to think that penser que **25**

  what do you think of . . .? comment trouves-tu...?, qu'est-ce que tu penses de...? **25**

third troisième **24**

thirsty: to be thirsty *avoir soif **30**

  are you thirsty? tu as soif? **10**

  I'm thirsty j'ai soif **10**

thirteen treize **2**

thirty trente **3**

  3:30 trois heures et demie **4**

this ce, cet, cette **26**

  this is . . . voici... **5**

those ces **26**

  those are ce sont **20**

thousand mille **6, 25**

three trois **1**

Thursday jeudi *m.* **8**

tie une cravate **25**

tights des collants *m.* **25**

time: at what time is . . .? à quelle heure est...? **4**

  at what time? à quelle heure? **4**

  what time is it? quelle heure est-il? **4**

to à **14, 22**; chez **22, 23**

  to (the) au, à la, à l', aux **22**

  in order to pour **29**

  to class en classe **14**

  to someone's house chez + *person* **22**

  to whom à qui **16**

today aujourd'hui **8, 31**

  today is (Wednesday) aujourd'hui, c'est (mercredi) **8**

toilet les toilettes **21**

tomato une tomate

  tomato juice le jus de tomate **10**

tomorrow demain **8**

  tomorrow afternoon demain après-midi **31**

  tomorrow is (Thursday) demain, c'est (jeudi) **8**

  tomorrow morning demain matin **31**

  tomorrow night (evening) demain soir **31**

  see you tomorrow! à demain! **8, 29**

tonight ce soir **31**

too aussi **2, 15**; trop **25**

  too bad! dommage! **15**

touring bus un autocar, un car **29**

tourist: tourist office office *(m.)* de tourisme

town un village **21**

  in town en ville **14**

track suit un survêtement **25**

train un train **29**

  by train en train **22, 29**

to **travel** voyager **13, 15**

trip: to take a trip *faire un voyage **16**

trousers un pantalon **25**

true vrai **20**

T-shirt un tee-shirt **25**

Tuesday mardi *m.* **8**

tuna le thon **33**

to **turn** tourner **21**

  to turn on *mettre **26**

TV la télé **B, 17**

  to watch TV regarder la télé **13**

twelfth douzième **24**

twelve douze **2**

twenty vingt **2, 3**

two deux **1**

ugly moche **25**

uncle un oncle **7, 24**

under sous **17**

to **understand** *comprendre **34**

  I (don't) understand je (ne) comprends (pas) **B**

unfashionable démodé **25**

United States les États-Unis *m.*

upstairs en •haut **21**

us nous **23**

  (to) us nous **35**

to **use** utiliser

vacation les vacances *f.* **29**

  on vacation en vacances **14**

  summer vacation les grandes vacances **29**

VCR (videocassette recorder) un magnétoscope **B**

veal le veau **33**

vegetable un légume **33**

very très **19**

  very well très bien **15**

  very much beaucoup **15**

videocassette une vidéocassette **B**

  videocassette recorder un magnétoscope **B**

videodisc un CD vidéo **B**

  videodisc player un lecteur de CD/vidéo

violin un violon **23**

to **visit** *(place)* visiter **15, 28**; *(people)* rendre visite à **28, 36**

volleyball le volley (volleyball) **23**

to **wait (for)** attendre **28**

walk une promenade **22**

  to take (go for) a walk *faire une promenade à pied **16, 22**

to **walk** *aller à pied **22**; marcher **17**

walkman un walkman **17**

to **want** *avoir envie de **28**; *vouloir **34**

  do you want . . .? tu veux...? **9**

  do you want to . . .? est-ce que tu veux...? **13**

  I don't want . . . je ne veux pas... **13**

  I want . . . je veux... **13, 34**

  I want to je veux bien **34**

  what do you want? qu'est-ce que tu veux? **9**; vous désirez? **10, 25**

wanted voulu *(p.p. of* *vouloir) **34**

warm chaud **12, 31**

  to be warm *(people)* *avoir chaud **30**

it's warm *(weather)* il fait chaud **12**

was été *(p.p. of* *être*)* **31**

to **wash** laver **29**

to **waste** perdre **28**

watch une montre **17**

to **watch** regarder **15**

to **watch TV** regarder la télé **13**

water l'eau *f.* **33**

mineral water l'eau minérale **33**

to **waterski** *faire du ski nautique **29**

waterskiing le ski nautique **29**

we nous **14, 23;** on **28**

to **wear** *mettre **26;** porter **25**

weather: how's (what's) the weather? quel temps fait-il? **12**

it's . . . weather il fait... **12**

Wednesday mercredi *m.* **8**

week une semaine **8, 29**

last week la semaine dernière **31**

next week la semaine prochaine **31**

this week cette semaine **31**

weekend un weekend **29**

last weekend le weekend dernier **31**

next weekend le weekend prochain **29, 31**

this weekend ce weekend **31**

weight: to gain weight grossir **27**

well bien **15**

well! eh bien! **26**

well then alors **19**

everything's going (very) well ça va (très) bien **3**

went allé *(p.p. of* *aller*)* **32**

what comment? quoi? **17;** qu'est-ce que **16**

what color? de quelle couleur? **20**

what day is it? quel jour est-ce? **8**

what do you think of . . .? comment trouves-tu...?, qu'est-ce que tu penses de...? **25**

what do you want? qu'est-ce que tu veux? **9;** vous désirez? **10, 25**

what does . . . mean? que veut dire...? **B**

what does he/she look like? comment est-il/elle? **17**

what is it? qu'est-ce que c'est? **17**

what is there? qu'est-ce qu'il y a? **17**

what time is it? quelle heure est-il? **4**

what would you like? vous désirez? **10, 25**

what's . . .'s name? comment s'appelle...? **6**

what's he/she like? comment est-il/elle? **17**

what's his/her name? comment s'appelle-t-il/elle? **17**

what's that? qu'est-ce que c'est? **17**

what's the date? quelle est la date? **8**

what's the price? quel est le prix? **25**

what's the weather? quel temps fait-il? **12**

what's your address? quelle est ton adresse? **21**

what's your name? comment t'appelles-tu? **1**

at what time is . . .? à quelle heure est...? **4**

at what time? à quelle heure? **4, 16**

when quand **16**

when is your birthday? c'est quand, ton anniversaire? **8**

where où **14, 16**

where is . . .? où est...? **14**

where is it? où est-ce? **21**

from where? d'où? **23**

whether si **C**

which quel (quelle) **26**

white blanc (blanche) **20**

who qui **16**

who's that/this? qui est-ce? **5, 17**

about whom? de qui? **16**

for whom? pour qui? **16**

of whom? de qui? **16**

to whom? à qui? **16**

with whom? avec qui? **16**

why pourquoi **16**

wife une femme **24**

to **win** gagner **28**

window une fenêtre **B, 17**

to **windsurf** *faire de la planche à voile **29**

windsurfing la planche à voile **29**

winter l'hiver *m.* **12**

in the winter en hiver **12**

with avec **14**

with me avec moi **13**

with you avec toi **13**

with whom? avec qui? **16**

woman une dame *(polite term)* **5;** une femme **17**

to **work** travailler **13, 15;** *(referring to objects)* marcher **17**

does the radio work? est-ce que la radio marche? **17**

it (doesn't) work(s) well il/elle (ne) marche (pas) bien **17**

would: I'd like je voudrais **9, 10, 13**

to **write** *écrire **36**

wrong faux (fausse) **20**

to be wrong *avoir tort **30**

Y

year un an, une année **8**

he/she is . . . (years old) il/elle a... ans **7**

I'm . . . (years old) j'ai... ans **7**

to be . . . (years old) *avoir... ans **18**

yellow jaune **20**

yes oui **2, 14;** *(to a negative question)* si! **18**

yes, of course oui, bien sûr **13**

yes, okay (all right) oui, d'accord **13**

yes, thank you oui, merci **13**

yesterday hier **31**

yesterday afternoon hier après-midi **31**

yesterday morning hier matin **31**

English-French Vocabulary

yogurt le yaourt **33**
you tu, vous **14, 23;**
 on **28**
 you are . . . tu es +
  nationality **2**
 and you? et toi? **1**

(to) you te, vous **35**
your ton, ta; tes **7;** votre; vos
 24
 what's your name?
  comment t'appelles-tu? **1**

young jeune **17**

Z ▬▬▬▬▬▬▬▬▬

zero zéro **1**

R49

Photo Credits